Praise for *The Kennedys*

"This extremely readable biography not only examines one particular immigrant family but also sheds light on the larger story of Irish-Americans from the early twentieth century onward." —*Booklist*

"A fascinating new perspective." —*Houston Chronicle*

"[T]he door is open and the time is right for another serious, multigenerational history of America's most fabled clan. *Newsday* reporter Maier answers the need quite well with this fascinating account." —*Publishers Weekly*

"A colossal work. . . . *The Kennedys* is a pleasure to read and a legitimate page-turner." —BookReporter.com

"A hefty, well documented, glowing account of the Kennedys as a prime example of Irish Catholic experience in America. [Maier] paints a vivid picture of the anti-Irish, anti-Catholic sentiment that faced immigrants with brogues." —*Kirkus Reviews*

"Thomas Maier reminds us of a story we've forgotten: the Kennedys are not simply America's most famous family. They are an immigrant family, a family that struggled through poverty and oppression on both sides of the Atlantic. This highly readable book offers a new and powerful look at this storied clan. This is a Kennedy book with insights and observations you haven't read elsewhere." —TERRY GOLWAY, author of *So Others Might Live* and co-author of *The Irish in America*

"You can't understand the Kennedys unless you look at their Irish Catholic roots. Thomas Maier has gone far beyond earlier Kennedy biographers and historians to reveal ties that shaped the Kennedys long after they left Ireland. And he's done it in a lively, readable way." —EVAN THOMAS, author of *Robert Kennedy: His Life*

The Kennedys

Also by Thomas Maier

Dr. Spock: An American Life

Newhouse:
All the Glitter, Power and Glory
of America's Richest Media Empire
and the Secretive Man behind It

THOMAS MAIER

BASIC
BOOKS

A MEMBER OF THE PERSEUS BOOKS GROUP
NEW YORK

The Kennedys
America's Emerald Kings

Copyright © 2003 by Thomas Maier

Published by Basic Books
A Member of the Perseus Books Group

Designed by Brian Mulligan

The Library of Congress cataloged the hardcover edition as follows:

Maier, Thomas, 1956–
    The Kennedys : America's emerald kings / Thomas Maier.
        p.   cm.
    Includes bibliographical references and index.
    ISBN 0-465-04317-8 (hc)
    1. Kennedy family.   2. Kennedy, John F. (John Fitzgerald), 1917–
1963.   3. Politicians—United States—Biography.   4. Irish
Americans—Biography.   5. Irish American families.   6. Catholics—
United States—Biography.   I. Title.

E843.M35 2003
973.922'092'2—dc21
ISBN 978-0-465-04318-7 (pbk)

                                                            2003010426

10 9 8 7 6 5 4 3

To my sons—
Drew, Taylor and Reade

"All of us of Irish descent are bound together by the ties that come from a common experience; experience which may exist only in memories and in legend but which is real enough to those who possess it. The special contribution of the Irish, I believe—the emerald thread that runs throughout the tapestry of their past—has been the constancy, the endurance, the faith that they displayed through endless centuries of foreign oppression—centuries in which even the most rudimentary religious and civil rights were denied to them—centuries in which their mass destruction by poverty, disease and starvation were ignored by their conquerors."

—SENATOR JOHN F. KENNEDY, 1957

"Be more Irish than Harvard."

—ROBERT FROST,
INSCRIBED IN A BOOK OF POEMS
GIVEN TO JFK AT THE 1961
PRESIDENTIAL INAUGURATION

Contents

Part III: Rise to the Presidency

Part IV: The Rites of Power

Part V: The Emerald Thread

Preface to the New Edition

*"Once I thought to write a history of the
immigrants in America. Then I discovered that
immigrants were America."*

—HISTORIAN OSCAR HANDLIN, AS QUOTED BY
JOHN F. KENNEDY IN *A NATION OF IMMIGRANTS*

THE 2008 PRESIDENTIAL CAMPAIGN offered many reminders for Sen.
Edward Kennedy of the barriers his brother faced in 1960 in becoming the
first and only U.S. president from a minority background. With a sign from
Dunganstown, Ireland, hanging in his Senate office, a reminder of the famine-
ravished farm where his ancestors began, Ted always seemed to understand that
the Kennedys were perhaps America's greatest immigrant story—overcoming
religious, ethnic, and cultural barriers to reach once unimaginable heights.

"My brother Jack wrote *A Nation of Immigrants* in 1958, and his words
ring true as clearly today as they did half a century ago," said Ted, a few
months before he was struck with a malignant brain tumor in spring 2008.
"I'm constantly reminded of my immigrant heritage." Indeed, Kennedy's
vision of *A Nation of Immigrants* transformed America forever.

Throughout 2008, presidential candidates from various minority backgrounds invoked the Kennedy name as a constant touchstone. The first major
female candidate for president, Sen. Hillary Clinton, drew endorsements from
Robert Kennedy's children, including Kathleen and Bobby Jr. The first major
candidate from a Hispanic background, New Mexico Gov. Bill Richardson,
echoed JFK in proclaiming, "We are a nation of immigrants." In a speech to
allay concerns about his Mormon religion, former Massachusetts Gov. Mitt
Romney harkened back to JFK's famous 1960 speech before the Houston
ministers, when many were fearful of a Catholic in the White House. Most
notably, Barack Obama, the U.S. senator from Illinois, possessed a style and
dignity particularly reminiscent of the Kennedy era. "People always tell me
how my father inspired them," said JFK's daughter, Caroline Kennedy, in
her endorsement. "I feel that same excitement now. Barack Obama can lift

America and make us one nation again." At a key moment in the primary campaign, Ted Kennedy publicly supported Obama who, in turn, said the Kennedy family always stood for "what is best about America." Obama's campaign faced many tests similar to those that Kennedy endured in 1960. As a minority, born to a black father and white mother, Obama had to overcome code words and subtle biases historically applied to African Americans. Like Catholic hard-liners who complained that Kennedy wasn't "Catholic enough" in 1960, Obama was sometimes criticized within the black community for not being "black enough" in 2008. And yet when the media made it seem Obama had been attacked for his minority status, African Americans rallied to his support, just as Catholics did in 1960 for JFK. Ted Kennedy's dramatic embrace of Obama's candidacy carried a powerful symbolism, one of the last significant acts of his distinguished career before he fell ill.

The Kennedys' legacy from a minority background demands greater understanding of the cultural forces that they both represented and overcame. From today's perspective, it is increasingly clear that John F. Kennedy was the Jackie Robinson of American politics, paving a way for presidential candidates from other minority backgrounds. For future generations, the transcendent appeal of JFK's 1960 success meant that other discounted Americans could possibly overcome the hurdles of ethnicity, race, religion, and gender. As this book recounts, the religious bigotry Kennedy faced in 1960 could have easily embittered a candidate with less personal grace and poorer awareness of this nation's history. But JFK's idealistic belief in America's greatness was clearly stated in *A Nation of Immigrants*, which reflected so much of his family's story. The essence of this little-known, little-studied book became the 1965 Immigration Reform Act, which ended the discriminatory preference given to white Europeans and opened the door to millions from Latin America, Asia, Africa, and around the world. First proposed by JFK in July 1963, a few months before his assassination, the bill was passed in his memory, pushed by his two brothers in the U.S. Senate. No law in our lifetime has done more to change America, and it is arguably the Kennedy family's most lasting legacy to our country.

THIS BOOK TAKES a new look at the Kennedy saga over five generations, exploring the impact of religion, race, and cultural identity on their public and private lives. Too often, previous historians ignored these powerful forces and portrayed JFK as a Harvard-educated Anglophile, the perfect specimen of a secular, assimilist, "melting pot" view of American history. As a result, dozens of Kennedy books routinely ignored, or gave only a passing nod to, the underlying forces of ethnicity and religion that so often influenced the Kennedy family's actions and outlook. In death, JFK's reign was lionized as "Camelot" by his widow and those who grieved. But a comparison to British royalty hardly seems proper for the great-grandson of an Irish migrant worker who fled from his Dunganstown, County Wexford, farm during the Great Famine. Only with the passage of time, and the recent availability of many personal documents at the John F. Kennedy Presidential Library, does a more complete and accurate portrait emerge. In reexamining the record, we gain a fresh understanding of the Kennedy family's sense of their own immigrant heritage, their epic encounters with religious bigotry, and how the complex dynamics of their family life reflected the Irish Catholic experience in America.

From Patrick and Bridget Kennedy fleeing famine-stricken Ireland among the great wave of emigrants in the 1840s to efforts in the 1990s by Ted Kennedy and his sister, U.S. Ambassador Jean Kennedy Smith, to bring peace to their ancestral homeland, their sense of being Irish, Catholic, and members of a family coming from an often oppressed immigrant minority— indeed, the very Irish notion of a Kennedy clan, as they often referred to themselves—carried through from one generation to the next.

Though this book is not intended as a policy analysis, it is nevertheless striking how much of the Kennedy family's cultural background played a role in such issues as civil rights, Vietnam, poverty, immigration, terrorism, and the fight against communism. Certainly, the Kennedy relationship with the Roman Catholic Church was far more extensive than the public perceived of the 1960 presidential candidate, elected as he was by vowing a strict separation between church and state. Private letters illustrate the family's deep political and financial ties to the church, both in America and with the Pope's right-hand man at the Vatican. These documents detail Joe Kennedy's secret role as a go-between for President Franklin D. Roosevelt and the future Pope Pius XII, why he felt that FDR harbored a bias against Catholics like himself, and how the Kennedys battled behind the scenes with the church's hierarchy during JFK's historic presidential campaign. Joe Kennedy's decades-long friendship with the suave, discreet Vatican administrator, Count Enrico Galeazzi, offers a fascinating venue into the Kennedy family's influence in Rome. Their correspondence during the 1960 presidential campaign provides a running commentary on the family's frustration with anti-Catholic bigotry and anger with the conservative bishops in their own church—something the Kennedys dared not show to the American public.

We also gain new insights into the personal side of the Kennedys, the often profound and pervasive impact of their cultural background beyond the sheer exercise of power and money. Volumes of family documents—from typed formal correspondence to handwritten comments on funeral Mass cards or scribbled St. Patrick's Day greetings—reveal their struggles with faith after so many tragedies, and reconciling matters of marriage and sex within the church's teachings. We learn of figures such as Jesuit priest Richard McSorley, who in recent years spoke for the first time about Jacqueline Kennedy's depression and thoughts of committing suicide in the wake of her husband's 1963 assassination. In a typical Kennedyesque setting—while playing tennis in Bobby and Ethel's Hickory Hill backyard—Father McSorley advised and comforted Jackie as she wondered aloud about a God who would claim the lives of both her husband and their infant son, Patrick, within just a few tragic months. We get a much more realistic picture of the traumatic impact of these events on the widowed first lady, who appeared silent and stoic to the American public from behind her black veil.

This book focuses on what JFK called the "emerald thread" between two nations—for so much about the Kennedys in America can be understood and appreciated only by first studying what happened to them in Ireland. Interviews and documents detail the Kennedys' long involvement in the quest for Ireland's independence, including how some family members in Ireland were tied to the Irish Republican Army. It recounts JFK's celebrated 1963 visit to Ireland, including the home of his elderly Irish cousin who, unknown to the unwitting White House, had once been a local gunrunner for the IRA's women's branch. As former Maryland Lieutenant Governor Kathleen Kennedy Townsend explains, the Kennedys' sense of being Irish Catholics—both as outcasts in Ireland and as outsiders in the Brahmin world of Boston—would affect their politics for decades to come.

Though some call them "America's royalty," a more apt analogy may be the Irish chieftains of old, the kings of an emerald isle who, according to legend, inspired and led large groups of followers. This book's title alludes to the chieftain notion mentioned by several people who were interviewed, and occasionally, by the Kennedys themselves. These qualities emerged first among the Kennedy men who achieved fame and power, but also, tellingly, in recent years with the family's prominent women. From the broadest vantage, the Kennedy story reminds us of the glories and the limits of America's melting pot and those histories that paint people from minority groups in familiar "just-like-us" tones. We gain a better grasp of the Kennedys' appeal beyond Irish Catholics—to countless other immigrant and minority groups who share a dream of ascendancy in America. In this context, our understanding of the Kennedys becomes richer, more complex, and of greater historical significance to this nation of immigrants that

JFK wrote about. It recalls how far we've progressed as a country since the 1960 election, and yet how many barriers still remain today.

MANY PEOPLE ARE to be thanked for their help in my efforts to bring this work to fruition, particularly Basic Books publisher Elizabeth Maguire, who edited this book in its original 2003 version. Liz died far too young, in 2006, but her memory lives on in all whose lives she touched. Editor Amanda Moon oversaw this reissued version and updated preface, which is being jointly released with a new documentary about the Kennedys based on this book. Robert Kline, producer of the new documentary, is particularly to be thanked for his friendship and help in putting together this joint effort. My agent, Faith Hamlin of Sanford J. Greenburger Associates Inc., has been a bedrock of support, finding the right venues for three successive, sometimes controversial, books about American life in the twentieth century.

Writing is a solitary endeavor, but I relied continually on my family for help along the way. My wife, Joyce McGurrin, provided constant encouragement with her knowledgeable insights, thoughtful ear, and nightly cups of tea. In Ireland, Joyce's family and her own intuitive awareness of Irish sensibilities proved invaluable for this New York native. This book is dedicated to the joy of our lives—our three sons, Drew, Taylor, and Reade—whom we love very much. The boys spent two weeks in Ireland with their parents during the early stages of research, alternately learning how to play hurling at the Kennedy homestead and how to look up material in the National Library in Dublin. Mostly, they gained a sense of their own history. Because they were teenagers with an abundance of intelligence, charm, and Irish wit, Drew and Taylor, known as "the redheads," likely learned the most from this experience. They spent hours with their father pulling books and sifting through archives. Reade, a bit younger but with the same gifts, probably had the most personally affecting experience.

For Easter 2001, we spent the weekend with Joyce's cousins, the Brennans, at their eight-hundred-acre sheep farm in County Donegal; there, Reade met a cousin who shared the same birthday and looked just like him. The two boys hit it off like twins. They were mirror images of each other, one Irish, the other American. It was a gentle reminder that we can all recognize a little of ourselves in the Irish and how much we might learn by looking back at where we've been.

—T.M.
Long Island, New York
May 2008

Part I

From Ireland to
Irish-American

"I am an Irishman and I have not forgotten."

—GEORGE BERNARD SHAW

Chapter One

The Boys of Wexford

IRELAND APPEARED STRANGE AND NEW, yet hauntingly familiar. From inside the presidential helicopter, hundreds of feet above the ground, John Fitzgerald Kennedy gazed out at the beautiful land below and reflected upon his journey. Something about this ancestral homeland stirred him deeply. "Ireland is an unusual place," he'd say before departing, "what happened five hundred or a thousand years is as yesterday."

The president's entourage took off that morning from Dublin and headed south along the rocky coastline of the Irish Sea on their way to Wexford County and the small town known as New Ross. From this place, Kennedy's great-grandfather had departed in 1848 to escape a land tortured by famine and oppression to seek a new life as an immigrant in Boston. As if coming full circle, as if completing some generational journey begun by his forefathers more than a century ago, Kennedy returned to Ireland for a state visit in June 1963, the only Roman Catholic ever elected to the White House and the first American president to come to the Emerald Isle while in office. His aides and the press had questioned the usefulness of stopping in Ireland as part of a much larger European trip in which Kennedy inveighed against the Berlin Wall and the evils of communism. But Kennedy insisted on adding his family's homeland to his itinerary. During the four days in Ireland, there would be plenty of political tasks, conversations about trade and diplomacy, though everyone recognized, including Kennedy himself, that the real reason for this Irish excursion was purely personal.

Out of the mist of this soggy day, Kennedy could see the lush farmlands of Eire—hundreds of acres stretched over long, sloping hills, carved majestically into the horizon by hedgerows, granite walls and crooked streams. Sliding by, almost in a blur, were scenes that seemed torn from picture postcards, the kind that Irish-Americans send to loved ones to remind them of what their families left behind: ruins of medieval churches and headstones lost in a meadow; cottages with thatched roofs; farmers feeding pigs or tending to sheep waiting to be sheared; old lighthouses, once kept by monks, perched along jagged beaches and grassy peninsulas whipped by waves. All were quiet reminders of an ancient land, culture and religion that Kennedy possessed in his bones but often kept from public view. On this trip, however, the young and often reserved president would hide neither his roots nor his enthusiasm.

Through his window, Kennedy tried to recognize certain landmarks, sites he remembered from his trips to Ireland before he became president. While in the helicopter, the president ordered the pilot to fly by Lismore Castle in Waterford County, the stone castle where his sister, Kathleen, once lived as the widow of the Duke of Devonshire and where he had stayed as a young congressman during his first visit to Ireland in 1947. The whirling bird hovered momentarily over this ancient castle as the president stared at its massive square towers and battlements, lost in his own thoughts. For some Irish, Lismore Castle, built on a giant rock, symbolized the oppressive presence of the British, a site with its own history of bloodshed in the struggle for liberty and political control of the isle. For Kennedy, though, the beautiful castle surrounded by gardens of magnolias and yews undoubtedly brought back memories of his dead sister and a different time in the Kennedy family's lives together. In such a short time, Ireland had changed and so had Jack Kennedy himself. The president's craft lingered for what seemed the longest time and eventually swooped away; it glided over the tops of trees to the River Barrow.

WAITING AT NEW ROSS, where the mouth of the river opens, were a throng of schoolchildren, all dressed in white sweaters and assembled on the thick green turf of an athletic field, newly named Sean O'Kennedy Football Field in honor of the president. From fifteen hundred feet above, Kennedy's entourage of aides and family members could see the children in a formation that spelled out *Failte,* the Gaelic word for "Welcome." The town soon made good on its promise. When the helicopter landed, Kennedy stepped out gingerly—immediately recognizable in his deep blue business suit, his thick wave of auburn hair and the smiling squint of his eyes—and was swarmed by well-wishers. Because first lady Jackie Kennedy was home tending to a troublesome pregnancy, the president was accompanied by his two sisters, Eunice and Jean, and his sister-in-law, Lee Radziwill. "He was just so thrilled how they responded," Jean recalled years later. "I never saw him so excited. It was so touching, such a poetic experience."

A choir from the local Christian Brothers school soon broke out in a song, "The Boys of Wexford," a rousing tune commemorating the 1798 rebellion in that county in which many Irishmen, including members of Kennedy's own family, died or were injured attempting to end England's long-time presence in their land. Kennedy immediately recognized the song and began tapping his foot lightly. When a copy of the lyrics was handed to him, he joined in the chorus:

We are the Boys of Wexford,
Who fought with heart and hand,
To burst in twain the galling chain
And free our native land.

When they finished, the president asked the children to sing it again. The tune would linger in Kennedy's mind for the remainder of his Irish trip and beyond. Another reminder of his own legacy came in one of the many gifts he received that day—a special vase of cut glass made by the nearby Waterford crystal firm, inscribed with his family's Irish homestead, an immigrant ship and the White House.

Some fifteen thousand people, many of them young schoolgirls holding American flags, cheered wildly as Kennedy slowly rode by in a limousine, standing and waving to the crowd from the car's half-opened bubble top. Despite a drizzle, the crowd roared its approval as the car moved into the heart of the town. "Kennedy . . . *Kennedy,*" they chanted without pause as the presidential parade car arrived at the quay. Beside the ships docked along the harbor, a special speakers' platform had been constructed, but it had been built only after much bickering. At the heart of the dispute was New Ross's town board chairman, Andrew Minihan, a gruff, opinionated man who knew what he liked and spared no remark for that which he didn't. Minihan was, in the words of one writer, "a man whose integrity is as bristly as the whiskers and rough tweeds that cover him." The Secret Service and some of JFK's White House aides definitely rubbed him the wrong way.

Minihan first became annoyed with the endless debate about where to place the speaker's dais on the quay. "Every man must justify his own existence somehow," Minihan proclaimed to a group of reporters assembled in a bar before the president's arrival, "but I've better ways of justifying my own than standing around with your American G-men and arguing whether the northeast corner should be *there,* or *there.*" And he moved his toes barely four inches to drive home the point. But Minihan's biggest gripe stemmed from the argument over a dung heap, a sizeable and fragrant pile of muck and animal excrement, often used as fertilizer, located within smelling distance of the speaker's dais. The Secret Service told Minihan, in no uncertain terms, that the pile of shit must go.

"Remove it?" he replied, indignantly. "I've no plan at all to remove it!"

Not one to be pushed around, Minihan staged his own rebellion by upping the ante. "As a matter of fact, we thought to add to it," he mused. "It would be good for the character of your mighty President to have to cross a veritable *Alp* of dung on his way to the New Ross speaker's stand."

Now that wasn't funny, not in the eyes of the sober–minded Secret Service men. The security detail argued that the dung heap posed a threat to the president. The agents insisted that the wives of the town council stay off the dais and banned a local marching band from appearing beside the platform. Their haughtiness only calcified Minihan's position. "I'll not live to see a sight more ridiculous," Minihan brayed to the press, "than your G-men combing out dung piles to see if we'd planted bombs and merciful God only knows what else in them." Eventually, the American ambassador, Matthew McCloskey, and some top brass at the foreign office in Dublin spoke privately with Minihan, telling him that his obstinacy would not do. Minihan let them know that he'd planned all along to have the dung carted away but objected to the airs put on by the Americans. As for the wives and the marching band, they got to stay.

When the big day arrived, Kennedy's aides feared that Minihan might be a wild card, a party pooper who could easily spoil the president's grand homecoming. He didn't disappoint. In introducing the president at the podium, the microphones suddenly went dead. "Can you hear me?" he asked. The crowd roared that they couldn't. Minihan, known for his hot temper, turned red and stewed. "We're in trouble right now," Minihan yelled. "Some pressman has walked on the communications."

When the sound system returned, Kennedy seemed nonplussed, almost amused. Word of Minihan's local rebellion, captured in humorous press accounts about the dung heap, had come to his attention. As he got up to speak, the president introduced his two sisters, Jean and Eunice, then recalled his family's ties to the thousands of Irish who had fled the Famine's death and despair, his great-grandfather Patrick Kennedy among them, and journeyed from places like New Ross to find a new home as immigrants in America.

"It took a hundred and fifteen years to make this trip, and six thousand miles, and three generations, but I am proud to be here," the president told the crowd. "When my great-grandfather left here to become a cooper in East Boston, he carried nothing with him except two things: a strong religious faith and a strong desire for liberty. I am glad to say that all of his great-grandchildren have valued that inheritance."

In passing, though, Kennedy couldn't resist a teasing reference for the locals.

"If he hadn't left, I would be working over at the Albatross Company," Kennedy quipped, nodding over to the local fertilizer company across the quay. The crowd burst into laughter.

"Or perhaps for John V. Kelly," the president added, referring to a well-known pub in Wexford, which earned him even further applause.

For on that day, all the Irish present—including the mayor, Minihan—recognized John F. Kennedy as one of their own.

TODAY, ALONG THE NARROW, WINDING ROADS from New Ross, you can see hundreds of acres of farmland, most covered by barley and hay swaying in the cool, raw winds from the Irish Sea. In early spring, the damp air and the low-flying clouds moisten your skin with a chilling touch. The breezes whip and tussle your hair, and your lungs expand and your eyes tear until you feel completely enraptured by nature, as if some supernatural force were at play and beyond your command. "The gods whistle in the air," novelist Sean O'Faolain wrote of his native country. "The Otherworld is always at one's shoulder." Undoubtedly, there is a sense of the past in Ireland and—in the rapid change of weather, in the stories of chieftains and kings and heroes who died as martyrs for their religion or for Irish freedom—a tumultuous free spirit to the land.

In the valley of the River Barrow, which runs parallel to the path leading from New Ross to the farms in the outer locale of Dunganstown, you can sense what life was like in the 1840s for a young man named Patrick Kennedy. The muddy waters filled with boats are much today as they were then. The bridge across the Barrow, originally built by Norman conquerors in the thirteenth century, is nearly the same as the one that Patrick Kennedy crossed to get to market. In those days, New Ross was a shipping port easing toward Waterford Harbour and the ancient stone lighthouse at Hook Head. In the 1840s, the town boasted four tanneries, three timber yards, two bacon cellars and some fifteen thousand residents. Among three local brewers in town was the Cherry Bros. Brewery, where Patrick often stopped his horse-drawn cart with fresh supplies of barley from the Kennedy family farm in nearby Dunganstown, about six miles south of New Ross. At Cherry Bros., the owners also ran a cooperage where wooden barrels for whiskey were bent and shaped by the men who greeted young Kennedy when he sauntered into New Ross two or three times a week.

Although no record of his image exists, family members believe Patrick Kennedy possessed the reddish-brown hair common in their clan, as well as a physical strength needed to lug about sacks of produce and barrels. From the cooper's tools and remnants of wooden barrels with "Cherry Bros." carved into their sides—which can still be found today on the Kennedy Homestead in Dunganstown—you realize that Patrick Kennedy probably learned the trade of coopering while in New Ross rather than, as some historians say, in the New World. Irish whiskey, called *Uisce Beatha,* "the water of life," by the populace and sometimes consumed in excess, was distilled from malted barley gathered by farmers like the Kennedys and kept in oak casks made by coopers.

On the hardscrabble farm the family cultivated, but did not own, a young man like Patrick commonly worked seventy hours over six days each week. The vein of granite running throughout their thirty-five-acre farm didn't allow for potatoes to be grown as much as it did barley. From his father, James, and two older brothers, John and James, young Patrick Kennedy learned to be a farmer. While they toiled in the fields, his mother, Mary, and older sister, Mary, tended the house. But it was in the bustling town of New Ross where Patrick, the youngest of four children, learned of the world beyond the surrounding countryside and of its desperate troubles.

Throughout Ireland, the smell of putrid potatoes overwhelmed the land, cutting off some four million Irish from their main—and sometimes only—source of sustenance. More than 900,000 acres devoted to potatoes had turned sour. Although this plague would spread farther and more cunningly in other parts of the nation, County Wexford suffered almost immediately from the potato blight and impending starvation. As early as August 1845, during a mild summer that appeared to promise an abundant harvest, an oppressive stench filled the air, bringing sickness and death. The *Wexford Independent,* the regional newspaper, reported "a fatal malady has broken out among the potato crop," warning that putrid potatoes plucked from the soil were "unfit for being introduced into the stomach and has often proved fatal."

By 1848, the same year Patrick Kennedy would make a fateful decision for his family and himself, some 298 poor souls in Wexford had died from starvation and its accompanying diseases. In New Ross, the number of destitute people seeking emergency relief climbed higher than in any place in the county. The Famine soon became another reason—perhaps the most devastating one of all—to leave a land where the Kennedys were once kings, yet now their misery seemed to know no bounds.

Chapter Two

Heirs of Brian Boru

THE KENNEDY ROOTS sink deep into Ireland's past. In preparing for the 1963 presidential visit, the Library of Congress worked with genealogical sleuths to trace the family's lineage back to the chieftains in Ormond and, at one time, the ancient kings of Ireland. In the native Gaelic tongue, the clan's name was *O'Cinneide,* "hard-headed" or "ugly-headed." (When told of that translation, President Kennedy quipped with a wry smile, "Let's keep that quiet.") Probably a more accurate translation, historians suggest, is "Head of the Clan." According to these accounts, the O'Cinneide clan was an important part of early Irish history, and their most celebrated member, Brian Boru, a heroic part of the nation's lore. As any pub crawler knows, hundreds, if not thousands, of those with Irish blood in their veins trace their roots to Brian Boru and other long-ago chieftains. For years, Irish historians have been as divided as Ireland itself in trying to decipher truth from myth. Regardless of the factual accuracy of their claims, these fables of lost majesty, of heroes who die tragically and leave behind a people yearning for freedom, were an important part of the Irish character. Intuitively, Kennedy seemed to understand the power of these myths on the imagination, and at times he paid homage to them. For these legends and folklore, as much as the gentle farmland or surrounding villages, provided the background for the Kennedy story in Dunganstown. And they would resonate within the family for many years to come.

IN ANCIENT IRELAND, the role of family was crucial, serving as a source of identity and protection for each individual. Several families of the same ancestry often formed a "sept"—a tribe of extended families—led by a chieftain who watched over their interests and protected them from invaders. The O'Kennedys made their home in Ormond in County Tipperary, about twenty miles west of New Ross, and demonstrated a greater degree of independence than other Irish clans. The ruins of stone castles from the O'Kennedy sept still dot the countryside in Tipperary. For centuries, the clans had participated in pagan traditions of the Druids, the ancient Celtic people who worshipped various gods in nature and believed in the immortality of the soul. As Ireland became more Christian—the faith introduced in A.D. 432 by St. Patrick, who used three-leaf shamrocks to describe the Trinity—the clans decided who would be kings and thus became increasingly part of Ireland's power structure.

The Danes became the first of Ireland's oppressors after the golden age of monks and monasteries, which had kept Western culture alive by producing such manuscripts as *The Books of Kells*. For two hundred years, the island nation existed under Danish domination until Brian Boru, chieftain of the O'Cinneide clan and the larger *Dal gCais Sept*, defeated the Norsemen in 1014 at the battle of Clontarf, near Dublin. Brian Boru, the King of Munster, the southernmost province of Ireland, emerged as the first Christian king of all Ireland and earned the title *Ard Ri*, "High King." According to these ancient scrolls, Brian Boru became king by picking up the mantle left by his brother, Mahon, who was assassinated by the Danes after a long period of peace. A glorious victory by Brian Boru ended that Irish generation's burden of being ruled by outsiders who ravaged their villages. In the style of a great chieftain, Brian Boru brought a new era of enlightenment for his people. "He restored and built churches," one historian said of Brian Boru's era. "He built and set in order public schools for the teaching of letters and science in general and every territory he took from the Danes by the strength of his arm, he gave it . . . to the tribe to whom it belonged by right."

When Brian Boru died, his heirs' dreams for national unity fell apart. Over the next several decades, Ireland was torn by political infighting among the clans, rendering it vulnerable to military and economic control from the country across the sea. In 1169, the Norman barons of England invaded Wexford and soon ruled the countryside, opening the door for what would become centuries of British domination. This particular invasion received the blessing of the Roman Catholic Church and from Pope Hadrian IV, who happened to be an Englishman. Though many loyal Catholics lived in Ireland, Hadrian IV decreed that England's King Henry II could seize Ireland as his own so long as the church received in return a pension of one penny for every Irish house. Surely, as the Vatican reasoned in this fateful exchange, the Catholic King of England would be preferable to the unruly and somewhat heretical natives of Ireland. "We are well pleased that you should enter that island," the Pope wrote to the British monarch, instructing that the Irish "should receive you with honor and venerate you as their master."

Under Norman rule, the Irish lost their own lands, and laws were passed that made them social outcasts. During this time, the family's Gaelic name was Anglicized to O'Kennedy, the "O" eventually dropped. The Kennedys moved into southeastern Ireland; eventually, they were reduced to serfdom and worked as tenants on farms they would never own.

BY THE LATE SIXTEENTH CENTURY, Ireland was a pawn in a larger religious struggle between the British monarchy and the throne of Saint Peter. When the Pope refused to annul Henry VIII's first marriage, the king broke away from Rome and formed the Church of England. Henry and his heirs converted Great Britain to Protestantism, setting off decades of strife. The austere Puritans, a group particularly intent on ridding England of its Catholic vestiges, replaced altars and rituals from the Latin Mass with the *Book of Common Prayer*. When the Irish Catholics attempted rebellion in the early 1640s, the British response was bloody and became even more oppressive.

Oliver Cromwell, a bold and ruthless leader, arrived in Ireland in 1649 to crush the rebels. A fervent Puritan during the Protestant reign of King Charles II, Cromwell believed that God oversaw and justified his every move, even those "regrettable" acts of violence that might become necessary. He possessed a relentlessness in demeanor and appearance. He wanted the British Empire "purified" of Catholicism. As a political leader, he envisioned the isle to the west freed of Rome's influence and colonized by English Protestants.

Cromwell's hatred of Catholics became a blood-lust in Ireland. His armies marched north to Drogheda, massacring some three thousand people. At Drogheda, the Irish tales of horror included Jesuit priests pierced with stakes, young virgins decimated and children used as shields as Cromwell's troops assaulted the church and city. "This is a righteous judgment of God upon these barbarous wretches," Cromwell wrote back to England after this annihilation. "It will tend to prevent the effusion of blood in the future." Then Cromwell turned south to Wexford, where he again showed no mercy, killing more than one thousand. When three hundred Catholic women in Wexford took refuge near a cross in a public square, their actions sealed their fates. Instead of invoking Christian sympathy from the soldiers, the women were butchered.

The Irish chose as their military leader Owen Roe O'Neill, an experienced field general whose father had fought for Eire's liberty. O'Neill won a stunning initial victory at the battle of Benburb, even though British troops outmanned his own. As legend has it, the Irish looked to O'Neill, the gallant, auburn-haired warrior, as their savior after years of violence. But their resistance to Cromwell faded that same year when O'Neill died suddenly (probably of illness, though many believed he was poisoned), leaving them without a leader. In song and poetry, Owen Roe O'Neill would long be remembered by the Kennedys and generations of others for his tragic fate and the unanswered prayer of Irish independence. Nearly two hundred years later, Thomas Davis, a poet and nationalist leader himself, wrote his own lament for what was lost:

We thought you would not die—we were sure you would not go,
And leave us in our utmost need to Cromwell's cruel blow—
Sheep without a shepherd, when the snow shuts out the sky,
Why did you leave us, Owen? Why, why did you die?

In Wexford, Cromwell marched to New Ross, where the local population surrendered rather than fall victim to the same bloodbath. Though Cromwell spared them from certain death in return for immediate surrender, he prohibited Catholics from all future practice of their religion. "I meddle not with any man's conscience," Cromwell insisted. "But if by liberty of conscience you mean a liberty to exercise the Mass, I judge it best to use plain dealing, and to let you know, where the Parliament of England have power, that will not be allowed." Incensed by the support of Irish priests and clergy for the rebellion, Cromwell denounced the Roman Catholic Church in strong, often violent terms, deriding the priests as "the intruders" in Ireland. "Is God, will God be, with you?" Cromwell asked, as his campaign wiped out all hope of Irish independence. "I am confident He will not." Cromwell's name was a curse word in Ireland for generations to come.

RESTRICTIONS ON the Irish became broader and more institutionalized, especially after the Catholic King James II put together an army in Ireland and was defeated by William of Orange and his Protestant forces at the historic 1690 battle of the Boyne. To make sure the Irish remained under its thumb, the British Parliament passed laws that reduced the Irish ownership of farms and granted large tracts of land to those, mainly Protestants, who had been loyal to the Crown. When lands were confiscated from Catholics and given to English squires, the fate of the Kennedys living around New Ross was dictated by these edicts. In 1704, the Irish Parliament, with the Crown's blessing, passed one of several "penal laws"—this one called "the Act to Prevent the Further Growth of Popery." It not only made the practice of religion illegal for Catholics but also offered a bounty for turning in priests.

Intended to break the back of rebellion, these penal laws enslaved the spirit of a people. No Catholic could own land, vote or hold public office. Catholics couldn't work in the civil service, nor could they send their children to school or seek education for themselves. Catholics were banned from the military, weren't allowed to own horses or other property worth five pounds or more. No Catholic was permitted to carry a sword or own other types of weapons. No Catholic could practice as a lawyer, doctor, trader or any professional. No Catholic could earn more than a third of the value of his crops. And all Catholics were compelled to pay a tithe to the Anglican Protestant Church. Irish Catholics became untouchables in their own land. "Papists" were forbidden to marry Protestants, and Catholic orphans were converted. Trinity College, the finest learning center in Dublin, was reserved for Protestants. For the Irish Catholic people, the infamous penal laws became, as Edmund Burke later observed, "a machine of wise and elaborate contrivance and as well fitted for the oppression, impoverishment, and degradation of a people, and the debasement in them of human nature itself, as ever proceeded from the perverted ingenuity of man."

Despite these shackles, the Irish survived and membership in the Catholic Church actually flourished. Religious persecution turned Irish Catholics into the Vatican's most devoted followers; they no longer worshipped at poorly attended and loosely organized churches influenced by the pagan rituals of old. During the 1700s, and for much of the next century, Catholics attended church in the outdoors, where large "Mass rocks" served as altars. In Dunganstown, where the Kennedys lived, Catholics built a small thatched building with mud walls in 1743 to serve as a church. It was later burned down. Though some Irish championing independence were Protestants, notably Wolfe Tone and Jonathan Swift, the move to rid Ireland of British control and its oppressive laws became linked with Catholicism. As historian Robert Kee later wrote: "The fact that the Church was able to surmount them strengthened not only the Church itself but also its bond with the vast majority of the population of Ireland who, deprived of all political and many other rights, saw the Church as the one representative organization they had."

The Irish wish to be rid of English domination, freed of its penal laws and its brutal restraints, could be heard in song, verse and prayer.

> *Oh, Paddy dear! and did ye hear the news that's goin' round?*
> *The shamrock is forbid by law to grow on Irish ground!*
> *No mor St. Patrick's day we'll keep; his color can't be seen,*
> *For there's a cruel law ag'in the Wearin' o' the Green!*

For the Kennedys in Dunganstown, and for all the Catholics in Ireland, the English penal laws effectively eliminated their hope of reclaiming the lands they had owned before Cromwell. Much of New Ross and its environs was given away to the Tottenham family, descendants of the Normans who became members of Parliament for decades to come. These British owners didn't visit their property holdings, nor did they care much about the occupants other than to demand that they pay an extortionate amount of rent. Compared to other absentee landlords, the Tottenhams had the reputation of being benevolent, almost mildly sympathetic to the Irish people, but never enough to enlist in their cause for independence. In County Wexford, the Tottenhams would eventually control as much as twenty thousand acres. They were the beneficiaries of laws in Dunganstown that stripped the Kennedys and many other Catholics of their holdings and kept them as tenant farmers. The Kennedy family lived in a farmhouse built of stone and covered on the inside and out with lime mortar, certainly better accommodations than the shanty cabins housing landless laborers and fishermen. They paid their rents to Colonel Charles George Tottenham, but bitterly despised it. For the Kennedys and their neighbors, the penal laws denied them basic human justice and the most fundamental dignities, even regarding their children's future. In Dunganstown, for example, a retired sailor named Fitzpatrick, disabled from scurvy contracted while at sea, was seized from the school where he taught local children. He was tortured by the military for violating the penal laws against educating Catholics. It was a lesson meant for all.

This British suppression, often sadistically administered, bred uncontrollable resentment and ultimately more violence. By 1798, the revolutions in America and France had inspired many Irishmen to dream once again of their own independence, to throw off the yoke of English rule. Rebel priests such as Father John Murphy and other men of the cloth—despite the indifference of Rome or the tepid direction of their church superiors—became leaders in this growing movement. Some fought to their deaths to establish an Irish republic. The most violent confrontations occurred in County Wexford and likely included members of Patrick Kennedy's family. "All of the Kennedys were very republican—the whole family," explains Thomas Grennan, a cousin who lives in the River Barrow valley and has studied the family's history extensively. "It was very likely that they were involved in the '98 uprising."

They were heady days at first. The United Irishmen, a nationwide band of rebels led by Wolfe Tone, openly resisted the British overlords, who reacted by flogging and torturing the Irish. Contemporary historians—attempting to sift fact from partisan myth—would later underscore that many United Irishmen were Protestants and not just Catholics. In Wexford, young rebels, sometimes called "Croppies" for their closely cut hair, managed to win a victory against the local militia from North Cork, then set another town ablaze before setting up a main camp at Vinegar Hill in Wexford County. The madness inspired by years of suppression erupted in a violent fury. At a farmhouse in a place called Scullabogue, some two hundred mostly Protestant men, women and children were set on fire, shot or piked to death—apparently in retaliation for a bitter loss by the rebels at New Ross.

SEVERAL KENNEDY relatives, friends and neighbors took up arms in the Rising of '98, historians say; very likely they were part of the "Boys of Wexford" who, as the famous folk song would recall, "fought with heart and hand" to break the British grip over their lands. At the battle of New Ross, two uncles of Patrick Kennedy fought, and one was struck by bullets. The second uncle left the battle scene with his wounded brother and dragged him home to the safety of their family farm in Dunganstown. Other accounts say that one of President Kennedy's relatives died in the crushing defeat at Vinegar Hill. The rebels' dead bodies were so mutilated that many were buried in a mass grave. Aware of the strong links between rebellion and religion in Ireland, the English troops burned some thirty-three Catholic chapels, including the small altar in Dunganstown.

Some thirty thousand Irish men and women lost their lives in the '98 rebellion. The short-lived but bloody conflict caused lasting repercussions. Some Irish decided to emigrate to America, a land where they believed they would be free to practice their religion, only to be met by nativist hostility. In Boston, for example, Congressman Harrison Gray Otis, a Federalist, complained that he did "not wish to invite hoards of wild

Irishmen, nor the turbulent and disorderly of all parts of the world, to come here with a view to disturb our tranquility, after having succeeded in the overthrow of their own governments." The fear of insurgent immigrants arriving on American shores led to the passage of the Alien and Sedition Acts of 1798, which attempted to restrict naturalization and blunt the political impact of these newcomers. But for the Irish who stayed, the failed rebellion doomed them to several more decades of oppression and control by the British. The Kennedys of Dunganstown had lost nearly everything except, as their famous descendant later noted, their sense of liberty and their religious faith.

Chapter Three

The Starvation

"Let any Englishman put himself in the
position of an Irish peasant, and ask himself whether, if the case were his own, the
landed property of the country would have
any sacredness to his feelings."

—JOHN STUART MILL

NO RECORDS EXIST of Patrick Kennedy's birth and baptism in 1823.
With the stifling system of penal laws still in effect, priests in Wexford
secretly performed sacraments throughout the county. But no official documents could be kept by clergymen without endangering their own lives
and their parishioners' well-being. The arrival of Irish infants such as
Patrick Kennedy, the third son of a poor tenant farmer, simply didn't seem
to matter.

Even when the penal laws began to be repealed, starting in 1829 with
the Catholic Emancipation, life in Dunganstown for the Kennedys barely
improved. Six generations of oppression had taken their toll. Nearly all the
farmland in Wexford was owned by non-Irish property holders; the
Catholic Church and clergy were still harassed by authorities, and most
local residents, including the Kennedys' neighbors, were illiterate. Not
much is known about Patrick Kennedy's father, James, except that he inherited the right to run the farm from his father, John, and that he married a
woman named Maria, who died, according to the headstones in the local
Whitechurch graveyard, on February 16, 1835—when young Patrick was
twelve years old. As Patrick grew older, he likely received a meager education by attending one of the "hedge schools," usually conducted in a damp
ditch beside the roadway.

By the time Patrick reached adulthood, both his parents were apparently dead and the family homestead was controlled by Patrick's older brother. Local land tax records show the lessee to be John Kennedy, more than a dozen years Patrick's senior, who was already married and the father of four children. Under these circumstances, the tiny family house in Dunganstown was surely cramped. Relatives say it's likely that Patrick spent some nights out in the loft of their barn with the horses and pigs.

In mid-nineteenth-century Ireland, families produced an average of six children; some died as infants, others were encouraged to emigrate as they became adults. Commonly, the eldest son inherited whatever claims existed to the family's farm, and a sufficient dowry was accumulated for one daughter to marry. Because of the life-threatening scarcity of food and resources, the rest of the children, such as third son Patrick Kennedy, usually were expected to leave for the New World. Emigration happened to such an extent that, as historian Ruth Ann M. Harris later commented, "Children became another of Ireland's exports." Not much is known about Patrick's sister, Mary, except that at a young age she married a man named James Molloy and presented the world with a daughter, Maria, in 1838. Patrick's other brother, James, remained unmarried until his mid-thirties. He became the tenant of another nearby farm, run cooperatively with the family's homestead farm. It was leased under the name of Patrick Kennedy for reasons that aren't clear. Perhaps, as some family relatives speculate, James Kennedy faced some sort of financial difficulty or legal trouble, or perhaps Patrick planned to run the farm on his own someday. But this second farm eventually became the home of James Kennedy, who married and raised his own family. His two oldest daughters later made their way to America, but the rest of his children stayed.

Patrick's life as a farmer in Dunganstown consisted mainly of cutting and tying bundles of grain by hand, and planting and tilling potatoes for his family's own consumption. This routine varied only when he ventured into New Ross with supplies of barley, and when the family attended Sunday Mass about a mile away. Life was often sheer drudgery for tenant farmers like Patrick. When they could, local townspeople gathered for regular evenings of music and dance—called a *ceilidhe* in Gaelic—where young people mingled and flirted, and the older ones engaged in storytelling by the fire. On long summer evenings, the men competed in great hurling matches, a passion among the Irish. The young women arrived at gathering places, located at every major crossroad, where dancing, music and skittles filled the air with laughter. One of the liveliest places was called The Hand, less than a mile from the Kennedy farm. "Romances made and broken there are still talked about in the district," Irish chronicler Tim Pat Coogan later explained. Yet, with each passing day in Ireland, the prospects for happiness dimmed.

Rebellion, once again, was in the air. Daniel O'Connell, Dublin's Lord Mayor, often known as The Liberator, slowly managed to achieve the first genuine political freedoms in centuries for Irish Catholics. Driven by a deep faith in democracy and nonviolent agitation, O'Connell galvanized the Irish to his cause. His followers organized huge but well-behaved rallies at what O'Connell called his "Monster Meetings." One of these gatherings attracted many thousands of people on the royal Hill of Tara, north of Dublin, the venerated place where, legend holds, the earliest Irish kings once ruled. The Liberator seemed destined to transform Ireland into a free republic. Unfortunately, O'Connell died in 1847, before his dream could be realized. His cause was taken up by a more confrontational group, known as Young Irelanders, who had far less success.

They gave voice to the Irish unrest coming from the farmlands. On "Gale Day," the Kennedys and other tenant farmers were expected to pay their British landlords ever-higher rents without any chance of ownership. When tenants were unable to keep up with these payments, many were evicted and thrown into poverty, a situation that lead to the murders of several British property owners. A commission investigating these killings concluded that "the motive for all was the wild justice of revenge" by ousted farmers against their landlords. But a wary government in England perceived this violence as a sign of political rebellion against which immediate steps had to be taken. The object of British wrath became the Young Irelanders, who refused the pledge against violence or armed rebellion that O'Connell and his "Old Ireland" group had made. The Young Irelanders were led by William Smith O'Brien, a Protestant patriot who claimed to be a direct descendent of Brian Boru; Thomas Francis Meagher, a Catholic son of Waterford's mayor, who preached a fiery call for armed rebellion; and John Mitchel, an inspirational writer for the *Nation,* a pro-independence publication. In 1848, on hearing news of a popular uprising against France's king, the Young Irelanders burned with desire for independence on their own native soil. Bonfires were lit in Wexford, and a banner calling for freedom waved in Waterford. Word of such excitement undoubtedly reached Patrick Kennedy's ears outside New Ross.

Unlike the revered Daniel O'Connell, the Young Irelanders didn't enjoy the clergy's support. Pope Pius IX specifically instructed the Irish priests to avoid political ties "and in no way to mix themselves up with worldly affairs." The British rushed in troops to quell whatever chance of rebellion might exist and arrested the three Young Irelanders leaders, forcing them to leave the country like "wild geese," as they had become known. Meagher was shipped to Australia, but then found his way to America, where he became the distinguished leader of an Irish Brigade fighting for the Union during the Civil War. Mitchel went to New England, where he later wrote about the Catholic bigotry of the Know-Nothing Party and the tar-and-feathering of a Jesuit priest in Maine. William Smith O'Brien tried to rally support for rebellion in Wexford and other southern counties, but he failed in this region, which still remembered the cruelty of the British sword· in '98.

In Dunganstown, Patrick Kennedy, upset about his family's fate under the control of British landlords, was most likely sympathetic to calls for rebellion, though there's no evidence that he took part in political activity. By 1848, whatever hope existed for Irish independence had faded with O'Connell's death and the crushed dreams of the Young Irelanders. Yet most devastating of all was the insidious arrival of a potato blight and, accompanying it, starvation.

BARLEY AND MALT were the grains by which the Kennedys paid the rent, but potatoes were the daily staple of their diet, the staff of life for untold thousands in Wexford and throughout Ireland. Potatoes had been introduced to the nation by Sir Walter Raleigh, who brought the vegetable back with him after discovering its use by natives in the New World. Potatoes were consumed at nearly every meal. Breakfast might consist of potatoes with milk; and dinner, potatoes with perhaps some goose or mutton. In Wexford before the famine, a cartload of potatoes cost only a shilling, making the foodstuff affordable to even the most modest homesteaders. Potatoes became central to Ireland's agrarian economy, employing thousands. When the blight came, a telltale spot on the leaf of the potato plant formed a white moldy substance that crept into the potato buried in the soil. Ripe edible spuds turned into rotten pulp encased in black. Carried by wind, rain and insects, the mold spores soon infected entire crops. Large expanses of healthy farmland turned into a putrid mess. No one knew what caused it—frost, summer thunderstorms, even the moon were suggested as culprits—though the killer was later identified as a fungus called *phytophthora infestans.*

Death and illness soon consumed the countryside. In Dungarvan, some thirty miles down the coastline, starvation and extreme poverty left many dead, their bodies scattered on the ground or in their homes, sometimes pulled apart by starving dogs. Within a few years, the population of Dunganstown sank by 21 percent. Similarly, in the parish where the

Kennedys lived, the number of baptisms plummeted, a sad testament to the preponderance of death and lack of births. In the 1830s, baptisms averaged about 115 a year, records show, and went up to 133 in the early 1840s. But as the famine took hold, baptisms in the parish dropped to around 70 in the 1850s and even lower, about 47 a year, during the 1860s, the same records show.

"Deaths from famine had been numerous . . . caused by the utter want of food," reported the *Wexford Independent* in January 1847. The next month, a Board of Works inspector for County Wexford wrote in his journal that farmers on plots of land the size that the Kennedys tended were "very badly off," and some were forced to leave their farms and seek employment with public works projects to avoid starvation. By February 1847, more than twenty thousand people in Wexford relied on public works to earn their daily bread. The local curate for the region, including the Kennedys' hometown, estimated that in his district there were "2,500 human beings without a morsel to put in their mouths unless they obtain[ed] from the public works." The number of paupers in the New Ross workhouse, a place known for its hellish conditions, rose to 1,006, including women and children; because most suffered from famine-related disease, the death toll reached eighty-two in one week. Suffering in Wexford became widespread and prompted one writer in the *Independent* to observe:

> The numbers of unfortunate creatures begging relief are surprising and many a dishevelled form, the emaciated face, the tottering step which tells a tale of poverty, misery and hunger indescribable by words, with cheeks like scorched leather, eyes sunken and a voice sounding as if from a tomb, beseech you, in accents almost inaudible from weakness, for relief for God's sake.

Famine caused great desperation throughout Wexford. Shocked and numbed by so many destitute people, so many starving in the streets, one contemporary physician described the agonizing process of watching a human die from starvation—first the headaches, bloody noses and pain in the limbs; then the "delirium and raving" convulsions of the face muscles; and finally, "the entire body changed to a deep livid or black colour as if scorched by gun-powder." With the rotting of the potato crops, and constant searching for anything to eat, some suggested a halt to malting in Wexford—a move that would still further reduce the meager income the Kennedys made from barley. With typhus, cholera and other diseases running rampant, New Ross authorities considered closing off the bridge across the Barrow to stave off the spread of illnesses from neighboring County Kilkenney. Undoubtedly, illness weighed heavily on Patrick Kennedy's thinking about the future, perhaps as much as famine itself.

The Famine posed a crushing blow to the Kennedys, as it did to many Irish farmers, and changed the composition of their family forever. No longer would all their children remain on the farm, succeeding one generation after the next. Nor would their prayers for freedom be answered any time soon. Once the Kennedys, some of whom fought with the Boys of Wexford in 1798, had dreamed of Irish independence and political and social equality for Catholics. Those days were now gone, effectively starved to death. Some histories suggest that the Kennedys in Dunganstown were more prosperous than most dirt-poor tenant farmers and that their region of Ireland was not much affected by the Famine. However, local newspaper accounts chronicling the Famine's devastating impact in Wexford, as well as a review of records in Ireland that document the Kennedy family's meager finances, suggest otherwise. In her well-documented history of the famine years in County Wexford, Irish historian Anna Kinsella wrote: "The spirit of a people, which forty years earlier had set up the Wexford Republic, was broken. The county was destitute and depopulated. Here, as elsewhere in Ireland, death and emigration had taken its toll."

At age twenty-six, Patrick Kennedy had few options before him. Whether for reasons of starvation or illness or because he knew that a third-born son had virtually no hope of running his family's small, failing farm—nor any other parcel of land for that matter—Kennedy decided to leave. Ireland could no longer sustain his hopes for the future. His good friend at Cherry Bros. Brewery in New Ross, Patrick Barron, who taught Kennedy the skills of coopering, had come to that conclusion months earlier and left on a ship bound for America. In October 1848, in love with Barron's cousin and with a plan to wed, Patrick Kennedy decided to follow.

Chapter Four

American Wake

"They are going, going, going and we cannot bid them stay,
Their fields are now the stranger's, where
the stranger's cattle stray."

—ETHNA CARBERY,
"THE PASSING OF THE GAEL"

ON THE NIGHT BEFORE Patrick Kennedy's departure, his family and friends likely held an "American wake" for him at the family homestead in Dunganstown to wish him farewell.

Wakes for the dead were all too plentiful in Ireland during the Famine, so much so that coffins were in short supply. Emaciated corpses were often buried in unmarked graves or, in some cases, with makeshift wooden burial boxes with hinges on the bottom for multiple use. Traditionally, Irish wakes, rooted in old pagan customs, were frolicking affairs, the shock of death defied by the living with acts of drunkenness and sex. But the so-called "American wakes" were different. The dearly departed were very much alive—emigrants leaving behind the only life they had ever known and being kissed and hugged goodbye by family and friends who would stay behind. These wakes were for those trying to avoid the death and destruction wrought by Ireland's famine. Despite this understandable attempt at self-preservation, there was much to mourn. No longer would Patrick Kennedy work with his two brothers in the fields, tending the crops and feeding the cattle together, nor would he share another laugh or meal with them. His departure, and the departures of all those who fled the Famine, carried the implicit message that Ireland was a dying nation, and that those left behind were the doomed—too old or too young to start a new life in America.

As part of this wake, Patrick Kennedy would seek the emigrant's blessing from his local priest, Father Michael Mitten, whose parish's thatched-roof chapel had burned down in the '98 rebellion. At the quay on his day of departure, Patrick stood dressed in warm clothes and waited with a crowd of emigrants for their ship to begin boarding. It is likely that he heard the emigrant's prayer repeated by his loved ones: *Go dtuga Dia slan sibh,* they'd wish in Gaelic. The literal translation, "May God bring you safely," only hinted at the true danger and uncertainty of crossing the Atlantic. In leaving his homeland, they were probably the last words Patrick Kennedy heard. *Go dtuga Dia slan sibh.*

NO ONE IS QUITE SURE of Patrick Kennedy's exact route from Ireland. Some early Kennedy histories suggest that Patrick left New Ross directly for Boston (a claim repeated by the White House press corps during JFK's 1963 visit); but the manifest for the ship that arrived in Boston in April 1849 with Patrick Kennedy aboard shows he left from Liverpool, England. Interviews with Kennedy relatives, and more recent accounts by Irish historians, indicate that Kennedy took the more complicated route to America, one that mirrored the common experience of many other poor tenant farmers from Ireland.

Nearly six months passed from the time Patrick Kennedy left Irish soil to the day he set foot in Boston. Though some suggest he departed from Cobh, the port of County Cork frequently used by emigrants, more convincing evidence suggests he left from New Ross, closer to his family's farm, where he knew the condition and cost of ships entering this harbor. Although he might have hopped aboard a barge to nearby Waterford before traveling across the Irish Sea to Liverpool, it appears more likely that Patrick went directly to England on a cross-channel boat, one of many using New Ross as a home port. The flow of emigrants from New Ross was nearly as great as it was from Dublin and nearby Wexford Town. Watching their young people leave in such droves caused remorse and bitterness among the Irish. "The landlords of Ireland, taken as a body, have, in their mad career of spoilation and oppression, left the people without confidence or hope," editorialized the *Wexford Independent.* "They are, therefore, flying from the land, even to commit themselves to chance upon other shores." If Patrick Kennedy thought he was leaving a land of misery, he soon learned that even tougher days lay ahead.

The ten-shilling ride to Liverpool could be brutal. In the cold, snappish winds of October 1848, hundreds of Irish emigrants—sometimes as many as a thousand—were packed into the upper deck of these transport ships, their main mission being to carry produce to England. One of the bitterest ironies of the Famine was that these ships bearing the masses of Irish fleeing starvation also carried tons of foodstuffs from Ireland—sacks of wheat and oats, firkins of butter, bales of bacon, boxes of eggs, as well as dozens of live lambs, cattle and pigs—more than enough to feed the native Irish population and relieve their suffering. Ireland was the breadbasket for Great Britain, and the empire's needs were not to be denied. In just one month, from late May to early June 1847, 163 tons of wheat, 570 shiploads of oatmeal, 481 sacks of flour and a cornucopia of other produce arrived in Liverpool on these ships.

On these trips, the Irish were "unwanted produce," extra money to be earned by the steamer companies. They remained in a standing-room-only section, exposed to the elements for from thirty to thirty-six hours, yet pigs and other livestock were sheltered on the decks below. The Irish passengers were often seasick, stuffed together so tightly that they could barely reach the sides of the boat to vomit. Official complaints about the conditions on these Liverpool steamers went unheeded, and the passengers were in no position to seek redress. Upon arriving in Liverpool, the Irish often waited weeks, sometimes months, for passage to America. Huddled in decrepit lodging houses, they became the targets of swindlers intent on stealing their victims' last sums of money; sometimes the emigrants resorted to begging on the streets. In the British House of Lords, a petition from Liverpool complained that, out of the some 150,000 destitute Irish deposited in the city, only 40,000 had moved on to the New World; the rest were lingering on their streets, ridden with crime, poverty and disease.

In this sea of misery, young Patrick Kennedy roamed the neighborhoods of Liverpool, living by his wits, until he could secure passage to Boston. More than a million Irish emigrated during the Famine years. Although many Irish headed for America, others took ships to Quebec, often with calamitous results. Cramped inside windowless decks, with little food and almost non-existent hygiene, passengers quickly fell victim to rampant disease and death. On the *Virginius,* for instance, 158 of its 476 passengers on the voyage from Liverpool to Quebec died during its nine weeks at sea. Overall, an estimated eight to nine thousand people died en route to America, and many more on the way to Canada. Nevertheless, the business of transporting human cargo became quite competitive. In Boston, the Shawmut Bank of Boston negotiated with Sir Samuel Cunard to make the Massachusetts port city into the terminus for his Liverpool-based fleet of packet ships. By 1840, the first ships were crossing the Atlantic, offering a fare of twenty dollars.

On the morning of March 20, 1849, Patrick Kennedy stepped onto the *Washington Irving,* a nine-hundred-ton packet ship, after buying his ticket at the offices of Train & Co.'s on Waterloo Road in Liverpool. Nearly six months had passed since he left Dunganstown. It was common for Irish emigrants, many of whom still spoke Gaelic, to be mislead or hoodwinked by unscrupulous passenger ship companies. Kennedy couldn't have known much about the operators of this ship. "Important to Emigrants!" proclaimed the company's advertisement, calling itself "the only established line" between Boston and Liverpool. The same ad, however, disclosed that the previous operator of this line, Messrs. Harden & Co., had "ceased" running their agency on January 1, three months earlier, for unknown reasons.

Day and night, the *Washington Irving*'s sails remained up, fully extended by the ocean breezes, as was the custom for American packet ships. The company and its captain, Daniel P. Upton, wanted to complete their voyage to Boston as quickly as possible, in about thirty-one days. On board were scores of passengers, but their experiences vastly differed. Those in cabin class—British or Scottish passengers for whom the company's "personal attention" was undoubtedly directed—dined in the ship's saloon, white linen, fine china and silvery cutlery adorning the tables. In steerage, located in the crowded, airless bowels of the boat, Irish emigrants were squeezed in like the animals accompanying them on their voyage. At best, an emigrant might get to eat a salt herring, a piece of moldy cheese and a stale biscuit. On the voyage carrying Patrick Kennedy, records show that one woman gave birth to a child. Another forty-year-old woman died and was buried at sea. The conditions on Kennedy's voyage are not clear from these records, but the following year, Vere Foster, an Irishman who spent most of his life abroad, complained bitterly about the horrendous treatment of Irish emigrants he had witnessed on the *Washington Irving*. When he gathered 128 signatures from passengers attesting to the abuse from the ship's crew, his plea drew attention from the press and the British government.

SQUALID CONDITIONS on these vessels—known as "coffin ships," from which dozens of dead bodies were thrown into the ocean like refuse—underlined for the world the awful consequences of England's callous indifference to its Irish subjects. No longer were the British guilty of merely suppressing a people, the quelling of insurgents seeking independence. Increasingly, in the eyes of their contemporaries and the judgment of history, the British policy toward Ireland amounted to genocide by starvation—an indictment still strongly contested today.

At the outset of the potato blight, British Prime Minister Robert Peel thought Irish farmers like the Kennedys might be exaggerating their plight and appointed a government commission to study the worsening crisis. To his credit, Peel allowed the shipment of Indian corn from America and set up a system of public works so the Irish might be able to pay for their food. But the crisis became deadly when Prime Minister John Russell took over the British government in June 1846. Russell and Charles Trevelyan, England's head of the treasury, both believed the Irish should not be subsidized by the British coffers, and that free-market forces would eventually straighten the economy's course without their intervention. Sharing many prejudices, both men feared government handouts would only make the Irish lazy and dependent. As soon as Russell took office, Trevelyan cancelled a shipment of Indian corn bound for Ireland. In closing down the public works program, the British effectively stole the life raft from a drowning citizenry. "These things should be stopped now, or you run the risk of paralyzing all private enterprise and having this country on you for an indefinite number of years," lectured Trevelyan. Whatever legal obligations England had to its Irish subjects were ignored.

The *Times* (London), after first rejoicing that the Irish had "gone with a vengeance" to the New World, realized the horrors wrought by the Famine and began criticizing the government's monstrous response to the death toll. Though the newspaper carried its fair share of vitriol against the Irish, its opinion makers still could not justify in their Victorian hearts the visions of coffins ships and mass starvation reported by its correspondents. In an editorial in September 1847, the *Times* described the vastness of the Irish tragedy:

> More than a hundred thousand souls flying from the very midst of the calamity into insufficient vessels, scrambling for a footing on a deck and a berth in a hold, committing themselves to these worse than prisons, while their frames were wasted with ill-fare and their blood infected with disease, fighting for months of unutterable wretchedness against the elements without and pestilence within, giving almost hourly victims to the deep, landing at length onshore already terrified and diseased, consigned to encampments of the dying and of the dead, spreading death wherever they roam, and having no other prospect before them than a long continuance of these horrors.

TALES OF EXTRAORDINARY DESPERATION—such as the *Times*'s account of a starving man extracting the heart and liver of a shipwrecked human body "that was the maddening feast on which he regaled himself and his perishing family"—only perpetuated the image of the Irish as something subhuman.

"It will be difficult for most of our readers to feel near akin with a class which at best wallows in pigsties and hugs the most brutish degradation," sniffed the *Times* in one editorial. The distrust and racism toward the Irish, so rampant in British public opinion, were implicit in the *Times*'s warning about their mass emigration to the United States. "If this [exodus] goes on, as it is likely to go on . . . the United States will become very Irish. . . . So an Ireland there will still be, but on a colossal scale, and in a new world. We shall only have pushed the Celt westwards. Then, no longer cooped up between the Liffey and the Shannon, he will spread from New York to San Francisco, and keep up the ancient feud at an unforeseen advantage."

Historians still debate whether Britain's intent was genocidal or simply misguided, though for the Irish, the intent of Lord Russell and his Whig government in denying an adequate food supply for the Irish poor couldn't have been clearer. As one writer observed in the *Galway Mercury*, "Almost the entire rural population . . . believe that the Government are determined to systematically put to death one half of the people." Before the Famine, Ireland had 9 million people and was one of Europe's most densely populated nations; but as starvation, illness and massive emigration claimed an entire generation, the population eventually dwindled to 2.8 million, the only nation in Europe during that period to see a decline. "Can we wonder if the Irish people believe—and believe it they do—that the lives of those who perished, and who will perish, have been sacrificed by a deliberate compact to the gains of English merchants," the *Dublin University Magazine* asked in April 1847. "Britain is now branded as the only civilized nation which would permit her subjects to perish of famine, without making a national effort to supply them with food." Watching from America as these events unfolded, New York's Roman Catholic Bishop John Hughes railed against the immorality of the British government for employing "famine as their most effectual instrument and ally in the work of subjugation." In a long lecture in 1847 about the causes of the Irish famine, Hughes recited a history of Irish troubles at the hands of the British, pointing to the long-running penal laws that outlawed generations because of their Catholicism. The New York bishop expressed outrage at Lord Russell's determination not to provide emergency food supplies to Ireland's starving masses. In particular, he took issue with the suggestion that the famine was God's retribution against the Irish people for their perceived sins. "It has attracted the attention of the whole world, and yet they call it God's famine, No! no!" Hughes thundered. "God's famine is known by the general scarcity of food. There has been no scarcity of food in Ireland, either the present, or the past year, except in one species of vegetable." Instead, Hughes

charged that England "multiplies deposits of idle money in the banks on
one side of that channel, and multiplies dead and coffinless bodies in the
cabins, and along the highways, on the other." .

What had happened could not be forgotten. The historic oppression of
their religion, the mass starvation of people and their flight from their own
homeland became ingrained in the works and letters of Irish Catholics on
both sides of the Atlantic Ocean—what James Joyce described as a "bowl
of bitter tears." In his 1963 trip to Ireland, President Kennedy repeated
Joyce's description and imagined the conflicting emotions for immigrants,
including his great-grandfather, Patrick Kennedy, in making such a journey.
"They came to our shores in a mixture of hope and agony," explained JFK.
"They left behind hearts, fields and a nation yearning to be free."

It is impossible to fathom what lingered in the heart and mind of Patrick
Kennedy as he left Ireland. Generations later, the lessons out of Ireland were
still recalled by his family and became part of their lore. "Political passion
came naturally to a deeply religious race for whom the distinction between
political and religious martyrdom had blurred during eight hundred years of
British occupation," Robert F. Kennedy Jr. observed near the millenium's
end. "From their arrival in America, the Irish took to politics as starving men
to food; stifled for centuries, as they were by rules that forbade them from
participating in the political destiny of their nation." Patrick Kennedy's own
destiny in America would be both tragic and sweet, though his hardships
would never end.

AFTER A MONTH on the ocean, the packet ship carrying Patrick Kennedy
and hundreds of other Irish immigrants neared Boston's harbor. The brisk
April air in New England still held the harshness of winter. The barren trees
and grassy hillsides were dormant and gray. After being slowly pulled into
the wharf, the ship allowed its cabin-class passengers to walk out first onto
the docks before unloading the rest of its human cargo. Several passengers,
sick and emaciated from the journey, were likely stopped and quarantined.
Inspectors found the young man from New Ross healthy enough to enter.
Several passengers from Ireland told the port authorities that they possessed
the needed skills for such jobs as mason, blacksmith, painter, butcher, "rope-
maker" and "engineer." All forty-nine women, in a way that belied their
status, were listed as "servants." When asked, Kennedy stated his occupation
as "labourer"—the most common, least skilled and lowest-paid job possible
for the Irish.

Kennedy biographies often claim that Patrick Kennedy and Bridget
Murphy met aboard their Boston-bound ship and fell in love during the

voyage. This romantic notion was part of the family legend which JFK's aunt and family historian, Loretta Connelly, helped perpetuate when speaking to interviewers. But the reality was probably a bit more complicated. There are no indications that Bridget Murphy sailed on the same ship as Patrick Kennedy. The manifest filed by the ship's captain spells out Kennedy's complete name, but not hers. The passenger list also carried the surnames of two young female passengers called "Barron," but their ages were not the same as Bridget's. More probable, say relatives in Ireland and local historians, the couple met in County Wexford and carefully planned their migration to Boston with the intent of marrying soon after they arrived. "It is unlikely that he married his best friend's cousin in six months (after arriving in Boston)," explains Patrick Grennan, the cousin who today operates the family's farm in Dunganstown. "It's more likely [Barron] introduced Patrick to his cousin before he left for Boston."

Maybe at a social at the crossroads near the Kennedy farm, or perhaps one day at Cherry Bros. Brewery while with his friend Patrick Barron, Patrick Kennedy met Barron's cousin, Bridget Murphy, and soon began courting her. By the mid-1840s, both Patrick and Bridget, a year younger, were of the age when young people thought of getting married and starting families of their own. Bridget grew up on a farm about eight miles southeast of the Kennedy home, near an area called Gusserane, where the Barron family maintained a farm. Patrick could read and write, but Bridget could only read. Between the Barron place and the Kennedy Homestead lay Sliabh Coillte, a densely wooded hillside, not easily traversed, so it is likely that the lovers met at some formal event. In a similar way, Bridget's own mother, Mary Barron, met her future husband, Philip Murphy, at a local fair while selling pigs. The Famine, however, dictated that nothing would be normal for this generation of Irish young people. And so the courtship of Bridget and Patrick Kennedy didn't come to fruition until they reached Boston.

For most Irish immigrants, walking down the gangplank to the dirty, crowded docks at Noddle's Island provided the first vista of the New World. These so-called greenhorns found work as carpenters, laborers and stevedores, many of them with the Cunard Line, the shipping company building piers and warehouses on this largest of five islands in Boston's harbor. Many immigrants from Irish farms, unaccustomed to America's language and customs, were duped by con artists or exploited in backbreaking jobs by American employers who paid one dollar for a fourteen-hour workday. The Famine created a new kind of immigrant, different from those who sought religious freedom or economic opportunity, the traditional magnet for American immigration. The waves of Irish flooding the ports of Boston, New York and other North American cities became a new kind of refugee, a generation of "wild geese," forced to flee their homes against their will. As historian Kerby Miller pointed out, the Irish farmers—many of whom spoke Gaelic as their primary tongue—were unprepared for the rigors of New England life, and felt themselves to be "homesick, involuntary exiles." Alone, desperate for work, vulnerable and constantly searching for "missing friends" and relatives, the Irish congregated in the ghettos of Boston. To some degree, their clannishness reflected a sense of loss, the feeling of being unfairly pushed out of their homeland by circumstances they couldn't control, as well as the desire to remain with those like themselves. Emigrants from Ireland often felt guilty about the breakup of their families—the determination of who would go to America and who would stay in the starvation-stricken land. Many in America contributed money and actively engaged in the political push for a free and independent Ireland, as if somehow trying to rectify the root causes for their departure. To other Americans, this Irish clannishness became a defining trait.

In East Boston, Patrick Kennedy found shelter in a cheap boardinghouse near the terminus where the steam ferry carried people across the harbor for two-cent fares. Probably with Barron's help, Patrick Kennedy soon began work as a cooper at Daniel Francis's cooperage and brass foundry on Sumner Street on Noddle's Island, which made mostly beer, water barrels and some ship castings. Considerable skills were needed to make a barrel airtight, and Kennedy's training in Ireland served him well. Working twelve-hour days, seven days a week, Kennedy soon managed to earn enough to proceed with his plans of marrying Bridget.

On September 26, 1849, five months after arriving in America, Patrick Kennedy took the ferry to the mainland with his fiancée, Bridget Murphy, and they were married in the Cathedral of the Holy Cross, the grandest Catholic church in Boston. There wasn't a crowd of friends and family. Most of them still lived in Ireland. Besides the newlyweds, the only two attending the ceremony were Bridget's cousin, Patrick Barron, and another friend, Ann McGowan. The nuptial Mass was performed by a young serious-minded priest named John L. Williams, who later became bishop of Boston's diocese.

After their marriage, the Kennedys set up home on Sumner Street, not far from the shipyard where the *Washington Irving* had been built. Life in Boston for the young couple wasn't much better than it had been in impoverished New Ross. Patrick worked many hours at the cooperage, and Bridget earned extra money in various menial jobs. Dutifully, they started a family, the children arriving in rapid succession. As the church instructed, marital relations were a necessary obligation, not necessarily a means for pleasure or joy. A Catholic guide of the time advised wives to engage in sex with their husbands in a quick and purposeful way so as "to lessen its keenness, destroy its power, and to render it disgusting." The couple's first child, a daughter they named Mary, was born in 1851; the next year, another girl, Johanna, arrived. Their first son, John—named in honor of Patrick's oldest brother—was born in early 1854, and a third daughter, Margaret, arrived in July 1855.

By that summer, the immigrants' dream of Patrick and Bridget Kennedy appeared to be coming true. To survive the journey out of Ireland, find work in Boston and support a brood of children must have been an accomplishment of considerable pride to both parents. But two months later, their eighteen-month-old son, John Kennedy, died of cholera. This highly infectious disease struck many immigrant children living in the vermin-infested confines of East Boston. In the city, Irish Catholic children suffered by far the highest rate of illness and death. Once one child was infected, parents feared that all their children would die.

There was not another child for Bridget and Patrick until nearly three years later. On January 14, 1858, Patrick Joseph Kennedy was born at home. The family now lived on Liverpool Street, a marked improvement from their tiny tenement apartment. They called the baby boy P. J. to distinguish him from his namesake father. The family baptized the new infant at the Church of the Most Holy Redeemer in East Boston, the religious and social center for Irish immigrants in their community. Patrick Kennedy, almost thirty-five years old, wrote to his family in Dunganstown to let them know his good news.

Before the end of 1858, however, Patrick's vibrant strength—the same quality that had survived the long journey to America—suddenly fell apart, weakened by a raging fever and nausea. Illness couldn't have come at a worse time. That same year, Boston's economy was deteriorating, causing wide-scale unemployment that may have eliminated Patrick's job as a cooper. One indicator of the Kennedys' declining fortunes was the assessor's report for Ward Two in East Boston showing that the family income, reported as $300 in 1852, had dropped in 1856 to only $100. In a cruel twist, the American dream of greater opportunity and more prosperity eluded Patrick Kennedy. With a wife and four young children, Patrick couldn't afford to be sick. He had no steady job and little money. Kennedy had somehow contracted cholera, the same disease that took his first son's life and claimed hundreds of others in East Boston. Illness gripped his body, turning his skin dark and clammy. There would be no escape, no way out from this fate. Virtually penniless, the immigrant from Dunganstown died on November 22, 1858—a date that would bring somber resonance in the years to come.

Less than a decade after arriving in America, Patrick Kennedy's journey had come to a heartbreaking end, boding ominously for his family's future. The average Irishman who immigrated to America survived only fourteen years after arrival. Patrick died even sooner—nine years after he came ashore. Most immigrant Irish families suffering these hardships never recovered. They became another anonymous statistic in Boston's annual census of the dead. As winter descended in 1858, there was little reason to believe that widow Bridget Kennedy and her destitute children, alone in the New World, wouldn't suffer the same fate.

Chapter Five

Brahmins and Bigotry

FOR CHILDREN of Irish Catholic immigrants, the Boston City Census Report in the 1850s ensured that bigotry began at birth. Although these infants were born in the United States, the official tally didn't record them as real Americans. The Kennedy children, P. J. Kennedy and his older siblings, Mary, Joanna and Margaret, were officially classified as "foreigners"—in effect, strangers in their own land.

Their "outsider" status was spelled out in bureaucratic language: "*Although many of them were born in this country, yet, subject as they are to the control, instruction and associations of their parents, they properly belong to, and are under the influence of the foreign element,*" reported the 1855 Boston census. That "foreign element" included the Kennedys and many of their friends and neighbors. Foreigners in Boston—especially those landing from Ireland—soared 194 percent in the five years after 1850, the census determined, accounting for nearly all the city's growth in population. Ward Two, where the Kennedys lived in East Boston, had the biggest jump of all. To those in power, the political implications were clear. "This fact gives evidence of an awakened interest on the part of those born in foreign countries to avail themselves of the elective franchise," the census report noted, with bureaucratic understatement. For politics—this "elective franchise"—would help pull the Kennedys out of their poverty.

AS A WIDOW with four young children, Bridget Kennedy and her fractured family endured what must have been insurmountable hardships. The census recorded that the Kennedys took in two boarders—a common method for staying afloat financially—even before Patrick Kennedy's death. To keep her family from starving, Bridget cleaned for long hours as a maid, an occupation so often filled by Irish Catholic women that the jobs were known derisively as "bridgets" or "biddys." Maids were virtually invisible, stuck in the lowliest position, watching a life to which they could merely aspire and observe with envy. Yet even these jobs were difficult to get for the Irish. Newspaper ads for maids usually sought out only "Americans" or "Protestant foreigners." As was true of so many jobs for both sexes, "Irish Need Not Apply" signs and other restrictions pervaded Boston. Uprooted by the Famine, the Irish soon discovered that life in Massachusetts could be harsh and insecure.

They took jobs as railroad laborers, ditch diggers, hod carriers and garbage carters, or as workers in textile mills. A significant portion of their wages went back home to Ireland to help their parents and relatives still reeling from the Famine. Performing dangerous and sometimes deadly tasks, they swung hammers, climbed scaffolds, descended into sewers, hauled cargo as longshoremen and constructed buildings, usually with no safety protections. Dying in alarming numbers, Irish laborers were called a "perishing class" by Boston's renowned minister, the Reverend Theodore Parker. In an 1846 letter to Henry David Thoreau, Ralph Waldo Emerson mentioned his surprise at learning that Irish laborers sweated through fifteen-hour days for fifty cents. Emerson repeated Parker's observation: he rarely saw a "gray-haired Irishman" because they died so young. Irish women also became tragedies on the job. At the nearby Pemburton Mill in January 1869, 900 workers, most of them immigrant women from Ireland, were caught in a sweatshop fire that caused their overcrowded building to collapse, killing 88 and injuring 116. For the Irish in America, life was as cheap as their wages.

Bridget Kennedy found a relatively safe job at a stationary and notions store in East Boston. With the help of her three daughters and her son, P. J., she scrimped together enough money so that she could eventually buy the thriving establishment. Not far from the ferry, Bridget's store, housed in a three-story building where her family also lived, soon expanded to include a grocery that apparently sold liquor as well as food to local Irish laborers. With the money she earned, Bridget sent P. J. to Sacred Heart, a school run by the Sisters of Notre Dame, so that he would receive a Catholic education. The young man helped out at the store when not studying. Like his mother, P. J. was hardworking, a quiet teenager whose reserved manner masked his quick and ambitious mind. Based on her own hard experiences, Bridget determined that her only son should seek a better life, the kind she had observed as a lowly domestic working for affluent families in Boston's ruling Protestant majority. To do that, she and her family would have to overcome not only the bigotry towards Catholics but also the confinement of the immigrant ghetto where they lived.

BOSTON'S IRISH stressed the concepts of community and the family as vehicles for social improvement. This view often grew out of, and was largely supported by, the Catholic themes of pain, sacrifice and religious sacraments that were devoted to some greater good, an ultimate spiritual deliverance from their ordeal. Many immigrants to America during those years— Germans, Italians, Poles and Eastern European Jews—would rely on similar traits as a source of strength. But because the Irish were the first large wave, they set a standard for others to follow. By sticking together, by working as a group, families such as the Kennedys were able to survive the trauma of famine and the harrowing odyssey of the coffin ships. They overcame challenges in the New World that might have defeated them as individuals.

A certain fatalism among the Irish, a despondency about their circumstances, lent itself to further cultural separation. Alcoholism, self-destructive behavior and a stunted social life centered around drink undermined their climb out of the Wharf's ghetto. In nineteenth-century America, the caricature of a drunken Irishman became a common stereotype. The Irish appeared to lack—at least to the Puritan's eye—the enterprise and fortitude needed for success. Talk of England's oppression seemed a sorry excuse for Irish self-destructiveness. "Is the landlord's absence the reason why the house is filthy, and Biddy lolls on the porch all day?" asked British novelist William Makepeace Thackeray. "People need not be dirty if they are ever so idle; if they are ever so poor, pigs and men need not live together." A fundamentally different worldview existed between Irish Catholics, a lowly flock who deferred to the priest for guidance, and Protestants whose fiercely independent outlook derived largely from their power and success in America. Their basic difference was inherent in religious education and cultural traditions. As historian Kerby Miller observed: "The Catholic Irish were more communal than individualistic, more dependent than independent, more fatalistic than optimistic, more prone to accept conditions passively than to take initiatives for change, and more sensitive to the weight of tradition than to innovative possibilities for the future."

Nevertheless, such generalities usually failed to consider the devastating impact of bigotry—ethnic prejudices and religious intolerance—on Boston's Irish Catholic population. Just as in Ireland, the restrictions placed on their social and economic ascendancy were sometimes codified in specific laws.

Small suppressions were found in subtle phrases of discrimination and discreet gestures of rebuke. These actions delayed the full impact of Irish Catholics into the American mainstream for years, often for generations. They also seeped into the individual consciousness of many Irish families. The corrosive results were limits on what each could achieve, how they were perceived by others and often what they thought of themselves. The Kennedys were not immune.

From the outset, Boston's reception to the Irish was wary and distrustful. Mayor Theodore Lyman described the Irish as "a race that will never be infused with our own, but on the contrary, will always remain distinct and hostile." With thousands of new immigrants descending on its streets, the Yankee Boston of old became defensive, scorning these newcomers as if they were a plague of water rats. "Each wave would distrust the next," John F. Kennedy later observed about this constant flow of new immigrants. Boston had been accustomed to absorbing fewer than five thousand new immigrants a year; now, it became "the Dublin of America," as the Reverend Theodore Parker put it, accepting nearly forty thousand new arrivals alone in the year Patrick Kennedy landed. The "Paddyvilles" and "Mick alleys" became the first mass urban slums in the United States.

In the pecking order of Boston's society, the newly arrived Irish were on the bottom rung. Visiting Boston in 1860, Walt Whitman found the Irish were treated worse than Negroes, who lived free in Northern cities but were still enslaved in the South. W.E.B. DuBois, the black scholar, later recalled that, when he was growing up in Great Barrington, Massachusetts, in the 1870s, "the racial angle was more clearly defined against the Irish than against me." Some wondered how New England abolitionists— including Harriet Beecher Stowe—appalled by the evil of slavery, could be unmoved by the suffering of the famine Irish and the bigotry against them. The Irish immigrants were perennial outsiders in a town with a rich aristocratic Anglo-Saxon past. In the struggle for jobs and acceptance, they were often the last hired and the most unwelcome. "The Irish found all others united with the natives against them," observed historian Oscar Handlin. "A Negro was as reluctant to have an Irishman move into his street as any Yankee."

Anti-Catholic bigotry was not unique to Boston and stretched across much of America. For many Protestants, any endeavor involving Roman Catholics—employment, education, cultural institutions, politics and government—became suspect. During the 1840s, for example, Pope Pius IX followed the example of other European monarchs and sent a block of marble with his regards for the building of the Washington Monument. An angry crowd threw the stone into the Potomac River. In colonial Boston, the long history of anti-Catholicism included "Pope's Night," in which floats, wagons and exhibits were devoted to stirring hatred for Catholics, a night capped by burning the Pope in effigy. These views were far from a refuge of the ignorant, for many of New England's most respected citizens shared a deep-seated distrust of Catholic influence. A person no less than future President John Adams warned about the papists, asserting that the "Roman system" kept human beings "for ages in a cruel, shameful and deplorable servitude." Many years later, John F. Kennedy noted that Ralph Waldo Emerson, that famed American proponent of individual freedoms, in writing to his friend Thomas Carlyle, expressed worry about "the wild Irish element . . . led by Romanish priests, who sympathize, of course, with despotism." JFK also underlined that Samuel F. B. Morse, a painter and celebrated inventor of the telegraph, wrote a book called *A Foreign Conspiracy Against the Liberties of the United States*—a diatribe about an alleged papal conspiracy to infiltrate America with Catholics avowed to do the pontiff's bidding.

New England's history proved it could be a forbidding place to Irish Catholics. Violence dated back to the hanging of Goody Glover in 1688 on Boston Common, found guilty as a witch for saying the rosary in Gaelic while kneeling before a statue of the Virgin Mary. In the summer of 1834— a decade before the famine Irish arrived in droves—local Protestants, alarmed about growing Catholic influence, stormed a convent run by Ursuline nuns in Charlestown, outside Boston, and burned it down. Though most Bostonians were rightly shocked by this incident, religious bias against Irish Catholics persisted. In June 1847, handbills distributed widely in Boston called for the destruction of a hospital treating "foreign paupers"; the campaign was aimed at provoking an uprising of hate similar to the Charlestown convent fire. Even workers toiling as maids, as Bridget Kennedy had, were under suspicion. "Though Bostonians could not do without the Irish servant girl, distrust of her mounted steadily," observed Handlin. "Natives began to regard her as a spy of the Pope who revealed their secrets regularly to priests in confession."

The Kennedys arrived in America when rampant anti-Catholicism prompted the creation of the so-called Know-Nothing Party, a national political movement of hate that wrapped itself in the American flag. Starting in 1850, a secret patriotic society called the Order of the Star-Spangled Banner evolved into an open "American Party." They pledged to vote only for native-born Americans and resisted the influx of immigrants into the United States with a call for a twenty-one-year naturalization period. Their common name arose because members were instructed, when asked about their plans, to answer, "I know nothing about it." The "Know-Nothings" voiced the deepest fears of many Americans, including concern for out-of-control breeding by Catholics. They had no intentions of allowing papists to outnumber the majority and skew their hard-won culture. In 1854, the Know-Nothings elected six state governors and seventy-five congressmen. Two years later, when the party convinced former President Millard Fillmore to run under their banner, he garnered 25 percent of the vote.

Upset by the Know-Nothing Party's swift political rise, Abraham Lincoln in 1855 confided to a friend that "our progress in degeneracy appears to me to be pretty rapid." Basic freedoms outlined in the Bill of Rights, he warned, might be endangered. "When the Know-Nothings get control," Lincoln cracked, "It will read 'All men are created equal, except Negroes, and foreigners and Catholics.'"

Within the Kennedys' own state of Massachusetts, the Know-Nothings were quite successful, electing in 1854 Governor Henry J. Gardner, the entire membership of the state senate, and all but four seats in the state's lower house. A long-time nativist, Jerome Van Crowninshield Smith, was elected mayor of Boston. In the state legislature, the Know-Nothings passed laws to make reading the Protestant version of the Bible compulsory in public schools. Some wanted to pass a law prohibiting public office to anyone who expressed allegiance to the Pope. They also pushed anti-immigration measures, including a state literacy test for voters and the exclusion of paupers, that almost gained sufficient support. No Roman Catholic was above suspicion. In 1858, a state legislature committee launched a probe into nunneries to investigate unfounded rumors of sexual improprieties and "certain practices" taking place at Catholic schools, including two run by the Sisters of Notre Dame, the same order who taught at P. J. Kennedy's school.

Although various Irish leaders suggested keeping a low profile or reacting violently to such outlandish acts of discrimination, Boston's Bishop John Bernard Fitzpatrick, a prudent man, advised a different approach. Rather than remain defensive, he urged his parishioners to become naturalized citizens, to vote and to avoid retaliation. Boston would be slow to create a parochial school system because Fitzpatrick believed Catholic children should learn and play in public schools with those of other faiths. Eventually, rising passions surrounding slavery and the impending Civil War in the 1860s eclipsed the Know-Nothing Party, though heated rhetoric and bigotry toward Irish Catholics never went away.

In Boston, the more liberal citizenry were appalled by the Know-Nothings's hateful actions, but they followed another questionable course. They espoused a doctrine of acculturation for Irish Catholics that, in the words of some state legislators, stressed that the Irish "be as we are." Though not overtly bigoted, this high-minded appeal carried a subtle message of cultural superiority, an overriding belief that the essential wisdom of Anglo-Saxon society would enlighten and replace the parochial dogmas of Irish Catholics. Many proponents were wealthy and powerful leaders in Boston society—bankers, educators, churchmen and property owners—whom Oliver Wendell Holmes labeled "the Brahmins," a reference to the preeminent priestly class of the ancient Hindus in India. These Brahmin leaders intended to maintain their positions of power in this modern-day caste system, the implicit message being that the Irish should follow along for their own good. The urge to remake and redefine others in their own image would become a unique trait of American democracy. The Brahmins in Boston were among the first American practitioners of the "melting pot" ideal of assimilation, and for all their expressed good intentions, the difficulties soon became apparent.

Public schools provided the best hope for Brahmins to remake immigrant children in their own image. Even if their parents spoke Gaelic and were unreconstructed foreigners, these children could become ideal products of assimilation—second-generation Americans who would learn to share the values of the Puritans, aspire to the great achievements of the Founding Fathers and never hear of their shiftless ancestors in Ireland. But the Irish proved unwilling pupils. Too often, the Yankee teachers brought their own prejudices into the classroom, constantly ridiculing and harassing their Catholic pupils. When Boston's new archbishop, John L. Williams (who years earlier as a young priest had married Patrick and Bridget Kennedy), heard these complaints, he announced plans to create a parochial school system and pull as many Catholic children as possible out of the public schools. The Brahmins were upset, arguing that Catholic schools would only undermine educational standards and indoctrinate children's minds with religious catechism. The Massachusetts legislature, still controlled by Yankees, even proposed a law creating local education boards to oversee what was taught in Catholic and other private schools. The Brahmins presided with the same high-handedness in local politics. They embraced Protestant Yankee candidates who proposed "good government," and they resisted all advances by Irish politicians whom they believed to be interested solely in patronage and far too susceptible to graft.

Behind the Brahmin rhetoric of good schools and good government lay some ignoble fears. As Irish Catholics flooded into the city, as they slowly inched their way to power through the ballot box, the Brahmins seemed caught in a malaise of spirit, the realization that Boston might be no longer theirs alone. By the 1860s, to escape the people they wanted to see assimilated into their way of life, many Brahmins moved out to Milton and Brookline, then nearly rural suburbs of Boston. They sent their children to their own private schools and created their own insular worlds in affluent gentlemen's clubs. Inside these restricted communities, ensconced in such places as the Algonquin and the Somerset clubs, Brahmin society became more tightly organized and more impenetrable, and the Irish were kept safely at a distance well into the twentieth century. For many priests and politicians, the dividing line between the Irish and the Brahmins confirmed what the *Boston Pilot,* the diocese newspaper, concluded in 1850 when it said that "cooperation for any length of time in important matters between true Catholics and real Protestants is morally impossible."

P. J. KENNEDY, known as "Pat's boy" in their East Boston neighborhood, grew up in a world of newcomers who spoke with thick Irish brogues, had dirty hands pounded by hard daily labor and entertained ambitions of getting ahead. He never finished school as his mother intended, but in the family store, he learned the important life lessons of being an attentive listener and pleasing customers. As a lad, P.J. worked as a stevedore along the wharf and developed a lean, muscular physique to complement his fair skin, blue eyes and wavy brown hair. In later adulthood, his girth widened and he grew a large curled handlebar mustache that demanded respect. He heard of a failing saloon for sale in East Boston's Haymarket Square, bought it for a pittance and by the 1880s had turned the tavern into a thriving business that specialized in sales of lager beer. Kennedy became known for a friendly manner that went down easy with the hard-drinking laborers and neighborhood residents who tottered up to his bar. Soon, P. J. Kennedy bought interests in two other saloons and expanded his business into a retail and wholesale whiskey distributorship. He hired Tom Barron, the son of Bridget's cousin, to help him after Barron's own tavern failed.

In his establishment, P. J. Kennedy not only listened to stories about Ireland from his customers but also convinced them he was looking out for their interests by trading information about job openings or lending cash when they were in need. In its early stages, the Kennedy family's fortunes were fueled by profits from the business of drinking—the traditional bane of Irish existence—even though P. J. Kennedy and, later, his son, would remain tea-totalers, wary of the dangers of drink. As a successful tavern owner in East Boston, Kennedy possessed a position in the Irish Catholic immigrant community that "lent him power and prestige second only to the parish priest," as one of his son's biographers explained. Increasingly, P. J. became active in the politics of Boston's Ward Two, and brought his own chieftain-like qualities to his loyal and ever-larger group of supporters. By a landslide margin in 1886, P. J. Kennedy, at the age of twenty-eight, won a seat in the Massachusetts House of Representatives.

His political climb was accompanied by an elevation in social status. A year after being elected, P. J. married Mary Augusta Hickey, the daughter of an Irish immigrant from County Cork who listed on his entry papers the profession of laborer and rose to become a successful contractor in Boston. Because of their financial success, the Hickeys were more Americanized than the Kennedys. Mary Augusta, educated by the nuns at the Notre Dame Academy, projected a refined and genteel image that appealed to her unpolished husband. Mary Augusta was "lace curtain" Irish, the emerging elite within the East Boston community. Her own quick wit, deep religious faith and optimistic enthusiasm were a constant source of moral support for her husband in his endeavors. In September 1888, little more than a year after their wedding, the couple celebrated the birth of their first child, a boy, whom they named Joseph Patrick Kennedy.

If his private life was simple and content, the world of politics that P. J. Kennedy ruled from his Boston ward was byzantine and cutthroat—a constant clearinghouse for favors, job offers and other forms of patronage. The Irish now constituted nearly half of Boston's population, just as the Brahmins feared, and they were determined to seize their share of power. A man as realistic and sober-minded as Kennedy knew just how hard that could be. Writing a job recommendation to a friend for a young man who was Catholic, Kennedy confided: "It is particularly hard on one of our kind (I mean by this the Catholic boy) because there are very few cities in the Commonwealth that I know of that will give one of our boys a position if they know he is Catholic."

Though he was not quite as ambitious as his wife might have liked, P. J. Kennedy managed to get elected later into the Massachusetts State Senate, and he became very influential in his own community. He plowed profits from his taverns and whiskey business into neighborhood banks, such as the Columbia Trust Company, and into buying vacant land. As a Democratic leader, Kennedy became part of the Board of Strategy, an aptly named group headed by the city's ward bosses, who divvied up perks and wielded power during their luncheon sessions together. These bosses included

Martin Lomasney, the powerful Ward Eight boss dubbed "the Mahatma" both by his admirers and his detractors. "The great mass of people are interested in only three things—food, clothing and shelter," Lomasney said, encapsulating much of his political strategy with a distinctly practical Irish immigrant's view. Seated at this same table was John F. Fitzgerald, the ward boss of the North End, who would become an adversary for Kennedy and ultimately a family in-law. More reserved than most Irish pols and content to stay in the background, Kennedy managed to thrive in this world of ballot stuffers and money grabbers without taint. His oldest son later laughed in recalling the Boston election when two ward healers came to the door excitedly to tell his father, then an election commissioner, "Pat, we voted one hundred and twenty-eight times today."

A year before Kennedy's own election to the state legislature, Boston voted for Hugh O'Brien, its first Irish Catholic mayor, an event marking the most serious threat yet to Brahmin political dominance. Fearful of what the Irish might do, the Yankee-controlled legislature passed a measure to wrest control of the Boston police from city officials. The Irish politician that P. J. Kennedy most admired—as he later told his oldest son—was Patrick Collins, a naturalized Bostonian born in Ireland. In the 1880s, President Grover Cleveland appointed Collins as American consul general to Great Britain. For Kennedy, the idea of an Irish-American going off to England as America's representative seemed almost incomprehensible, a remarkable feat for a people so afflicted by the British. Collins, who later became Boston's mayor, was different from other Irish politicians. He didn't inflame the anti-Brahmin and anti-British resentments of his constituents for political gain. A thoughtful, courtly man who graduated from Harvard, Collins seemed to straddle successfully the divide between being Irish and being American. He didn't want to battle the Brahmins as much as cooperate and live with them. "I denounce any man or any body of men who seek to perpetuate divisions of races or religion in our midst," Collins once said, in endorsing a Brahmin candidate for governor. "Let me say now that there are no Irish voters among us. There are Irish-born citizens like myself and there will be many more of us, but the moment the seal of the court was impressed upon our papers, we ceased to be foreigners and became Americans. Americans we are and Americans we will remain."

Collins's words and actions resonated with P. J. Kennedy. He, too, considered himself fully American. And yet for Kennedy, like so many Irish-Americans, the familial ties to Ireland, the loyalties to an impoverished land his parents left behind, still beckoned. In fact, the Kennedys' connection to Ireland was never broken. Over the years, both Patrick and Bridget

Kennedy kept in contact with relatives in Wexford County, writing long letters telling of births, deaths and important details of their life in America. Undoubtedly, like many famine Irish, the Kennedys felt remorse about leaving behind loved ones, and these correspondences were a way of assuaging their guilt and sad memories. For P. J. Kennedy, Ireland was more of a romantic notion, a lost emerald homeland that he heard his widowed mother and other Irish immigrants speak of wistfully, but where he'd never set foot. With his success in business and politics in Boston, P. J. possessed more money than any Kennedys in Ireland had ever owned. The future for his growing family in New England appeared bright, and there was no cause to look back. Still, P. J. and his sisters remained in touch with relatives in Ireland, and heeded their call when the Kennedys who stayed behind were in trouble in 1888. Before this new crisis resolved itself, P. J. Kennedy would help save his Irish cousins from ruin.

BACK IN DUNGANSTOWN, the Kennedys faced jail and lost nearly everything because of their strong opposition to the British rule in Ireland.

The family's history of defiance reached back more than a century, to the Kennedys who shed their blood at the battle of Vinegar Hill in 1798. As the famine years subsided, farmers in Ireland who survived became convinced that they could no longer tolerate the English system of land ownership, which they believed choked the lifeblood out of their country. Tenant farmers such as the Kennedys could sweat and toil all their lives and have no chance of ever owning their farms. Certainly, Patrick Kennedy's oldest brother, John, who ran the homestead, felt that way until his death in 1864, and so did John's two sons, Patrick and James, who continued the family's tenancy of the farm into the 1880s. Those Kennedys who stayed in Ireland became resolute in the republican cause, fervent believers that Ireland must be free of the British before its people could prosper. In the 1880s, the two Kennedy brothers, Patrick and James, became strong political supporters of Charles Stewart Parnell, his drive for Irish independence and his Home Rule campaign against the British-run system of land ownership in Ireland.

In the pantheon of modern Irish heroes, Parnell holds an exalted place. *"He is dead / Our Uncrowned King is dead / O, Erin mourn with grief and woe,"* wailed James Joyce, who imbued almost Christ-like qualities on Parnell, the political hero of his youth. A Protestant Irishman whose mother was American, Parnell came from a family of wealthy landowners, but he championed the cause of the tenant farmers. After the scare of a potato crop failure in 1878, Parnell rallied the farmers into a new political movement called the Irish National Land League, with himself as president.

More than anyone since O'Connell, Parnell effectively pushed the British government to reform, not through violence but through negotiation with Prime Minister William E. Gladstone and the moral weight of his words. Because of the nature of his message, Parnell's movement was embraced by the Catholic priests, who hadn't always supported confrontation. Sympathetic Irish-Americans from Boston, New York and other U.S. cities sent more than $1 million to aid the Land League's activities. "The money that has kept the Land League together," reported the *New York Times* in 1881, "has come mostly from the day laborers and the servant maids of America." Some of these Irish-Americans also were connected by heart and wallet to the Irish Fenian movement, which was devoted to the violent overthrow of the British from Ireland. The church condemned the secret Fenian society's call for assassination and murder, and viewed Parnell as a welcomed alternative.

At a rally in New Ross in 1880, Parnell stirred the crowd, estimated at nearly twenty thousand, by underlining the evils of the British land system. "They know their only hope of maintaining their right to commit wrong lies in the maintenance of English power in Ireland," he proclaimed to cheers from the crowd of tenant farmers. He urged them to join him in the campaign "to destroy the system of landlordism which was planted here by England in order that she might divide Ireland's sons." On the carriage carrying Parnell into New Ross were garland and banners that read: "Let it ring out over hill and dale, God bless our noble chief Parnell!"

James and Patrick Kennedy enlisted in Parnell's cause. The Kennedy brothers became Land League organizers in Dunganstown and nearby Ballykelly, working with a well-known patriot priest, Thomas Canon Doyle, whose public exhortations pleaded for an end to the government's squeeze on tenant farmers. Both Kennedy brothers were assigned the task of collecting money, organizing and recruiting new members and representing their local branch in the larger organization. It is not clear whether the two acted with splinter groups of this reform movement responsible for some 2,500 acts of violence throughout Ireland, including their local Wexford area. This violence was usually intended to stop "land grabbers" who exploited the situation when their neighbors were evicted from their farms under the British laws. Much of the Land League's strategy called for Irish tenant farmers to withhold their rents to British landlords, resist their eviction when they defaulted and threaten or intimidate "grabbers or landlords" who would try to claim the farms being run by the tenant farmers. Although Parnell didn't publicly condone violence, it was not uncommon for local organizers to enforce their resistance to the "rack rent" system with terrifying acts of force. Eight "agrarian homicides" to landlords or their agents were recorded in Ireland in one year alone, as well as numerous mutilations, stabbings and other threats of violence and intimidation. The most dramatic local confrontation occurred in October 1887 at the house of a tenant farmer named David Foley, who ran a farm at Ballykerogue, about four miles from the Kennedys' place. The landlord insisted Foley pay his rent or face eviction. When ordered to leave, Foley refused. James Kennedy—a later photo shows him to be a burly man with a wide flattened nose and round jaw—also wasn't one to be pushed around lightly, nor his brother, Patrick. The Kennedys also withheld the rents on their homestead farm in protest. The two brothers rounded up nineteen other supporters of the Land League and jammed into Foley's house with him, fortifying the doors and windows. When the sheriff and police came to Foley's house for the eviction, the Kennedy brothers and the others resisted until more police were called, and the men were arrested. They were released on bail, the money put up by two other Land League supporters, and went to trial in January 1888. Each of the protestors, including James Kennedy, received a sentence of three months of hard labor at the Wexford jail for breaking the British laws at that time.

On his first night in jail, James Kennedy, then thirty one years old who, like his older brother, never married, wrote home expressing concern. The two brothers worried how their widowed seventy-five-year-old mother, Mary, and two sisters—Catherine Kennedy, a widow, and Bridget Kennedy, a "spinster," as one legal document called her—would manage the family farm while they were in jail for the better part of the spring. Fortunately, their incarceration didn't last long. After four days in jail, the Land League secured an appeal for the protestors, who were released on bail. Eventually, they were granted probation as first-time offenders, and released with a bond to keep the peace. But their British-sanctioned landlord didn't drop his own eviction campaign against the Kennedys.

In March 1888, while the brothers were fighting the Foley jail sentence, Colonel Charles George Tottenham, the British owner of vast tracts of Wexford farmland, including the Kennedy-run acreage, obtained a civil court order for payment of rent that the Kennedys had been withholding in protest for more than two years. If they didn't come up with the money, the court said, the Kennedys would be evicted. As local leaders of the Land League movement, the Kennedy brothers stayed true to the cause and refused payment, forcing the hand of the court. By summer's end, the

Kennedy family was thrown off the homestead farm—the same fields of barley and wheat that Patrick Kennedy had cultivated with his brothers before leaving for America.

For the next several weeks, the Kennedys were forced to depend on the charity of their relatives and neighbors for food and shelter. Under the law, those who helped the Kennedys were criminally liable. "This charity, typical of the time and the neighbourhood, endangered the kind people who gave it, because they left themselves open to charges of collaboration," local historian John W. Pierce observed. After decades of paying escalating rents on farmland they once owned, the Kennedys were now homeless. The fundamental inequity of the British-run land system—indeed the centuries of oppression and denial of basic liberties in their own land—became a painful reality, the sort that can distill into the deep-seated hatred shared by so many other Irish. During this time, no one moved in to claim the tenancy to the Kennedy Homestead. Apparently, potential land grabbers considered it unwise to seize the property of the local Land League chief. But the Kennedys were still desperately at a loss, without a home or the money to reclaim it.

News of the dire predicament in Dunganstown soon reached Boston, about the same time in late 1888 that P. J. Kennedy's mother, Bridget, was dying, and his first son, Joseph, was born. Though the details are no longer known, the letters between the two countries once again reunited the Kennedys in trying to save their family homestead. P. J. Kennedy, along with his sisters, all married to successful Irish-American men, sent a sum of money to Ireland large enough to pay off the debts of fifty pounds and regain the family's tenancy of the farm. Perhaps the money came from P. J.'s booming businesses or perhaps from the estate of Bridget Kennedy as one last gesture to the land she and her husband left. Under the existing British law, however, the Kennedys still couldn't buy what they viewed as their own property. For the rest of the century, James and Patrick Kennedy kept pushing for land reforms with their local Land League movement. After Parnell lost his leadership role (because of a sex scandal involving Kitty O'Shea, a follower's wife), the Kennedys were active with the new replacement organization, the Irish National Land League. In 1903, with the passage of the Irish Land Act, the Kennedys were finally able to buy the ownership of their homestead for £214, financed with credit from the Irish Land Commission, a debt paid off in installments until the 1960s.

The Kennedys of Dunganstown didn't forget the debt they owed America, just as their American cousin couldn't seem to get his family's homeland out of his mind. For many Irish-Americans like Kennedy, the process of assimilation stirred conflicting emotions and mixed loyalties. For all his considerable success in Boston, P. J. Kennedy—counted officially at birth as a "foreigner" in his own native land—still faced a world of bigotry and social barriers. Like so many other Irish Catholics in the United States, P. J. Kennedy claimed a spiritual foothold in both worlds—Ireland and America—aware of the many similarities that bound them together and the vast differences between the two lands.

Later in his life, P. J. Kennedy visited Ireland, talking for hours with his Irish cousins about what their lives had been like and what they might look forward to. Mary Ann Ryan, a Kennedy cousin who today lives at the Kennedy Homestead, says that her mother, Mary Kennedy Ryan, remembered being introduced as a little girl to the visitor from Massachusetts. "My mother would say P. J. came here for about a week," she recalled. During his visit, P. J. made sure to pay homage at Vinegar Hill, the battle site where his Kennedy relatives fought with the Boys of Wexford in '98. He carried back to America a greater sense of the injustices to the Irish, which he shared with his son, Joseph, as he grew up. When he returned to Boston, P. J. Kennedy wrote letters to Irish cousins in Dunganstown and sent a photograph of himself, which faded over time. In one correspondence, he thanked his Irish cousins for giving him the "copy book" his immigrant father, Patrick, used when he attended school. "My children were particularly interested in it," he wrote, "and you know how pleased I was . . . the fact that I had never seen my father to remember him." Years later in an interview, Mary Kennedy Ryan recalled how her own father took delight in reading her "the Boston letters coming from Patrick, the Senator."

One Sunday afternoon, long after P. J. Kennedy's death in 1929, Mary Kennedy Ryan and her husband sat in the living room of the main house on the Kennedy farm and pulled down the old box containing P. J.'s letters. By then, the Kennedys owned their farm and no longer feared losing it to the British landlords. Mary's marriage was a union of second cousins in the Kennedy family. Her grandfather, James Kennedy, was the younger brother of Patrick Kennedy, who emigrated to America. Mary's husband, James Ryan, was the grandson of John Kennedy, the oldest brother of immigrant Patrick Kennedy.

On that afternoon, Mary remembered the visits by P. J. Kennedy, Patrick's son, and the way he helped save their family farm. As was true of other Irish families who saw their loved ones drift away to America, the Kennedys of Dunganstown fell out of contact over time with P. J.'s son. As

Mary shuffled through the correspondence, perhaps she thought she'd never see her American cousins again. She decided to dispose of these old papers left in the house.

"We sat in front of the fire and read them," Mary Kennedy Ryan recalled, "and then we burned them, one at time."

Chapter Six

The Long Climb to Acceptance

AFTER NEARLY A HALF CENTURY in Boston, the Irish, unwashed and unwelcome, had not melded into the broader society. "The Irishman fails to fit into the complex of our civilization, apparently for the reason that his talents are too little interwoven with the capacities which go to make up the modern successful man," the *Atlantic* expressed with utter contempt in 1896. Elsewhere, the view of immigrants wasn't much better. In his *Harper's Weekly* cartoons, illustrator Thomas Nast portrayed the Irish as crass semi-illiterate drunkards, shiftless in action and violent by nature, given to all forms of graft and chicanery when elevated to power. Even those who once supported America's open-ended immigration policy, who believed they could forge the Irish and so many other "poor wretches of the old world" into a new nation, creating, in Emerson's words, "a new race, a new religion, a new state, a new literature," were no longer optimistic. What ailed the Irish-American, wrote *Atlantic* editor James Russell Lowell, a one-time enthusiast of immigration, was "something too deep for railways or transplantation to cure."

By the turn of the twentieth century, the dream of assimilation in America gave way to resentment among even the most successful Irish Catholics in Boston. Fading away were their more accommodating leaders, Patrick Collins and Archbishop John Williams, two men who had acted as temperate voices of reason with the Brahmins. (Archbishop Williams declined a cardinal's hat because he feared it would stir up too much bigotry.) In their place were such men as Mayor John Francis Fitzgerald, the boisterous dynamo from the North Side who rallied the Irish to City Hall and extended his message to include an array of Italian, German, Polish and Jewish immigrants. Fitzgerald embraced a career in politics—turning it into a vehicle for Irish ascendancy as well as his family's own ambitions—because, as he once claimed, "In business, I was held back by prejudice."

Another man who embodied this new assertiveness by Irish Catholics was Cardinal William O'Connell, a zealous defender of the faith unafraid to attack strongholds of Brahmin society. He voiced a separatist call for Catholics to attend their own schools and follow their own ways rather than bow to the New England culture in which they were perpetually second-class citizens. Ablaze with his own personal sense of injustice, O'Connell recalled the sting of bigotry he endured while attending public schools in Lowell, Massachusetts, and how he "sensed the bitter antipathy, scarcely concealed" of Yankee "schoolmarms" toward Irish Catholics like himself. "For any slight pretext we were severely punished," O'Connell remembered bitterly. "We were made to feel the slur against our faith and race, which hurt us to our very hearts' core."

Fitzgerald and O'Connell, both sons of Irish Catholic immigrants, understood their parents' struggle to survive in the New World, but they, as proud second-generation Americans, were determined not to remain docile or subservient to any of their countrymen. Though they could barely tolerate each other personally, the two men were bound by their common resentments and their great ambitions for the Irish. Each understood how important religion could be to politics, especially in Boston.

In his early years, John F. Fitzgerald seemed to personify that Brahmin ideal of "Americanizing" the children of Irish immigrants, certainly as much as Emerson or any other Yankee visionary might imagine. Fitzgerald graduated from the Boston Latin School—the renowned public institution attended by many sons of Yankee aristocrats—and he performed so well that he was accepted to Harvard Medical School. It was a remarkable climb for the son of immigrant parents, Thomas Fitzgerald and Rose Mary Murray, both of whom emigrated from County Wexford during the famine years of the 1840s and settled in Boston's bustling North End. Thomas was the last to leave his family's farm in Ireland, and he wound up working for six dollars a month as a farm laborer in South Acton, Massachusetts, before saving enough to buy a grocery store in their North End neighborhood. In his close-knit community of Irish immigrants and their children, John Fitzgerald became known as a smart, amiable young man. He gained notice as a good athlete and for helping the parish priests at St. Stephen's Church run sunlight dances, picnics and charity events. "My playgrounds were the streets and wharves busy with ships from every port of the world," this young man of boundless energy recalled years later.

When both his parents died at a young age, John felt compelled to drop his plans for medical school and went to work, hoping to keep his family of eight siblings together rather than, as a neighborhood priest suggested, seeing the younger ones sent off to an orphanage. The turmoil in Fitzgerald's early life resembled that of many other Irish politicians of his time—Patrick Collins, Martin Lomasney and P. J. Kennedy among them—all of whom were forced into the workplace as youngsters when their parents died at an early age. Blocked by "prejudice" in Boston's world of commerce, Fitzgerald explained, "I chose politics, the only field where I could get influence and opportunity."

His fortunes were helped along by Matthew Keany, then boss of the North End's Ward Six district, who appreciated the young man's organizing abilities and arranged for him a clerk's job at the Customs House. Keany supported Fitzgerald's first bid into politics, for the city's Common Council in 1892 and then the state senate the following year. Young Fitzie, as his friends called him, became "the social leader of a great section of the most sociable of folk—the Irish—surrounded on all sides by a socially hostile population," *Collier's* magazine later observed. Though unexceptional in stature, Fitzgerald possessed an outsized personality, piercing blue eyes, a large head with slick dark hair parted down the middle, a pointed nose and a droll mouth that always seemed ready to speak. At the slightest urging, he could sing "Sweet Adeline" to crowds of supporters with the gusto of an old vaudevillian. If P. J. Kennedy in Ward Two gained a reputation for quiet, almost stolid behind-the-scenes effectiveness, Fitzgerald practiced an affable, flamboyant political flimflammery mixed with genuine concern and a desire for programs of substance for his immigrant constituency. In a ward filled with Irish immigrants, some of whom still spoke Gaelic, Fitzgerald understood their desperate need for work. He used municipal government as a supply house for jobs that kept many families from the poorhouse. Eager to please, Fitzgerald claimed that his parents hailed from various parts of Ireland—Tipperary and Limerick, rather than, in truth, County Wexford—depending on whom he was talking to and in what county their Irish immigrant parents were born. "New England is more Irish today than any other part of the world except Ireland," Fitzgerald said, pointing out that Boston's population was made up of more than 60 percent Irish. As more Italian and Jewish immigrants filled Ward Six, Fitzgerald made sure they got their fair share of patronage and political perks.

When Keany died suddenly, young Fitzgerald stepped in as the chieftain in Ward Six and, through a consensus with the other ward bosses, managed to get elected to Congress in 1894—the same seat his grandson would later hold. Fitzgerald managed to push through federal money to revitalize the dormant Charlestown Navy Yard, the first major upgrade of Boston Harbor, and saved the old frigate *Constitution,* which was rotting at a New Hampshire pier. As one of the few Catholics in Congress, he tried unsuccessfully to secure federal funding for Indian schools run by Catholic missionaries (Protestants wanted the Native Americans taught in nondenominational schools), and pointed with pride to a $5,000 appropriation he did get for a Catholic-run orphanage in Washington, D.C. But perhaps his most significant action occurred one afternoon when Congressman Fitzgerald urged President Grover Cleveland to veto a bill requiring a literacy test for new immigrants. Passed with the political support of nativists who feared the swelling ranks of immigrants, the bill demanded that those entering the United States must show they could read and write, and also understand the U.S. Constitution. Fitzgerald, aware of how many illiterate and non-English-speaking immigrants could never pass such a test, objected to such discriminatory tactics. Immigration always remained a crucial issue for Fitzgerald—as it would for generations of family members to come.

CONGRESSMAN FITZGERALD was keenly aware of the renewed anti-Catholic and anti-immigration fervor sweeping across America. The forces pushing this immigration bill resided in many states, and the old Know-Nothing spirit had found new voice in such groups as the American Protective Association (APA), which claimed anywhere from 100,000 to 2.5 million members nationwide. Formed in the 1880s, the APA made each new recruit swear not to vote for a Catholic, to hire a Protestant when one was available over a Catholic and never to go on strike with a Catholic worker. "The determination of the Church of Rome to capture our great cities, those centers of life and power, rests on immigration!" declared the Reverend Daniel C. Eddy, also a legislator in Massachusetts. "Our dangers as a free people, dangers against which the wisest men of the world have warned us, spring from immigration." During this time, the APA built up several chapters in Massachusetts, including Boston, and deliberately provoked the Irish and other newly arrived groups with their anti-immigration message. Books and commentators accused immigrants not only of causing crime in the streets and corruption in government but also of a papal conspiracy to take over the United States and playing an alleged role in the assassination of Abraham Lincoln. An economic downturn in 1893 made some Americans fear immigrants were stealing their jobs. Three deadly riots linked to the APA broke out around the country. During an Independence Day celebration in 1895, the APA marched through East Boston, the heavily Irish ward run by P.J. Kennedy, with a float carrying a woman dressed in orange—the traditional symbol in Ireland of Protestant pride and unity against Catholics—an incident that incited fighting. On the street where Bridget Kennedy had once kept her store, a Protestant extremist shot into an angry crowd of Catholics, killing two men and injuring many others. Rather than remorse or reconciliation, a Baptist minister told the *Boston Post* that he prayed for God to "hasten the day when there should not be a Catholic priest on this continent."

With a growing amount of national concern about Catholics and immigrants, the American Protective Association pushed Congress to enact the literacy-test immigration bill. It was proposed by Republican legislator Samuel McCall of Massachusetts to weed out "undesirable" immigrants from southern and eastern Europe—exactly the same people coming to live in Congressman Fitzgerald's district. A similar 1888 immigration bill severely limiting Chinese immigration to America was signed into law by President Grover Cleveland under great political pressure. It was the first significant act to curb immigration into America and, if up to the nativists, would certainly not be the last. Newspapers such as the *Chicago Tribune* embraced this new anti-immigration measure, declaring the moral fiber of the nation was "being enfeebled by its absorption of the dregs of the Old World." The literacy bill passed overwhelmingly in the House, as did a similar bill in the Senate, Fitzgerald being one of the few voices against it.

He painted the bill as an assault on immigrants: "Thousands of Irish and Jewish girls, owing to the injustices and barbarities that have been heaped upon them by the English and Russian governments and the lack of opportunity offered by these governments in the education of their subjects, are unable to read and write," he said. If this law had been in place "at the time of the arrival of my own mother from Ireland into this country," he noted, "she would have been denied admittance." In early 1897, Fitzgerald placed these words into the *Congressional Record*, adapted largely from a speech supporting American immigration that he had given at an Independence Day celebration the previous year in Boston. Hardworking, industrious immigrants were to be welcomed and admired, he argued, and not met with scorn. "It is fashionable to-day to cry out against the immigration of the Hungarian, the Italian and the Jew, but I think that the man who comes to this country for the first time, to a strange land, without friends and without employment, is born of the stuff that is bound to make good citizens," he said.

On a Saturday afternoon soon after the vote, the Boston congressman wandered over to the White House, a far smaller and more informal place than the palatial compound of later years. With the president's secretary gone for the day, he happened to find Cleveland in his office, answering his mail in longhand. According to his biographer, Fitzgerald argued strenuously against the bill for the next half hour and told Cleveland that his veto would "bring millions of immigrants to these shores who would otherwise have been kept out." Fitzgerald found a receptive audience. The APA considered the election of Cleveland, a Democrat, as a triumph of "political Romanism." Cleveland shared the old democratic belief that illiterate immigrants could be assimilated and made into good Americans. In vetoing the literacy-test bill, Cleveland chastised legislators for giving way to prejudice. "If any particular element of our illiterate immigration is to be feared for other causes," the president decided, "they should be dealt with directly, instead of making illiteracy a pretext for exclusion."

Congress never mustered enough support to override Cleveland's veto, issued two days before he left office in March 1897. Although historians later praised Cleveland's veto as one of the most courageous acts of his presidency, most contemporaries agreed with his rival, Theodore Roosevelt, who said Cleveland's "last stroke was given to injure his country as much as he possibly could." Years later, however, Fitzgerald still counted his opposition to the immigration literacy-test bill as one of his finest moments in politics, a story that would be repeated to his grandchildren.

After three terms in the nation's Capitol, Congressman John F. Fitzgerald came home in 1901. The infighting of the Irish ward bosses in Boston, and his own need to make more money to support his wife, Josephine, and his five children, mandated his return and put his political career in doubt. Boston remained a deeply divided city: the Brahmins were in one camp, still controlling the economic and cultural institutions, and the Irish were splintered into various political factions, their hands around each other's necks. "Boston politics of this era was not unlike that in Ireland before the Anglo-Norman conquest," Fitzgerald's daughter Rose wrote decades later. "The Irish had their local chieftains, who often warred against one another for fancied glory and advantages for themselves and their followers. They made unstable alliances that could find one year's ally another year's foe. Yet they produced especially strong leaders, superchieftains who reigned as kings over large regions, in turn allying and defecting and forming new constellations as the winds blew."

In their yearning for acceptance, the Boston Irish rallied around the esteemed Patrick Collins for mayor, a drive strongly supported by Collins's friend and ally, P. J. Kennedy. Fitzgerald found himself one of the few ward bosses outside this coalition. Collins held a personal disdain for the syrupy pol who could weep on demand, and for another rising politician as well, James Michael Curley, considered, with more than ample reason, a crass local demagogue known as "the Purple Shamrock." "Patrick Collins had lived as nobly as he spoke; no scandal ever tarnished his name," Curley's biographer Jack Beatty recounted. Harvard's president even wanted to erect a statue to honor Collins. Although Fitzgerald was ridiculed in some quarters as a pathological glad-hander, he nevertheless represented the broad, sometimes coarse, but ultimately legitimate interests of Irish-American citizens looking for acceptance. They wanted to become enfranchised in the political process on their own terms, not someone else's. More often than not, the bigotry of the past and present against the Irish engendered a mix of wounded ethnic and religious pride, rather than the dispassionate high-mindedness of Mayor Collins so applauded by the Brahmins. Fitzgerald understood the effectiveness of this appeal and turned it into a fine art.

With typical energy, Fitzgerald gained control of a rundown newspaper called the *Republic,* which he aimed at Irish immigrants and sold on Sundays outside churches, quickly turning it into a moneymaker. "You know, sixty percent of the shoppers in Boston are Catholic and my newspapers are the only effective medium to reach them," he reportedly told George J. Raymond, one of Boston's largest advertisers. "Besides, if you want anything in the Massachusetts legislature or at City Hall, I can get it for you." After all, Honey Fitz had arranged a state senate seat for his brother, Henry, and helped get state-approved liquor licenses with no problem. Another newspaper, the *Sacred Heart Review,* complained that Fitzgerald improperly intimidated potential advertisers by claiming undue influence with priests and being the "authorized representative" of the Catholic Church. "Fitzgerald makes a business of trading on the Catholic name," the competing newspaper charged. "He has the hardihood to pretend that he represents Catholic interests, and speaks for the Catholic clergy." The *Republic* not only made Fitzgerald financially successful but revived and provided a new platform for his political ambitions. When asked by Mayor Collins about the newspaper's billboards featuring a photo of its owner, Fitzgerald smiled. "I'm just trying to promote *The Republic,*" he told Collins. "I want to make it a newspaper for the Irish."

When Collins, who had never appreciated the need for patronage among the ward bosses, died suddenly in 1905 during his second term, Fitzgerald seized upon this opening to City Hall. With barely a straight face, he fashioned a campaign for the Democratic nomination by attacking the city's ward bosses—even though he remained the power broker of Ward Six— and later won in the general election against a Back Bay Republican. On victory night, Fitzgerald paid emotional tribute to his dearly departed Irish immigrant parents and how they might relish their son's place in Boston history. "It would have been a great delight to them, for they were natives of a country where democracy could not be exercised freely due to English domination," he told supporters, many of them "Dearos," the shortened name for what Fitzgerald often called the "dear old North End" of his youth. "I am the first son of foreign parents to become Mayor of Boston, thus my parents were the first persons of immigrant stock to have a son as Mayor."

Rather than deny the stubborn bigotry in Boston, Fitzgerald con- fronted it head-on in his campaigns and transformed any whiff into a ral- lying cry for his troops. Indeed, his organization spread false rumors of bias against the Irish by his opponents so that he could express outrage and defend his people publicly. Fitzgerald later lost a two-year term to a Republican challenger but, after chronicling his trip to Ireland and other European countries for the Boston papers and planning a new strategy, he was reelected in 1910 to a four-year term as mayor. When his opponent in the 1910 campaign, James Jackson Storrow III, a wealthy reformer, held a well-attended rally, one of the featured speakers, former Governor Curtis Guild Jr., made a fatal blunder. "By what right does any candidate for high public office in this fair city dare to introduce the issue of reli- gion into a political campaign," Guild bellowed, his finger pointing to high heaven. Even though Fitzgerald's newspaper had declared three years earlier that Storrow didn't possess "any motive that can be fairly viewed as hostile to those of Celtic blood," candidate Fitzgerald seized on the gaffe so that he could defend the honor of the city's Catholics, who also made up the majority of the electorate. Police were forced to stop the fist- fights and near-riots that erupted during the rest of the campaign. At Honey Fitz's last rally in that race, the "Star-Spangled Banner" was inter- spersed with Irish songs, including the romping beat from "The Wearin' of the Green."

The theme of bigotry against the Irish remained a constant war cry for Honey Fitz, even after he left City Hall. He later ran for Congress, but was forced from his seat in 1919 because of voter fraud—including a ballot cast in the name of a dead soldier. Confronted with the evidence, Fitzgerald saw green instead of red. He wrapped himself in the Irish flag rather than deal successfully with charges for which he had no good answers. His accusers were guilty of "injecting the Irish issue to stir up the prejudice of the bigoted natures in the House," he countercharged. "I would sink into the ground before I would prostitute a cause that has struggled for centuries and is struggling now, and to which men and women of Irish blood have given their all."

DURING HIS PUBLIC CAREER, Fitzgerald not only represented the Irish Catholics in Boston but helped to transform their position in the city and their image of themselves. He railed against the "Puritan sons" who, he said, "cannot know the personal memories that hallow this scene of our fathers' struggles. . . . Our annals tell of villages emptied by famine, of crowded immigrant ships, of laborious lives in the new land, and the scanty reward of the laborers." In his orations, Honey Fitz complained about a "small knot of wealthy men" who controlled too much of Boston. In particular, he chafed at how the Irish were still largely barred by prejudice from Boston's banking and financial world. Once, as he told the story, he quizzed a banker why, with so many Irish depositors, there were no Irish on the board of directors:

"Well, a couple of the tellers are Irish Catholic," the banker replied, a bit defensively.

Indignant, Fitzgerald had proved his point. "Yes," he answered, his voice dripping with sarcasm, "and I suppose the charwomen are too."

Unlike other Irish leaders in Boston, Fitzgerald didn't genuflect to the Brahmin hierarchy and its gentile traditions. Certainly no such deference could be expected from a man whose home contained a stained glass window with his family's Irish coat of arms and his own self-styled Gaelic crest named *Shawn A Boo,* "John the Bold." Brashly, he suggested the great days of the Yankee colonists—the brilliant revolutionaries who carved a republic out of a wilderness, the bold capitalists who built industries and fortunes—had given way to a generation of reclusive coupon-collectors whose bloodlines were weak and instincts reactionary; people who were content to sit on their money. "Old Boston is cold and proud, wrapped in the mantle of Puritanism, not progressive enough," Fitz proclaimed. "It has been too long deaf to the aspirations of the young Irish, Italians, Jews and Frenchmen in our midst who are eager to make their way in business here."

By embracing all immigrants, Fitzgerald resisted the Irish tendency toward isolation in their own community, focused only on their own problems. With his remarkable panache, Fitzgerald made sure his campaigns appealed to new waves of immigrants beside the Irish, enabling him at times to overcome defections and rancor within the Democratic Party itself. It was a vision of Boston—indeed of America—not shared by many politicians of his time. When Russian and eastern European Jews moved into his beloved North End, stirring anti-Semitic feelings among some Irish Catholics, Fitzgerald welcomed the new voters into his coalition. He recognized from experience that patronage jobs and important city posts should reflect all the city's ethnic voting blocs. "Mayor Fitzgerald had a good rapport with Boston's Jews," historian Dennis P. Ryan noted. "Despite Yankee charges that he was giving official sanction to a quota system, he persisted in asserting that one of five positions on the School Committee should go to a Jew and helped one win election to the Committee in 1913." Similarly, Fitzgerald wooed Negro voters away from the ranks of the Republican Party by genuinely understanding the racism they faced in Boston and speaking out publicly about discriminatory practices. When his appointment of a Negro lawyer to head the city's Weights and Measures Department caused protests among workers, Fitzgerald accused them of bigotry and ordered their resignations. Appreciative of Fitzgerald's record, the *Guardian,* the city's leading African-American newspaper, declared the mayor "free from all color prejudice."

In his free-associating, audacious style, Fitzgerald traced his own family roots back to the Normans, claiming a little bit of French blood, a little Italian, a little Greek and part of just about any cultural heritage whose hall, church, temple or wake he visited. To his good government detractors, these statements seemed ludicrous. It was another example of Fitzgerald's over-the-top flimflammery, the kind expected of a big-city ward boss. Yet there was a progressive, inclusive spirit to Fitzgerald's politics that was heartfelt and authentic, born of his own past, that served as a model for the urban Democratic coalitions of the twentieth century. "When I was growing up in Boston, my grandfather, Honey Fitz, would often regale us with stories about my great-grandparents," remembered Senator Edward Kennedy. "He would also tell us about the famine and the waves of Irish immigrants who left for the hope of a better future in the United States—about how they made their marks in Boston and all across America—enduring hardships, building railroads, digging the canals, settling the West, manning the factories of a growing America. . . . Our own family history gave us empathy for other immigrants who had to face the same struggle."

In helping these new immigrants land jobs, obtain vital services and climb Boston's social ladder, Fitzgerald also never let them forget his name. His nemesis, Curley, who followed Honey Fitz to City Hall, once recalled a conversation with a new immigrant who was taking a naturalization class. Every time he was asked how things were done in America, the man replied: "John F. Fitzgerald." Astounded, Curley stopped the man when he gave the same name for the president of the United States. As Curley quipped: "I'm sure he would have gone on to tell me that John F. Fitzgerald drove the snakes out of Ireland and discovered America."

WHILE FITZGERALD'S BLUSTERY politics pushed Boston's Irish to a more expansive democratic approach, seizing for underdogs what was rightfully theirs in the political arena, the new Catholic prelate, William O'Connell, led his immigrant flock on a decidedly more separatist path, away from the Protestant influence of the Brahmins. Though he shared a past similar to that of the mayor, O'Connell urged all Catholics, particularly the Irish, to create their own culture, to go their own way. "The Puritan has passed, the Catholic remains," O'Connell proclaimed in 1908, at the diocese's centennial celebration. "They wrote the history of the last century; we must make the history of the coming one."

Appointed as bishop the previous year by the Pope, O'Connell wielded enormous power in Boston because of the sheer number of Catholic voters in the city, the influence of so many Catholic parishes, schools and fraternal organizations, and the sheer energy and command of the archbishop himself. Few politicians, certainly not Fitzgerald, dared cross him. But the outlooks and remedies of the two men could be quite different. Whereas Fitzgerald spoke generally about the bigotry of the past and present to work toward a more democratic future of shared power, O'Connell pinpointed the same prejudices as precisely the reasons why a Catholic should avoid anything having to do with Protestants. In his book of slights, O'Connell underlined the deep-seated bias of the Brahmin intelligentsia as well as the cruder nativism of the Know-Nothings, the APA and, later, the emerging Ku Klux Klan. O'Connell's prescription for Catholics in Boston called for shunning non-Catholics. Though this cultural isolation was a familiar tactic of the church, especially in Ireland, this view pushed back the progressive movement for Catholic immigrants in Boston for at least another generation. And because the prelate, soon to be elevated to cardinal in 1911, held sway with so many followers in Boston—including the Kennedy family— O'Connell's influence would help define the American Catholic Church for the next half century.

Growing up in Lowell, Massachusetts, the youngest of eleven children born to immigrants from County Cavan, William Henry O'Connell was expected by his family to become a priest—a tremendous honor in Irish Catholic families large enough to dedicate one of their own to the church. Perhaps appropriately for a defender of the faith, O'Connell was born in

1859 on December 8, the Feast of the Immaculate Conception, a holy day in the Roman Catholic Church and singularly different from the rituals of other Christian churches, some of which do not recognize the virgin birth of Jesus or venerate Christ's mother with the same devotion as Rome. As a public school student in Lowell, O'Connell remembered being ridiculed for his religion by his teachers and Yankee peers. He later graduated from the Jesuit College in Boston and studied for the priesthood in Rome, coming of age when the Vatican asserted a more authoritarian hand over its followers and the American church was beginning to emerge from its backwater status. In 1908, church officials lifted the "missionary status" of the United States, recognizing the growth and importance of American Catholics, even though Pope Leo XIII had earlier condemned "Americanism," the movement among Catholic lay people for more control of their parishes. The pontiff's move against the heresy of modernism—"ultramontane orthodoxy"—appealed to O'Connell's own authoritarian instincts: "There can be no true morality unless it is founded on religious principle," he demanded. His motto, *Vigor in Arduis,* envisioned life as a "struggle . . . through storm and tempest," a call perfectly tailored for a people who once arrived on famine ships.

O'CONNELL EXERTED the enormous influence he held in local politics with the subtle timing and punch of an Irish ward boss. He not only fought against a state lottery but also opposed birth control, which the diocesan newspaper condemned as "a practice which God Almighty has forbidden." He objected to baseball on Sundays, supported prohibition, chastised radio crooners and condemned the public discussion of scientific theories about relativity and the cosmos as a "ghastly apparition of atheism." As easily dismissed as these views might be in academic circles, O'Connell would have none of it. His gospel to Boston's Irish demanded that they stand up for themselves and no longer view themselves as victims. "The child of the immigrant is called to fill the place which the Puritan has left," he said, referring to the declining number of Brahmins in Boston. He cast a withering eye on American melting pot theories of assimilation and instead urged Catholics to establish their own culture in Boston. "There is, as you know, just one point of view, and that is, Catholic people should attend Catholic schools," he declared. Through his strident calls for autonomy and ethnic pride, O'Connell transformed the Irish self-image away from what biographer James O'Toole called a "preoccupation with discrimination, both real and perceived . . . the whine of self-pity" into "the confidence of self-assertion." And yet part of that self-assertiveness, as O'Connell defined it, would involve identifying those powerful figures or institutions who would discriminate against Irish Catholics. Most prominent on his list was Harvard University.

Plenty of anti-Catholicism festered behind the ivy walls at Cambridge, a rarified world of Anglo-Saxon Protestant intellectual life far removed from the hand-to-mouth existence of Boston's Irish Catholics. In many ways, Harvard's attitudes were merely an extension of the British view of the Irish, part of a stubborn bias engrained in American intellectual life for many years to come. In the early eighteenth century, the Dudleian lectures were established at Harvard, dedicated in part to the purpose of "detecting, convicting and exposing the idolatry, error and superstitions of the Romish church." With the turn of the twentieth century, Harvard's president, Charles Eliot, became an outspoken critic of Catholic doctrine and sacraments, the priesthood and the onslaught of Irish Catholic immigrants because of what it meant to the waning power of the Brahmins. Eliot insisted that Boston's children attend public schools. Although he shunned any suggestion of being a bigot, this Harvard president declared himself "an enemy of all that the Catholic Church inwardly stands for." He predicted America would change the Roman Catholic Church more than the church would his countrymen. At Harvard, Eliot instituted an entrance system for the law school that many Catholics considered discriminatory, designed to keep them out of the city's top law firms. Although some students from elite colleges gained entry to Harvard Law School without taking a test, graduates of Catholic colleges had to take a "special test," a mandate based on Eliot's view that their education was somehow inferior. He also ordered that these students must maintain higher grades than the rest to keep their places in class. The Jesuits at Boston College were infuriated by the "second-class status" accorded their graduates.

Harvard's actions confirmed in O'Connell's mind that Catholics should go it alone. The drive for money and assimilation at Harvard would only drive the Irish away from their families and church. Harvard lacked "the whole truth, the real truth, the fundamental truth" of religion, the cardinal advised, and its lack of moral underpinnings and its overt discrimination should be avoided—a message heeded by many Catholics, but not all. Some prominent Catholics attended Harvard because they hoped their presence in the Ivy League would bring about greater tolerance. Honey Fitz himself considered allowing his bright oldest daughter, Rose, to attend Wellesley College, one of the Ivy League's seven sister schools, until he consulted O'Connell, who upbraided him on the choice. Rather than face the cardinal's wrath, Fitzgerald steered Rose to a Catholic women's school, the

Convent of the Sacred Heart—a fateful decision that Rose later said was the biggest regret of her young life. "I was furious at my parents for years," Rose told a family member. "I was angry at my church. As much as I loved my father, I never really forgave him for not letting me go."

O'Connell's antipathy toward Harvard could be justified by the university's own actions. Many professors believed the Irish to be unworthy heirs of the American Revolution and incapable of performing in the leadership roles they coveted. "Our whole social system suffers from their weak personal characteristics," wrote one Harvard sociologist. And a 1911 *Harvard Lampoon* cartoon depicted a drunken Irishman with the caption: "The Glorious 17th of March." Alarmed by the tensions between Irish laborers and Anglo-Saxon business owners, scholars at Harvard and other leading universities wrote strongly worded treatises against immigration, or pushed pseudoscientific studies claiming a mental inferiority among the new immigrant groups. During Fitzgerald's tenure at City Hall, many Brahmins joined the Immigration Restriction League, an anti-immigration group put together by Harvard men, serving as the Back Bay's answer to the more crude and populous American Protective Association, from which it held its nose. The league aimed to crush the nation's immigration movement without getting its hands dirty or called any nasty names. "At home, Brahmin restrictionists never stooped to religious discrimination, but to aid restriction, they willingly co-operated with Know-Nothing nativists," historian Barbara Miller Solomon observed. As late as 1913, the league's prominent members included bankers, educators, rich philanthropists, New York publisher Henry Holt, and several college presidents, including Harvard's A. Lawrence Lowell. The duty of Brahmins, as Lowell asserted, was not only to dominate the Irish but to "absorb" them into the existing American culture until their separate Irish identity could no longer be detected.

But many league members were weary of good-government attempts to meld poor and uneducated Irish immigrants into their own society. Francis A. Walker, the president of the Massachusetts Institute of Technology and an early league member, said that even second-generation Irish immigrants were no more than "homemade foreigners," separated by religion, race, "clannishness" and "the jealousy of their spiritual teachers toward our popular institutions." Other league members, influenced by the rise of eugenics, argued against immigration on the grounds of mixing "inferior" bloodlines with the Anglo-Saxon. Overt or subtle, bigotry at Harvard—regardless of its patronizing assurances—continued for years against immigrants and their children. In reporting about the Brahmin concerns at Harvard in 1922, the *Boston Telegram* noted: "The Irish, not the Jews, present the real problem at Harvard. The new plan of class selection will cut down the number of Irish as well as Jews."

Although the league enlisted many influential people in its cause, none was more prominent than Henry Cabot Lodge, a Harvard man who revived a flagging political career with his anti-immigration message. Despite his words of support for the American democratic ideal, Lodge held a strong belief in the innate superiority of the Anglo-Saxon. "English to the last fibre of his thought," said his Harvard professor, Henry Adams, in admiration. Lodge feared the Brahmins would be doomed if they didn't step forward and close the door on immigration—a dagger, he said, aimed at the very heart of America. Lodge warned of "changing the quality of our race and citizenship through the wholesale infusion of races whose traditions and inheritances, whose thoughts and whose beliefs are wholly alien to ours and with whom we have never assimilated or even been associated with in the past." Elected to the U.S. Senate, Lodge shepherded through the Capitol the literacy-test immigration bill, which Congressman John F. Fitzgerald helped convince President Cleveland to reject in 1897. But Lodge continued his campaign against the flow of "undesirable" immigrants into America—the very same people filling Fitzgerald's ward and Cardinal O'Connell's parishes. Neither man would stand for it.

Though controversial and outspoken, O'Connell built up a strong parochial school system in with Boston, with the number of church-run elementary schools more than doubling, and Catholic high school enrollment soaring. When James Michael Curley, perhaps the most outlandish Irish pol in Boston, thought of challenging incumbent Mayor Fitzgerald, he asked the cardinal to support his bid for City Hall. O'Connell refused because he would not abide a challenge to the incumbent Mayor Fitzgerald. It would be bad for the Irish, he told Curley in so many words. By going it alone, Catholics in Boston saw their power increase to form an insurmountable voting bloc in the city's electoral process and turn Boston into what many called the most Catholic city in America. After having seen his flock so long denied, O'Connell was determined not to see the Irish fail. As he often implored: "It is time for Catholic manhood to stand erect, square in the shoulders, look the world in the eye and say, 'I am a Roman Catholic citizen; What about it?'"

Fitzgerald benefited greatly from the rise in Irish fortunes, though the divisions in Boston were still painfully obvious. With his showmanship and blarney, Honey Fitz became the personification of the Boston Irish during his tenure in City Hall, his much caricatured persona sometimes glossing over genuine achievement. Worse, greed and corruption in Fitzgerald's administration perpetuated the Brahmin belief that the Irish couldn't be trusted to run government in a fair and honest way. In favoring Lodge in the 1916 Senate race, the *New York Times* complained the election was "turned into a joke" with the Democrats' selection of Fitzgerald as their candidate. "To this amiable kisser of the Blarney Stone, warbler of 'Sweet Adeline,' rider of Florida sharks, a butterfly flitting unconcerned around the solid men of Boston, famed in song, is given the uncontested honor of nomination for Senate," the newspaper sneered.

Fitzgerald remained true to his immigrant family's origins. Though he paid his dues to the cultural conservatism of Cardinal O'Connell, Fitzgerald's politics reflected a far more liberal view than heard in Sunday sermons. They were closer to the real views of his immigrant constituency. In City Hall, Fitzgerald pushed Boston to become more diverse, more willing to embrace the newest immigrant arrivals. His "Old Home Week" festival, ostensibly for the Brahmins, who refused to attend, turned into a celebration of Boston's immigrants. "A great public holiday of the foreign people of the city," as one journalist at the time described it. The mayor gave fifty speeches, often mixed with a line or two of poetry. "If my car were as big as my heart," he bellowed from his large, open touring automobile, "I'd give you all a ride!" The mayor's commitment to the famine Irish was never forgotten. "He was always involved in the Irish question," remembered his granddaughter, Jean Kennedy Smith. "My grandpa Fitzgerald was a very loyal Irishman. I think all of that was about immigration too." He managed to translate the experience of his Irish immigrant family—and of so many other minorities—into the national debate. He fought against Know-Nothings and the restrictive leagues; and twice he challenged Henry Cabot Lodge on immigration, once in the Congress and again when he lost a bid in 1916 for Cabot's Senate seat.

In a story he fondly told, and probably embroidered, Fitzgerald recalled encountering Lodge, the senator from Massachusetts and a prime sponsor of the literacy-test immigration bill who blamed Fitzgerald as the culprit for President Cleveland's veto.

"You are an impudent young man," said the senior senator. "Do you think the Jews or Italians have any right in this country?"

"As much right as your father or mine," replied Fitzgerald. "It was only a difference of a few ships."

Chapter Seven

The Family Enterprise

THEY FELL IN LOVE during a family outing. In the sand and saltwater of the Atlantic, they frolicked and shared laughs as their unsuspecting parents looked on. Rose Fitzgerald, the sixteen-year-old daughter of Boston's mayor, realized she cared for Joseph Patrick Kennedy at Old Orchard Beach, Maine, in August 1907. Joe was a tall, handsome young man, a year older than she, with light reddish hair, engaging eyes and a quick lively wit. They were brought together by their families' common passion—politics.

As a way of ingratiating himself to a potential rival, Mayor John F. Fitzgerald invited Joe's father, P. J. Kennedy, the East Boston ward boss, to share the same summer holiday with him and some other power brokers. "Not surprisingly, practically all of them were Irish Catholics from Boston," Rose later recalled. These two men were very different in temperament, and at times Kennedy opposed Fitzgerald's political plans. Still, Fitzgerald figured the relaxing summer days at the Maine resort, playing a friendly game of baseball, or just taking a dip along the oceanfront, would deepen bonds between the two elected officials and their families. If he hoped this trip might pay off politically, he certainly had no idea to what extent.

A photograph taken during that holiday shows the two families in bathing suits stretched out on the sand as if on a picnic blanket. Honey Fitz, his jaw jutting and his bantam-like physique on display, is seated beside his beautiful daughter, Rose, her raven black hair tied behind her head. P. J. Kennedy, his thick hair curled by the surf, reclines in the sand behind them. Off to the side, Joe Kennedy, with his long legs and broad shoulders, gives a discreet smile. "I shall always remember Old Orchard as a place of magic," Rose sighed long afterward. "For it was the place where Joe and I fell in love."

In that idyllic setting, the teenagers began a summer romance that would eventually turn into marriage and a large extended family, becoming the lasting foundation for one of the most unique dynasties in U.S. history. Over the next several decades, this family would achieve an extraordinary political and economic success never seen before by Irish Catholics in America. In their words and actions, the Kennedys defined their lives not in historic milestones but around the concept of family and their sense of belonging to an entity greater than themselves; it was cultivated by more than two thousand years of Irish history and prized by the Roman Catholic Church, an institution that viewed the family as the prime expression of hope and love in a dark and dangerous world. "Long before it ever became a slogan," Joe Kennedy explained simply, "my family and I had togetherness."

Like many American dynasties engaged in empire building, Joe Kennedy's family enterprise would employ rapier-like techniques learned on Wall Street while propagating an all-American image burnished in Hollywood. But its core was based on a set of precepts and values that were distinctly foreign, other-than-American. Indeed, the basic underpinnings of the Kennedy family—the large and sprawling brood inspired from those languid summer days in Old Orchard Beach—reached back to the Celtic roots of both their families and the unique experience of Irish Catholic immigrants, people who often relied on the family as the essential vessel into the New World. "The origin of the Kennedy sense of family is the holy land of Ireland, priest-ridden, superstitious and clannish," adduced Gore Vidal, the novelist (and Jackie Kennedy's stepbrother) in 1967. "Because the Irish maintained the ancient village sense of the family longer than most places in the West and to the extent that the sons of Joe Kennedy reflect those values and prejudices, they are an anachronism in an urbanized, non-family-minded society."

At times, the sense of familial duty and obligations for individual Kennedy members, especially for women such as Rose, could be an emotional straightjacket as well as an abiding source of strength. But in defining their lives around the concept of family, there was no doubt of its origins. Nearly a century later, Rose would insist that her grandchildren read the novel *Trinity* by Leon Uris so that they'd understand what drove so many out of Ireland and why such sweeping bittersweet emotions accompanied the exodus. At his mother's funeral in 1995, Senator Edward Kennedy cast the history of Rose Fitzgerald very much in this light: "She was the grand-daughter of immigrants who saw her father become the first Irish Catholic congressman from Boston and her son and grandson succeed him. She saw the son who proudly carried her Fitzgerald name become the first Irish Catholic president of the United States," the senator eulogized. "As we gathered to share memories of Mother, grandchild after grandchild stood to tell anecdotes about Mother—different stories with one common theme. She had instilled in the next generation the bonds of faith and love that tie us together as a family."

THE FAMILY SPAWNED BY Rose and Joseph Kennedy almost never happened. After their summer in Maine, Joe asked Rose to accompany him to the first dance that fall at Boston Latin, the same school Honey Fitz had graduated from. But the mayor refused to let his daughter go. For the next few years, as both Rose and Joe attended school, they conspired to meet secretly at other dances, or at friends' parties or even at the Boston Public Library. The romance was given some naughtiness because it flourished under the nose of the city's mayor. When Honey Fitz's favorite daughter, the one who accompanied him on so many political outings, announced that she intended someday to marry Kennedy, her alarmed father shipped her off to a convent school in Europe.

Honey Fitz simply adored Rose. No one seemed good enough for her. "He seems to have regarded me as a miracle, an impression from which he never really recovered," she wrote years later in her memoir. Rose graduated at the top of her class from Dorchester High School, a coeducational public school, and was handed her diploma by her father, the mayor, brimming with pride. Young Miss Fitzgerald was considered the most beautiful girl in Boston, at least outside the Brahmin circles where the Irish were trying to carve out their own social world. Rose helped form the Ace of Clubs, the top Catholic social club, created as a mirror image to the Boston society from which the Irish were excluded. Their club aspired to feature distinguished lecturers to stimulate the mind rather than copy the purely frivolous events of the restrictive Junior League. Their aspirations were ridiculed. "The *greenbloods,*" the Brahmins gibed. Like her father, Rose Fitzgerald remained painfully aware of the crippling stereotypes of the Irish as an inferior race not worthy for inclusion in society's upper echelons. "I remember my father saying that the typical picture of an Irish politician was a man with a glass of whiskey in his hand and a pipe in his mouth," Rose recalled. "So my father never took a drink in public, and he never smoked anyway. So I think that particular generation was an effort to counter the image of the Irish who were drunkards and boisterous."

The Catholic Church loomed large in the lives of the Fitzgeralds. The mayor's wife, Josephine Hannon Fitzgerald, a quiet woman of deep and devoted faith and possessing none of her husband's gregarious personality, grew up in a Protestant farming community where her family was keenly aware of being in an Irish Catholic minority. A special room in the Fitzgerald house was transformed during Lent into a flowery shrine to the Blessed Virgin, a quiet reflective place where Rose became a believer. "Sometimes I wondered why I should be doing all the kneeling and studying and memorizing and contemplating and praying, but I became understanding and grateful," Rose wrote. The growing power of the Catholic Church in Boston, personified by Cardinal William O'Connell, also changed the course of Rose's life when her father sent his cherished daughter to the Convent of the Sacred Heart, the most prestigious Catholic school in Boston for young women. The connection with this Catholic order of nuns would extend through two more generations of Kennedy women. This school, as Louise Callan wrote in her history of the Society of the Sacred Heart, intended to do "for young Catholic women much the same work that Vassar and Wellesley do for non-Catholics." These institutions were established as a solution "to one of the most pressing problems the Church has to deal with in the New World, that of securing for Catholic young women the benefits of college education without the sacrifice of faith." To make sure of this task, Callan wrote, Cardinal O'Connell kept a watchful eye at the Sacred Heart school in Boston and "loved to make surprise visits."

Rose's rigorous academic studies were accompanied by lessons in religious doctrine, French culture, "domestic science" and piano lessons, a curriculum designed to teach young women how to be good Catholic wives. Though she attended public school early in life, Rose's enrollment in Sacred Heart seemed to reflect the mixed feelings of many successful Irish families. At the same time that they pursued acceptance in the secular institutions controlled predominantly by Protestants, many Irish Catholics in Boston believed their cardinal's remonstrations that they were better off in their own schools. Historian Paula Kane, in her study of Catholic cultural separatism in Boston, suggests the young women from these convent schools often "internalized the Church's outlook on female subservience and embraced its obsession with bodily disciplines, contenting themselves with self-renunciation in order to achieve some higher, communal goal."

Rose absorbed this lesson well. To widen her experience in this parochial world, she attended the Sacred Heart school at Manhattanville in New York and spent a year with her sister Agnes at the Convent of the Sacred Heart in Blumenthal, Prussia, where she mixed with daughters of European aristocrats. During her stay in Blumenthal, Rose received her medal as a Child of Mary, the highest honor bestowed on the laity by the Sacred Heart order. "I am an angel," she wrote home. "I arise at six o'clock (fifteen minutes earlier than the others) and go to meditation nearly every morning. So you see my piety is increasing."

Rose took to heart the duties of the Children of Mary, which required that she march forth into the world spreading Christ's teachings into everyday life. For this vivacious young woman blessed with the same social skills as her father, the ascetic lessons of sacrifice, confession and spiritual reflection were a strong and lasting counterpoint to the more frivolous sides of her personality. Years later, her call for prayer and acceptance of God's will, no matter how tragic or cruel, seemed to emanate from her time with the Sacred Heart nuns. She promised "in the face of changes of fortune, to hold my soul free." If she left Boston with any hint of bitterness about her father's actions, she resolved to overcome them and seek out her own path. "I decided to forgive them all—all of them, my father, the bishop, the church, politics, I was not going to rebel against my faith but become its advocate, to become truly a Child of Mary. And I would marry Joe, too, no matter what anyone thought or said."

DESPITE THE YOUTHFUL DEVOTION of Joe and Rose to each other, their path to the altar was paved with difficulties. Although he curried favor with P. J. Kennedy, Mayor Fitzgerald didn't want his lace curtain daughter to marry the ward boss's son. P. J. Kennedy's contempt, though masked in his usual reserve, came from his uneasiness with the mayor's vulgar vaudeville mannerisms. His son's lack of regard for Honey Fitz was even greater. He felt the mayor was a caricature of an Irish political hack, a relic from an earlier age when the Irish sacrificed their dignity to get the political gains they wanted. Honey Fitz was exactly the kind of blustery character that well-bred Brahmins pointed at to justify their exclusions of the Irish. In particular, Joe resented Fitzgerald's heavy-handed interference in his relationship with Rose. If anything, Joe Kennedy felt he represented what a modern Irish Catholic young man in America should strive for—acceptance into the finest schools and into the vaunted temples of high finance and power. Money, not votes, would be his key.

Joseph P. Kennedy had neither a brogue nor any other stereotypical characteristic of Irish-American life of old. Even his name reflected these changes. Joe didn't receive his father's moniker because his ambitious mother, Mary Augusta Hickey, felt "Patrick" could be identified too easily by the bigots. She wanted a "less Irish" name so that her middle-class son could meld more quickly into Yankee society. (Unlike other Irish women bounded by the moral conscription of the church, Mary showed a fair degree of independence and, according to one obituary, was "always interested in woman suffrage" along with her other political concerns in East Boston.) Until the eighth grade, her son attended a neighborhood parish, the Assumption School, and then Xaverian School run by the Christian Brothers, before transferring to Boston Latin, one of the finest public schools in the nation. Its alumni included Ralph Waldo Emerson, Cotton Mather and four signers of the Declaration of Independence, John Adams, Benjamin Franklin, John Hancock and Thomas Paine. Mary Augusta, in particular, didn't want her boy's ambitions stymied by the narrowness of a Catholic parish school. With his quick mind and athlete's skills, Joe Kennedy excelled at Boston Latin. He became captain of the baseball team and won the city's batting title. It earned him a trophy from Mayor Fitzgerald. In the meritocracy of Boston Latin, Joe Kennedy flourished. "To strangers, I could not possibly convey the reasons for the powerful and sweet hold which the School has on my affections," Kennedy explained years later at Boston Latin's tercentenary dinner in 1935. "It would be like trying to explain to strangers why I love my family."

Although they were good Catholics, the Kennedys didn't agree with Cardinal O'Connell's view that a Harvard education "does more harm than good." If Harvard held out the same promise as Boston Latin—reward and recognition through achievement—then Kennedy had nothing to fear. But to his dismay, the closely guarded social rankings within Harvard, with its relatively few Catholic and Jewish students, presented barriers that even Joe Kennedy couldn't leap. Within the confines of Harvard Yard, the lanky red-haired young man from East Boston seemed ill at ease. His roommate, Bob Fisher, a football all-American and a favorite among the Brahmins, reminded Kennedy that "he was always being watched for any lapse that would justify the anti-Irish prejudice of snobbish classmates." His grades mediocre, Kennedy managed to join a handful of respected clubs, including Hasty Pudding; but the top fraternities, where membership was still guided by social standing as much as merit, were denied him. For years afterward, Joe Kennedy remembered the day he didn't make the Porcellian Club, the most desired in his mind, realizing that none of the Catholics he knew at Harvard had been selected. Rather than deny his heritage or smooth over his rough edges, Kennedy remained cocksure, defiantly emphasizing in his speech and manner those crass traits attributed to the Irish.

Upon graduation in 1912, Joe Kennedy, with some help from his father's political connections, landed a job as a state bank examiner. The job allowed him to look at the books of financial institutions throughout eastern Massachusetts, a guided tour of how to make money. When Columbia Trust Company in East Boston, one of Pat Kennedy's modest holdings, was threatened with takeover by another bank, the boss of Ward Two rounded up as much capital as he could from friends and associates and enlisted his son in the effort to save Columbia. The bank was a favorite in the Irish immigrant community, and Joe's successful intervention earned him its presidency at age twenty-five and established him as America's youngest bank president. The publicity surrounding Kennedy's financial acumen also impressed Honey Fitz. He dropped his opposition to Rose's suitor.

Fitzgerald was no longer in a position to tell his daughter how to con duct her life. A few months earlier, Mayor Fitzgerald had ended his bid for reelection against James Michael Curley after his relationship with Elizabeth "Toodles" Ryan—who worked at a gambling roadhouse as a cigarette girl and was about the same age as Rose—was threatened to be exposed. Rose and her mother, who had received an anonymous letter about the affair, waited at the door one night when Fitzgerald came home and confronted him. Distraught about being caught, Fitzgerald dawdled in defeat, hoping the crisis might pass over. After all, Honey Fitz and his wife were rarely seen together in public, and wagging tongues talked knowingly about the mayor's wandering eye. In Massachusetts, Irish Catholics had learned to be as intolerant of weaknesses of the flesh as the Puritans. P. J. Kennedy may have been aware of the mayor's libertine ways in arriving at his disdain for His Honor. But Josie Fitzgerald didn't seem to want to know the truth about her husband's unfaithfulness. Only when Curley, clearly a snake displaced from Ireland, announced a public lecture titled "Great Lovers in History: From Cleopatra to Toodles" did Honey Fitz finally drop out of the race.

For Rose Fitzgerald, a young woman devoted to the church, the revelations about her father must have been severely disappointing, if not shattering. Undoubtedly, she believed such a fate could never happen to her. Over time in her own marriage, though, she would adopt the same distinctions as her mother between sex and love, between the lasting obligations of family and the none-too-discreet urges and gropings of the moment. After that night in the doorway, John Fitzgerald's reservations about his future son-in-law were gone. On September 20, 1914, the social page of the *Boston Sunday Post* carried a short notice, headlined "Simple Wedding for Daughter of Ex-Mayor," that said the couple's "romance has been one of the most closely and confidentially watched" in Boston. Three weeks later, in the small private chapel of Cardinal William O'Connell, with her sister, Agnes, as the maid of honor, Rose Fitzgerald married Joseph P. Kennedy. The presence of the cardinal, who shared a private disdain for Honey Fitz similar to that of the groom's father, nevertheless underlined the political clout of the two families who were now joined as one. "I always wanted to be married by a Cardinal," Joe crowed years later, "and I was."

AFTER A TWO-WEEK HONEYMOON, Rose and Joe Kennedy moved into a modest gray frame house on Beals Street in Brookline, a quiet, tree-lined suburb where the Kennedys were one of the few Irish Catholic families. Their home exhibited plenty of signs of their heritage, including the guest room bedspread with its harp and shamrocks, a gift from Mayor Fitzgerald after a trip to Ireland. It was a sign of progress that this couple didn't consider living in the Boston enclaves where their fathers had made their mark. Brookline, with nearby streets named "Harvard" and "Crowninshield," was far different from East Boston, where Irish immigrant families worked a variety of odd jobs to put bread on the table. Rose and Joe were both well educated, a modern couple adhering to the customs of contemporary American families. As a wife, Rose was focused on the daily demands of raising a family while her husband pursued a business career. Like a firm with clear lines of authority drawn, they both fell into their jobs with characteristic single-minded enthusiasm. "We were individuals with highly responsible roles in a partnership that yielded rewards which we shared," Rose later explained in a remarkably detached tone. "There was nothing that he could do to help me in bearing a child, just as there was nothing I could do directly in helping him bear the burdens of business."

After an initial success in local banking, Joe Kennedy expanded his financial empire to shipbuilding and later the liquor distributing business. By several accounts (none terribly well substantiated, as his grandchildren later pointed out, but repeated so much that they became part of the Kennedy lore), Joe was a middleman in the underground liquor industry, reaping another fortune as a bootlegger. He dealt with so many mobsters during Prohibition that some elder Mafioso would later remember him by name.

During the Roaring Twenties, America's swearing off booze created one of the most bizarre social experiments in the nation's history. Prohibition had its peculiar class distinctions, shutting down the taverns and saloons of immigrants and the social life surrounding them, while providing enough loopholes and leeway for the rich to stash away their bottles in their wine cellars or country clubs for a quick nip of the hard stuff. Kennedy reportedly made a bundle from his large-scale bootlegging endeavors, which included shipments of Irish whiskey and Scotch from England. When Prohibition was repealed a decade later, he turned his interests into a legitimate liquor distributing business. He became the U.S. agent for Haig and Haig, John Dewar and Sons and Gordon's Dry Gin. Ironically, Joe Kennedy didn't drink at all himself, just like his father, who owned the East Boston tavern which begat their financial and political fortune. There was something quite delicious about making money from this duplicitous social policy, imposed by the same people who refused him memberships to their exclusive clubs—the Cohasset Country Club and the Somerset Club. "Those narrow-minded bigoted sons of bitches barred me because I was an Irish Catholic and son of a barkeep," he fumed years later. "You can go to Harvard and it doesn't mean a damned thing. The only thing these people understand is money." Making a fortune was his best revenge; he even named his liquor company Somerset Importers.

A YEAR AFTER the couple's 1914 wedding, a boy was born and christened Joseph P. Kennedy Jr. He was followed in succession by John Fitzgerald Kennedy in May 1917, and a daughter, Rose Marie, about whom one newspaper said "a brilliant future is predicted" given her socially prominent parents. Though Joe Jr. grew up a vibrant, healthy boy, little John, named in homage to Rose's father, suffered from a variety of illnesses. Their eldest daughter, later known as Rosemary, was slow to respond to the simplest tasks. Her parents eventually realized that she suffered from mental retardation.

Often left alone with her children, her husband engrossed in business affairs, Rose felt worn down by the responsibilities of motherhood. Although she had a maid and a nursemaid to help, she found herself pregnant again with a fourth child and unable to manage her overwhelming responsibilities. During this time, Rose apparently got wind of her husband's randy social life without her. Whatever the reason, in an act of desperation early in her marriage, Rose Kennedy left her husband and children and moved back into her parents' house in Dorchester. After a very long two weeks in January 1920, the former mayor informed his daughter that she must return to her own home. "You've made your commitment, Rosie," he told her. If she needed more household help, or more time to herself, she must take it, he advised. But both knew divorce was unthinkable in an Irish Catholic family, and such a long separation placed an unfair burden on her husband and children. "So go now, Rose," her father urged, "go back to where you belong."

Before she returned home, Rose went for a few days on a religious retreat, sponsored by the diocese, to pray for the inner strength she felt so lacking in herself. In quiet meditation, Rose found strength in her church, and recalled the instructions for a life of sacrifice and self-denial that she had learned in the Sacred Heart convents. From these moments on, Rose's approach to her family life would bear the stamp of Madeleine Sophie Barat, the founder of the Sacred Heart order later anointed a saint, who taught that the family unit was the essential bulwark of society and that women were its captains. Barat's schools rejected the Jansenism of her native France, with its severely threatening and demanding image of God, absolutely convinced of humankind's sinfulness. Instead, women were encouraged to see God as warm, generous and just. The tragedies and tribulations of life could be overcome through prayer, usually in private, constant and heartfelt. Though she was a tough, complicated woman who came of age during the French Revolution, Barat's legacy appealed to Rose, a young Irish-American woman with many of the same characteristics herself. In rearing children, Barat said, mothers must keep in mind that "in this love, there must be neither weakness nor familiarity, it must be lofty, pure, disinterested, aiming only to gain souls to the Heart of Christ."

Through her religion, Rose found a way to cope, and she approached motherhood as both her church and the baby experts proscribed. During strolls with her children, she would stop into nearby St. Aidan's Church to say her prayers, her children silently in tow. At times, she'd pass time under the hairdryer while saying her rosary beads, or dash off reminder notes to the children about upcoming holidays of the saints or holy days of obligation. As a Catholic mother, she intended to form the habit of "making God and religion a daily part of their lives." Rose also followed many of the "scientific" theories espoused by Dr. L. Emmet Holt. His guidebook—the "bible" of American parenting during the early part of the twentieth century—instructed mothers to follow a precise schedule of feeding and sleeping. Wary of contagious diseases, Dr. Holt frowned on all signs of affection by parents. "Infants should be kissed, if at all, upon the cheek or forehead," Dr. Holt advised, "but the less of this the better." Through this combination of forces, Rose, the bouncy young girl with a wide smile who enjoyed being her father's favorite child, could at times be an emotionally reserved parent who would love her children but, as she was told, in the distanced manner that all good mothers should demonstrate.

About this same time, another crisis tested the faith and strength of the Kennedy marriage. Just as Rose gave birth to their fourth child, Kathleen, their little boy Jack became deathly ill with scarlet fever. If Joe Kennedy had not been already humbled by his wife's desertion and the realization of great trouble in his marriage, the threat of seeing his second oldest son die before his eyes seemed more than he could bear. In the past, he had regularly attended Sunday morning Mass, dressed like a peacock, his wife at his side for all the parishioners to see. But now Joe Kennedy, the hard-nosed entrepreneur with the go-go career, could be seen slipping into church during the middle of the day to pray fervently that God might spare his son. If only his son lived, Kennedy beseeched, half of his money he'd donate to some charity doing the work of the Lord. When Jack recovered from his long illness, Joe Kennedy made out a check to the Guild of St. Apollonia, providing dental care to children in Catholic schools. The scenario calls to mind the Old Testament tale of an omnipotent Yahweh who spared Abraham's son from death. Perhaps Joe Kennedy had this biblical parable in mind when recounting this experience years later, and with his usual bravado, to friendly reporters. But for even the most skeptical eye, it seems reasonable to conclude these family traumas shook Joe Kennedy to his emotional core. As he recalled, "During the darkest days, I felt that nothing else mattered except his recovery."

Although his relationship with Rose was never quite the same again, this tycoon decided the family would be the centerpiece of their lives together, that he'd never become the absentee landlord of his children's hearts. "After Jack's illness, Joe was determined to keep up with every little thing the children were doing," Rose later wrote. "It made me feel that I had a partner in my enterprise."

Chapter Eight

Hard Lessons

WITHIN THE KENNEDY HOUSEHOLD, Rose usually handled matters related to school. She made sure that homework assignments were completed. She checked preparation for tests and consulted with teachers. She also supervised religious instruction at home. For a time, Joe Jr. and Jack served as altar boys, and later so did Bobby and Ted. When other children whispered loudly in church, young Jack shushed them into silence. "I wanted all of the children to have at least a few years in good Catholic schools, where along with excellent secular education they would receive thorough instruction in the doctrines of their religion and intelligent answers to any doubts or perplexities," Rose explained.

In deciding what school their boys should attend, however, Joe Sr. debated strenuously with his wife, arguing that Catholic classes were too limiting. They received sufficient religious training at home, he contended. His boys were headed for a world of power and money, and he wanted them fully prepared. "If Joe wouldn't accept a Catholic school," Rose later recalled, "I thought they should go to public school. They could have seen that some of those boys were even brighter than they were. But as it was, Joe took responsibility for the boys while I took charge of the girls." Joe proposed a third option—sending their sons to the long-established private academies favored by the Brahmins and well-to-do Protestant families, a place most Irish Catholics had never dreamed of attending.

While the family lived in Brookline, the Kennedy boys went to the exclusive Noble and Greenough School, attended by the sons of many prominent Bostonians, including James Jackson Storrow III, the grandson of the Yankee banker that Honey Fitz beat for mayor in 1910. Joe and Jack were likely the school's only Irish Catholic pupils. One day, a group of Protestant boys decided to shove Joe around until he dashed away and stopped in the doorway of a Catholic church. "This is a shrine!" Joe shouted, his fists curled in a ball. "You can't touch me here!" The boys never entered. But there were other ways bigotry could hurt. One summer when Joe was thirteen, he became enchanted with a beautiful young girl, a Unitarian from California, who was visiting her Boston relatives for an extended vacation with her mother. After they went sailing a few times, the girl's hosts became upset that she was seeing an Irish Catholic boy, and she soon left for home. Joe spent the rest of the summer heartsick. "I have been thinking about you ever since you went away," Joe wrote to his first love. "Really I love you a lot." He never saw her again, though bittersweet memories of the experience remained.

When their sons grew older, the Kennedys sent Jack to the Canterbury School in New Milford, Connecticut, a boarding school for upper-class Catholic students, where Rose hoped her son's inquisitive mind and his restless soul would be inspired. At Canterbury, Jack's health suffered terribly, with constant fevers for unknown reasons. A frail thirteen-year-old freshman with barely skin on his bones, Jack tired of being treated by the school's doctor for weeks on end; at dinner, rather than chatting with the rest of the kids, he sat quietly next to the doctor and the headmaster's wife, hardly any fun. Jack's eyes gave him constant trouble, his sight weak enough that for a time he wore glasses. In his letters home, though, he kept a generally upbeat and humorous tone, recalling how he tried to sing Catholic hymns—the "Kyrie Santus [sic], Agnus Dei, and so on"—while his voice cracked. The Agnus Dei comes at the most solemn portion of the Mass, the consecration, when the school's choir would chant in Latin, *"Lamb of God, Who takest away the sins of the world, have mercy on us."* The teacher suspected Jack of fooling around irreverently until he got a good listen at this hormone-stricken youth. "My voice must be changing because when I go up, it sounds as if Buddy (the dog) was howling," he wrote to his parents. "I go up another note and Buddy is choking. Another note and Buddy and me have gasped our last." His report card at Canterbury for the fall of 1930 was a disappointment. Although he earned "Good" grades in math, science and English, he received only a "Fair" grade of 75 in religion, and a nearly failing grade in Latin. "He can do better than this," Nelson Hume, Canterbury's headmaster, wrote on the report to Kennedy's parents, underlining the Latin grade. "In fact, his average should be well into the 80s." Aware of his mother's religious concerns, Jack started another letter to her by underlining that he'd just finished breakfast and "am going to chapel in about two minutes." Canterbury students such as young Jack Kennedy not only learned the central beliefs of the Roman Catholic Church but also reflected on their meaning and how they might apply to their own lives. "We have religious talks on Tuesday and Catacism [sic] on Wednesday," he informed his mother. Rose noticed the Catholic school teachers were not helping her son's poor spelling. "We have chapel every morning and evening," Jack wrote, "and I will be quite pius [sic] I guess when I get home."

Jack's difficulties at Canterbury were endured not only in the classroom and the doctor's office but on the sports field as well. Unlike some teenagers who already possessed adult bodies, Jack hadn't grown yet, and his small stature only added to his problems. "Football practice is pretty hard and I am the lightest fellow on the squad," he wrote home. "The heaviest is 145 pounds—five pounds heavier than Joe. My nose, my leg, and other parts of my anatomy have been kicked around so much that it's beginning to be funny." Another Canterbury student, Robert Sargent Shriver Jr., who would become Jack's brother-in-law, remembered Jack as a "very wiry, energetic, peppy youngster . . . who did extremely well playing on the lightweight football team." Despite his jaunty tone, though, Jack wasn't well. Before the year ended, he was forced to drop out of Canterbury because of illness. Though Jack's difficulties as a teenager at Canterbury are hardly mentioned by his biographers, the disappointment of that year led to one of the most significant decisions in the life of the future president. He would never attend a Catholic school again.

THE FOLLOWING YEAR, after catching up with the help of a private tutor, Jack joined his older brother at Choate, one of the nation's most exclusive private schools and patterned after Eton, the elite British boarding school. His parents, though, still feared for their son's almighty soul.

During the summer of 1934, after a short stay by the two boys at the Gabriel Laymen's Retreat in Brighton, Massachusetts, the priest in charge wrote a letter to Rose, generally praising her "fine manly boys—so sincere" before getting to the point. He confessed to Rose that he feared for their piety. Far more than mere apostates, Father Nilus McAllister warned Rose, her boys might become indifferent to their faith or, worse, doubters. Shaken by the priest's concerns, Rose sent the letter to her husband, who was away on business, and he sent his own reply back in the mail. In his estimation, the two boys were "very critical and rather of an inquisitive frame of mind," Joe explained to the priest. He further mentioned that Joe Jr., two years older than Jack and already a Choate graduate, had started that fall at Harvard and would be in contact with the St. Paul Catholic Club on campus where he'd meet "people of a more rational point of view." But there was no sense in defending his younger son. "As far as Jack is concerned, I am very worried," Joe admitted to the priest. "I did try him at the Catholic school—Canterbury—and feel I completely wasted a year of his life. We made every effort to interest parish priests near the Choate School, which he attends, but with no help or cooperation whatsoever—a fact, I believe, to be a disgraceful proceeding on the part of the clergy." Expressing his appreciation to Father Nilus for his warning and enclosing a further check "to defer" the retreat's expenses, Joe Kennedy promised that he and his wife would be "more insistent on attention paid to this obligation" with their boys in the future.

Joe Sr. began to bear down on Jack, aiming to rid him of his carelessness and instill more order into his life. His son's dismal year at Canterbury was in stark contrast to Joe Jr.'s success at Choate, where he excelled as a student and an athlete. In cheering his eldest's overall performance, Joe Kennedy told his namesake: "There is not much that a father can do to make his boy's career a success—it rests entirely upon the boy." His parents didn't have to worry much about Joe Jr. He showed the kind of industriousness, the stick-toitiveness, prized by his father and the unquestioning religious faith valued by his mother. When Joe Jr. later studied at the London School of Economics with the brilliant socialist Harold Laski, he was quizzed about the Catholic Church during a discussion with Laski's wife, Frida. "I don't know the answers to all those questions but I know the Catholic Church is right, anyway!" young Joe insisted. (Laski was bemused by young Kennedy's talk of becoming America's first Catholic president. During their class trip together to Soviet Russia, Frida recalled young Joe Kennedy's "RC reaction at the museum of anti-religion. I can see him to this day in all amazement.") To his parents, Joe Jr. was a true defender of the faith. Rose encouraged religious training for her sons as well as her daughters because it provided "a sense of responsibility and a sense of security," and a set of moral guidelines so they "knew exactly what they were expected to do." Seeking to assure his mother that he was being a good boy at Choate, Jack signed off one letter he wrote home in 1932 by asking, "P.S. Can I be the Godfather to the baby?"—little Edward Moore Kennedy born that year. Rose and her husband were still concerned about their second son. Young

Jack had changed from a "funny little boy" who loved life, Rose recalled, into a youth who was "generally a nuisance and wasting his time and the time of a lot of the (school) masters."

THE EXCHANGES BETWEEN Joe Kennedy and his sons reflected his high expectations for them. In writing to his eldest son, the Kennedy patriarch mentioned traveling up to Choate to watch Jack compete in a football game against Deerfield. "Jack plays tackle and played very well, but still has that careless indifference of his," wrote his father. At Choate, Jack's actions were monitored by a coterie of teachers, including Russell Ayres, a former classmate of Joe Kennedy's at Harvard, who promised to keep an eye on the boy. In this large Irish clan, Joe Jr. took naturally to the role often designed for the oldest child—protector of the small ones—and was treated as a surrogate parent. Joe Jr.'s place as the anointed one, the son most like the father, most likely to succeed and realize his father's ambitions, are implicit in Joe Kennedy Sr.'s letters. They also expressed strong misgivings about his second son: "Mr. Ayres told me that he [Jack] has one of the few great minds he has ever had in history and yet they all recognize the fact that he lacks any sense of responsibility and it will be too bad if with the brains he has he really doesn't go as far up the ladder as he should. If you can think of anything that you think will help him, by all means do it."

Joe Kennedy's letters to his second son cut him no slack. One well-written letter from Jack was notable in his father's judgement because, as he later wrote back, "there seems to be a forthrightness and directness that you are usually lacking." Yet, Joe Kennedy also could be a thoughtful parent, careful not to push his son too hard. His remonstrations were designed to kick-start Jack's ambition. "Now Jack, I don't want to give the impression that I am a nagger, for goodness knows I think that is the worse thing any parent can be, and I also feel that you know if I didn't really feel you had the goods I would be most charitable in my attitude toward your failings," he wrote in a December 1934 letter. "I am not expecting too much and I will not be disappointed if you don't turn out to be a real genius, but I think you can be a really worthwhile citizen with good judgment and good understanding." Although Joe was judicious in his comments about Jack's best friend at Choate, Kirk LeMoyne "Lem" Billings, a bespectacled pal who became Jack's lifetime friend, he subtly implied that Billings wasn't always the best influence for his son. "After long experience in sizing up people, I definitely know you have the goods and you can go a long way," Jack's father implored. "Now aren't you foolish not to get all there is out of what God

has given you and what you can do with it yourself." His language resonated with the biblical adages that Rose taught the boys—especially St. Luke's
instruction: "To whom much is given, much will be expected." In the spring
of that school year, Joe showed little patience with his son's poor performance. "Don't let me lose confidence in you again, because it will be pretty
nearly an impossible task to restore it—I am sure it will be a loss to you and
a distinct loss to me," Joe reminded him. "The mere trying to do a good job
is not enough—real honest-to-goodness effort is what I expect." Aware of
their parents' expectation, both Joe and Jack Kennedy faced additional hurdles as Catholics at Choate. Pupils were required to attend Protestant chapel
services daily, the Catholics standing mute as psalms were recited. (Roman
Catholicism was not the only religion tracked. As apparently part of the
screening process, Choate asked each applicant's guardian: "Is the boy any
part Hebraic?") With other Catholic students, Joe and Jack had to attend
Mass at a church in downtown Wallingford while the religious needs of
their Protestant peers were tended to on campus.

Jack's biggest crisis at Choate was caused by his wiseacre behavior, which
upset George St. John, the school's headmaster. In his sermons dedicated to
upholding the ideals of Choate, St. John routinely derided the "muckers"
who caused problems in the school. Kennedy, Billings and their pals conspired to form their own "Muckers Club." When the Choate headmaster
found out about the boys' mockery, he summoned Joe Kennedy to a meeting at the school about his son's poor behavior and threatened to expel the
impudent young man. During the meeting, Kennedy scolded his son, who
was seated by his side, but reminded the headmaster that the term "muck-
er" was for many years a slur used against the Irish. Years later, the headmaster still couldn't help noting the family's ethnicity. "Jack's father didn't
hold back—in fact, he spoke very, very strongly, and also with Irish wit,"
wrote St. John about the meeting. Privately, Joe radiated with anger toward
his son, but kept a cool head while convincing the headmaster not to throw
Jack out. Shaken by the experience, Jack nevertheless graduated on time
and, despite his mediocre grades, was voted "most likely to succeed" by his
amused classmates.

Generally, the Kennedy boys fit amiably enough into life at Choate,
though their status as Irish Catholics remained an unspoken barrier. At
Choate and later at Harvard, another bastion of Brahmin culture, the
Kennedy boys sought friendships mainly with Irish Catholics. Jack roomed
with Torbert Macdonald, a Boston Irish Catholic from a modest family, and
Joe's best friend was Ted Reardon, another Boston Irish Catholic, who

worked his way through college. Bobby's roommate and closest friend at Harvard, Ken O'Donnell, was an Irish Catholic from Worcester. "A sociologist or a psychiatrist might make something out of a study of the friends that the three older Kennedy boys sought at Harvard," commented writer Joe McCarthy in his 1960 book about the family. "Selecting such friends at Harvard instead of continuing an association with the upper-crust types in their own wealthy economic level whom they had known in prep school, the Kennedys made an interesting reaching grasp at the racial, social, religious family roots from which they had been removed as children." McCarthy contended this assimilation process went only so far with this generation of Kennedys: "You can take the boy out of Irish Boston but apparently it is difficult to take the Irish Boston out of the boy."

At Harvard, Jack couldn't gain acceptance into any of the elite clubs because of his religion. "Jack Kennedy was part of the Irish contingent, the Catholic contingent, and that set him apart somewhat," recalled a former fellow student Donald Thurber. "The class was, in those days, just dominated by a WASP atmosphere. And Kennedy didn't fit into the mold at all. Do I think Jack Kennedy ever suffered ethnic prejudice? Well, yes, I think so—because he was such an obvious Boston-Irish type." To many at Harvard, the Kennedys were Wall Street hustlers rather than old money, and Mayor Fitzgerald the very epitome of outlandish Irish ethnicity beyond the ivy walls of Cambridge. Joe Jr. endured the same treatment at Harvard. But Jack's friends prevailed on one group, the Spee Club, to let him in. "It's wrong that Jack Kennedy can't get in a club," said Bill Coleman who, along with Jimmy Rousmaniére, insisted that the club accept them as a threesome or not at all. Jack remained particularly grateful to Bill Coleman, reared in an Episcopalian and Republican family, for helping him overcome this social barrier, a feat neither his father nor brother ever accomplished. Torby Macdonald, despite his popularity and athletic accomplishments, didn't get into the Spee Club because he was perceived as too Irish, certainly not as polished as his roommate. As the first, Jack learned how to make himself acceptable to the WASPs at Harvard, in his polished speaking manner, his stylish appearance and engaging yet deflective sense of humor—all skills he'd later employ on a grander scale.

It is understandable why teenagers from a minority group, away from home for months at an institution sometimes hostile to their religion, would find comfort with friends who shared the same cultural touchstones. In this world, the Kennedy sons seemed to find comfort in the shared Irish Catholic background of their inner circle of friends—a pattern often repeated within the family. In his own pursuit for wealth and acceptance, Joe Kennedy relied on a rear guard of Irish Catholic cronies, such as Eddie Moore, an Irishman educated in the public schools of Charlestown. (The *New York Times* once described Moore as "Irish as a clay pipe.") These men were born several rungs down from the Kennedys on the social ladder, and yet, through some alchemy of similar heritage and experience, they could be trusted with the most intimate secrets of their Kennedy friends. This pattern of friendships would continue into the White House, where Jack's "Irish Mafia" of confidants, including O'Donnell, existed on a parallel plane to the tweedy official world of State Department experts and Foreign Service diplomats.

JACK KENNEDY'S SENSE of ethnicity and religion, like other aspects of his personal character, was always hard to decipher. Each version of reality, as attested in the numerous volumes written about him, seemed to depend on who was doing the looking. When she wrote her 1974 autobiography, Rose Kennedy asked Jack's best friend at Choate, Lem Billings, to recall their school days; he claimed the worst thing they ever did, besides the Muckers Club fiasco, was to keep a messy room and sometimes arrive late for class. "Some of our [Muckers Club] members, I expect, did break the school code of conduct by going into town and smoking, drinking and so forth," he allowed. Two years later, in a biography of JFK written by an old Harvard friend and his wife, Lem Billings revealed another, quite different escapade, which happened while the Choate students were on vacation: "Another time I remember, when Jack first got laid. What a night!" enthused Billings, recalling how Kennedy and another pal, both seventeen, lost their virginity in a Harlem whorehouse ("they were white girls of course") and then panicked at the thought of contracting venereal disease. Lem accompanied them to a hospital for treatment. "These salves and cremes and a thing shoved up their penis to clean it out," Billings recalled. "They came home, still sweating. They couldn't sleep."

For a young man steeped in the conservative mores of the Catholic Church, the secrecy and shuffling surrounding sex—as well as the fear of punishment—were all part of the thrill for Jack Kennedy. His handwritten letters to Billings, now entombed in the Kennedy Library, were replete with adolescent musings about sex, masturbation and his exploits with women, paid or not. Although the tales are undoubtedly exaggerated, given his bad back and sickly body, young Jack one summer still dreamed of the nurses who came into his hospital room while he was being treated at the Mayo

Clinic and serviced him sexually as well as medicinally. In Kennedy's world, with its images of madonnas and whores, there were good girls for marrying and bearing children—exemplified by his mother, Rose—and other girls for partying and quick sexual encounters. Lem and Jack knew the rules and delighted in breaking them without getting caught. Kennedy seemed convinced that his Saturday night excesses could be forgiven if he said enough prayers at Sunday morning Mass.

Sex outside marriage loomed as a mortal sin, the most serious offense against God. Catholics were taught by the Irish priests that sex served God as an act of procreation—adding to the splendor of divine creation—and never solely for the pleasure of the participants or the enjoyment of the act itself. If eating meat on Friday, missing Mass on Sunday and going to restricted movies were all mortal sins, as the priests commanded in the 1920s and early 1930, then surely Jack Kennedy's reveries were taking him along the road to hell. If that was his eternal fate, he'd surely meet some of the other men in the family on the way. (Year later, when told his father was seen chasing after some young woman at a racetrack, JFK could only say, "When I'm sixty, I hope I'm just like my father.")

This stern condemnation of sex by the Catholic Church in America differed from the old Irish view. The ancient Celts enjoyed bawdy Gaelic songs and imagery, and in the Irish countryside, well into the nineteenth century, the roadhouses were places of sexually charged dancing and delights. "Rural Ireland was a highly sexual society, with sexual tensions resolved by early marriages," observed Charles R. Morris, in his history of the American Catholic Church. "Nudity or seminudity were not uncommon, and visitors were surprised to see young Irish men and women bathing within sight of one another." All that changed in Ireland with the arrival of Cardinal Paul Cullen at the time of the Famine. Influenced by the Puritan strains of Jansenism, he enforced a strict and foreboding view of sex. Inside the marriage bed, sex had solely a utilitarian function—to produce enough sons and daughters to maintain a farm properly, attend Mass as faithful followers and ideally contribute one or more children to the Mother Church as priests, nuns and monks. "In a society where feckless reproduction had just led to catastrophe, the newly rigorist doctrine of sexual purity and the Church's carefully fostered cult of the Blessed Virgin found receptive ears," Morris noted. "Sex even among the married was shamefaced and fleeting." Cullen's influence spread widely among the Irish who sought new lives in America, where Puritanism and its hell-and-brimstone condemnations of sex were already deeply rooted. The American Catholic Church fathers proved every bit as conservative in sexual matters as their Protestant brethren, an attitude that intensified as the twentieth century progressed.

Rose Kennedy shared the church's view of sexuality as a matter of her extended faith in all its teachings. Her schooling at the Sacred Heart convents prepared Catholic women for a future as mothers, but implied that the lust of men was a chore for wives and was to be handled neatly, like diaper changing or putting out the garbage. Good girls like Rose might preen and keep themselves attractively attired in the latest Paris fashions but, once married, the vibrancy of their sexual union was of little matter, certainly not compared to the more pressing needs of the family. As part of her family building with Joe, Rose Kennedy extended herself to her husband repeatedly and with the devotion that only a brood of nine children can attest to. But the romance of their youth, perhaps shattered by Joe's early acts of infidelity, never matured into a sexually fulfilling relationship. After the birth of her last child, Rose demanded separate bedrooms and refused any more sex, according to historian Doris Kearns Goodwin. Goodwin quoted Marie Greene, an old family friend who played cards with the Kennedys on Friday nights, who recalled Joe Kennedy's pleas: "Now listen, Rosie, this idea of yours that there is no romance outside of procreation is simply wrong," Joe urged in this account. "It was not part of our contract at the altar, the priest never said that and the books don't argue that. And if you don't open your mind on this, I'm going to tell the priest on you."

Instead, a false veneer arose with the Kennedys, who often spent a surprising share of their lives apart, sometimes for business reasons, but often in Rose's case for purely personal reasons. Her trips to Europe, Florida and California seemed to be covering over a deep hurt. When confronted with evidence of cheating, she reacted as her mother, the good politician's wife, had before her and simply looked the other way. Rose extended this same denial and sanitizing technique to her son Jack, preferring not to dwell on his sins and failings. Instead, she repeated the selective remembrances of his best friend, Lem Billings, who is quoted in her book as saying, "Never can I remember Jack not saying his prayers on his knees every night before going to bed."

The most glaring example of these contradictions in the marriage of Rose and Joe Kennedy involved his relationship with actress Gloria Swanson. This affair came at the height of his business career. During the 1920s, Joe Kennedy mastered the art of making money on Wall Street. He amassed a fortune in the world of speculation, and then moved into Hollywood movies, which he declared a "gold mine." Portraying her husband's struggle in familiar ethnic terms, Rose would later recall: "When he went to Hollywood, there were predictions that this Boston Irishman soon would be sadder and poorer." He soon controlled three studios. During the production of his most ambitious film, *Queen Kelly,* Joe began an affair with its star, Gloria Swanson, to whom Kennedy acted as an independent financial advisor. The new-money world of Hollywood was far different from the old established one he knew in Boston. "The Cabots and the Lodges wouldn't be caught dead at the pictures or let their children go," he explained to Swanson. "And that's why their servants know more about what's going on in the world than they do. The working class gets smarter every day, thanks to radio and pictures. It's the snotty Back Bay bankers who are missing the boat."

The fabulously attractive Swanson, a sophisticated independent woman already married to her third husband, carried an allure that Rose Fitzgerald Kennedy couldn't match. Swanson's expressive blue eyes, underlined with mascara, and her de rigueur sleek, tight clothing carried tremendous allure. Joe's intense sexual relationship with Swanson became an open secret in Hollywood, acknowledged by virtually everyone but Rose herself. Mrs. Kennedy carried on an acting tour de force worthy of an Oscar, ignoring both hints and clear evidence of her husband's infidelity with the movie actress, whom she treated as a treasured family friend. In an extraordinary visit, Kennedy invited Swanson to his summer home so that she could meet Rose and all the kids. "If she suspected me of having relations not quite proper with her husband, or resented me for it, she never once gave any indication of it," Swanson wrote years later. "Was she a fool, I asked myself as I listened with disbelief, or a saint? Or just a better actress than I was?"

When Swanson moved to divorce her husband, as she later claimed in her autobiography, Joe sought special permission from Cardinal William O'Connell to separate from Rose and set up a household with Gloria. Swanson said she soon got a knock on the door from the cardinal himself.

"You are not a Catholic, my child, therefore I fear that you do not grasp the gravity of Mr. Kennedy's predicament as regards his faith," explained the churchman. She recalled that his eyes were "filmy" behind his thick glasses. "I am here to ask you to stop seeing Joseph Kennedy," O'Connell insisted. He informed her that Kennedy had met with some top Catholic officials in an attempt to legitimize their illicit affair without luck. Irked by the cardinal's invasion of her privacy, Swanson questioned whether he'd violated the confessional or was just repeating gossip. The cardinal emphasized

Kennedy's position "as one of the most prominent Catholic laymen in America" and that this affair exposed him to scandal if she persisted. "Every time you see him, you become an occasion of sin for him," O'Connell lectured. "As a Catholic, there is no way Joseph Kennedy can be at peace with his faith and continue his relationship with you." Swanson, not easily intimidated, suggested the cardinal address his concerns to Kennedy himself.

In an indirect way, the church did rupture Kennedy's relationship with the movie star. At the time, many Catholic officials, including those in Boston, pressured regulators to oversee what they called the morally offensive and sexually titillating content of movies. "Everyone knows what Hollywood is—it is the scandal of the world," proclaimed O'Connell. With Catholics making up a sizeable portion of the American population thanks to decades of immigration, the clergy threatened to ban the faithful from films that didn't conform to their standards. By 1929, the film industry set up its own censor, Will H. Hays, to bring about a decency code. Halfway through *Queen Kelly,* it became obvious to both Swanson and Kennedy that their star director, Erich von Stroheim, had structured the film around scenes that would never get past Hays's review. The script called for Swanson to play a poor Irish convent girl who falls in love with a crown prince, but some scenes were so salacious that Kennedy decided to fire von Stroheim and can the film without ever showing it. (Snippets from the film appeared years later as an "inside joke" in Billy Wilder's *Sunset Boulevard,* starring Swanson as an aging film star and von Stroheim as her former director turned butler.) This disaster soon ended Kennedy's affair with Swanson and his dream of becoming a major Hollywood magnate.

For her own reasons, Rose never mentioned whatever evidence existed of her husband's sexual involvement with Swanson. A few years later, though, Rose recounted for her children how she bumped into Swanson's former husband, Henri de la Fallaise, at a French restaurant in New York, and how he introduced her to his new wife, a woman from Colombia "who looked very sweet in her French frocks." Rose couldn't help but note the comparison. "As he [de la Fallaise] was never properly married before, he is now married to a Catholic so his mother is very happy."

WHILE TENDING the mess he wrought in Hollywood, Joe Kennedy learned that his father had died. P. J. Kennedy, the son of Irish immigrants, never wandered far from home in East Boston, either physically or emotionally. Unlike his father, Joe considered himself far more American than Irish and was eager to prove it so. In settling his father's estate, Joe found in his possessions a bundle of Republic of Ireland bonds issued in 1920 that were now worthless.

Many contemporaries viewed Joe Kennedy as an amoral hypocrite, a capitalist shark who jumped at the first sight of blood in any field or endeavor, then posed after Sunday morning Mass with his smiling family outside the church. "Yes, he was amoral, sure he was," declared Arthur Krock, the Washington bureau chief of the *New York Times*, who for decades traded favors with him. "I think only a Roman Catholic could possibly describe how you could be amoral and still religious. That is, how you can carry an insurance policy with the deity and at the same time do all those other things." But other observers suggested that Joe Kennedy was still fighting the Irish immigrant's battle for acceptance, only at a much higher level. "Where does the Kennedy competitive drive come from? Most probably it stems originally from the chafing, frustrating atmosphere of anti-Irish and anti-Catholic prejudice in Boston fifty years ago that made the young Joe Kennedy determined to push himself and his children to a place at the top of the world where they would not have to take a back seat to anybody," explained Joe McCarthy, the journalist who later collaborated with Dave Powers and Ken O'Donnell on their memoir of the Kennedy White House years. "Resentment probably burned hotter in Joe Kennedy than in most Boston Irish of his generation because he associated more closely with the Yankee Brahmins than did most Irish of his time. Consequently, he was more exposed to slurs, more aware from first-hand experience of the cool condescension with which Beacon Hill looked down on people of his religion and racial background."

In Boston, Joe Kennedy had attempted to break into the Brahmin world of finance on State Street, but was only able to enter banking with the Irish-controlled Columbia Trust. Twice Kennedy was rejected as a new member of the board of trustees for the Massachusetts Electric Company. When he finally made it to the board in 1917, the company president apologized for the two earlier turndowns, which he blamed on the company's discrimination of Irish Catholics. The feeling of Irish resentment seeped into the consciousness of his own children, seemingly perfectly assimilated, one of whom commented to a friend while walking along the cobblestone streets of Beacon Hill, "Those aren't cobblestones—they're Irish heads." In suburban Brookline, the Kennedys weren't much better off; they realized that the Kennedy girls, despite the family's wealth, would never be invited to the top debutante cotillions of Boston. After spending several summers in the primarily Catholic enclave of Nantasket, where Mayor Fitzgerald kept a summer home, the Kennedys moved to the more fashionable Cohasset. When Joe applied for membership in the local country club, he was blackballed after a belabored and humiliating process.

Joe Kennedy was an anomaly who wallowed in Irish sentiments while rejecting all trappings of them. He didn't want power as a ward boss in East Boston or as mayor of the town. He wanted to build a fortune big enough for his outsized family so that they could never again be treated as less than American, their birthright. He set up trust funds for each of his children so they'd never be intimidated by the rich, and could even "spit in my eye" if they wished. "Big businessmen are the most overrated men in the country," he told his sons. "Here I am, a boy from East Boston, and I took 'em. So don't be impressed." He became convinced that Boston—the cradle of American democracy—could no longer contain his dreams. The Brahmins still hated the Irish pretensions to social acceptance and their exercise of power in City Hall, and the Catholics led by their Cardinal O'Connell were steadily retreating into their own segregated communities. He decided to move to New York. Not only could Wall Street provide more money for the Kennedy coffers, its New York social world didn't appear as strangulated as Boston's, nor as restrictive to his children.

In 1927, the Kennedys relocated from Brookline to Riverdale in the suburban-like outer reaches of New York City. In a parting boot in the pants, Joe declared that Boston "was no place to bring up Catholic children." As he explained years later, "I didn't want them to go through what I had to go through when I was growing up there. . . . At that time, the social and economic discrimination was shocking. I know so many Irish guys in Boston with real talent and ability that never got to first base only because of their race and religion." Honey Fitz bemoaned the departure of his beloved daughter, blaming anti-Catholic prejudice as the cause. The Kennedys, as strivers and very much pioneers in untested waters for Irish Catholics, were still hitting their heads upon what historian William V. Shannon called the "glass ceiling of religious bigotry" in Boston. Driving through the city years later with a journalist from a well-known and esteemed Boston family, Rose turned and asked, "When do you think the good people of Boston will accept us?"

Part II

The Family Faith

"I think that the Irish in me has not been completely assimilated, but all my ducks are swans."

—JOSEPH P. KENNEDY

Chapter Nine

Happy Warriors

> "It is possible for a man in public life to
> separate his religious beliefs from his polit-
> ical activities."
>
> —GEORGE NORRIS

ALFRED E. SMITH'S presidential bid in 1928 contained a sense of yearning for Irish-Americans, an inestimable influence on their collective imagination. The New York governor was a Democrat, a Catholic and a "wet"
who favored repeal of Prohibition's drinking laws. If Smith could make it
to the White House, so could any child of immigrants.

Smith's candidacy had considerable impact on the Kennedys. Years later,
Rose remembered the feeling of pride that one of their own kind was running for president, and the bigotry he faced in such states as West Virginia.
In his Pulitzer Prize–winning book, *Profiles in Courage,* John Kennedy lauded
Senator George Norris, a Republican from Nebraska, for supporting
Smith—the first Catholic ever to run for the presidency—and arguing that
no American should be discarded simply because of religion. For his courageous stand, Norris ranked in JFK's political hall of fame as "an idealist, an
independent, a fighter—a man of deep conviction, fearless courage, sincere
honesty." But on the subject of Al Smith, Kennedy's own father was never
so forthright. In fact, it's not clear whether Joe Kennedy even voted for
Smith. At a time when thousands of Irish Catholics were rushing to Smith's
support, hoping for an electoral miracle, Joe Kennedy cagily stepped back,
gauging his own prospects and acting in his own self-interest. Nonetheless,
the ill-fated campaign of Al Smith in 1928—crippled by a nationwide tide

of anti-Catholic bigotry—would hold a profound impact on the Kennedy family's political fortunes.

For most of the 1920s, Joe Kennedy cared more about making money than about politics. He flirted with the Massachusetts Republican Party, and in 1924 he gave a sizeable contribution to the Progressive Party presidential campaign of Robert LaFollette. He adopted a similar contradictory role in 1928. In early September, Franklin Delano Roosevelt, then Smith's floor manager at the Democratic Convention, sent a letter to Joe Kennedy asking for his "suggestions and counsel." It seemed natural that Kennedy favored Smith, already denied the 1924 Democratic nomination because of his religion. Both men were conservative Democrats who had grown up in working–class Irish Catholic neighborhoods and worked diligently to reach the pinnacles of American society. Back in his native Boston, Kennedy's father-in-law, former Mayor John F. Fitzgerald, strongly supported Smith's election. And Kennedy, a newly arrived resident of New York State, would likely need Smith's help someday. In Joe Kennedy's private correspondence, however, a friendly letter suggests he favored Herbert Hoover, the Republican candidate for president. Dated April 1929, Kennedy's letter complimented Hoover's new secretary of the navy, Charles Francis Adams, whose selection, he wrote, "was reason enough for President Hoover's election and sufficient justification for a good Democrat like myself to vote for him again." Perhaps Joe Kennedy simply lied to flatter Adams or to curry favor with a new Hoover administration. If his letter expressed the truth, though, why did Joe Kennedy abandon the first Irish Catholic to run for president—the standard-bearer of his father's party and a candidate promoted at rallies by his father-in-law in Boston? Some of the answers undoubtedly lie in what compelled Joe Kennedy into public life in the first place.

AL SMITH's ascension to power in New York resembled the rise of Honey Fitz in Boston and other Irish politicians around the nation who emerged from immigrant neighborhoods to stake a claim at City Hall or in the statehouse. "Immigrants and city dwellers recognized that he was someone in higher politics who stood up for them, accepted them as equals, and above all, who gave them respectability," wrote Robert Slayton, one of Smith's biographers. Smith was a progressive, often brilliant politician who made no effort to hide his origins; with his brown derby hat, street-map complexion and a honking Lower East Side voice, he personified his theme song, "The Sidewalks of New York." As New York's governor, he championed educational reforms, built better housing and hospitals, and, with the help of a young aide, Robert Moses, created parks and playgrounds. Increasingly, the political coalition of various ethnic and religious groups built by Smith and other urban politicians, enfranchising thousands of immigrants as new voters, would invigorate the Democratic Party and redefine the nation during the twentieth century—even if these efforts came too late for Smith himself.

Smith's entry into presidential politics became a rallying cry for the Ku Klux Klan, the most widespread hate organization in the Republic's history. Notorious for lynching blacks in the South, the Klan also perpetuated vile claims and frauds against Catholics, and in 1924, it worked hard to block Smith's attempt for the Democratic presidential nomination against William G. McAdoo. The dispute forced the party to settle, on the 103rd ballot, for a compromise candidate, John W. Davis, who lost miserably to Republican Calvin Coolidge. Four years later, Smith tried again for the nomination and succeeded.

But the 1928 candidacy of Alfred Emanuel Smith devolved into what his biographer Slayton called "the worst example of cultural wars in American presidential history." The prospect of a Catholic in the White House rekindled the old nativist conspiracy theories and inspired pamphlets warning of a plot by the Pope to take over America. A photo of the newly constructed Holland Tunnel, connecting New York to New Jersey, became the so-called evidence of a secret passageway being built across the ocean to the Vatican. Governor Smith received bundles of angry letters, some threatening assassination. In Oklahoma City, fertile ground for the Klan, a Baptist minister declared, "If you vote for Al Smith, you're voting against Christ and you'll all be damned."

Some made a fuss when Smith knelt to receive a visiting cardinal's blessing and kissed the prelate's ring as a sign of respect. Other critics, aware of Smith's immigrant heritage, bemoaned the loss of a time when America was "of one blood as we were of one tongue." In a sense, Smith's bid became a plebiscite about newcomers, those not of Anglo-Saxon blood, already within the nation's borders. Many Democrats, particularly in the South, opposed their party's candidate for the basest religious reasons. With the big cities growing, Al Smith came to represent "the urban stranger who was the symbol of the new America," wrote Oscar Handlin, one of Smith's biographers. The ugliness of 1928 spread throughout the land. The *Christian Century,* the largest and most respected Protestant journal in the nation, argued that a "reasonable voter" wasn't a "religious bigot" for rejecting

Smith. The magazine conceded that it, too, shared the concern of "seating a representative of an alien culture, of a medieval Latin mentality, of an undemocratic hierarchy and of a foreign potentate in the great office of President of the United States." Hoover avoided mentioning religion, but his wife, Lou Hoover, a well-educated woman who spoke out forcibly against racism toward blacks, nevertheless shared the religious bigotry of large swaths of the American electorate. "There are many people of intense Protestant faith to whom Catholicism is a grievous sin," she said. "And they have as much right to vote against a man for public office because of that belief" as anyone else, without being charged with "persecution."

With the electoral equivalent of a burning cross on his front lawn, Smith realized he needed to address America's distrust of Catholics. In an eloquent article for the *Atlantic,* he outlined his belief in the strict separation of church and state. To make sure he wouldn't alienate Catholics, he asked New York's Cardinal Hayes to review the article beforehand for errors in church doctrine. While affirming his own Catholic faith, Smith declared: "I recognize no powers in the institutions of my Church to interfere with the operations of the Constitution of the United States or the enforcement of the laws of the land. I believe in the absolute freedom of conscience for all men and in equality of all churches, all sects, and all beliefs before the law as a matter of right and not as a matter of favor." Other publications came to Smith's defense, underlining his credentials as an effective governor of the nation's then-most populous state and what it might mean if he was rejected for the presidency purely because of religion. "Who has a right to expect Americanization of an immigrant people if we persist in setting before them so flagrant a case of anticonstitutionalism and antitolerance?" asked *Commonweal,* the magazine published by Catholic laity.

Smith's loss of several then-traditionally Democratic states, such as Virginia, Florida, North Carolina, Tennessee and Oklahoma, was regarded as proof that anti-Catholicism was a major factor in Smith's demise. John W. Davis, the defeated Democratic Party nominee of four years earlier, blamed the nation's religious biases for Smith's 1928 loss. "Maybe twenty-five years from now . . ." Davis sighed to one reporter. The widespread vitriol against Catholics left Smith shaken, just as it did for a generation of Americans not far from the immigrant experience. "It was disturbing to be forced to wonder whether his conception of Americanism was at fault," summarized Handlin about Smith's reaction to the election outcome. "Could it be that he had not read aright the lesson of his own life? If Americans were not really willing to accept an Irish Catholic as fully their equal, where then did he belong?"

His defeat became a source of bitterness for many Catholics, particularly in Boston, where Honey Fitz sang "Sweet Adeline" at Smith rallies. "The saliency of the religious issue in Al Smith's loss in 1928 rankled Boston Catholics, whose attachment to Smith bordered on hysteria," observed Jack Beatty, biographer of Mayor James Michael Curley. As their oldest son prepared for the presidency in 1960, the Kennedys still remembered Al Smith's crushing experience. Handlin noted that Smith's defeat "made a sharp impression" on John F. Kennedy, who carefully read about Smith before starting his own campaign. Rose and Joe had often felt the sting of anti-Catholic slurs and slights, and they worried that their religion might become a political liability too hard to overcome for their sons. "True, there was now a new generation, and religious tolerance had grown," Rose Kennedy later wrote in her memoir. "But how much, how far, and how effectively was debatable. There were strong feelings, and in some cases strong convictions, among Catholic as well as Protestant and Jewish leaders that Jack's Catholicism would prove to be too severe a handicap. Political leaders dislike backing losers." Perhaps that fear of backing a loser—a great sin in the Kennedy political catechism—was why Joe Kennedy sat out the 1928 election, unwilling to aid the first Catholic to run for president.

EVER THE swift appraiser, Joe Kennedy spotted a winner in Franklin Delano Roosevelt. By 1932, the Depression had knocked out the underpinnings of the U.S. economy, causing a national crisis that Hoover, the engineer turned politician, seemed incapable of fixing. Many Irish Catholics, including Joe's father-in-law, John F. Fitzgerald, still supported another bid by Al Smith, but Kennedy remained convinced that the country needed a drastic change. Kennedy believed that Roosevelt—Smith's replacement as governor—was the only one up to the task. He also appeared convinced that Roosevelt would considerably further his own political success.

More than a decade earlier, Kennedy had lost a rancorous dispute with Roosevelt, then assistant secretary of the navy, over shipment of battleships from the Fore River shipyard. "Roosevelt was the hardest trader I'd ever run up against," Kennedy recalled. "When I left his office, I was so disappointed and angry that I broke down and cried." But this rare experience at losing—and the sage words of several friends who admired Roosevelt—only reinforced Kennedy's conviction that the Hyde Park aristocrat whom he had once denigrated as "just another rich man's son" could pull the country out of its dilemma. As biographer Arthur Schlesinger Jr. noted, FDR thought of himself as an upstate New Yorker, a country gentleman from Dutchess County, not a city dweller with recent immigrant roots. Annoyed at his inability to attract ethnic voters in urban neighborhoods, Roosevelt once complained: "Al Smith is good at that. I am not."

During the 1932 campaign, Kennedy worked tirelessly for Roosevelt, contributing $25,000 himself and soliciting more than $100,000 in anonymous donations. He was rewarded not with his first wish—the Treasury Department—but with an appointment as the chairman of the new U.S. Securities and Exchange Commission, overseeing Wall Street. When some complained privately about the choice, Roosevelt summarized his strategy with a quip: "Set a thief to catch a thief." Kennedy viewed his entry into government in far grander terms: it was part of a dynastic plan, something that Roosevelt clearly understood. "I told him that I did not desire a position with the Government unless it really meant some prestige to my family," Joe explained to his oldest son. With his wide array of interests and contacts in many fields, Joe Kennedy proved himself helpful to the new president, whether he was twisting the arm of publishing magnate William Randolph Hearst to support Roosevelt editorially or writing his own 1936 book, *Why I'm for Roosevelt*.

During FDR's first term, Joe Kennedy also became an important liaison between Roosevelt and the Catholic Church, whose congregants formed a vital voting block for the New Deal. Since his days in Boston, Kennedy had nurtured an amiable, businesslike relationship with Cardinal William O'Connell and a mutual alliance with another rising church eminence, Auxiliary Bishop Francis Joseph Spellman. As Roosevelt's reelection campaign neared in 1936, Kennedy finessed an extraordinary arrangement between the Vatican and the U.S. president that, with the help of the two churchmen, would ensure Kennedy's status as the leading Catholic layman in America for decades to come.

Cardinal O'Connell, like Kennedy, was an Irish Catholic of many contradictions. Built like a football linebacker, the bald, barrel-chested O'Connell ran the Archdiocese of Boston as if it were his own corporate fiefdom. His proud, defiant stature demanded attention and respect from the powerful entities who had so often abused Irish Catholics in the past. Dating back to Mayor Fitzgerald's tenure, O'Connell wielded extraordinary power over Boston's political and social life. The cardinal became a symbol of upward mobility for the Irish, casting a disdainful view on certain elected officials. In one election, he dissuaded the faithful from voting for Mayor James Michael Curley, known as the "Purple Shamrock," because of his graft and outlandishness.

In the cardinal's eyes, however, the Kennedys were different. His niece and nephews, Joe O'Connell and Mary O'Connell Ryan, were friends of Rose and Joe, Joe O'Connell having served as godfather for the Kennedys' firstborn, Joe Jr. For all the cardinal's rant against Harvard and the movies, Kennedy was the kind of successful Irish Catholic he truly respected. Joe Kennedy's thousands of dollars in Catholic donations made him more special. Even if Kennedy strayed in his marriage, he wouldn't let this trespass get in the way of greater glories to God.

THE COMPLEXITIES in Cardinal William O'Connell, enough to rival any wayward politician in Boston, went to extremes when it came to matters of money, spirituality and sex. During the Depression, he used the tithes and donations of working-class families to buy an oceanside summer estate in Marblehead and a winter home in the Bahamas, and he motored around the diocese in a customized Pierce Arrow. He'd been caught pocketing $25,000 in diocesan funds from his earlier assignment in Portland (returned only after his successor questioned it). While in Boston, he built a palatial residence complete with a private golf course. Though a tough-minded administrator and a high-minded public moralist, O'Connell didn't seem much interested in religion, rarely said daily mass and galloped through services at a pace that sometimes shocked those in the pews.

But his most extraordinary deception involved his nephew, James O'Connell, a priest who was named chancellor and oversaw the diocesan finances. At some point, James O'Connell broke his priestly vows and married a divorced woman who lived in New York. Like some double agent, he divided each week between his dual role: that of a priest in Boston and of a married man using an assumed name in New York. Another priest, an editor of the diocesan newspaper and a friend of James O'Connell's, also married a woman who didn't realize he was a priest using an alias. The cardinal looked the other way because his nephew threatened to expose evidence of financial chicanery with church funds and "proofs of the Cardinal's sexual affection for men," according to his biographer, James O'Toole. Eventually, word of this scandal reached the ears of Pope Benedict XV, who summoned the cardinal to Rome and asked him directly about the whole affair. "O'Connell foolishly tried to bluff his way through," wrote O'Toole, who recounted how the angry Pope produced documents to back up the allegations, including the nephew's marriage certificate. "The cardinal was seriously embarrassed at having been caught in a lie." Eventually, O'Connell's nephew and the other priest were forced to resign, but the cardinal, as testimony to his power and influence, survived the scandal.

Boston's Irish Catholics, accustomed to deferring to the church's hierarchy, remained oblivious to the contradictions in O'Connell's personal life. The cardinal now turned his attention to other threats to the soul. O'Connell condemned government programs that, he believed, smacked of communism or "Bolshevism." He was one of several conservative American Catholic clergy appointed by Rome who echoed the concerns about socialism that were expressed in papal encyclicals, dating back to Leo XIII's *Rerum Novarum,* "On the Condition of the Working Class," of 1891. These themes were reiterated again in 1931 by Pope Pius XI, who stressed the need for a fair and adequate "family wage" for all workers, but rejected atheistic communism. In Depression-stricken America, many Catholics looked to liberal politicians such as Roosevelt to help provide their daily bread. But the church kept a wary eye out for God-less, state-driven movements of the kind that swept through Russia and drove Catholics underground. Instinctively, Joe Kennedy shared the cardinal's worry about creeping socialism. By the mid–1930s, he also shared another concern with O'Connell—the rise of an outspoken priest from the Midwest, Father Charles Coughlin of Michigan, who accused Roosevelt of a host of evils, including sympathy for communism.

From the Shrine of the Little Flower in Royal Oak, outside Detroit, Father Coughlin's radio broadcast on Sunday afternoons became immensely popular throughout America, especially in regions with large Catholic populations such as New England. Mayor Curley, with his finger to the wind, called Boston "the most Coughlinite city in America." At first, Coughlin, a bespectacled priest with a fiery delivery, espoused the doctrines of social justice found and embraced in Roosevelt's New Deal. "I will never change my philosophy that the New Deal is Christ's Deal," he told listeners, inflecting certain syllables with a brogue. Coughlin based many of his sermons for social justice—a harmony between workers and owners—on the same papal encyclicals that warned of communism. Coughlin had started his broadcasts as a way of addressing anti-Catholic hate after the Ku Klux Klan burned a cross on the front lawn of his Royal Oak parish. Initially, Roosevelt welcomed the priest's support and encouraged top administration officials who were Catholic—including Joe Kennedy—to visit Coughlin and keep him in the fold. Kennedy befriended the priest, flattered him with praise and jocular ribbing (he once called Coughlin a "jackass" to his face) and wrote him friendly letters. "Joe was fascinated by Coughlin's talent on the radio," recalled James Roosevelt, the president's son and close friend of Kennedy. "He recognized it as demagoguery, but reveled in what the priest could accomplish. He was intrigued by Coughlin's use of power." In his notes to fellow New Dealers, Kennedy appeared critical of the priest, perhaps more so than he actually was. By December 1933, Kennedy predicted to his friend, future Supreme Court Justice Felix Frankfurter, that Coughlin was "becoming a very dangerous proposition in the whole country" and could be stopped only through the Vatican's intervention:

> He has the most terrific radio following that you can imagine and to my way of thinking he is becoming an out and out demagog [sic] with a rather superficial knowledge of fundamentals, but a striking way of making attacks that please the masses, with a beautiful voice that stirs them frightfully. Of course, I believe that if Roosevelt would turn against any of the policies that Coughlin is advocating, Coughlin would turn at once against Roosevelt unless he felt that the Apostolic Delegate in Washington might demand his silence.

Cardinal O'Connell was among the first to criticize Coughlin. He warned of "almost hysterical addresses by ecclesiastics," prompting a flurry of angry letters from Boston parishioners, many of whom were Coughlin's most faithful listeners. Some even stopped placing money into the church's collection baskets in protest. O'Connell argued, somewhat disingenuously, that priests should not get involved in politics and that "the Catholic Church does not take sides with the rich or the poor, the Republican or the Democrat." Like Kennedy, O'Connell feared Coughlin would become a clarion for a new totalitarian state in America. Increasingly, Coughlin's broadcasts reeked of nationalism, Roosevelt diatribes and anti-Semitism. Coughlin had a strange and disturbing grip on the sentiment of Irish Catholics. In their struggle for acceptance, the Irish could be remarkably intolerant of other striving immigrant groups, notably Jews. Coughlin's sermons roused ancient and ugly anti-Semitic tendencies in the history of the Catholic Church itself. "My dear friends, we . . . believe in Christ's principle of Love Your Neighbor As Yourself, and . . . I challenge every Jew in this nation to tell me he does not believe in it!" he boomed to a Cleveland audience. Politically, Coughlin aligned himself with Huey Long, the Louisiana governor and rabid critic of Roosevelt, posing a serious threat to the president's 1936 reelection campaign. By one Democratic estimate, an independent ticket put together by Long and Coughlin could steal away as many as six million votes from Roosevelt, assuring victory for the Republicans.

Despite his rabid attacks on FDR, Coughlin managed to keep a warm spot for Joe Kennedy, whom he called "the shining star among the dim 'knights' of the Administration." With a strained smile on his face, Kennedy tried to woo Coughlin at the president's instruction. "Thanks for all the kind things you are saying about me," Kennedy wrote back to the priest in August 1936. "I feel like the fellow on his vacation who sends the postal card to his friends saying, 'Wish you were with us.'" By then, however, Roosevelt decided that he could no longer ignore or graciously dismiss Coughlin and his corrosive impact on the electorate. With Kennedy as the architect, a plan would soon be launched to silence the troublesome priest.

FOR YEARS, Joe Kennedy's family had cultivated its ties with Cardinal O'Connell. But by the mid-1930s, Kennedy realized that another figure in the Boston diocese possessed even more clout with the Vatican— Bishop Spellman, who served under O'Connell. Spellman spent several years studying as a priest in Rome at the North American College, a training seminary, where he learned the byzantine ways of the Vatican power structure. When he returned to Boston in 1932, Spellman, an Irish Catholic from Massachusetts who had graduated from the Jesuit-run Fordham University in New York, hoped to ascend quickly through the church hierarchy. O'Connell disliked him immediately, sensing the young prelate's overweening ambition. In many respects, the two churchmen were very much alike—authoritarian by nature, delighted by publicity, raconteurs of power and money in their expressed mission to build their church. After Joe Kennedy's family moved to New York, Spellman came to his attention, and the two men became friendly. "In Spellman he found a churchman who met him on his own terms," noted Spellman's biographer, John Cooney. "Neither man minded being used by the other, as long as they both benefited." Although O'Connell's public statements against Coughlin were important, Kennedy realized that Spellman could be even more effective as a behind-the-scenes agent in the effort to stop the radio priest.

Spellman's chief source of power in the Vatican was Cardinal Eugenio Pacelli, the Vatican's secretary of state, a smart, sophisticated man who held a strong antipathy toward communism. Many observers—including Spellman, who first met him in 1927—believed quite correctly that Pacelli would someday become Pope. The fifty-year-old career Vatican diplomat was impressed with the shrewd, calculating mind of the younger American, and admired Spellman's ability to maneuver through the Vatican bureaucracy to get things done. While Spellman was in Rome, he became a close confidant of Pacelli's, saying Mass with him and traveling across the countryside to visit churches and convents. Spellman also developed good friendships with two top Pacelli aides, Mother Pascalina, a nun who oversaw Pacelli's household, and Count Enrico Galeazzi, a layman often called a "Vatican architect," but more accurately described as Pacelli's top administrator. Within a year of his return to America, Spellman introduced Galeazzi to Joe Kennedy; the two would share a long friendship and correspondence lasting for nearly thirty years.

Often hidden from public view, Count Galeazzi, a thin, balding man with a slight mustache and a Continental air, knew all the confidences in Pacelli's life. His half brother, Ricardo Galeazzi-Lisi, an eye specialist, became Pacelli's personal physician, even though many thought of him as a quack. When Pacelli became Pope Pius XII, Galeazzi-Lisi was appointed the Vatican's doctor. (At one point in his career, an Italian court ordered Galeazzi-Lisi to pay the equivalent of more than $10,000 to colleagues who improperly drafted medical articles under his name. He was later expelled from several medical societies for his improper actions, and roundly criticized and fined for selling deathbed accounts when Puis XII died, including selling photographs of the dead pontiff to the press.) Nevertheless, even if his half brother's medical skills were dubious, Count Galeazzi's skills at Vatican intrigue were beyond reproach. His influence with the new Pope proved invaluable. As a key financial advisor, Galeazzi oversaw matters involving the Vatican bank and important church projects, and acted as a discreet diplomat for the Holy See with other nations. He'd become a top official in the Knights of Columbus, the large Catholic fraternal organization with hundreds of chapters around the world. The Kennedys marveled at his insider's knowledge and ability to get things done without being noticed. Decades later, on a 1961 trip to Rome, Ted Kennedy observed Galeazzi's skills up close. He described them in admiring detail to the president: "Jack, our problem is not lack of ideas, but lack of good men to carry them out," Teddy urged. "Let's look for more Galeazzis."

For nearly twenty years, the count remained the liaison between the Vatican and those in America, such as Spellman and Kennedy, who had committed themselves to protecting Pacelli and the church's interests. Churchmen in America who didn't have a relationship with Galeazzi, including Cardinal O'Connell, didn't have much influence in Rome. Both Spellman and Kennedy knew how to plant an idea or a recommendation with Galeazzi that would mysteriously become a papal decree or initiative.

In 1936, both men became the key brokers in putting together a deal between the president of the United States and the future Pope.

BEFORE BOARDING the liner *Conte di Savoia* in the port of Naples, Cardinal Pacelli explained the intent of his trip to the United States. "I am going to America simply on a vacation," he told the press on September 30, 1936. "There is no political aspect to my trip whatever." Few accepted Pacelli's statement on face value. On both sides of the Atlantic, newspapers speculated about the real reasons for Pacelli's visit, the first time such a high-ranking Vatican official had ever arrived on American shores. With Pope Pius XI in his seventies and in poor health, Pacelli could only be leaving Rome for a serious reason. As the *New York Times* suggested, Pacelli's mission would "separate the Vatican's responsibilities from Father Coughlin and prove to the world that the Catholic Church as a body is in no way hostile to the policies with which President Roosevelt is identified."

On the same day Pacelli departed from Italy, Spellman met secretly at the White House with President Roosevelt, who lambasted Coughlin and the church officials who had allowed him to run amok. In the midst of a difficult reelection campaign, Roosevelt believed the steady drumbeat of criticism from Coughlin's broadcast—calling Roosevelt a "liar," an "anti-God" and a Communist—would cost him thousands of Catholic votes, an essential part of the New Deal's political coalition. Spellman explained that the church could not be seen as taking sides in an American presidential election. However, Spellman confirmed what Joe Kennedy had already indicated to the president on the telephone: Pacelli would be willing to meet Roosevelt during his extended tour and make a genuine effort to repair whatever damage existed with the administration. Press reports of Pacelli's plans with Roosevelt, an implicit sign of Vatican support for the president in the upcoming election, sent an important public message to Catholics in America.

Right after his meeting with the president, Spellman rushed to contact Pacelli on the liner, still far out in the ocean, and relayed Roosevelt's deep concerns. Pacelli implored Spellman to keep everything quiet and not speak to the press. Joe Kennedy, working on Roosevelt's behalf, went to Washington in early October to finalize the arrangements for Pacelli's meeting. Though not quoted in any accounts, Kennedy was likely a source in the news accounts underlining the church's concerns about Coughlin. "The campaign looks to me distinctly Roosevelt, but it will be by no means an easy fight," Kennedy wrote that month to Robert Worth Bingham, the wealthy publisher of the *Louisville Courier* who was then serving as Roosevelt's ambassador to the Court of St. James. "Father Coughlin has definitely made bother [sic] in the states that we need to carry, and the Communist cry has been raised rather successfully among the Catholics, I believe to the damage of Roosevelt."

The president knew he could count on Kennedy. Having just ended his stint at the Securities and Exchange Commission, Kennedy was momentarily back in private life, so his actions were less likely to be traced directly to the White House. More than any Catholic in the administration, Kennedy possessed an insider's knowledge of the church's power structure. He wisely set up the secret meeting for the president with Spellman, still only an auxiliary bishop, because of his special ties to Pacelli. To the chagrin of O'Connell and other U.S. church figures, Pacelli had indicated that he preferred working with Spellman, who leaped at the offer to act as the cardinal's guide to America. He never strayed from Pacelli's side during his monthlong visit. Kennedy served as an important booster for Spellman by helping to overcome whatever reservations Roosevelt still retained about the often pushy prelate. (During World War I, Roosevelt, as assistant secretary of war, had refused to grant a chaplaincy to Spellman, then a young priest in Boston, because of his brashness.) With a foot in both camps, Kennedy acted as a broker between Spellman's orders from Rome and Roosevelt's own demands from the White House.

THE VATICAN knew how to drive a hard bargain as well. During his trip, Pacelli sought an important concession from the United States government. He wanted Roosevelt to appoint a U.S. representative to the Vatican, the same way in which thirty-five countries—some predominantly Catholic and some not—were represented, including Great Britain and Japan. Despite its large Catholic population, the United States refused for long-standing political reasons to send an envoy. To Joe Kennedy and Bishop Spellman, this absence was a painful reminder of the depths of anti-Catholic sentiment in America. "To the American Catholic it seemed that his government was avoiding the normal course of action at the dictation of bigotry," recalled the Reverend Robert Gannon, a president of Fordham University, in his authorized biography of Spellman.

From the Revolutionary War until 1847—a time when Catholics were an insignificant portion of America's population—the U.S. government had sent consuls and counsels general to the papal states with little political repercussion. In 1847, the American government raised the appointment to a legation, complete with a chargé d'affaires. But during this period, the Know-Nothing movement, spurred by the huge influx of Irish and other Catholic immigrants, altered the American government's view of the church. When President Franklin Pierce was asked to accept a Vatican-appointed nuncio in Washington, D.C., anti-Catholic sentiment prevailed and Pierce refused. After the Civil War, Congress refused any further funding for a U.S. representative at the Vatican. For the next seven decades, a U.S. representative at the Vatican was too provocative for any Congress or president to consider seriously.

With Europe's worsening political condition in the 1930s, the Vatican was determined to overcome America's isolationist mood and improve the church's relationship with the U.S. government. The Soviet Union's Communist revolution and the rising tide of Bolshevism routing and dismantling churches across the Ukraine and other places of Russian influence had greatly alarmed the Vatican. As a way of building its own strength in a troubled time, Pacelli attempted to secure diplomatic relations with every nation in which a sizeable number of Catholics lived, signing concordats even with Hitler's Nazi Germany. These diplomatic agreements were viewed in Rome as a vital shield against communism. Upon his return to America, Spellman lobbied hard with sympathetic supporters about the need for stronger ties with Rome and convinced Joe Kennedy to bring the Vatican matter personally to Roosevelt's attention. While planning their strategy, both Spellman and Kennedy kept in contact with Galeazzi, the unofficial voice for Pacelli. To their delight, Kennedy reported back that Roosevelt was receptive, and they should try to work out a meeting in which their mutual interests could be settled. Negotiations were carried on during Pacelli's visit. By October 24, 1936, Kennedy had convinced the White House to invite Pacelli to the president's Hyde Park home in upstate New York for a visit on November 5, immediately after Election Day. As a matter of protocol, Spellman suggested that Roosevelt issue a formal luncheon invitation. The White House agreed to do so, even though the Vatican was not recognized as an independent state. It was a coup for Joe Kennedy. By successfully arranging this historic meeting between the church and the American government, he had ended a century-long breach.

UP ALONG the Hudson River, a private railroad car arranged by Kennedy carried Cardinal Pacelli and his official entourage to Hyde Park, including Spellman, Galeazzi and Kennedy's wife, Rose. The crisp, clear autumn air, the spectacle of leaves turning crimson and gold along the Catskill

Mountains, and the high spirits from Roosevelt's overwhelming reelection victory earlier in the week filled the railcar with great expectations.

Rose Kennedy remembered the ride to Hyde Park as a poignant personal journey, keenly aware of being in the likely presence of the next Pope. Pacelli's appearance was striking to Rose. Physically, he was a thin, average-sized man "of rather dark and sallow complexion and dark eyes behind rimmed spectacles set on a Roman nose," she recalled. But Pacelli's demeanor and his preference for wearing flowing red cardinal's robes rather than a simple black suit and Roman collar, added to his aura. When the train stopped at Hyde Park, where limousines were waiting to take them to the president's house, Pacelli took time out to greet hundreds of school-children waving American and papal flags. Pacelli ministered the Sign of the Cross, smiled and patted the children on the head. "He was not a handsome man, yet his eyes shone with such intensity and compassion, in his bearing there was an unearthly sense of important purpose that I truly felt I was in the presence of a mortal who was very close to God," Rose recalled.

At Hyde Park, the entourage was greeted by Roosevelt and his mother, Sara Delano Roosevelt, who acted as a hostess in first lady Eleanor Roosevelt's absence. All the servants in the Roosevelt home who were Catholic were given the privilege of meeting Pacelli and, on their bended knees, of receiving the cardinal's blessing. Outside the door, a gaggle of reporters begged Pacelli for a comment. The American press accorded Pacelli far more publicity than a visiting Catholic clergyman had ever before received. Spellman barked and shooed them away like an anxious guard dog. Near a large fireplace at the far end of the house's great living room, the American president and the Vatican secretary of state chatted alone for more than an hour, a dialogue that dealt with the problem of Father Coughlin as well as the church's desire for a U.S. representative in Rome.

The results of their talks soon became apparent. On the same day of the visit, Coughlin announced that he'd no longer continue his radio broadcasts, attributing his decision to Roosevelt's huge electoral victory and not a directive from church officials. But years later, Coughlin admitted he'd been silenced. "Cardinal Pacelli visited America and had conversations with our high government officials, which conversations could be regarded as a type of informal pact," Coughlin wrote to Spellman's biographer, Father Gannon, in a 1954 letter. "Small as I was, it was necessary to silence my voice." However, it would take a long time for that promise to be fully realized.

On the way back from Hyde Park, Cardinal Pacelli stopped for tea at the Kennedy home in Bronxville. The visit was the most tangible public expression of thanks Pacelli could make to someone who had done the church's bidding. Rose and the children were thrilled, and Joe beamed with pride. Outside their home, the cardinal spoke with some of the neighbors and "prominent citizens of New York" who came to greet him. When he entered, Pacelli blessed the house and conversed in French with the older Kennedy children. Relaxing in the Kennedy living room, Pacelli sat on a sofa and little Ted Kennedy, then four years old, wandered over and sat on the cardinal's lap. Teddy played with the large pectoral cross hanging from a long chain around the cardinal's neck, and everyone, including Pacelli, was amused. "He had a wonderful way with little children, and he loved them, I believe, as Jesus did," Rose remembered. "I have regretted that we didn't have a camera in the house at the time to record the scene." For many years after, the sofa where Pacelli had rested became a venerated treasure, and was eventually moved to the Kennedy compound in Hyannis Port. "No one was allowed to sit on it because that's where the Pope once sat," Joseph Gargan, Rose's nephew, recalled fondly.

Shortly after the presidential visit, Pacelli left for Rome aboard a ship. A week after this departure, Spellman informed Pacelli about Kennedy's follow-up discussions with the White House. Clearly, the church had responded to Roosevelt's concerns about Father Coughlin, and they were determined to make sure the historic promise of a U.S. representative at the Vatican also came true. As Spellman entered in his diary: "Wrote letter to Cardinal Pacelli that Joe Kennedy had conversation with President Roosevelt and the President had practically determined to recognize the Vatican. This conversation was held at my suggestion and request." At month's end, Spellman vacationed in Florida at the Kennedys' Palm Beach winter home, as a guest of his new and powerful friend.

FOR JOE KENNEDY, the Cardinal Pacelli visit showed Roosevelt his ability to wend his way through the thorniest assignment. He had cemented his status within the church, no longer just through financial contributions, but by boosting his friend Spellman's stature with Roosevelt and cultivating his own relationship with Pacelli. Kennedy and Spellman realized tremendous benefits from the success of Pacelli's trip. In influence, Spellman leaped over his superior, Cardinal William O'Connell, emerging, thanks to Kennedy, as the favored Catholic clergyman consulted by the White House on policy issues. Spellman rose swiftly through the American church's hierarchy, his sights set on its most valued prize, and soon reaped his reward. In early 1939, Joe Kennedy called to tell Spellman about receiving a Vatican honor for his service to the Pope. As they talked, Kennedy assured him not to worry about his own future. "Enrico is in there fighting for you all the time," Kennedy said. Less than a month later, in April 1939, Spellman was chosen to lead the New York archdiocese, a selection made by Pacelli as Pope Pius XII.

During his long, controversial tenure in New York, Spellman became known as "the American Pope" and remained close to the Kennedys for years. Perhaps his biggest favor to Joe Kennedy involved an introduction to the archdiocese's ace real estate broker, John J. Reynolds, a savvy Bronx Irishman who promised to make Kennedy a bundle of money. At Reynolds' suggestion, Kennedy gobbled up various commercial buildings. He immediately doubled their fees, earning an estimated $100 million before World War II and prompting tenants to complain of rent-gouging. The best buy suggested by Spellman's real estate man was the Merchandise Mart in Chicago, which Kennedy bought from Marshall Field for $12.5 million, less than half the construction cost. It soon turned into the jewel in Kennedy's personal fortune.

Joe Kennedy learned that money, power and intrigue were not the sole province of government or Wall Street. Though founded on a rock of faith, the egos and human frailties within the Roman Catholic Church were enough to rival those of any institution. Kennedy understood the faults and weaknesses of men such as Spellman and O'Connell, but his fidelity to the church of his forefathers remained unquestioned. At times, Kennedy's life mirrored so many contradictions within the American Catholic Church— the different educational standards for men and women, the clash between monetary and spiritual needs, the ascendancy from a rejected immigrant clan to a respected family in the upper echelons of American society. Like any good Irish Catholic, Joe Kennedy attended Mass on Sundays with his wife, and they raised their children according to the moral guidelines of the nuns and priests who taught them. But the Kennedys were a different kind of Irish Catholics, much better prepared for modern American society than the old emigrants from Eire. As "one of the nation's leading Catholic laymen," to use his wife's phrase, Joe Kennedy mastered the intricacies of his own church, resisted anti-Catholic discrimination and privately influenced the American government in ways so discreet that they would remain unexplored for years by historians. He avoided the brassy, political machine methods of Al Smith, the unpolished Democratic Party candidate, whom a bigoted nation viewed as leading a horde of unwashed foreigners into the White House. Instead, Joe Kennedy and his family maneuvered smartly through the established corridors of Washington and Rome to make their own mark. "They were something new in America—the immigrants' final surpassing of the blue bloods," observed historian James MacGregor Burns.

In this inexorable march toward his ultimate goal, the church became an instrument, a means for gaining more power and influence. Joe Kennedy was determined not to fail.

Chapter Ten

An Irishman in the Court of St. James

IRISH POLITICIANS GATHERED in Boston for a showing of the green at the Clover Club's annual St. Patrick's Day dinner in 1937, an event started fifty-five years earlier when Famine emigrants were still digging holes and driving stakes to survive in their adopted city. Though life in Boston was much better than before, even the most successful Irish-American tended on this holiday to look back with nostalgia.

Inside the Somerset Hotel, judges, businessmen and government officials listened appreciatively to a program of Irish music, poetry and drama, including the city's Mayor Frederick W. Mansfield, an Irish Catholic who would later work as counsel for the archdiocese. The Clover Club's famous glee club sang a parody titled "If Roosevelt Ruled Ireland." And the featured presentation reenacted the last hours of Michael Collins, the sainted hero of the 1916 uprising who created the Irish Free State only to be murdered by his own. Former Mayor John F. Fitzgerald, decked out in a tuxedo, smiled approvingly.

Boston was now an Irish Catholic town. Though restrictive immigration laws and the Depression had reduced the flow of newcomers, the Catholic population was more than one million in the late 1930s, a number surpassed only in New York and Chicago. Slowly but inevitably, the last bastions of Brahmin-controlled culture, education and finance, yielded to this reality. With parochial schools booming, vocations on the rise and the number of parishes doubling, Cardinal O'Connell's dream of a separate Catholic culture in the city appeared to be coming true.

At this dinner toasting the Irish, the evening's main speaker, Joseph P. Kennedy, rose to offer a distinctly different view. Kennedy surprised the crowd with a message that the days of Irish power were almost over, that Irish Catholics were no longer to be hyphenated Americans, but melded into American society without regard to their Celtic race or Roman creed.

"As we listen to the song and story and hear the haunting melodies of the homeland of our fathers, it is not easy to appreciate the great change in the status of the Irish in America," Kennedy said. "The melting pot process implicit in a democracy will fashion, and is already fashioning, a new and different people. The evolution will absorb and mold the offspring of even the most unregenerate Fenian. Thus the influence of the Irish culture in this country must be recognized as on the wane. Nor is it likely that anything or any person can change this process of cultural absorption."

Kennedy's salute to American assimilation that evening, while giving slight credit to the eclipsed Yankee culture, made it clear that the Kennedy clan and other families of immigrant heritage were the rightful heirs to what their ancestors had wrought in the New World. "The Irish in Boston always suffered under the handicap of not possessing family traditions adequate to win the respect and confidence of their Puritan neighbors," he said. "This Yankee pride of ancestry developed a boastfulness and a snobbishness which, although difficult to understand, explains many of the strange idiosyncrasies of Boston. To the descendants of the early settlers, the newer races meant annoyance, a class to be endured but never treated as equals. The inevitable happened. At first a political and then an economic change occurs to improve the status of the late comers."

After the speech, some mistook Kennedy's intent as a call for the Irish to be more like the Brahmins, which he later took pains to deny and clarify. In his own mind, though, the loyalties of Joe Kennedy often weren't clear. Kennedy's adult life had been predicated on the belief that he would be accepted in American society, go as far as he could on his brains, drive and constant persistence—the stuff of Horatio Alger legends and modern-day fortunes like his own. Always aware of his Irish Catholic roots, Kennedy didn't like to be reminded of them, especially by white Anglo-Saxon Protestant men whose money or positions of power he coveted. Two months after this speech, Kennedy complained bitterly to *Fortune* magazine about an upcoming profile that he believed revealed a "social prejudice against my origin."

This tension between striving and acceptance, this undercurrent of inferiority and resentment, lay beneath the surface of his complicated relationship with Franklin Delano Roosevelt. No matter how much money he raised, no matter how many problems he fixed, deals he negotiated or arms he twisted, Kennedy sensed the president saw him in a box, defined by his religion and ethnic background. That feeling existed from the very first job offer Roosevelt made to him—as U.S. ambassador to Ireland. Years later, President Kennedy joked that he'd support any presidential candidate who offered him this same job when his second term ended in 1968. It was also the same position that his daughter, Jean Kennedy Smith, eagerly sought and accepted when it was offered by President Clinton in the 1990s. But in 1934, going to Ireland seemed like a step backward to Joe Kennedy. Unlike his father, he'd never been to Ireland, and he considered himself a full-blooded American. He didn't want to be perceived simply as another Irish politician tending to his own ethnic group, but as a new breed, different from the Honey Fitzs and the Curleys of the world. Supporting FDR, rather than Smith, had seemed to be his ticket out of this confining world. Roosevelt's first offer of a job in Ireland must have been a disappointment.

When Roosevelt's son, James, relayed his father's offer of Ireland, Kennedy refused to consider it. Shortly afterward at the White House, the president summoned Kennedy to talk again about Ireland. As Kennedy related in a letter to his oldest son in 1934: "He (Roosevelt) said that he thought I had an obligation to do something, and then suggested that I go to Ireland as Minister because there is a very strained situation between the Irish Free State and the English Government. He thought it would be a very nice thing for me to go back as Minister to a country from which my grandfather had come as an immigrant. But Mother and I talked it over, and we decided that this wasn't of any particular interest, and I told him so." Even years later, Roosevelt contended that Kennedy, as he recorded in his diary, "was the only one who could straighten out the Irish problem."

CHARMED AND SLIGHTLY awed by Roosevelt, Kennedy accepted his offer to oversee the Securities and Exchange Commission (SEC) and later the U.S. Maritime Commission, important positions that gained him recognition for a job well done. However, the plum assignment Kennedy hoped for—the one to add prestige to his family—took nearly four years to obtain and came only after considerable lobbying. During a conversation with James Roosevelt, who served as his father's aide, Kennedy mentioned the idea of becoming ambassador to England. "Oh, c'mon, Joe, you don't want that," he replied.

Kennedy persisted. "I've been thinking about it and I'm intrigued by the thought of being the first Irishman to be ambassador from the United States to the Court of Saint James." They both chuckled at the prospect, but mindful of Kennedy's service and friendship, James Roosevelt agreed to mention the idea to his father.

When he heard of Kennedy's latest idea, the president "laughed so hard he almost toppled from his wheelchair." But before his son could call Kennedy, the president changed his mind; he was, he said, "intrigued with the idea of twisting the lion's tail a little," and instructed Kennedy to come see him.

When Kennedy arrived at the White House, he was greeted with a broad hello from the president, who then made what seemed like a friendly request. "Joe, would you mind stepping back a bit, by the fireplace perhaps, so I can get a good look at you?"

Taken aback, Kennedy nevertheless complied.

The president continued his instructions. "Joe, would you mind taking your pants down?"

Neither Kennedy nor Roosevelt's son could believe their ears. After being assured they had heard him correctly, James Roosevelt recalled that Kennedy "undid his suspenders and dropped his pants and stood there in his shorts, looking silly and embarrassed."

The president explained that he knew someone who had once seen Kennedy in a bathing suit and claimed that he was bowlegged. Now that it was confirmed with his own eyes, Roosevelt said this awkward condition preempted Kennedy from consideration as the new British ambassador. "Don't you know that the ambassador to the Court of St. James has to go through an induction ceremony in which he wears knee britches and silk stockings?" he teased. "Can you imagine how you'll look? When photos of our new ambassador appear all over the world, we'll be a laughingstock. You're not right for the job."

Kennedy, desperate not to be turned down, asked for a two-week grace period so that he could get approval from the British monarch to wear a cutaway coat and striped pants instead for the ceremony. Roosevelt laughed and agreed. When Kennedy produced his promised letter, the president appointed him the new ambassador to Great Britain.

FROM A HISTORICAL vantage, the idea of Joseph Patrick Kennedy—an Irish Catholic from Boston, the grandson of an immigrant pushed out of Ireland during the Famine—going to Great Britain as the new U.S. ambassador seemed too fanciful to believe, almost like sweet revenge. As the *Times* of London had warned a century earlier when British policies caused a massive emigration to the West, America was now filled with Irish descendants who remembered the foul treatment by the British. Would Kennedy avenge his forefathers in some subtle ways, as skeptics in London wondered. As

British historian David Nunnerly flatly declared, "Irish-Americans, particularly those who live in the Boston area, are almost to a man staunchly anti-British." Some in America also had their doubts about the appointment. "I do not believe you can promote peace on earth by sending an Irishman to London," Senator James F. Byrnes of South Carolina confided to Arthur Krock, the *New York Times* reporter who broke the exclusive story. Harold Ickes, a Roosevelt aide, couldn't understand Kennedy's obsession with London. "You don't understand the Irish," explained Thomas Corcoran, a speechwriter for FDR. "London has always been a closed door to him. As Ambassador of the United States, Kennedy will have all doors open to him."

Well aware of the historical ironies, Roosevelt called his choice of Kennedy "a great joke, the greatest joke in the world." In Boston and New York, Irish Catholics were delighted by his selection. Honey Fitz declared the British ambassadorship "the most important job that the Administration has to give out", and Al Smith called Kennedy "Mr. Irish-American." Despite all his claims of being fully assimilated, Kennedy realized he had been chosen by his president partly for what he was, rather than who. "In many quarters," Kennedy later wrote, "my appointment was applauded for the very reason that my Irish and Catholic background, my self-made qualities and lack of homage to old-fashioned protocol, my bluntness and outspokenness, would render me proof against British wiles."

In London, the Kennedy family attracted great attention. Ambassador Kennedy's wide-ranging speeches (extolling the virtues of America's freedom of religion, for instance, or suggesting the British study American history in the same way U.S students imbibed Shakespeare and English history) inspired numerous newspaper articles, and his ebullient, photogenic clan made plenty of news. "He is Irish and Roman Catholic, and proud of it," profiled the *Times* of London. "The appointment would have created quite a stir some years ago, when the Irish question was an obstacle to better Anglo-American relations. Now it will provoke little more than wonder that it has not occurred before." In the past, the U.S. embassy was filled with esteemed Brahmin names such as James Russell Lowell, Joseph Choate, Whitelaw Reid, Frank B. Kellogg. (In suggesting that Kennedy employ both his Harvard-educated oldest boys as aides, Felix Frankfurter reminded the new ambassador of the experiences of his predecessors, John Adams and Charles Francis Adams, who served Washington and Lincoln, respectively, and viewed the London post as an excellent foreign policy training ground for their sons.) But the *Times* profile did hint that Kennedy's heritage might be too parochial for the job.

As an Irishman, he represents the new Boston which has grown up within the last 50 years and has come increasingly to conform to the type of northern American cities having a large proportion of Irish in its citizenship. As Roman Catholics and as racial exiles these people have formed strong political coteries, often crowding together in the more humble parts of the city, and keeping mostly to themselves in religion, education and politics.

INSTEAD, THE KENNEDYS surprised everyone. "London will be grand," Joe predicted to a band of reporters upon landing with his family. They immersed themselves in British culture, the genesis for many future Anglophile theories about individual family members. While Kathleen Kennedy partied and enjoyed the company of young British squires, her brother John devoured lessons about the aristocracy from his English friends and from such books as *Pilgrim's Way* by John Buchan, later named Lord Tweedsmuir for his services to the Crown. In a reversal of their treatment in Boston, where the Kennedy girls were not invited to the Junior League balls, the ambassador's daughters were embraced as debutantes by London society. The Kennedys lived lavishly in the six-story embassy residence at Prince's Gate, with its twenty-seven bedrooms and staff of some two dozen maids, butlers and other servants. Invited to Windsor Castle for a splendid weekend with the king and queen, Joe couldn't resist crowing to his wife, "Well, Rose, it's a hell of a long way from East Boston, isn't it?"

In his own independent style, Ambassador Kennedy quickly ended the embassy's practice of presenting upper-class American young women to the British monarch, rejecting what he called an "undemocratic" selection process. He also refused to follow the tradition in which American ambassadors appeared at court functions in knee breeches, silk stockings and formal black coats. "Not Mrs. Kennedy's little boy," he remarked. Yet some biographers and analysts of the Kennedys have insisted this American family, arising from new money and Irish immigration, were transformed by English immersion into would-be royalty. In these accounts, the Kennedys were enlightened by—and recognized the superiority of—the same British culture that had once forced their Irish grandparents to rebel or emigrate. So weak and secondary was the Irish Catholic culture to the Kennedys, according to these accounts, that a miraculous transformation took place in London before the eyes of the world. Yet in the late 1930s, there were plenty of reminders for the Kennedys, both home and abroad, of their minority background. At an exclusive London bottle club, a journalist for the London

Daily Express came up to Joe Kennedy Jr. and asked "whether Kennedy *pere* had a chance of becoming President despite the fact that he is a Roman Catholic." Young Joe, surrounded by friends, replied that everyone had assumed his father's religion would bar him from the ambassadorship but they were wrong. Another reminder came when Ambassador Kennedy returned to America in late spring 1938 to attend his eldest son's graduation at Harvard. No doubt at Kennedy's urging, the newspapers predicted that his alma mater also would bestow an honorary degree on the senior Kennedy, recognizing his prominence in Britain. (Two years earlier, Kennedy's bid for appointment to the Harvard Board of Overseers had been rejected because of what he privately considered bias against Irish Catholics.) But when Kennedy learned that no honor would be forthcoming, he told reporters he'd "declined" the offer. "Can you imagine Joe Kennedy declining an honorary degree from Harvard?" Roosevelt laughed.

Despite his public embrace of America's melting pot theories, Joe Kennedy's private sensitivity to perceived ethnic slights and tribal resentments seemed unlimited and at times unfounded. There was often a kind of connect-the-dots undercurrent in the Kennedy family's statements about bigotry that set forth their case without directly claiming they were victims. In this instance, the Harvard committee refusing the honorary degree to Kennedy was headed by Charles Francis Adams, who apparently believed an ambassadorship to the Court of St. James to be "an insufficient mark of distinction," even though Adams's grandfather and great-grandfather had once held the same post. In her memoir, Rose didn't mention this Harvard incident but described Adams as "the most patrician of all Back Bay Bostonians." And in the portion dealing with this time period, she goes out of her way to quote Adams's none-too-subtle remarks at a Chamber of Commerce testimonial dinner for Honey Fitz's seventy-fifth birthday:

> At times in your past, you, John F., have found it politically expedient to say things about my class that have sometimes hurt. You have even called us degenerate sons of splendid ancestors. Quite possibly that is true. But it takes a man of supreme gifts to tell us a thing like that without arousing rancor. Yet, it was said so pleasantly, with such good humor, that no one could take offense, or long be angry with a man of the charm of John F. Fitzgerald.

ALL THIS UNSUBTLE joking makes the reader wonder whether maybe Adams really did have it in for old Joe and his Irish clan, just as he suspected.

Despite his trip across the Atlantic, Joe Kennedy didn't attend his oldest son's graduation because, he claimed, he was monitoring the ill health of his other son, Jack. The memory of rejection, similar to his undergraduate disappointment with the Porcellian Club, turned him bitter toward Harvard. He never returned, even after Jack was elected to the Board of Overseers. "Of all the boys, Jack likes Harvard best," the old man admitted. "I guess I have the old Boston prejudice against it."

KENNEDY'S NEED for acceptance, some kind of recognition for all he had achieved, found another forum. Shortly after returning from America, the ambassador received an invitation to Ireland for an honorary degree at the National University in Dublin. The summer before, Rose and Kathleen and Joe Jr. sauntered over to Ireland in 1937 to see the sights and even take in a horse race. Rose took several laconic photos of the Irish scenery, from the isolated, stoic rocks along the western coastline to street scenes of old men in tweed caps tending to their mares. Someone, probably Joe Jr., snapped a picture of Kick as she leaned backward to kiss the Blarney stone. But the senior Kennedy's journey would be different. Remarkably, given the number of U.S. citizens of Irish descent, Kennedy's trip marked the first official visit to Ireland by the American ambassador to Great Britain. Young Joe came along and the two journeyed to Wexford, where they visited the Kennedy Homestead in Dunganstown, and Clonakilty on the coast, where the family of the ambassador's mother, Mary Hickey, had come from a century earlier. The beauty of the land, the simple farmland and cottages where his ancestors once lived, stirred him. He'd never before visited Ireland. Yet at its sight, Kennedy's sense of Irishness, an affinity for the forgotten homeland his father twice returned to see, beckoned him. During his trip, he heard from relatives, and those who welcomed him, about Ireland's travails. He listened to those who remembered the bloody fight for Irish freedom a decade earlier, and the brutal repression by the Black and Tans—the British occupying force—during Ireland's fight for independence. When asked why he didn't like certain Englishmen, Kennedy replied that "he could not forgive those who had been responsible for sending the infamous Black and Tan into rebellious Ireland."

At a state dinner in Dublin, after receiving his honorary degree, Kennedy became quite emotional, so much so that he feared he might cry. "My parents and grandparents talked ever of Ireland, and from my youth, I have been intent upon this pilgrimage," Kennedy told the packed audience at Dublin Castle, his son seated nearby. Though he considered himself 100 percent American, Joe Kennedy still showed interest in his roots. The Irish abundantly exhibited their pride and sense of kinship with him, the sort of public reverence his own father, P. J. Kennedy, once held for Patrick Collins, the Irish Catholic who served as general consul in Britain. "We are proud that men like you not merely do honor to your country, but honor our race," proclaimed Eamon De Valera, the Irish prime minister.

"Dev," as De Valera was known by the Irish, was the president of Sinn Fein ("Ourselves Alone" in Gaelic), who fought successfully for the creation of the Irish Republic from Britain in the early 1920s. De Valera had survived that conflict and the murderous civil war that followed to become the head of the Free State. He was born in New York and stayed in frequent contact with Irish-Americans amenable to his cause. Much of the money and guns for the independence fight came from America, where Irish immigrants contributed out of a fervent hatred for England and its policies, just as they had during the Fenian movement of the 1880s. A hard bargainer himself, De Valera vowed not to rest until the northern section of Ireland—the six counties of Ulster still under British rule—were reunited with the south.

As part of his mission from Roosevelt, Kennedy was instructed to explore a peaceful resolution to the disputes between England and Ireland, especially as the prospect of war with Germany loomed on the horizon. "I have taken the course of asking my good friend, Mr. Joseph P. Kennedy, who sails today for England to take up his post as Ambassador, to convey a personal message from me to the Prime Minister, and to tell the Prime Minister how happy I should be if a reconciliation could be brought about," Roosevelt declared.

Ultimately, Kennedy helped finalize a treaty between England and Ireland, a settlement that neither side particularly liked. The proposed treaty didn't unify Northern Ireland with the south under Dublin's control, as De Valera had sought. And England gave up control of the Irish ports at Berehaven, Lough Swilly and Queenstown—so critical to their defense in time of war—to men such as De Valera, who despised the British. Kennedy's determined negotiating style and his growing friendship with British Prime Minister Neville Chamberlain smoothed over the rough edges between the two sides. As war loomed, Kennedy inquired about Ireland's safety and whether the British planned to supply planes to Eire. "Every country wants planes and ammunition," Chamberlain replied. "Trouble is we can't supply enough for ourselves."

Some felt that London had gone too far. Winston Churchill, a staunch critic of Chamberlain's policies, wondered aloud whether Ireland's neutrality would prohibit the use of the crucial Irish ports if Britain went to war. "Many a ship and many a life were soon to be lost as the result of this improvident example of appeasement," Churchill later lamented. From a broad perspective, this agreement would leave the north-south partition of Ireland unresolved, a matter to be decided for another day. But with the treaty's signing, Kennedy could point to a significant achievement for those back home, particularly in the eyes of Irish-Americans.

Chapter Eleven

The Vatican Go-Between

TO HIS SURPRISE, JOE KENNEDY soon met Ireland's Eamon De Valera again. In March 1939, they were both in Rome, seated near each other for the coronation of Cardinal Eugenio Pacelli as the new Pope Pius XII. While waiting for the ceremony to begin, De Valera, representing the independent Republic of Ireland, chatted with Rose and Joe about ending the partition of Northern Ireland from the south. De Valera worried how his actions were perceived by Irish-Americans. "I never understood this but I could see he was whipping himself into his campaign for U.S. [sic]," Kennedy recorded in his diary. "He thought there would be many Irish against him in U.S.A."

On this day, however, religion mattered more than politics. Rose insisted that all the family attend the Mass and ceremonies for the new pontiff, who three years earlier had been a guest in their home. President Roosevelt granted Kennedy's request to be the official U.S. representative for the papal event, but only after some long-distance lobbying. Emphatically, Joe thanked Sumner Welles, the undersecretary of state, for convincing FDR on his behalf. "Dear Sumner: I can't tell you how much I appreciate your kindness," he cabled from London. "If I have one real virtue I never forget." Some in the White House thought a Protestant should be sent, but Roosevelt remembered Kennedy's close ties to the new Pope. Years earlier, Kennedy had predicted that Pacelli would rise to Pope, although Vatican secretaries of state generally did not reach this position. With war fast approaching, the Roosevelt administration welcomed a pontiff with Pacelli's worldly experience.

Kennedy wanted to avoid American participation in an impending European conflict with the Nazis. Some of Roosevelt's aides criticized Kennedy as disloyal, a potential wild card in a sensitive post. But Kennedy's impressive portfolio of contacts kept him in FDR's good graces. From the embassy in London, Kennedy acted as an occasional go-between with the Vatican and White House, an important consideration in both domestic and international politics. In April 1938, for example, Kennedy copied a "strictly confidential" memorandum prepared by Pacelli and sent it along to the president's son, James, at the White House, suggesting that it would be "of interest to the President and yourself." The Pacelli memo assured Kennedy that local church leaders had been threatened into cooperating with Nazi leaders in Austria and that the Vatican would never approve.

FDR realized that a way of rewarding Kennedy for his service was to send the ambassador and his large family to the Vatican for the 1939 papal coronation. Only Joe Jr., caught in Spain, was unable to attend. After arriving by train, the Kennedys stayed at the Excelsior on Rome's Via Venetto. At dawn, the Kennedys and their children traveled in four separate cars to St. Peter's Basilica. Count Galeazzi joined Rose and Joe in the first car. For twenty-one-year-old John F. Kennedy, the Vatican trip was one of several European experiences during that exciting year when he took leave from Harvard to work as his father's aide. During this extraordinary tutorial on world politics, young Jack ventured through the Middle East to Istanbul and Moscow, and then across Hitler's Germany. While touring Paris with his friend Lem Billings, Jack insisted they attend Mass at Notre Dame Cathedral to hear Pacelli give a sermon.

Pacelli's coronation was something special for the Kennedys because it underlined their father's unique position with the government and their church. With the intervention of his good friend Galeazzi, Kennedy had received several honors over the years from the Roman Catholic Church; he was made a Knight of Malta, a Grand Knight of the Order of Pius IX, a Knight of the Equestrian Order of the Holy Sepulchre and a member of the Grand Cross Order of Leopold II. They were mostly honorific titles, but they underscored Kennedy's influence. Joe and Rose believed Pacelli would be a wonderful Pope, a transcendent force for good in a troubled world. "Besides being a most saintly man, he has an extensive knowledge of world conditions," Kennedy informed State Department official J. Pierrepont Moffat. "He is not pro-one country or anti-another. He is just pro-Christian. If the world hasn't gone too far to be influenced by a great and good man, this is the man."

Inside the basilica, Kennedy attended the coronation Mass in a prominent seat alongside his children. Unfortunately, the presence of so many Kennedys pushed other invitees out of their chairs and into less desirable gallery seats. Count Galeazzo Ciano, the son-in-law of Italian dictator Benito Mussolini, was particularly incensed by the overflow crowd of Kennedys. "He (Ciano) began to protest, threatening to leave the Basilica and to desert the ceremony," remembered Cardinal Giovanni Battista Montini, who later became Pope Paul VI. Boston's Cardinal William O'Connell was highly amused by the ruckus caused by his long-time friends. When another ambassador commented on the Kennedys, the cardinal smiled and said, "Oh, will Joe ever learn!"

In a private session with the new Pope that day, Kennedy planned to discuss the pontiff's desire for formal recognition of the Vatican by the American government, a proposal that O'Connell and other American cardinals opposed because it would undercut their own power. When he arrived in Rome, O'Connell stopped by Kennedy's hotel to give him some advice. As Kennedy recorded in his personal diary, the cardinal told him "1. Don't trust anyone in Rome. No one was your friend. 2. Do as I wanted to, of course, but Cardinal hoped I'd be against USA affecting diplomatic relations with Vatican." Kennedy thanked O'Connell, but said nothing more. "The Hierarchy, I think, are afraid they will lose some influence," he concluded in his diary.

Cardinal O'Connell apparently had no idea that his direct underling, Bishop Spellman (as he was then), was already pushing for his own promotion with the lobbying aid of Galeazzi and Kennedy. This threesome had worked hard to bring about Pacelli's wish for a U.S. representative to the Vatican. When the old pontiff, Pius XI, died in early 1939, Kennedy sensed the ground shift and immediately dashed off a letter to Galeazzi. "The death of the Holy Father was a great shock and I was concerned regarding the future of our friend," wrote Kennedy. In numerous letters exchanged over three decades, the two men referred to Spellman in the cryptic, ambiguous phrase of "our friend." While Spellman was still in Boston, Kennedy told Galeazzi how he had spoken highly of Spellman to President Roosevelt during his recent trip back to America. "I talked with the President about it before I left and it was his sincere hope that great honor would come to him," he wrote, referring to Spellman's ambition to become cardinal in New York. "I know that the wish of the President is his wish too."

When he finally met the new pontiff in private, Kennedy discussed the possibility of a U.S. envoy to the Holy See. He suggested that American cardinals weren't in agreement with Rome because they were afraid of losing power. "No, of course not!" replied Pius XII. "Let America send [a] representative to [the] Vatican."

During their chat together, the Pope showed genuine affection for the man who had set up his meeting with FDR three years earlier. Count Galeazzi, who remained in the room throughout Kennedy's visit, spoke only at the conversation's end. "You know, the Ambassador comes from Boston," he interjected.

As Kennedy recalled, the hint was Galeazzi's way of "wanting to put in a boost for his friend Bishop Spellman of Boston," just as Kennedy was doing for their friend with Roosevelt.

"I took the hint and made a speech for Spellman," Kennedy later wrote, "and the Pope said, 'He is a good man and a good friend.'" Kennedy felt the same way. He later sent a cable to Sumner Welles summarizing his talks with the new Pope. "He is far from having any political prejudices," Kennedy determined, "except a subconscious prejudice that has arisen from his belief that the tendency of Nazism and Fascism is pro-pagan and, as pro-pagan, they strike at the roots of religion."

As the forty-five-minute confidential talk with Pius XII ended, Rose and the Kennedy children were brought in. They clutched numerous rosaries and holy items to be blessed, and the Pope greeted them like old friends. He even recalled that during his visit to the Kennedy home in Bronxville, Teddy had climbed on his knee and asked about his crucifix and ring. From a side table, the Pope pulled out rosaries of his own and gave one each to the Kennedy children. "He gave me the first Rosary beads from the table before he gave my sister (Patricia) any," little Teddy, a chubby-faced seven-year-old informed the press afterward. "He patted my hand and told me I was a smart little fellow." Rose also received a gift of rosaries from the Pope. "He talked with her so much and so kindly and intimately I thought she would faint," Joe remembered.

Outside the church, Kennedy posed with his smiling family sandwiched by two Swiss Guards, and Rose and her older daughters dressed in ceremonial black dresses and veils. To the press, the ambasador said the new Pope "had a great admiration for President Roosevelt because he always admired his stand for religion." Galeazzi then introduced Kennedy to other Vatican clergy and they were ushered through the Sistine Chapel, gazing at the wondrous, heavenly art by Michelangelo and Raphael. The count then showed Joe the room where the cardinals met in secret to vote for a new Pope. With great intrigue, Galeazzi recounted how "he had been selected to make a thorough search" of the room for hidden microphones attached to Dictaphones, and actually found one connected to the overhead wires. Only he and the Pope knew of this covert device. Galeazzi explained to Kennedy the secret balloting leading to Pacelli's selection as Pope. On the first ballot, Pacelli had received votes from ten Italian cardinals and all those from North America except O'Connell's, but it was not enough. On the third ballot, Cardinal Pacelli finally received the forty-two votes that ensured his elevation to the Holy See. During their tour that day, the Kennedys met another cardinal who posed for a picture with the ambassador. Unwittingly, Jack came up to the cardinal, got on his knees and started to kiss his ring as the cameras clicked. "Jack said if that [photo] ever appears in USA goodbye to Martin Luther [supporters]," his father wrote.

During this same trip, Teddy received his first Holy Communion from the Pope—the first for an American from this pontiff—inspiring visions in Rose's head that her last born might someday have a vocation. "I thought that with such a start he'd become a priest or maybe a bishop," Rose wrote years later, "but then one night he met a beautiful blonde and that was the end of that." For this special honor, young Teddy wore a blue suit with a white rosette on his left arm. In a private chapel in the Vatican, a small room with red walls and a white marble altar that was filled with lilies and lighted candles, the Pope served Communion to the young boy. The Kennedys noticed the pontiff had a touch so light that they barely knew the consecrated wafer had touched their tongues.

After the Mass, a group of nuns brought over a box with a small gift inside, a memento of the papal coronation, and the Pope handed it to Teddy. "This is a souvenir of your First Communion," he said, and then blessed the young boy in front of his family. The Pope turned to Eunice and Pat, standing near Jack, and told them, "I had such a nice time in your villa in New York." Galeazzi informed the Pope that the girls had traveled all night from Naples to be at the early morning Mass. "I thank you very much," the Pope said humbly, to the family's amazement. Then he turned to Teddy again, made the Sign of the Cross on his forehead, and said, "I hope you will always be good and pious as you are today."

Before he left Rome, Joe Kennedy gave Galeazzi a gift of fifty thousand lire for the Pope, who seemed to him "awe-inspiring, majestic, kindness personified and with the humility of God." Even his second son was impressed. On arriving back in London, Jack recalled his "great time" in Rome to his friend Lem Billings, who'd been at the Kennedys' Bronxville home in 1936 when Pacelli visited. "Pacelli is now riding high, so it's good you bowed and groveled like you did when you met him," Jack wrote his friend. "He gave Dad and I communion with Eunice at the same time at a private mass and all in all it was very impressive. . . . They want to give Dad the title of Duke which will be hereditary and go to all of his family which will make me Duke John of Bronxville and perhaps if you stuck around sufficiently I might knight you."

EVENTUALLY, the breach between Joe Kennedy and the president who sent him to England could no longer be papered over in platitudes and gestures such as a trip to Rome. Roosevelt resented Kennedy's freewheeling style and his penchant for expressing isolationist views far different from the administration's position. Almost from the moment he arrived in London, Kennedy became associated with the "Cliveden set," those British intellectuals and aristocrats sympathetic to Neville Chamberlain who believed the German threat could be dealt with through negotiation rather than war. Roosevelt, aware of Kennedy's own ethnic heritage, became incensed by this alliance. "Who would have thought that the English could take into camp a red-headed Irishman?" Roosevelt fumed to Henry Morgenthau. "The young man needs his wrists slapped rather hard."

Aside from their growing differences in policy and political outlook, Kennedy began to believe that the patrician Roosevelt was a bigot, someone who looked down his nose at him in a way that set off all Kennedy's ethnic and religious defenses. Such sentiments are not discussed much by historians or the biographers of either man, but these concerns were in the mind of at least one of them. As Kennedy later wrote in his diary, "I got the impression that deep down in his heart Roosevelt had a decidedly anti-Catholic feeling. And what seems more significant is the fact that up to this time he has not appointed a prominent Catholic to any important post since a year ago last November." Kennedy also believed "this [anti-Catholic] feeling [was] firmly imbedded in the Roosevelt family," a claim he'd heard that Alice Lee Roosevelt Longworth had made to a friendly newspaper columnist about her father, former President Theodore Roosevelt. The president's wife, Eleanor Roosevelt, seemed ill at ease with Catholics and the church's authoritarian prelates. She particularly disliked Spellman, who was brought to the White House's attention by Kennedy. "Eleanor still believed the anti-Catholic nonsense she heard during her childhood," later explained her cousin, political columnist Joseph Alsop.

Although FDR was viewed as a champion of the underdog, his perspective remained distinctly patrician. It was the same tone that Kennedy's Brahmin professors at Harvard commanded. "Buried just beneath those noble aims was the inherited assumption that America, its ideals and its form of government, had been made by the good Anglo-Saxon and Dutch Protestant stock that had first reached its shores and to which Roosevelt belonged," FDR biographer Ted Morgan concluded. "The others, the immigrants, the Catholics, the Jews, the latecomers to an already formed society, were not quite up to snuff." As Roosevelt once exclaimed to Leo T. Crowley, an economist who was Catholic and became an administration official: "Leo, you know this is a Protestant country, and the Catholics and Jews are here on sufferance." Crowley later confided to Treasury Secretary Henry Morgenthau that he'd never been so shocked in his life.

Rose Kennedy tried to simmer down her husband's temper, reminding him that "the President sent you, a Roman Catholic, as Ambassador to London, which probably no other President would have done." This cauldron of resentment may have existed only in Kennedy's mind, though other Catholics serving in the Roosevelt administration, notably James Farley, sometimes suggested similar sentiments. It is difficult today to determine the truth of this suspicion. Historically, it must be said that Roosevelt's administration relied on several Catholics and Jews to serve in top positions, a significant political stepping-stone for minorities who were a crucial component of his New Deal coalition. But clearly, as his private papers indicate, Kennedy's sensitivity to religious and ethnic slights from the president were never far from the surface.

In writing to Roosevelt about a meeting with Kennedy in London, Rabbi Stephen Wise, president of the American Jewish Congress, recalled the ambassador's pride in being "the first Catholic to hold the London Embassy post." During their friendly chat in early 1938, Wise called Kennedy's attention to the large portrait on the wall of former Ambassador Joseph Hodges Choate, who had served during Teddy Roosevelt's administration.

"I suppose you know, J.K., that Choate was nastily anti-Irish at times?" Wise noted.

Kennedy responded quickly. "I'll ring for the porter and have the portrait removed at once," he said.

Both men laughed at the painting, which showed a stern-looking Choate dressed in a red gown, and commented that, as Wise recalled, "Choate was frowning at us, Joe for being an Irish Ambassador, and at me on general principles as a Jew and Rabbi." Joe must have shared the story about Choate's anti-Irishness with his father-in-law. On the day after St. Patrick's Day, Honey Fitz sent him this one-line cable: "Hope you will be able to do what Choate wants."

GIVEN HIS PUBLIC STATURE and his private sensitivities to ethnic in-sults, Joseph Kennedy's anti-Semitism seems at first confounding—an infectious prejudice that spread to some of his children. Kennedy's views were reflective of the sentiment of many Irish Catholics of his generation. For decades, Irish immigrants found themselves competing for jobs and social opportunities with Jews, whose assimilation into American society was often faster and more successful. Unlike the Irish, who created their own cultural isolation, Jews generally embraced America's public school system and were more willing to adapt to their new environment. Feeling left behind, the Irish sometimes lashed out. During the Depression era of the 1930s, Father Coughlin's tirades gave voice to a misdirected anger at other ethnic groups, particularly Jews. Cardinal O'Connell in Boston per-petuated an underlying tone of anti-Semitism, complaining about the "doubt about God" caused by the revolutionary theories of Albert Einstein and Sigmund Freud, intellectual giants with a Jewish background. "Anti-Semitism was common among American Catholics and if the cardinal never publicly voiced such sentiments, he was not immune to the anti-Jewish bias that thrived among his people," observed James M. O'Toole, O'Connell's biographer.

Although he strained not to be stereotypically Irish, Joe Kennedy carried some of the same biases as uneducated Irish immigrants in East Boston who suspiciously treated the newly arriving Eastern European Jews as a threat to their jobs and religious culture. He learned to couch his bias against Jews with the same phrases and condescension that America's affluent WASP culture used—the same segment of society that Kennedy bitterly felt had acted unfairly towards him as an aspiring, ambitious grandson of immi-grants. Hollywood was run by a "bunch of ignorant Jewish furriers," Kennedy complained. He chastised Jews for supposedly controlling too much of the press and public opinion. The crisis in Germany evoked a strange indifference from Kennedy and a lack of understanding about the plight of Jews in Nazi-controlled lands. His own family's history as victims of bigotry and religious persecution seemed oddly irrelevant in assessing the threat to Jews. In writing to his son, Joseph Jr., who echoed his father's sen-timents about Jews, Kennedy asked about Adolf Hitler: "If he wanted to re-unite Germany, and picked the Jew as the focal point of his attack, and con-ditions in Germany are now so completely those of his own making, why then is it necessary to turn the front of his attack on the Catholics?"

After the vicious *Krystallnacht* attacks against Jews by Nazi mobs in Germany, Kennedy proposed a plan of action that called for the mass migration of thousands of Jews out of Germany to relocation in unpopulated areas of Africa and South and North America. Although he was criticized as an appeaser to Hitler and unresponsive to the plight of Jews, this plan in 1938 gained Kennedy favorable attention in the American press. "Kennedy is rated the most influential U.S. Ambassador to England in many years," commented *Life,* one of the most popular magazines of its day. "If his plan for settling the German Jews, already widely known as the 'Kennedy Plan,' succeeds, it will add luster to a reputation that may well carry Joseph Patrick Kennedy into the White House."

Privately, Kennedy helped arrange the transport of some individual German Jews fleeing Hitler's terror, but the huge effort he had proposed never got off the ground. The estimated cost of $150 million to $600 million seemed astronomical, and neither the British nor the American governments backed the plan. American Jews didn't like the plan because it conflicted with the ideal of a proposed homeland in Palestine. Roosevelt and his top aides in Washington avoided showing support for their ambassador in London, whom they viewed as a foreign policy maverick with his own political agenda. In America, columnist Walter Lippmann and other press critics questioned Kennedy's motives and actions, prompting a response tinged with anti-Semitism from both Kennedy and his children. Writing a rebuttal to Lippmann, thirteen-year-old Bobby Kennedy dismissed the columnist's views as "the natural Jewish reaction," and Joe Jr. had a similar heated response. In a note to his wife Rose, Kennedy wrote: "Walter Lippmann is around saying he hasn't liked the U.S. Ambassador for the last 6 months. Of course the fact he is a Jew has something to do with that." And to a top aide of press baron William Randolph Hearst, Kennedy later wrote that "75% of the attacks made on me by mail were by Jews, and, yet, I don't suppose anybody has worked as hard for them as I have or more to their advantage."

Whether Joe Kennedy worked hard enough to save Jews from Hitler's genocide is debatable; certainly the overall response from the American government, the Catholic Church and the world community at large was tepid. The extent of Hitler's racist policies, his imprisonment of thousands of Jews and his campaign of extermination would become brutally clear as World War II progressed. But even a sympathetic assessment of Kennedy can't explain the upsurge in anti-Semitic views expressed by the ambassador during this period, a coarse response to public criticism that took a particularly ugly tone in private. Disparaging comments about "jews" and other anti-Semitic references are found in the ambassador's private notes and numerous letters between Kennedy and his family and circle of intimates. "The belief that he was under attack in influential Jewish circles for his reported anti-Semitism, indifference to the refugee issue and support of appeasement seems to have prompted him, curiously, to record his views on Judaism and on some of his Jewish colleagues far more explicitly and pejoratively than he had ever done before," observed his granddaughter, Amanda Smith, a half century later. "Almost entirely absent from his papers before his ambassadorship, such comments would afterward become commonplace among his writings."

Joe Kennedy's FBI file makes clear his willingness to expose and recruit Jewish acquaintances in the government's campaign to uncover Communists in the film industry. "Mr. Kennedy is a devout Catholic and is very well versed on Communism and what it might possibly mean to the United States," reported Edward A. Soucy, the FBI's special agent in charge in Boston, in a confidential memo to FBI chief J. Edgar Hoover in December 1943. "He has said he has many Jewish friends in the moving picture industry who would furnish him, upon request, with any information in their possession pertaining to Communist infiltration in the moving picture industry." As he told the FBI, Kennedy "fears that the Communists and their fellow travellers have succeeded in obtaining for themselves many key positions" in Hollywood. Hoover and his bureau knew they had a friend in Kennedy.

IF FRANKLIN DELANO ROOSEVELT chose not to seek an unprecedented third term in 1940, then Joseph P. Kennedy wanted to make history of his own—as the first Catholic elected to the White House. By May 1938, only a few months after arriving in London, Kennedy's long-term political ambitions were being touted by the press. "Will Kennedy Run for President?" asked *Liberty* magazine, and noted that "he is a Roman Catholic," one of his "weak points." The *New York Times* ran a similar political story, speculating about a Kennedy candidacy if Roosevelt served only for two terms, traditional for every American president since George Washington. The *Washington Post* predicted that Kennedy held "an excellent chance to be the first Catholic President," and other publications suggested that Kennedy was sent to London for international grooming as Roosevelt's heir apparent. Nothing could have been further from the truth.

Increasingly, Roosevelt eyed Kennedy with suspicion, both as a potential political rival and as a harping critic who privately eviscerated the president and his policies to just about anyone in London who would listen. When Kennedy came to Washington for a visit that June, James Roosevelt met him aboard the *Queen Mary* as it pulled into New York harbor and warned him about the president's anger. "If I had my eye on another job, it would be a complete breach of faith with President Roosevelt," Kennedy assured the press at the dock. At Hyde Park, the president and his ambassador discussed the worsening situation in Europe, but both men silently realized that a Kennedy candidacy faced the longest odds. As Kennedy later wrote in his diplomatic memoir: "No one can lightly turn away a serious suggestion from his friends that he is worthy of succeeding to the presidency of the United States. There were many reasons that militated against my candidacy for that office, including my Catholic faith, but these might (perhaps) be overcome. But I knew that the time was not propitious." Kennedy scratched out the last line about "propitious" timing and instead wrote in "did not desire the Democratic nomination." Soon after the Hyde Park meeting, the White House leaked to the *Chicago Tribune* that Roosevelt believed Kennedy to be disloyal and cited "positive evidence that Kennedy hopes to use the Court of St. James as a stepping stone to the White House in 1940." When Kennedy learned of the story, he offered in a fury to resign. "It was true Irish anger that swept over me," he said. Kennedy returned to London, but he knew his days were numbered. After the ambassador had left Washington to return to his post, Roosevelt lunched with a top aide and pooh-poohed "the idea that Joe Kennedy could be elected President."

Nevertheless, Roosevelt didn't sever ties but instead kept Kennedy dangling at a distance in case he was needed politically. Talk in Washington suggested that Roosevelt's potential rival for the 1940 nomination, Vice President John Nance Garner, might join forces with another former ally-turned-rival, Postmaster General James Farley, to form a separate ticket. Farley, a Catholic from New York, could be expected to pull away many Irish, Italian and other immigrant votes—a major segment of Roosevelt's winning Democratic Party coalition. Under these circumstances, the president might be forced to call upon his wayward ambassador. "In that event, the President might have to turn to Joe Kennedy as a candidate for Vice-President," recalled Interior Secretary Harold Ickes in his published diary. "That would match a Roman Catholic against a Roman Catholic. While Farley would be able to command certain undoubted political advantages, Kennedy would be able to command the great conservative business support and his campaign would be well financed since he himself is a very rich man."

Instead, Kennedy urged his friend, Senator James F. Byrnes of South Carolina, to consider running for president in 1940. "The only thing that could bring me into active political life again would be to hear that you were going to be a candidate for President," Kennedy wrote. "If you go, I declare myself right here and now unquestionably and unqualifiedly for you and I don't give a damn who is against you." Byrnes didn't run but he was considered briefly by Roosevelt for vice president. Like Kennedy, Roosevelt personally enjoyed Byrnes's company, but the president's aides discouraged any thought of Byrnes because of opposition among labor, his racial views and his religion. Byrnes was born a Catholic but left the church. As a top aide to Roosevelt put it during the vice presidency deliberations, Byrnes has "a double-disadvantage politically; for not only would anti-Catholic bigots oppose him, but Catholics themselves might resent his change of religion."

Little more than a decade after Al Smith's 1928 debacle, politicians such as Kennedy, Byrnes and even Jim Farley recognized that any hint of Catholicism still posed an obstacle to national office in America, regardless of their credentials. The religious recriminations faced by Smith seemed to dissuade an entire generation of Catholic politicians from trying for the nation's top office. But Kennedy felt himself prepared to assume the presidency. As *Collier's* magazine observed in 1939, "There is slight doubt that Joe, despite the political handicaps of his religion, cherishes the hope that he may be President." Kennedy was enough of a realist to recognize his long-shot chances. In his own estimate, natural constituent groups for a conservative-minded Democrat like himself—such as the business community—seemed foreclosed. His ambitions were also effectively blocked by Farley, who actively pursued the 1940 presidential nomination. In Boston, Irish Catholics still devoted themselves clannishly to candidates from their own ethic and religious group, and many backed Farley rather than the incumbent president. One of those supporters was Kennedy's eldest son, Joe Jr., elected as a delegate to the Democratic National Convention by those who flocked to Farley. Joe Kennedy Jr., a handsome gregarious young man with a seemingly bright political future ahead of him, resisted lobbying efforts by Roosevelt's forces to switch his vote. The president's team even called the ambassador in London and asked him to pressure his son, but he refused. "DO WHAT YOU THINK BEST," he cabled his son. Joe Jr. voted for Farley, even though Roosevelt won the nomination on the first ballot.

THERE WERE MANY IRONIES late in the fall 1940 campaign when President Roosevelt visited Boston and embraced the Kennedy clan. A few nights before, Joe Kennedy had given a radio speech in support of the president, allaying fears of defections by Kennedy and many other Catholic voters to the Republican candidate Wendell Wilkie. In a gesture typical of their relationship, Roosevelt smoothed Kennedy's riled feathers by inviting him to dinner at the White House, where he charmed Rose, flattered the ambassador and, most important, implied that he'd help Joe Jr.'s budding political future. (In return for his own support in 1940, Joe Kennedy later suggested he'd worked out a deal for FDR's support of a gubernatorial run for Joe Jr. in Massachusetts.) In his radio speech, Kennedy vouched for the president; any claim that he was "trying to involve this country in the world war" was "false"—even though Kennedy deeply suspected it to be true. His endorsement's most effective part, however, was also his most heartfelt line: "After all, I have a great stake in this country," Kennedy concluded. "My wife and I have given nine hostages to fortune. Our children and your children are more important than anything else in the world. The kind of America that they and their children will inherit is of a grave concern to us all."

When the president's train arrived in Boston, Jack and Joe Kennedy Jr. went with their grandfather, Honey Fitz, to meet Roosevelt, who welcomed them with open arms. At the Boston Garden, before a packed audience, Roosevelt introduced his headstrong envoy as if they were old friends. "Welcome back to the shores of America that Boston boy, beloved by all of Boston and a lot of other places, Ambassador to the Court of St. James . . . Joe Kennedy!" The crowds roared their approval and, with the specter of war looming on the horizon, they listened to their president give his solemn vow.

"And while I am talking to you mothers and fathers, I give you one more assurance," Roosevelt said. "I have said this before but I shall say it again and again and again. Your boys are not going to be sent into any foreign wars."

With his own two boys beside him, Joe Kennedy listened to the president's promise with a faint smile, knowing in his heart that it was all a lie.

The isolationist views of Ambassador Joseph Kennedy were different from those of most American politicians. A long history of geopolitical isolation—keeping the United States out of foreign entanglements in Europe and the rest of the world—existed in nearly every American political party, from the Progressives to conservative Republicans, and dated back to the Republic's birth. This strain of isolationism in the heartland often found itself intertwined with a similar anti-immigrant sentiment, a distinct aversion to anything perceived as foreign. Among Kennedy's own friends and acquaintances, Charles A. Lindbergh, the celebrated aviation hero who became prominent in the America First movement, was a typical American isolationist of his time. But the origin of Kennedy's views was different.

Despite his money and power, Joe Kennedy had spent his whole life trying to remove the hyphen from the "Irish-American" attached to his name. "I was born here, my children were born here," he said on more than one occasion. "What the hell do I have to do to be an American?"

Isolationism was one of Kennedy's answers. By protecting America's shores, performing their patriotic duties, Irish immigrants and their descendants had proved their allegiance to their new country. Kennedy wasn't immune. "A need to assert and reassert his Americanism may have helped to motivate Kennedy to take the most narrowly American approach in foreign policy," said biographer David Koskoff. "Isolationism helped to identify Kennedy with traditional America, and proclaimed that his only concern was for America." Even though he and his family enjoyed their stay in London, Joe never intended to help England, certainly not at the expense of young Americans like his sons. "I hate to think how much money I would give up rather than sacrifice Joe and Jack in a war," he wrote to Honey Fitz from London. To say the Kennedys were Anglophiles fails to account for their actions in England when the empire truly was at stake. During the worst times, when bombs were falling on London, Kennedy sent his family home to the safety of America, far from the reach of foreign powers. He endured the remainder of his tenure largely alone. "For Christ's sakes, stop trying to make this a holy war because no one will believe you," Kennedy burst out in one meeting in London with British officials. "You're fighting for your life as an Empire, and that's good enough." In the estimation of British officials, especially Winston Churchill, now prime minister, Kennedy's isolationism was nothing more than defeatism and, as they murmured behind his back, sheer cowardice. A British foreign office memo about Kennedy's position explained that Roosevelt owed much of his political success to the "East Coast Irish," which it characterized as "about the most dirty group of politicians in the country." To "pacify" the Irish, it reported, the president felt compelled to appoint one of their own. As the memo concluded: "From Mr. Kennedy's point of view he owes his position to the fact that he represents a Catholic, Irish, anti-English group."

Within Roosevelt's administration, several other top officials who were Irish Catholic shared a reluctance to join Great Britain in the war. They perceived the state visit in 1939 of the king and queen, for example, an ominous sign. "The announcement of the royal visit infuriated the Irish at the White House," recalled Thomas Corcoran, FDR's speechwriter and confidant. "It signalled an impending alliance and we interpreted it to mean that America would soon be at war." Frank Murphy, Roosevelt's attorney general and later appointed to the U.S. Supreme Court, felt that some of the president's advisers who were Jewish, such as Felix Frankfurter and Ben Cohen, also were pushing a physically weakened president into the war. "Murphy regards the Jewish influence as most dangerous," Kennedy recorded in his diary. After attending a Notre Dame football game, Kennedy listened to Murphy as he ticked off a litany of Roosevelt aides who were either Jewish, married to Jews or sympathetic to Communists. "We can't have both Catholics and Communists," Murphy insisted. "We must have one or the other." Clearly, Murphy had found a receptive audience for his anti-Semitic diatribe in Kennedy. A few months later, Kennedy would repeat the same litany in his own diary: "The four men who followed me to Europe: [Harry] Hopkins had a Jew wife and 2 Jew children. [Averell] Harriman a Jew wife. [Ben] Cohen a Jew. [Charles Harold] Fahey—lawyer—a Jew mother."

The virulent anti-Semitism shared by Kennedy and Murphy expressed a wider attitude within the Catholic Church. Despite assurances to Roosevelt in 1936, the hate-spewing Father Coughlin managed to remain in the public eye as late as 1940. Even after he was off the air, Coughlin continued publishing his reactionary magazine, *Social Justice,* which editorialized against "communistic Jews" and published the phony *Protocols of the Elders of Zion,* a forged "plot" by Jews to gain financial control of the world. Kennedy's own professed distance from Father Coughlin must be questioned. In February 1939, *Social Justice* devoted its full cover page to a picture of the Kennedy family and designated the ambassador its "Man of the Week." When war erupted in Europe, Coughlin urged his followers to form into a "Christian Front," a small but violent group of mostly Catholic men in New York, Boston and other cities who sometimes beat up Jews in the streets, just as the Nazis did. Coughlin pushed hard for American isolationism, expressing disdain for the English and admiration for Hitler's policies in Germany. "Had we Christians enforced the discipline and produced the good accomplished by the Nazis for a good end, we would not be weeping at the wailing wall," Coughlin cried. Only after Pearl Harbor, when Roosevelt threatened sedition charges against him, did Coughlin finally end his tirades. What is so disconcerting is that the Catholic Church allowed Father Coughlin to fester this hatred for such a long time and, as the historical record shows, that America's radio priest expressed views that weren't too far from those privately held by the ambassador to the Court of St. James.

JOE KENNEDY'S BITTERNESS about impending war, well known to his circle of intimates, soon spilled over. Within days after Roosevelt's Election

Day victory in 1940, Kennedy granted an interview while home in America to a reporter who published his candid comments without any self-censorship. In this interview, Kennedy's true feelings were exposed for the world to see. "Democracy is finished in England," he said. "It may be here." Contradicting the spirit of his recent radio speech in support of Roosevelt, Kennedy instead painted a damning picture of Great Britain's chances against totalitarianism, and expressed support for American isolationists. "Lindbergh's not so crazy either," he added. Though his comments were tucked into a *Boston Globe* article with a quiet, almost misleading headline, the content caused a sensation worldwide. Nailed by his own words, Joe Kennedy seemed almost disoriented by the outcry, especially from the British. In a long letter to his father, twenty-three-year-old Jack Kennedy made several lengthy suggestions about how to write a speech that would extricate Joe Sr. from the mess. "I think it is important that you write in a very calm and a judicious manner, not as though you were on the defensive," advised his son. But his words came too late.

At a meeting in Hyde Park before Thanksgiving, Roosevelt accepted Kennedy's letter of resignation. After a short contentious meeting, the president asked Kennedy to step out of the room. "I never want to see that son of a bitch again as long as I live," the infuriated president told his wife. "Take his resignation and get him out of here!"

Although he agreed to stay in London until the president named a replacement, Kennedy's ambitious political career was essentially over.

Tortured Souls

ON CHRISTMAS DAY 1943, alone and feeling blue, Kathleen Kennedy poured out her soul in a letter home. Using the nickname by which everyone knew her, she signed it "much love to all from Kick." Apart from her family in America, and the young Englishman she loved who was fighting in the war, Kick Kennedy longed for a future still so far away.

Her romance with Billy Hartington—William Cavendish, Marquess of Hartington, the future Duke of Devonshire—compelled Kick to return to England during the height of World War II. She had left her newspaper job in Washington to work as a Red Cross volunteer. In her Christmas letter, she talked about wartime hardships, and mentioned the decline of some of the old English manor houses, including Chatsworth, the palatial 150-room mansion where she thought Billy might live someday. So much of the "grandeur, tradition and strength that is very much a part of England" would be lost if those beautiful mansions disappeared, she explained to her family. Then, in the very next line, Kick seemed to remember her other self—the young woman born and reared as an Irish Catholic in Boston—who could not forget her own history.

"I know my little brothers will think 'Kick has gone more British' than ever," she admitted. "My persecuted Irish ancestors would turn over in their graves to hear talk of England in this way but I don't care. I think a landed aristocracy can be an instrument of good as much as of evil and when it is the former than—'Perserve [sic] it.' (You'd better not let Grandpa Fitz see the above.)"

During World War II, the Kennedy family faced several tragedies and moral dilemmas that tested their faith and their family loyalties, and played upon their Irish sense of fate's cruel ironies. The war that Joe Kennedy had tried so hard to prevent, the conflict that had ruined his own political chances, now threatened the lives of his children. Rather than run for office in Massachusetts, Joe Kennedy Jr. enlisted in the navy and volunteered as a pilot for dangerous bomber flights over Europe. Instead of continuing his budding career as a writer, Jack Kennedy also joined the navy, becoming the skipper of a torpedo boat in the Pacific. But no Kennedy was more conflicted than Kick, the vivacious daughter so much a focus of the Kennedy family life. She followed the dictates of her heart and returned to war-torn London—a place where her father was vilified as an appeaser, willing to see the British Isles collapse in defeat to Hitler so long as his own country was spared war. Kick felt differently. "I feel that my devotion to the British over a period of years has not been without foundation and I feel this is a second home more than ever," Kick wrote to her brother Jack that same year. This extraordinary time would define the Kennedys for years to come, not only in the public image of this Irish Catholic clan but in the subtle and often profound ways they related to their God and religion, their sense of love and fidelity to each other, and the random, often tragic events that neither their mother's prayers nor their father's wealth could keep them from confronting.

KATHLEEN KENNEDY, the fourth child of Joe and Rose Kennedy, had inherited differing traits from each of her parents, though she could arguably be called the favorite of both. Kick possessed the charm and social graces of her mother—with what Rose described as a "glowing, lightly pink Irish complexion"—as well as the sly, quick wit of her father. In an intriguing combination, she was a smart, poised young woman with curly brown hair, a wide dimpled smile, and a sweet sense of naughtiness. "Sir Francis says that ninety percent of the people who write on newspapers haven't a bit of talent," she observed as a cub reporter for the *Washington Times-Herald* in 1942. "Well, brother, another member has joined those ranks." She appreciated her family's Gaelic ancestry and understood the Irish quest for social acceptance in all forms of American life. "Green was very prominent around the *Times-Herald* on St. Patrick's Day," she wrote home. "I think Irishmen must have a great weakness for newspapers." She possessed the fondness of many Irish-Americans for discovering someone with the same heritage. One afternoon in the newsroom, "a rather cultured gentleman" called up with an idea for her boss, and Kathleen was asked to take the message. When she asked the caller's name, he said his identity didn't matter. "Just an old Irish name," he replied.

Kick's curiosity was piqued. "Tell me, because I certainly have an Irish name," she insisted.

"What is it?" the man asked.

"Kennedy," she answered proudly.

There was a pause on the other end, and then the voice continued. "I've liked every Kennedy I've ever known—except Joe Kennedy."

Kathleen's "ears perked up" at this reply, as she later recalled, and she continued her inquisition. "Why don't you like him?" she asked sweetly, "I hear he's quite a nice guy."

The voice would have none of it. "I *know* him," the man growled. "I went to college with him."

Kick never did get the man's name, but the story of her conversation was so amusing that she repeated it in a letter to her parents.

LIKE HER SISTERS, Kathleen Kennedy's education followed the path set by her mother. Rose made certain her daughters learned their Catholic catechism along with their mathematics and a foreign language from the Sisters of the Sacred Heart at their convent school at Noroton, outside Greenwich, Connecticut, a tony enclave on the Long Island Sound. Mrs. Kennedy didn't want her daughters socializing with boys from the public schools in Bronxville but rather improving their minds with purposeful study and cultivating their souls through prayer. Irish Catholics, even at the Kennedys' strata of the American economic pyramid, still were not found in significant numbers at the select all-girls boarding schools or the Ivy League's seven sister schools of the 1930s. Instead, these successful children of Irish immigrants, usually more than a generation removed from the mother country, created their own social world around the church. At Noroton, young women were instructed by nuns who molded students to show "distinctively feminine qualities: tact, quiet courage, and the willingness to subordinate her will to another's gracefully and even gaily." In this small, private elite school for the daughters of wealthy Catholic families, Rose and her daughters met families—such as the McDonnells and Coakleys—who set a social pace that the Kennedys found hard to match. As a "First Irish family" in New York, the McDonnell patriarch refused to let his daughter Charlotte date Jack Kennedy because of his father's controversial past. When Charlotte McDonnell married a few years later, Rose wrote to her daughters: "Mrs. McDonnell rather hints that I am long on education and short on match-making as far as my children are concerned."

The Kennedy women showed more independence than most Irish Catholic women in their social group, none more so than Kick. Because she was so much like Jack, Kick loved and admired her brother. His breezy style and devil-may-care antics were such a change from the subdued, controlling atmosphere of the convent. "She really thinks you are a great fellow," their father wrote to Jack when both siblings were still in boarding school. "She has a love and a devotion to you that you should be very proud to have deserved. It probably does not become apparent to you, but it does to both Mother and me. She thinks you are quite the grandest fellow who ever lived and your letters furnish her most of her laughs in the Convent." In 1935, Kick went to a Sacred Heart convent in Europe for a year, just as her mother had, to further her education and devotion to the church. She raved to her mother that her first Solemn High Mass at Notre Dame Cathedral in Paris was "the most impressive thing I have ever seen." A highlight was her visit during March break to the Vatican with four other students and a chaperone. Her father's friend, Count Enrico Galeazzi, helped Kick and her friends receive an audience with the Pope.

Though a fine student, Kick didn't possess the same religiosity as her younger sister, Eunice, whom many thought might become a nun. Eunice, a smart, energetic young woman deeply devoted to her faith, embodied the ideal sought by the Sacred Heart nuns. In her teasing manner, Kick would poke a little fun at her sister's vaunted reputation. She told her family that Hugh Fraser, a potential beau just back from the war, had inquired about Eunice. Fraser, the playwright who stayed friendly with Jack and the family for decades, was one of several Catholics in the Kennedy's British social circle. "He asks a lot about her," Kick relayed, "and hopes and prays that she is not taking herself into a nunnery." In a similar vein, Jack teased Eunice about her religiosity. "I hope everything is going nicely at the Convent, and that the novenas etc. are going off on schedule," wrote Jack. "It always seemed to me that if you worried less about your chances of getting into heaven and more about your chances of getting a man, which are slimmer and slimmer as you get fatter and fatter—it would take a great load off your brother's mind."

Despite their different styles, Kick and Eunice were still very much products of their mother's influence and direction, counsel that taught them how to be Irish Catholic women in a world that sometimes looked askance at their heritage. Rose's instructions would stretch across generations among the Kennedy women. "She was the one who would tell the stories about the discrimination against the Irish," observed her granddaughter, Kathleen Kennedy Townsend (née Kathleen Hartington Kennedy), who was named for her aunt. "She was very well aware of her place in history. Her faith in the Catholic Church taught her a great deal and had a lot to say to her, and that it should be adhered to."

AT AGE EIGHTEEN, Kick met Billy Hartington, a tall, brooding Englishman two years her senior, while living in England during her father's time as ambassador. When she was forced to return to America because of the war, Kick stayed in contact with Billy through letters, even though she dated other men in the United States and he became engaged, for a short while, to another woman. "It was a very long time before I gave up all hope of marrying you," Billy later explained in a letter. Eventually, in July 1943, Kick left for England, ostensibly to work for the Red Cross but with the intent of renewing her love affair with Billy. She assured her family that she saw no future with the future Duke of Devonshire. "Of course I know he would never give in about the religion and he knows that I never would," she wrote to Jack. "It's all rather difficult as he is very, very fond of me and as long as I am about he'll never marry." She sent the same reassurances to her mother. "Billy and I went out together for the first time last Saturday. It really is fun to see people put their heads together the minute we arrive any place," she wrote. "There's heavy betting on when we are going to announce it. Some people have gotten the idea that I'm going to give in. Little do they know."

On the surface, the couple appeared as opposites attracting. Their own backgrounds seemed to preclude all chances of a serious relationship. The Cavendishes were Protestants with a long history of Irish Catholic bias. Many of their lands were confiscated from Catholics by King Henry VIII and bestowed upon Sir William Cavendish, who opposed the ascension of the Catholic king, James II, in a bloody rebellion. On Billy's maternal side, another relative, Robert Cecil, chief minister to James I, objected to the Prince of Wales's marriage to the Spanish Infanta because she was a Roman Catholic. Billy's grandfather, Lord Salisbury, had, as prime minister, ridiculed the idea of Irish self-government. But much of their ill will toward the Irish stemmed from one violent act. Billy's paternal granduncle, Lord Frederick Cavendish, was appointed chief secretary for Ireland in 1882 by Prime Minister Gladstone. History would record Gladstone as a British ruler who showed more sympathy for the Irish than most, yet his new man in Ireland wasn't greeted warmly. "We will tear him in pieces within a fortnight," promised an Irish Party leader. The Irish were true to their word: Cavendish was murdered within his first week of arrival, hacked to death by assassins wielding twelve-inch surgical knives. Cavendish's body was found in a pool of blood outside Phoenix Park in Dublin. His killers were later traced to a secret Irish nationalist group headed by an Irish-American ex-Fenian and called the Invincibles. Five were hanged for the plot and three imprisoned. To many horrified British people, Cavendish's assassination justified their ill will toward the Irish and their opposition to Ireland's long-held desire for self-rule. This event would be seen quite differently in the Kennedy family, particularly by grandfather John F. Fitzgerald. When he visited Dublin with his daughter Rose in 1908, Honey Fitz—a Fenian at heart if not in secret membership—pointed out the site of Cavendish's murder as "a Catholic monument." (One Irish Republican newspaper would claim years later that Fitzgerald and other prominent Boston Irish Catholics were involved in a secret society named for an Irish patriot that helped to procure surplus arms from American police departments and then ship them to the rebel Irish Republican Army (IRA) during the fight for independence. Guns from America were said to be hidden in the false bottoms of coffins, trunks and crated farm tools sent to Irish ports. However, no other evidence points to Fitzgerald's involvement in such efforts.)

Like his forebears, Billy's father was proud of the Cavendish family's long anti-papist legacy. He was a Freemason, part of the secret society opposed to Catholics and condemned by the church for more than two centuries. "I think it's fair to say that my father was a bigoted Protestant," Billy's brother, Andrew, later conceded. "My father and mother both felt very strongly that Catholics proselytized. And that our family had a long tradition opposed to Catholicism." Indeed, in a self-published pamphlet, the duke warned about a papal scheme to "re-Catholicize" their country by encouraging Catholic women to marry into the British upper classes, including his fellow English noblemen. In Kick, the duke recognized her danger as well as her beguiling charm. "She is very sharp, very witty, and so sweet in every way," the duke described. "The Irish blood is evident, of course, and she is no great beauty, but her smile and her chatty enthusiasm are her salvation. I doubt, of course, she'd be any sort of a match for our Billy even if we managed to lure her out from under the papal shadow."

Most members of the British social circles entertaining the Kennedys, particularly those on the Cliveden estate, shared a similar view about Catholics. Though they could be personally gracious to the Kennedys, and shared much of the ambassador's political wish to negotiate with the Germans rather than fight them, there was an air of privilege and tradition among the so-called Cliveden set that necessarily cast Roman Catholics in an inferior light. Lady Nancy Astor, who hosted these gatherings on her family's estate, befriended the Kennedys in a generous way, yet her views about their religion were evident. In a letter home, Kick recalled how a friend "spent the night at Cliveden and [did] nothing but argue with Lady Astor about Catholicism. Although I don't think he is a very strong Catholic himself, he was going to get a list of books for her to read on the subject." Lady Astor, a Christian Scientist, harbored deep suspicions about the Roman Catholic Church and its ways—what she called "the candlestick plot." When their friend David Ormsby-Gore, a British lord with nearly the same pedigree as Hartington, decided to marry Sissy Lloyd-Thomas in a Catholic Church, Astor asked: "How *could* you, David?" But Kick's romance brought a different response. Lady Astor decided that if the Kennedy family back in America disapproved of this match, she would become its biggest booster in England. As an American-born woman, "Aunt Nancy," as Kick called Lady Astor, identified with Kathleen's situation. "Of course, she still hopes I'll marry Billy and keeps telling me I'll only be happy in England," Kick wrote home.

Though she preferred things light and gay, Kick was compelled by events to face her own set of beliefs. In many ways, she remained eager to please her parents, and she shared their outlook, particularly the strong Catholic antipathy toward communism. "Father [Fulton J.] Sheen who speaks on 'The Catholic Hour' was up a week ago Saturday," she mentioned in one letter to her mother. "He spoke on communism and was really marvelous." In a letter to his eldest son shortly after Kick's arrival in London, Joe Kennedy relayed a story from a U.S. Army friend about seeing one of their hard-bitten sergeants in church with Kick. As her proud father recounted: "On inquiring as to how it came about, he said that he hadn't been to Mass for a year and Kathleen at the Red Cross had urged him to go, and he said he would go if she'd go with him, so it seems like she's still working on the side of God." Kathleen Kennedy also shared her father's prejudices. In mentioning to her parents that she had attended an Oscar Levant concert in which the well-known entertainer refused to play anything but Gershwin, Kick commented: "The Hebes stick together even in death."

On her return trip to London in July 1943, as her ship carrying Red Cross volunteers bobbed between enemy submarines in the Atlantic, Kick managed to find time to pray daily. "We have had Mass every afternoon at 3:30—a wartime measure and guess where we have it—in the synagogue," she wrote to her family in her first letter from London. "I have been serving Mass as the soldiers didn't seem to show up. We are allowed to go to Communion then and yesterday we had Mass on the deck under the most crude circumstances." While spending a weekend with Billy Hartington and other English friends soon after her arrival in 1943, Kick found how difficult it could be as a Catholic in this crowd. "Of course on Sunday morning, there was a great problem of my going to church," she recalled in a letter. "They all told me that the church was miles away and I couldn't possibly go. I think they would have considered it a moral triumph if I hadn't so I was determined to get there no matter how far away it was. Had a chat with the priest who said it was about four miles each way and it was just according to my conscience whether I should attend mass. Finally hoppped [sic] on a bike and was there in twenty-five minutes. I must say it would have been a bit far to walk."

Some accounts portray Kick as a headlong romantic, but her letters reveal a deep ambivalence about the religious difficulties she'd face in her relationship with Billy. In her jaunty, joking way, she was keenly aware of the prejudices aimed at her. "It is really funny how worried and how much talking is being done, by all those old Cecil and Devonshire spooks," she wrote home. In another letter, she repeated the same thought, almost word for word, as if repetition might convince her that the situation was truly humorous. "Some of those old Devonshire and Cecil ancestors would certainly jump out of their graves if anything happened to some of their ancient traditions," she commented. "It just amused me to see how worried they all are." Certainly, Billy's father wasn't amused. For her birthday in February 1944, Kick received "a lovely old leather book" from the Duke of Devonshire. As she began to unwrap the gift, Billy's mother rushed toward her.

"The Duchess said she had nothing to do with it and when I opened it up I knew why," Kick recalled.

The gift was a copy of the Church of England's *Book of Common Prayer.* Typically, Kick laughed it off, and thanked the duke very much. But his thinly veiled joke was transparent: Kathleen Kennedy must renounce her religion and embrace the Anglican church if she wanted to marry his son.

AS THEIR love affair turned more serious, Kick and Billy searched for ways to uphold their family traditions and please their parents while still being able to marry. At her parish church on Farm Street in London, Kick consulted the Reverend Martin Cyril D'Arcy, a highly influential Jesuit philosopher and priest who, she thought, was most likely to be sympathetic to her cause. If anyone could arrive at a wise and equitable answer to her dilemma, she felt it would be this extraordinary priest.

Many of the Kennedy family friends belonged to a group of British Catholics who turned to Father D'Arcy for spiritual guidance. During Sunday Mass, the Kennedys were enthralled by D'Arcy, who was lionized as England's favorite Catholic at a time when allegiances to Rome could hardly be considered a social enhancement. Erudite and witty, D'Arcy personified the highly distinguished cadre of Catholic intellectuals who carved a small but commanding niche in British society in the 1930s. He counted Albert Einstein, T. S. Eliot and Bertrand Russell among his friends. D'Arcy gave invigorating radio sermons and wrote several critically acclaimed books. His most famous work, *The Mind and the Heart of Love,* tried to reconcile the passionate love of Eros with the selfless ideals of Christian love. Father D'Arcy became a central figure in the movement by some British intellectuals to convert to Roman Catholicism—their fervent response to the "wasteland" of secular modernism. "His urbane charm and cultivated mind," *Time* magazine later commented, "have influenced a quarter century's crop of Oxonians and helped bring many a British highbrow into his broad-browed church." The Oxford-educated Jesuit helped convert novelist Evelyn Waugh, a social acquaintance of the Kennedys, and Dame Edith Sitwell to the faith. In *Vile Bodies,* Waugh used D'Arcy as the prototype for the character called Father Rothschild, who knew "everyone who could possibly be of any importance" in London. Waugh was one of a handful of British writers—including G. K. Chesterton and the poet Maurice Baring, also converts—who blended their strong Catholicism with a sense of British aristocracy. This atmosphere was the perfect blend of influences for the Kennedys. Kick embraced the work of Maurice Baring and socialized with Waugh. Their friend Hugh Fraser's mother, Laura, would later write a biography of Baring and their days up to the start of the war. Baring's poetic sensibility became deeply engrained in these young Kennedys. When Bill Coleman, Jack's good friend from Harvard, was killed in the war, Kick wrote to his grieving sister and suggested that she read a book of Maurice Baring's poems to soothe her grieving soul. "I know what a sock in the eyes it will be for you because I have never heard you talk so well of anyone as you did Bill," Kick consoled Jack in a letter.

But though Father D'Arcy had helped many fellow Catholics in London, Kick misjudged him on her pressing matter. With the full force of a priest long convinced that he could convert the most ardent skeptic, D'Arcy warned that marrying Billy would mean leaving the church, living in sin and being forever separated from the God of her Catholic heritage. He reminded her of what the catechism she learned from the Sacred Heart nuns said about mixed marriage: "Instead of a blessing, the guilty parties draw down upon themselves the anger of God." D'Arcy referred her to a friendly bishop to seek a dispensation, but, as she wrote to her parents, "I suppose it will [be] practically impossible."

On the home front, Kick's search for an answer proved equally unsuccessful. In America, intermarriage among Catholics and Protestants was not common, and in Boston it was rare. Teachings from the church hierarchy certainly counseled Irish Catholics to marry among themselves, and the hostile reception from Brahmins only reinforced this cultural alienation. Rose Kennedy's opposition to her daughter's impending marriage is often discounted as simply a prejudice of her own, a tribal acrimony against Protestants. For example, as Barbara Gibson, one of several aides to write of their Kennedy days, contended: "It horrified Rose, as a Child of Mary, to think that her daughter could become the example cited by other Catholics in love with other Protestant boys. Nothing could be worse than Kathleen's marriage to a man of the wrong faith." However, the available letters and documentation give little if any evidence to support the notion of Rose's alleged bias as they do, say, Joe's obvious anti-Semitism. Most historical accounts of this fated Romeo and Juliet romance rarely explore the overt bigotry faced by the Kennedys that obviously exacerbated their response and barely mention the extensive anti-Catholic history of Billy's family. Yet given the repeated instances of religious bias mentioned in Kick's own letters, it doesn't seem unreasonable for Joe and Rose Kennedy to be quite concerned about their daughter's decision to marry into a family holding such rancor toward their faith.

Rather than make a frontal attack on Billy's religion, Rose took a different tack. She attempted to sway her daughter's decisionmaking by appealing to their own cultural heritage. In her view, Kick not only learned the church commandments but possessed a "gift of faith," and understood what the Catholic Church meant to their family and Irish ancestors. As Rose later argued in her memoir, the Catholic Church "had, in fact, as I think historians of almost any persuasion would agree, been the main cohesive force, more than language, custom, any circumstance that had enabled the Irish people to survive and in some ways prevail during the course of many centuries of domination by the English." If Kathleen made a choice based on her religion—similar to the one Rose's father made for her with Wellesley—she would learn to accept it over time.

In one letter in late February 1944, Rose composed a subtly manipulative message to her daughter about staying true to her religion. After a breezy salutation, she told Kick of getting a letter from a Boston friend "whose third cousin watches you go to Communion frequently, so the news has been carried across the waters." Of course, the underlying message was not only parental approval of Kick's continued religious observance but also the hint that she was being watched by an ever-present army of her parents' minions, not to mention Almighty God. "It is Lent now and I am praying morning, noon and night, so do not be exhausting yourself and running your little legs off going to Church, as your first duty is to your job," Rose instructed. "The little verse—'Do your duty, that is best; leave unto the Lord the rest' may be Protestant or Catholic, but it really teaches us that our first responsibility is towards our immediate job." In a direct reference to their internal struggle, Rose cast doubt about the outcome of Joe Kennedy's effort to secure special Vatican approval for her marriage. "Galleazzi's [sic] pal said of course the authorities were always the same and frankly I do not seem to think Dad can do anything," reported Rose. "He feels terribly sympathetic and so do I and I only wish we could offer some suggestions." Then Rose underlined her view with a brief sermon. "When both people have been handed something all their lives, how ironic it is that they can not have what they want most," she commented. The detached pose here, the mention of irony, is remarkable given Rose's expressed sympathy for her daughter in the previous line. While expressing empathy, Rose underlined what Kick's decision would mean for the family, and placed the ethical dilemma equally on Billy's shoulders. "I wonder if the next generation will feel that it is worth sacrificing a life's happiness for all the old family tradition. So much wealth, titles, etc. seem to be disappearing. But I understand perfectly the terrific responsibilities and the disappointment of it all."

The duke was no help. He pressured his son increasingly to abandon his quest to marry the Irish Catholic girl from America. Without an easy solution of her own, Billy's mother offered many of the same words as Rose. "Had a long chat with the Duchess and she is very sympathetic," Kick wrote back to her parents. "She said to me, 'It's a shame because you are both so good and it would please everyone so much.'"

As in most Kennedy family crises, Kick turned to her father to search for an answer. Joe Kennedy wasn't inclined to find a solution through prayer or divine intervention. Rather, he preferred to rely on his contacts with powerful clerical figures, hoping that they could discover some special dispensation so that his favorite daughter could stay in her church and still marry the man she loved. "Please try and discover loopholes although I keep feeling that the particular parties involved would make compromise impossible," Kick implored. "The Catholics say it would give scandal. This situation, Daddy, is a stickler."

IN THEIR secret code across the Atlantic, they called him "Archie Spell." Because of the wartime censorship of letters, the Kennedys referred to

Archbishop Francis Spellman of New York by this rather flippant moniker. "Archie Spell has made investigation—there & here," telegraphed Rose to her daughter. "Can you write or cable what concessions your friend will consider—Hoping for some solution but looks extremely difficult."

Spellman, vicar of the most powerful Catholic diocese in the United States, welcomed the opportunity to help Joe Kennedy with his troublesome personal matter, even though he knew it would do little good. As America's top churchman and the church's most influential layman, they traded favors, big and small. Two years earlier, Spellman had written a glowing letter of recommendation for Eunice to attend Stanford University. In his letter of thanks, Joe Kennedy relayed how much Rose wanted the archbishop to say Mass at their house. When the diocese's chancery needed expanded offices, Kennedy sold a block of houses on Madison Avenue near Spellman's residence at terms very favorable to the church. But Kick's request was different, far more complex. At the urging of his daughter, and aware of the possible political consequences for his sons, Kennedy requested a private visit with Spellman in April 1944 to determine whether the church might somehow recognize Kick's marriage to the Marquess of Hartington. "One of our closest friends among the Catholic clergy in America was Francis Spellman," Rose later recalled. "We enlisted him as our adviser and also as our friend at court, so to speak, with Pope Pius XII." In a lengthy meeting, Spellman listened to the ex-ambassador pour out his heart about his daughter; during the same meeting, the archbishop pursued his own political agenda.

Spellman had gained stature with President Roosevelt following the Pacelli visit arranged by Kennedy. Since then, he'd pursued his own kind of foreign policy, acting as a liaison between the Vatican and the White House. During the war, the Pope relied on Spellman for advice and to deal with war-time leaders such as France's Charles de Gaulle and such sensitive issues as the Allied bombing around Rome (for which the Vatican wanted U.S. reimbursement for its damaged properties). Roosevelt also enlisted Spellman's help in a variety of ways, including a well-publicized mission to Ireland in 1943 to secure support for England in the Allied effort, particularly the use of Irish ports for British ships. Ireland remained determined to keep its neutrality. At a dinner at Ivegh House, the seat of Irish government, Prime Minister Eamon De Valera introduced the archbishop and underlined his Irish Catholic ancestry. But Spellman, as he did in private talks with De Valera, made sure that Ireland realized whose side he was on. The archbishop raised his glass in a toast. "To the President of the United States," the Archbishop proposed, "and the cause he serves!" De Valera remained unmoved.

Undoubtedly, some of the archbishop's political concerns were discussed during his meeting with Joe Kennedy. As Rose later wrote in her diary, Joe "talked with him about three hours but not all about Kick." Rather than fuss and fume about intermarriage as other prelates might, Spellman "did not seem unduly excited" about the prospect of Kathleen marrying a Protestant. Spellman's placid response, in Rose's estimation, caused her to second-guess her own view. She thought of Kick's engagement as "a blow to the family prestige," and her husband bemoaned all those lost votes in Boston, where newspaper rumors scandalized his daughter's romance with the British lord. "I thought it would have such mighty repercussions in that every little young girl would say if K-Kennedy can—why can't I?" Rose inscribed in her diary. "No one seemed to be as excited about that as I." On the scale of world events, Spellman considered this concern very small indeed. Later, in another conversation with the archbishop, Joe Jr. received the same impression as his father. "His [Spellman's] attitude seemed to be that if they loved each other a lot, then marry outside the Church," Joe wrote to his father. "He didn't seem to be disturbed about it creating a bad example."

Nevertheless, in their common language of political bartering, Spellman promised Kennedy he would try somehow to gain Vatican approval for Kick's marriage, just as Count Galeazzi assured his American friend that he'd attempt to find a solution. Spellman asked Archbishop William Godfrey, the first apostolic representative to Britain since the Reformation, to intercede with Kathleen and discuss the religious ramifications of her plans. Rose prayed that her daughter might change her mind. "Feel you have been wrongly influenced," Rose cabled her daughter. "Sending Archie Spell's friend to talk to you. Anything done for Our Lord will be rewarded hundredfold." But Godfrey's premarital advice reflected more of Spellman's practical view than Rose's hope for a miraculous turn of events. "The Bishop told me that it would put the Church in a very difficult position for us to get a dispensation," Kick explained to her family, "and it would be better if we went ahead and got married and then something might possibly be done afterwards. Of course, he wouldn't guarantee that anything could be done, but I'm quite sure that if we wait to see them about a dispensation we might have to wait years." Godfrey later sent a telegram back to Spellman saying that he had done the archbishop's bidding but "in vain." After his conversation with Kick, the Vatican's man in London became convinced that only Rose could influence her. "Mother could try again with all her power," Godfrey cabled from London. "Am convinced this only chance."

As Kick agonized over her choices, however, she also faced the religious terms insisted by her future husband and in-laws. For Billy's family, the ideal solution would be for Kick to convert and, not too subtly, they pressured her to do so. During a weekend trip to Churchdale, the Duchess of Devonshire arranged for Kick to meet a family friend, the Reverend Ted Talbot, a chaplain to King George VI, who explained the history of the Cavendish family in the Church of England and why Billy could never bring up his son as a Roman Catholic. As Kick recounted in a letter home, Talbot outlined the "fundamental differences" between the two religions. "Of course, I explained that something one had been brought up to believe in and which was largely responsible for the character and personality of an individual is a very difficult thing for which to find a substitute," Kick wrote in a section of her missive marked "THIS IS FOR MOTHER AND DADDY ONLY." She admitted that "it seemed rather cheap and weak to give in at the first real crisis in my life." Both the duchess and "Father Talbot," as she wrote, "don't for a minute want me to give up something. They just hoped that I might find the same thing in the Anglican version of Catholicism."

Ultimately, Kick decided not to convert, though in just about every other way she had given in. At least one of Kick's confidants, Sissy Ormsby-Gore, felt that Billy's demands were unreasonable, almost selfish. Her own husband, David, a cousin of Billy's, had compromised far more with her spiritual needs. "Sissy wondered if Billy really understood what he was asking Kick to do," observed Lynne McTaggart, a biographer of Kathleen Kennedy. "He was going to give up nothing, while she was going to be made to give up so much." In her own opinion, Kick felt that Billy had been placed in a nonnegotiable position. "Poor Billy is very, very sad but he sees his duty must come first," Kick explained to her parents. "He is a fanatic on this subject and I suppose just such a spirit is what has made England great."

In a letter dated April 30, 1944, Billy finally addressed the religious issue with his future mother-in-law. Beginning on a conciliatory note, he apologized for not writing sooner. "I have loved Kick for a long time, but I did try hard to face the fact that the religious difficulties seemed insurmountable," Billy confessed. After spending his first Christmas with Kick in years, Billy said he could not bear to let her go ever again. The war only made their desire to marry more pressing. "I could not believe, either, that God could really intend two loving people, both of whom wanted to do the right thing, and both of whom are Christians, to miss the opportunity to be happy, and perhaps even useful, together because of the religious squabbles of His human servants several hundred years ago," he observed. And yet, Billy had no intention of bending his adamant stand, nor did he attempt to ameliorate the "religious squabbles" separating him from the Kennedy family's Catholicism. His perceived duty to country superceded duties to his future family. His references to Kick's religion were at best patronizing, and he made no indications that he might compromise in any way. Instead, he made it quite clear who would be in charge of their children's upbringing. As he informed Rose:

> I do feel extremely strongly about the religion of my children both from a personal and from a national point of view, otherwise I should never have asked Kick to make such sacrifices in agreeing to their being brought up Anglican. I know that I should only be justified in allowing my children to be brought up Roman Catholic, if I believed it to be desirable for England to become a Roman Catholic country. Therefore, believing in the National Church of England, as I do very strongly, and having so many advantages, and all the responsibilities that they entail, I am convinced that I should be setting a very bad example if I gave in, and that nothing would justify doing so.

BY THE TIME Billy Hartington sent his letter, Kick had already decided to acquiesce to her future husband's wishes. She'd fallen in love not only with Billy but with the idea of becoming the Duchess of Devonshire, of having a castle in Ireland, and another in Scotland, in Yorkshire and in Sussex. Unlike most other Kennedys, she had learned to love Great Britain and all its long-held traditions. "I can't really understand why I like Englishmen so much as they treat one in quite an off-hand manner and aren't really as nice to their women as Americans but I suppose it's just that sort of treatment that women really like," Kick teased her brother, Jack, a few months earlier. "That's your technique isn't it?" But months of emotional turmoil had drained the humor out of Kick. She relied on the only other Kennedy in Europe—her older brother Joe Jr.—to meet with the Devonshire lawyer and read over the marriage settlement. The terms spelled out how much of the Devonshire fortune Billy would receive in annual income, how much Kick would receive if she became his widow and how much their children would have for education and maintenance. "All of this is conditional on them not becoming Catholics, which would automatically cut them out of the gift and the income," Joe Jr. relayed to his parents. After his perusal, Joe expressed surprise that Billy had no capital of his own and that his future income "depends entirely on the Duke, and there is nothing automatic about it." The duke exerted increasing pressure on the bride and groom to conform to his religious dictates, urging them to agree to a blessing from the Archbishop of Canterbury, which Joe Jr. rejected in his negotiations. "Kick did not sign a paper saying that she would bring the children up as Anglicans, though I think the Duke did want her to do it," her brother reported. When young Joe went to see him, the duke—"a shy old bird," as he called him—conversed in a strained way about the whole matter but assured young Kennedy that he wasn't trying to pressure Kick to become an Anglican. In her own letter home, Kathleen tried to put the best face possible on a difficult situation.

> Of course the Dukie is very worried about having A Roman Catholic [sic] in the family. In fact, he's fanatic on the subject. In their eyes, the most awful thing that could happen to our son would be for it [sic] to become a Roman. With me in the family that danger becomes immediate even though I would promise that the child could be brought up as an Anglican. The Church would not marry us and the result would be that I would be married in a registry office. I could continue to go to Church but not Communion. How long this state would continue is impossible to say. I certainly am not going to count on everything being made okay—I shall only hope for it.

ONE CAN only imagine what Joe and Rose Kennedy said to each other about their daughter's predicament. Though their letters and telegrams to Kathleen were carefully composed to avoid offending or inciting emotions, they had to be distressed, particularly over the underlying bigotry of Billy's family. As Rose later recalled, "The only way for Kick to marry Billy within the sacraments of the Catholic Church—and even this would be a civil ceremony—would be for Billy to agree that their children would be raised as Catholics; and, of course, he could not agree to that." Even after the fact, Rose continued to discuss the idea of an annulment with Archbishop Spellman. Back in America, both Bobby and Eunice, perhaps Kick's most religiously orthodox siblings, expressed displeasure with Kick's decision. Jack thought Billy should make some concession to Kick's religion, to a degree that surprised the ambassador. However, in writing to his friend

Lem Billings, Jack commented, "You might as well take it in your stride and as sister Eunice from the depth of her righteous Catholic wrath so truly said: 'It's a horrible thing—but it will be nice visiting her after the war, so we might as well face it.'"

With the battle lines drawn, Joe Kennedy surrendered atypically. Though his dislike for the British and his own sense of Irish Catholic aggrievement were more sharply etched than his wife's, Joe couldn't bring himself to dislodge his favorite daughter from his heart. In one letter urging Kick to find the right choice, Joe mentioned her success at inspiring converts to Catholicism. "Maybe if you made enough of them a couple of them could take your place," he quipped. "If Mother ever saw that sentence I'd be thrown right out into the street." He trod down every avenue, right to the Pope's door, to find a special dispensation to accommodate his daughter's love and his wife's faith. Realizing its futility, however, he could only wish his beloved daughter Godspeed. As a father, Joe Kennedy experienced one of his shining moments. In a telegram, he encouraged Kick to continue writing letters, and assured her of their confidentiality. "I feel terribly unhappy you have to face your biggest crisis without Mother or me," he admitted. But in a lasting touch, he let his daughter know just how much he cared for her. "With your faith in God you can't make a mistake," he ended. "Remember you are still and always will be tops with me, Love, Dad."

WITHIN TEN MINUTES, inside the sparse and cramped red-brick Chelsea Register Office building, Billy and Kick married in a civil ceremony in which no religious words were exchanged. The room was filled with vases of pink carnations from the Chatsworth estate. Kathleen Kennedy was given away by her oldest brother. After the couple exchanged vows, Billy slipped a family heirloom on Kick's finger. They both signed a contract and were done. As they left on the morning of May 6, 1944, a small group of photographers, reporters and onlookers caught the couple off-guard and snapped the bridal party's picture. To his sister, Joe cracked that he would be "finished in Boston" when his potential Irish Catholic constituency spotted that photo. With war-time restrictions in full effect, the reception featured a chocolate cake with no icing, offered to a crowd of some two hundred people. "Everything went over quite well considering the problems," Joe wrote home. "Once she had definitely made up her mind to do it, I did the best I could to help her through. She was under a terrific strain all the time, and as the various wires came in she became more and more upset. It is extremely difficult over here to tell exactly what everyone there thought about it."

The newspapers carried the message from America. The ancient rifts and traditional schisms between Catholic and Protestant were emphasized in many of the accounts from Boston. "The marriage of the Boston girl and British nobleman," reported the *Boston Globe*, "is now providing a choice morsel of gossip for the dowagers, matrons and debutantes of Mayfair, as well as the crusty and tweedy set of the British squirearchy." If the Kennedys felt a vicarious thrill at their daughter's marriage into the aristocracy, it was quickly chilled and tempered by her alleged conversion. "Kick's apostasy is a sad thing," declared Evelyn Waugh. "It is second front nerves that has driven her to this grave sin and I am sorry for the girl." When the announcement of their engagement was made two days before the wedding, gossips on both sides of the Atlantic howled. "Parnell's ghost must be smiling sardonically," said London's *Evening News*. "It was the Lord Hartington of the 'eighties who headed the Liberal-Unionist revolt that wrecked Gladstone's Home Rule Bill. Hartington it was who moved the second rejection of the Bill, and the hopes of Parnell and Irish-America vanished in the division lobbies. Now a Hartington is to marry a Catholic Irish-American who comes from one of the great Home Rule Families of Boston."

Caught off-guard by the engagement announcement, the Kennedys in Boston denied the marriage plans to the local press. Honey Fitz, even further out of the loop, conceded the marriage plans but "did not know whether the British nobleman, a member of one of the leading Protestant families of history, would embrace the Catholic faith," reported the *Boston Herald*. Fitzgerald confidently predicted his granddaughter's wedding would take place in a Catholic church. "When non-Catholic young people were week-end guests at the Kennedy home," the former mayor recalled, "Kathleen would take them all to Mass every Sunday morning." With the scent of scandal in the air, the inquiring press quizzed Honey Fitz extensively about his granddaughter's religious beliefs. In his own way, he was defending Rose as much as Kick. "Although Kathleen and the young man have been friends for some time, the announcement has come in a rush," he explained. "Quite apart from her family training, she is by choice and conviction a Catholic."

Billy's family provided their own version of the nuptials. In a long dispatch about the wedding, the *New York Times* described the new marchioness's "frock of pink suede beneath a short jacket of brown mink and a small hat of blue and pink feathers" and then made reference to her future religion. "Within the next day or so it was learned tonight from acquaintances of the Marquess, a private religious ceremony will be held in the drawing room of Compton Place," the *Times* reported. "The family has not yet confirmed this report. The nature of the ceremony could not be learned but it was assumed that it would be Protestant. The erroneous suggestion of religious conversion was based more on wishful thinking by Billy's father than by any concrete promise from Kick or her brother. There was never a religious ceremony after the marriage contract was signed. News to the contrary, however, spread rapidly.

After the wedding, the Kennedys were bombarded with questions about Kathleen's future as a Catholic and whether she was renouncing her faith—inquiries that landed like stones on her mother's psyche. "May the Blessed Mother give her the necessary grace to see the error of her ways before many weeks have passed," one priest friendly with the family wrote to Rose. On the afternoon after her daughter's wedding, the Kennedy matriarch, dressed in black, funereal clothing, took an airplane to New York on her way to a "much-needed rest" in Hot Springs, Arkansas. Rose spent a few days "under medical care" at the New England Baptist Hospital, more for her frayed nerves than a physical ailment. When reporters at the airport asked her to share a good word about her daughter, she declined to say anything, citing ill health. "I'm sorry it has to be this way," she muttered.

WITHIN DAYS after the wedding, the Kennedys began slowly to repair the internal turmoil caused by Kick's marriage. After standing up for his sister, Joe Jr. sent a bold but eloquent rebuke to his family. "THE POWER OF SILENCE IS GREAT," he cabled to his father. Never before had Joe Jr. expressed such disagreement to his parents. "As far as Kick's soul is concerned, I wish I had half her chance of seeing the pearly gates," Joe wrote home. "As far as what people will say, the hell with them. I think we can all take it. It will be hardest on Mother and I do know how you feel Mother, but I do think it will be alright."

Alarmed by reports of her mother's illness, Kick assumed her decision was the cause. Three days after her ceremony, Kick wrote that she "was very worried" that her marriage had prompted Rose's illness, and pleaded with her mother not to be too upset. "Please don't take any responsibility for an action which you think bad (and I don't). You did everything in your power to stop it. You did your duty as a Roman Catholic mother. You have not failed. There was nothing lacking in my religious education. Not by any means am I giving up my faith—it is most precious to me." She expressed hope that the church might sanction her marriage at some later date. "Until that time I shall go on praying and living like a Roman Catholic and hoping. Please, please do the same," she urged. Aware of her mother's unspoken social sensibilities, Kick knew that her decision could bring some scorn from the McDonnells and other "First Irish" families. "My very best love to Mother and pray just like I do every morning and evening and no matter what the McDonnells think just tell them not to judge anybody," she implored. "God does that." Kick also gave a glimpse of the hate mail and emotional battering she had received for her decision to marry a Protestant, a response perhaps fueled by the Kennedys own taciturnity. "Of course it was too bad that the papers made such an issue of the religious question. However, I must admit that I expected it," she said. "Letters continue to pour in from irate Catholics saying I have sold my soul for a title. Billy is very busy answering them all."

The transatlantic dialogue between mother and daughter continued through their letters that spring and summer. In one exchange, Kick described talking with a local Catholic priest near her hotel who expressed sympathy for her situation. "He confessed that he was unorthodox, but he said he admired my courage and he sympathized with my stand," Kick recounted. "He went on to say that I would be amazed at the number of people who felt the same way. He told me not to worry and he was quite sure that prayer and trust in God's holy will would bring everything right." In her correspondences, Kick offered her own form of confession, not for some terrible sin in marrying Billy but for a graver transgression among the Kennedys—upsetting their family dynamic. "I knew you would be upset, but I felt sure you would see the ultimate good," Kick explained to Rose in a letter for her birthday that July. "I knew you would never forbid anything if you felt it meant my happiness. It must have been hard for you to resign yourself to the idea of my doing something quite against all your principles—I repeat, the one thing I don't want you ever to think is that my religious or moral education has been lacking. You have done more than enough to show me the gateway to Heaven. Please God I can do half as well for the little Cavendishes." From her new home in England, Kick could view her happy youth more appreciatively than ever before, and gave thanks to her mother in a way that undoubtedly healed some wounds. "You are the most unselfish woman in the world," she praised. "Any house where we have all been has been difficult to run and you have always put us before any of your own desires or pleasures. We all have happy personalities and get along with people far easier than most people—This is due to the happy atmosphere which has always surrounded us. When I see some homes I marvel at you more and more."

Despite its storybook overtones, Kick conceded that her new life in Great Britain would be troublesome. The shock of marrying an Irish Catholic reverberated in the old English castles and estates of Billy's family.

"All the old relatives and servants continue to give me the eye, but now I feel I can stand anything," she wrote after a weekend with Grandmother Salisbury and Billy's uncle, Lord Robert Cecil. In her own bemused style, Kick tried to present the best picture possible of her young marriage to a man about to return to the war after their honeymoon, and a father-in-law who remained "very difficult in ways" and viewed her with a certain suspicion. "The funny thing is that he thinks Billy has given in as the one thing he has always dreaded is that one of his sons should marry an R.C.," admitted Kick, surprised and hurt that such an attitude could extend after their wedding. "Even though his present daughter-in-law has acquiesced to his demands he always sees within me a sort of evil influence. I shall just have to prove myself over a period of years, I suppose."

More than a month after the wedding, Rose composed a letter from the family's summer home in Hyannis Port. It reflected her acceptance of what had happened, even if the results were not to her liking. The idea that her daughter would marry a Cavendish, with all their history of hatred toward Irish Catholics, had seemed unthinkable. Some of Rose's doubts were assuaged with the personal kindness found in the letters to her from the Duchess of Devonshire, who tried to bridge the gap created by her husband's bigotry with a gentle understanding for the young couple's moral dilemma and a genuine fondness for Kick. In a letter written shortly after the D-Day invasion that June, Rose assured her daughter that both she and Billy would be embraced by the Kennedys and that she longed for the day when the newlyweds could visit America. As war raged across the world, which undoubtedly added to the tensions leading up to her daughter's marriage, Rose looked to the future and wished happiness for both families. She had no idea how much more suffering they would still endure.

"It was all quite a surprise and a shock," Rose conceded. "I really didn't expect that you would be married until after the invasion or at least until I knew more definitely of your plans. However, that is all over now, dear Kathleen, and as long as you love Billy so dearly, you may be sure that we will all receive him with open arms."

Chapter Thirteen

Hero Worship

As an Irish-American, John Fitzgerald Kennedy seemed far different, temperamentally rooted on the other end of the emotional spectrum, than his namesake. Grandfather John F. Fitzgerald, the avuncular "Honey Fitz," the spreader of blarney and a product of the Irish Catholic immigrant machine in Boston, could bloviate and entertain, a true artist in the theater of politics. He was a master of the "Irish switch"—the ability to shake the hand of one voter, smile at another and look to queue up a third—all expertly executed with the seemingly utmost sincerity. Honey Fitz truly loved crowds, the press of flesh, the telling of a good story or joke. Irish to the core, Fitzgerald brought his ethnicity to bear in all forms of life, and even death. In the middle of World War II, Honey Fitz interrupted an otherwise sensible letter to his grandchildren to make this observation: "Reading through the names of the boys who have been injured or killed, the Catholic element in New England is standing up admirably."

If Honey Fitz's parochial absurdities annoyed Joe Kennedy (perhaps because they cut too close to the bone), they amused his grandson. John Kennedy, educated and trained at the finest Brahmin schools, was removed enough from the immigrant experience that he could appreciate his grandfather with almost historical perspective, as if he were an artifact from a bygone era. Yet, in their own ways, both grandfather and grandson succumbed to the allure of Ireland.

In the early 1940s, Jack Kennedy seemed destined for the life of a writer. Jack dashed off several articles as a newspaper foreign correspondent and turned his Harvard senior thesis into a book called *Why England Slept,* which became a bestseller partly because of the bundles of copies bought by his father. In 1941, Jack wrote an analysis for the *New York Journal American,* and other Hearst newspapers with a large Catholic audience. His position was sympathetic to Ireland's wartime neutrality and the Free State's position regarding Great Britain's use of its naval bases. Jack understood Ireland's unique history far better than most Irish-Americans. "In Ireland's long struggle, the aid that poured from America has been decisive and the ties that bind the two countries together are as strong now as ever," he began. As if it had been explained to him by a Dunganstown forebear, Kennedy recognized the deep roots of Ireland's bitterness toward England and the wariness with which such heroes as Winston Churchill were viewed by the Irish. "It must be remembered that the British quarrel with Ireland has been going on for over six hundred years, while the German-British fight is a comparatively modern one," he explained. Kennedy's point of view was hardly that of an Anglophile:

> Ireland has bitter memories of the last war. England made large prom-ises to Ireland at that time in return for her support and Ireland paid a tragic price—she sent a greater number of soldiers in proportion to her population than any other unit of the British Empire. And except for France, this army suffered a greater percentage of killed and wounded than any other country in the war. For this great sacrifice the Irish received nothing. Instead the Lloyd George Government, in which Winston Churchill was Minister of War, dispatched the Black and Tans who scourged Ireland for three years. Ireland has not for-gotten this, and remembers further that in 1938 Mr. Churchill also led the group who opposed the return of the ports to Ireland. They do not feel they can depend on him to restore them once the war is over.

After reading Jack's dispatch, his old Harvard roommate, Torby Macdonald, a fellow Irish Catholic, wrote back his approval. "Your article on Ireland got rather less play than I anticipated," he observed. "It seemed to me that you gave Ireland a little of the better of it, but perhaps that is due to fact that actually their view has the best reasons behind it."

JACK'S WAY OF LOOKING at the world, his intellectual bent and fondness for the written word, could be easily misunderstood. His sense of humor, his ironic outlook on the twists and foibles of human existence, were distinctly rooted in that Gaelic black humor, a combination of natural wit and fatalism, as much as any young Irish writer might claim. Though overt gestures and the political rostrum didn't seem to be his forte, the blood of an Irish pol still flowed in his veins. When Honey Fitz, for elaborate political reasons, endorsed his old Boston adversary in 1938, Jack could only comment with pluck: "Tonight is a big night in Boston as the Honorable John F. Fitzgerald is making a speech for his good friend James Michael Curley," he wrote bemusedly to his father, then in England. "Politics makes strange bedfellows." Usually, their grandfather railed against his old adversary.

Because of his casual air, Jack became a family favorite. Joe Jr. and Jack kidded each other in constant, if always competitive, banter. Kick loved her brother's charming honesty in a world of humbugs and protocol. "Jack just returned to Harvard after being home a week," Kathleen wrote to her parents. "He really is the funniest boy alive. He had the Irish maid in fits the whole time. Every time he'd talk to her he'd put on a tremendous Irish brogue." After receiving one of his mother's round-robin letters to the entire family, Jack wrote back, "Thank you for your latest chapter on the '9 little Kennedys and How They Grew' by Rose of Old Boston. Never in history have so many owed so much to such a one—or is that quite correct?" Jack's comments to his mother could be jocular and, as a later generation might term it, condescendingly sexist, but they were also affectionate and sophomorically humorous. "My health is excellent—I look like hell but my stomach is a thing of beauty—as you are, Ma—and you, unlike my stomach—will be a joy forever," he penned in 1941, shortly before America's entry into the war.

After Pearl Harbor, Jack took a dim view of what war might mean for the world's future, particularly for the British Empire. During his time in London, Kennedy enjoyed the social entree that his father's position brought them. Several historians, when not fashioning Kennedy into a Boston Brahmin, have made much of Kennedy's interest in British manners. These scribes seemed unaware of the dour note he wrote to Kathleen, the only real Anglophile in the clan, when he predicted in 1942 that it was "time to write the obituary of the British Empire." Like the fall of the Roman Empire, "When a nation finally reaches the point that its primary aim is to preserve the status quo, it's approaching old age," he commented. "When it reaches the point where it is willing to sacrifice part of that status quo to keep the rest, it's gone beyond being old, it's dying—and that is the state of mind England reached some time ago."

Despite his mild English affectations and sharp Harvard accent, Jack still retained a bit of the green, even a sense of Irish roguishness, to those who knew him well. Soon after entering the navy, Jack was assigned to the Office of Naval Intelligence in Washington, where he met Inga Arvad, a beautiful Danish woman who had been friends with Kathleen when they worked together at the *Washington Times-Herald*. For several weeks, Jack engaged in an affair with this non-Catholic divorcee who, much to his father's chagrin, was under investigation as a Nazi spy. When rumors of the affair reached the navy brass and nearly became public, Jack was quickly shipped out of Washington. He reported first to a naval station in South Carolina and eventually to officer's training school in the Midwest before heading to the Pacific. (Ever the dissembler, Joe claimed in a letter to his oldest son that Jack had "become disgusted with the desk jobs and all the Jews," without mentioning any other factors in his transfer.) Arvad, whom Jack affectionately called "Inga Binga," had learned enough about her paramour to kid him about his secret desire for the White House. She predicted success for Jack because he was "brainy and Irish-shrewd." As she quipped, "You have more than even your ancestors and yet you haven't lost the tough hide of the Irish potato."

During his first weeks in the Pacific, Kennedy detected a certain standoffishness from fellow Ivy League officers because of his Irish background. One of these officers, recalling how he had heard the Ambassador Joseph Kennedy on the radio, said he "was surprised that he didn't speak like the rest of the Irish trash from Boston." Furious over the comment, Kennedy confided to a friend that he had wanted to punch the oaf right in the nose. Jack's first letters from the Pacific were matter-of-fact, stuffed with details of a navy man's everyday life. As the correspondence developed, and as he saw more action, Kennedy's letters became more thoughtful and aware of the fragility of life. One of the first shocks was the death of George Mead, scion of an Ohio paper manufacturer and an old friend from their days of socializing in Washington with Kick. At Guadalcanal, Meade died trying to rescue one of his men. Jack later wrote home after visiting his friend's grave: "He is buried near the beach where he fell—it was extremely sad." In most of his letters from the Pacific, however, young Jack Kennedy tried not to break a sweat, not to loose his cool observant humor as he sought to make sense of the destruction he was witnessing. Though he might be loath to admit it directly, Jack's Catholicism remained a touchstone in his letters from the Pacific. Some were self-mocking, while others hinted at a genuine spiritual struggle.

"May I first express my appreciation for the manner in which you have kept in contact with your broken-down brother & to know that all nuns and priests along the Atlantic Coast are putting in a lot of praying time on my behalf is certainly comforting," he began one letter home. "Kathleen reports that even a fortune-teller says that I'm coming back in one piece. I hope it won't be taken [as] a sign of lack of confidence in you all or the Church if I continue to duck." Like his siblings, Jack never failed to mention to his mother his steadfast church attendance, the most obvious indicator of his faith: "P.S. Mother—Got to Church Easter—they had in a native hut—and aside from having a condition red 'enemy air-craft in the vicinity'—it went on as well as St. Pat's," he wrote in May 1943, an apparent reference to the majestic St. Patrick's Cathedral, the home base of the Kennedy family's diocese in New York.

Some of Jack's spiritual concerns, though, could venture beyond the mandates of church attendance and the simple adherence to doctrine. He was hardly an overnight seminarian, yet he could pose thoughtful questions about what it meant to be a Catholic, particularly in a predominantly Protestant nation. At the navy yard in Charleston, South Carolina, in 1942, a city still very much a part of the Deep South, he wrote to Rose: "They want me to conduct a Bible class here every other Sunday for about 1/2 hour with the sailors. Would you say that that is un-Catholic? I have a feeling that dogma might say it was—but don't good works come under our obligations to the Catholic Church. We're not a completely ritualistic, formalistic, hierarchical structure in which the Word, the truth, must only come down from the very top—a structure that allows for no individual interpretation—or are we?" Then, as if catching his breath, Kennedy reverted to the familiar crutch of any young Catholic of his era confounded by questions about faith. "Just send me Father Conway's Question Box as I would like to look through it," he requested.

The best-selling book, *The Question Box,* first published in 1909 by the Paulist Press and periodically updated by its author, the Reverend Bertrand L. Conway, a New York–based priest, answered virtually every imaginable question about Roman Catholic doctrine. This handy book of apologetics armed Catholics against the inquisitive arrows flung by nonbelievers, disbelievers or amoralists—discussing not only the central tenets of the faith, but arcania such as how to spot signs of the devil and whether a divorcee might have sufficient terms for an annulment. Young Kennedy may have needed *The Question Box* as a bulwark from his own doubts or those posed by others. After all, a Roman Catholic leading a prayer get-together may not have gone down easy with his navy brethren, particularly in a place where the Ku Klux Klan remained quite active. Most historians have ignored this letter from young Kennedy, or suggested that it represents, as one wrote, "just a matter of doubt accumulating over time as his adult mind tried to reconcile and understand some of the illogical teachings he had learned as a child." However, Jack's letter and other missives suggest there was a bit more at play here that shouldn't be so easily dismissed. The acquisition of *The Question Box* (assuming, of course, that his mother sent it to him) was an intriguing choice. Its author, Father Conway, roamed the United States for forty years, seeking converts to Catholicism with remarkable success. At the time of his death, Conway, whose other books included *The Virgin Birth* and *Studies in Church History,* was credited with actuating some six thousand souls into the Mother Church—a gargantuan effort at proselytizing, exactly the activity Protestants feared most from Rome and its avowed army. In this crusade, *The Question Box* served as Father Conway's most powerful weapon, with more than four million copies distributed since its original publication. Though often consulted by Catholics, its expressed purpose, as the *New York Times* later observed, was as "a book designed to explain Catholicism to non-Catholics." Was Jack Kennedy intent on the same purpose—the teaching of Catholic doctrine to a group of unsuspecting Protestant navy men? Given his future, it's an amusing scenario to consider: Jack Kennedy—Converter of Souls. But the request for *The Question Box* was clearly sincere; and so, apparently, was his intent to do his best as a Bible class leader.

In his own irreverent way, Kennedy found himself struggling not only with the mortality of his young friend Mead, but his own wonderment about fate and the eternal verities raised by death. He was a doubter who needed convincing, and he wasn't sure whether that would ever happen. Still, he clung intuitively to the symbols and conventions he'd learned from his Irish Catholic heritage. In his letters, Jack appeared to find it easier to express this conundrum in the form of a joke—the amiable needling the Kennedys all shared with one another as a universal language—than in some sober, ponderous meandering. "Mother, you will be pleased to know that their [sic] is a priest nearbye [sic] who has let all the natives go—and is devoting all his energies to my salvation," he teased in July 1943. "I'm stringing along with him—but I'm not going over to [sic] easy—as I want him to work a bit so he'll appreciate it more when he finally has me in the front row every morning screaming halleluyah [sic]." One could hardly picture skinny Jack Kennedy at a church meeting, hands shaking like a tambourine and shouting "Hallelujah," nor full of fire and brimstone and condemning his fellow mariners for their off-shore immoralities. But evidently, Kennedy as well as his colleagues felt comfortable enough for him to lead a group of Baptists, Lutherans, Episcopalians and any others in a Bible class, at least for a time, under a category he considered "good works."

In the Pacific as commander of a PT boat, Kennedy quietly practiced his religion despite the near impossible conditions of war. In one letter from a friend, Joe Kennedy heard of a priest who served as a naval chaplain in New Guinea, and passed along his admiration for young Kennedy. "His son, Jack Kennedy . . . was one of my parishioners—fine, upstanding lad, guts, brains, courage to give away, generous, worshipped by his lads. He does his Dad credit," as Joe's friend relayed. Confronted by random violence and the unfairness of dying far before one's time, Jack's voice in his letters home consistently maintained a mix of good humor leavened by occasional deeper references. "Your old brother looks a bit different these days—for one thing I've got a beard—a red, bristly unattractive-looking thing," he wrote to his youngest sister, Jean, in talking about his next visit. "When I shall get there is extremely hard to say—whenever they send someone out to relieve me. I sometimes wonder if he is even born yet. In your prayer, you might pray that it is a boy and that he grows up fast and gets out here as soon as possible." All Jack Kennedy's thoughts about death and war and God—and his own family's prayers—would soon be put to the test.

The bonhomie of the Kennedy letters belie a certain nervous dread, as if they suspected that somehow fate might call one of their own. In a remarkable letter to her family in 1942, Rose observed that Jack's "whole attitude about the war has changed and he is quite ready to die for the USA in order to keep the Japanese and the Germans from becoming the dominant people on their respective continents, believing that sooner or later they would encroach upon ours. He also thinks it would be good for Joe's political career if he died for the grand old flag, although I don't believe he feels that is absolutely necessary."

On the night of August 2, 1943, while cruising in dark, mist-shrouded waters with his small crew, Kennedy's PT boat was sliced in half by a passing Japanese destroyer. "This is how it feels to be killed," Lieutenant Junior Grade Kennedy later said he thought to himself. Two men lost their lives immediately and the inept circumstances of the accident lent to some serious consideration of disciplinary charges. But Kennedy's heroic actions helped save the rest of his crew—and his reputation. During the next few days, Kennedy swam with his ten surviving men to safety on a small island; there, they carved a message of distress into a coconut shell and convinced some native fishermen to carry it back to the Allies. For his injuries and genuinely gallant actions, Kennedy later received the Purple Heart and the Navy and Marine Corps Medal, as well as a citation from Admiral William Halsey that read: "His courage, endurance and excellent leadership contributed to the saving of several lives and was [in] keeping with the highest traditions of the United States Naval Service."

When they were all picked up by another PT boat, Kennedy's crew of survivors, battered, burned and bruised, bellowed a hymn to celebrate their survival. Their skipper, gaunt and with six days of beard growth, chimed in with his creaky Irish tenor:

Jesus loves me, this I know
For the Bible tells me so;
Little ones to him belong,
They are weak, but He is strong,
Yes, Jesus loves me; yes, Jesus loves me . . .

Back home, Kennedy's ordeal raised fears of the worst. Shortly after the PT boat's remains were found, Joe Kennedy received a telegram about Jack's disappearance, but he kept it a secret from his wife and family. For a few days, he carried out his everyday routines as though nothing had happened, but finally he told Rose. When he heard a report on the car radio that Jack had been found, Joe became so excited that he nearly drove off the road. Rose knew of no other way but to thank God and the mercy he had shown their son. As she inscribed in her diary: "He is really at home— the boy for whom you prayed so hard—at the mention of whose name your eyes would become dimmed—the youngster who you would think dead some nights & you would wake up with sorrow clutching your heart. What a sense of gratitude to God to have spared him."

Several biographers insist on portraying Kennedy as an absurdist hero who had no regard for religion. But Jack's letters home after his rescue gave thanks as can only someone who nearly met his maker: "I can say that I am well and thanking my St. Christopher, my St. Elmo and my St. Clair. One of them was working overtime." Jack typically made light of his actions. "Dear Folks: This is just a short note to tell you that I am alive—and *not* kicking—in spite of any reports that you may happen to hear. It was believed otherwise for a few days—so reports or rumors may have gotten back to you. Fortunately, they misjudged the durability of a Kennedy—and am back at the base now and am O.K." Recalling later for friends how he swam virtually naked through the Blackett Strait during this ordeal, he claimed to worry that sharks might feast on his genitals. "I swam a lot of backstroke," he quipped. But the brush with death did chasten his devil-may-care attitude. In discussing the PT boat incident with friends, he admitted that he had feared dying in the strong currents. "He said, seriously, 'I never prayed so much in my life,'" recalled a girlfriend, Bab Beckwith.

His friends in the Pacific were also concerned about Jack's whereabouts, and they noticed some changes when he returned. "I remember when I heard the 109 was lost, I was very upset," recalled Johnny Iles, one of several Catholic and Irish pals who were part of Kennedy's circle in the navy. "I went to the Catholic chaplain, Father McCarthy, and I asked him to say a mass for Jack." A devout Catholic from Louisiana who seemed in awe of the Kennedy family, Iles remembered going with Jack to midnight Mass on Christmas 1943. At times, though, he questioned Jack's faithfulness to church doctrine. When Lt. Kennedy was shipped back to America and entered a Boston hospital because of his ailing health, Iles visited him with a group of their friends. Rose Kennedy had just left the hospital room. "He was lying in bed," Iles recalled. "The first thing I noticed was a rosary hanging on the bedpost. And I said, 'Well, boy, it looks like you got back into favor.' And he just looked at me and grinned and didn't make any comment at all." When Iles told Kennedy how he asked the priest to pray for him when he was reported missing, the anticipated response of thanks didn't transpire. "He was furious," recalled Iles. "He read the riot act to me. He said he wasn't ready to die just yet and why the hell had I given up hope?" Kennedy no doubt had in mind the experience of his fallen crewmate, Andrew Kirksey. Two weeks before the PT-109 incident, Kirksey had been with Kennedy when a bomb landed near their boat without detonating. The nearness of death seemed to unnerve Kirksey, who began to fear he'd never survive the war. "He never really got over it; he always seemed to have the feeling that something was going to happen to him," recalled Kennedy, unusually sensitive to the fatalism of others. Intuitively, Kennedy felt that such guys would bring bad luck. He resolved to leave Kirksey—who had a wife and three kids—at the home base at the next available opportunity, which of course never came. "When a fellow gets the feeling that he's in for it, the only thing to do is to let him off the boat because strangely enough, they always seem to be the ones that do get it," Jack later explained. "I don't know whether it's coincidence or what."

The vicissitudes of fate, the loss of two crewmates and the nearness of death sobered Kennedy, a twenty-six-year-old who suddenly felt much older. He was touched by a letter written by the wife of one of the men he had helped save, Patrick McMahon, who was badly burned. With McMahon in a life preserver, Kennedy swam with the jacket's strap between his clenched teeth and pulled his crew member to safety. McMahon's wife later told Kennedy that his intervention had saved more than one life. "I suppose to you it was just part of your job, but Mr. McMahon was part of my life and if he had died I don't think I would have wanted to go on living," she admitted. Kennedy's experience with death in battle curbed his hunger for more bloodshed. It made him wary of powerful men who established war policy and spoke with grand bellicose visions. "People get so used to talking about billions of dollars and millions of soldiers that thousands of dead sound like a drop in the bucket," he wrote home. "But if those thousands want to live like the ten I saw—they should measure their words with great care. Perhaps all that won't be necessary—and it can all be done by bombing."

Jack, the affable good-time boy, now noticed the suffering of others in ways that he'd never done before. Sometime in late 1943, Jack and his brother Joe were among a group of several men in uniform who visited the Mott Street headquarters of the Catholic Worker in Manhattan, a small storefront soup kitchen run by the revered Dorothy Day and others. As Day recalled, the Kennedy brothers and their friends listened with interest to the Catholic Worker ideals, which included pacifism and a commitment to helping the poor. A former leftist journalist who had converted to Catholicism, Day would champion many of the social causes of liberal American Catholics from the Depression of the 1930s through to the Vietnam era. Her penny-a-copy newspaper, the *Catholic Worker,* was read by thousands; its writers included John Cogley and Michael Harrington, both of whom influenced Jack Kennedy in later years. That night in 1943, Day recalled, she and the Kennedy boys went to a nearby restaurant to discuss "war and peace and man and the state."

During this visit home, Jack flew to Palm Beach, where his old friend, Chuck Spalding, met him; they immediately grabbed some dinner at a favorite restaurant. "I can still see him sitting there in that restaurant, the war running through his head, and certainly through a lot of his body—he was pretty well banged up," recalled Spalding. "He didn't say a thing." During the meal, Kennedy stared out at the crowd, his grayish eyes fixed on the men and women in formal attire, all laughing without a care. "He just sat there, looking and thinking. And you could just tell what was going through his head—the terrific discrepancy between people at home dressed in white jackets with bow ties, looking like asses . . . and thinking of the nonsense of people being killed, somebody having his leg blown off. You could see the anguish in his face as he was trying to put it together. We stayed there an hour and I don't think he said one word, not one word."

THE STORY OF Kennedy's exploits soon became legend, though not necessarily of their own volition. Joe Kennedy seized upon his son's unfortunate accident as a public relations bonanza, turning the episode into an ocean-faring myth of Melvilleian proportions, a virtual Jack Kennedy and the Argonauts. The *New York Times* and the Boston papers all carried front-page stories about Kennedy and PT-109. Within weeks, Jack's old girlfriend, Inga Arvad, penned a newspaper column in San Francisco about his heroic exploits on the PT boat (privately he told her the navy was deciding "whether they were going to give him a medal or throw him out.") The most remarkable coup for Kennedy père was writer John Hersey's saga published in the *New Yorker* and reprinted in *Reader's Digest,* where it enjoyed an even wider popular audience. Ironically, Jack knew Hersey (who married an old flame of Kennedy's) and envied his accomplishments as a writer. Now, Hersey was making Kennedy into a national hero with an account that read like a gripping adventure story. Increasingly, Jack felt uneasy about all the attention, especially because two men had lost their lives on his watch, and he also suffered from guilt that heroism by others had been ignored or given short shrift. When asked how he became a hero, Jack gave a wry response: "It was involuntary—they sank my boat."

Joe Kennedy would have none of that false modesty. Some of his enthusiasm surely sprang from the sheer glee and thanksgiving of a father who had feared his son dead only to see him return alive. But undeniably, Joe Kennedy recognized the political capital to be gained from having a war hero in the family, even if he wasn't running for office. Many months later, when the PT-109 account grew to true epic proportions, Kennedy marveled how his father had worked in some aspect of the story to appeal to everyone. "My story about the collision is getting better all the time," Jack commented dryly to a friend. "Now I've got a Jew and a Nigger in the story and with me being a Catholic, that's great." When Jack expressed his concerns to his father, Joe Kennedy barely paused to consider them. "Jack's only concern is that it may be building him up too much," the elder Kennedy wrote to Hersey, "but I told him that if you and the editor, in your judgment, thought you had a story, he could rest assured that it was one." Of course, Joe Kennedy had already negotiated with the *New Yorker's* editor, Harold Ross, about how the piece would be presented. With this crafty letter of his own to Hersey, Joe Kennedy accomplished two goals: he acknowledged his son's misgivings about the hype, but he also firmed any soft spots of doubt that Hersey may have had in building up the PT-109 affair, especially if Hersey gave any credence to Jack's self-effacing account. Joe Kennedy had fought like hell to avoid war, but now that the conflagration was on, he was damned sure to have his son declared a hero. "We have the PT boat picture and mother is having it framed and saving it for you," he wrote to Jack.

With one son rescued in the Pacific and the war winding down in Europe for the other, Joe Kennedy felt remarkably fortunate, as though some heavenly light that had guided him to a fortune also enveloped his sons and protected them from harm. By February 1944, he could extend his condolences to another father with the impression that the worst was over for his family. "I have just heard today of the loss of your boy," he wrote to one friend, Harry Hogan. "As one father to another, who, although he has not had the total loss, has had his boys missing in action, I can feel in a small way how you must be suffering," Joe began. "Regardless of what some of us older fellows feel about the war, the reasons for it, and what it is to accomplish, we all know that our youngsters have had a firm determination to make the world a better place. It is small satisfaction for you, but God in his justice, will soften the blow."

THE FAMILY celebrated Jack's return from the Pacific with immense gratitude and pride. In Hyannis Port, Bobby, nearly of age to enter the military himself, received an overflow of congratulations from neighbors who thought he was Jack. They "rushed up to him with effusive words of praise," recalled their mother, and "Bobby was so bowled over that he didn't have time to explain." For a while, Jack rested in Florida and then flew to Boston to attend a testimonial for Honey Fitz, who didn't know of his grandson's plans. By then, the well-publicized story of Kennedy's PT-109 travail was known to virtually all Bostonians. The highlight of the Parker House reception, marking the former mayor's eighty-first birthday, featured a noticeably gaunt but gleaming Jack Kennedy, who walked into the room as a surprise. The mayor, with tears in his eyes, embraced his namesake while the crowd stood and applauded. "I haven't seen this boy for more than a year," Honey Fitz told everyone, "and he's been through hell since that time." In the span of a few years, Jack had become both a best-selling author and a war hero. In her round-robin letters, Rose told the rest of her children that "we have all been terribly excited about Jack's feat of glory in the Pacific." Later that summer, she wrote that "we still meet people every day who congratulate us on Jack's achievement, and we receive letters from all over the country, and of course, we are more proud and more thankful than words can tell to have him such a hero and still safe and sound."

At this point in the war, however, Rose didn't make lighthearted comments about the political future of her sons. The war in Europe would soon be over, and she didn't want to see her family run any more risks. In her letter, she recalled an encounter with two long-time family friends who said "they always knew Jack would do it and they always felt that Joe had the same sort of stuff, which is all very wonderful for a mother to hear." But Rose didn't encourage such talk. As she admitted: "I believe I would be just as happy though if Joe did not have to risk his life in such a fashion."

Chapter Fourteen

Blood Brothers

THE KENNEDYS WERE collectors of priests. The clergy who were friends with Joe and Rose Kennedy and their clan were scattered across the eastern seaboard from New England to Florida. Joe Kennedy's roll call of monks, nuns, priests, monsignors, bishops and cardinals reached as far as distant Rome. In her memoir, Rose specifically named eleven clergy members, and mentioned many more in her letters and diary.

Joe Jr., a more orthodox and conscientious Catholic than his younger brother Jack, followed in his parent's footsteps. While serving as a cadet at the Jacksonville Naval Station, a huge and stifling-hot base in northern Florida, Joe became buddies with Father Maurice Sheehy, a gregarious priest; the two cemented their friendship by playing several rounds of golf together. Sheehy was already known to Joe Sr. While he was working as assistant to the rector of Catholic University in Washington, D.C., Father Sheehy, a broad-shouldered man with a full, jowly face and engaging manner, had been friendly with President Roosevelt, helping smooth out problems between the Catholic community and the administration. Privately, he provided information and advice to Joe Kennedy about other politicians. He soon became another priest embraced by the family.

With the outbreak of war, Sheehy was appointed chaplain of the navy compound at Jacksonville. A man of demonstrable faith, Sheehy nevertheless knew how to relax and have a good time at a restaurant or nightclub. "Father Sheehy seemed to get a great kick out of all the entertainment," Rose recalled. "He's very interesting and full of anecdotes and made a great hit with everyone. Of course, he wore his uniform and so fitted in very nicely in the party." In Washington, Kathleen shared the family enthusiasm for this gregarious priest. "Father Sheehy called me yesterday with all the news on the golf games of Brother Joe and Daddy," she wrote. As she did with any close family friend, Rose extended a standing invitation to the priest to come by on future holidays. During a 1942 New Year's visit to the Kennedy winter home in Palm Beach, Sheehy explained that their eldest son had passed successfully through the most dangerous part of cadet training and earned himself other distinctions. "Joe seems to be sailing along now quite happily," Rose wrote after her debriefing by Sheehy. "His father is delighted that he is the President of the Cadets' Club and says he is probably the only Catholic in the country to hold that honor."

Joe Jr., an equally handsome young man both taller and stronger than Jack, didn't hide his religion. As president of the Holy Name Society on the base, he took upon the responsibility of waking up the Catholics for early Mass. Sometimes he extended that morning call beyond his faith. When some of the Jewish servicemen in the barracks complained of Kennedy's antics, Sheehy spoke with him.

"Don't they have souls?" young Kennedy asked about the Jews in his ranks. "Aren't you interested in saving them?"

Sheehy didn't appreciate Kennedy's attempt at sophomoric humor. "I don't think you're making friends for the Church by dousing them with water at five in the morning."

With his gleaming white teeth, Kennedy smiled like a zealot. "The trouble with you, Father, is you're anti-Semitic," he countered.

The thread of anti-Semitism shared by many co-religionists was only a part of young Kennedy's Catholicism, a more parochial variety than his brother Jack's. Rather than compose thoughtful letters home about the strictures of the church as Jack did, Joe's narrow interpretation of his religion didn't venture very far into the shadow of doubt. Typical of Joe Jr. was his arcane, almost childish inquiry to his mother about whether the church frowned on eating candy during Lent. "My suggestion would be that you say a Rosary occasionally or stop a Coca-Cola or two," his mother recommended. On a visit to Rome in the late 1930s, Joe went to the Vatican and met with the Pope thanks to his father's connections. He later wrote that he had "climbed the holy stairs on my knees," a reference to the famous Scala Sancta, the twenty-eight marble steps shipped to Rome that, according to tradition, were climbed by Jesus before being crucified by Pontius Pilate. Joe Jr. was one of many pilgrims who prayed a Hail Mary as they ascended each step as a sign of their devotion. It was the sort of intense, outward religiosity that Jack studiously avoided. If his brother's liberalism reflected the American church of the future, Joe Jr.'s faith remained firmly ensconced in the church of the moment, conservative in doctrine and its application. He was deeply devoted to the church and made no secret of his desire to become the first Catholic elected president.

Joseph P. Kennedy Jr. became his ambitious father's great political hope. The ambassador envisioned his eldest riding to glory on votes from the Irish and other immigrant descendants. Although they disagreed at the 1940 Democratic Convention, Joe Sr. respected his son's decision to back James A. Farley, the darling of Irish Catholic voters in Massachusetts. When his father pushed Honey Fitz, then seventy-nine, to run once more for the U.S. Senate in 1942, it was part of a Machiavellian plan to keep a potential rival, Joseph Casey, another Irish Catholic candidate backed by Roosevelt, from possibly blocking Joe Jr.'s future political path. This strategy required calling attention to Casey's personal life. "Honey Fitz has thrown his hat into the ring," Jack wrote to Lem Billings. "It seems his opponent—Casey by name—had a baby six months after he got married and Mrs. Greene and the Catholic women . . . are busy giving him the black-ball for it." Joe Sr. sent a similar message to his eldest son, noting that the woman Casey had married was also a Protestant. "Politics is a great game!" Kennedy advised his oldest son in July 1942. "You better be sure to marry yourself a nice Irish Catholic girl."

Around that time, Joe and Rose heard rumors of Joe's interest in a young Protestant woman. Father Sheehy, whose friendship with Joe involved keeping his wealthy parents informed of his activities, discounted the seriousness of the romance. As if determined to firm up his faith, however, Rose quickly put his name on a year's subscription to the *Catholic Digest*. Papa wasn't taking any chances with his prized son, either. In a letter that summer, the senior Kennedy advised: "You wouldn't think this was very important but it definitely is, and I am thoroughly convinced that an Irish Catholic with a name like yours and with your record, married to an Irish Catholic girl, would be a pushover in this State for political office." He even enlisted Father Sheehy in the cause and asked him to help find a Catholic girl for his son. Sheehy, hoping to obtain a baptismal font for his local church, hinted that the Kennedys might give him one, all in the name of friendship. "Father Sheehy wrote me that you defeated him at golf and he is very chagrined," Joe Sr. began one letter. "He also said that you didn't respond very eagerly to his suggestion about the Baptismal Font on the ground that you have no girls in view, but mother thinks if you give it to him you may have good luck with the girls."

No one ever feared Joe Jr. would become an apostate. At Harvard, when a fellow student made a snide comment about Honey Fitz, his Irish temper flared and he swung at the offending student. Joe and his siblings adored their grandfather, his songs and stories, and relished his legacy. "*To Boston's best Mayor, and the next Mayor of Heaven, on his 73rd birthday, from his grandsons, Joe and Jack*" they engraved on a silver bonbon dish for the occasion. Joe Jr.'s religiosity was guided by his own sense of family, the expectation by his parents that he would lead his younger siblings by example. "I wish you could make First Fridays like your father did for years," Rose urged, referring to the practice among devout Catholics of attending Mass on each initial Friday of the month as well as on Sundays.

In her letters, Rose seemed to bring her oldest sons into the decision-making about the education of the two younger ones, Bobby and Teddy. As an adolescent, Bobby started out at St. Paul's, an Episcopalian-run school in Concord, New Hampshire, its headmaster a former Harvard classmate of Joe Sr.'s. But by 1939, Rose was worried about her son's religious education. That year, Joe Sr. was still in London, and he supported his wife's decision to switch Bobby to the Catholic Portsmouth Priory School in Rhode Island. After three unsatisfactory years at Priory, however, Bobby was sent to the Milton Academy, near Boston. Rose's letter in late 1942 to her sons in the military, Joe and Jack, showed the ambivalence she felt about Catholic education for her sons—a view heavily influenced by the opposition of her husband and far different from her own unequivocal support of Catholic schools for her daughters.

Catholic education had transformed Rose's own life. As she later recalled, "When I had children of my own I wanted to pass those beliefs and values on to them as they had been passed to me." She didn't consider herself particularly religious but "just an ordinary, staunch believing Irish Roman Catholic." All the Kennedy girls, without exception, attended church-affiliated schools as part of their education. But the decision to pull Bobby out of Priory was "a wise one," Rose explained to her older sons, because Bobby didn't like the headmaster and because he "did not show any particular effort according to the reports from all the different masters." Though Rose liked the exposure to Catholic faith and training for her most devout son, Priory seemed to suffer from the chronic lack of funds endured by most parochial and private schools. In education, as in many other facets of life in America, the separatism of the Irish was beginning to wane. Though many Irish Catholics in Boston, New York and Chicago sent their children to parish schools or diocesan high schools, an increasing number of Catholic parents didn't heed the call of their bishops and chose instead to send their children to public schools or, if they could afford it, to private schools such as Milton Academy. Parents like Rose Kennedy were torn increasingly between their loyalties to the Catholic culture and their obligation to seek the best possible education for their children. "They were always rather handicapped at the Priory on account of lack of money and I felt that this year the food and the accommodations might be even less good than other years," Rose wrote. "I also felt that he had had the advantage of a Catholic school training for three years and as he had reached the age of seventeen under those circumstances he ought to be able to hold his own as far as his religion is concerned." This is a rather odd comment to be made to her eldest sons, who spent even less time in a Catholic school. But it reflects a certain rationalization by Rose with a decision that carried her husband's imprint.

Joe Sr. believed that "a child learned faith and morals at home" and was better prepared for life in America by meeting children from other religious backgrounds at an early age. Young Teddy was shipped off at an early age to the Fessenden School in the greater Boston area. "There does not seem to be any good Catholic boarding school for young boys," she explained. "I plan to send him to a Catholic school when he is about thirteen." Teddy later spent a short time at a Jesuit school in western Massachusetts, but most of his education came from outside the Catholic school realm. For his confirmation as a Catholic, Teddy favored taking the name Anthony, but was talked out of it by his mother and siblings. "Much to our surprise and embarrassment, the Priest asked them confirmation questions at the ceremonies in the church before the assembled congregation," Rose recounted in an March 1942 letter to her elder children. "He gave Teddy rather a hard one—'What is the Church?' Teddy faltered a little but he said he knew most of it."

IN THE KENNEDY FAMILY, all the children looked up to Joe Jr., his father's favorite. As the dutiful eldest son, Joe Jr. shared his parents' emotional bonds between church and family. Only his familial loyalty to his sister Kathleen could allow him to see beyond the dictates of church law and to support her marriage to Billy. Because of his closeness in age to Jack, Joe felt a perpetual tug from his brother, a contest heightened by their parents' expectations. At times, Rose could foster the rivalry between her two eldest boys as much as her husband. "Jack brought me a miniature Torpedo Boat done in silver in the form of a tie clip," she wrote. "He is really terrifically jealous of the fact that I wear Joe's gold wings all the time and is bound that I have one of his insignias, and so I am to turn this tie clip into a pin some way or other." As the chronically thin, often sickly younger sibling, Jack grew up watching the exploits of his brother with a mix of pride and awe, usually from an emotional distance. The family competitiveness probably cost him any real closeness with his elder brother. "I suppose I knew Joe as well as anyone and yet I sometimes wonder if I ever really knew him," reflected Jack afterward. "He was very human and most certainly had his faults: a hot temper, intolerance for the slower pace of lesser men, and a way of looking—with a somewhat sardonic half smile—which could cut and prod more sharply than words. But these defects—if defects they were—were becoming smoothed with the passage of time."

After enlisting in the navy rather than finishing his last year at Harvard Law, Joe's service in the war quickly became dangerous. He shared his father's isolationist politics, but also felt the swell of patriotism traditionally shown by Irish-Americans when America entered wars. The young Kennedy's gung ho attitude and fearlessness (recklessness, some crew members suggested privately) seemed a way of answering his family's critics. As if to prove himself, Joe flew dozens of missions in Europe, his planes repeatedly hit by flak from the enemy. Although Joe's military assignments were more dangerous than his brother's maneuvers in the Pacific, Jack walked away with a medal. His younger brother, who'd been often ill, lackluster and seemingly without direction, was now a figure of considerable esteem. It didn't seem fair, but Joe could only resolve to try harder. Before leaving for England after a short training stay in America, Joe traveled to Hyannis for his father's fifty-fifth birthday celebration, where Jack's exploits were the talk of the evening. A prominent judge at the affair rose to make a toast: "To Ambassador Joe Kennedy, father of our hero, our *own* hero, Lieutenant John F. Kennedy of the United States Navy." Seated at the dais in uniform, Joe Jr. smiled faintly but seethed with fury. Recalling that night, former Boston Police Commissioner Joseph Frances Timilty, a family friend who drove down for the occasion and stayed at the Kennedy home, remembered that Joe was terribly upset before falling asleep. As Timilty recalled, the young man sat on a nearby bed, clenching and unclenching his fists, and, as if cursing his fate, said, "By God, *I'll* show them."

DIVINE INTERVENTION, the vagaries of fate and their own survival were nagging thoughts for the Kennedys during this time, as their letters indicate. The emotional tumult from Kathleen's wedding reminded them all of what it meant to be a Catholic, and the war underlined how uncontrollable their lives had become. For Joe Jr. each flight held the risk of sudden death.

He remained a devout Catholic, regularly serving Mass for Father Gallery, the Catholic chaplain at Dunkeswell Airdrome, the English air base for Joe and his crew. Each night, he dropped to his knees in prayer, an act so conspicuous and yet so sincere that it never drew a remark from his fellow aviators. His parents, greatly upset by Jack's ordeal in the Pacific, worried about their eldest son's fate as well. "We were considerably upset that during those few days after the news of Jack's rescue we had no word from you," his father chastised. "I thought that you would very likely call up to see whether we had had any news as to how Jack was."

After realizing how close they had come to losing a son, the Kennedys employed every method possible to ensure their other son's safety. Joe Kennedy drew upon the conventions of his church for comfort and the protection that money couldn't buy. "Enclosed is a medal which your Mother bought here in Hyannis, and which has been blessed," Joe wrote to his eldest. "This is an inexpensive medal and is being sent to you only because the gold medal, which was ordered from Boston, was late in arriving here. . . . In the event the gold medal and chain doesn't reach you before you leave, I'm sure this silver medal and chain—while not as attractive as the other will give you just as much protection. Good luck to you—and may God protect you and bring you home safely."

Joe Jr. was hell-bent not to leave the conflict. "Theoretically, I have only two more missions to go, but it still looks like it will be about the first of July before my handsome face is seen around Hyannis Port," he dispatched in March 1944. Back in a hospital bed for further treatment, Jack urged his brother to return home with the rest of his crewmates, as he was entitled to do. But young Joe insisted on pushing ahead, accepting even more assignments. By June, when most of his old crew had opted to depart, Joe decided that "after staying over here this long, it would be foolish to return home." Somberly, he described his crew's part in the massive D-Day invasion into France, admitting that "though we haven't played a very sensational part, I guess we have done what was expected of us." The comparisons to Jack—the family's new yardstick of achievement—were implicit in Joe Jr.'s comments about his exploits. "I now have 39 missions and will probably have about fifty by the time I leave," he wrote. "It is far more than anyone else on the base, but it doesn't prove a hell of a lot." In a late July 1944 letter, with still more to prove to himself and to his family, Joe mentioned an ominous new assignment. "I am going to be doing something different for the next few weeks. It is secret, and I am not allowed to say what it is, but it isn't dangerous so don't worry. So probably I won't be home till sometime in September. I imagine you are a bit disappointed that I haven't gone home, but I think when I tell you the whole story, you will agree with me."

With the war in Europe rapidly drawing to a close, Joe Kennedy Jr. seemed desperate to become a war hero. "When news came about Brother John's PT-boat activities I think it inspired him to try harder," Jack Degman, chief of their squadron, later told biographer Hank Searls. "I don't think anyone was any more intent on seeking out the enemy and meeting him than Joe Kennedy." A day or two before this special mission, Joe told his friend and occasional racetrack companion, Frank Moore O'Ferrall, that his odds of returning safely were no better than fifty-fifty. "And that's a darned sight better than most of the horses you gave me," he added. As he walked back to camp after Sunday Mass with O'Ferrall, a friendly dark-haired horse breeder serving in the Irish Guards, Joe reminisced about his family and plans for the future. Just before leaving on his mission, Joe seemed intent on righting things at home, especially any hard feelings about his role in supporting Kick's marriage. His parents would later became aware of their son's relationship with Pat Wilson, a married woman with three children, whom he talked of marrying after the war. Shortly before departing, Joe called a friend and asked her to pass along a message. "I'm about to go into my act," Joe said, "and if I don't come back tell my dad—despite our differences—that I love him very much." He seemed to realize this mission bordered on the suicidal.

By late in the afternoon on August 12, 1944, the sky had become cloudless. There was no further threat of delay or thought of turning back. Joe Kennedy's plane, loaded with explosives, climbed into the air shortly before six that evening. His supersecret mission, called Project Aphrodite, required that Kennedy and his copilot transform their plane into a flying bomb; it was aimed directly at the bunkers in Belgium where the Nazis launched the V-1 buzz rockets that so terrorized Britain. For many months, the bunkers had survived repeated Allied bombing attacks, and a similar air force mission had failed only a week before. The navy plan called for Kennedy to fly the craft near the target and then, at a synchronized point, bail out with his crew after handing off control of the craft to a nearby mother ship; the plane would then be guided into the target by way of remote control in the aircraft's nose. Kennedy managed to fly the heavy plane without interruption over the English Channel. Within moments of the hand-off, however, a flash ignited the sky. The shock was so powerful that those in accompanying planes suffered concussions. There was no doubt of the outcome about the first plane. Joseph Patrick Kennedy Jr. was dead.

After Mass on a hot Sunday morning, Father Francis O'Leary returned to his room in Boston and received a message to report to navy headquarters downtown. A gruff heavyset Irish priest who had served as a chaplain in the Pacific aboard the USS *Brooklyn,* O'Leary received a particularly tough assignment that day, under direct orders from Secretary of the Navy James Forrestal. As the highest-ranking Catholic chaplain in the area, O'Leary was instructed to travel by small plane out to Cape Cod and inform Ambassador Kennedy that his beloved oldest son was missing in action.

Inside the house at Hyannis, the Kennedy family was nearly all together. They had finished a picnic-style lunch on the porch, and Teddy and his cousin Joe Gargan were playing quietly. Rose was reading the Sunday newspaper, and the younger girls, Jean and Pat, attended to their own affairs. Bobby, a seventeen-year-old anxious himself to see military action like his brothers, had come home on a short leave from the navy R.O.T.C. And Jack, still yellowish with jaundice from his bout with malaria, had returned to convalesce after his stay at the Chelsea Naval Hospital, where he had endured an agonizing back operation to relieve the pain from his war injuries. When the bell rang at the summer house, a butler answered and summoned Rose Kennedy. Father O'Leary asked to speak with Joe Sr., but Rose, thinking that he and an accompanying priest wanted to discuss another charitable gift to the church, asked him whether the matter could wait because her husband was taking an afternoon nap.

"This cannot wait," O'Leary said, indicating the matter concerned their oldest son.

Rose rushed upstairs and shook her husband awake. At first, she just hovered over him, unable to say anything, and then she blurted out the message from the priests. Joe leaped out of the bed and hurried downstairs. He ushered the two priests into an anteroom and quizzed them about the circumstances. He hoped their "missing in action" description for Joe's flight might somehow turn out as miraculously as Jack's fate in the Pacific. The details of the secret mission were still quite sketchy, but O'Leary and the other priest made it clear that there was no hope, that their son most certainly did not survive.

As the priests expressed their condolences and departed, the children realized that something awful had happened. Joe and Rose gathered them on the porch, away from their fun and frolicking of that summer afternoon, to let them know about their oldest brother's death. With his arm around Rose, Joe fought back tears. He explained what he knew about the accident, that Joe Jr. had volunteered for the assignment. He urged the children to follow through with their plans for sailing that afternoon, just as their brother undoubtedly would've wanted them to do, and most of them dutifully complied. "We've got to carry on," Joe declared stoically. "We must take care of the living. There is a lot of work to be done." This response couldn't have been more Irish in nature. And then he added, "I want you all to be particularly good to your mother."

Jack chose not to set out upon the water, and instead walked aimlessly along the shoreline near the house, lost in thought about his brother. Jack couldn't bring himself to believe his vibrant, energetic older brother was dead; later, he said he didn't fully grasp that finality until he saw the black-inked newspaper headlines. Inside the house, Joe and Rose sat together, holding each other close, and "wept inwardly, silently" for a few minutes. As Rose later recalled, her tears were shed for "the death of our first born who had shown such promise and had always been such a joy to us and the other children." As the afternoon passed, Rose prayed with her rosaries for her lost son while Joe made a series of telephone calls. Eventually, he reached the widow of Joe's copilot, Lieutenant Wilford "Bud" Willy, left in Fort Worth, Texas, with three small children. He offered whatever financial assistance she might need. (She declined, but over the years accepted his generous offer to send two of her sons to college.) Joe also called his sister, Loretta, and wept uncontrollably. He later retreated alone to his room and listened to symphony music on the radio.

Young Joe's death forever added tragedy into the family's equation of success, money and achievement. The golden aura of the Kennedys, the air of invincibility that had permeated their lives in London and New York, seemed no longer to exist with Joe gone. In the past, they had endured other tragedies, such as the early death of Rose's young sister Eunice and, more recently, the botched frontal lobotomy on Rosemary Kennedy, the eldest and mildly retarded daughter whose condition worsened as a result of her father's mistaken medical intervention. In Rosemary's case, he played God and it failed horribly. Because Joe Kennedy was alarmed by Rosemary's budding sexuality ("the thing the priest says not to do" as Kick called it), and her frustrated rages, he sought to control her behavior, much as he did other aspects of his children's lives. For the rest of her life, Rose harbored regrets about Rosemary's risky and unnecessary operation, which had resulted in her being placed in various institutions. Among the Kennedys, Rosemary faded from the everyday thoughts in their letters and conversations as though she were no longer alive. But Joe's sudden, violent death was different, a sorrow never felt before by the family. It was the event by which all future tragedies would be measured.

In the first few moments, Rose said she couldn't stop thinking of the boy she loved and had nurtured into adulthood, the son who had died in the sky "splintering into a thousand pieces." While she was consumed in grief, her husband acted as the strong one, making all the funeral arrangements. But after days of prayer, after supportive letters and calls from friends, several of them nuns and priests, Rose discovered in herself a transcendent faith that somehow bolstered their collective spirits and lent a kind of moral courage when her family most needed it. She rededicated herself to the daily activities of life and maintained an almost undaunted cheerfulness in her round-robin letters to her family. ("We are having some little prayer cards made out for Joe which we will send along to you as soon as they arrive," she wrote a few weeks afterwards to her children.) Some chroniclers later suggested that, after Joe's death, Rose fled unthinkingly into the shelter of her religion, barely showing emotion. In her own memoir, though, Rose indicated that she never fully got over her eldest son's death. "It has been said that time heals all wounds. I don't agree," she wrote. "The wound remains. Time—the mind, protecting its sanity—covers them with some scar tissue and the pain lessens, but it is never gone." Years later, during a campaign appearance for Jack, she mentioned her own son's death as she commiserated with the mothers of soldiers killed in the Korean War. Then she lost her composure and left the platform in tears.

THE FAMILY'S most tangible attempt to make sense of Joe's death came from Jack. He put together a small volume of reminiscences about his brother titled *As We Remember Joe*. Threads of Joe's Irish Catholic background were woven throughout these recollections, particularly by family members, as they sorted through matters of life and death. "It is God's will— He knows best," declared Honey Fitz, a veteran of numerous wakes among the Dearos, his Irish immigrant constituents in Boston. "Joe is gone—and we shall never look again on that dear face or hear that laugh or see that wonderful smile." In her essay, Kick recalled her brother's leadership as the oldest sibling and his "moral courage" in the days before her wedding when he had acted as a "pillar of strength" in supporting her decision. "Without Joe there will be always a gap in the Kennedy family circle, but we are far, far luckier than most because there are so many of us," she wrote. "One thing Joe would never want is that we should feel sad and gloomy about life without him. Instead he'd laugh with that wonderful twinkle out of his Irish eyes and say, 'Gee, can't you all learn to get along without me.'"

Father Sheehy, the navy chaplain who became Joe's friend and golfing buddy, underlined how much church and family were tied together for young Joe. "The faith of many generations of Kennedy's and Fitzgerald's was revealed in the humility of this favorite son of fortune whenever he went to Confession," Sheehy wrote. In the introductory essay, Jack Kennedy recalled his brother's commitment to his younger siblings' development. "If the Kennedy children amount to anything now or ever amount to anything, it will be due more to Joe's behavior and his constant example than to any other factor," wrote Jack. "Through it all, he had a deep and abiding Faith—he was never far from God—and so, I cannot help but feel that on that August day, high in the summer skies, 'death to him was less a setting forth than a returning.'" At Kick's suggestion, he ended the book with a verse from a British poet who had converted to Catholicism, someone with whom they were both familiar—Maurice Baring, who captured the sense of loss among the young in the previous world war.

When Spring shall wake the earth,
And quicken the scarred fields to the new birth.
Our grief shall grow. For what can Spring renew
More fiercely for us than the need of you?

The private letters sent to Jack from so many Kennedy friends and family were filled with religious references, and undoubtedly they reflected some of his own difficulties in reconciling his brother's fate with any sense of God. "Death like that just doesn't seem anything but a nightmare, but God is good and will give you all the strength and courage needed at this dark hour in your lives," assured the sister of Torby Macdonald, one of Jack's best friends. Some letters expressed the hope that young Joe might still be found alive. "I am saying prayers to the Lady of the Miraculous Medal that they will find out that Joe bailed out to safety," wrote one family friend. John "Mac" Maguire, one of the survivors of PT-109, arranged for a Mass to be said in Joe's name. "Words seem so futile," wrote Dick Flood, a friend and roommate of Joe's at Harvard Law School, who had lost his own brother a year earlier. "I know that great things were awaiting Joe, but God must have a still greater mission for him." For the living still in their twenties, not only was coming to grips with death an extraordinarily difficult task but it also made them nostalgic for earlier days before the war. "It seems such a short time ago, Jack, we were all happy and this terrible thing was such a long way off," sighed one friend. "It is inevitable that some of us have to be hurt and we can only pray for the strength and courage to carry on." Another college friend decried: "Each day I learn of some new boy becoming a casualty from the Harvard group and it makes me feel bad to think how few of the old faces will be present at the future class days after this is all over." When Kick flew home after the news of Joe's death, she was stunned at the airport by Jack's haggard and sickly appearance. Later, before returning to the hospital for corrective treatment on his back, Jack asked Kick to go with him to St. Francis Xavier, the local church in Hyannis Port, to talk with the pastor and soothe their ailing souls.

Jack's new status within the family was mentioned subtly in bereavement letters and recollections. In expressing sympathy and prayers for Joe, Owen Hanley, Jack's teacher at the Catholic-run Canterbury School, mentioned his pride in his former student's accomplishments. "What changes since those—your care-free days," Hanley wrote. "You certainly have made good in all your endeavors." Kick's essay referred to the family's pecking order. "I know Joe would always feel that Jack could easily take over the responsibility of being the oldest," she said. The dream of an Irish Catholic elected to the U.S. presidency—the great ambition of Joe Kennedy for his eldest son—now seemed passed along to a successor. A family friend, Max O'Rell Truitt, after speaking twice with Joe Kennedy following Joe Jr.'s death, sent a sympathy note to Jack when he was in the hospital that made reference to his father's intent. "And for you, Jack, may you soon be healed of your own afflictions so that you may be able to carry on—yes, carry on with some of those parental hopes and aspirations which had, with great affection and care, been planned for Joe." After making a biblical reference to the mystery of God's intervention in life, Mike Grace, another friend from Harvard, put it even more bluntly: "Joe has left behind to you a great responsibility for when God calls one of us away from a job it is so another can do it alone."

The pain in the senior Kennedy was visible, palpable, for all to see. "The death of Joe Jr. was the first break in this circle of nine children nearly all extraordinary in some way: handsome, intelligent, with a father and mother to whom they were devoted and who were devoted to them," wrote Arthur Krock, a Kennedy ally and Washington bureau chief of the *New York Times,* in his memoir. "It was one of the most severe shocks to the father that I've ever seen registered on a human being." Because Joe kept busy with the logistical details surrounding his son's death, the hard reality took weeks to seep in fully. "Joe's death has shocked me beyond belief," he confided in a private note to Jim Farley after receiving his letter of condolence. "All of my children are equally dear to me, but there is something about the first born that sets him a little apart—he is for always a bit of a miracle and never quite cut off from his mother's heart. He represents our youth, its joys and problems. For this reason, the shock of Joe's death and the effect it has had on his mother have caused me real grief."

Rose remembered that her husband's psyche seemed to shatter when, many days after young Joe's death, they received the last letter their son had written home from Europe; in it, Joe mentioned his secret mission and gave the assurance that "it isn't dangerous so don't worry." As he finished his son's letter (with an ending assuring his parents that "the Kennedy clan on this side of the Atlantic is doing OK"), Joe threw the letter down on a table and collapsed into a chair, as if he had suddenly been struck by the awful finality of his son's death. Though he tried in vain several times, Joe also couldn't bear to read the book of recollections prepared by Jack, certainly not without crying. "Every night of my life, I say a prayer for him," he later said of his son's memory. "Joe is now, and always will be, another part of my life." So many of his ambitions, his preparation and his drive were rolled into his oldest son. Though he had received the sacraments and followed the traditions of his religion, Joe Kennedy's faith seemed overwhelmed by his son's death, a calamity almost incomprehensibly cruel. Krock observed that Joe Kennedy "is, I'm sure, religious. At least we used to go to Sunday Mass together whenever and wherever I was visiting him." But in this personal crisis, while her husband's spirit remained lost, only Rose's "supreme faith," as her husband almost enviously called it, seemed capable of providing comfort from tragedy. Imbued with Irish charm and luck for most of his life, Joe Kennedy couldn't find an answer, couldn't unlock the mystery of why his favored son should be claimed by death. "When young Joe was killed," he later reflected to a friend, "my faith, even though I am a Catholic, did not seem strong enough to make me understand that after all, he had won his eternal reward without having to go through the grief of life. My faith should have made me realize this and I should not have indulged in great self-pity the way I did."

On Labor Day weekend, only a few weeks after Joe's death, the Kennedys gathered at Hyannis Port, as they had in the past. Jack invited some of his navy friends to share the holiday with them. They had dodged death together, though Jack, home from the hospital again, still suffered from the injuries of war. Throughout the day, Jack's group of friends played golf and shared laughs; at dinner, they were quizzed by Joe Kennedy about the day's contests. Throughout the dinner, Rose smiled graciously but without response, as if the jokes about navy life were flying over her head. She remained quiet, with an underlying sadness to her. After dinner, Jack and his friends continued their chatter outside on the porch, telling stories that ended with loud laughs.

Suddenly, an upstairs window flung open. "Jack, don't you and your friends have any respect for your dead brother?" Joe yelled in a pained voice.

Jack and his friends were stunned and stared at the old man in a hushed silence. "You get in here!" his father continued. "You're making a nuisance of yourself with the neighbors!"

As if to counter death, Joe Kennedy had instructed his family to stay busy, to keep up their hectic pace of activities, to laugh and not let young Joe's death subsume their lives. But as his outburst showed, it was an emotionally impossible demand that he couldn't sustain himself.

KICK, ALWAYS SPRY AND full of life, spent hours helping her father try to overcome his grief. After hearing the news about her brother, she rushed home from England and decided to stay with her family in the United States until her husband, Billy Hartington, returned from the war. During the Labor Day weekend with Jack's friends, she chatted with Kate Thom, the wife of one of Jack's crewmates. "We talked a lot about the war and religion and Joe," recalled Thom. "She had been the last one to see Joe. I was also married to a non-Catholic and we talked about that."

At home for the first time since her marriage, Kick tried to mend fences with her mother and slowly convince her of the wisdom of her decision. She and Billy had spent barely a few weeks together before he was shipped off again to battle. As an officer, Billy Hartington fought valiantly against the Germans during the summer, leading his men through Normandy and into Belgium. With the Allied forces marching across Europe, the war seemed likely to be over soon. Perhaps Billy and his bride could then finally begin their lives together. But in mid-September, Hartington was killed during fierce hand-to-hand combat in a tiny village. A sniper shot him through the heart. When the Duke and Duchess of Devonshire were informed of their son's death, they attempted to contact Kathleen in America. It fell upon Joe Kennedy to break the news to his daughter. Kick was devastated. The last vestiges of her lively spirit drained from her. Within two months, her eldest brother and the man she loved had been killed, among the dead in the last stages of the European war. After all the emotional tumult surrounding their wedding and the question of religion, she had hoped and prayed to God that her Billy would be spared. "I can't believe that the one thing I feared most should have happened," she confessed to her diary. "Life is so cruel."

Kick knew she must return to England, and the British government arranged for a flight back to London. It was difficult to hear the spiritual counseling from her mother, who advised that "God did not give us a burden more than we can handle." In the name of religion, she had been made to believe that somehow her love for Billy was improper, that she had lost her soul as well as repudiated her Irish Catholic heritage. After Joe's death, she accompanied her mother to Mass every morning, hoping to heal the rift between them, but to no avail. Billy's death contained a bitter irony, as though her mother's wish for her to return to the church had been accommodated. "I guess God has taken care of the matter in His own way, hasn't He?" she remarked coldly to a friend.

Back in America, Rose expanded her morning prayers at Mass to include Billy, as though in death she had finally granted her approval. In a fit of emotional exhaustion, she even sought the sympathy and refuge of the Sacred Heart nuns at Noroton for a night. "I have been to Mass for Billy frequently," she wrote to her daughter. "After I heard you talk about him and I began to hear about his likes and dislikes, his ideas and ideals, I realized what a wonderful man he was and what happiness would have been yours had God willed that you spend your life with him." Rose's letter suggested that her daughter's romantic love for Billy was temporal, whereas devotion to the church should be eternal. "A first love—a young love—is so wonderful, my dear Kathleen, but, my dearest daughter, I feel we must dry our tears as best we can and bow our heads to God's wisdom and goodness. We must place our hand in His and trust him."

After the funeral for Billy, Kick decided to stay in England, a guest of the Cavendishes, while she grieved; weeks later, she returned to the Red Cross as a volunteer. Kick's English friends were not only emotionally supportive but aware of the religious difficulties she faced at home in America. "Among Kathleen's Anglican circle," wrote her biographer, Lynne McTaggart, "it was rumored that Mrs. Kennedy believed not only that there was a causal relationship between Kathleen's sacrilege and Billy's death but that God in His wrath had struck down both Joe and Billy, for plotting the unholy marriage together. By killing Billy, God, in effect, was giving Kick another chance." Though this view was overly melodramatic, Kick's close British friends, Lady Nancy Astor among them, did harbor their own suspicions and prejudices. "I know you realize that we who believe in the Christ message can't really believe in death," Lady Astor wrote to Rose soon after young Joe's death. But the following month, Lady Astor refused to attend her own son's wedding when he married a Catholic. Well aware of the irony, Kick dropped a congratulatory note to the bride "welcoming" her to the "club" of mixed marriages. In her own mind, Kick had never left the church, even though, during her marriage to Billy, she couldn't receive its sacraments. Only her closest friends knew how much this breach tormented her. During the early summer, before these tragedies shattered her life, Kick attended Mass several times with her friend, Sissy Ormsby-Gore, whose husband, David, drove them to the church but didn't enter. As Sissy rose from the pew and joined the rest of the congregation in receiving Communion, Kick remained kneeling, mortified and angry with her ostracism. "Every week her exclusion from Communion served as a fresh reminder of her sacrilege, and no amount of prayer, charitable work, or good intentions would alter her state of sin in the eyes of the Church," McTaggart wrote. "It infuriated Kathleen to be so humiliated."

Among the Cavendishes, resentment that Billy had married a Catholic now melted away, replaced with affection for his lonely young widow. Kick spent a quiet Christmas in England with her husband's family and tried to come to grips with Billy's death and the war's destruction. Kick confided to Jack that she felt directionless and asked for advice on what to do next. "I know that there were a lot of difficulties for me if Billy had lived but somehow now none of those things seem to matter," she explained. "It just seems that the pattern of life for me has been destroyed. At the moment I don't fit into any design." To Jack, who came back nearly a cripple, Kick freely expressed her frustration. Her natural wit turned acrid in noting the hypocrisies of war. "I just read in the paper this morning that Archie Spell brought back a tremendously high decoration to Daddy," she wrote to Jack about the New York prelate. "What was that for? His children's war record."

None was so lost as Joe Kennedy, who tried to remain strong for his family while mourning its shining star, the boy with his name. Just as he had feared, his son was killed while saving England from destruction. Yet to suggest that his son's death—or any of the events of the war—had ended Joe Kennedy's faith is as wrong as it is to claim that he had never possessed it to begin with. In his letters and telegrams, there is enough documentary evidence to suggest a deep and thoughtful struggle about God and the greater meaning of tragic events in human lives. Though not as doctrinaire as his wife, Kennedy drew upon his religion enough to provide some comfort to his children. Writing to his widowed daughter just before Christmas, Joe Kennedy sent a telegram summing up his view: "Darling 1944 has been a difficult year for all of us," he cabled, "but as you have well said we still have lots for which to thank God." To close friends, however, there was no denying his heartache. "I still find it very difficult to get over Joe's death," he wrote a year later to one intimate. "God in His wisdom ordained so well that the young soon forget the sorrow of the death of older people, but I don't think that the older people ever get over the death of the younger ones."

Father Maurice Sheehy, his lost son's friend and golfing buddy, the priest who had gotten to know the Kennedys so well, realized the depth of Joe Kennedy's anguish and sent a booklet of Catholic teachings just before Christmas to help lift him from his abyss. Attached was a handwritten note from Sheehy, by then a navy chaplain stationed in San Francisco:

Dear Joe:

Enclosed is a little pamphlet which might bring you some consolation. I know that this is a dark Christmas for you—but it is, I believe, young Joe's first Christmas in heaven; and God has been extravagantly generous to you in surrounding you with people who love you. Others have lost their only son.

When the day comes that your tragedy can be seen in its greater light, I hope to visit you and Rose again.

Sincerely yours, Maurice S. Sheehy.

After the holiday, Joe composed a note of thanks to Father Sheehy. Once again, he invited the priest to visit the Kennedy home in Florida, just like the old days. "We would love to see you," he wrote, cheerily. "Let me know if there is anything I can do for you out there." But in this same letter, Joe conceded that "the whole mess of this war and all its attendant troubles just make me sick at heart." No pamphlet nor catechism was going to help him find a way out of this morass. Though his wife could follow the spiritual path suggested by priests and nuns, he seemed determined to find his own way. As he admitted to Father Sheehy, "Of course, it is inevitable that the day will come when we can regard Joe's tragedy in, as you say, 'its greater light,' but it is still a long way off for me."

Chapter Fifteen

A Lighter Shade of Green

AFTER WORLD WAR II, the Irish in Boston were ready for a change. The wave of immigrants from Ireland, the haggard unskilled day laborers and maids with brogues desperate for any job, were now two or three generations removed, and their children formed the city's emerging middle class. Many Irish worked in civil service positions—police officers, firefighters and teachers—and spoke of college for their own children. Still, for Irish Catholics living in places such as Boston, there remained two constants deeply rooted in their culture. "In the old days, your life centered around one or two things," Congressman Thomas P. O'Neill recalled about the district in which he grew up. "It centered around the Democratic Party or it centered around the Catholic Church. Those were the two organizations where they would run festivals, they would run social affairs, your whole social life was around them." Politics and the church had helped both P. J. Kennedy in East Boston, and particularly John F. Fitzgerald among the "Dearos" in the north, and these two potent forces were at play in the 11th Congressional District when their grandson, John F. Kennedy, sought election in 1946. Unlike Honey Fitz, twenty-nine-year-old Kennedy ran for Congress not as a stepping-stone to becoming the city's mayor—the usual prize for ethnic politicians in American cities—but with an eye toward something grander.

Kennedy's campaign enlisted the full power of Boston's Catholic Church in a way that not even his grandfathers could have imagined. In previous elections, Honey Fitz and James Michael Curley had curried favor with the clergy, hoping some favorable mention from the pulpit might pay off at the ballot box. Generally, though, the church hierarchy, in accordance with Vatican directives, did not allow themselves or church-affiliated organizations to become directly involved in such temporal matters as political endorsements. Cardinal O'Connell deliberately distanced himself from both Curley and Fitzgerald when they implicitly sought his support. Even Spellman, for all his courtier intrigue with politicians, still tried to keep church matters from the local Caesars.

Kennedy's campaign was different. As other histories have shown, money from the Kennedy family helped buy the support of an influential newspaper and eliminate the only serious competition that Jack Kennedy faced in winning the congressional seat. But unknown to most, Kennedy money also bought the Roman Catholic Church's support for his 1946 candidacy and subsequent campaigns through a large dispersal of funds donated to Catholic-run organizations. The close working relationship between the Kennedys and key church figures can be found in financial documents and letters. Each donation to a Catholic parish, nursing home or charitable organization was calibrated by Joe Kennedy's key aides—mostly Irish Catholics themselves—to maximize the church's support for Jack's political efforts, to raise his visibility in a place where he had never lived as an adult and to broaden his support among other immigrant Catholic groups.

In turn, church figures signaled their support of Kennedy. In particular, Archbishop Richard Cushing, far more than any prelate before him, became an active promoter of his candidacy—a financial and emotional investment that would pay dividends throughout Jack Kennedy's career. Cushing's enthusiasm for Kennedy not only derived from large donations but, as several letters indicate, also from Joe Kennedy's clout with powerful figures at the Vatican, particularly Count Enrico Galeazzi, the Pope's right-hand man. Indeed, Joe Kennedy encouraged the perception that he might be able to affect Cushing's elevation someday to cardinal.

Increasingly, the Kennedy campaigns made the transition from patronage machine politics to a new era driven by money and media. Far from keeping a distance between church and state, Jack Kennedy's early political career relied on church-related donations funneled through Kennedy-controlled charities to bolster and augment his political organization. His first campaign in 1946 was not orchestrated by navy buddies and Harvard roommates, as some early histories have suggested, but by an Irish organization of machine-bred pols much closer to the immigrant experience than Jack. Like Boston itself, Kennedy's campaign that year contained the old and the new, serving both as further evidence of Irish Catholic ascendancy in the city, and, more important, as a harbinger of diverse and profound changes taking place in postwar America.

To REMEMBER his fallen son, Joe Kennedy planned several memorials. He pushed hard for a Congressional Medal of Honor for his martyred boy, but received instead the Navy Cross in his honor. In a well-publicized ceremony, Jean Kennedy, the youngest Kennedy daughter and Joe Jr.'s godchild, christened a new navy destroyer, the USS *Joseph P. Kennedy Jr.*, upon which Bobby served for a time. At St. Francis Xavier, the small white frame church where the Kennedys worshipped in Hyannis Port, the family donated a new altar. It featured a sky-blue background in which a pair of gold navy wings were depicted between images of England's St. George and France's St. Joan of Arc. But the most extensive tribute was the charitable foundation created in young Joe's name. "My father—still in his grief—decided he wanted to build a memorial to his son," Eunice later recalled. "He had never believed much in building buildings. He wanted to invest in men. He asked us all at the table one day what could be done to best perpetuate Joe's memory." Eventually, they decided that the foundation should focus on mental retardation, an area largely ignored by government and other charities. In an unspoken way, the decision seemed to atone for the Kennedys' own remorse about daughter, Rosemary Kennedy, whose condition they still did not acknowledge publicly. Over the next several decades, the Joseph P. Kennedy Jr. Foundation built several facilities for retarded children, symbols of the family's genuine commitment to the cause. But in its early years, the foundation also served another purpose—the intention of helping John F. Kennedy get elected.

Wrapped often in hyperbole, the story of Jack's entry into the political arena sounds like some Irish legend, of one chieftain lost in battle being replaced by another. The theme of a brother picking up the mantle for his fallen sibling recurs throughout Irish history in heroes such as Brian Boru or in the battle legends of Vinegar Hill. According to most popular accounts, Joe brought the family together in Hyannis Port and informed Jack of his destiny. "I got Jack into politics—I was the one," his father explained years later. "I told him Joe was dead and that it was therefore his responsibility to run for Congress. He didn't want it. He felt he didn't have the ability but I told him he had to." To most chroniclers of this saga, the idea of Jack Kennedy picking up the gauntlet of his fallen brother seemed gallant, almost romantic, like the plot concocted for some B-movie adventure produced by Hollywood's Joe Kennedy. Ted Sorensen and Arthur

Schlesinger, in their own paeans to their former commander in chief, suggest that Jack Kennedy entered politics of his own volition as an extension of his liberal views, though the record of JFK's misgivings and the elder Kennedy's repeated admissions certainly undermine this claim. A bit more plausibly, other biographers suggest that Jack's entry was merely a manifestation of Joe Kennedy's unrelenting megalomania. In American presidential history, there was no precedent for the Kennedy brothers (other previous dynasties, such as the Adamses, were handed down one generation to the next, though the current Bush family is more comparable). Yet in popular accounts of this brotherly succession—such a powerful dynamic in the Kennedy family's future—there remains little examination of the past to find its root causes.

Joe Kennedy's familial control over his adult sons was reflected in many examples of Irish Catholic family life. Like his older brother, killed near age thirty, Jack was still unmarried at age twenty-eight. The center of his emotional life remained focused on the large family created by his parents, a common Irish trait as observed by the Reverend Andrew Greeley and other social historians. In Boston, many Irish politicians and others in the Kennedys' circle of friends didn't start families of their own until later in life. Without a wife to counsel him, Jack was particularly susceptible to his father's influence. "I was drafted," Jack told a journalist. "My father wanted his eldest son in politics. 'Wanted' isn't the right word. He *demanded* it."

An air of destiny hung over this brotherly succession. Jack's future plans as an individual would give way to duty and the greater needs of the clan. Somehow, it seemed that all of the slights and resentments endured by the Irish in America would be redeemed if one of their own became president, and Joe Kennedy was determined to see that his son would be that one. It was more than just a father-son directive: the entire family seemed vested in this legacy. "When we lost our oldest son and Jack assumed his mantle, I thought it was great," Rose confirmed.

Before his brother's death, Jack had some interest in politics, but expected his career would be spent mainly as a writer. For newspapers owned by his father's friend, William Randolph Hearst, Jack toured through Europe in the summer of 1945, ostensibly to cover the British elections. While in London, he met with several British politicians and attended a rally where Harold Laski, the socialist and his brother's venerated former teacher, gave his views. After a private chat with Laski, Kennedy wrote in his diary that "these Leftists are filled with bitterness" and that Laski's bitterness came "not so much from the economic inequality but from the social." Kennedy seemed well aware of the class distinctions made by the

British in dealing with Jews as well as the Irish. In this regard, one particular remark from Laski during their friendly chat seemed to resonate with young Kennedy. "In speaking of Boston, he [Laski] said, 'Boston is a state of mind—and as a Jew, he could understand what it is to be an Irishman in Boston,'" Kennedy wrote in his diary. "That last remark reveals the fundamental, activating force of Mr. Laski's life—a powerful spirit doomed to an inferior position because of race—a position that all of his economic and intellectual superiority cannot raise him out of." Could this be Jack's fate, too? Rather than castigate Jews as his father did in private, Kennedy seemed to understand the frustrations and similar troubles faced by minority groups in dealing with a dominant culture different from their own.

AFTER SPENDING A WEEK writing in England, John Kennedy crossed the Irish Sea. In Dublin, he also filed a dispatch about the Irish situation, but, though bearing a London dateline, the vantage was hardly that of an Anglophile. Instead, Kennedy wrote an eloquent description of the Irish plight. His feature, headlined "De Valera Aims to Unite Ireland," described Eamon De Valera's attempt to bring the six counties in Ulster under the same flag as the twenty-six counties in the south forming the Republic of Ireland. Perhaps most surprising about the essay was Kennedy's point of view.

During World War II, Ireland steadfastly held on to its neutrality and denied the Allies access to military ports in the south—to the everlasting annoyance of English leaders. It turned out just as Winston Churchill had warned before the war, when Neville Chamberlain gave up control of the Irish ports as part of a deal brokered by Joe Kennedy. The position of Kennedy's son was now even more surprising. A former U.S. Navy lieutenant planning to run for Congress, particularly one who had lost a brother a year earlier while fighting over the English Channel, might be expected to agree staunchly with the British position—but not John Kennedy. His essay made De Valera's position seem reasonable to an American audience. He described De Valera, born in New York to a Spanish father and an Irish mother, not as a radical or a terrorist but as a freedom fighter. As leader of the "powerful" Fianna Fail Party, he said, De Valera was a "brilliant, austere figure" trying to bring all of Ireland together.

"De Valera is fighting politically the same relentless battle they fought in the field during the uprising of 1916, in the war of independence and later in the civil war," wrote Kennedy. "He feels everything Ireland has gained has been given grudgingly and at the end of a long and bitter struggle. Always it has been too little and too late." Kennedy detailed the Irish struggle for independence in the same glowing terms as the American Revolution and described the men around De Valera—such as Sean Lemass, the deputy prime minister—as sort of Founding Fathers of Irish freedom. "All fought in the war of independence against Black and Tans and later in the civil war of 1922," he recounted. "All have been in both English and Irish prisons, and many have wounds which still ache when the cold rains come in from the west. They have not forgotten nor have they forgiven. The only settlement they will accept is a free and independent Ireland, free to go where it will be the master of its own destiny."

In his article, Kennedy conscientiously informed readers that De Valera's position for total unification was opposed not only by the British but by more cautious members of the Irish Dail, who felt it better to join the British Commonwealth and work together in mutual trust for the end of partition in Ireland. Yet Kennedy made clear that De Valera owned the Irish hearts and minds on this matter. "One is a strong stand and supported by the great majority of the people," he observed. "The other is willing to compromise in view of present world circumstances." Clearly, Kennedy's perspective looked beyond the "present world circumstances" to the long history of Ireland in its quest for freedom. "De Valera is determined to end this partition, as it is called, and to that cause he has dedicated his life," Kennedy wrote. "In this cause, all Irishmen of the south are united." Undoubtedly, these words sounded more like an Irish Catholic politician preparing to run for office in Boston than the son of a former U.S. ambassador to Great Britain, though his father likely agreed with every point.

In his private diary of the trip, Jack Kennedy wrote with fascination about De Valera and his appeal throughout the Irish countryside. In his diary, Kennedy recalled how young De Valera was ordered to jail and sentenced to death for his part in the uprising of 1916, a week-long revolution crushed by the British occupying force that set the stage of Irish independence. The older Irish leaders were shot "one or two a day" by British soldiers as a warning against further uprisings. "Public indignation had come to a fever pitch in America and Ireland due to the daily executions," Kennedy wrote. The worldwide outrage prompted the English to reduce De Valera's sentence and send him to a British jail for safekeeping. Kennedy recounted in detail the story of De Valera's eventual escape. "Michael Collins, the great Irish hero, arranged for keys to be sent to De Valera in jail in a cake and went to England himself to aid the escape," recalled Kennedy, who enjoyed such courageous tales. "One of the keys broke but at the last minute Mr. De Valera was successful in breaking out."

Young Kennedy listened one day to the sharp criticisms of De Valera by David Gray, the U.S. minister appalled by Ireland's neutrality during the war. Yet Kennedy seemed to distance himself from Gray's caustic comments. He recognized the deep, almost spiritual desire among the Irish to end the partition of their country and gain their own fully realized independence. His diary notes underline the linkage between De Valera's commitment to a united Ireland and the Catholic hierarchy's view of their nation. "The Cardinal believes that Ireland was created by God—a single island and people, and partition is therefore an offense to God," observed Kennedy, well aware of the intermingling of church and state in Irish politics. "Because of De Valera's appeal to nationalism and his mystic hold on the hearts of the people and his practical politics, he did not lose control."

Though sympathetic to the Irish historical quest for freedom, Kennedy also noted in his journal a quote intended for "Irishmen abroad" from Thomas D'Arcy McGee, a Canadian of Irish descent, which seems to apply to himself: "While always ready therefore to say the right word and do the right act for the land of my forefathers, I am bound above all to the land where I reside."

FOUR MONTHS LATER, when he returned to Massachusetts, Kennedy reworked his article and diary notes into what would become his first public speech. On November 11, 1945, Kennedy appeared at the Crosscup-Pishon American Legion Post, one of the largest in New England, and added even more comments about his Irish allegiance and admiration for De Valera. His talk abounded with ironies.

It was a night for showing Jack Kennedy in a greener tint than usual. Among Boston's Irish, the speech was meant to shore up lingering questions about Kick Kennedy's marriage to a Cavendish and to demonstrate Kennedy's affinity for Ireland. The tall, thin war hero regaled the crowd with stories of meeting General Richard Mulcahy, who served as chief of staff of the Irish Republican Army (IRA) during the 1919 war for independence from Britain and was then leader of the Fine Gael (United Irish Party). In glowing terms, Kennedy described Mulcahy as "that able warrior who proved his toughness in the wars against the Black and Tans." Jack spoke of the Black and Tans with the same contempt as his father. Of Mulcahy, Kennedy commented that "he looked like the soldier he was—he was a man of strong opinions. When an Irish politician gives you his views on his country's position, you know that they are not lightly held and that he has probably shed some blood in their defense."

Indeed, Kennedy's description of Mulcahy, particularly his familiarity with violence, seemed deliberately downplayed. Through sheer will, Mulcahy had whipped ragtag Irish soldiers into a credible army that would not fail in 1919, not as Irish resistance had done so many times before to British tyranny. Mulcahy survived imprisonment as an Irish freedom fighter and waged a tightly organized guerrilla war for the IRA. As a biographer later concluded, Mulcahy "epitomized the political and cultural nationalist whose vision of a free and independent Ireland was a synthesis of traditions: Gaelic and English, constitutional and revolutionary, modern and traditional." In the civil war that erupted, Mulcahy, who served as minister for national defense for the new provisional government, employed brutal counterterrorism methods, including the execution of prisoners. None of these messy details were in Kennedy's speech.

Instead, Jack Kennedy, the budding Boston pol, skated carefully between the two Irish factions, careful to praise both sides without alienating the other. His audience knew enough of modern Irish history to recognize the general's name. In his speech, Kennedy recalled sitting with Mulcahy in his small office full of books, a large portrait—"the most impressive object in General Mulcahy's room"—of the fallen Michael Collins adorning the wall. "If Michael Collins had lived," the old man told Kennedy, "the history of Ireland would be different." Kennedy said he talked for "several hours" with Mulcahy about the legacy of Michael Collins.

In the pantheon of modern Irish heroes, Michael Collins's tale is perhaps the most charismatic and tragic. During the war for independence, Collins rejected the idea of a large-scale rebellion against vastly superior armed forces. Instead, with the help of Mulcahy, he brilliantly forged a campaign of hit-and-run guerrilla tactics. He arranged for secret loans to finance the struggle and set up a complex web of spies to learn of the British military's strategy. Once victory over the British was attained—in the form of a negotiated settlement that drew a partition line through Ireland—Collins tried to convince his fellow freedom fighters of the treaty's merits, but to no avail. The Irish civil war became a cross for Collins to bear. "Think, what have I got for Ireland? Something she had wanted these past seven hundred years," Collins wrote a friend about the treaty, which he called "my death warrant" because he knew it would be untenable for those who wanted their freedom from England complete. Soon after the treaty signing in 1922, Collins was assassinated; his memory became a treasured part of Irish history.

"This young man who was killed in his early thirties looms as large today in Ireland as when he died," John F. Kennedy declared about Michael

Collins in this November 1945, speech. Decades later, others would compare Michael Collins to a fallen leader in America. In his history of Ireland, Robert Kee said that Collins "has assumed, in Irish consciousness, a place not unlike the place that John F. Kennedy has in American consciousness. A young, attractive and dashing individual shot down at a young age, shortly after his greatest triumph. Like Kennedy, the perception in Ireland is, that if Collins had lived, Ireland's future could only have been different and better."

IN HIS SPEECH that day, Kennedy offered a debatable interpretation of the past. But his take on recent Irish events was even more noteworthy. He suggested that De Valera—who had asked Collins to negotiate with the British and then vehemently rejected the treaty—would be the one to "finally settle the problem of Partition." He pointed to De Valera's success in getting the British to relinquish their naval ports at Berehaven, Queenstown and Lough Swilly to the Irish without mentioning his father's part in the arrangement. He also avoided Churchill's criticisms of the deal and its impact on the war effort. Instead, he focused on praise for the Irish leader. "De Valera has a unique hold on the hearts of the Irish people," Kennedy told the crowd. "There is no compromise in De Valera's firm, ascetic face. He has a passionate intensity and a single-mindedness in the course he is taking that brooks no opposition."

Before these Irish-American war veterans sitting in Massachusetts, Kennedy forgave Ireland for not fighting with the Allies in World War II, citing its ancient antipathy for the imperialist Brits. He explained away De Valera's stance as "identifying neutrality with freedom from England, which will always win support" with the Irish people. As Jack certainly realized, the wish to avoid war was one that De Valera's friend, Ambassador Joe Kennedy, tried in vain to affect for his own country. With his intense, oracular manner, De Valera managed to cast a spell on the Kennedys, as he did much of the Irish people.

Understanding De Valera was much like deciphering a mystic. He showed great strength and cunning to gain Ireland's long-sought independence from its great oppressor, England. Rather than look forward as the new nation's leader, however, De Valera insisted that Ireland return to its roots. He promoted an agrarian economy, rather than develop the cities, clung to an isolationist policy and instructed that native Gaelic be taught as Ireland's first language. Keenly aware of the simmering prejudices of the British toward his country, De Valera never trusted Churchill, who thought briefly of taking back the Irish ports by force during the war but was prevented from doing so because of the Irish lobby in America. "De Valera is quite content to sit happy and see us strangle," Churchill complained bitterly to Roosevelt. After the war, the British prime minister lambasted the Irish leader for not allowing Ireland's ports to be used by the Allies, a stand that he said resulted in needlessly lost lives. In reply, De Valera pointed to his country's own history. "Could he not find in his heart generosity to acknowledge that there is a small nation that stood alone, not for one year or two, but for several hundred years, against aggression?" De Valera said of the British prime minister. "Mr. Churchill is justly proud of his nation's perseverance against heavy odds. But we in this island are still prouder of our perseverance for freedom through all the centuries."

That the Kennedys, both father and son, should find such affinity with this champion of Irish freedom seemed unlikely, and yet his words struck a chord in both of them. Indeed, Jack Kennedy's deference to De Valera was so complete that he could even excuse the Irish leader's decision to express his condolences at the German embassy in Dublin when Adolf Hitler died. "He is extremely conscious that his visit to the German Legation on Hitler's death caused unfavorable comment in America," explained young Kennedy. "He discussed it with me at some length. He was determined to carry out Eire's policy of strict neutrality to the end, and carry it out he did. To all critics he answers, 'I kept Ireland out of the war.'"

JOHN F. KENNEDY's appearance before this American Legion post was a remarkable way for a future American president to begin his political career. Though the National Archives records this talk as JFK's first public address, few historians have examined it in any great detail, even though Kennedy's comments were exceptional. To be sure, De Valera's positions were hardly acceptable to most American politicians after the war; nor were they acceptable to the press: "No act of Prime Minister Eamon De Valera's public life had evoked more world-wide criticism comment than his call upon the German Minister in Dublin to express his condolences upon the reported death of Adolf Hitler," observed the *New York Times*. "In many places it was decried as a first-class blunder." The newspaper also sharply criticized De Valera's courtesy call in an editorial: "Considering the character and the record of the man for whose death he was expressing grief, there is obviously something wrong with the protocol, the neutrality or Mr. De Valera." Three months after his son's speech, Joe Kennedy received a letter from an old friend at the U.S. embassy in Dublin that urged him to separate from De Valera's decisions "placing this country on record as a protector and an apologist for the Nazi regime. If I were an American of Irish descent, I would very much resent such a policy."

But neither Joe Kennedy nor his eldest surviving son had any plans to disassociate themselves from the Irish leader, even after De Valera's questionable call on Hitler's death. For the predominantly Irish Catholic crowd gathered that day at the American Legion post, Jack Kennedy's comments were not considered particularly controversial or politically adventurous. Many were Irish immigrants or descendants strongly allied with the Irish cause who viewed De Valera as a folk hero. Though Jack Kennedy carefully crafted a moderate image on financial and domestic matters in the United States, this speech proved that when it came to Irish freedom, he was no middle-of-the-roader. Somehow, it seemed fitting that, in his first public address as a soon-to-be candidate, Jack Kennedy underlined his natural affinity with the Irish.

ALTHOUGH JOE KENNEDY had left Boston behind in disgust nearly two decades earlier and moved his large, ambitious family to New York, the Kennedys, in a sense, never left Boston. Both the Kennedys and the Fitzgeralds were too engrained in the fabric of Boston's political life not to recognize the electoral advantage for Joe's sons. Joe Jr.'s selection as a 1940 Democratic Party delegate from Boston and Honey Fitz's own last hurrah as a 1942 Senate candidate in Massachusetts were preludes to Joe Kennedy's grand political scheme. After Joe Jr.'s death, the senior Kennedy pursued a relentless campaign of speeches for the Massachusetts Commerce Department, ostensibly reviewing business conditions around the state, but, in effect, extending the public's awareness of the Kennedy name; indeed, publicity about the Kennedys often made it appear as though they had never left Boston. Yet Joe Kennedy, still nursing the slights of yesteryear, never denied his ambivalence. "That's exactly why I left Boston," he admitted in the late 1950s, when asked about the anti-Catholic prejudice in the city of his birth. Only as a postscript did he add, "They tell me it's better now."

During the ensuing years, Joe Kennedy had learned a hard lesson in politics—even with millions of dollars at his disposal, the path was too difficult alone. To the Roosevelt administration, he was just an Irish Catholic with his own portfolio, a man lacking any real political organization or geographic base behind him to compel action. After the 1942 election, Kennedy met with FDR and "point[ed] out to him that he had failed to appoint an Irish Catholic or a Catholic to an important war position since

1940," an omission, he emphasized, that was "not conducive to strengthening the Democratic Party." Yet, without a well-organized constituency of his own, Kennedy could be ignored. Early that year, his father-in-law, Honey Fitz ("John F," as Joe called him), urged Boston Congressman John W. McCormack to speak to Roosevelt about appointing Kennedy to a post in the Defense Department. When McCormack brought up the subject at the White House, Roosevelt "at once replied that as far as he was concerned personally, he had great affection for me, but I was of course a tough Irishman and very stubborn," as Kennedy recorded in his diary. Roosevelt claimed that Kennedy was one of the few who didn't offer his services when America jumped into the war. Kennedy had indeed offered to help, but he didn't see the point now of arguing with the White House. Certainly by the mid–1940s, Kennedy realized that to achieve political success for his sons—the heirs to his political ambitions—he'd have to rely on a different approach.

Money would become the lubricant of politics in postwar America, though politics in Boston in 1946 still depended very much on ward healers and fixers. Patronage and graft were often the only means to get ahead at City Hall. The Kennedys realized that their plans to return to Boston would depend in part on the clannishness of the Irish and an organization of men and women, most of them Catholics, who were very familiar with the city's parochial politics. Starting with this first campaign for Congress, each campaign for Jack Kennedy would envelope two distinct camps—the Irish and the non-Irish. There were Jack's navy buddies, Harvard roommates and intellectual-minded liberals in Cambridge who reflected part of Kennedy's psyche, as if it were one side of the brain. And then there was the Irish crowd—generally more practical, more socially conservative, more politically intuitive, and, in a real sense, more loyal personally. They might not be asked into the strategy sessions, or become congressional staffers, but they could be counted on to share a joke or accept a particularly odious task. They could take a buck from the old man's payroll, but they also shared his dream to elect Jack the first Irish Catholic president of the United States, as if it were some ancient quest to crown a king.

Given Jack's degree of education and worldliness, what was perhaps most remarkable was his ability to relate to the old-school pols who remembered the days when Irish immigrants were fresh off the wharf. As historian James MacGregor Burns observed: "Some politicians might have broken away from the immigrant world and embraced the more edifying, more sophisticated, and more exciting world of liberal intellectuals. But for Kennedy this would have meant breaking away not just from a remote background

The Kennedy Clan. The entire family of U.S. Ambassador to Great Britain Joseph P. and Rose Fitzgerald Kennedy, all gathered together in London in the late 1930s, before so many of the triumphs and tragedies that they would share together. From left to right: Kathleen, Joseph Jr., Robert, Eunice, Edward "Teddy," Joseph Sr., Patricia, Rose, Rosemary, Jean, and John. *Kennedy Family Private Collection*

P. J. Kennedy. From a modest beginning, Kennedy started a successful tavern, displaying the chieftain-like qualities that allowed him to get elected as a Massachusetts State Senator. *Kennedy Library*

Saving Dunganstown. In the 1880s, James Kennedy was jailed and faced the loss of the family's farm in Ireland when he objected to the high rents enforced by the British. His American cousin, P. J. Kennedy, sent money to help him and later came for a visit. *Courtesy Kennedy Homestead*

Giant's Causeway. On a tour of Ireland, former Boston Mayor John F. Fitzgerald and his daughter, Rose, visited this famous site in Ulster. *Kennedy Family Private Collection*

The King of Boston Politics. After serving as a Congressman, "Honey Fitz" moved back to Boston and became mayor, beating his Brahmin challenger. To celebrate the city's anniversary in 1907, Mayor Fitzgerald (middle of second row) posed with the city's other political leaders, including P.J. Kennedy (third from left on top row). *Kennedy Library*

Love and Politics. When Honey Fitz invited P.J. Kennedy on a summer vacation in Maine, a romance blossomed between the mayor's daughter, Rose, and Kennedy's son, Joe. The couple eventually were married by Boston's Cardinal William O'Connell. *Kennedy Library*

Rose and Joe. Though their marriage was marred by her husband's infidelity, Rose found solace in both her family and religion. Joe Kennedy proved himself an active and engaged father to their nine children. "It made me feel that I had a partner in my enterprise," Rose said. *Kennedy Library*

Fathers and Sons. Joe Kennedy, the hard-driving businessman who became a millionaire, encountered a more sophisticated form of bigotry than his father, P.J. (seen here with grandson, Joseph P. Kennedy Jr.) "I think that the Irish in me has not been completely assimilated, but all my ducks are swans," he later confided. *Kennedy Family Private Collection*

Immigrants and Nativists. As the first great wave of immigrants, Irish Catholics faced religious bigotry and anti-immigrant sentiment. The fear that "Uncle Sam may be swallowed by foreigners" was expressed in this 1880s cartoon that caricatured both Irish and Asian immigrants. *The Library of Congress*

Papists and Know-Nothings. Catholics were often scorned in America's predominantly white Anglo-Saxon Protestant culture of the 19th Century. This 1853 cartoon captures the bigotry of this era when the Know-Nothing Party, concerned about the influx of "papists," garnered 25 percent of the U.S. presidential vote. *The Library of Congress*

Jack. Unlike his sisters who attended all-girls schools run by nuns, John F. Kennedy attended a Catholic school for only one year, an experience similar to his other brothers. With a white sash on his sleeve, Jack Kennedy smiled while celebrating his First Holy Communion. *Kennedy Family Private Collection*

The Kennedy Brood.
Claiming Boston "was no place to bring up Catholic children," Joe Kennedy moved his growing family to New York, probably more for business reasons than bigotry. By the late 1920s, the Kennedy clan included, from left to right, Jean, Bobby, Patricia, Eunice, Kathleen, Rosemary, Jack and Joe Jr. Brother Ted was born in 1932. *Kennedy Library*

Togetherness. Influenced by their heritage, the Kennedys defined their lives around family, the sense of belonging to an entity greater than themselves. "Long before it ever became a slogan, my family and I had togetherness," said Joe Kennedy, seen here playing in the Atlantic with Jack and his other children. *Kennedy Family Private Collection*

Minorities. Though the Kennedys were keenly aware of religious and anti-Irish discrimination, they grew up with little contact with other minorities, particularly African-Americans. Negroes were encountered as porters and servants (as seen here in the 1930s with young Ted Kennedy) while Jews were often derided in private. *Kennedy Family Private Collection*

Al Smith. The New York Governor, seen here in a public appeal for tolerance on the religious issue, faced a great deal of anti-Catholicism during his unsuccessful 1928 run for president. *Library of Congress*

Franklin Delano Roosevelt. After turning down FDR's offer to go to Ireland, Joe Kennedy urged his own appointment as Ambassador to the Court of St. James. As his White House relationship soured, Kennedy wrote in his diary: "I got the impression that deep down in his heart Roosevelt had a decidedly anti-Catholic feeling." *United Press International*

Heirs to Power. Joe Kennedy's interest in running for president in 1940 was thwarted when Roosevelt announced for a third term and Kennedy's private criticisms about Europe's war were publicized. He would focus his energies on the political careers of his sons, starting with his eldest, Joe Junior. *Kennedy Library*

Father Coughlin. From the Shrine of the Little Flower outside of Detroit, Father Charles Coughlin's radio broadcasts were popular throughout the United States, especially in regions with large Catholic populations. Initially a supporter of Roosevelt, the radio priest became a bitter critic of the New Deal, his comments sometimes laced with anti-Semitism. Joe Kennedy later arranged with church officials to help silence Coughlin. *Library of Congress*

Good Friends. Joe Kennedy set up the 1936 meeting between President Roosevelt and Cardinal Eugenio Pacelli, then Vatican Secretary of State who later became Pope Pius XII. FDR wanted the church to quiet Father Coughlin, while Pacelli convinced the U.S. to send an envoy to Rome, ending nearly a century of America's refusal. This success cemented the friendship between Kennedy, little-known Boston bishop Francis Spellman (seen behind Kennedy), and Pacelli's top aide, Count Enrico Galeazzi (left). *Wide World Photo*

Ireland's Eamon DeValera.
He bitterly opposed Ireland's partition in the 1920s after its war for independence against Great Britain, and knew the importance of cultivating Irish-Americans like Kennedy. After Kennedy was rebuffed by his alma mater, Harvard, DeValera (right) granted him an honorary degree in Dublin. DeValera's neutrality during World War II, including his condolences to the Germans following Hitler's death, were sharply criticized—but not by the Kennedys.
Wide World Photo

Princes of the Church. To Joe Kennedy's delight, FDR sent his British ambassador in 1939 to the coronation of Cardinal Pacelli as the new Pope Pius XII. Inside the Vatican, the pontiff recalled his earlier visit to the Kennedy's home in New York and offered young Ted his first holy communion. *Kennedy Library*

Billy Hartington. Kick's romance with Billy—William Cavendish, the Ninth Marquis of Hartington and future Duke of Devonshire—seemed star-crossed from the start and became increasingly complex as they wed. "I do feel extremely strongly about the religion of my children both from a personal and from a national point of view, otherwise I should never have asked Kick to make such sacrifices in agreeing to their being brought up Anglican," he wrote Rose Kennedy, who opposed the marriage. *Kennedy Library*

Lismore Castle. For many Irish, Lismore Castle in County Waterford was a reminder of British control of their homeland, but for Kathleen, it was one of her in-laws' country estates. "I know my little brothers will think 'Kick has gone more British' than ever," she wrote home. "My persecuted Irish ancestors would turn over in their graves to hear talk of England in this way but I don't care... (You'd better not let Grandpa Fitz see the above.)" *Library of Congress*

The Bride's Brother. Aware of the family's disagreement back home, Joe Jr. (seen here with Kick on her wedding day in 1944) defended his sister's decision to marry Billy Hartington. "The power of silence is great," he cabled to his parents. Before the war's end, both Billy and Joe Jr. were killed in action. Kick died in a 1948 airplane crash. *Wide World Photo*

Family Ties. Young Jack Kennedy returned from the South Pacific as a war hero and, urged by his father, ran for his grandfather's old seat in Congress (seen here together). Kennedy relied heavily on his family's money and political connections in Boston's Irish-American community. When Jack won in 1946, Honey Fitz predicted he'd become the first Catholic elected U.S. President. *Kennedy Library*

Road to Dunganstown. During a trip in 1947 to see his sister Kick at Lismore Castle, Jack Kennedy decided to visit his distant Irish cousins at the family's ancestral home in Dunganstown, County Wexford. A bit lost, he asked Robert Burrell (pictured) for directions to the Kennedy farm. *Library of Congress*

Mary Kennedy Ryan and Irish Kin. After tea and swapping stories, Congressman John F. Kennedy took this snapshot of his third cousin, Mary Kennedy Ryan, and her family and friends, outside their barn. Mary recalled as a child meeting P.J. Kennedy during his visit, and told JFK about other aspects of their shared history. Reflecting on his family's success in America, Jack "thought about the cottage where my cousins lived, and I said to myself, 'What a contrast'." *Courtesy of Kennedy Homestead*

"Archie Spell." The Kennedy family's private nickname for the powerful Cardinal of New York, whom they viewed as a close friend. The influence of Spellman (seen here marrying Edward and Joan Kennedy in 1958) extended from land deals to fighting international Communism and gaining favors with the Vatican. *Wide World Photos*

Grudge Match. Jack Kennedy's upset victory in the 1952 U.S. Senate race against incumbent Henry Cabot Lodge drew upon his family's old grudges. Decades earlier, Honey Fitz battled Lodge's grandfather over the immigration issue and later lost an election to him for the Senate. The 1952 contest marked a watershed for Brahmin statewide political power in Massachusetts. *Kennedy Library*

Church and State. Religion and ethnicity were a potent part of the Kennedy appeal in Boston. Joe Kennedy influenced Boston's Cardinal Cushing (right) through donations administered by his aide, Francis X. Morrissey (left), and with his clout at the Vatican. "Who the hell does he think he is?" Joe once asked in a fit. "If he wants that little red cardinal's hat, he'd better shape up because I've got a hell of a lot more friends in Rome than he does." Though wary of the senior Kennedy, Cushing proved a genuine friend to the Kennedy family, particularly Jack. *Kennedy Library*

Houston Ministers. Hounded by anti-Catholic critics in 1960, John F. Kennedy decided to attend a gathering of Protestant ministers in Houston, where he flatly promised to keep his religion out of his political decision-making. "I believe in an America where the separation of church and state is absolute," JFK declared. "I do not speak for my church on public matters, and the church does not speak for me." *Paul Schutzer/Timepix*

Al Smith Dinner. In 1960, at the annual event named for the former New York Governor, Jack Kennedy used humor to mask his anger at Cardinal Spellman's all-but-formal endorsement of Republican Richard Nixon. But Joe Kennedy, who counted on Spellman to help his son's candidacy, felt betrayed and let their mutual friend at the Vatican, Count Galeazzi, know of his feelings. *Kennedy Library*

but from a dominant family whose powerful way of life was still strong within him. And symbolizing that family—standing guard, as it were, over the links between him and the Fitzgeralds and the Kennedys—was his father . . . the example of a self-confident man of affairs who had succeeded as a Catholic and an immigrant's grandson." Dave Powers, a young man recruited by Jack from the Charleston neighborhood who became perhaps the closest of the "Irish Mafia" around him, agreed that the skinny rich kid with the charming manner was a hybrid. "It was a strange thing," Powers said later, "while Jack Kennedy was a completely new type of Irish politician himself, having come from such a different background, he was, at bottom, very Irish and he could never hear enough of the old Irish stories."

The master storyteller of the 1946 campaign was also its tactical mastermind—Joseph L. Kane, Joe Kennedy's sixty-six-year-old cousin, the son of P. J. Kennedy's sister from a considerably less affluent side of the family. Curt and easily agitated, Kane had toiled in the grimy vineyard of Massachusetts politics for forty years. He knew everybody and every favor. Usually seen wearing a fedora and chomping a cigar between his false teeth, Kane provided a tutorial on Boston politics for Joe Kennedy's son in the same way that Jack earlier had attended the London School of Economics for lessons in political economy. An obituary years later described Kane as "one of Boston's most colorful political figures," and "a familiar figure in the cafeterias around City Hall." In her memoir, Rose Kennedy admitted that "Cousin Joe was quite a rough diamond, with an abrasive style of thought and speech. My husband wasn't sure how he and Jack would get along, but they hit if off quite well. Jack was surprised, entertained and informed."

Joe Kane had seen it all. In 1937, he served as a campaign manager for another Irish-American, Maurice Tobin, elected to City Hall, and helped run the 1942 Senate bid for Honey Fitz. Back in 1918, while working for Peter Tague, a bitter Fitzgerald opponent, Kane contested the congressional race in which Honey Fitz seemed to squeak by with 238 votes but was removed from his seat because of voting irregularities. Somewhat to Joe Kennedy's secret delight, his cousin and his father-in-law remained political enemies for years. To the public in 1946, Honey Fitz appeared the éminence grise behind his grandson's candidacy, even sharing the same address at the Bellevue Hotel in downtown Boston. But in reality, Kane was the relative providing the best advice. "He was quite old, but he was a very wise, wiley figure," Bobby Kennedy recalled of Kane. "My grandfather, of course, felt very strongly about it, and he felt very close to my brother. But I think that his effectiveness, in some of these areas, was not overwhelming."

At an early strategy session, the octogenarian Honey Fitz unexpectedly showed up, ready for action, as if breathing in new life from a room filled with smoke. Kane immediately turned to a gofer.

"Get that son of a bitch out of here," he demanded, in the direction of the former mayor.

Overhearing it, the candidate was shocked.

"Who?" Jack asked. "*Grampa?*"

Kane nodded, insisting the old man leave the room. When Jack later relayed the story, Joe Kennedy agreed with his cousin's decision. Kane also convinced him that Jack should run for Congress rather than as lieutenant governor—a wise choice in a year when the Democrats would wind up losing the statewide races to the Republicans.

As tough-talking as he seemed, Kane's nimble mind immediately assessed the political chances of the young candidate. "Your Jack is worth a king's ransom," Kane told the candidate's father. "He has poise, a fine Celtic map. A most engaging smile." Joe Kennedy was amazed by his son's political transformation, his willingness to shake hands for hours. "I never thought Jack had it in him," he marveled. Kane advised his cousin that he should "buy him in" and fork over the money for a first-class campaign. "It takes three things to win," Kane taught his pupils. "The first is money and the second is money and third is money."

Along with the neighborhood galoots and the professional pols enticed by cash, the Kennedy campaign employed sophisticated advertising and one of the nation's top election polling firms to gauge the candidate's strengths and weaknesses. Despite his old-school manner, Kane thought up the campaign's forward-looking slogan: "*A New Generation Offers a Leader.*" It exquisitely matched Jack Kennedy and the image they wanted to project. In a crowded Democratic field of ten candidates, cash helped eliminate the competition. One candidate served as a stalking horse, given $7,500 by Kane to "stay in or get out" of the race, depending on how he was needed. When long-time city council member Joseph Russo jumped into the race, Kane found another Joseph Russo and convinced him to put his name on the ballot to confuse the electorate and siphon off votes from the real thing—a ploy that Honey Fitz remembered from the old days. (Faced with a similar situation in 1907, Fitzgerald issued campaign ads that warned: "*Vote for the original John F. Beware of substitutes!*") Kennedy's campaign wasn't the only one employing underhanded tactics. In some predominantly Irish districts, one candidate charged erroneously that Jack's sister, Kathleen, had married a relative of Oliver Cromwell, the hated British foe, and brought up the Massacre at Drogheda and memories of Cromwell's Irish victims.

Not to be outdone, Joe Kennedy enlisted an old Irish pol, Michael J. Ward, who years earlier as Boston's School Committee chairman had proposed half seriously that Eamon De Valera be imported as the city's new superintendent of schools. At the tea parties and other affairs sponsored by the campaign, another Irishman, Joseph F. Leahy, sang Irish songs, and Jack in particular enjoyed hearing renditions of "Danny Boy." The Harvard boy, never distant or haughty, reveled in the company of these old Irish pols and their tales. Patsy Mulkern, a crusty pol brought in by Kane, showed Jack how to work a crowd in taverns, hotel lobbies and street corners. On their first day of campaigning together in East Boston, Mulkern upbraided the millionaire's son on his appearance. "For the love of Christ, take the sneakers off, Jack," exclaimed Mulkern, who wasn't too fond of Jack's pink Oxford shirt, either. "Are you going to play golf, or are you a candidate?" Mulkern was "one of the Damon Runyon characters that you'd get from the South End," recalled Frank Morrissey, another Kennedy aide. "A real Irish talker, or whisperer or wailer, but he could really talk and he would be in an out with Jack to give him an understanding of how the rougher element in the particular Congressional district worked."

BY 1946, THE BOSTON of Kennedy's youth was rapidly changing. Within two years, the city's two most familiar Irish Catholic figures had faded from their positions of authority.

James Michael Curley, the nemesis of Honey Fitz during his own career at City Hall, was old and broke, forced to pay a huge sum of money after being convicted of fraud. He'd spent several years in the political wilderness, but managed to win the 11th Congressional District seat in 1942. His need for cash convinced him not to stay long in Washington. Joe Kennedy, mainly through Kane's intervention, offered to pay off Curley's debts, estimated at around $40,000. He'd also finance an upcoming mayoral campaign to the tune of $100,000, if Curley would relinquish the congressional seat being eyed for his son. Curley took the money. He predicted the young man taking his place possessed a "double-barreled name" sure to win the election. As he assessed, "With those two names, Fitzgerald and Kennedy, how can he miss?" Though Curley won his last hurrah for City Hall in 1945 (the thinly veiled novel of Curley's life, *The Last Hurrah,* was eventually made into a movie starring Spencer Tracy), the Purple Shamrock was convicted for mail fraud and sent to federal prison. The man of a thousand comebacks would never recover.

Another constant in the lives of Boston's Irish Catholics—Cardinal William Henry O'Connell—died in his bed at age eighty-four. A stalwart of orthodoxy and ethnocentricity, O'Connell's devotion to the cause of Irish freedom was nearly as great as it was to the church. Both a confessor and a protector of the Kennedys, O'Connell was succeeded by his top aide, Bishop Richard Cushing, a son of South Boston Irish immigrants, who would become even more of a family intimate. At first glance, Cushing, with his lantern-jaw, gravelly voice and rugged appearance, seemed every bit as conservative as his predecessor. Like O'Connell, Cushing warned Catholics early in his career about the dangers of secularism, preferring the faithful to remain in parochial school rather than attend public institutions. Cushing, educated at the Jesuit-run Boston College, also portrayed Harvard as a citadel of anti-Catholicism and shared similar views as Joe Kennedy about the treatment of Irish Catholics in Boston. "The only place for an Irishman in Boston was in the church or in politics," Cushing recalled of his options as a young man. "As far as banking was concerned, the 'Irish need not apply.'"

As Cushing exerted his influence over Boston, however, his views and policies parted significantly from those of his predecessor. He spoke out strongly against incidents of violence and bigotry directed against Jews and other minorities, crimes perpetrated mainly by Catholic youths. Eventually, he helped create a Catholic-Jewish committee to foster dialogue and work for the city's benefit. "Cushing was more than a new man in town with a different way of doing things," wrote Thomas O'Connor in his history of the Boston Irish. "He helped define a new level of human relations in an archdiocese theretofore noted for bitter sometimes violent conflicts among people of different religious, ethnic and racial backgrounds." From the pulpit and in public sessions, Cushing promised to refrain from "all arguments with our non-Catholic neighbors and from all purely defensive talk about Catholicism." But Cushing's emerging liberal views did not sit well with church conservatives such as Cardinal Spellman, an old rival from the time when they had worked together as auxiliary bishops for O'Connell in Boston. From his powerful position in New York, Spellman used his close ties with the Pope in Rome for more than a decade to keep Cushing from being named cardinal. Cushing would overcome that obstacle with the help of the Kennedys.

DURING THE 1946 CAMPAIGN, Cushing often introduced Jack Kennedy during appearances at parochial schools, Knights of Columbus gatherings and in church meeting halls. The prelate first met Jack and his brother, Joe, during their college years. Not one to show his religious convictions openly, Jack admired the down-to-earth manner of Cushing, whose faith

appeared rooted in good works rather than in ceremony or dogma. Like
Kennedy himself, Cushing came to represent the intentions of many
post–World War II Catholics, generations removed from the immigrant
experience, who wanted to avoid the class and ethnic divisions of the past.
"The Archbishop had a great feeling of affection for Jack because he represented integrity and capacity and the best that we had as far as the Irish
Catholics were concerned; that he was a credit to his faith; he was a credit
to his people," recalled Morrissey, who often served as a conduit between
the two. For the next decade, the major connections between Cushing and
the Kennedy political organization were handled by this short, fast-talking
firecracker of a man. Morrissey had gotten to know Cushing, the diocese's
chief fundraiser and head of the Society for the Propagation of the Faith,
and enlisted the churchman in Kennedy's cause. "I brought Jack over and
we developed, through the father, a tremendous affection that started right
before the Congressional fight, that maintained itself all through the years,
down to the time that Jack became President," Morrissey recalled years
later.

Although Rose and Joe Kennedy knew many priests and bishops,
including the Pope himself, Cushing was different. Though tending to their
family's spiritual needs, O'Connell and Spellman were almost too diplomatic, always keeping up a barrier of protocol and decorum. Cushing had
no such reserve toward the Kennedys in his manner, which was genuine
and sincere. He became the spiritual counselor "for all the family,"
Morrissey said. "He had a simpleness and a deep compassion and understanding, so every crisis that they sought spiritual comfort, the Cardinal
was always there—always."

Money became another form of communion between Cushing and the
Kennedys, serving their mutual interests. Though once a discreet donor,
Joe Kennedy increasingly made sure the family's charitable largesse was
noticed by the public. During the early 1940s, when Rosemary's behavior
after her botched lobotomy turned sullen and erratic, Cushing helped the
family find a suitable Catholic-run home for their daughter at a Wisconsin
institution for the mentally retarded. When the foundation set up in Joseph
Kennedy Jr.'s memory decided to focus on mental retardation, one of
its most sizeable donations went to a new hospital for retarded children in
the Boston area overseen by Cushing's diocese. To avoid attention to
Rosemary's condition, Cushing claimed the hospital would be dedicated
to helping "poor" children. In August 1946, a few months before the election, the diocesan newspaper, the *Boston Pilot,* ran a photo of John
Kennedy, now thin, almost emaciated-looking, and his mother as they

handed over a $600,000 check to Cushing for the new facility named in Joe Jr.'s memory.

Repeatedly, the Kennedys used donations to church-run and Catholic-affiliated organizations to build up Jack's political reputation. A memo prepared by Morrissey for his boss, the senior Kennedy, listed each group and the amount given, and included such names as United Catholic Charities, St. Mary's Hospital, Franciscan Sisters of Mary, Christ Child Society, Catholic Women's Club, Mother Damman Memorial, League of Catholic Women, Convent of Our Lady of the Cenacle and Guild of the Infant Savior. Although these donations undoubtedly did much good, they also expanded the political awareness of Kennedy's name. Joseph Casey, the 1942 Senate candidate picked by FDR and hurt by Joe Kennedy's money, later called the foundation's gifts "perfectly legitimate" and even "laudatory," but nevertheless insisted they were "political currency."

Over time, Morrissey and the senior Kennedy judged some donations almost solely for their political impact. Morrissey used his wide contacts within Cushing's diocese, including many priests, monks and nuns, to build up support among the Italians and Poles as well as the Irish. For example, in deciding on two requests for money from the Home for Italian Children and the Don Orione Rest Home, Morrissey provided a stark analysis to his boss about their possible political benefit. "Monsignor Haberlin wanted to be remembered to you personally and he feels [Jack Kennedy] is still in excellent shape as far as the Italian vote is concerned," he concluded to Joe Kennedy in one memo. In a follow-up note, Morrissey recalled how the monsignor became overjoyed when he said the Kennedys were thinking of a $65,000 donation for the Don Orione Home. "I think on this gift to the Don Orione Home, Mr. Kennedy, with your permission, I can build this up to a tremendous thing among the Italians in making sure that Jack gets a maximum amount of publicity on it," Morrissey explained. "I have already planted a couple of thoughts with the good people over there but I have not stated that you would definitely give that amount to them as yet."

With Morrissey as his right-hand man, Joe Kennedy wielded the foundation's money as part of a carrot-on-the-stick approach. One Franciscan monk, desperate for funds for his seminary, showed up at the wedding of Jack's sister, Patricia, hoping to get the attention of the senior Kennedy. "As you may recall, Rev. John J. Trella . . . is the little Franciscan who attended each of your weddings and has been trying desperately to present the case of the Franciscans to you," Morrissey began, detailing how he met with the friar after the wedding. The Franciscan said he had met with the superiors of his religious order and offered an exchange to the Kennedys. According to Morrissey, the friar "feels that he could make you or Jack a member of the Franciscan Order giving you the title of O.F.M. which he says has been given only to two people in the United States. He claims that if any assistance is given the Franciscans, that they will announce it in each of their churches that he has listed in the letter and would bring it to the attention of all their friends at the big banquet. He also enclosed a magazine that they publish in which he states that they would give the Foundation or the Senator [Jack Kennedy] or anyone you desire a write-up." Morrissey argued the money should be dispensed to bolster established areas of political support. The priest at the Assumption School in East Boston, which Joe attended as a youngster, was delighted to learn of a gift, Morrissey reported, and "stated very clearly that not only would there be a placque [sic] there in honor of your father and mother but that he would announce it from the altar and through the East Boston newspapers."

Joe Kennedy kept in constant contact with Cushing about how the foundation money should be dispensed around Boston. "I would like to find out how the Archbishop feels about this organization," he instructed Morrissey. Over time, Kennedy realized that nearly all the family foundation's donations were invested in the church. "I would like to do something for some charities that are not Catholic, because 96 or 97 percent of what money we give goes to Catholic causes, but I don't want to do anything for them unless they really help as they should," he directed. Morrissey responded by letting the boss know of some "negro" groups that were being "buttered" with Kennedy largesse.

Although ostensibly working for Jack, Morrissey spent a large amount of time dealing with the archbishop and the senior Kennedy, no easy task to be sure. Both men possessed very similar personalities—outspoken and direct, Morrissey remembered, which sometimes caused difficulties. Unlike the condescending manner of a Cardinal O'Connell, Cushing seemed to defer to Joe Kennedy's power and money, as did nearly everyone in his world. As Cushing himself later admitted, "At first, Joe and I didn't hit it off at all."

Their most intense clash occurred over the foundation's funding for the Joseph P. Kennedy Jr. Memorial, the hospital for retarded children. A newspaper article in the *Boston Post,* based on a public talk given by Cushing, suggested that the Kennedys had welched on a promise of more funding for the facility. In fact, the foundation gave $725,000 to create the hospital with the agreement that Cushing would find other donors for the rest of the construction and operating budgets. "The archbishop expressed the belief that the Kennedy Foundation should make a contribution for this purpose since it bears the Kennedy name," the *Post* reported. As soon as he spotted the story, Cushing knew he was in trouble. He hurriedly contacted the reporter, who sent Cushing a handwritten letter of apology; it was then forwarded to Kennedy with a more formal letter of explanation from Cushing himself. "Having read his article, I was shocked to put it mildly," the archbishop confessed. When he arrived home in New York from Chicago, Joe Kennedy erupted over the archbishop's reported comments. "Needless to say, Mrs. Kennedy and I—indeed, the whole family—were deeply shocked and grieved by your reported remarks," he began unforgivingly. Despite Cushing's denials and apologies, Kennedy told the archbishop that he had heard rumors to the same effect. "Naturally, [I] gave them no credence at the time, nor even thought it necessary to bring them to your attention, in view of the clarity of our understanding of your relationship and that of the Foundation to the operating problems of the Memorial." Kennedy took this occasion to demand that his own aides review the church's finances at the hospital to find out why it needed more money and to make it operate "on an efficient and business-like basis."

Cushing never forgot his lesson. When dealing with the elder Kennedy, Cushing acted warily. Joe Kennedy didn't want to be perceived, in Cushing's phrase, as "a Santa Claus." The Kennedy patriarch insisted upon getting value for his charitable dollar, both in this world and the next. "If one has been fortunate enough, with God's help, to amass a fortune, one comes to a sense of realization that God must have meant him to give so that he could make it possible, in a measure, for his noble workers, like yourself, to carry on His charity," he explained to Cushing. In thanking him for another $250,000 check in the mid–1950s, the archbishop passed along praise for Kennedy from the FBI director, J. Edgar Hoover, for whom, FBI records later showed, the prelate acted as a government informant. "He certainly has tremendous admiration and esteem for you," the archbishop told Joe. "It is really a remarkable thing that the only Catholic layman in this country, in my estimation, who is mentioned by the highest leaders of the country is yourself. That is a tremendous tribute to you but it is also a manifestation of our own weakness. Would that we had hundreds like you."

Aside from hefty donations, Cushing knew Joe Kennedy also wielded other power over him. For more than a decade, Cushing waited for Rome to appoint him a cardinal, a fairly common move after an archbishop had served for a while in a diocese as large as Boston. But Cushing knew that Spellman had put a damper on his elevation and was grateful for any assistance that Joe Kennedy could provide. When Joe Kennedy visited with the

Pope in Rome, Frank Morrissey quickly relayed to Cushing back in Boston that his boss had put in a good word for him. "You will never know how grateful I am for your thoughtfulness in speaking so laudatory about me and the activity of the Archdiocese to His Holiness," Cushing wrote to Joe. "I really feel that you were the only man in the Church who could speak adequately and effectively to the Pope about the status of our sector of the vineyard. . . . Confidentially let me tell you, that I never had a satisfactory Papal audience and I had no one close to His Holiness to say a kind word for us."

When he returned to America, Kennedy wrote back to say that he was "deeply touched" by Cushing's candid admission and tried to buck up his spirits in the same way he might for one of his family. Kennedy told him of his talk with his long-time friend, Count Enrico Galeazzi, "who, as you know, next to the Holy Father's nephew, Prince Pacelli, is the closest man to the Holy Father and sees him every day." Because of his talks in Rome about Cushing, Kennedy added, he was hopeful of "some visible sign of the Holy Father's great satisfaction of the work being done by you." Kennedy subtly underlined just how much effort he had made on Cushing's behalf. "This may seem like stepping into a situation that is none of my business, but I made it very clear that as a Catholic, as a Bostonian, as a man who recognizes such a magnificent contribution to the Church's work, I feel completely justified in my attitude." For this successful intervention with Rome, Kennedy earned the undying gratitude of Cushing, who became a cardinal in 1958.

Joe Kennedy appreciated Cushing's own contribution to the spiritual life of his family, and became indebted for his many kindnesses. The cardinal counseled Rose and encouraged her efforts at public speaking, and he befriended Jack, whom Cushing called his "best friend." In politics, Jack Kennedy continued to receive blessings from his association with Cushing, such as the time he recited the rosary with him on a radio program. "I believe this is the only time a layman has ever had this privilege," gushed the president of Assumption College, a small Catholic school in Worcester, in a letter to Joe Kennedy. Cushing, though not a formally declared partisan, couldn't help showing his public support for Jack. "He has a hard fight but I am very optimistic about his success," he wrote to Joe about his son's upcoming election. The old man himself recognized Cushing's contributions to his fallen son's memorial and promoting the Kennedy name among the voters of Boston. "To see an idea brought to fruition under the guidance of a great church man like yourself, must give to anyone the same satisfaction that it gives to Rose and me," Joe wrote. "Your interest in Jack and Bobby and Teddy has so touched our hearts that we do not feel that we can ever repay you in any way whatsoever."

THE EXTENSIVE TIES between religion and politics in Jack Kennedy's early success in Boston remained largely unknown. The campaign's fresh-faced volunteers, many of them pushed to the forefront by Joe Kane, obscured the truth of who was really responsible for its success. Kane, Morrissey and Dave Powers already knew, and other newcomers such as Mark Dalton, hired as a speechwriter, found out when they got their marching orders. "He'd be sitting in his hotel room, somewhat in shadow," recalled Dalton about the candidate's father. "With him would usually be Joe Timilty, former Police Commissioner, and Archbishop Cushing. In this sense he was surrounded by the powers sacred and secular, both of them subordinate to him. I remember once when he got mad at Cushing and yelled, 'Who the hell does he think he is? If he wants that little red cardinal's hat he'd better shape up because I've got a hell of a lot more friends in Rome than he does.' It was strong stuff for a young Catholic man like myself. Going to see Mr. Kennedy in those days was like going to visit God."

When the November 1946 election returns came in, the Irish Catholics in Boston were disappointed. In the U.S. Senate race, the Democratic incumbent David Walsh, the state's first Irish Catholic elected to the post, lost to Republican Henry Cabot Lodge Jr. The Democrats' ticket of Maurice Tobin and Paul Dever, running for governor and lieutenant governor, also lost decisively to the Republican ticket, headed by Robert Fiske Bradford, in what one writer called "a direct confrontation between the Catholic Irish and the Brahmins." For the most part in Massachusetts, the Brahmins won. But a Democratic win in the 11th District was never in doubt. Twenty-nine-year-old John F. Kennedy, who had beaten a crowded field in the party's primary contest in mid-June, handily defeated the Republican, Lester W. Bowen, by nearly a three-to-one margin. On primary night, Jack, once a cool, detached observer, shook the hand of every campaign worker he could find and, with tears brimming in his eyes, expressed thanks. Honey Fitz, who had introduced his grandson each Sunday to dozens of parishioners at St. Stephen's Church—and had also taught him to remember each name with the face—was overjoyed. He jumped up with a jig on a table and began singing his trademark, "Sweet Adeline."

Jack Kennedy won by embracing his roots, a move of political necessity in Boston and, perhaps more than his critics realized, of personal choice. His campaign employed virtually every aspect of Irish politics in Boston, and yet somehow pushed its possibilities into a different era, leaving behind the days of Curley, Cardinal O'Connell and his own Honey Fitz. When the election results were announced, his grandfather predicted that Jack would become the first Irish Catholic elected as president—the dream his father had cherished for his lost brother. Not until days after Election Day did it all seem to sink in. At an Armistice Day ceremony at an American Legion hall in Charlestown, Jack gave his usual political speech, moving along gracefully until he hit one particular line: "No greater love has a man than he who gives up his life for his brother." Suddenly, Kennedy started to cry.

"He broke down and was unable to finish the speech," recalled Mary McNeely, a supporter. "An elderly little woman, Mrs. Lillian Keeney, got up to carry on for Jack. While I played the piano, she sang 'Too-Ra-Loo-Ra-Loo-Ra.' And whenever I met Jack after that, he always asked for that."

The song, as Kennedy well knew, was an Irish lullaby.

Chapter Sixteen

Eire

No FINER CASTLE IN IRELAND existed than Lismore, and for Kathleen Kennedy, there was certainly no grander tribute to her dead husband than the ancestral estate with eight thousand pastoral acres in the heart of Waterford County, just south of Tipperary. Like some fairy-tale castle, Lismore's vast stone structure, with its massive square towers and turrets, loomed above a rocky bluff resting along the River Blackway, silently attesting to the many decades the Cavendishes had presided over the valley.

In a postcard sent home to Massachusetts, Lismore Castle emblazoned on its front, Kick scribbled a little arrow pointing to a small window in the mammoth building, whimsically adding the words, "My room."

During his first summer as a congressman in 1947, Jack decided to visit Lismore as a guest of his widowed sister, known to all as Lady Hartington. Lismore possessed a fascinating past for a history buff like Jack. In 1185, King John of England built a stone castle on the grounds, originally the site of a monastery for Catholic priests, monks and nuns, and later turned it over to the church for use as a bishop's palatial residence. In 1589, Sir Walter Raleigh bought the castle, and when he was imprisoned for high treason a decade later, he sold it to Richard Boyle, the first Earl of Cork. During the reign of Cromwell, Irish Catholic confederates sacked both the town and Lismore Castle, but eventually the British gained control and the castle fell into the hands of the Cavendish family, starting with the fourth Duke of Devonshire in 1753. Billy's forebear, the sixth Duke of Devonshire, a patron of Charles Dickens and William Makepeace Thackeray, restored the ancient castle to its almost magical quality. Inside were paintings by the masters,

Flemish tapestries, several dozen bedrooms, a massive fireplace in the draw-ing room and a church-like banquet hall. Lismore served mainly as a sum-mer home for the wealthy Cavendish family and their guests, including Adele Astaire, the widow of Billy's uncle and sister of the American enter-tainer Fred Astaire, who sometimes paid a visit. Captivated by its beauty, Kick wondered in a letter home just how far away her own forebears, the Irish Kennedys, once lived from this castle. "The food is terrific. I shall burst before returning to England," she explained to her parents, writing on Lismore Castle stationary. "The people are so charming as ever and I wish I knew where our ancestors came from."

During Jack's 1946 congressional race in Boston, Kathleen was one of the few family members (other than the disabled Rosemary) who didn't help in the effort. The Kennedys kept her far from the limelight because of concern for the political consequences of Kick's marriage to a British Protestant marquis. Though they fought side-by-side with the British dur-ing the war, many Irish-Americans could not forget Great Britain's past with Ireland. Before she arrived home for a visit in September 1945, Kick wondered whether she "might give some lectures" in Boston on the work of the Red Cross in Great Britain. "What does Daddy think of the idea?" she asked, to no avail.

From his room inside the Hotel Bellevue, Jack and his band of Boston Irish political advisers worried that his family might be appearing a bit too Anglophile. With his usual wit, Jack wrote a note addressed "Dear Family" and began, "Just a question to ask whether you're all with me." He cited newspaper accounts about Rose Kennedy and Lady Astor appearing together, a photograph of Kick identified as "Lady Hartington" and a speech by his father suggesting that the United States forgive its British loans.

"Let's not forget," Jack reminded them,

"1. That they read the papers here.

2. That I'm running for Congress, not Parliament."

From the other side of the Atlantic, Kick cheered when she learned Jack had won the election. In a letter to her brother, Kick gushed "how terrifi-cally pleased I am for you. Everyone says you were so good in the election and the outcome must have been a great source of satisfaction." With the wry sense of humor they both shared, Kick alluded to her brother's pro-Irish views in the congressional race in Boston and how that perception was so different abroad. Somehow, Jack managed to benefit from people's perceptions of him, regardless of the reality. "Gee, aren't you lucky?" she wrote a month after his victory. "The folks here think you are madly pro-British so don't start destroying that illusion until I get my house fixed. The painters might just not like yóur attitude!"

ENGLAND WAS A pleasant memory for the rest of the Kennedys, but for Kathleen, the war-battered nation became a permanent home. During her brief stays in Massachusetts, Kick felt a distance from her mother, as though Rose could not bring herself to forgive or forget her daughter's marriage into a family with such an anti–Irish Catholic history. Despite her vaunted faith, Rose could not overcome her daughter's actions, and England became a spiritual refuge for Kick as much as a place to live. After Billy's death, Kick seemed committed to returning to her religion, hoping to please her parents. "Dearest Mother," she wrote home in one letter, "You will be glad to hear that I am writing this from the convent where I have been for the last two days making the annual retreat." At this religious gathering for British Catholics—a small but active band of converts and born believers in London—Kick enjoyed the company of her friend and fellow Catholic, Sissy Ormsby-Gore. "As the weather has been amazingly warm and convents are so peaceful and tranquil I depart tomorrow feeling blessed in both body and soul," Kick told her parents. To her brother Jack, she acknowledged her difficulties. "How are Pa and Ma? I hope they are better," she wrote a few months later. "Since my short trip to the convent things somehow look much better."

Though she was busy reestablishing her relationship with her family and the church, Kathleen learned to cast a wary eye on the Irish. Her stays at Lismore Castle were relaxing ("a peaceful atmosphere which Mother would love"), but her hectic trips up to Dublin gave her the chance to observe Ireland close up. "The Irish certainly can go wild," she observed after attending a few parties on the small island called Ireland's Eye, a bit north of the capital. A friend of her father's took her to the racetrack, where she was introduced to "all the government people, who by the way all look like gunmen, as 'Joe Kennedy's daughter.'" When Jack visited briefly in 1945, he mentioned the possibility of buying an Irish thoroughbred as a gift for their father to run at the Hialeah track in Florida. The historic struggle between the Irish and the British, so much a part of her own family history, held little meaning for Kick except in the most personal terms. After staying with family friends at the U.S. embassy at Phoenix Park, Kick learned that the residence had been the site where Billy's relative died many years earlier when he was assassinated by knife-wielding pro-IRA men. "Another thing which I didn't know about this house then," she wrote.

"Lord Frederick Cavendish, Billy's great, great uncle, was brought in here, dying, when shot [sic] by Irish patriots in 1882." The thought of political assassination by Irish terrorists, no matter what Grandpa Fitz's views, was repugnant to Lady Hartington.

In her letters home, Kick tried to maintain a girlish quality in her voice, never letting on to her parents about the complexities of her personal life. Lonely and at times despondent, Kick contemplated marriage to Richard Wood, scion of the politically connected Halifax family, who owned their own huge estates in England and Ireland; but again, there were nettlesome questions of a mixed marriage to a Protestant. Wood received a large catechism text, *Apologetics and Catholic Doctrine,* and, like a schoolboy, dutifully studied at Kathleen's request. The book, published in Dublin and popular among many young Catholics, was written in understandable yet devout terms by Archbishop Michael Sheehan, an Oxford-educated priest born in Waterford who also favored a return to Gaelic in Irish life. Sheehan's aim was virtually the same as Rose Kennedy's intent—*"not only to teach children religion but also to teach them to be religious; not only to teach them what they must believe and do in order to be saved, but also to help them love Our Lord and Saviour with a great, personal love, and to love the Church he founded."* Whether Sheehan's book was given to her by Father D'Arcy, sent by her mother or obtained on her own, its presence underscored Kick's intent to make some rectification with her church, even if the realities of her own life fought against it. Unlike Billy, Richard Wood told her that he wouldn't object to their children growing up as Catholics if they married. Wood couldn't accept some central mysteries of the church, however, such as the Immaculate Conception of the Virgin Mary and the infallibility of the pontiff. "But that's what I was taught," Kick insisted. For whatever reasons, her talk of marriage to Wood ended soon after she met a married man, Peter Fitzwilliam.

Her attraction to the Earl of Fitzwilliam, a dashing older man of thirty-seven with a commanding presence and an alcoholic wife, would soon prove overwhelming. She flung herself into a deeply passionate love affair for perhaps the first time in her life. A handful of friends in Britain who learned of her secret trysts with Fitzwilliam tried to dissuade her, some because of Peter's superficial nature, and others, among them Sissy Ormsby-Gore, because of the renewed religious conflict such a marriage would portend. Kick didn't breathe a word of the affair to her family, not even when her mother and sister Patricia visited Lismore Castle. She would wait to tell Jack when he arrived in Ireland late that summer in 1947. If anyone would understand, it would be her brother.

The cost of being Irish was sometimes more than Jack Kennedy could bear. During the 1946 campaign, he resisted wearing the fedoras pushed on his head by Joe Kane, making an allowance only once, quite briefly, at a parade where he knew he'd see his mother, who also favored the old-fogey chapeaux worn by every Irish Catholic male in Boston of a certain age. At a St. Patrick's Day celebration, Jack donned a fedora as he passed Rose in the parade, then quickly ditched it. A more troublesome price of Irish politics in Boston came due in the matter of a man who seemed born to wear a fedora—James Michael Curley, the imprisoned mayor, whose yes-men and lickspittle roused enough political support to circulate a petition for a presidential pardon, some kind of amnesty that would spring the Purple Shamrock from his jail cell. When John McCormack, the head of the congressional delegation and an old Curley supporter, brought it up on the House floor with the new congressman, Kennedy looked nauseated. "Has anyone talked with the President or anything?" Kennedy asked. McCormack, irked by his response, told him curtly that he didn't have to sign the petition if he didn't want.

Kennedy, though barely more than a beginner in Boston politics, knew that his failure to sign the petition would have serious consequences. Curley, for all his shenanigans, reflected much of the Irish Catholic experience in Boston: hardscrabble, tough, ambitious, clannish and keenly aware of slights from Brahmins and those who would look down their noses at the Irish. His lifelong dream, to be appointed by FDR as the American representative to the Vatican, was short-circuited because he was a Catholic at a time when only a Protestant would do. Sitting in Danbury federal prison, he stewed about the dead president he had once helped elect. "Am enclosing a clipping about another victim of FDR," he wrote a friend. "This list of victims of his sadistic tendencies continues to *grow,* and strange to relate all are Irish Catholics, Smith, Farley, Kennedy, Kelly, Nash, Hague, Walker, Walsh, Curley and others." More than 100,000 Bostonians petitioned President Truman to grant clemency to their hero, who claimed to be too ill for incarceration. Old Joe urged his son to come to the aid of the embattled mayor, reminding him that Curley had given up the seat Jack now occupied. Archbishop Cushing also urged compassion. But Jack, claiming to have checked out Curley's health problem and found it phony, was the only one in the Massachusetts delegation to refuse. Though his young supporters viewed Kennedy's decision as the idealistic mark of a new leader, it could very well have been an old-score settling for the family, a payback for Curley's part in sabotaging Honey Fitz's political career years earlier. By late summer 1947, with the Curley issue still heating up, Jack Kennedy was ready to escape by taking a long junket to Ireland.

For her brother's arrival, Kathleen made sure that Lismore Castle was filled with vivacious and interesting people. As she later recalled for her father, "I have never enjoyed a month so much and I think Jack has enjoyed it too." Anthony Eden, the dashing war hero and foreign minister during Churchill's Conservative government, "arrived loaded down with official-looking" documents but soon "got into the Irish spirit," and made fast friends with Jack. Sir Shane Leslie, a writer and a cousin of Winston Churchill's who converted to Catholicism and became an Irish nationalist, stayed for a time, and so did old friends—Tony Rosslyn, a member of Parliament, and the playwright William Douglas-Home, who had dated Kick before the war. With its lush accommodations and lively conversations, Lismore became a summer idyll—"one of the loveliest spots in the world"—for the two young Kennedys. "The newspapers never arrive, the telephone can barely work so it doesn't take long to get into the real old Irish atmosphere," Kick wrote home. "I could really spend six months of the year. Daddy, you simply must come next year."

Despite his ailing back, Jack couldn't keep still. As part of his congressional trip, Jack intended to investigate economic conditions, and met for an hour in Dublin with De Valera to discuss the Irish economy. On this trip north, he also visited a familiar haunt—Mulligan's on Poolbeg Street, where he had pushed back a creamy pint or two during his visit as a Hearst columnist in 1945. He'd first read of the musty old pub in James Joyce's *Dubliners,* and he had enjoyed its dark corners and the animated conversation of fellow journalists and the actors from the Theater Royal nearby. Jack Kennedy's interest in Irish lore also extended to the origins of his own family. Before he left America, he consulted his father's sister, Loretta Kennedy Connelly, in preparation for a visit to the Kennedy Homestead in Dunganstown, County Wexford. Back in the 1920s, Aunt Loretta, the family historian on the Kennedy side, had accompanied Jack's grandfather, P. J. Kennedy, when he visited relations in the old country, and she never forgot the trip. With a letter of introduction from Aunt Loretta, who was also his godmother, in his pocket, Jack set out one day to find his Irish cousins, whom he called "the original Kennedys."

AT FIRST, the drive in Kathleen's shining new American-made station wagon didn't seem that bad as Jack and a friend cruised from Lismore through Waterford and into New Ross, the river port city where his great-

grandfather had left with hopes of landing in America. Kick and her aristocratic friends thought Jack was crazy. They preferred to hit golf balls on a
nearby course that wasn't very well manicured but was good enough to
wile away some free time. With his bad back, Jack couldn't swing a club easily and, besides, he had harbored thoughts of this journey for a long time.
"I researched before I came over where the original Kennedys come from,"
he explained before leaving. "And it's not so far away, only about one hundred miles or so. And I'd like to go." He convinced one of Kick's friends,
Pamela Churchill, a beautiful woman recently divorced from the former
prime minister's son, to come along for the ride. As they turned south from
New Ross, the unpaved roads became muddier and narrower, barely wide
enough for one car to pass, let alone two. After consulting Aunt Loretta's
directions, Jack still couldn't find his way through Dunganstown, and rolled
down his window when he came upon a passerby, an older man named
Robert Burrell.

The American in the car inquired where the "Kennedy" family might
live. Burrell paused, thought for a moment, and then sent the traveler and
his companion to the only place he knew with a Kennedy name—the farm
of James Kennedy, about a half mile from the original Kennedy Homestead.
They pulled up to a farm not far from the banks of the River Barrow, and
were met by James Kennedy, his wife, Kitty, and their children, including a
spry, red-headed eight-year-old son, Patrick, who had been working in the
fields. All were a bit soiled that day from their work. Wearing casual clothes,
as if on a college outing, Jack introduced himself as a Kennedy cousin from
America and began almost immediately asking questions about their family heritage. "He was very thin and tall," remembered Patrick, more than
five decades later. "He had a camera and he took our picture. Unfortunately,
we didn't have a camera." Kitty prepared a cup of tea for their visitors, and
they chatted for nearly an hour with the young man who, unpretentiously,
mentioned his important job back in America. As they chatted, Jack realized his error. When he stopped the passerby, "he asked for the name
'Kennedy' and we were the only ones with the same name," explained
Patrick Kennedy. And so James Kennedy, ever gracious to his appreciative
American cousin, escorted the congressman to the old family homestead
where his great-grandfather had once lived.

Jack's mistake was easy enough to make. In the years since 1888—when
Patrick Kennedy's brothers successfully fought their eviction from the family homestead with the help of their American cousin, P. J. Kennedy—the
thirty-acre Kennedy Homestead had become known as the Ryan place.

During these years, Patrick's two brothers, James and John, had managed to resist eviction from the British landlord, Colonel Tottenham. Eventually they gained back rights to the property in the early twentieth century, which was passed down to the next generation of Kennedys. Several of the Kennedy cousins remained unmarried, and some emigrated to America. Ownership of the Kennedy Homestead wound up in the hands of second cousins, James Ryan and Mary Kennedy Ryan, a married couple who both had family ties to the original Kennedy owners. A man with a receding hairline and some features similar to those of his millionaire American cousin, James Ryan was the grandson of John Kennedy, the oldest brother of Patrick Kennedy, who had emigrated to Boston. His wife, Mary Kennedy Ryan, was the granddaughter of James Kennedy, Patrick's other brother, who also remained in Eire during the Famine. When Jack Kennedy arrived that sunny late summer day in 1947—nearly a hundred years to the day after his great-grandfather had left the farm for America—it was his cousin, Mary Kennedy Ryan, who came to the door.

"I'm John Kennedy from Massachusetts," he said, almost apologetically. "I believe we are related."

Mary Ryan, an ever practical woman, thoroughly eyed the stranger up and down, and cast an even more dubious gaze at the well-dressed British woman in his company before deciding whether to bother her husband, James Ryan, who was tending the fields beyond. If it weren't for the presence of her nearby cousin, James, she might have shown even more skepticism. But Mary Ryan did the Christian thing, welcoming her uninvited guests into her small farmhouse, and beckoned her husband. For the next two hours, while sipping more tea, Jack learned about the Kennedys who stayed in Ireland.

NEVER BEFORE had the long journey of the Irish diaspora seem so real, so personal, to Jack Kennedy than during this visit to the modest, almost primitive farm still toiled by his Kennedy cousins. Instead of a massive summer house by the shore in Hyannis and a winter place in Palm Beach with its own swimming pool, the home of these Kennedys was a simple whitewashed stone house with a thatched roof. Without electricity, most chores were performed manually. The barn sheltered five or six cows, a few pigs, three horses for the field and a pony to pull a wooden cart carrying bags of barley to market in New Ross. Though hardly an agricultural combine, the Kennedy Homestead, with its barnyard smells and Irish authenticity, exuded a distinct charm in Jack's eyes. He had found what he came looking for. Just how much was revealed about his family's history in Ireland is unclear.

At age forty-eight, Mary Kennedy Ryan looked very much like the hardworking farmer's wife that she was. She ruled a household made up of three young children—two daughters and a younger son, all under the age of ten. Her matronly clothes and her corpulent, bosomy figure suggested a gentle nature, but her wide, muscular hands and tough, determined stare stated otherwise. Indeed, as a young adult, Mary Kennedy had been a devoted and active member of the Irish Republican Army's women's auxiliary organization known as the Cumann na mBan, and had secretly carried guns and other weapons. With every bit of her fiber, Mary Kennedy Ryan despised the British oppression of her country and its crushing effect on her family. Two decades earlier, she and her husband had taken considerable risks for Ireland's independence and in the resulting civil war. "The IRA was her god," recalled Mary Ann Ryan, her eldest surviving daughter. "It never dissipated in my mother. She took that feeling to the grave with her."

The Kennedy family had supported the Republican cause for several generations, long before Mary Kennedy Ryan and her husband came along, stirred by their own unjust treatment from the British. Her uncle, James Kennedy, went to jail over the land eviction in the 1880s and barely managed to hold on to the farm. That indignity was not soon forgotten. "Mary Ryan was very aware of the way the British treated the Irish here," said her cousin, Patrick Kennedy, who tagged along as a boy in 1947 with his father, James, when they accompanied JFK to the family homestead. Both he and Mary Ryan's children attended St. Bridget's Church in Ballykelly, the same parish where JFK's great-grandfather, Patrick Kennedy, likely attended classes, at least for a few years, despite the provisions preventing Catholics from gaining an education. "I'm sure that the feeling (against the British) stretched back to Patrick Kennedy and his time," said his great-grandnephew, sitting in the kitchen of the old homestead many years later.

Though the Kennedys knew and grew to like Robert Burrell—the man who gave directions to Jack Kennedy—they were also well aware that Protestant families such as the Burrells had gained their choice farmland from the British. Mary's husband, James Ryan, a man considerably older than herself, had refused to bend his will to the British overseers while growing up in Wexford. As a lad, according to the story his family tells, Ryan was reprimanded for not tipping his hat to some high-ranking

Englishman as he passed by on a horse cart. He accepted the punishment as a badge of honor.

During the bloody era from 1916–1922, as Ireland convulsed and was split into two by treaty, the Kennedys in Wexford remained firmly in the Republican camp of De Valera, opposed to the treaty and the new government that would enforce it. Though the Catholic clergy condemned the violence and brutal tactics of the IRA, many young men such as James Ryan in Wexford were swept up by the group's nationalist outlook and its determination to rid Eire of its imperialist neighbor. Without missing Mass on Sundays, these Catholic young men enlisted in the fight to unite Ireland once and for all. The family remains oblique about what exact role James Ryan performed as a volunteer for the IRA during the fight for independence and the civil war. But when James Ryan passed away two years after Jack Kennedy's visit in 1947, he was given a military funeral in the custom of the IRA, and shots were fired over his grave, his daughter said. While speaking about her father, Mary Ann Ryan pulled out the medal with its green and gold ribbon that her father had earned with the IRA. Inscribed on its face were the words "Eire" and *Cogadh na Saoirse,* "The Fight for Freedom," with a crest of the four provinces and a soldier standing at attention. On the back, her father's name was etched along with his Wexford outfit: "J. Ryan, B.COY, SW Brigade, Old IRA." She displayed it affectionately as she sat at the kitchen table with her cousin, Patrick Kennedy, his fiery red hair now flecked with gray.

John W. Pierce, a local historian who has known the Dunganstown Kennedys for years and wrote a small book about the family, said that JFK's great-grandfather, Patrick Kennedy, had brothers and uncles actively involved in the Irish nationalism movement. "The sympathy of the family with the Republican cause was known and their house was open to provide safe haven for activists 'on the run,' and members of the family supported the nationalist side," Pierce wrote, without elaboration. In an interview, Pierce told the story of how the Kennedys provided refuge to Dan Breen, a notorious gunman in the IRA who years later became a member of the Irish Parliament. During the war for independence in 1919, Breen and another IRA member shot two policemen while helping to free an imprisoned Irish volunteer. A wanted poster for Breen printed by the British police, offering a reward of a thousand pounds, described Breen as having "grey eyes, short cocked nose and stout build" and a "sulky bulldog appearance; looks rather like a blacksmith coming from work." While on the lam during the Irish civil war, Breen made his way to Dunganstown with the aid of IRA underground members. Breen, like De Valera, opposed the treaty fashioned by Michael Collins, and his violent actions left him trying to evade the Irish Gardai, the police of the new Irish Republic. In his autobiography, Breen later recalled his guerilla fight for Irish freedom with "an army at one's heels and a thousand pounds on one's head." As the story goes, the Kennedy farmhouse near the River Barrow, the same one visited by JFK in 1947, became a temporary hideout for Breen. When the Gardai came knocking unexpectedly one night, Breen supposedly hid under the covers in a large bed, nestling between two young female Kennedy cousins who acted as though they were asleep. A history of Breen's colorful life makes mention of his flight into Wexford, but no specific documentation collaborates Pierce's tale of local color.

Similar tales of wartime courage involving Mary Kennedy Ryan are shared by her surviving daughter, Mary Ann. In an interview, she said her mother proudly joined the IRA's women's group, Cumann na mBan, like many other young women in the surrounding community. The group said its mission was "freedom for our nation and a complete end to all forms of discrimination against our gender." While resisting the British at every turn, the group's published ideals called for proper housing, better education, a return to Gaelic customs and free health care for all who needed it. "We in Cumann na mBan are working for an Ireland in which not a few individuals—but ALL shall enjoy the maximum amount of happiness which God permits in this passage of suffering and sorrow," it declared. Mary Kennedy Ryan stayed a committed member of the Cumann na mBan well into the 1930s, said her daughter. Though De Valera paternally instructed the group to act mainly as helpers with first aid and cooking for his male volunteers, Mary Kennedy Ryan, certainly no wilting flower, and other women got involved in the smuggling of armaments. "My mother would carry guns and money," recalled Mary Ann, whose soft voice underscored the boldness of her mother's actions. She carried the cash and materiel, either in carts or under her clothing, from a smuggling contact in New Ross to a secret hiding place not far from the farm of James Kennedy. Though some women were caught by the Gardai, Mary Kennedy Ryan had a knack for avoiding detection. "The women would be stopped and searched, but not my mother," said Mary Ann. "She was never stopped once."

DURING HIS two-hour visit, Jack Kennedy chatted amiably about the family's past with Mrs. Ryan and his other Irish relations, though it's not certain how much, if any, of their political activities were revealed to their third cousin from the United States. Mary Ann Ryan said that while her visiting American cousin may have gotten some inclination of her parents' views, it's unlikely the future president knew of his relatives' involvement with the IRA. "I don't think he knew," she concluded. Pierce, however, said it would be difficult to recount the past of the Kennedys in Ireland without mentioning their Irish Republican participation. He stressed that the IRA of Mary Kennedy Ryan's young adulthood, fairly commonplace among her contemporaries, was far different from the terrorist group of today. "I think the President was aware of his family's history and I don't think he would have held it against Mrs. Ryan," Pierce said. "She'd not have been an outcast like the current-day IRA people."

Whatever he learned, Jack Kennedy drove away that afternoon in 1947 enchanted by his visit with the Kennedys of Dunganstown. "Jack kept pressing on about his ancestors going to America and so on, trying to make the link," recalled Pamela Churchill, who did not share Jack's enthusiasm. After a long drive and a laborious afternoon listening to Irish stories, the former daughter-in-law of the famous British prime minister had heard quite enough. She waited patiently as Jack finished his tea and walked around the farm. In front of the barn, with the chickens milling around, Jack snapped a photograph of Mrs. Ryan, her children and their relatives, a copy of which he later sent to them. The faded black-and-white photo, still kept by the Ryans, shows the little girls in ponytails and the towheaded boys in dirty overalls; they had an austere, impoverished look reminiscent of American farm families during the Depression.

When they finally got into the car, Pamela Churchill issued a withering remark about Jack's Irish relatives. "I spent about an hour there surrounded by chickens and pigs, and left in a flow of nostalgia and sentiment," Kennedy recalled a decade afterward. "This was punctured by the English lady turning to me as we drove off and saying, 'That was just like Tobacco Road!' She had not understood at all the magic of the afternoon." In another, blunter assessment, Jack admitted, "I felt like kicking her out of the car."

When he returned to Lismore Castle, Jack relayed enthusiastically to his sister all he had witnessed: the sights, the sounds and the stories of their family. In one afternoon, Jack Kennedy had discovered his Irish roots, a visit he'd remember for the rest of his life. But Kick couldn't be more indifferent. Dinner had already been served at the castle and Jack and her friend Pamela were terribly late back from their excursion. In her best aristocratic tone, Kick listened to her brother and then quipped dismissively, "Well, did they have a bathroom?" As he dined inside the plush Irish castle of the

Devonshires, Jack couldn't help thinking of how much his own Irish-American family had accomplished in a century, and how things remained so different for his Kennedy relatives in Ireland. Reflecting on his own wealthy environs, Jack "thought about the cottage where my cousins lived, and I said to myself, 'What a contrast.'"

BEFORE JACK LEFT for America, Kick confided in him about her affair with Peter Fitzwilliam, the Englishman she intended to marry as soon as he gained a divorce. Jack, often a libertine in his own actions, appeared sympathetic while listening to her, yet remained almost priggish in his advice, the same tone he'd adopted in the past for such matters. In March 1942, aware of Kick's intent to return to London and marry Billy, Jack had cautioned: "I would advise strongly against any voyages to England to marry any Englishman." Though neither as orthodox as Eunice nor as righteous as young Bobby, Jack nevertheless remained guarded as he listened to Kick talk about her newest affair. They both knew what their parents' reaction would be. Though a loyal brother and a good listener, Jack knew when to keep quiet.

Near the end of his European trip, Jack became terribly sick, collapsing while in London and learning from doctors that he suffered from Addison's disease, an incurable condition he would keep secret for the rest of his life. "That young American friend of yours, the brother of Lady Hartington, he hasn't got a year to live," his London doctor confided to Pamela Churchill. The specter of an early death—always a very real possibility during the war—continued to haunt Jack Kennedy, enduring private pain from a host of illnesses while projecting a public image of youthful vigor. In the gloomiest times, Jack and his sister were very much alike in their defiance of death, insistent on the passions of life, even though so many of their contemporaries and loved ones had died. If Kick could find true love with Fitzwilliam, a man she obviously adored, how could he condemn her?

During 1948, while Jack ran for reelection, Kick struggled with her feelings and finally resolved to tell her parents. When she came home and broke the news, the reaction was far more severe than even she had anticipated. Her father's words were disappointing and disapproving, though he was nowhere nearly as emotional as her mother, Rose, who threatened to banish her from the family. Kathleen's scandalous affair with a married man not only would ostracize her from the church once again—undermining all her halfhearted claims of reconciliation with her faith after Billy's death—but have a deleterious impact on the political career of her brother. Kick's adultery was not only seen as socially and politically mortifying but as a particularly selfish act, as if falling in love should be gauged for its impact on her family's ambitions. To dissuade her, Eunice arranged a meeting for Kick with Bishop Fulton Sheen, a clergy member her older sister admired. At the last minute, though, Kick canceled her appointment. After her daughter left for England, Rose soon followed and confronted Kick at her London apartment, determined to win back her soul for the family and church. But they were too far apart for any resolution, and Kick could only shudder and cry. She hoped her father could somehow make things right for her.

Joe Kennedy, who at times believed he could bend the church to his will with enough money and persuasion, undoubtedly was alarmed by his daughter's behavior, and even more by its impact on his son's political ascension. Rose's admonishments, though motivated by her own religious fervor, clearly had his blessings. Joe suggested a convoluted plan in which Fitzwilliam would claim that he'd never been baptized and then gain the church's approval for his marriage by agreeing to certain stipulations. Kick knew that neither the church nor her proud future husband would ever go for such a ruse. Nevertheless, correspondences suggest that Joe Kennedy contacted his old friend in Rome, Count Enrico Galeazzi, to come up with some type of arrangement for his daughter that might be acceptable to the church. Kick convinced her father to meet Fitzwilliam and arranged for a meeting in France when her father visited in May 1948. At a Fitzwilliam family dinner where he announced his intention to marry Kick, Peter attempted a strained joke about the situation. "We're going off to try and persuade old Kennedy to agree to our getting married," he mentioned to a cousin. "If he objects, I'll go to see the Pope and offer to build him a church." After they married, he told Kick, they'd live in Ireland.

DESPITE WARNINGS of inclement weather, Fitzwilliam insisted the pilot of the small plane they rented in Paris fly them to Cannes for a meeting with Joe Kennedy. In the darkened skies, the plane flew fitfully through the wind and rain and smashed into the hills of the Rhone Valley, killing Kathleen Kennedy, Peter Fitzwilliam and all the others aboard. Rescue workers found her body crushed and in her luggage only a few possessions, including a photo album of her family and a string of rosary beads. Newspaper accounts of the crash in May 1948 identified the Earl of Fitzwilliam as a friend who had offered Kick a ride on the plane, but suggested nothing more. The rumors swirling around their affair were stilled.

In a hotel room, the elder Kennedy awoke to the news of his daughter's death and performed the sad task of identifying her body. Over the next several hours, all the Kennedys learned of the death of Kathleen, the daughter whose verve and wit had filled their hearts even at her most maddening. Rose chose to stay in Hyannis Port and leave the funeral arrangements to her husband. Though only a few weeks earlier she had rushed to London to confront her daughter about her impending marriage, Rose could not bring herself back to England to bury her. The Mass card Rose sent out for her daughter asked for prayers that suggested her daughter's soul might be in purgatory, an act that infuriated some of Kick's British friends. Other friends of the Kennedys, among them Lem Billings, suggested that Rose viewed her daughter's death "as a matter of God pointing his finger at Kathleen and saying *No!*" By today's standards, Rose's behavior can't be seen as anything but cold and condemning, a rigidity of faith that virtually cast Kick out of the family for her cardinal sins. In the context of Rose's Irish Catholic background in Boston, however, Kathleen's embrace of the Cavendishes, a notoriously anti-Catholic family and a scourge of Ireland, and then her romance with Fitzwilliam, a married British lord, were unforgivable offenses. What Rose had been taught about the Protestant cruelties in Ireland, about the strictures of the church that forbade marriage outside the faith, about the shame surrounding divorce and sex outside of marriage, had hardened her heart to the love her daughter had found, perhaps even made her envious. Certainly, if her heart was broken, Rose found herself unable to express it.

After several days of discussions in Europe, Joe Kennedy decided to accept the offer of the Duchess of Devonshire and have Kick buried next to Billy in the Cavendish family plot in England. A funeral Mass at Kick's favorite church, on Farm Street in London, was attended by dozens of her friends as well as top British officials and associates of the former U.S. ambassador to the Court of St. James, now a forlorn old man who sat by himself in a front pew, the only Kennedy family member there to say goodbye. At this church, the same Jesuits who once counseled Kick—long but ultimately fruitless discussions about how she might stay within the constraints of her church—now sprinkled holy water and incense on her flower-filled casket and administered the church's final rites of forgiveness.

BACK IN WASHINGTON, Jack learned of Kick's accident through a call to his home in Georgetown. He had been listening to the haunting, Irish-inspired melodies of the musical *Finian's Rainbow.* When a second call confirmed her death, Jack stared blankly at Billy Sutton, the tough Boston pol who became an aide. The brother and sister who were his contemporaries were now dead, like so many of his friends from the war. Kick's death seemed particularly senseless and cruel, for he loved her more than anybody. On the record player, a particular favorite filled the room with its sad lament:

I hear a breeze, a River Shannon breeze,
It may well be it's followed me across the seas.
Then tell me please:
How are things in Glocca Morra?

As the music played on, he didn't say anything about Kick's death. Instead, Jack made a brief remark to Sutton about what a great voice the song's singer, Ella Logan, possessed. Then he turned his head away. "When the news came that the fatal accident happened, he—you know, his eyes filled up with tears," Sutton recalled years later. "You know, when they say that the Kennedys never cry, don't believe that. They do. I saw them. He cried that morning for his sister, Kathleen."

For the rest of his days, Jack seemed accepting, almost with an odd detachment, about the capriciousness of human existence. At times, he engaged in morose, fatalistic discussions about death, ruminated about his almost certain prospects of dying young and wondered what were the best ways to die. With Lem Billings and other close friends, he questioned how a loving God could be so cruel. "The thing about Kathleen and Joe was their tremendous vitality," Kennedy explained years later. "Everything moving in their direction—that's what made it unfortunate. . . . For someone who is living at the peak, then to get cut off—that's the shock." He resolved to live at the peak himself. As if to make up for the premature deaths of his two siblings, Jack adopted a carpe diem strategy, wringing every bit of fun and excitement and good times from the life granted him. Time became a precious commodity, a gift he wouldn't squander. "Death was there—it had taken Joe and Kick and it was waiting for him," his pal Chuck Spalding observed. "So whenever he was in a situation, he tried to burn bright. . . . He had something nobody else did. It was just a heightened sense of being; there's no other way to describe it."

LEAVING HIS daughter's body behind, Joe Kennedy flew back to America a shattered man. Once home, he finally thanked Billy's parents for all their kindness in arranging Kick's funeral. "The only thing that helped me retain my sanity was your understanding manner in the whole sad affair," he wrote to the Duchess of Devonshire at summer's end. Billy's family put together the service at the graveside, presided over by a Catholic priest. Joe could not bear to acknowledge those around him. The duchess composed the epitaph on her gravestone: "JOY SHE GAVE JOY SHE HAS FOUND." In this hallowed ground of the Cavendish family, there were several reminders of the contradictions in Kick's life, including a wreath from Joe's old nemesis, Winston Churchill. In some of his letters, Joe tried to make sense of these conflicts.

"I realize that people say, 'You have so many other children, you can't be too depressed by Kick's death,' and I think that, to all intents and purposes, no one knows that I am depressed," he confessed to the duchess. "In fact, I have never acknowledged it even to Rose who, by the way, is 10,000 percent better than I am. Her terrifically strong faith has been a great help to her, along with her very strong will and determination not to give way."

Joe admired his wife's faith, something he knew he didn't possess, certainly not to the same extent, no matter how many times he attended Mass. In these tragic moments, Rose was tougher than he; the church more of a rock for her than for him. Joe found himself adrift in grief and melancholia. From the very outset, he struggled to make sense of his daughter's death. "We know so little about the next world we must think that they wanted just such a wonderful girl for themselves," he scribbled less than an hour after hearing the news of her death. "We must not feel sorry for her but for ourselves."

Because of who they were in politics, the Kennedys received numerous calls of sympathy and letters of condolences from the powerful, in Boston and around the nation. Because of who they were, Irish Catholics striving in a world of bigotry and resistance, Joe would be well aware of the clash of religion and cultures inherent in his daughter's death, and be perceptive enough to note at least some of the ironies. "If Kathleen had lived, I'd be the father of the Duchess of Devonshire, and father-in-law of the head of all the Masons in the world," he'd later say. Because of who they were within the church, Joe Kennedy received a letter from Rome saying that the Pope was praying for the Kennedys in their bereavement, "so terribly tried by the inscrutable God's Providence." In a letter to his old friend, Count Galeazzi, Joe made sure the Pope accurately understood his daughter's status within the church at the time of her death. He pointed out, as if talking to God's intermediary, that though his daughter had married the future Duke of Devonshire, a Protestant, he had been killed in the war. "So for the last three years Kathleen has been a widow and a devoted child of the church," he noted.

To Galeazzi, who knew that his friend's pride and love for his children was its own religion, the eldest Kennedy could acknowledge the depth of his own grief. The deaths of his son, daughter and son-in-law Billy seemed at times more than he could bear. "I know I have never recovered from the shock of Joe's death, and yet, it was in the war when so many other people were sharing equally devastating losses," Joe wrote. "However, the loss of Kathleen leaves me almost without spirit. . . . The sudden death of these three children has, as you can well imagine, left its mark on me and my hopes for the future."

Part III

Rise to the Presidency

"I have heard the statement that there will never be a Catholic President, this is all nonsense. When the right man is presented, the United States will choose him and not discriminate because of his religion."

—ARCHBISHOP JOHN IRELAND, 1917

Chapter Seventeen

The Irish Brahmin

HENRY CABOT LODGE JR., heir to one of the most patrician names in Massachusetts, looked unbeatable in 1952. With his slick clipped hair, modulated voice and chiseled chin, the dapper fifty-year-old legislator was "almost the archetype of the cultured, well-born and well-to-do New Englander," the *New York Times* observed, his very presence a reminder of where power still resided. The Irish might dominate Boston's inner-city wards, but statewide victories remained few and far between. Like some family heirloom, Lodge seemed destined to keep his seat in the United States Senate, the ultimate club, for a long time.

During early 1952, Lodge served as a campaign coordinator for Dwight D. Eisenhower's presidential effort; he was a respected figure on the national scene and virtually ignored his own situation back home. Six years earlier, he easily won election to the Senate and he felt no compelling need in this race to campaign before necessary. Lodge's political image so dominated the Massachusetts landscape that incumbent Governor Paul A. Dever, after carefully weighing his options, chose not to run against him. Only then did an opportunity open for another Democratic challenger, the young Congressman John F. Kennedy, who didn't seem to have any chance of winning.

Lodge's name was legend, as much for the deeds of his forebears as for his own. His family's history boasted, ever so discreetly, of six U.S. senators, including his grandfather, Henry Cabot Lodge, who held the same seat continuously from 1893 to 1924. Lodge's other ancestors included George Cabot, the nation's first secretary of the navy, appointed by President John

Adams; John Davis, who'd been both the state's governor and a U.S. senator; and a roster of distinguished relatives that included a brigadier general in the Civil War, secretary of state and even a candidate for vice president of the United States. When his father died at an early age, Lodge's grandfather oversaw his training and education. Lodge went to Harvard (where he captained the school's crew team) and worked for a time as a journalist (filing dispatches for the *New York Herald Tribune*). As the boy wonder of Massachusetts politics in 1936, he managed to grab the Republican nomination and then beat James Michael Curley in a surprise victory for the Senate (underlying the differences in their backgrounds, the Purple Shamrock referred to Lodge as "Little Boy Blue," but Curley's support among the Irish was undermined by a third-party candidate put up by Father Coughlin's Union Party). Lodge won reelection in 1942, but resigned from the Senate two years later to serve in World War II. When he returned, he ran again for the Senate, overwhelming a second Irish Catholic opponent, David Walsh, in 1946. Politically, Lodge adopted a decidedly more moderate and internationalist view than his grandfather. Nevertheless, his name stirred up visions of the retrenched Brahmin power, the kind that Jack Kennedy's family remembered all too well.

As a CONGRESSMAN in the 1890s, Honey Fitz had battled the "Old Senator" Lodge's attempts to pass legislation calling for literacy tests and other anti-immigrant measures. Years later, the former mayor lost a close race with Lodge for his U.S. Senate seat in a campaign that reprised their old fight over immigrants and Lodge's nativist views. Joe Kennedy harbored his own resentments against the Lodges. "All I ever heard when I was growing up," he later recalled, "was how Lodge's grandfather had helped put the stained glass windows into the Gate of Heaven Church in South Boston, and they were still talking about those stained glass windows in 1952." Joe Kennedy's objection seemed strictly territorial: the only ones to buy their way into the hearts of Boston's Irish Catholics would be his family, not the Lodges.

Differences in ethnicity and religion were underlined subtly by Lodge's 1952 campaign, but they were mentioned overtly and repeatedly by the press. In a profile of the two candidates, *Time* magazine identified Lodge's opponent as "Catholic Jack Kennedy," but made no similar reference to the senator's religion. In the same article affirming Senator Lodge's Brahmin background ("whose family tree is rooted in the neighborhood of Plymouth Rock"), the *New York Times* reported that "Representative

Kennedy is Irish Catholic to the core, but strictly of the 'lace curtain' variety, in view of the wealth and distinction of two or three generations of forebearers in this country." The national media, contrary to their later view of him, portrayed Jack Kennedy as a young Irishman, well educated and buoyed by his father's millions, but essentially just a new edition of the same old machine that had produced his grandfather and so many other Irish pols in Boston. Kennedy's personal proximity to the immigrant experience was presumed to be a major part of his appeal. As the *Times* concluded:

> A factor adding unusual zest to this struggle is that, in a purely local sense, it boils down essentially to a tug of war between two antithetical religious and ethnic groups—the predominantly Catholic immigrant group on the one hand, made up of people of comparatively recent Irish, Italian, French, Polish and other European ancestries, and the largely Protestant Yankee group on the other, mainly Anglo-Saxon in origin or so long in this country as to have submerged its Celtic or Latin affinities. . . . If not all the Irish, Italians and Poles in industrial Massachusetts today are [economically] "depressed," most of their immigrant parents and grandparents were, and they have taken their politics from them.

THESE DESCRIPTIONS of Jack Kennedy's 1952 campaign were understandable. His previous elections had been local efforts that still relied heavily on the Joe Kanes, Patsy Mulkerns and Francis X. Morrisseys of Irish machine politics. Aides such as Billy Sutton and Dave Powers were part of the trusted inner circle who shared the same ethnicity and cultural background as Kennedy (much as his father had assembled a similar coterie of Irish-Americans in his private business enterprises), though their usefulness was questionable. "He amused my brother," Bobby said of Sutton, "but he didn't contribute very much." The Senate campaign proved different and would change Jack Kennedy as a candidate. Step by step, his organization separated from the traditional Democratic Party in Boston, the vehicle used by an earlier generation of Irish Catholic politicians to get ahead. Instead, Jack relied on his father's huge fortune to finance his own organization—in effect, creating the Kennedy Party of Massachusetts, his younger brother being its tactical boss and "ruthless" enforcer. Even if he was "Irish Catholic to the core," as the *Times* put it, Jack's public veneer would be increasingly WASPish. He became an "Irish Brahmin," as one of his fellow Democrats said, only a bit admiringly. To realize his father's ambition, Kennedy kept his distance from the stereotypes of his Irish heritage and hoped that the prejudices of the past might not cloud their dream.

YEARS LATER, Thomas P. O'Neill Jr., a local politician known to the world as "Tip," remembered his original impression of Jack Kennedy. The bushy-haired young man with the gleaming smile seemed only a slightly updated version of a familiar big-city Irish pol. In a way that would make his grandfather proud, Kennedy showed "a real yen for patronage," recalled O'Neill, describing how Kennedy had prodded President Truman for his share of federal plum jobs to give out like some neighborhood chieftain. "He wanted to take care of this one; take care of that one." The 1952 campaign demanded something different, however, far more than a local approach to politics, and the Kennedy camp responded in a way that amazed even a hand as seasoned as O'Neill.

Propelled by innovative tactics and sophisticated mass media, Jack Kennedy pushed beyond the limits of any Irish Catholic politician from Boston before him. He wasn't some timeworn candidate who had worked his way up through the Democratic Party, beholden to the paybacks and favors of every hack on the greasy pole of politics. The family set up independent committees "in every city and town in the Commonwealth which was known as the Kennedy organization," recalled O'Neill. "And believe me, they were resented, for the most part, by the regular Democratic organization. But they were effective. You've got to admit, they were effective." Joe Kennedy hired top pollsters and publicity people for his son's challenge, and made sure local Kennedy groups received enough funds to project his message to the electorate. Rather than the "Irish switch" of old, the candidate was trained in such new political skills as looking earnestly into the eye of a television camera. Key strategists and organizers, such as Kenny O'Donnell, Bobby's long-time friend who became a top aide to JFK, were rewarded not with political jobs but with offers of plum jobs in the private sector arranged through Joe Kennedy's network of contacts. Different from the traditional political machine, those who worked for Kennedy were loyal only to him.

The Irish reliance on politics as a means of social ascendancy in Massachusetts reached its epitome in Jack Kennedy's 1952 campaign. Understanding the Irish need for acceptability and status, the Kennedys held a series of social teas around the state—large events in hotels and catering halls attended by hundreds, often thousands, of voters. Rose and her daughters—Eunice, Pat and Jean—acted as hostesses, capped off with a few words by the candidate himself. These teas were aimed at women voters, satisfying the same kind of social aspiration the Ace of Clubs fulfilled in Rose's youth. Each voter received an engraved invitation and was treated to a grand afternoon of high and lofty pretensions. It was the kind of affair many Irish imagined they would never attend, or even learn of, in a Brahmin world. Lodge's dismissive comments about the teas only reinforced this impression of social barriers. "Many of the attendees were working-class women of Irish immigrant descent who sought the social prestige of hobnobbing with a representative of arguably the most prestigious Irish-American family in the country," wrote Thomas J. Whalen in his history of this campaign.

During this campaign, Jack Kennedy's sexual attractiveness—the undercurrent of excitement that ran throughout his political life—became abundantly clear. No longer a scraggly 145 pounds, Kennedy was invigorated; the cortisone shots, prescribed for his various illnesses, had added about 15 pounds to his frame and a glow of health to his demeanor. ("Jack really looks like a tackle for Notre Dame in that picture you sent me," Joe marveled in a letter to Dave Powers. "You fellows must be taking good care of him.") At the various teas around the state, the response by swarms of women who almost swooned while in the receiving lines were noted by many observers. "Unmarried, wealthy, Harvardishly casual in dress, and with a distinguished war record in addition to his other attainment, he just about bracketed the full range of emotional interests of such an all-feminine group—maternal at one end and romantic at the other—irrespective of what it may have thought of his politics," wrote journalist Cabell Phillips. Not typical of his kind, this young Irishman named Kennedy was more than acceptable, the *Times* underscored in its cultural shorthand, he was downright "*Harvardishly.*"

Unlike those brutal contests endured by his grandfather, when the Irish were still a distinct minority, Jack Kennedy stood to benefit from the tide of immigration of more than a hundred years in Massachusetts; it had slowly, inexorably transformed the state's electorate, and, by 1952, more than half of the state's voters were decently educated middle-class Irish Catholics. To these voters, old-style Irish candidates like Curley were a sentimental embarrassment, thieves who would rally Celtic pride on their way to jail. But Jack Kennedy was more of an aspirant than a candidate. He embodied their ambitions and how many Irish Catholics wanted to be perceived in a society still not completely accessible to them. Kennedy appealed to their better instincts, a cerebral candidate better suited for debate on television than for ranting on a soapbox. Jack Kennedy, like some historical imperative, marked the high-water crest of Irish Catholic power in Massachusetts. Lodge, who nurtured good relations with the Irish Catholic community in Boston and took pains to reject the anti-immigrant measures of his grandfather, understood that it was only a matter of time until the Irish politicians of old gave way to a new generation. As Lodge later said, "All along, I always knew if there came a man with an honest, clean record who was also of Irish descent, he'd be almost impossible to beat."

ROBERT KENNEDY, a twenty-six-year-old Justice Department lawyer, didn't expect to get involved in his brother's campaign. He was more interested in setting out on his own course. When the campaign manager resigned in a huff, Bobby was summoned to take the position, almost as a family obligation. "The campaign began as an absolute catastrophic disaster," remembered Kenneth O'Donnell, one of Bobby's friends from Harvard recruited for the effort. Joe Kennedy, hell-bent on seeing Jack elected to the Senate, became unbearable, prompting campaign manager Mark Dalton to quit. "He was such a strong personality that nobody could—nobody *dared*—fight back," O'Donnell said. "The only time the campaign got any direction was when John Kennedy, who was then a Congressman in Washington, was able to get up to Massachusetts to overrule his father." O'Donnell convinced Jack that the only one to oversee the campaign was Bobby, who could work with his father's complete trust.

Although Jack assumed the political life his father had envisioned for Joe Jr., the Kennedy patriarch always felt that Bobby resembled him "much more" than any of his children. "Bobby is like me," he boasted. "Bobby's hard as nails." He once was quoted as saying that Bobby resembled him "because he hates like me," though he later denied it. Both were high-strung, intense men with coldly calculating heads, but their hearts could spill out with emotion when provoked or inspired. Bobby's political skills were recognized by more than his father. In February 1952, long before the fall campaign against Lodge was under way, Joe Kennedy received a note from a friend. Attached to it was a newspaper clipping mentioning that Robert Kennedy might run for political office. Joe's friend suggested that the source of the reporter's article was a Kennedy cousin, Joe Kane, who had orchestrated Jack's first campaign six years earlier. The elder Kennedy quickly squelched the rumor about Bobby. It wasn't his turn yet. "Joe Kane is very enthusiastic about him and definitely wants to get him into the political arena, but I think we have one good contest coming up this year," the senior Kennedy insisted.

When he got the call for help, Bobby wasn't pleased. He'd been working on his first big investigation for the Justice Department and didn't want to be pulled away.

"I don't know anything about Massachusetts politics," Bobby argued. "I don't know any of the players, and I'll screw it up."

O'Donnell urged him to help out or his brother might lose. After a week, Bobby relented and joined the campaign. His decision helped cement a close, almost symbiotic, working relationship between the brothers that would last for the rest of Jack's life. Bobby threw himself, heart and soul, into working for his brother's success. He toiled endless hours in tasks ranging from late-night strategy sessions to going door-to-door with leaflets extolling Jack's virtues. To his family's delight, Bobby proved himself to be a natural in politics.

ROBERT FRANCIS KENNEDY'S sense of family and faith were deeply engrained from youth, with a fidelity befitting his status as a former altar boy. Under the spiritual tutelage of his mother, Bobby attended Mass as much as three times a week and became Rose Kennedy's most devout son. A shy, awkward and diminutive boy growing up, Bobby understood Catholicism in his bones, beyond the mere recitation of psalms and vespers, beyond the cultural appreciation of religion adhered to by his father and older brothers. At St. Joseph's Church in Bronxville, a parish nun, Sister M. Ambrose, suggested to his parents that Bobby "might have a religious vocation." Many years later, the same nun wrote a letter to Bobby in which she recalled how, after being moved by a sermon about the poor given by a Caribbean bishop, he marched home, broke his piggy bank and donated its contents to the charity mission. In a household of many children, Bobby gained recognition and approval, particularly from his mother, for his earnest faith. "He worked hard at it," recalled his sister, Pat. "I used to go into his room to hear his Latin. Then mother would come in, too, so he could show her how much he learned." After attending a succession of schools, including a disappointing time spent at the Portsmouth Priory School run by the Benedictine monks (where neither the educational nor spiritual standards met his parents' approval), Bobby found himself among a handful of Irish Catholic adolescents at the Milton Academy, a private school in Connecticut with a student populace distinctly destined for the upper crust of American life. "My first impression of him was that we were both, in a way, misfits," recalled David Hackett, who became a lifelong friend from Milton. "I think that was because his name was Kennedy and he was an Irish Catholic and Milton Academy was basically a WASP school." Interestingly, several biographers later repeated Hackett's "misfit" description as a psychological condition without relating it to Kennedy's ethnic and religious background.

Unlike his brother Jack, Bobby could never smooth out the rough edges of his ethnicity, nor did he seem willing to downplay his religion to gain approval. Rather than find a comfortable place in a parochial school for affluent Catholics, where Bobby would be likely treated deferentially because of his family's prominence, his parents instead had placed him in a setting where his snoot would be rubbed raw by not-so-subtle bigotry. In this higher social strata, Bobby, the runt of the Kennedy family, tried to find his way. Like other Kennedys at various times, the idea of proselytizing—convincing others to Catholicism, hoping others would become like him, rather than being assimilated himself into the dominant Protestant culture—was cited in letters sent home. While at the private academy, Bobby wrote to his mother: "Am now leading an underground movement to convert the school, and am taking a lot of the boys to church on Sunday." In such an Anglophile atmosphere as Milton, "Bobby Kennedy liked to play the tough Irish 'mick,' especially around Brahmins," wrote biographer Evan Thomas. "The elder boys had been by and large accepted into the Protestant elite. But Bobby, defiantly Irish, had his father's outsiderness, the drive that comes from resentment." This tough outer shell, the sense of estrangement, didn't limit his ability to feel empathy and compassion, and perhaps enhanced it. When Bobby heard the bad news about another Milton friend, Sam Adams, whose father was killed in a car crash two weeks before Christmas break in 1942, he went to Adams's room to comfort him. "We sat on the bed and talked about faith," Adams recalled. "I said to him, 'I wish I had your acceptance, your conviction. I wish I could believe that it's not all over when you die, and that I would see my father again.' Bobby was very sure. He believed that very surely."

During their quiet conversation, as Adams packed to return home, Bobby discussed how faith might overcome such a personal tragedy. Adams wasn't Catholic, and under different circumstances might have been offended by such suggestions after losing a parent. But Kennedy's words were so sincere that Adams, through his own grief, still remembered them many years afterward. "He told me that faith would get me over this great burden," Adams told biographers Lester and Irene David. "Not his faith, but mine. Even though I had no particular religious belief, and he knew it, he said that I *can* find faith, and that I could find comfort in it."

BOBBY'S DEEP religious faith manifested itself in a social conscience that showed signs of personal growth and independence as well as a penchant for fervid moral righteousness. At Harvard, where the student body became increasingly diverse after World War II, he'd been invited to join the Spee Club—the same fraternity that had rejected his father and Joe Jr., and barely admitted Jack. Jack was delighted to be in their presence, but Bobby quit when he concluded that an Irish Catholic had been blackballed because of his heritage. In lieu of the Spee Club, Bobby hung around with his friends on the football team, several of whom, such as Kenny O'Donnell, were Catholics. Perhaps the most remarkable act of moral independence, however, came with Bobby's reaction to Father Leonard Feeney, a notorious Jesuit eventually excommunicated by the church.

Father Feeney, a poet, writer and talented orator, served as chaplain for a storefront ministry near the Harvard campus. He seemed to be an unlikely radical, but toward the mid-1940s, he became increasingly conservative and anti-Semitic. He appealed to a segment of Catholicism that had agreed with Father Coughlin's diatribes a decade earlier. Feeney pushed his central message—*extra ecclesiam nulla salus,* "outside the Church there is no salvation" — well past church doctrine into an absolute declaration that only Catholics could enter the gates of heaven. Protestants and Jews need not apply. From the St. Benedict Center in Cambridge, Feeney preached his reactionary doctrine to Harvard students who wandered into the former bookstore looking for spiritual enlightenment. A sampling of Father Fenney's rants, according to those who witnessed them, included his claims that "the Jews have taken over this city" and "I would rather be a bad Catholic than any Jew in existence." At a time of increasing incidents of anti-Semitic violence by Catholics in Boston, Feeney's sermons proved incendiary. Some who enlisted in his cause withdrew from Harvard, Boston College and other schools to work for Feeney; others were appalled and alerted church authorities about his outrageous statements. Evelyn Waugh, the British writer who was a convert to Catholicism, walked away from a meeting repulsed by this "stark, raving mad" priest.

Each Thursday evening, Father Feeney presided over an audience at St. Benedict or gave a Sunday sermon to even larger crowds on the Boston Common. During one lecture, Bobby Kennedy, a Harvard undergraduate, confronted the priest in a boisterous argument, glowering with contempt for such a hateful screed. He argued that church's doctrine taught just the opposite, and that his Catholic teachers had never preached such exclusionary lessons. The confrontation was remarkable for several reasons. More than any of her sons, Rose Kennedy's seventh child revered authority figures, never acted up in school, and remained particularly deferential to clergy wearing the Roman collar. To engage a priest in such a hostile challenge must have taken an extraordinary act of will by the former altar boy now in his early twenties. The confrontation with Feeney marked a subtle rite of passage for young Kennedy. Though still a conservative by nature, his action departed from the old, reactionary "Coughlin" world and showed a willingness to draw his own moral conclusions. A half century later, his cousin Joseph Gargan marveled at Bobby's gall and strength of conviction in confronting the renegade priest. As a harbinger of things to come, it demonstrated his willingness to stand up against powerful figures when he felt them wrong.

By 1949, Archbishop Richard Cushing came to the same conclusion and officially silenced Feeney, directing Catholics to steer clear of the St. Benedict Center. Feeney responded by calling the archbishop a heretic. Nevertheless, Rose Kennedy was horrified to learn that her devout son had displayed such disrespect to a priest. Good Catholics, in her mind, just didn't do such things. Only when the Pope decided to excommunicate Feeney in 1953 did her mind ease on this matter. "Bobby was right," Rose admitted to a friend. "When the Vatican excommunicated Father Feeney, I knew Bobby had been right."

ONCE DIPPED into the political waters of Boston, Bobby Kennedy immersed himself completely. During the 1952 campaign, his wife, Ethel, pregnant with their second child, also knocked on doors, passed out leaflets and socialized at the teas as if she had been born a Kennedy. Her devotion to religion and family matched her husband's. Before agreeing to marry, she had considered becoming a nun. "How can I fight God?" Bobby wondered.

Ethel Skakel Kennedy grew up in a wealthy Connecticut family. In the heat of the 1952 battle against Lodge, her father was asked to contribute and line up a quick $100,000—like some political dowry—for the Kennedy campaign. "Anytime now you could get us twenty individuals or a smaller amount if that is not possible, we could use it in the campaign," Joe Kennedy urged his son's new father-in-law. "As an individual cannot give a total of more than $5,000 and cannot give more than $1,000 to a committee, I am enclosing herewith a list of five committees to whom checks could be made payable." George Skakel, of the Great Lakes Carbon Corporation in Manhattan, signed a check for $5,000 before leaving for a hunting trip and promised he'd line up the rest when he got back. Though he remained out of the public eye, Joe Kennedy's fingerprints were all over the levers of his son's juggernaut. The old man's political instincts, however, were far from impeachable. He assumed the Republican presidential candidacy of war hero, General Dwight D. Eisenhower, would fizzle with no impact on his son's Senate bid. "I think his campaign will break in seams in the next six weeks," he predicted confidentially in early February 1952. When he heard the rumor of former FDR aide and Postmaster General James A. Farley making a bid for the White House, Joe Kennedy quickly dismissed it. "Very few, if any, would believe that the time has arrived for a Catholic to be that candidate," he wrote, "and therefore, I doubt very much if, as worthy as Jim Farley is, he would receive any serious consideration."

Joe Kennedy's political handicaps extended beyond his poor prognostications. In Brookline and other Boston neighborhoods with sizeable Jewish populations, he was viewed as a German appeaser during World War II and a long-time anti-Semite—a generally accurate assessment that posed a considerable obstacle for his son's chances. To beat Lodge, Jack Kennedy needed the overwhelming support not only of Irish Catholics but of voters from all immigrant groups and minorities, including Jews, Italians and blacks. In a campaign appearance for his fellow Republican, Jacob Javits, a prominent New York politician who was Jewish, gave a speech that strongly suggested Jack Kennedy was anti-Semitic like his father, pointing to his amendment on the House floor to cut appropriations for the fledgling state of Israel. In one of the more interesting twists of the campaign, John McCormack, whose congressional district encompassed many Jewish neighborhoods in Boston, came to Jack Kennedy's defense. McCormack's own brother, Ed "Knocko" McCormack, was a longtime Curley crony. He was still peeved with Kennedy for not signing the petition to spring His Honor from jail. But soon after Javits's visit, McCormack gave an impassioned speech at a Kennedy rally held on Blue Hill Avenue in the heart of a Jewish neighborhood. Earnestly, McCormack explained to the crowd how Jack Kennedy had offered the amendment, at his suggestion, only to stop efforts by Israel's detractors in Congress to eliminate funding entirely. "It will cut the budget some, but we will save the remainder of the money for Israel," McCormack said, recounting his conversation with Kennedy before his hometown constituents. His virtuoso defense of Kennedy was utterly convincing. The reputation of McCormack—whom some Irish called "Rabbi" because they felt he was too deferential—counteracted Javits's visit and became conventional wisdom within the Jewish community.

None of McCormack's account was true. His story of a supposedly secret deal concocted with Kennedy to keep Israel from its enemies was created out of whole cloth simply for the benefit of Jewish voters. "Of course, it was a figment of McCormack's imagination; it never happened that way whatsoever," attested Tip O'Neill, who recalled how Kennedy told him the truth later on. Jack seemed to admire McCormack's fidelity to another Democrat from the same Irish political machine. "When the chips were down, because I was a Democrat, he was up in the fire lines for me," Kennedy admitted to O'Neill. "He did something for me that I never could have done for him."

Politics increasingly became a family affair with the Kennedys, especially between the two brothers. Winning was a crusade that took on its own moral imperative. Together, they worked as a team, adding ballast to their father's heavy-handed advice with their own growing, self-assured political judgment. Sometimes they agreed with the old man; other times they quietly but effectively dismissed his judgments. "He doesn't require it," Bobby said about his father's approval, when an aide, Ed Guthman, once asked. The troika of Kennedy men, forged in the 1952 race, would work diligently, almost single-mindedly, for one goal during the next decade. Among the threesome, as Guthman observed, "there was a great deal of love and respect." As a campaigner, Jack learned to keep his own distance from his ever-aggressive and relentless brother. Bobby sometimes bumped against too many heads, including then Governor Paul Dever, who was in his own fading quest for reelection. "I know you're an important man around here and all," Dever warned the ambassador over the telephone, "but I'm telling you this and I mean it: keep that fresh kid of yours out of sight from here on in." Stung more than once by the Kennedys, it was Dever, the product of a working–class Irish Catholic family, who later called Jack "the first Irish Brahmin" and saddled Bobby with the moniker "the last Irish Puritan." There was more than a little truth in both sobriquets.

ELECTION NIGHT brought sweet vindication. The upstart Kennedy beat Senator Lodge by more than 70,000 votes. With a record 90 percent turnout, the Republicans prevailed throughout the state and country, and Eisenhower won the first of what would become two terms in the White House. The GOP swept races against Dever and other Massachusetts

Democrats. But Lodge never recovered from his slow start, not enough to overcome Kennedy's lead.

Campaign headquarters of the two candidates were located across the street from each other. As election night dragged on, Bobby and Jack stayed with only a handful of the faithful. Patsy Mulkern, ever the blunt assessor of political odds, went across the street, stood outside the window of Lodge headquarters and yelled, "You're dead! You're finished! Give up! Give up!" But the senator didn't concede until seven the next morning. Bobby knew it was over when a glum-looking Lodge left his headquarters and "walked across the street, right in front of our window."

The Irish wards in Boston voted heavily for Kennedy, the margins five and six to one. The historical ironies and a bit of a grudge match were evidenced by the family's reaction in victory. Jack sang a few bars of "Sweet Adeline," as a tribute to Honey Fitz's memory. John F. Fitzgerald had died two years earlier, but had lived long enough to see his namesake enter Congress and envision the potential for even higher office. The same tensions between the Irish and Brahmins that toppled Honey Fitz in his 1916 race against the old Senator Lodge were still present in the 1952 campaign, though this time with different results. "At last, the Kennedys have evened the score!" Rose rejoiced, only half joking. Joe Kennedy, triumphant at last, thought of another lost family member and how things might have been different. "This is probably one of the jobs that I thought Joe would have filled, but we are more than fortunate to have Jack come along with the same hopes and ideals," the senior Kennedy wrote to a friend. "His victory was, next to Eisenhower's, the most sensational in the United States because he defeated a Republican that has never been defeated for anything in Massachusetts before." Young Joe's old friend, Father Maurice Sheehy, sent a note of congratulations with a similar reference. "How proud his brother Joe would have been of him!" the priest wrote to their father. "Jack is destined to do great things for his country and his Church."

The old resentments eased for only a few moments. In assessing Kennedy's impressive victory, the press weighed in uniformly with a lament for the fallen Senator Lodge, a politician who had valiantly tried to steer the national party of Lincoln away from right-wing extremists and pave the way for the steady and trustworthy Eisenhower, yet was knocked off at home by what seemed a political lightweight. Implicit in these accounts was the subtle impression that Lodge was worthier, more fundamentally American than this scion of Irish immigrants. No journalist recognized this victory for what it was historically: the end of the Brahmin era in

Massachusetts and the rise of a new wave of politicians, mostly Democrats, whose forebears had come on boats from Ireland or Italy or places other than the Back Bay. With his own ethnic sensitivities always in gear, Joe Kennedy still could perceive a slight in such wonderful news as his son's election to the United States Senate. "After reading the Boston papers and most of the papers in the country," old Joe wrote to a friend, "I have almost come to the conclusion that as far as they are concerned Jack has committed the unpardonable social error of beating Lodge."

Chapter Eighteen

A Child of Fate

ROBERT KENNEDY'S WRITTEN confidential request to his father, dashed off in a kind of quick Kennedy shorthand, contained references understood only by each other. But in the deeply personal matters of marriage, sex and the church, he knew that if anyone could come up with a solution, it would surely be his father.

As Bobby explained, the wife of an old law school chum had asked how she might be granted an annulment from the Catholic Church. The exact circumstances surrounding the young woman's troubled marriage—spelled out in the letter passed along to his father—are lost to history. But Bobby's note in February 1958 indicated his own view. "The letter speaks for itself and I don't know if anything can be done but it certainly appears the girl deserves a break on this one," he concluded. "As a Papal Count married to a Countess, I am sure you will have the answer."

Bobby's closing line referred to the unique honor bestowed on his mother a few years earlier and, in a more subtle way, to his father's own influence with the church. In late 1951, the Vatican recognized Rose Fitzgerald Kennedy as a papal countess for her "exemplary motherhood and charitable works." A small article in the widely circulated *Boston Post* proclaimed that she was only the sixth woman chosen for such a distinction. In the *New York Times*, Spellman upped the ante with his claim that "only two other American women hold the title." Money provided the entree for such an award, especially the $2.5 million grant from the Kennedy Foundation to open a home for troubled children in the Bronx. Spellman presided over the ceremony and gave Mrs. Kennedy a scroll conferring the "extraordinarily high" honor to her. Some church critics objected to Vatican decrees that turned a rich donor into a "countess" or bestowed other such honors, practices not unlike the old discredited process of selling indulgences. But for Rose, the lifelong bonds between church and family came to a magnificent culmination with this special recognition from Pope Pius XII—the same pontiff she had welcomed into her home two decades earlier on his trip to America. As much as any of her children, Bobby appreciated his mother's fealty to the church, shared her inviolate loyalty to the idea of family and carried on many of the Catholic traditions in his own household. He was also aware of his father's hand in such a unique selection by the Pope, of his close ties to powerful Vatican figures such as Count Galeazzi and his ability to make things happen behind the scenes. His father's reply to the annulment request again reinforced this belief.

In a letter from Palm Beach, Joseph Kennedy assured his son that he'd help out, particularly when it reached the highest levels of the church. "To get an annulment, it takes time, even though the matter is as simple as this seems to be, since the one seeking the annulment has never been baptized," his father replied. He said the woman should file the necessary annulment papers with her local bishop in Hartford where she lived, then send it on to the Archdiocese in New York and eventually it would reach Rome. "I think that we might be able to expedite it once it gets its way to New York," Joe explained, without explicitly mentioning his long-time friendship with Cardinal Spellman. Bobby knew that "New York" was shorthand for the cardinal, much as Kathleen had delighted in referring to him as "Arch Spell" in her wartime letters. "I would think that if she had somebody get the Bishop of Hartford to hurry it along," his father ended, "we will then do the best that we can thereafter." His reply suggested this was not the first such favor requested of Joe Kennedy, nor surely would it be the last.

FOR THE ADULT KENNEDY CHILDREN, even for those who were married and parents of children of their own, the emotional and financial pull of their parents still dominated much of their lives in the 1950s. Indeed, for all their affluence and worldliness, the Kennedys at times resembled some Irish family in the bog, the adult children staying on the proverbial farm until well into adulthood. Perhaps most paradoxically, Jack, elected to the U.S. Senate at age thirty-six but still unattached, seemed caught in the orbit of his family, the gravity of its demands.

Rose's incessant notes and reminders to her adult children about all sorts of personal matters—reinforced by the moral strictures instilled through the culture of the church—fashioned many of their own beliefs, like some religious superego looming over all they would do. Those acts that specifically defied or rejected her religious teachings, be they cardinal sins or merely carnal desires, seemed to take into account some omniscient Mother Church in their lives. If one parameter of the church was delineated by Rose's high-minded spirituality, the other extreme—a more worldly, bricks-and-mortar morality—was exhibited by their father. Joe's influence sprung from his bankroll, the scope of which few in America had ever witnessed, and the knowledge of an Irish cynic ever hopeful, ever optimistic for his children. He once called them "hostages to fortune," but their fates seemed more directly tied to his own wishes. Rather than going their own way, the adult children of Rose and Joe Kennedy were increasingly viewed by the public—and just about everyone who knew them personally—as one entity, a sprawling familial force of raw ambition that sometimes showed its teeth. After the 1952 Senate campaign, the idea of the Kennedys as a "clan," the word they themselves used, was sealed in the public imagination forever.

IN THIS ERA after World War II, the Catholic Church struggled to define itself. The old bigotry of nativism and anti-Catholicism still simmered, most typified by Paul Blanshard's best-selling 1949 book (*American Freedom and Catholic Power*) warning about the evils of Catholic influence on American society. By today's standards, Blanshard's writings seem replete with cultural stereotypes and rank bigotry. Blanshard warned that Catholics could someday become the majority in the United States because they were "outbreeding the non-Catholic elements in our population." In Blanshard's diatribe, Boston was a hotbed of trouble. "Boston is aggressively Catholic largely because it is aggressively Irish, and it is aggressively Irish because its people have not quite overcome their sense of being strangers in a hostile land," Blanshard wrote. Blanshard summarized his outlook in the *Atlantic Monthly* in his reply to a critic: "[He] does not try to deny that the Roman Catholic Church is a complete dictatorship in which American Catholic people have no participating control; nor does he specifically attempt to justify . . . the celibate rule on birth control, the theological coercion applied to Catholic parents to maintain a segregated Catholic school system, or the treatment of non-Catholics as second-class citizens in mixed marriage. . . . Liberal Catholics have almost no voice or forum within the

Catholic system of power. . . . They cannot reach their fellow Catholics through any existing organs of the Church."

NUMEROUS CATHOLIC theologians and partisans howled over Blanshard's assessment, but several liberals applauded his treatise, including John Dewey, who praised its "exemplary scholarship, good judgement and tact." When portions of Blanshard's critique appeared in the *Nation,* Cardinal Spellman insisted bitterly that the New York City public schools remove the offending article from their libraries. Spellman's crude attempt at censorship soon made the newspapers, and a committee of civil libertarians and liberals, including former first lady Eleanor Roosevelt, condemned the cardinal's action. Their support confirmed for many Catholics that overt bigotry existed not only in reactionary quarters but also tacitly in the more educated, more refined sectors of America.

The Blanshard book and other writings about American Catholics in the mid-century caused some painful self-evaluation. To some observers, the insularity of the immigrant experience and the steadfastness to church traditions caused a parochialism that impeded progress by Catholics in America. Too often, they were viewed as mundane, unimaginative thinkers, too caught up in the mechanics of the catechism and ill-equipped for the diverse challenges of a pluralistic society. Though Catholics were among the most heterogeneous group in the nation, they remained dominated by a hierarchy almost exclusively Irish, male and decidedly conservative. Historians later commented about a kind of infantilism afflicting the church and its flock during the 1950s—a period still far emotionally and spiritually from the reforms of Vatican II.

These contradictions were reflected in the Kennedy family itself. For the Kennedys, the church could be a source of spiritual strength and moral courage, the impetus for some of their finest moments; but it also became an institution that curiously constricted the voice of its adult members, justified the second-class status of women and encouraged the hiding of intellect behind emotion. Similarly, the Kennedys' idea of family also differed from that of the emerging American ideal. In a nation where mobility and independence was a birthright, the family reared by Joe and Rose Kennedy seemed to live by a creed fashioned by their father. Regardless of their popularity or wealth, the Kennedys—with their kindred, us-against-them perspective—remained unsure of anything but themselves. Although thoroughly modern American in public, Joe Kennedy still insisted on building up his family in the most familiar way, an approach undeniably Irish Catholic. As Jack's best friend, Lem Billings, later explained: "Mr. Kennedy also built within the family a real loyalty to each other. . . . It's very unusual the way the members of this family, all of them in their middle years, still have this very clan family feeling. . . . Mr. Kennedy always said that the family should stick together. He said the family would be happier as one unit than if they broke up into separate individual families."

This oneness among the Kennedys, the idea of family, emanated from their religion and cultural heritage, as their own words in public and private show. Journalists and historians would note this dynamic in their profiles—"The Remarkable Kennedys!" declared *Look* magazine—as if the family were some oddity bucking the national trend. The American public seized upon this clannishness of the Kennedys as something terribly unique. With their numbers big enough for a scorecard, the Kennedys presented a different ideal beyond the sanitized two-parent, two-child (preferably a boy and girl) WASPish family prototype found on television or in women's magazines in the postwar era. The Kennedys, often photographed by wide-angle lenses overflowing off the page, reflected the accomplished immigrant family in American culture, defining itself on its own terms and redefining society in the process. Those of immigrant heritages—whether from Italian, German, Hispanic, Jewish, African or a myriad of other minority groups in America—could find a little piece of themselves in the upwardly aspiring Kennedys. As Irish Catholics, this high profile family signified the subtle but dramatic revolution taking place in the American church, particularly the struggle to maintain faith and traditions in a meaningful, up-to-date way. If the church of their parents was focused on parochial concerns, the Catholicism of this new generation of Kennedys gradually became more outward-looking. The words of St. Luke were transformed into their own social compact. Each Kennedy found his and her own way of doing what was expected, including the future president of the United States.

EUNICE KENNEDY'S work reflected the progressive spirit of a Dorothy Day in the Catholic Church. Eunice was a highly energetic and intelligent woman with a twig-like figure and prominent cheekbones of a Katharine Hepburn. After college, she moved to Washington and, with her father's help, landed an important job in the federal Justice Department's program for fighting juvenile delinquency. Her older sister Rosemary's mental retardation and devastating lobotomy inspired Eunice to devote herself to that cause as well. She visited Rosemary, institutionalized in Wisconsin, as often as possible and sometimes shared vacations with her. Eunice would not forget her. Jack's congressional aide, Billy Sutton, recalled how Eunice would invite troubled girls, teenagers from her government program, to her home for dinner. She did the same with mentally impaired youngsters. Since her days in the convent schools, Eunice had tackled each new assignment with vocation-like tenacity. And yet, like most women of her era, she had been taught to defer to male authority. Despite her obvious abilities, Eunice was never groomed for the top-tier jobs her father sought so desperately for his sons. "If that girl had been born with balls, she would have been a hell of a politician," her father boasted, with barely a trace of the fundamental inequality inherent in his statement. With laser-like intensity, Eunice contributed tremendously to her brother's 1952 Senate campaign. Her effort ranked second only to Bobby's. "Eunice is a lot like me," observed her brother Jack, who shared a Georgetown apartment with her during the late 1940s. "She's just as competitive as the boys."

Eunice adored her father, though she remained very much her mother's daughter. She embraced her family's religious beliefs wholeheartedly and, before transferring to Stanford, she practiced her acts of faith at Manhattanville College, the women's college operated by the Society of the Sacred Heart nuns. The brand of Catholicism at this school was not cloistered or hermetic but aggressively social-minded. One day a week, the students at this plush school journeyed downtown to work with children at the Barat Settlement in the Bowery and at a Casita Maria in East Harlem, a shelter for Puerto Rican youngsters founded by two Manhattanville students. Intermittently, students were sent to Dorothy Day's Catholic Worker in Manhattan and other urban ministries serving the poor and needy. At Manhattanville, Jean became fast friends with the fun-loving Ethel Skakel and introduced her to Bobby. In the years to come, the Kennedy women carried on the lessons learned at Manhattanville.

Although the foundation named for her fallen brother was used by others to drum up political support, Eunice never lost sight of its mission among the truly needy. She gave an impassioned sermon at the South Side Catholic Women's Club about the effectiveness of the homes for the mentally retarded opened by the Kennedy Foundation in Illinois, New York City, Wisconsin and Massachusetts, and the Kennedy Memorial Hospital in Brighton, facilities that treated and researched illnesses afflicting children. Eunice placed her family's charity firmly in the context of the church's good works. She relied on religious imagery and allusions her brothers would likely shy away from in private, and certainly be disinclined to use publicly. "Jesus set up an entirely new standard," Eunice insisted. "His famous words are: 'For as much as ye have done to the least of these, you have done it unto Me.' As a result, with us, the test of a community's worth is not how well the most privileged people make out—but, rather, what provision is made for the least, for those who are 'exceptional' in their need for our kindness." Her speech bore an uncanny resemblance in cadence and idealistic substance to the speeches that would make her older brother famous. Those who witnessed Eunice's endless devotion and effort to these causes never questioned her sincerity.

Though she had the heart of an ascetic, Eunice appreciated the church's rituals and sense of theater. When she married R. Sargent Shriver in 1953— the official Kennedy press release called the nuptials "one of the most important and colorful weddings ever held in America"—Cardinal Spellman presided at St. Patrick's Cathedral, along with three bishops, four monsignors, nine priests and an apostolic blessing sent by Pope Pius XII. Shriver shared many of the traits of his bride's parents: the ambition and gregariousness of her father, and the cultural interests and sense of faith of her mother. To her wedding guests, Eunice declared: "I found a man who is as much like my father as possible." Shriver came from an old and distinguished Catholic family in Maryland. After graduating from Yale, he was introduced to the Kennedys and began working in Joe Kennedy's business empire. Shriver was soon dispatched to Chicago to oversee the Kennedy-owned Merchandise Mart and was immediately established as an important economic and political figure in the Windy City.

Both Eunice and her husband were profoundly thankful to Joe Kennedy. "Jack is right," Eunice wrote to her father. "We may all get our 'drive' from our mother but from whom better could we receive the gift of generosity than you, Love and hugs, Eunie." Sarge Shriver, a polished, articulate man, seemed almost prostrate in his solicitousness to his father-in-law. "Actual politicians are now asking me to run (senators, previous candidates) & the business community seems favorably disposed," Shriver wrote to Joe Kennedy in a long letter on Merchandise Mart stationary. "Even if nothing comes of the talk, it indicates at least for my personal satisfaction that all your confidence in me, the effort and the support you have given me, have not been misplaced. This means much to one who is indebted to you for so much." Though Joe Kennedy was undoubtedly supportive of his daughter's new husband, it is unlikely the family patriarch ever encouraged Shriver to pursue a political career. In fact, part of Shriver's role in Illinois was to act as a political scout for Jack's eventual run for national political office, not to create a staging area for a candidate who was only an in-law.

Stephen Smith, a Georgetown graduate from a wealthy Irish Catholic family in upstate New York, adopted a similar role in the Kennedy family a few years later. He married Jean, the youngest of Joe Kennedy's daughters, in a wedding also presided over by Cardinal Spellman. Soon, Smith became a trusted political aide and eventually a campaign manager for his brothers-in-law's election campaigns. Before marriage, Jean worked for no pay with Father James Keller, the Maryknoll priest who started the Christopher movement of Catholic public service. Keller's newspaper column and *The Christopher Hour* television show made him one of the most famous church figures in America. Though she had heard Father Keller speak when she attended the Noroton convent school, Jean decided to volunteer her hard work while chatting with the priest at the wedding of her brother Jack. Father Keller had created the Christophers as a bulwark against corruption and communism "by urging Christians to enter professions where Communists most often operate—in the fields of government, education, labor relations, literature and entertainment." In 1956, John F. Kennedy won a Christopher Award for using "his God-given talent in a positive way" with his book, *Profiles in Courage.* By joining Father Keller's cause, Jean lived out the religious faith espoused by her mother and underwritten by her father with money donated from the family's foundation. "The idea of doing something for other people came from my parents," Jean explained to author Laurence Leamer. "They both believed very strongly that those to whom much is given have responsibility. They both felt that we had a real responsibility for some kind of public service."

THERE WERE OFTEN painful resonances for Joe Kennedy of the children he had lost, and he harbored a wariness of the potential for tragedy just around the bend. His Irish fatalism crept into a 1952 letter discussing the high costs of constant plane flights by his daughters, pointing out that it "becomes a matter of danger in that after having travelled as much as folks have, your chances of not having an accident are that much worse." Joe Kennedy had long ago realized that his millions could not save his children from their own destinies, yet often he exerted a subtle control not only over his adult children but over their spouses as well. The emotional and financial strings were particularly evident in the marriage of his daughter Patricia to the actor Peter Lawford.

In a whirlwind romance, the couple decided to marry in 1954 after dating for only two months. The young and virginal Patricia, perhaps the most beautiful of the Kennedy daughters, was smitten by the suave charm and Hollywood good looks of the British actor, though the relationship began immediately with some difficulties. Peter was not a Catholic, and his widowed mother, Lady May Lawford, viewed the Kennedys as "barefoot Irish peasants" who were nouveau riche not worthy of her esteem. Nor were Patricia's parents overly impressed. "If there's anybody I'd hate worse than an actor as a son-in-law, it's a *British* actor," Joe reportedly said. Nevertheless, when the couple married in April 1954 inside an Upper East Side Manhattan church, not St. Patrick's Cathedral, Peter agreed to raise their children as Catholics. "Is there any chance of getting the Pope's blessing for our marriage, or does it have to be an all Catholic ceremony?" Pat wrote to her father that same month.

The couple moved to Los Angeles, and Pat quickly became pregnant. She even consulted her father on the choice of obstetrician-gynecologist, and whether the doctor she chose was a Catholic. (When considering a non-Catholic OB-GYN recommended by a friend, Pat informed her father, "He himself is not a Catholic but does work at St. John's Catholic Hospital for patients.") Drawing upon his own Hollywood experience, Joe Kennedy was asked to provide long-distance career counseling for Lawford, who patterned himself more as a Malibu surfer boy than an English squire. After receiving a long letter from Pat about the tribulations of her husband's show biz career, Joe wrote back advising his pregnant daughter to worry less about such matters.

"I think it's too bad you both have to be bothered with this contract at a time when you are looking for a house and expecting a baby," her father wrote from Palm Beach. "My first interest would be that baby, second the contract, and third the house. . . . I have had enough experience in forty odd years to realize that anything you can settle with money is not worth losing a night's sleep about because there is always a ways to fix it up." Yet there was something about Peter Lawford's character that left Joe and Rose unsettled, never quite comfortable with their son-in-law, as if marrying a Kennedy was just a fortuitous move for a rakish cad. Peter seemed more interested in Joe's advice about the latest television or movie offer than in anything else. "Last night your father talked to Peter and after he finished, Peter mentioned that Pat and two other people had been listening in on the conversation," Rose confided to her youngest son Ted. "It seems to me that it is almost as bad as having your wire tapped."

At age sixty, Rose Kennedy appeared well suited to Roman Catholicism, with its allusions to saints, its penchant for sacrifice and its medieval view of the human condition. Her own life—a mighty cathedral of passions and ideals devoted to family and religion—contained its own contradictions and ironies as well as its abiding truths and love. She did not issue firebrand sermons or wholesale condemnations, yet she was neither a dupe nor a complete innocent. "She may look as fragile as a violet, but don't be deceived for a minute," said her close friend, Marie Greene. "If Rose had been a boy, she—not Jack—would have been the first Catholic president of the United States."

Her son's 1952 Senate campaign showcased Rose's political skills, still the daughter of Boston's ever-gregarious Honey Fitz. She could tell a good story, dress up anecdotes to the Irish Catholic audience about the British royalty she'd met during her days in England and spin yarns about rearing such a large brood. She always managed to underline, in a matter of fact way, why her family was so special. After the election, Rose asked Archbishop Cushing about setting up speaking engagements for her among Catholic organizations. Cushing's response was hardly enthusiastic. He gingerly suggested that she begin with talks to the Catholic Women's Club but not other groups because he sensed trepidation from elsewhere in the Kennedy family. Eventually, Rose garnered an invitation from her alma mater Manhattanville. She spoke about being a Catholic woman in America and the challenges of faith in the world. In a letter of thanks to the college's president, Mother Eleanor M. O'Byrne, Rose admitted that she was "thrilled" by the size of the audience for her "speaking debut." When she returned a few years later for a similar address at Manhattanville, Rose mixed in family tales with her own point of view "so full of faith and the practical expression of devotion to the Sacred Heart," as O'Byrne later described it. The nun marveled over how "very brave" and "deeply moving" Rose was in talking before seven hundred people about her deceased daughter, Kathleen. "I am sure that Kathleen was sending a great current of prayer through the so sure bond of the Communion of Saints," wrote Mother O'Byrne, "a current of prayer which sustained and up-held her mother."

Rose Kennedy embraced the earthly demands of this world with the spiritual expectations of the next. She kept herself thin and attractive well past her youth, certainly not looking like a woman who had born nine children. She indulged herself in designer clothes that placed her on best-dressed lists, and she took long vacations without her husband, traveling with female companions such as her niece Ann Gargan, who for a time became a nun. As was true in many Irish families, the Kennedys had a clear division between the sexes. There was the men's realm, Joe and his sons; and the secondary world inhabited by Rose, her daughters and eventually her daughters-in-law, deferential to the needs of their men. Rose's spiritual life was truly her own, however, a place her husband respected and dared not invade. She wrapped herself in prayer and devotion to God, convinced of an afterlife where all of the departed Kennedys would someday be united, and actively encouraged family members and their siblings to join her at religious retreats. She could use her faith like a buckler, shielding her from the hurts and disappointments in life. At Hyannis Port, Rose maintained a tiny house along the shore where she could sit, read, meditate and pray—a shelter from her storms. Like many Catholic women of her generation who were educated and trained by nuns, Rose aspired to combine elements of a good Catholic home with those of the convent. She sought out religious retreats that would somehow reveal a new and even deeper insight into God. Some of her children, such as Bobby and Eunice, intuitively grasped her religiosity; those with far less devotion, such as Jack, learned to respect it, even if they shook their heads a bit defensively. "She was terribly religious," said Jack to an early biographer. "She was a little removed, and still is, which I think is the only way to survive when you have nine children. I thought she was a very model mother for a big family."

For all her seraphic ways, Rose understood the sinner, the weaknesses of the flesh, especially the animal cravings of men. Particularly if these cardinal sins occurred in her own family, Rose could excuse, apologize and look the other way with extraordinary grace and self-denial. She did so with her father, then with her husband and again with her own children. Sex for her had been largely a duty, far more for procreation than for recreation, an integral part of the progression of the species, the marvelous extension of God's plan as agreed to in her marriage vows. She did not refuse her husband's insistent attempts at family making, but she didn't engage in much more than necessary. Though often a crude practitioner, Joe's interest in sex was more catholic than Catholic, a man whose far-flung tastes ran from showgirls and starlets to the young women his adult children brought home as friends, according to his detractors. They attested that he could be a grabber, a cajoler and a boor, sometimes pushing himself on women when he wasn't wanted.

At times, Rose adopted a strange, almost distant approach to her husband's sexuality, as though he suffered from a glandular problem. For instance, in a letter to her daughters in 1949, Rose tried to fob off as cute a rather mortifying comment from her husband to Teddy's girlfriend that summer: "She stayed here last night," Rose recounted. "She is really very pretty but looks about fifteen. Your Father made the startling announcement to her that when she was about eighteen he would be waiting for her. As she is already eighteen, she was really dumbfounded." Joe's letters to his sons contained a jocular air about the opposite sex. "I haven't seen all those beautiful girls that everybody talks about being here in the South of France, but maybe when Jack arrives here next week he'll find them," he wrote to Teddy in 1955 from the Riviera. He mentioned a girl "very anxious to see" Torby Macdonald, Jack's friend from the Harvard football team, adding that "I don't know whether it's with a gun or a lawyer's letter."

The church's anathema toward sex outside of marriage carried the unintended consequence of covering up and perpetuating this behavior by Joseph Kennedy and men like him who struck a firm distinction between marital relations at home and the pleasures they sought on the road. There were the Madonnas these men had married, who slept in separate bedrooms as shrines to their shriveled sex lives; and then there were the randy unattached women aroused by Joe Kennedy's bankroll and those whom Joe allegedly paid for introductory services to Jack and Robert at an East Harlem whorehouse. In the world of Catholic imagery and Jansenist restrictions, sex for men was dirty and illicit and made all the more exciting by the condemnations of their religion and the belief their wives weren't looking.

Clearly Rose knew about or suspected much of this lasciviousness but refused to worry or complain, trusting in the Lord that her family life would never be sunk by her husband's infidelities. Whatever dalliance he found outside her purview would never disturb their permanent bond in life, the sanctity of a marriage consecrated by the church. Even in Hollywood, with her husband "surrounded daily by some of the most beautiful women in the world, dressed in beautiful clothes," she didn't fret, but rose above the muck and mire of her husband's carnal desires. "One of the characteristics of my life with Joe was that we trusted one another implicitly," avowed Rose, the ideal wife for a compulsive philanderer. "If he had occasion to go out with theatrical people, he told me that he was going and he went. There was never any deceit on his part and there was never any doubt in my mind about his motives and behavior."

ROSE WAS NOT BLIND to the way women at various campaign teas gazed upon her handsome son Jack. After the election, the press certified the junior senator from Massachusetts as one of the most eligible bachelors in America. Jack enjoyed a randy bachelorhood, a fast-and-loose approach to women shared and encouraged by his father. In one letter during the war, Joe Kennedy bragged to his son how he had come across "a very beautiful blond in New York who was looking for some help to get a job on the stage . . . and said she got into the country through the help of my very attractive son, Jack," he wrote. "It strikes me that you and Joe must have done some great work over there when I wasn't looking."

For the men of the family, sex—playful, active and frenetic—became the indoor version of the kind of games, like touch football, they played on the lawn with such intensity. Even when referring to so-called nice girls, Jack spoke in a kind of adolescent, almost misogynist patter with dear old Dad, as though he were shooting the breeze with another school chum. Years earlier, when he accompanied one of his sister's friends, Charlotte McDonnell, to a 1940 Princeton football game, Jack told his father that it "will be my first taste of a Catholic girl so will be interested to see how it goes." At that time, Charlotte's family reigned as one of the leading Irish Catholic families in New York, part of a social circle with houses in Southampton who looked down their noses at the upstart Kennedys from Boston. Though some viewed Charlotte as a potential fiancée for Jack, he wasn't particularly interested, nor was Charlotte's father approving of young Kennedy as a potential suitor for his daughter. After Jack had attended a Saturday night party with Charlotte and his sister Kick, the threesome stayed up so late that they wound up going together to seven o'clock Mass on Sunday morning. "If the subject of marriage came up," Charlotte remembered, "Jack would never talk about it directly." Several years after serving in Congress and preparing for his Senate race, Jack's blithe love life began to be viewed as a potential liability, as even his father recognized. At the overripe age of thirty-five, he needed to become a family man, not an overaged Casanova or worse. "I understand brother Johnny is on his way to Notre Dame next Sunday by way of Jamaica," Joe wrote to Eunice. "I know he'll almost go insane when he hears that the Associated Press carried a front page story last night that 'he had gone to Jamaica for a short vacation.' That should furnish plenty of material for his constituency, particularly Mr. Lodge. With Congress just reconvening, that's rotten publicity. After all, he's over 21 and he knows what he's doing."

The Kennedy family rejoiced when Jack started seriously courting Jacqueline Bouvier, a beautiful, dark-haired woman with a whisper of a voice and an intelligent, sensitive manner. The couple met at a dinner party but their romance escalated after they attended an inaugural party for the new president, Dwight Eisenhower. Jackie came from a wealthy Catholic family familiar with the estates of Southampton and Newport. As a young girl, her parents divorced—a rare event for Catholics—because of the numerous affairs of her father (called "Black Jack," a descriptive, if somewhat dark, term of endearment), which biographers suggest left Jackie emotionally shaken but still attached to her daddy with the wandering eye. Her mother soon married a wealthy older man, Hugh Auchincloss—who doted over his stepdaughter and her sister, Lee; the new Mrs. Auchincloss moved with her daughters to the Auchincloss estate in Newport, Rhode Island. Jackie's education took place not in the Catholic convent academies attended by the Kennedy women but in a private secular school in Connecticut, then on to Vassar, the Sorbonne in Paris and graduation from George Washington University. She was working as a photographer for the *Washington Times-Herald* when she met Jack Kennedy. Their relationship evolved as part fairy tale and part press release; it developed privately on dates and publicly in glossy photos taken by the popular magazine *Life*.

When Jackie's mother met with the Kennedy parents in the summer of 1953, a certain competitive air, the jockeying for the high ground of class and stature, took place. The Bouviers liked to give the false impression of being related to French royalty, and Jackie's mother, Janet Norton Lee, suggested that her origins were with the famous Lees of Maryland. In fact, her grandparents were famine Irish who lived in the slums surrounding New York City, and her grandmother spoke with a brogue. To the Kennedys, Jackie gave no hint of her heritage and, as her cousin John H. Davis later claimed, she "did everything possible to hide her Irish background." Joe Kennedy, who had FBI reports on the backgrounds of his sons-in-law sent to him when they became serious suitors, never had a clue about the Bouvier lineage, nor did his eldest son. They were both smitten by Jackie's charm. In Jack's marriage proposal was the unspoken prospect of moving up socially by marrying a Catholic woman whose family was seen as part of the old money, blue-blood set in Newport. At times with the regally poised Jackie, the Kennedys' feeling of social inferiority, of still being somehow part of the Irish immigrant class, became transparent. The Kennedy girls mocked Jackie's upper-class affectations. Jack sensed that the Kennedys were perceived in Newport as somehow wild and uncultivated. "I'm afraid that they feel that their worst fears are being realized," Jack quipped, after he and two friends improperly played a round of golf at Auchincloss's exclusive club without permission of a member. "The invasion of the Irish Catholic hordes into one of the last strongholds of America's socially elite is being led by two chunky red-haired friends of the groom."

The religious compatibility of Jack's fiancée proved an important factor in gaining Rose's endorsement. One account of the wedding noted, undoubtedly with Rose's approval, that the bride was related to Mother Katherine Drexel of Philadelphia, a nun who had founded the Order of the Blessed Sacrament in Pennsylvania. "Joe and I could not be more thrilled to know that Jack had won such an outstanding bride who is so charming, so cultured and such a devout Catholic," Rose wrote to Jackie's mother. "We shall welcome her with all our hearts and we shall always try to make her very happy." The Auchincloss parents, who hosted the wedding reception at their Hammersmith Farm estate in Newport, were taken aback by the onslaught of press and relented only after much disagreement to the Kennedys' demand that reporters and cameramen be allowed to attend in the background. "I had no idea what it was like to be in politics!" Jackie's mother bemoaned. Nevertheless, Janet Auchincloss reaffirmed her daughter's commitment to the young senator and his family. "We are perfectly delighted that Jackie has chosen to marry a man whose mind and whose religion and whose great charm give them so much in common," she concluded.

Rather than Cardinal Spellman of New York, Jack asked Boston's Cushing to officiate at his wedding at St. Mary's Church—a wise political choice for Massachusetts' leading Irish Catholic politician but also a decision more in touch with his own brand of Catholicism. Jack didn't exude any great religious fervor, certainly not the increasingly conservative, confrontational kind practiced by the New York prelate. In Cushing, he saw a gentler soul, one who appreciated Kennedy's love of life, his wit and his fundamental optimism. In words and deeds, Cushing became Kennedy's family priest and political adviser. During the heat of Jack's 1952 Senate battle, when Cushing baptized Bobby Kennedy's first child in a well-publicized special ceremony, "that cut the heart right out from us," a Lodge man complained. Years later, when Robert Kennedy was asked about the "good deal of publicity" gained from Cushing's christening his first son a week before the 1952 election, Bobby conceded, "We were aware of that." Now, little more than a year later, Cushing presided over another important day for the man about whom he spoke with such great hope and anticipation, as if Jack were the Great White Hope of Irish Catholicism. In Cushing's view, Kennedy represented the very best his tribe had to offer. As he once told a crowd at a Communion breakfast attended by the senator, "If it pleases God, we shall follow [Kennedy] to the most exalted heights that are within the power of the people of the United States to give him."

After the couple exchanged vows, Cushing read a special blessing from the Pope. Then he extended his own wish for the couple's future "with its hopes and disappointments, its successes and its failures, its pleasures and pains, its joys and sorrows [which] are hidden from your eyes. You know that these elements are mingled in every life and are to be expected in your own."

Amidst the prayers and pomp of the wedding ceremony, Luigi Vena sang the "Ave Maria," a beautiful rendition that Jacqueline Bouvier Kennedy would remember throughout her marriage to Jack.

As part of the Kennedy clan, Jackie felt the almost suffocating embrace of her husband's expansive family. She couldn't keep pace with the rah-rah enthusiasms of the other Kennedy women, including Bobby's wife, Ethel. As sort of a tutorial for her new daughters-in-law, Rose imparted her own experiences in being a Kennedy wife. "I warned them [Jackie and Ethel] in the beginning, there would be rumors," she later explained. "There would be letters, anonymous letters. There'd be all sort of stories. That was part of the political spectrum. I tried to explain to them as soon as they were thinking of getting married." Of course, she didn't mention any practical solutions should these rumors and anonymous letters suggesting infidelity prove to be true. Instead, Rose counseled a different tack; she took her vision of things to a higher plane, even if she seemed naïve or simply foolish. Her devotion to God, church and family had buoyed her own spirits in the most difficult times. Repeatedly, she urged Jackie to do the same, suggesting her daughter-in-law attend a Catholic spiritual retreat. One year, she dropped a note to Jackie about a Lenten retreat. "Please do a little work on it, dear Jackie," she urged, as though she were the mother superior of her daughter-in-law's soul. In another letter, Rose offered more of an explanation for her push toward religion. "I believe sincerely it will open up new vistas of inspiring ideas to you," Rose suggested, "and you will have a better understanding of life. Not that I would change you, dearest Jackie. It is just that I have spent a long, happy life with a few baffling as well as tragic moments, and I have found that these spiritual signposts along the way have helped me tremendously."

On a more earthly plane, Joe Kennedy provided his own lessons about family and fate. In one heartfelt letter written on vacation from the South of France, Joe indulged Jackie as he might one of his own daughters, telling her that he'd pay for whatever horse she'd like to buy. "Honestly, I can't see the point of saving a couple of thousands of dollars and not having a winner," he declared. "If you're going to have a horse get yourself one that will give you the satisfaction of winning whatever you go after. You know all of us Kennedys don't like second prize. So get the horse you like and send me the bill."

Joe had paid heavily to ensure Jack's success so far. As if part of a long, daunting pilgrimage, he kept putting together the political advisors and priests and press pundits and segments of the American public who increasingly believed his son would become the first Catholic elected to the presidency. Now, he delighted in another step taken—his son's selection of a wife whose beauty, charm and intellect seemed the perfect match for his outsized ambitions. He advised Jackie not to let the political battles bother her, that destiny would somehow take care of his son. Jack was someone special, he assured her, someone who'd survive the slings and arrows aimed his way. "Remember I've always said he's a child of fate," he explained to her about Jack, "and if he fell in a puddle of mud in a white suit he'd come up ready for a Newport ball."

Chapter Nineteen

Articles of Faith

COMMUNISM STRUCK FEAR in the hearts of Americans in the 1950s. The growing titans of the Soviet Union and "Red" China—spreading global communism like some dread disease throughout large swaths of Europe and Asia—transfixed America as few other obsessions in the nation's history.

In this Cold War, the United States competed in a nuclear arms build-up of mammoth proportions. Politicians worried aloud about a missile gap with the Russians. At home, the fervent and often excessive hunt for Communists within America's borders created all sorts of watchdog government panels, such as the House Un-American Activities Committee. In seeking to sniff out Reds in their midst, the committee abused civil liberties and ruined many citizens. Whatever sanguine thoughts that some liberal Americans harbored from the 1930s of social justice through Marxism were largely crushed by the brutal totalitarian regimes of Stalin and Mao.

For Catholics, the fear of communism ran even deeper. The atheistic principles of the Communist bloc nations, denying the practice of religion with a philosophy that venerated socialism, almost as a deity, convinced church leaders both in the United States and in Rome that it faced a struggle for survival. The priests closest to the Kennedys were often in the forefront of this battle. "The Communist strategy of 'divide and conquer' is nowhere more apparent than in the field of religion," warned Monsignor Maurice S. Sheehy, an old friend of Joe Kennedy Jr.'s from their navy days, after visiting the Soviet bloc nations of Poland, Hungary, Czechoslovakia and the Balkans in 1956. "Since religion, of whatsoever form, is the only power that the Communist leadership fears, it must be destroyed."

On television and in his book, *Communism and the Conscience of the West,* Bishop Fulton J. Sheen, the charismatic national director of the church's Propagation of the Faith office, urged Catholics to resist communism passionately. In Boston, Archbishop Richard Cushing called communism one of the "greatest evils" ever to threaten Western civilization. With biblical imagery, Cushing declared that communism "is revealed as a false religion—the religion prophesied by the precursors of Stalin, namely, the religion of the Man-God in place of the religion of the God-man. The Christian symbol of this kind of religion, which is no religion at all, is Antichrist." Taking its cue from church leaders, the Massachusetts State Legislature created a Committee to Curb Communism to root out any "Communist Party and communist-front organizations" in the Bay State.

The Kennedys, like many Irish Catholics in America, believed communism posed an unacceptable menace. In this era, even cool heads such as Jack Kennedy learned to embrace the hot rhetoric of the Cold War, casting the struggle in terms of good and evil. Long after many liberal Democrats like himself had disavowed the anti-Communist excesses, Kennedy could still conjure up an epic vision of confrontation for America's soul. "I believe religion itself is at the root of the struggle, and we forget that the essence of this struggle is not material, but spiritual and ethical," Kennedy said in a little-publicized talk at the Columban Fathers' Seminary in Milton, Massachusetts, in 1958.

Kennedy's anti-Communist ardor reached back at least a decade when, as an aspiring congressman, he spent time in 1946 being prepped on the Soviet threat by a Catholic priest, Edward Duffy, who reflected the church's teaching on this grave matter. Duffy had been influenced by the writings of another priest, John F. Cronin, an anti-communism expert who served as a back channel informant to the FBI and later became a close friend and associate of another young Republican congressman, Richard Nixon. (Father Cronin became known nationally after he took a key position with the National Catholic Welfare Conference and became the church's chief protagonist against the threat of communism in America.) In 1948, Jack passed along to his father a proposal by the national Catholic War Veterans to produce films designed to fight communism and promote "a clear understanding of Christian social thought" based on two papal encyclicals.

As a politician in an overwhelmingly Catholic district, Congressman Kennedy maintained a strict anti-Communist posture, loathe as a "fighting conservative" to bend to the fuzzyheaded liberals in his own party. Kennedy blamed President Truman for allowing Communists in China to overwhelm the nationalist government of Chiang Kai-shek and saw that his 1952 Senate candidacy focused criticism on Lodge's support for Truman's policy. Some liberals viewed the young congressman as almost reactionary in his espousal of a hard-line anti-Communist diatribe. In embracing the 1950 Communist Control Act, Kennedy declared, "We are faced with an enemy whose goal is to conquer the world by subversion and infiltration or, if necessary, by open war." But for Catholic voters, Kennedy's rhetoric adopted an almost religious tone in its support of the church's deep antipathy toward communism. In a 1950 graduation day speech at the University of Notre Dame, Kennedy underlined the sharp philosophical distinction between Catholicism and its view of government only as a protector of human freedoms and natural law as opposed to communism with its all-encompassing belief in the powers of the state. "You have been taught that each individual has an internal soul, composed of an intellect which can know truth and a will which is free," he told graduates. "Believing this, Catholics can never adhere to any political theory which holds that the state is a separate, distinct organization to which allegiance must be paid rather than a representative institution which derives its powers from the consent of the governed." Fulton Sheen could not have said it better.

Jack's family members felt even stronger about communism. All his adult life, Joe Kennedy inveighed against the threat of Marx upon the soul and the pocketbook. He applauded fellow anti-Communist fighters such as the FBI director, J. Edgar Hoover, who, when talking to Archbishop Cushing (who himself provided information to the FBI), praised Kennedy as the most outstanding Catholic layman in the United States. Joe Kennedy's vehement anti-communism undoubtedly affected his earlier accommodation of fascist states such as Germany and Italy, which had presented a Hobson's choice as the lesser of two evils. "True, I was pessimistic as to the meaningfulness of any kind of a victory that might result eventually from that war, even after Hitler's attack on Russia," he later conceded, "for I foresaw then that the result of war would be the destruction of many of our democratic institutions and the rise of Communism." Historians often point to Kennedy's anti-Semitism as a possible cause for his policy of appeasement toward the Axis powers, but part of it likely stemmed from the anti-Communist stance of the Vatican, which saw its churches disassembled in Eastern Europe and deeply feared its further spread. "Of the polarities of totalitarianism, as a Catholic and a capitalist he objected more strenuously to communism, which he feared would grow unchecked in Europe in the wake of the defeat of fascism," wrote his granddaughter Amanda Smith more than a half century later. As a self-described "prophet" warning of these dangers, Joe Kennedy said the postwar world of communism on the march turned out precisely as he had warned.

Bobby Kennedy enlisted wholeheartedly in his father's cause. After a 1948 visit to Hungary, Bobby wrote an article for a Boston newspaper describing the Communist persecution of Cardinal Josef Mindszenty, who was arrested for being a Western spy, including an alleged collaboration with New York's Cardinal Spellman. The embattled prelate—"uninfluenced and uncorrupted by temporal power," as young Kennedy described him—had been jailed by the Nazis in 1944, and now was suffering as a Catholic in a Communist bloc nation. Bobby's own Catholicism and his sense of moral outrage rang out in this piece. "As a ranking official of an organization which is [a] direct antithesis of Communism, he [Mindszenty] naturally has been a symbol about which the opponents of this 'type of democracy' have rallied—but he has been far more than that," wrote young Kennedy. "He was Faith, Hope and Charity personified." During his stay in Hungary, the government suspected Kennedy of spying for Cardinal Spellman. "The only premises upon which they based this fantastic suspicion seemed to be that my father and Cardinal Spellman were close personal friends," he wrote.

In the mid–1950s, during a trip through Central Asia with a family friend, Justice William O. Douglas of the Supreme Court, Bobby reprised his critique of communism's impact on religion. "Today, religion and the family unit, which mean so much to the Moslem, have been destroyed," he observed in the *New York Times Magazine*. "The parents have been replaced by the state-operated nurseries and Youth Pioneer camps." To young Kennedy, this system struck at the heart of his own family's most cherished beliefs, and his moral objection was palpable. In the Soviet bloc, he saw the intense struggle between the Communists and the church. In Leningrad, he found the Communist government operating "a museum which is devoted completely to ridiculing God and people's religious beliefs," he told *U.S. News and World Report* disgustedly. "For instance, as you enter they have God sitting on top of the cross, wearing a top hat, smoking a cigar and portrayed as a capitalist while a working man is bent over carrying the Cross and Him."

During their trip, Douglas recalled, young Kennedy "carried ostenta-tiously a copy of the Bible in left hand" like a missionary. Yet Bobby responded to the poverty and loss of freedom in a humane way, Douglas recalled, despite his "violent religious drive" against the apparatchiks. The suffering he witnessed in the Soviet empire was further proof for Kennedy of the evils of communism.

FOR THE KENNEDY family, the personal and ideological came together in their friendship with the man who embodied the era—Senator Joseph McCarthy.

The Republican from Wisconsin, a genial fellow in private but in public a demagogue with a straining voice and indiscriminate conscience, seized on the Red Scare in 1950 when he held up a sheaf of papers and claimed they contained the names of 150 Communists in the State Department. He rode the issue mercilessly. In pure humbug fashion, McCarthy seized on the fear of subversion in America not to preach a deeply held conviction but rather to create an issue that would get him reelected. He jumped on the idea suggested to him initially by the Reverend Ed Walsh, a Jesuit priest at Georgetown. McCarthy's foghorn of alarm about the Communist threat struck a chord among many Catholics in America, who heard similar warnings from the pulpit. At first glance, this unique link between McCarthy and Catholics, particularly Irish-Americans, could be explained as some form of ethnic politics, the pride of an immigrant people about one of their own rising to an esteemed position of power. For a long time, this glow overshadowed the questionable motives and tactics behind McCarthy's effort to rid the countryside of all hidden Communists. "The grandiloquent gesture, the blarney, the do-or-die bravado, the inability to forget slights and humiliations, as well as the drinking and affinity for lost causes: it is not possible to understand McCarthy's career without this ethnic component," observed biographer Arthur Herman, who pointed out that McCarthy didn't lose his Irish brogue until he attended law school.

But McCarthy's prominence illuminated another schism among American Catholics. For all the progressive individuals associated with the church who were working toward social justice and enacting Christ's word in the world, just as the Sacred Heart nuns would have it, there was another side. The hidebound institutional church, particularly the all-male hierarchy of mostly Irish descent, was far more conservative. They instinctively agreed with McCarthy's anti-Communist crusade. The senator's actions were applauded by the Catholic clergy closest to the Kennedy family. In New York, Cardinal Spellman publicly backed McCarthy's crusade long after its Red-baiting excesses were exposed. "He is against Communism and he has done, and is doing, something about it," Spellman declared. "He is making America aware of the danger of Communism." A few Catholic prelates, notably Bishop Bernard J. Sheil of Chicago, condemned McCarthy's tactics, but many Catholic clergy, including Archbishop Cushing, still viewed the Wisconsin senator as doing God's work. "It all depends on what they think of Communism," explained Cushing in late 1953. "Despite any extremes or mistakes that may have been made, I don't believe anything has brought out the evils and methods of Communism more to the American people than the investigations." When Ralph E. Flanders, the Republican senator of Vermont, suggested that McCarthy's charges were upsetting his church as well as the nation, Cushing came to McCarthy's defense. "He certainly is not dividing the church," Cushing rebuked. "There is no Catholic attitude on the issue and Catholics can go the way they will."

Regardless of Cushing's disclaimer, the American leaders of the church sent a message portraying McCarthy as a defender of the faith as well as the nation's security. In the early 1950s, McCarthy became the most prominent Catholic in American political life since the days of Al Smith. At the same time, though, McCarthy stirred deeply imbedded tensions throughout the country between Catholics and the Protestant majority, some of whom resented the inquisition like tactics of this Irish Catholic ideologue. In his study of this period, Donald F. Crosby, a Jesuit priest, observed, "Many Protestants began to see in Joe McCarthy the lurid image of everything they had come to fear in American Catholicism: like many Catholics he showed a certain disinterest in civil liberties, he demanded conformity to his own set of opinions, he was intolerant of all opposition, he dogmatized mindlessly, and he made a shambles of the democratic process by abusing the witnesses who came before his congressional committee. In sum, Joe McCarthy had come to represent what the Roman Catholic church had always seemed to be." Many wondered whether McCarthy hoped to become the "first Catholic President." He discounted such a possibility. As he told the press, his religion made it virtually impossible.

THE KENNEDY FAMILY'S affinity for Joe McCarthy was inexplicable unless viewed in the religious and ethnic complexity of its time. McCarthy's "rough-hewn Irishness, his unsophisticated Catholicism, and his resentment of the establishment," as a writer for the *New Yorker* later put it, appealed greatly to young Bobby Kennedy. As a University of Virginia law student, Bobby proudly arranged for his appearance at a school forum. McCarthy embodied the cultural conservativeness of many Catholic voters who were enrolled in the Democratic Party of their immigrant ancestors, but increasingly agreed with the concerns of Republicans. Joe Kennedy developed a personal friendship with McCarthy, inviting him on vacation to the Cape. McCarthy genially took part in the family's softball games and boat outings, and even dated Kennedy's daughter, Pat. The two Joes were birds of the same feather. "In case there is any question in your mind, I liked Joe McCarthy—I always liked him," Kennedy told an interviewer years later when his son was president. "I thought he'd be a sensation. He was smart. But he went off the deep end."

Even though McCarthy was a Republican, Joe Kennedy contributed generously to his political coffers. This investment of money and friendship paid dividends for the Kennedys in the 1952 Senate race. Several Republicans urged McCarthy, by far the most influential national figure at the time, to campaign for the party's candidate in the close Massachusetts race. An appearance by McCarthy would undoubtedly boost Henry Cabot Lodge's reelection chances in the Boston area, cutting into Jack Kennedy's crucial core support among Catholics. But out of deference to old man Kennedy and his clan, McCarthy never showed for Lodge. "I told [the Lodge campaign] I'd go up to Boston to speak if Cabot publicly asked me," McCarthy later boasted to fellow conservative, William F. Buckley Jr. "And he'll never do that—he'd lose the Harvard vote."

Jack's relationship with McCarthy was amiable enough. During their early days in Washington, McCarthy occasionally socialized with Jack and his sister, Eunice, and the friendliness lasted for several years. As young congressmen elected after the war, both were ardent anti-Communists. As Catholics, both senators made certain they found time in their Sunday schedules to attend Mass each week, though neither practiced their religion in a showy way. The Kennedys viewed Joe McCarthy as one of their own. Bobby and Ethel even considered asking McCarthy to stand as godfather for their first child, Kathleen. At a centennial celebration for Harvard's Spee Club in 1952, when a speaker likened McCarthy to Alger Hiss, Jack uncharacteristically became upset. "How dare you couple the name of a great American patriot with that of a traitor!" he bellowed, storming out before he could finish dessert. Early in McCarthy's campaign against Communist subversion, Jack shared his father's view that the senator "may well have something." During Jack's 1952 campaign, when a liberal aide, Gardner "Pat" Jackson, unveiled a potential announcement attacking McCarthyism, the candidate's father erupted in fury, knocking over a table as he sprang to his feet. "You and your friends are trying to ruin my son's career!" he shouted. The elder Kennedy railed against Jackson and "your sheeny friends," who included unionists, liberals and Jews on his son's staff. The next day, when Jack attempted a consoling comment to his shaken aide, Jackson asked him to explain his father's behavior. "Just love of family," Jack replied, pausing to add, "No—pride of family."

For the rest of that campaign, Jack tried to steer a fine dividing line, careful not to bring up McCarthy's name for fear of pitting one portion of his constituency against the next. His campaign literature promised to fight against "atheistic communism" and yet promised his liberal supporters that he wouldn't do so at the expense of civil liberties. He mastered the art of balancing himself on a very thin line.

Soon after the 1952 election, Joe Kennedy implored McCarthy to find a place on his staff for his son Bobby, fresh from his triumph as Jack's campaign manager. McCarthy already had a chief counsel for his Senate Permanent Subcommittee on Investigations—Roy Cohn, a wiry and crafty aide-de-camp who shared his boss's taste for savaging reputations with baseless lies. The senator offered Bobby a job as deputy counsel. Cohn later recalled watching McCarthy nod his head dutifully during a prolonged telephone conversation and wondering who was on the other end.. "Joe Kennedy," McCarthy mouthed to his aide, as if being held captive. Every minute or so, McCarthy would reply, "Sure, Joe . . . I see. . . . That's a good point." Exasperated, McCarthy finally waived over his aide and, while still on the telephone, wrote out a note to Cohn: "Remind me to check the size of his campaign contribution. I'm not sure it's worth it."

The Kennedys were major backers of the senator's anti-Red jihad. As the national controversy around him mounted, McCarthy's support remained firm among Catholics, his words carrying the political imprimatur of New York's powerful cardinal. "Congressional inquiries into Communist activities in the United States are not the result of any mad legislative whim," insisted Spellman. "There are strong reasons for these inquiries and we thank God we have begun while there is still time to do something about it." One Spellman aide told a Catholic war veterans' Communion breakfast that a $5 million anti-McCarthy war chest had been raised "to kick Joe out" and that "the reason is solely because of his Catholic ideals." Firefighters in New York were instructed by their Knights of Columbus affiliate to come to Washington for a McCarthy rally. Some clergy suggested that an attack on McCarthy smacked of anti-Catholic bigotry. "Protestants know that in some Catholic circles being pro-McCarthy is somehow considered a test, if not of faith, at least of loyalty to the Church," warned *Commonweal*. "We do not want to see the Church forced into a shotgun wedding with the far right-wing of the Republican Party."

As a practical political matter, however, Jack expressed dismay when his brother joined McCarthy's staff. He recommended Bobby not do it, as did other friends. "McCarthy could prove your mother was a Communist by his way of reasoning," Kenny O'Donnell argued with Bobby. "By using his methods of proof, the Pope could be a Communist." Nevertheless, Bobby jumped at the chance with the same enthusiasm as he had his earlier work. Joe Kennedy, who sometimes acted as a behind-the-scenes intermediary between Spellman and McCarthy, also gave his blessings. Soon, all three Kennedys rued this decision.

Bobby's first major assignment produced a well-received report that showed American allies were trading with the Chinese at the same time the mainland Communists were fueling the war in Korea against American soldiers. Within a few months, however, Bobby realized that McCarthy's sloppy recklessness would cost the committee all shreds of its remaining credibility. In one fiasco, McCarthy's director of investigation wrote a magazine article that declared "the largest single group supporting the Communist apparatus in the United States today is composed of Protestant clergymen." Howls of outrage by President Eisenhower and many distinguished religious leaders led to the aide's swift dismissal. After his own feud with Cohn, Kennedy quit, only to return a few months later, in early 1954, as the Democratic counsel to McCarthy's committee.

The televised 1954 hearings into alleged Communist infiltration of the U.S. Army turned into a watershed disaster. McCarthy unraveled before the nation's eyes with an endless stream of unfounded and blatantly false accusations. Kennedy's anger focused on Cohn, rather than McCarthy, for whom he still retained some fondness. But both Joe and Bobby Kennedy concluded McCarthy's power was declining. The most prominent Irish Catholic on the national scene in years was bound for disgrace. Personally, the Kennedys remained loyal and defensive. "All this poppycock about McCarthy having any effect on America's standing in Europe is the biggest lot of dribble," Joe wrote to a rather dubious Jack. "The masses haven't the slightest idea of what McCarthy stands for, what he does and what's wrong with him."

The army hearing debacle resulted in a censure vote in the Senate. In October 1954, this thumbs up or down on McCarthy's fate created a complicated moral dilemma for Jack Kennedy, already in the throes of a great personal crisis. His chronic back problem, traceable to the PT-109 accident and other injuries, had left him hobbling on crutches most of the time. Hoping to cure his aching spine and regain some degree of normalcy, the young newlywed senator agreed to a risky operation that his doctors promised would make him better if successful. Three days after surgery, a severe staph infection in his body, already weakened from his undisclosed

Addison's disease, forced him into a coma and nearly killed him. "Jack's dying," Joe Kennedy moaned aloud to his newspaper confidant, *New York Times* columnist Arthur Krock, his vibrant blue eyes reddened with tears. A priest gave Jack the last rites of the church.

A more cautious person might not have accepted the odds of such a dangerous operation, but Kennedy's intimacy with death and his hunger for the pleasures of life compelled his choice. Slowly, he recovered and faced weeks in a hospital bed trying to regain his strength. He even sent messages to girlfriends involved in his extramarital escapades to assure them that he'd soon be back in business. During this period, the Senate moved toward a censure vote against McCarthy, but Kennedy ducked it by saying he was too ill to cast a vote. He later conceded that a public rebuke of McCarthy was just too difficult, both personally and politically. By coming out against the most prominent Irish Catholic in national politics, Kennedy would alienate a large proportion of voters back home. "I was rather in ill grace personally to be around hollering about what McCarthy had done in 1952 or 1951 when my brother was on the staff in 1953—that's really the guts of the matters," Jack later told biographer James MacGregor Burns. Critics suggested that Kennedy lacked the courage to stand up to McCarthy and used his illness as a shield to avoid public rebuke from his pro-McCarthy constituents. When he had refused to sign a petition for Curley's release from jail a few years earlier, he thought he had committed political suicide. He certainly wasn't going to take a second risk again in Massachusetts by criticizing McCarthy. In both cases, family considerations—Curley perceived as an enemy of the clan and McCarthy as a friend—were crucial to understanding Jack's decisions. Many liberal Democrats, Eleanor Roosevelt among them, had little sympathy for Kennedy's predicament. Mrs. Roosevelt suggested that Jack placed political expediency before moral principle with the McCarthy vote. "I think McCarthyism is a question on which public officials must stand up and be counted," said the former first lady when asked specifically about Kennedy. "I cannot be sure of the political future of anyone who does not willingly state where he stands on the issue."

But the Kennedys never really gave up their emotional ties to Joe McCarthy. Though they were appalled by his blunders and excesses, they believed McCarthy understood the worldwide threat of communism and that he was the only American doing something about it. Long after he left the committee, Bobby visited the senator's office to reaffirm his abiding friendship. At a 1955 Junior Chamber of Commerce dinner honoring him as one of the ten most outstanding young men of the year, Bobby walked out because one of the speakers was Ed Murrow, the television commentator whose documentary exposed McCarthy's reckless ways. "His Irish conception of loyalty," as Arthur M. Schlesinger Jr. later characterized it, "turned him against some he felt had treated McCarthy unfairly." When McCarthy collapsed into alcoholism and eventually died in 1957, Bobby genuinely grieved, so upset that he dismissed his staff for the day. In his journal, he scribbled: "It was all very difficult for me as I feel that I have lost an important part of my life—even though it is in the past." Joe Kennedy viewed McCarthy as a fallen comrade-in-arms in the fight against communism. "Shocked and deeply grieved to hear of Joe's passing," the senior Kennedy wrote to McCarthy's widow, Jean Kerr McCarthy. "His indomitable courage in adhering to the cause in which he believed evoked my warm admiration. His friendship was deeply appreciated and reciprocated."

McCarthy's fall from grace confirmed the stereotype of Catholics held by so many Americans. In particular, Irish Catholics seemed all too willing to follow such demagogic figures as McCarthy and Father Coughlin before him. For Jack Kennedy, the McCarthy connections could only hurt his chances for the White House.

Chapter Twenty

A Nation of Immigrants

DUBLIN, WITH ITS ANCESTRAL HISTORY and fond personal memories, proved just the tonic for Jackie Kennedy and her husband. In late September 1955, the senator and his wife stopped for a week's vacation in Ireland, the last leg on their journey home from a fact-finding trip to Poland. Their marriage had suffered terribly in its first years—not only with Jack's near fatal back surgery, his long absences and the whispers of infidelity, but also with the miscarriage of their anticipated first child. Ireland beckoned as the perfect place for a respite together.

During this visit, Jack and Jackie stayed at the Shelbourne Hotel, perhaps the grandest address in Dublin. As part of its storied past, the hotel played host in the 1920s when the Irish Free State's leaders composed their new constitution inside a first-floor suite. Jack could barely get around without help, but he insisted on visiting the city's pubs and exploring its nightlife. The public events of their unheralded stay were arranged by an old friend of Jackie's, a priest who had given her so much spiritual comfort in the past.

Father Joseph Leonard of All Hallows College in Dublin invited Jack to give a rousing, extemporaneous address about the suffering of Catholics at the hands of Poland's Communist state. During his talk at All Hallows—a training school for Irish priests, many of whom were sent abroad to America—Kennedy echoed the church's concern about the dismantling of religion in that Soviet bloc nation. On his way to Poland, Kennedy's commitment to the church's struggle against communism was underlined by his brief stop in Rome for an audience with Pope Pius XII. Several years earlier, Jacqueline Kennedy had met Father Leonard during a trip to

Ireland. A relative had known the priest since the 1920s and urged Jackie to look him up when she visited Eire with her stepbrother, Hugh D. Auchincloss Jr. Since their meeting, she'd kept a regular correspondence with Leonard, who sometimes sent books of prayers and religious meditations to inspire her.

While in Dublin, Jack attended a luncheon in his honor given by Liam Cosgrave, the minister for external affairs. The Irish-American from Boston peppered everyone with questions about Irish history and politics. "At that time [Kennedy was] moving around on crutches, and instead of giving him the lunch anywhere else, we arranged that it be given in the Shelbourne," Cosgrave recalled. Father Leonard sat near Jackie at the front table. Cosgrave and their other Irish hosts impressed upon Kennedy their concerns about a divided Ireland and the need to end the partition of the north. Kennedy exhibited a keen interest in Irish affairs. For example, he expressed interest in Roger Casement, a hero of the Irish Rebellion in 1916, hanged as a traitor in England for his part in smuggling German arms to the Irish rebels—a controversy still debated today.

Jackie renewed her friendship with Father Leonard, a clergyman whose faith didn't seem cloistered or ethereal but rooted in everyday reality. "Father Leonard's spirituality was not merely unobtrusive, it was wholly sane," wrote an observer. "He had no use for mere pietism, or for the 'dangerously devout.'" Like Cushing in Boston, Father Leonard possessed an approachable manner that helped him make fast friends with Jackie's husband as well. (When their first son was born a few years later, Jackie would ask Father Leonard to come to America to baptize him—a request the Irish priest couldn't honor because of failing health. When Cosgrave later came to the United States, he spotted Kennedy at a reception; the senator smiled with recognition and said, "Father Leonard," then inquiring about his wife's friend.)

Before the Kennedys left Ireland, Father Leonard inscribed a recently published book he had translated from the French, a biography of St. Vincent de Paul, the patron saint of the hopelessly sick and downtrodden. "To Jack and Jacqueline with love and admiration," he wrote inside the cover. Leonard gave Jackie another book, a biography of the English Catholic writer, Maurice Baring. "*For Jacqueline,*" he penned. "*Dublin: September 29–October 2.*" Over the years of their friendship, Father Leonard sent Jackie other books, including Baring's biography of Mary, Queen of Scots, and the works of another contemporary English Catholic writer, Ronald Knox. These titles sent by Father Leonard included *Layman and His*

Conscience and *Retreat for Lay People*. In her own quiet undemonstrable way, Jackie seemed to have adopted some of her mother-in-law's Catholic spirituality, and she developed her own counselors in faith. A decade earlier, Jack had finished his privately published tribute to his dead brother, *As We Remember Joe,* with a poem from Baring.

BOOKS HELD a special meaning for these Kennedys. During his seven-month convalescence, Jack lay flat on his back and read stacks of volumes taken from the Library of Congress, and also put together the manuscript for a best-selling history, *Profiles in Courage.* Joe Kennedy always impressed upon his son that his reputation would be burnished, the public's esteem for him enhanced, by publishing a book under his own name. For *Profiles in Courage,* Joe Kennedy acted as agent, producer and promoter even more so than he had with his son's earlier effort as a young Harvard graduate. *Profiles in Courage* was published in early 1956 and won the Pulitzer Prize after intense lobbying by his father's journalism fixer, Arthur Krock, a long-time member of the Pulitzer board. (Joe Kennedy's private papers are replete with ethical compromises made by the *Times* man. "It needs punch and polish," Kennedy once directed Krock about a rough draft of a speech he planned to give. "Will you look it over, shape it up, and then send me what you think will do the most good for us.") Despite the family's angry denials, a succession of journalists and authors would claim, with considerable evidence, that a coterie of staffers and advisers had done the heavy lifting for young Kennedy.

Whatever its origins, the book indisputably helped John F. Kennedy's political fortunes and lifted him from the realm of cultural stereotype. During the 1950s, several critics, notably Paul Blanshard, wrote about the lack of intellectual life among American Catholics and blamed the church and the insular nature of immigrant life for its underdevelopment. The rants of Senator McCarthy only reinforced this die-hard stereotype of Irish Catholics, particularly among liberals and intellectuals, a significant segment of the Democratic Party and the press. In writing his book, Kennedy twisted the old archetypes on their head to create his own new standard. Here was an Irish Catholic who didn't look like Al Smith or a bleary-eyed big-city hack; instead, he was a Harvard-educated young man who got himself elected to the Senate and managed to win a Pulitzer to boot. His respectful tribute to the Senate's white Anglo-Saxon Protestant politicians—several of whom probably would have prohibited the Kennedy clan from entering this nation had they been given the chance—pushed

Kennedy back toward the middle of the political spectrum, away from the extremes of McCarthy. He was no longer touted as "a fighting conservative"—the phrase that Colonel McCormick's *Chicago Tribune* used to describe him—but as a thoughtful, moderate senator who wanted to be president someday. "Today the challenge of political courage looms larger than ever before," Kennedy assured his readers. "Our public life is becoming so increasingly centered upon that seemingly unending war to which we have given the curious epithet 'cold' that we tend to encourage rigid ideological unity and orthodox patterns of thought."

As if repenting for his silence during the censure vote, in his book Kennedy embraced old American virtues based on individual liberties and devotion to the democratic institutions. "The ultimate source of political courage in a nation, Kennedy was saying in his book, lay in the extent that independence, unorthodoxy, and dissent were tolerated among the people as a whole," observed historian James MacGregor Burns, one of several experts credited in the preface. "This conclusion was of particular importance, for he was arguing that the toleration of unorthodoxy is a matter not merely of democratic rectitude, but a matter of democratic survival." Kennedy's heroes paid homage to the traditional separation between church and government, though they remained always answerable to a higher power. Kennedy suggested that this same spirit of openness should apply not only to orthodoxy in politics but also to choosing a politician with an unorthodox religion.

By EARLY 1956, John Kennedy's name was being circulated among the Democratic conventioneers as a potential running mate for Adlai Stevenson of Illinois, the odds-on favorite as the party's presidential nominee. Four years earlier, Stevenson lost badly to Eisenhower and his chances didn't seem any brighter this time against the Republican incumbent. Joe Kennedy considered Stevenson a sure loser; he advised his son to be patient and not take a possible vice-presidential bid, even if the opportunity were offered. The senior Kennedy, still mindful of Al Smith's 1928 loss, worried that Jack's Catholicism might be blamed unfairly as a reason for the ticket's failure. Such a scenario would be worse than just a single defeat; for at least another generation it could dissuade any Catholic from seeking the presidency. Stevenson himself wasn't sure that running with a Catholic would help his chances for the White House. Several of his allies wondered whether under all Kennedy's polish lay the beastly heart of a Red-baiter willing to abuse civil liberties at any cost.

Other advisers exuded the faint whiff of anti-Catholicism found in intellectual circles. Plenty of anti-Catholic and anti-Kennedy mail found its
way to Stevenson, and several national figures, including national chairman Frank McKinney (a Catholic himself), advised Stevenson against
asking Kennedy because it would mean certain defeat. In one of the private letters he received, Agnes Meyer, a Stevenson friend married to the
publisher of the *Washington Post,* warned that such a selection would
unleash a more sophisticated and more powerfully organized opposition
than the 1928 election saw because the Protestant clergy was more formidable than in Smith's day. She clipped a newspaper article quoting a
prominent Protestant clergyman in New York who vowed not to vote for
a Roman Catholic on any national ticket "because of the authority the
Roman Catholic Church holds over its members."

As the summertime convention neared, Jack took his father's progno-
sis under advisement. "While I think the prospects are rather limited," he
admitted to his father before the convention, "it does seem of some use
to have all of this churning up." At the same time, though, Jack made sure
that his brother Bobby would be working on his behalf on the convention floor. The senator called his friend Tip O'Neill, who had taken over
Jack's old congressional seat, and asked for credentials for his brother. Told
it was too late, Kennedy persisted. "My brother Bob is the smartest politician I have ever met in my life," Jack implored. "You know you never can
tell, lightning may strike at this convention out there, I could wind up as
vice-president."

Boston's Irish Catholic politicians with a sense of history, such as O'Neill
and future Speaker of the House John McCormack, were well aware that
Kennedy had traveled farther and faster than any of their kind before.
Despite his sophisticated and often witty manner, he knew how to be an
organization in-fighter, a party chieftain, just like his two grandfathers.
Earlier in the year, Kennedy had won a struggle to wrest control of the state
Democratic Party from those allied with Curley and McCormack. "He and
his millions don't know what decency means," complained state party
chairman William Burke, after being ousted by Kennedy's hand-picked candidate. On the national scene, however, Boston's pols were inclined to root
for Kennedy, even if they did resent the family's power and money. O'Neill
knew what he must do. He agreed to turn over his own seat at the convention to Bobby.

As the buzz about Kennedy increased, *Look* magazine published an
article that questioned whether any Democrat could win with a Catholic

on the ticket. In a survey of thirty-one Democratic officials in thirteen Southern states, more than half said a Catholic would hurt the party's chances in their states. Only three said it would help. "You know, you guys have got this Catholic thing all wrong," Kennedy told *Look* magazine reporter Fletcher Knebel after the article appeared. "I think a Catholic would run better for vice president, maybe not president." Jack directed his chief strategist Ted Sorensen to prepare a memorandum about why Kennedy's religion would help the Democrats that year. The memo argued that Catholics, regardless of age, residence or social class, would vote in "high proportion . . . for a well-known Catholic candidate or a ticket with a special Catholic appeal." It relied heavily on statistical analysis gleaned from top pollsters and published academic studies. The Kennedys mailed the report to top party leaders around the country under the signature of Connecticut's Democratic boss John Bailey (and thus dubbed "the Bailey report") to avoid having their fingerprints directly on the document's creation.

The so-called Bailey Report wasn't the first time Sorensen's work had benefited Kennedy. If the Irish pols surrounding him in his congressional races reflected one side of Jack Kennedy's background, the hiring of Ted Sorensen for his tenure in the Senate reflected another part of Kennedy's personality and ambitions. In effect, Sorensen became Kennedy's Brahmin alter ego, the sober-minded tactician not swayed by ethnic pride or prejudices but committed as a liberal to helping a like-minded politician try to win favor in a Protestant nation. Before being hired in early 1953, Sorensen was warned by a well-placed Washington lawyer that he wouldn't get the job because of his religion. "Jack Kennedy wouldn't hire anyone Joe Kennedy wouldn't tell him to hire," the lawyer told him, "and with the exception of Jim Landis, Joe Kennedy hasn't hired a non-Catholic in fifty years!" Wary of Kennedy's father, Sorensen also thought Bobby Kennedy was "militant, aggressive, intolerant, opinionated, somewhat shallow in his convictions . . . more like his father than his brother."

A native Nebraskan, Sorensen understood the prairie lands, where Catholics were a rarity and looked at askance. As he later wrote, "Having been raised in a Unitarian and civil liberties atmosphere that looked with some suspicion on Catholic political pressure, I could help the Senator understand the more reasonable fears he encountered." Before accepting the Senate staff job, Sorensen inquired about Kennedy's religion. "We had another interview and this time I asked the questions—about his father, Joe McCarthy and the Catholic Church," he recalled. Kennedy quickly put to rest his young aide's concerns. "There is an old saying in Boston—'We get our religion from Rome and our politics at home,'" Kennedy replied.

In surveying the 1956 political landscape, Sorensen built his argument for Kennedy with a strong dose of numbers and revisionist history. Rather than a defensive treatise, arguing for religious liberty and tolerance, Sorensen instead crafted a memo that underlined why Catholics—many of them first- and second-generation children of Irish, Italian, German, Polish and other immigrants—were a pivotal part of the Democratic Party's strength. Without the margin of victory provided by Catholic voters in the 1940 presidential campaign, the report noted, states such as Pennsylvania, Wisconsin, New Jersey, Illinois and even New York—Franklin Roosevelt's home state—would have been lost to the Republicans, changing the entire outcome of the election. After World War II, as Catholics moved to the suburbs and integrated into the mainstream of American life, some defected to the Republicans, the report pointed out. By 1952, many groups such as Irish Catholics—who normally voted 65 percent Democratic—voted by a 53 percent margin for the GOP's Dwight Eisenhower. In this report, Sorensen contended that putting a Catholic on the 1956 ticket would regain this traditional bloc of Democratic voters.

The Bailey Report also addressed "the Al Smith myth"—the historical contention that Smith's Catholicism posed an insurmountable hurdle for his presidential candidacy. Instead, the report argued that in the 1928 election, the prohibition of alcohol was three times more important as an issue than religion, and Hoover, a "dry" candidate, reflected public sentiment more than a "wet" like Smith. More significantly, the report insisted that America was now different, had grown past the bigotry of yesteryear. "The nation has changed since 1928," Sorensen concluded. "There are more Catholics—their political role, as seen above, is more crucial—their leadership in the Democratic Party and in the statewide offices from California to Maine is both frequent and accepted—and the nation is considerably more tolerant on religious matters."

Despite its compelling arguments, the Bailey Report didn't sway Stevenson enough to put Kennedy on the 1956 ticket. He did ask the young Massachusetts senator to give a nominating speech on his behalf, however, which Kennedy did effectively before a television audience. Without warning, Stevenson then threw the vice-presidential decision open to the delegates. Kennedy's troops, led by his brother and a handful of state leaders, made a last-minute effort, but he fell short of the sufficient number of votes, the party instead nominating Senator Estes Kefauver of

Tennessee. Before the full convention, Kennedy made a gracious concession speech that marked him as a future contender for the top spot on the ticket. He dutifully campaigned for Stevenson, but he didn't forget the dismissive reaction he heard in the voice of one of Adlai Stevenson's relatives—"Oh, those poor little Catholics." In 1956, Kennedy's political achievements and his success with a best-selling book brought him great acclaim. But the question of religion underlined how difficult it would be for him to seek the presidency.

AFTER THANKSGIVING dinner in 1956, the Kennedy patriarch held a long discussion at the family's home in Hyannis Port about his son's political future. Though he'd been against the idea of Jack's running for vice president with Stevenson, Joe Kennedy now proposed that his son pursue the 1960 presidential nomination. Laboriously and cautiously, Jack went through each major hurdle, each of which his father assured him could be overcome, including religion. Years later, Rose recounted her husband's pep talk, which took on the dramatic overtones of a quest.

"Just remember, this country is not a private preserve for Protestants," Joe concluded. "There's a whole new generation out there and it's filled with the sons and daughters of immigrants from all over the world and those people are going to be mighty proud that one of their own is running for President. And that pride will be your spur, it will give your campaign an intensity we've never seen in public life. Mark my word, I know it's true." Old man Kennedy, though tart and cynical, still burned with a certain idealism when it applied to his son and his country. Perhaps the glass ceiling in American life could be broken, and Joe took heart when Jack was elected to Harvard's Board of Overseers in 1957. "Now I know his religion won't keep him out of the White House," he declared. "If an Irish Catholic can get elected as an Overseer at Harvard, he can get elected to anything."

IMMIGRANTS AND THEIR children were the untapped potential for Kennedy. The symbolism of his candidacy represented far more than the potential acceptance and toleration of Roman Catholicism in the United States; it extended into the realm of opportunities and possibilities for all minority groups. Joe Kennedy surely didn't see his son as the messianic leader of all minorities in America, and surely his politically prudent son didn't, either. But Joe's keen grasp of the facts and figures outlined in the Bailey Report made him aware that immigrants and minorities held the key to Jack's potential victory. "Catholic voting strength is currently at its peak, in view of the maturing of the offspring of the Italians, Poles, Czechs and other former immigrant elements," according to a voter survey quoted in the report. These "immigrant elements" would form the stone and mortar of Kennedy's presidential campaign.

Immigration remained a constant in Kennedy's politics. Like grandfather John F. Fitzgerald, he paid particular attention in Congress to matters concerning immigrants. For all of his considerable cautiousness in politics, Kennedy became a maverick on this issue. During his six years in the House, Kennedy consistently favored immigration reforms along with other liberal domestic issues that balanced his hawkish anti-Communist foreign policy. His concerns were sensible local politics in a congressional district with many recent émigrés from around the world. Massachusetts then contained a greater percentage of foreign-born residents than any other state in the union. In the Senate, Kennedy's interest in immigration broadened even further, both in proposed legislation and his own public writings. He fought hard for reforms to the McCarran–Walter Immigration and Nationality Act of 1952 by seeking to end racist restrictions that favored "Caucasian" immigrants and restricted entry for those from Asia and Latin America. In strong moral tones, he criticized the national origins quota system that kept many immigrant families, apart for years, from coming together.

Kennedy's objections to the nation's immigration system, its fundamental unfairness, struck a deep chord within him. In late 1958, Kennedy published a small book, almost pamphlet-sized, called *A Nation of Immigrants*, in which he provided an enlightened history of America's immigrants and carefully picked apart the problems of the current system. "I know of no cause which [Jack] Kennedy championed more warmly than the improvement of our immigration policies," observed Robert Kennedy, who later said the book was "deliberately designed to provide those who were unfamiliar with this aspect of our history with an appreciation of the enormous contributions to American life made by immigrants."

Far more than Jack Kennedy's two earlier books, *A Nation of Immigrants* had very personal roots. Kennedy's heritage allowed him to perceive changes in America that other Anglo-American thinkers might not pick up. His sense of history made him see a universal quality to America's immigration.

Years later, Senator Edward Kennedy would agree that this small book, often ignored by biographers, had sprung from some of his brother's most deeply held values. "It was very important to him," Ted recalled. "He was very proud of his Irish heritage and while growing up came to realize how the Irish in Boston made great contributions to the life of the city. He came to see that immigrants from many other nations enhanced America and helped the nation to move forward into the future. He knew that there were misconceptions about immigration and immigrants. . . . So he wrote that book to show how much immigration helped America and how much it was needed and should be appreciated."

IN LANGUAGE suitable for a Boy Scout manual, Jack Kennedy saluted America's cherished beliefs in democracy, equal opportunity and the melting pot of disparate cultures brought by immigrants. Invoking Walt Whitman, he surveyed a land enlivened by a constant flow of new blood in all walks of life. "There is no part of our nation that has not been touched by our immigrant background," he praised. "Everywhere immigrants have enriched and strengthened the fabric of American life." To draw strength for his argument, Kennedy quoted probably the most patrician character his father ever knew, President Franklin D. Roosevelt, who told a convention of the Daughters of the American Revolution (DAR), "Remember, remember always, that all of us, and you and I especially, are descended from immigrants and revolutionists."

As part of his argument, Kennedy quoted Harvard historian Oscar Handlin and his Pulizer Prize–winning book, *The Uprooted,* about immigrants from long ago ("Once I thought to write a history of the immigrants in America," wrote Handlin. "Then I discovered that the immigrants *were* American history.") But Kennedy also included more recent immigrant experiences in his tribute. "In our own day, for example, anti-Semitic and anti-Christian persecution in Hitler's Germany and the Communist empire have driven people from their homes to seek refuge in America," Kennedy observed. "Minority religious sects, from Quakers and Shakers through the Catholics and Jews to the Mormons and the Jehovah's Witnesses, have at various times suffered both discrimination and hostility in the United States." Intolerance became universal in immigrant life, as Kennedy depicted it, a suffering they all shared.

Kennedy displayed his own understanding of Irish-American history in this book. "The Irish were in the vanguard of the great waves of immigration" during the 1800s, he wrote, many of whom "were mostly country folk, small farmers, cottagers and farm laborers"—just like Patrick Kennedy, his great-grandfather. These young Irish workers became a supply of "cheap labor" for the most menial, dangerous jobs. He explained how the Irish gravitated to civil service jobs in government, helped establish the Catholic Church in America and overcame the "handicaps of illiteracy" by setting up their own parochial school system and Catholic-run colleges. Above all, Kennedy emphasized their place in American history: "The Irish were the first to endure the scorn and the discrimination . . . inflicted . . . by already settled 'Americans.' In speech and dress they seemed foreign; they were poor and unskilled; and they were arriving in overwhelming numbers. The Irish are perhaps the only people in our history with the distinction of having a political party, The Know-Nothings, formed against them. Their religion was later also the target of the American Protective Association and, in this century, the Ku Klux Klan."

IN THE WHITE-BREAD atmosphere of the 1950s, Kennedy's book offered a remarkably different perspective. In prose and pictures, it celebrated a broad mosaic of American immigration—Poles, Chinese, Italians, Czechs, Germans, Armenians, Danes and Laplanders. But it also contained examples of America's less than glorious past, including pictures of a Klan rally with two burning crosses. Kennedy's book seemed to equate, or at least find common ground, in the experiences of all minorities in America. He reminded readers that as their numbers increased, so did nativism and the level of hostility "against the Irish, who, as Catholics, were regarded as members of an alien conspiracy."

Kennedy held a more qualified view of the American "melting pot" ideal than the prevailing popular doctrine of the 1950s presented. It differed even from the views of some academics and political aides surrounding him. The Irish Catholics he knew—certainly those like his grandfather and own father—did not wish to become Brahmins as much as to be accepted for what they were and not have to adopt someone else's religion or culture. In Kennedy's concept of assimilation, public schools became a critically important tool for preparing immigrant children to get ahead in American life, but he emphasized that it should not come at the loss of self-identity. "The ideal of the 'melting pot' symbolized the process of blending many strains into a single nationality, and we have come to realize in modern times that the 'melting pot' need not mean the end of particular ethnic identities or traditions." In an eloquent, almost philosophic way, he emphasized why immigrants were so central to the American dream. As he wrote:

> Immigration is by definition a gesture of faith in social mobility. It is the expression in action of a positive belief in the possibility of a bet-

ter life. It has thus contributed greatly to developing the spirit of personal betterment in American society and to strengthening the national confidence in change and the future. . . . The *continuous* immigration of the nineteenth and early twentieth centuries was thus central to the whole American faith. It gave every old American a standard by which to judge how far he had come and every new American a realization of how far he might go. It reminded every American, old and new, that change is the essence of life, and that American society is a process, not a conclusion.

NO TRUER, MORE simply stated expression of John Kennedy's fundamental liberalism exists. Undoubtedly, *A Nation of Immigrants* was created in response to Joe Sr.'s tactical advice that immigrants and their descendants could hold the key to electoral success in the 1960 race for the White House. Surely the treatise would curry favor with many minority groups whom Kennedy needed desperately in a winning coalition. But Kennedy's book went further in scope than could ever be expected from a mere campaign pamphlet. At that time, the notion of immigration as an active agent in the "process" of an ever-changing America was far different than the worldview of many Americans who insisted that newcomers become just like them—in effect Anglicized and devoid of their cultural beliefs. Kennedy's book stressed that America would be better off if it understood and embraced its remarkable immigration history rather than ignore or deny it. This testament of faith formed the basis for Kennedy's strong opposition to U.S. immigration policy and his determination to reform it.

In later chapters, Kennedy unsparingly dissected the racism and religious bigotry that had existed within American immigrant policy since the nation's founding. By 1921, America had in place a "radically new policy" that set a cap on the number of immigrants allowed to enter each year; entry was determined according to a rigid formula based on the "national origins" of those foreign-born citizens already here. Immigrants from Britain, Ireland and Germany had few problems, but those from Italy, Hungary, Poland and the Baltic states faced huge backlogs, the number of applicants far greater than the number allowed to enter. This "national origins" system was still largely in place when Kennedy wrote his book. "The national origins quota system has strong overtones of an indefensible racial preference," Kennedy charged. "It is strongly weighted toward so-called Anglo-Saxons." Such language was remarkable for someone already planning to run for president and aware of the bigotry he might encounter. Kennedy called for a new immigration system judged not by race or ethnicity but by the need for each immigrant's skills as well as by an immigrant's ties to family members already living in the United States. In summarizing his plea, Kennedy harked back to Boston and the wisdom of an Irish Catholic immigrant who edited the archdiocese's newspaper during Honey Fitz's era. "We must avoid what the Irish poet John Boyle O'Reilly once called 'organized charity, scrimped and iced / In the name of a cautious, statistical Christ,'" Kennedy concluded. "Immigration policy should be generous; it should be fair; it should be flexible. With such a policy, we can turn to the world, and to our own past, with clean hands and a clear conscience."

John Kennedy's manifesto, his paean to the pulsing, flowing heart of America, drew little attention when published in 1958. Many press accounts, influenced by the Kennedy publicity machine, portrayed the candidate and his family as all-American success stories, often with little examination of their cultural background. Certainly Jack's version of American history, recounting as it did instances of hatred and bigotry, was not flattering to a Protestant nation he would soon ask to vote for him. What's extraordinary about *A Nation of Immigrants* is that it existed at all. Its political usefulness was questionable and its potential to backfire loomed over the whole project. It never became a bestseller of the magnitude of *Profiles in Courage,* and could, by the Kennedys' must-win standards, be considered a failure. Though later editions after Kennedy's death were printed by a major publisher, the first edition of *A Nation of Immigrants* was distributed by the Anti-Defamation League of B'nai B'rith. Most notable books about Kennedy—written in the post-assassination era of "Camelot" imagery by well-known biographers—ignore *A Nation of Immigrants.* It's a remarkable omission, for this book provides the clearest, most historically rooted raison d'être for John Kennedy's presidency.

IN THE 1950S, Kennedy gave public talks for the descendants of immigrants, who, like himself, were some generations removed but understood and appreciated the Irish experience and its link to contemporary America. "All of us of Irish descent are bound together by the ties that come from a common experience; experience which may exist only in memories and in legend but which is real enough to those who possess it," he said as a guest of honor at a January 1957 Irish Institute dinner at the Hotel Commodore in New York.

But the special contribution of the Irish, I believe—the emerald thread that runs throughout the tapestry of their past—has been the constancy, the endurance, the faith that they displayed through endless centuries of foreign oppression—centuries in which even the most rudimentary religious and civil rights were denied to them—centuries in which their mass destruction by poverty, disease and starvation were ignored by their conquerors. . . . Let us here tonight resolve that our nation will forever hold out its hands to those who struggle for freedom today, as Ireland struggled for a thousand years. Instead we will recognize that whether a man be Hungarian or Irish, Catholic or Jew, white or black, there forever burns within his breast the unquenchable desire to be free.

Earlier in Chicago, Kennedy gave a similar speech for St. Patrick's Day 1956, invoking the same "emerald thread" imagery, with a deep appreciation for the transcendent themes of liberty and struggle for independence contained in Irish history. With the same Republican spirit his cousins in Wexford might express, Kennedy noted that "all of the classic weapons of oppression were employed to break the will of the Irish. Religious persecution was encouraged—mass starvation was ignored. . . . Even assassination was employed to end resistance." Only in retrospect does Kennedy's allusion to "assassination" grab the ear. For in the next breath, Kennedy seemed to recognize the devastating impact of a young leader taken by an early death. "Listen, if you will, to the wild melancholy of the Irish after the murder by Cromwell's agents of their beloved Chieftain, Owen Roe O'Neill," Kennedy said, hushing the crowd of Chicagoans before reading from the poem, which ended:

We're sheep without a shepherd, when the snow shuts out the sky—
Oh! Why did you leave us, Owen? Why did you die?

To Kennedy, this "emerald thread" extended across the Atlantic, from the migration out of famine Ireland to the political and social barriers still faced by immigrants of all kinds in post–World War II America. His understanding of immigrant history in this country—and the fierce bigotry and sometimes violence it evoked—provided some personal perspective as he embarked on his presidential bid. Kennedy wouldn't view anti-Catholic bigotry and ethnic slurs as a personal affront as Al Smith did in 1928, nor would these attacks wound Kennedy in quite the same way. Instead, this historical perspective provided a kind of ballast that kept his candidacy afloat and on course, without being swamped by rancor or resentment. As his small book proclaimed, America was indeed a nation of immigrants, and in many ways, John Kennedy was determined to become their heir, the first of their kind as president.

Matters of
Church and State

IN JUNE 1950, President Harry Truman left a frustrating cabinet meeting concerned with the Korean War and hurried to another White House appointment. He'd been up since 4:30 A.M., worried about the Russian expansion in the Baltic states. This noontime meeting would require a delicate balancing act and it promised even more headaches for him. The president had agreed to talk privately with Joseph P. Kennedy, the Vatican's most powerful advocate in America.

"The Russians have no God and no morals," Truman fumed, as he entered the room, "and I'll be damned if I would trust anyone who did not have both." For a few moments, the president and Kennedy chatted about tensions with the Soviets before turning to discuss their main business.

The Roman Catholic Church, with its millions of faithful living throughout the United States, still felt very much like a second-class entity, the object of lingering bigotry at home and of disdain abroad. Though many Catholics were Democrats in Northern industrial states, Truman's party also encompassed many Southerners deeply suspicious of the Pope in Rome. Truman weighed both factors in listening to the church's requests. For the past several years, the Vatican had pushed without success for reparations from the U.S. government for damages caused by Allied bombing during World War II. Some U.S. officials adamantly opposed paying any money to the Vatican.

But most of the conversation between Truman and Kennedy centered on an even thornier and more pressing issue—whether the U.S. government would replace its special emissary at the Vatican, a position Kennedy himself had persuaded FDR to fill. In 1939, Roosevelt had appointed Myron C. Taylor, an Episcopalian, as his personal representative to the Vatican. Taylor was the first U.S. emissary to the Holy See in nearly one hundred years, and his appointment resulted from a deal brokered by Kennedy himself back in 1936, when Pacelli came to the United States, escorted by Count Enrico Galeazzi and Spellman. Though Kennedy wasn't thrilled with Taylor (in his meeting that afternoon with the president, he called Taylor a "horse's ass"), he lasted in the job until January 1950, stepping down without a replacement.

Once again, opposition to the Vatican post arose from several quarters, including Methodist Bishop G. Bromley Oxnam, president of the Federal Council of Churches of Christ in America, who expressed concern about Cardinal Spellman's undue influence on public policy. Protestants and Other Americans United for the Separation of Church and State (POAU), an anti-Spellman group with many allies in the Democratic Party, also urged no new Vatican appointment. As Truman explained to Kennedy, even top Democratic congressmen—some of whom were Catholic—advised him to wait. "They all felt it would defeat Democratic Senators and Congressmen in the Bible Belt if it were done right away, so Truman decided to do it after the election," the senior Kennedy recorded in his diary. "He pointed out that [Massachusetts Congressman John] McCormack, a Catholic, was very insistent on this as a plan. . . . As far as the Vatican is concerned, he [Truman] is not going to take all the abuse that the Protestants and Oxnam have been heaping on him all the time for keeping Taylor there."

For Joe Kennedy, the Vatican vacancy meant more than just reneging on the hard-fought original deal but symbolized the lack of clout many American Catholics still felt with their own government. Truman afforded the former ambassador time to air his views, largely as a personal courtesy. Though no admirer, the president was mindful of Joe Kennedy's religion and his family's sizeable political influence. But, Truman, like most Americans, was unaware of the depth of Joe Kennedy's alliances with the church.

IN THE DECADE FOLLOWING World War II, the Kennedys frequently blended matters of church and state. The former ambassador and his eldest son, a rising star in Congress, acted on several measures advocated by the Catholic hierarchy. Some were proposed pieces of legislation, though many were actions taken out of view of the American public. On the surface, the

Kennedys' involvement extended merely to generous contributions to Catholic-run charities and a tip of the hat to local clergy, the kind of deference often accorded by Irish Catholic politicians of their era. Most perceived the Kennedys's advocacy of church causes as just part of the ethnic politics found throughout America, a polyglot of interests and pride common among many groups. Few had any idea about the Kennedy influence with the Vatican.

For Joe Kennedy, the direct pipeline to the Vatican remained Count Galeazzi, the aide-de-camp to Pope Pius XII. After more than two decades of working together on church-related issues, Galeazzi had become one of Kennedy's truest confidants, a man to whom he confided his ambitions and resentments. The church could not wish for any more devoted advocate than Joe Kennedy, as he promised in his letters. A year before his meeting with Truman about the Vatican, Joe Kennedy made clear his fidelity to Rome. "Of course, with the problems of the world now centering to a great extent at the Vatican, I realize what a terrible burden the Holy Father is under and how he must depend on you for help," he wrote to Galeazzi in 1949. "I don't know what I can continue to do to be of any assistance to him, but you know all you have to do is command me and, if it is humanly possible, I shall do it."

The duality of Joe Kennedy's interests—his combined loyalties between his church and his government—were evident in negotiations over the Vatican appointment. Shortly after Taylor left his post, Kennedy requested the meeting with President Truman. "I am writing you not as a Catholic but as the man more responsible than anyone for the suggestion of establishing the so-called Taylor mission at the Vatican," Joe Kennedy plainly stated to Truman. "I feel there is a great deal more to this appointment than its religious aspect."

But as his letters indicate, Kennedy was committed privately to serving as a negotiator for the church hierarchy, consulting with Cardinal Spellman before his Friday meeting with the president. After his White House chat, he dispatched a note to Count Galeazzi in Rome. Detailing his conversation with Truman, Kennedy wrote: "I was quite critical of the sudden manner in which the Vatican office was closed and he told me that he had personally sent word to the Pope and that Taylor has also informed the Pope three months ahead of time that the office was to be closed. Cardinal Spellman certainly is not of that opinion, I am sure, and did not give me this impression." He explained Truman's reasons for not filling the post immediately and mentioned that, after the 1950 election, the president had promised to submit "the name of a Protestant Republican as Minister to the Vatican."

Kennedy knew the lack of Catholic political influence, even among the Democrats, did not bode well for his son's chances for the White House, and appeared anxious to do something about it. "I still believe, as I told the Pope, and as I told you, that until the day comes when the hierarchy of the United States makes up their mind that they should have political influence, we are not going to fare very well in this country, and unless we do it right away, the opportunity will be lost," he wrote. Then showing his own biases, Kennedy added that, by comparison, "a Jewish minority group, well-organized, gets whatever it wants and we get nothing." In closing, Joe Kennedy emphasized to Galeazzi that he remained at the Pope's disposal: "If there is anything you want me to do, all you have to do is ask," Kennedy ended. "Please convey my deepest respects to His Holiness and tell him I am prepared to do anything he suggests in this matter."

Eventually, in October 1951, Truman did live up to his promise. He selected General Mark Wayne Clark, who had led a bloody capture of Rome during World War II, to become the first U.S. ambassador to the Vatican since 1868. The announcement caused an uproar among hundreds of Protestant clergymen. Their calls and letters of protest doomed Truman's decision, which needed the confirmation of Congress to take effect. The reaction illustrated the strong undercurrent of anti-Catholicism still imbedded throughout the United States. At a Washington rally attended by hundreds, the Reverend Carl McIntyre, president of the International Council of Christian Churches, not only attacked the proposed appointment but the Catholic Church as well. "Communism is the enemy we are all against— but we have another enemy, too, older, shrewder," McIntyre proclaimed. "It is Roman Catholicism and its bid for world power. In the United States, it is called 'Spellmanism.'"

After several weeks of religious rancor, Clark withdrew his name from consideration, though the issue continued to burn. Leaders of several Protestant denominations vigorously attacked the very idea of an ambassador to the Vatican, and with nearly as much antipathy as the Know-Nothings of yesteryear. Truman retreated from the issue, and so did Stevenson, the Democratic presidential nominee in 1952, who warned such an appointment "would be highly incompatible with the theory of separation of Church and State."

Watching his long-time hopes and hard work for a U.S. embassy at the Vatican fade away, Joe Kennedy could only express his true frustrations to

Galeazzi. For years, they'd worked together with Cardinal Spellman for what Kennedy believed was the good of the church in America. But the three were no longer united on this issue. For all his bluster and candor with President Truman, however, Kennedy failed to comprehend, quite naïvely, Spellman's change. After all, the cardinal had united Joe's children in marriage and baptized his grandchildren; he had also accepted thousands of dollars for his favorite charities. Kennedy felt he could count on Spellman, the same way he had been able to manipulate and count on the support of Cushing in Boston.

As the premier Catholic figure in America, however, Spellman didn't want to share power or prestige, certainly not with another American figure with close links to the Vatican. A U.S. representative to the Holy See could go over the cardinal's head directly to the Pope, rather than deal with Spellman in New York. Though he chatted amiably about the issue with Kennedy and shared correspondences, Spellman discreetly did everything he could to undermine the effort. He ignored the Vatican's directive to push for the measure with American Catholics and only halfheartedly lobbied other politicians about the matter. The subterfuge was pure Spellman. "Though nearly twenty years earlier Spellman had worked diligently for such an appointment, he no longer wanted an American official at the Vatican," biographer John Cooney later observed. "If an effective ambassador were named to replace Myron Taylor, he would undercut some of the Cardinal's influence, both in Rome and Washington."

In Rome, Vatican officials detected Spellman's sleight of hand. One of the Pope's top aides later sent a letter to the New York archdiocese blaming him for the whole mess and the new tide of anti-Catholicism evidenced in the United States. As late as June 1955, however, Kennedy was writing letters to the cardinal marked "personal and confidential," evidently unaware of Spellman's role in sabotaging the Vatican's plans. Enthusiastically, Kennedy recalled his meetings in Rome with the Pope and their good friend Count Galeazzi, and wondered how they all might make the pontiff's dream come true for an American representative in Vatican City. "The Holy Father, as I have found out in my last four visits with Him [sic], is still incensed that nothing is being done in America," Kennedy wrote. "He repeated again that personally Mr. Taylor was a nice man but the operation, including the closing, was an insult 'not to me but to the Holy See.'" In a transparent allusion to his own political aims, Kennedy claimed the Pope "was vitally interested in why no Catholics seem to be appointed to important posts in the United States. I told Him I thought it was because the Catholics did not swing any political weight and I doubted if anybody, outside of yourself, could call the

President or any high official on the telephone and get any service whatever, and I doubted whether you felt you could accomplish much along this line even with all your friends in the government. This perplexed him no end and then he asked me what I thought could be done." Kennedy proposed a plan to merge the interests of church and state by using the National Catholic Welfare Council or some other Catholic agency "to alert every diocese in the United States and they, in turn, to alert the people when there is a problem that affects the Church." Using his old prejudiced baseline of comparison, Kennedy again said he "pointed out the success of the Jews in working on these problems 365 days of the year."

Without revealing much, Spellman listened politely to Joe Kennedy's reports and took his telephone calls. He recognized that Kennedy maintained a remarkable connection to the Vatican, and that his son's presidential ambitions could possibly affect the church in America. When Jack Kennedy nearly won the 1956 vice-presidential nod, Spellman forwarded pleasantries ("Jack is a great credit to us all") and even indulged Joe in his father's moment of pride. "I believe if you have what Jack has, you should try for the big job, then if you're licked, at least you've had a shot at it," Joe boasted to the cardinal. "Trying for the second best never appealed to me."

Surely when the time was right, Joe Kennedy believed, Cardinal Spellman would support him on another quest—the effort to get Jack Kennedy elected as the first Catholic to the American presidency. Only then would Kennedy and his family realize how little they could trust Cardinal Spellman.

A Friend in Rome

THE FAVORS, big and small, between Enrico Galeazzi and Joe Kennedy extended to their children. When Jack breezed through Europe with his friend Lem Billings in 1937, Galeazzi managed to arrange a private audience for the twenty-year-old American with the Pope, who immediately asked about Kennedy's parents. At dinner that night, Galeazzi "gave me quite a talk about the virtues of fascism and it really seemed to have its points," Jack recorded in his diary. When young Kennedy returned in 1947 as a congressman, his father cabled him: "Spellman arranging with Galeazzi in Rome your appointment." Joe Kennedy returned the favors by helping Galeazzi's daughter and her husband, Dr. Roman Antonelli, immigrate to the United States. In particular, Kennedy felt indebted to Galeazzi for gaining the Pope's special blessings following Kathleen's fatal plane crash (to "help her in her eternal life," as Galeazzi put it). "Rose and I and all the children are again, as so many times in the past, greatly indebted to you for your most unusual kindness and generosity," Kennedy replied. "It has been my privilege to have met a great many men and women in my life, but none have left me with the gratitude I feel towards you for your consistent kindnesses to us all. It is one of the bright spots in a very unkind, cynical world—and I don't exaggerate."

Kennedy probably didn't know much more about Galeazzi's personal life, nor the full extent of the intrigue within the Vatican walls. For example, though Kennedy had been introduced to Mother Pascalina, the beautiful nun who served as the Pope's assistant and ran his household, he was most likely unaware of the extent of her influence over Pius XII and her close relationship with Galeazzi. Behind the scenes, Mother Pascalina, Galeazzi, and Cardinal Spellman—friends from their days together in the 1930s when Spellman served in Rome—wielded tremendous clout over the church's decisions and, in Galeazzi's case, over its finances. Throughout the 1950s, Joe Kennedy was one of their most constant allies in the United States. He shared their ardent anti-communism, their increasingly conservative outlook and their devotion to the consolidated power of Pope Pius XII in Rome.

Prominent Catholics in America who wanted a favor from the church found they could seek out Kennedy to make it happen. When Ed Sullivan, the famous television host and newspaper columnist, went to Rome, he asked Kennedy to arrange a papal audience. "I dislike bothering you with these things," he relayed to Galeazzi, after explaining Sullivan's prominence in America, "but there are some important people who are helpful when we want to get something done here." Sullivan helped secure the support of Protestant clergymen for Jack Kennedy in 1960 and created a committee designed, in Joe's words, to "offset some of the bigoted spokesmen." When the *New York Times* political columnist James Reston wanted to forward some confidential information to the Pope concerning the Russians and India, he used Kennedy as a courier. Within the church, Kennedy became a sponsor and advocate for other prominent clergy (especially those not particularly in Spellman's favored circle), acting as a godfather for their aspirations. Before the president of Notre Dame University, the Reverend John J. Cavanaugh, left for Rome, Kennedy dashed off a letter calling Cavanaugh "my closest friend in the entire priesthood in the United States" and urging Galeazzi to contact him during the trip.

In his lengthy correspondences with Galeazzi, Joe Kennedy revealed numerous private insights about himself, his growing family and the ever-changing status of Catholics in postwar America. Kennedy confided some of his own doubts about still feeling like an immigrant's grandson in America. "I think that the Irish in me has not been completely assimilated," he acknowledged, "but all my ducks are swans." Increasingly, Joe Kennedy's neatly typed letters also reflected his escalating hopes for Jack's political career and the implicit belief that the church would be a powerful force in their success. During the 1952 Senate campaign, Joe Kennedy mentioned the possibility of victory for his son, adding that presidential candidate Adlai Stevenson could still win "if the Irish Catholics would swing back the last week" before Election Day instead of deserting for the Republican, Dwight Eisenhower. Stevenson would make a fine president, he explained to Galeazzi, but some Catholics objected to the Democratic nominee because he was divorced and was surrounded by too many leftists. When Jack nearly died from his back surgery in 1954, Cardinal Spellman alerted Galeazzi and suggested the Pope send a get-well message to the young senator with his blessing. "I can't tell you how happy I was to have John receive the cable from the Holy Father," Joe Kennedy wrote to his friend. "John is feeling better. He had two very close calls with death but now seems to be recovering."

Each letter spun its own tale about the Kennedys, a carefully crafted version of partial fact and fiction, just as Joe wanted the Pope to hear it. In the summer of 1956, Joe mentioned to his old friend that "Jack's wife had a miscarriage after seven months." Then he speculated that "very likely the strain and excitement of the [1956 Democratic] convention caused it and it's a terrible blow to both of them." After Democrats suffered a landslide defeat in the 1956 election, Joe told Galeazzi of his relief that Jack wasn't selected as the vice-presidential nominee with Stevenson. "It would have absolutely set back the possibility of a Catholic in the White House for another fifty years because the defeat would have been blamed on the Catholic [sic]," he insisted, his eye always on the prize. In the late 1950s, as Bobby became more directly involved on the Senate Rackets Committee and its fight against organized crime, Joe echoed his son's zeal. "We are doing nothing about the fact that the racketeers and the gangsters are the most powerful influence in American Labor," the senior Kennedy claimed, without the slightest bit of irony or self-consciousness about his own Prohibition days. "Under the leadership, for the most part, of gangsters and racketeers, the United States has many many problems."

Joe Kennedy's letters were composed with his usual cold and calculating eye. The subtleties of intent, the feeling of manipulation, were evident throughout. And yet there was an equally undeniable candor with Galeazzi in many parts—a shared worldview, a history of personal and professional experiences together, a unity in their commitment to the church. Joe Kennedy's belief in the pontiff remained unshakable, both as an indicator of his own religious conviction rooted in his Irish Catholic heritage and in his own assessment of communism's threat and what plagued the world. Like many Irish Americans of his generation, the essence of his Catholicism was built on a respect for the church's traditions and structure, a conviction based on visible magisterial powers on earth as much as in the heavenly visions of a hereafter. For the Pope's eightieth birthday, Kennedy sent a cable to Galeazzi extolling the Holy See's influence on the world. "There are those who ask why God permits communism to destroy so many of his creatures and there are those who answer, of which I am one, that the Catholic Church has increased its influence throughout the entire anticommunistic world because of the confidence that all have in the Holy Father," Kennedy wrote. "He may not have the battalions or the guided missiles but this man has a force greater than all."

Both Joe and Rose considered their family very fortune to be in the Vatican's good graces, as though they'd been selected by some higher force for a transcendent task or mission. At Christmas, surrounded in Hyannis Port by his large and handsome family, Kennedy reminded them how privileged they were to have the Pope so concerned, so aware, of their welfare. "We had eight of the grandchildren here for the holidays and all of my own children and in a talk when we got together one night, I told them what a wonderful gift it has been to have been so close to the Holy See during the past twenty years, a privilege, I am sure, not given to any other family in the world and it is all due to you," he thanked Galeazzi. "You can imagine how grateful the Kennedy family feels toward you."

In turn, the Pope's chief administrator reinforced Kennedy's vision of his own family's uniqueness, that providence had chosen the Kennedys, particularly his eldest son, for some fateful destiny. Whether Pope Pius XII actually shared this belief is not clear, though the pontiff's actions by awarding both Joe and Rose Kennedy special church honors and Galeazzi's own letters suggest it was so. "I was happy to have from you interesting clippings about Jack," Galeazzi wrote in 1958 after the Kennedys were featured in *Time*. "Please have someone in your office select a few clippings once in a while to allow me to follow the development of this great battle, which after all is the natural logical consequence of a long series of wonderful achievements and providential mysterious events that have happened to your family in a steady sequence." Though signed with a florid and familiar "Enrico," this letter on Vatican stationary could have been written for Joe Kennedy in the hand of God. With all the religious conviction he could muster, he felt sure these "providential mysterious events" would lead his son someday to the White House.

THE KENNEDYS bolstered their claims to the church, their constant exchange of favors, with an uninterrupted flow of cash. In the private realm, Joe Kennedy could be quite generous with his own funds; his financing of the underground discoveries at the Basilica of Saints John and Paul, a pet project of Cardinal Spellman, was one such instance. To move that work along, he sent installments of $20,000 to keep the workers digging. With another favorite Spellman project in Vatican City—the Arch of

Constantine—Kennedy was a virtual spendthrift. "I told His Eminence, Cardinal Spellman that I didn't think very much could be done with the figure he talked to you about—$100,000," Kennedy wrote to his friend in Rome. "I sincerely want to make this a really worthwhile job so don't worry about any cost within a reasonable figure."

As a congressman, Jack Kennedy could be equally generous in satisfying the church's needs, sometimes by using the American taxpayer's money. For several years, the request for U.S. reparations to repair Vatican properties at Castel Gandolfo, damaged by Allied bombing during World War II, remained an unsettled sore point. In a 1946 assessment prepared by Galeazzi, the Vatican said that $850,000 worth of damage occurred at the Pontifical Villas, and another $788,000 from damages to another papal building. During the next several years, the Vatican and the United States wrangled over the correct amount of money for the damages, the Apostolic Delegate twice asking the State Department for the funds with still no resolution by 1954. In 1956, Senator John F. Kennedy helped push through legislation that eventually allocated nearly a $1 million in federal funds for damaged church properties at Castel Gandolfo, the Pope's summer residence at the Vatican, but also provided $8 million for schools in the Philippines. "As you know, the authorization for the Vatican bill passed the Senate unanimously yesterday," Jack wrote in a June 1956 note to his father. "I think the appropriation bill will be all right too." Church officials expressed their indebtedness to Kennedy for arranging this federal compensation. "You have been wonderfully cooperative and wonderfully successful both in obtaining reimbursement to the Vatican for the damages caused during the war and also in obtaining funds to help pay for the damages to institutions in the Philippines," Cardinal Spellman applauded Senator Kennedy the following month in a note signed "your sincere friend."

Throughout his early political career, Jack Kennedy acted as a stalwart supporter of the church, both for calculated political reasons and out of his own convictions. His public statements and behind-the-scene efforts reflected not only Rome's view about international communism but the American church's position on such domestic issues as education. As a Massachusetts congressman, Kennedy tried to maintain a careful line—some would say a nonexistent one—between matters of church and state.

Parochial schools formed the heart of Boston's archdiocese, a place where, as Kennedy wrote, thousands of Catholic immigrant families first learned the language and what it meant to be an American. During congressional debate over a 1950 federal aid-for-education bill, Kennedy not only supported assistance to public schools but also contended that parochial school students should be entitled to federal aid for bus transportation and health services. Kennedy worked with Spellman and other Catholic leaders to ensure a fair share of funds for Catholic schoolchildren. "The principles are still clear but, unhappily, the prejudices remain powerful," observed the *Boston Pilot,* the archdiocese's publication, in the midst of this effort. "Standing out as a white knight against the crepuscular haze, we are very proud to note, is our own Congressman John F. Kennedy." Another Catholic publication, the *Sign,* noted that "Boston's boyish congressman was in the thick of the adroit intra-committee maneuvering over the boiling hot federal aid to education issue." This publication said "much credit is due" to Kennedy, a "Galahad in the House," for helping to block one bill that would entirely prevent aid to Catholic schoolchildren, and another bill backed by President Truman that left the eligibility of Catholic schools for aid up to the states.

Ugly prejudices surfaced often on this issue, and at least once they angered Kennedy. At a 1947 House subcommittee hearing, Kennedy listened politely to the testimony of Elmer E. Rogers, assistant to the Sovereign Grand Commander of the Freemasons in the South, who suggested that Catholics were under orders from the Pope to undermine the traditional American divide between church and state. At one point, Rogers declared the church wanted "to destroy our liberties and further expand their theocracy as a world government." He said that American Catholics felt a split allegiance to the Pope as well as to their country. When Rogers claimed Catholic parents would be excommunicated if their children didn't go to parochial school, Kennedy challenged him.

"I never went to a parochial school," Kennedy insisted, a statement based on the fact that Canterbury was run by Catholic laymen, not the local archdiocese or parish. "I am a Catholic and yet my parents were never debarred from the sacrament, so the statement is wrong."

Rogers didn't relent. "You are pretty prominent people up there in Massachusetts," he replied. "I know something of the prominence of your father, and the bishops are pretty diplomatic and have good judgment about such things."

The confrontation was extraordinary. Indeed, Kennedy's father did wield a great deal of influence with the Catholic hierarchy, quite evident from the abundance of photos and news clippings showing him and his son awarding gifts and donations to church-run hospitals and orphanages. But the ugliness of Rogers's comments seemed to startle. Jack knew of the Freemasons' historic criticism of the Catholic Church, though never had he confronted it in such personal terms.

"The statement is wrong because you have a living example," Kennedy stated. "I do not want to get in an argument about Catholic theology, but you do not want to make statements that are inaccurate. . . . Now you don't mean the Catholics in America are legal subjects of the Pope? I am not a legal subject of the Pope."

At a public hearing, Rogers, with his obvious hidebound rants, could be dismissed easily as a kook. Though clearly perturbed, Kennedy still kept his cool when confronted with such intolerant views. Yet in this exchange, what Kennedy found perhaps most disconcerting was the nagging suspicion that many other Americans harbored views similar to those Rogers had expressed, a none-too-subtle bigotry that marginalized Catholics, cast them as a subversive threat to American freedoms and, in effect, allotted them second-class status in society.

THESE FEARS about Catholic power extended beyond the reactionary realm of the Freemasons and included several prominent Protestant clergymen. In particular, G. Bromley Oxnam, a bishop of the Methodist Church and leader of Protestants and Other Americans United for the Separation of Church and State (POAU), complained loudly and bitterly about attempts by the Catholic hierarchy to gain a portion of federal monies for their students. "The Church not only wants public funds for private purposes," Oxnam charged, "but must know that to drain off vast sums from public education is so to weaken it as eventually to destroy it." In a letter to the *New York Times,* three other religious leaders complained about "the political activities of members of the Roman Catholic hierarchy who, as representatives of a foreign power, have been carrying on unceasing propaganda and utilizing continuous and insistent pressure on press and radio and state and federal officials to break down our United States constitutional guarantee of separation of church and state."

The lightning rod for this criticism was Cardinal Spellman, the Machiavellian-like prelate who virtually glowed with resentment. His words echoed the rhetoric of his former boss, Cardinal O'Connell of Boston, who had once rallied his embattled flock with sermons about Brahmin oppression. "Once it was the tremendous influx of Catholic immigrants which stirred the attack on the Catholic Church," fumed Spellman. "Now it is the growth and expansion of Catholic education which is claimed to be a constant threat to the supremacy of public education in the United States. Why is Catholic education thus attacked? Is it because in fact the public schools are Protestant schools, or at least schools which consciously or unconsciously are directed along Protestant lines? . . . Is it not clear that when a

Catholic schoolchild is denied the use of a public school bus an injustice is done not to the *Catholic* child, but to an *American* child who happens to be a Catholic?"

MANY LIBERAL DEMOCRATS, a natural constituency for Jack Kennedy, expressed their own reservations about the church's intent in seeking federal aid for its schoolchildren. The most notable critic was former first lady Eleanor Roosevelt. In her newspaper column called "My Day," Mrs. Roosevelt inveighed against any federal aid for Catholic schools and poked the cardinal with a few thinly veiled jabs. ("Sometimes, I think church organizations are foolish because they do things that lead people to believe that they are not interested mainly in the spiritual side of the church, but that they have a decided interest also in temporal affairs," she wrote.) Mrs. Roosevelt, though taking the high road, had a fondness for alluding to the church's inquisitorial past in Europe. To prove she wasn't a secularist, she even suggested that "it might be possible to devise a prayer that all the denominations could say" in public schools—exactly the kind of notion a religious minority would fear in a pluralistic society. Spellman reacted bitterly with a crude personal attack. "Whatever you may say in the future, your record of anti-Catholicism stands for all to see—a record which you yourself wrote on the pages of history which cannot be recalled—documents of discrimination unworthy of an American mother!" he charged in a letter released to the public.

Though Joe Kennedy probably agreed with Spellman's position—both on federal aid and on the whiff of anti-Catholicism from the Roosevelts—his son avoided the open warfare exhibited by the cardinal with the former first lady, as did virtually every Catholic politician in the Democratic Party. Spellman's attack on Mrs. Roosevelt drew criticism from many quarters of American life; it prompted even more anticlerical harangues from such groups as the POAU. Senator Kennedy consistently made it clear that he favored federal aid only for "auxiliary" educational services such as buses, not a wholesale subsidizing of religious schools—exactly what Spellman later enunciated in a "clarifying" letter forced upon him by the Vatican. But, despite the efforts of Jack Kennedy and others in Congress, the public uproar doomed a federal aid-for-education bill.

SENATOR KENNEDY'S reputation as an advocate of causes close to the heart of America's Catholics, while winning praise back home, created unease among those who questioned his ability to distinguish between matters of church and state. The Kennedy family's alliance with Spellman suggested that the young, ambitious politician came from a conservative sector of the church, intolerant of dissent and repressive by nature. They took note when Joe Kennedy quickly endorsed Spellman's move to censor the movie *Baby Doll,* even though he'd never seen it. Liberals wondered about Jack Kennedy's opposition to any government assistance for birth control—and whether U.S. bishops had influenced his stand. Could Kennedy be trusted to keep black-robed clergy out of the inner sanctum of government?

Conversely, many Catholics wondered whether Senator Kennedy would have to make too many compromises, be forced to disavow his own Irish Catholic roots if he ran for higher office. In taking on this extraordinary challenge for a Catholic in America—given the still painful memory of Al Smith's debacle thirty years earlier—Jack Kennedy's own religious precepts would be questioned incessantly. Whether he liked it or not, he became the uber-Catholic, a focal point for a discussion about the role of church and state in America, about tolerance and the rise of immigrant minority populations, that went far beyond his own personal merits or beliefs. As history unfolded, Kennedy became not only a candidate for president but a de facto defender of his faith, a vessel of transforming hope and power for the immigrant experience—a kind of political Jackie Robinson for those Irish-American kids who dreamed of the White House. By inclination and design, Kennedy aimed to break the hold of white Anglo-Saxon Protestant men on the Oval Office by appearing as unthreatening and non-ethnic as possible—in short, just like a WASP. (Even his hair—once rough and tumbly like Bobby's unruly locks—was now as smooth and neat as a corporation chief's approaching the summit of his career.) Both Kennedy and his father spent most of their public lives deliberately avoiding the traditional stereotype of the rowdy Irish pol, the roly-poly Big Daddy of big-city machine politics and patronage with the smell of alcohol on his breath. Ironically, press clips and television commentators now made Jack's religion an identifying trait and repeatedly referred to him as "the Catholic running for president."

There was something terribly amusing about his predicament. Among the Kennedys, Jack wasn't perceived as particularly religious at all. Jack's sister Eunice and brother Robert were considered far more devout. Jacqueline Kennedy believed it odd that her husband's bid for the presidency would revolve so much around religion. "I think it's so unfair of people to be against Jack because he is a Catholic," Jackie quipped to a family friend at a Washington party. "He's such a poor Catholic. Now, if it were Bobby, I could understand it: he never misses Mass and prays all the time."

As a Catholic, Jack Kennedy was quite ordinary; and he kept his church practice deliberately out of the limelight, a prudent political judgment as the 1960 election neared. Unlike other Irish Catholic politicians, he didn't routinely pose with nuns and priests, just as he didn't like marching in St. Patrick's Day parades. As a result, some historians dismissed Kennedy's sense of religion altogether. But friends and relatives said Kennedy's Catholicism contained more than that simple assessment. He celebrated Mass regularly, prayed faithfully and observed the sacraments. Although he remained imbued with the culture and traditions of the Catholic Church, he clearly enjoyed the modern world and its obsessions with sex, power and money. To many Americans, Jack Kennedy didn't fit their own stereotype of how a Catholic should look and behave. But undeniably, Kennedy was a Catholic for all to see if they wanted.

Jack was a believer with a healthy dose of skepticism, recalled Lem Billings, whose numerous adventures with Jack ranged from their visit to a Harlem whorehouse to meeting the Pope. Though Jack surely didn't fall prostrate at holy sites during a late 1930s European tour, he showed an avid interest in the culture and history of the church. "I think it was a bit difficult for Jack to buy a lot of the miracles which we were shown in Rome, for instance Veronica's veil or the steps down which St. Peter's head is supposed to have fallen. . . . He assured me that it wasn't necessary to believe this in order to be a good Catholic," said Billings. "I don't think he was a dedicated Catholic like his mother and sisters, but he was a good Catholic. I cannot remember in my life when Jack Kennedy didn't go to Church on Sunday. . . . I never, never, never remember in my life Jack's missing his prayers at night on his knees. He always went to confession when he was supposed to."

Though the world around him increasingly identified Kennedy as a Catholic, his aides detected only a slight undercurrent in his thoughts and actions. "John Kennedy was a faithful adherent but he did not talk about it," recalled Sorensen, forty years later in an interview. In his book on the Kennedy years, Sorensen's comment that JFK "cared not a whit for theology" has been repeatedly quoted by historians, though the rest of his explanation rarely follows. "He felt neither self-conscious nor superior about his religion but simply accepted it as part of his life," Ted Sorensen added. "He resented the attempt of an earlier biographer to label him as 'not deeply religious'; he faithfully attended Mass each Sunday, even in the midst of fatiguing out-of-state travels when no voter would know whether he attended services or not." From a similar perspective, Arthur M. Schlesinger Jr. observed: "Though Kennedy spent only one year of his life in a Catholic school, he assimilated a good deal of the structure of the faith, encouraged probably by his mother and sisters. He often adopted the Catholic side in historical controversy, as in the case of Mary, Queen of Scots; and he showed a certain weakness for Catholic words of art, like 'prudence,' and a certain aversion toward bad words for Catholics, like 'liberal.'"

Decades later, his cousin Joseph Gargan recalled Jack Kennedy's sense of religious identity as quite common for his time, what some today might call "traditional." In his own way, Gargan echoed Schlesinger's assessment: that Catholicism was engrained in Jack Kennedy's soul, a cultural touchstone that could not be erased in prep school or at Harvard. Gargan seemed to acknowledge his cousin's faults as well as his graces: "Jack Kennedy was a humble sort of fellow—he didn't wear his religion on his sleeve. . . . I can remember going often with him to St. Francis Church. . . . He was very much aware of the rules of the Catholic Church. . . . But like all of us, he was a human being and all of us have failures, defects of character and frailties, and Jack Kennedy would be the first to admit he had many. But as far as the Catholic Church is concerned, Christ wouldn't have had to die on the cross if we were all saints. Jack Kennedy would say simply, 'Join the club, we're all sinners, we're all in the same boat.'"

These testimonials hardly account for the paradoxes in John Kennedy's character and the mystery of his beliefs, perhaps the most abstruse aspect of an individual's life to document. Yet in this respect, Jack resembled so many young American Catholics returned home after World War II who remained loyal to the church but held misgivings about its teachings, including some tenets that for Kennedy threatened to become political land mines in a national election. A bundle of contradictions rolled up into one engaging package, Jack Kennedy possessed the affectations of a Brahmin but the inclinations of a liberal Irish Catholic. His favorite priest was not New York's powerful and vainglorious Cardinal Spellman, so rooted in the intrigue of Rome, but rather the far simpler, unassuming Cushing of Boston, whose earthy manner and plainspoken English appealed to him. At night, Kennedy said his prayers in a routine way, and might occasionally have meant them. Whatever his private religiosity, however, it was overshadowed by his public identification as a Catholic.

OVER THE NEXT several months, Jack Kennedy would be confronted with his own Catholicism probably more than ever before in his life. As he crisscrossed the country as a potential presidential candidate, he began to realize his ineluctable fate—that the upcoming 1960 election would become a test of his faith, in name as a Catholic and perhaps in spirit as well. Before large audiences and in press interviews read by millions, he explained his religion patiently and respectfully, careful not to show anger or resentment as he tried to assuage the prejudices of a suspicious nation. "I am a strong Catholic and I come from a strong Catholic family," he avowed in April 1959, while being quizzed about his beliefs by Bishop Oxnam's group of Methodist ministers on tour in Washington, the first of what would become many such public encounters about his religion.

Before the primaries started, the Kennedys learned that some who didn't want Jack to run could be found in the Catholic Church itself. Joe Kennedy was incensed to discover that the hierarchy was neither ready for the challenge posed by his son's candidacy nor willing to assume the risks imposed by a Catholic running for president. As he fumed in his letters to Count Galeazzi, Kennedy simply couldn't get over what he viewed as an unforgivable act of betrayal. For decades, the Kennedys had been loyal and faithful to the church, with their millions in charitable donations, their honorary titles and secret entreaties to the White House on the Vatican's behalf, as well as with their genuine devotion to the faith. Joe had spent his adult life preparing for this moment, striving to achieve a breakthrough in America that he assumed everyone in the church wanted—from the pontiff who had once visited his home to his confidant Cardinal Spellman to the nun in the school yard. His son's best chance was now. Jack could not afford to wait for another day, for another distant opportunity. The tone of Joe Kennedy's letters to his old friend suggested that Galeazzi might influence the Holy See on this crucial matter in the same way they had collaborated for years. But things in Rome were no longer the same.

KENNEDY NEVER DOUBTED Enrico Galeazzi's loyalty. After reading news clippings about Jack's impending candidacy, Galeazzi encouraged Joe to continue "working steadily and quietly for the great goal which is ahead." For years, the two old friends had dreamed of this quest—a Kennedy running for president—and they would not be deterred by bigots and recalcitrants. To Galeazzi, the benefits to Rome of having a Catholic in the White House were obvious. "Of course the religious issue is beginning to show on front lines," Galeazzi scribbled in his familiar handwriting, "and that is why the fight will mean a great service not only to your country but to the Church also." In return, Joe Kennedy expressed his willingness to serve as a conduit between the Vatican and the White House. This liaison was underlined after Allen Dulles, then the CIA director and the brother of

Eisenhower's secretary of state, John Foster Dulles, came to visit the senior Kennedy at his Florida home. After Dulles's visit, Joe assured his friend in Rome that he'd be willing to act as a go-between with the American government's top spymaster if Galeazzi and the Pope so desired. "I think that if there is anything that you want me to do, you could let me know at once and I will contact him," Joe promised in an April 15, 1958, letter written from Palm Beach. "He [Dulles] is very aware of the fact that Jack may be the next President and while he has always been very friendly to me, I think that he is more than ever anxious to please."

Whether Jack Kennedy, well under way with his presidential plans, knew or approved of such an extraordinary promise by his father is not certain. To be sure, though, Jack's political opponents, if they were aware of this letter's existence, may very well have raised serious questions about the candidate's independence of Rome. The *quid pro quo* inherent in Joe Kennedy's letter was a bit of Latin that every American could understand. The letter clearly suggested that, in return for help from the Vatican in getting his boy elected, Joe Kennedy would help the church with "anything" it might want from his son's administration. The senior Kennedy believed that Galeazzi, whose power increased within the Vatican as Pope Pius XII became sick and infirm, could be counted upon to persuade the church hierarchy to all but formally endorse his son's candidacy. In the same letter, Kennedy alluded to a sum of money he had sent to Galeazzi as a gift. ("That remittance was yours to do with as you wish," Joe instructed. "I am sure that you can find plenty of personal things to take care of.") The message was unambiguous: Joe would be a benefactor to Galeazzi if the Pope's right-hand man took care of his son's political needs.

In October 1958, the death of Pope Pius XII, Galeazzi's long-time patron, left a power vacuum soon filled by an affable but aging churchman, Cardinal Angelo Roncalli, who became Pope John XXIII. Many expected the new pontiff—a compromise candidate among the bishops who elected him—to serve as a quiet interim choice for a relatively short time. But Galeazzi's power began to fade by early 1959, just when Joe Kennedy needed him to win support within the Vatican for his son's presidential run. Galeazzi's reputation suffered because of a bizarre scandal involving his half brother. When Pius XII succumbed to illness, Ricardo Galeazzi-Lisi, who served as the Vatican doctor, was caught selling deathbed accounts to the Italian tabloids, including a photo of the dead pontiff. The public uproar forced Galeazzi's half brother to give up his Vatican post; eventually he was barred from the practice of medicine in Italy. Enrico's stature was hurt by the scandal. In speaking with Cardinal Spellman, Kennedy indicated that he'd heard of Galeazzi's diminished influence with the new Pope, who clearly didn't trust the old inner circle surrounding Pius XII. As evidence, the senior Kennedy referred to a magazine profile about the changes in Rome. "After reading it, I just marveled at how stupid people can get in not realizing how great Pius XII was," he told Spellman. The same article confirmed the rumors he'd heard: Galeazzi's powers inside the Vatican were no longer what they were when Pius ruled. On Galeazzi's behalf, as a favor to his old friend, Kennedy offered to speak privately with other cardinals in Rome, including Cardinal Tardini, the Vatican's secretary of state.

But the Vatican's shift of power was also felt in America. One place where Joe Kennedy felt an Irish Catholic running for president could expect to do well—Notre Dame University, once presided over by his old friend the Reverend John J. Cavanaugh—was now run by the Reverend Theodore Hesburgh, who expressed some consternation about Jack Kennedy's ambitions. Joe vowed he'd "never forgive or forget" Hesburgh's disloyalty, or that of other clergy. "I am more than ordinarily bitter about the whole subject," he wrote to Galeazzi in March 1959. "I doubt very much if my relations with the Church and the hierarchy, with the exception of Cardinal Cushing, will ever be the same." With more than a little self-pity, Joe conceded to his old friend: "I really do not care now whether Jack is elected President or not and I have told him so. I certainly will never ask the hierarchy for anything ever again—not that I have ever asked them for much."

When Kennedy complained, Galeazzi insisted that none of the hierarchy's opposition came from Spellman, whom he described as "the truest and most loyal and faithful friend we can shape in the best of our imagination." Gradually, however, Joe Kennedy suspected otherwise. Spellman, at odds with the new, more liberal-minded Pope, set out on his own conservative course, particularly as it applied to American politics. To his friend in Rome, Joe Kennedy expressed his sense of being double-crossed. "I value your suggestions and advice, but I am really more than annoyed or upset— I am downright disgusted!" Joe Kennedy wrote, underlining "the weakness of some of the hierarchy for not speaking out, at least in some measure, in Jack's defense." Though Jack generally maintained his public composure in the national debate about religion, Joe Kennedy knew his son was privately annoyed about the matter. "I am satisfied that Jack is less affected than I am by it all," he told Galeazzi, "but he is definitely upset."

In August 1959, Joe Kennedy decided to address a fawning letter to Cardinal Tardini, a long-time friend of Galeazzi and Spellman but still in the Pope's good graces, to ask that he pass along "my steadfast sentiments of loyal devotion and obedience" to the new Pope. Carefully, he invoked

Galeazzi's name high up in his missive, and then made his main pitch: a plea for the Vatican to direct the U.S. bishops "to avoid any discussion on the religious issue" at its upcoming conclave, and not to get in the way of his son's chances for the presidency. Surely, he reasoned, the Holy See would recognize the importance of this turning point for Catholics in America. "It will not be easy, for many many years to come, to find another Catholic with so many exceptional qualifications for such an office, the fundamental Catholic sentiments of his whole family being one of the most important outstanding qualifications," Joe Kennedy implored. "I thought it was my duty, Your Eminence, to call your attention to the above facts. The stake is too great for the Catholic Church in the U.S. . . . It was been 30 years since Al Smith, a Catholic, tried for the Presidency."

But Pope John XXIII had a different agenda, one that favored a spiritual revolution rather than temporal matters of politics. He was determined to end the secretive, autocratic power plays of his predecessor and his cadre of minions. The Kennedys realized if the Catholic Church was going to help in their upcoming campaign, it would have to come from places other than Rome or the "powerhouse" in New York.

Primary Lessons

DINNER CONVERSATION with the Kennedys that night in 1959, inside their elegant nineteenth-century Georgetown town house, touched lightly and gracefully upon many topics before inevitably settling down to politics. Eugene McCarthy, his wavy hair still more dark than gray, relaxed and enjoyed the insights and humor of his host and the company of his beautiful wife, Jacqueline. At the table was another invited guest, columnist Joseph Alsop, a long-time Kennedy family friend.

McCarthy wasn't here to be converted. As a Minnesotan, McCarthy had committed himself firmly to the state's favorite son, Senator Hubert Humphrey, expected to run against Kennedy for the Democratic Party presidential nomination. The two young senators not only enjoyed each other's company but also shared a common background. McCarthy's ancestors came from Ireland just as Kennedy's did, his great-grandfather leaving Ireland in 1803, well before the Famine, and his family had settled in the cold but fertile farmland of Minnesota by the 1860s. Casually but clearly interested, Jack wondered aloud how McCarthy, an Irish Catholic, had managed to pull off a victory in a predominantly Protestant state. "It wasn't a place where Catholics were running for the Senate," McCarthy recalled in an interview a half century later. "It was a success if they were running at all." Without using the hard sell, Kennedy asked him "not for advice but a description of what happened in Minnesota. . . . He assumed Minnesota was a Protestant state and he wanted to talk about the fact that I was the first Catholic to get elected in Minnesota in a hundred years. He felt there was something that I could tell him about how to do it."

McCarthy knew he could be frank with Kennedy. In the scramble for vice-presidential votes during the 1956 convention, Kennedy had sent Ted Sorensen over to the Minnesota delegation to try to pick up some more support. "All we have are Protestants and farmers," then-Congressman McCarthy told Kennedy's aide. In his own 1958 Senate contest, McCarthy faced a Republican incumbent, Senator Edward Thye, a Lutheran married to a Catholic. Yet obvious attempts were made to interject religious differences into that race. As he shared anecdotes at dinner with Kennedy, McCarthy pointed out that Minnesota's Catholics were not looked upon with much suspicion or rancor. "I told him religion wasn't a major factor in Minnesota," he remembered. "I said the states where you'd have the most trouble is where you have 15 or 20 percent Catholic. If you have 35 or 40 percent, a lot of people know them; if you have 2 or 3 percent, people don't know them. There's a range of about 20 percent Catholic minority—that's a problem for you." McCarthy was a darling of American liberals, particularly the subset who were Catholics. Alsop once told Kennedy that he had spotted McCarthy riding on a plane with his head buried in a large missal. "Well, Joe, there's an old saying in Boston politics," Kennedy replied with bemusement, "never trust a Catholic politician who reads his missal in the trolley car." At this private dinner, though, Jack didn't say much. He nodded politely, absorbing all that McCarthy had to say, and at the end of the evening thanked him for his help.

THE PUBLIC IMAGE surrounding Jack Kennedy's candidacy often focused on his large extended family and their devotion to each other. The genuine sense of family loyalty—a clannishness fostered by blood and supported for years by their parents—was now packaged, buffed and shining, for the cameras and the American electorate. Readers and magazine editors reacted enthusiastically, unable to get enough. "The Rise of the Brothers Kennedy," an eight-page spread in *Look* magazine in August 1957, featured a photo of the two brothers working side-by-side at a Senate hearing and relaxing on the beach with their wives. "Seldom in Washington annals have brothers come so far, so fast, so young," it reported, with the kind of hyperbole usually reserved for the trailers of Hollywood B-movies like those Joe Kennedy once produced.

With their religious and ethnic customs presented almost as eccentricities, the Kennedys were lionized as the all-American ideal, the triumph of family over rugged individualism—indeed, the type of family to which anyone sitting home alone might want to belong. Laughter and engaging conversation, touch football games played with gusto, handsome ambitious men and their beautiful wives, all in their prime, hordes of children and two smiling, lordly grandparents beaming in delight were all part of the image making, the raw stuff of legends. "At clan reunions, the din of argument is deafening, the enthusiasm overpowering," the magazine observed. Another carefully choreographed photo-essay in *Life* magazine in April 1958 pictured the Kennedys at a church baptism for Bobby and Ethel's newest arrival, Michael, amid a swarm of cherubic, energetic kids orbiting the couple in a chaotic but joyous procession. Whatever concerns may have existed about family privacy or the sanctity of the moment gave way to the need for positive publicity as Election Day neared. "Mother and father seemed to get so much happiness out of us that all of us want a big family too," said Jack, seen on the cover holding four-month-old Caroline. "Bob and Ethel will get there first, but all of us will be close behind." How Jacqueline Kennedy, with her history of miscarriages, felt about this proposition was not mentioned. Her husband's comment was chalked up to "Kennedy competitiveness." As if trading an aura of destiny around the Kennedys, *Life* reminded readers that it had been following this clan's exploits for more than twenty years. It reprised an old photo of the whole brood printed in a December 1937 issue, just before Joe Kennedy's appointment as ambassador. A similar article in the *Saturday Evening Post* titled "The Amazing Kennedys" described Jack as "a talented combination of scholar, lawmaker, and astute politician with a prodigious zest for work and an Irish flair for vote-getting."

In these stories, plentiful in the months before Jack's announcement, a carefully nurtured mythology began to develop around the Kennedys. These accounts never failed to mention the $1 million trust funds that Joe, the wise and wealthy father, had set up for each son and daughter so they wouldn't have the concerns of mere mortals and could devote themselves entirely to the cause of doing good. "Thus, they can repay, in some degree, the debt the family owes the nation for the blessings they've received since their hungry ancestors arrived in Boston as refugees from the great potato famine that ravaged Ireland in 1847," extolled the *Saturday Evening Post*. This account ends with a short bromide from the proud patriarch, Joseph Kennedy. "The measure of a man's success in life is not the money he's made," he insisted. "It's the kind of family he has raised. In that, I've been mighty lucky."

In a sense, the Kennedy's message was old-fashioned. It harked back to the kind of family life that might have existed before the masses of immigrants, before the flight of whites from city neighborhoods to the distant suburbs, before the reduction in family size through birth control, before women in the workforce and other modern socioeconomic factors, and before the fragmenting of families, the generations living apart from each other, often hundreds of miles away. The Kennedys, with all their toothy smiles and sprawling progeny, exuded a different, often fascinating ethos—faintly Catholic in tone but not too much so. Their sheer numbers underscored the obvious fertility of these Kennedy men and their women, as if potency in one area of life surely could extend itself to another. These laudatory press accounts might mention the family's ethnic and religious heritage, but clearly the all-American image they projected implicitly told readers that the assimilation process had worked for these Irish Catholics, that the Kennedys were just like any other happy-go-lucky WASPy family seen on 1950s television. Norman Rockwell could not have painted a more idealized portrait than the one greased and paid for with Kennedy publicity money. These stories seemed to say the Kennedys were "just like us"—or at least the vision of what we'd like ourselves to be. Yet without fail, these tributes to the Kennedy clan also mentioned their Irish Catholic heritage—"poor Irish immigrant stock," as a 1958 *New York Times Magazine* profile put it—and invariably the underlying religious conflict behind their political quest. In a nation where myth holds that every little boy grows up thinking he could become president, Jack Kennedy's ambition drew attention to one of the most accepted dirty little secrets of American politics. As *Look* concluded about Jack Kennedy: "He faces two obstacles: his youth, and a legend that no Catholic can be elected President."

THE TACIT BAN on Catholics running for the nation's highest office was more than a legend. Among Jack's political advisers, including several family members, the prevailing sentiment was to ignore the issue, not bring it up at all. Better to leave the demons of bigotry undisturbed than provoked. But the candidate himself disagreed, borne of his own recent experiences. While traveling aboard a ship from Europe months earlier, Kennedy engaged in a long conversation with Dr. Henry Knox Sherrill, at the time the presiding bishop of the Episcopal Church, who quizzed him extensively about his position on public aid to parochial schools. Sherrill's questions were sincere and, as he recalled it, his talk with Kennedy was "very pleasant." But Kennedy recognized that many fair and perfectly reasonable Protestants like Sherrill still held fundamental misunderstandings about Catholicism and the ability of Kennedy to separate his own views from those of the church hierarchy. He couldn't ignore this problem or wish it away. As 1959 began, he decided the best strategy would be to lance the boil early—make abundantly clear his arms'-length position on church and state—and then let the body politic adapt in time for the November 1960 election. As the perfect vehicle for this candor, the Kennedy strategists decided on *Look* magazine, a publication perhaps more enthralled with the Kennedys than any other. Jack expressed his views to writer Fletcher Knebel, whom the campaign considered friendly. Prior to Jack's 1956 bid, Knebel had written a piece called "Can a Catholic Become Vice President?" He spent many hours with Kennedy and became aware of his sensitivity about religious issues. "There was a chaplain of the Senate at the time, I forget his name, a Protestant who had made some passing comment to somebody about Kennedy's Catholicism. It just burned him up," Knebel recalled. "I had never heard such rough language as he said, 'That cocksucker,' stuff like that, with this poor chaplain. I said, if he gets elected, that chaplain better go to the House." In print, Knebel stayed away from the profane. He wrote an elaborately detailed piece that, essentially, allowed Kennedy to state his modest position. "In a capsule," Knebel summarized, "his theme is that religion is personal, politics are public, and the twain need never meet and conflict."

Kennedy's comments in the March 1959 issue of *Look* magazine saluted the flag rather than bowed to religion. "Whatever one's religion in his private life may be, for the officeholder, nothing takes precedence over his oath to uphold the Constitution and all its parts—including the First Amendment and the strict separation of church and state," he explained. "I believe as a senator that the separation of church and state is fundamental to our American concept and heritage and should remain so."

In its deferential tone, John Kennedy's approach bore some resemblance to the 1927 *Atlantic Monthly* article in which Al Smith stated his views on the same perilous subject. Once again, a Catholic aspiring to the presidency was asked to explain himself. Indeed, the *Look* headline declared: "A Catholic candidate would have to give his views on religion." But Kennedy, with his keen sense of history, remained aware of the pitfalls. Recently, he'd written a review in the *Washington Post* of a new biography of Al Smith authored by Oscar Handlin. In it, Kennedy somehow never mentioned Smith's Catholicism and its relationship to the disastrous 1928 election results.

As a candidate, though, Kennedy demonstrated that he had learned from Smith's mistakes in trying to explain his religious beliefs to other Americans without arousing their suspicions. In a masterstroke informed by history, Kennedy chose a different tack. "Smith in 1928 had defended his church, quoting clerics and encyclicals," Sorensen later explained. "Kennedy defended himself, and quoted his own record and views. He spoke only of legislative, not theological, issues, and he spoke only for himself."

In the *Look* piece, Kennedy sounded more like a Founding Father than a papist. His comments drew a sharp distinction between conscience and the Constitution. His affiliation with Roman Catholicism would have no direct bearing on his actions in the White House. He went as far in disassociating himself from the church and its demands for adherence by members as he could reasonably go. What little was left of the Irish Catholic congressman from Boston, the local pol praised in the archdiocese's newsletter, was now gone. He had reinvented himself and tailored his positions for the big time. "Kennedy notes that he has opposed a number of positions taken by Catholic organizations and members of the hierarchy," *Look* explained. In Congress, he favored aid to Communist satellite states, including Yugoslavia, a move opposed by the U.S. bishops. Kennedy didn't object, as the American hierarchy did, to the selection of a former Harvard president and critic of the Catholic school system, James B. Conant, as U.S. ambassador to West Germany. More significantly, Kennedy flatly ruled out federal funds to support private or parochial schools. "The First Amendment to the Constitution is an infinitely wise one," he said, giving an almost deistic description to the document. This stance was different from his earlier one. As a Congressman, he supported textbooks and buses for parochial school students, not to mention the private thank-you note he received as senator from Cardinal Spellman for helping to arrange public funds for Catholic schools in the Philippines and to rebuild Vatican property.

If the issue of church and state was going to be the major crisis of the 1960 campaign, it was remarkable that virtually no one examined the Kennedys' lengthy record in melding the two entities. With Joe Kennedy wisely keeping himself out of sight, and therefore out of the glare of public examination, no one looked at his close association with key church figures, both at home and abroad. For nearly a quarter of a century, Joe Kennedy had pushed and cajoled two American presidents to appoint a U.S. official at the Vatican, lobbying for the church with his son's help. Yet now, that same son, the prospective presidential candidate, took a completely different stand. "I am flatly opposed to the appointment of an ambassador to the Vatican," Kennedy declared. "Whatever advantages it might have in Rome—and I'm not convinced of these—they would be more than offset by the divisive effect at home."

Overall, Knebel predicted that Kennedy would face bigotry among "some Protestants as well as some who speak as liberals." He even quoted author Peter Viereck's axiom that "Catholic baiting is the anti-Semitism of the liberals," and underscored the Constitution's ban on a "religious test" for public office. Remarkably, *Look* magazine's closing statement echoed the same mixed message of hope and resentment that Joe Kennedy had given his son on Thanksgiving 1956, when they decided privately he would run: "The Democrats may erase this [religion] test next year, banishing the unspoken warning to presidential candidates: 'Protestants only need apply.'"

JOHN KENNEDY'S tactical move with *Look* magazine—"in the hope that the issue would lose some of its mystery and heat by 1960," as Sorensen put it—failed miserably. It didn't have any discernable effect on those who harbored doubts about a Catholic in the White House. More so, the move infuriated many Catholics, Kennedy's wellspring of anticipated support for the election. Several in the church's hierarchy and Catholic press took offense. Some attacked Kennedy's posture in the article because, they contended, he seemed to avoid or disavow his Catholicism. From a historical perspective, few realized the political necessity of Kennedy's arms-length detachment from the church in showing his independence to the American voters. For some, the prospect of another Catholic as a serious presidential candidate caused remarkable anxiety, as if they were still not sure of their place. "Catholic Americans in 1960 lived almost in a nation apart," political observer Michael Barone wrote decades later. "The descendants of Irish, German, Italian and Polish immigrants were still concentrated in industrial cities. They . . . ate fish on Friday and attended Mass every Sunday, shunned birth control and boasted of large families and sent their children to schools run by celibate priests and nuns. In this Catholic America, John Fitzgerald Kennedy was an aristocrat." So why was one of their own so distant, so cool in his rhetoric toward them? In the weeks that followed, their anger and hurt was palpable.

"Young Senator Kennedy had better watch his language," warned the *Indiana Catholic and Record,* which said his *Look* comments "have set Catholics fighting among themselves." Many thought Kennedy was striving too hard to dismiss his own cultural heritage. "We regret that Senator Kennedy, in his sweeping statement opposing Federal aid, did not think it appropriate to add his tribute to the enormous sacrifices that millions of his fellow Catholic citizens are making for their schools," lamented an editorial in *America,* the magazine published by the Jesuits, who operate numerous Catholic schools and colleges around the nation. "On the part of one who himself never went to a Catholic school, such a gesture would have been as gracious as it was obviously called for."

Kennedy's insistence that his actions would be ruled by the Constitution rather than his own conscience was ridiculed and called disingenuous. "Something does indeed take precedence over the obligation to uphold the Constitution—namely conscience. And this applies whatever the religion of the officeholder," lectured *Ave Maria*, another Catholic periodical. "To relegate your conscience to your 'private life' is not only unrealistic, but dangerous as well." Some pushed the analogies much further. "The Kennedy statement expresses fundamentally the same doctrine as the one used by Nazi torturers and assassins in the Nuremberg trials," howled the *St. Joseph Register* in Kansas City. "They argued that they could not be convicted of any crimes because they had acted in obedience to duly constituted superiors and the 'law of the land.'" Ironically, some criticized Kennedy for taking part in exactly what he sought to avoid—a religious test for the presidency. "One of the things that bothers me in relation to Mr. Kennedy is that he appears to have gone overboard, in an effort to placate the bigots," said Gerald E. Sherry of the *Catholic Review* in Baltimore, Maryland. "Unfortunately, despite lessening in tensions in many areas, a Catholic President is something quite a number of bigots still can't stomach." Some argued that Kennedy needed more moral courage in standing up to his detractors. "The Catholic does not have to put his religion aside if he runs for or holds public office," scolded the *St. Louis Review*. "He does not have to assure anyone that he will not let it interfere with his duty to his government because it never will."

When asked about the interview, Kennedy refused either to retract or to clarify his comments. The public uproar caused his father's temper to explode in private. "The only result of it can be to knock a Catholic out of the chance of getting the big job. . . . They don't deserve to have a President," Joe Kennedy wrote to Galeazzi. "I myself am thoroughly disgusted and if I were Jack, I would tell them all to go jump in the lake and call it quits."

The fallout from the *Look* magazine article, as Sorensen recalled, made Kennedy appear to be "a poor Catholic, a poor politician, a poor moralist and a poor wordsmith." In response to the bundles of critical mail, Kennedy's office sent out a standard letter restating his belief that a Catholic could serve as president and "fulfill his oath of office with complete fidelity and without reservation." Certainly, any hopes of putting the "religious issue" behind them were premature, if not impossible. Given the strong response from the Catholics, some editorialists in the mainstream media wondered aloud whether Kennedy could overcome the religious pull of his church, whether he could live up to his promise. His initial foray had plumbed only a small part of the deep morass of prejudice in America. "It would be a national tragedy if the question of a Catholic nomination for the Presidency produced a new wave of religious bigotry," worried *Commonweal*. "Unfortunately, reaction to the Kennedy statement provides ample proof that such an eventuality is entirely possible."

KENNEDY KNEW he couldn't rely on Cardinal Spellman, still the most visible Catholic prelate in America, to speak up for him. He would need the help of other theologians to craft a more finely tuned statement about his beliefs on church and state, one that wouldn't land him in trouble.

As the presidential campaign neared, the most consistent and trustworthy ally for Kennedy's cause proved to be Cardinal Richard Cushing of Boston. In Cushing's estimation, Jack was special, different from James Michael Curley and all the rest—the embodiment of every Irish Catholic immigrant's dream in America. "This is wonderful," he pronounced when Jack won the Pulitzer Prize, "I don't know when a Catholic was ever awarded such an honor. Thanks be to God." As he later concluded, "Jack is the only outstanding man that the local Democrats gave in my lifetime to the national picture."

Relative to his times, Cushing was progressive among American Catholic cardinals. Unlike his predecessor O'Connell, Cushing encouraged ecumenical dialogue by Catholics with those of other religions; he was particularly attentive to the Jewish community, as if atoning for the well-documented past sins inflicted by his own Boston flock. He applauded Protestant ministers who spoke out against "the renewed anti-Catholicism . . . sweeping America," and condemned statements that fostered stereotypes, including the belief that a Catholic couldn't be voted into the White House. "I believe that people of all faiths think the same, that religion has nothing to do with a man's holding public office, the highest or the lowest," the cardinal declared at the opening of the Joseph P. Kennedy School in Hyde Park in 1957. Cushing dismissed the idea that American Catholics should vote according to Vatican decree. "The only things Catholics agree on is the dogma mentioned in the Apostle's Creed," he quipped. Some have repeated Cushing's claim that the Kennedys didn't mix religion with politics. "The candidate explicitly asked the prelate not to involve the church in the campaign in any way," insisted one biographer. But outside the scrutiny of a wary and often bigoted nation, Cushing intervened at various points in the Kennedy campaign as a clear-cut partisan.

Symbolically, Cushing became convinced that the election of Kennedy would break the stranglehold of power in America that heavily weighed against minorities. Irish Catholics would be only the first of many to follow. "My idea was to do everything I could to help him," Cushing recalled. "I would have done the same for a Jewish . . . or a Negro candidate as long as I could break through what . . . was a sort of iron curtain." Publicly, Cushing's support of Kennedy's strict stance on the separation of church and state added ecclesiastical legitimacy to his views and quelled some of the complaints within the ranks of American Catholics. Behind the scenes, however, Cushing played a much more direct role in the Kennedy camp, helping to line up support among the clergy and elected officials who were Catholics.

In late 1959, Cushing promised to lobby on Jack's behalf with Bishop John Wright of Pittsburgh (his former top aide in Boston) so that "he will start a little aggressive talk among the folks in his area that will reach the ear of the Governor of Pennsylvania." Through his private consultations with the candidate's father, Cushing decided that Pennsylvania's Governor David Lawrence, also a Catholic, could be of tremendous help. But Lawrence worried that Kennedy's candidacy would only hurt the Democratic Party's chances of regaining the White House after eight years of Eisenhower's Republican rule. Like other state and local officeholders of the same religion, Lawrence remembered the painful legacy of Al Smith's defeat. With anti-Catholicism on the rise, he felt the timing was poor, that hopes would be raised among Catholics, only to be dashed by religious bigotry at the ballot box. But Cushing wouldn't be deterred. When he flew out to Pittsburgh for the installation of Wright as the new bishop in March 1959, the cardinal asked the mayor of Pittsburgh to arrange a private meeting with Lawrence. Along for the ride was Francis X. Morrissey, the Kennedys' long-time political aide. The cardinal and Morrissey urged Lawrence to end his reluctance; after some arm-twisting, Lawrence changed his mind and swung his ample political resources for Kennedy.

After years of courting Spellman in vain, Joe Kennedy suddenly found himself grateful to Cushing as his son's only true friend in the church hierarchy, as a prelate who "gave me confidence that there was somebody left in high places in the Catholic Church who saw something in this battle that Jack is making." A subtle change in their relationship occurred. Cushing had long been aware that Spellman didn't like him and had for many years used his clout within the Vatican to block Cushing's promotion to the rank of cardinal. Early letters between Cushing and the senior Kennedy contain a cautiousness that suggest the then-archbishop quite correctly assumed Joe Kennedy to be a Spellman confidant. Cushing preferred dealing with Jack rather than his father.

As the presidential election neared, however, the Kennedy patriarch couldn't understand the silence of American church figures. The reasons were quite proper and deeply rooted. Often during the church's history, priests and bishops were instructed by the Vatican to refrain from local politics and secular matters. In Ireland, some priests had inspired parishioners in their fight for independence and religious liberty; yet at other crucial times, the clergy were maddeningly passive and distant when the Irish seemed to need them most. Once again, the clergy had disappointed, or so believed Joe Kennedy. "Most of the hierarchy are so busy thinking they have a big struggle that they haven't the time to take a big look at the position," he complained.

Cushing couldn't agree more. When Joe Kennedy asked why the U.S. bishops didn't speak out, Cushing recalled that he explained their passivity didn't mean they weren't for Jack, "but I'm not sure Joe was convinced." Increasingly, Joe Kennedy felt grateful for Cushing's unabashed efforts. "We are again indebted to you for your enthusiastic support of Jack with their gentleman," Joe wrote, referring to the Pennsylvania's Governor Lawrence. "He is very, very important." Consistently in public appearances, Cushing shored up Catholic support and made sure that his co-religionists didn't abandon Kennedy over some intramural squabble. The cardinal's "courageous, generous speech on Jack's position" regarding church-state separation, wrote Joe Kennedy, saved his son from being picked apart by his own. "This letter really adds up to saying that if Jack stays in this fight, it will be you who has kept him in," Joe told Cushing. "If he wins, it will be you who has made it possible." Now by their desire to see Jack elected president, Cushing commiserated at times with Joe in his frustration. "It breaks my heart . . . to hear the defeatist attitude concerning the advisability of a Catholic becoming President," Cushing responded. "Despite all this, I have never had any doubt with regard to the ultimate victory." Arguably, the cardinal in Boston was Jack's biggest booster outside his own family members, a devoted member of the team. "I am glad that all things look well for the senator," the cardinal enthused to the candidate's father. "I wish this Democratic National Convention was over. I dream about it. It is my opinion that if we can get by the Convention with a victory, we are 'in.'"

THOUGH COVERT maneuvers were appreciated and private meetings welcomed, the Kennedys didn't always take up Cardinal Cushing's offers to help in public. During the fury over the *Look* article, some critics wondered aloud about Jack Kennedy's fidelity to Catholicism. His confident statements about the powers of the Constitution and the secular state made him appear to be a nonbeliever. "Cushing tried to silence a whispering campaign among Catholics themselves that the candidate was not a practicing communicant," recounted one of the cardinal's biographers, John H. Cutler. These rumblings so upset Cushing that when a national magazine offered to let him set the record straight, he wrote an article titled "Should a Catholic Be President?" Proudly, he submitted it to Kennedy for his prepublication approval. Initially, Jack thought enough of the piece to send it out privately for comment. Some readers were friendly but others included "the most outspoken Protestant critics of Catholic doctrine in the country." All who were consulted came to the same conclusion: Cushing's article could only hurt Jack's chances. They advised killing it immediately.

Kennedy telephoned the cardinal with the bad news. During the conversation, the senator praised the article as one of the best expositions about faith and governance that he had read so far. "But I don't want to get you involved," Jack said, putting it in personal terms, as one friend to another. "So forget the whole thing."

When it came to religion, Kennedy knew he must be more precise with his language, far more than he had been with *Look* magazine. Increasingly, he relied on influential figures within the Catholic Church who shared a similar outlook to guide him through the linguistic and theological minefields. In this respect, his father's connections again helped him. As early as 1958, Joe Kennedy consulted with his old friend, the Reverend John J. Cavanaugh, former president of Notre Dame, where Joe also served as a board trustee, "to see if he would prepare some answers to the Protestant interrogation" his son would face. One can imagine Joe Kennedy's indignant face, strained and seething, as he dictated the word "interrogation." Instead, Cavanaugh referred him to some of the best minds on the subject. "He suggests it would be a very good idea to get in touch with Reverend John Courtney Murray and Reverend Gustave Weigel at Woodstock," his father relayed to Jack. "Father Cavanaugh considers these men the top in the United States for answering this type of interrogation."

Kennedy's staff followed Joe's advice and put together a theological brain trust that included the well-respected *Commonweal* editor, John Cogley. Officially, the campaign called it their "Community Relations" branch which, as Cogley recalled, "was a euphemistic way of saying 'the religious issue.'" Cogley represented the quintessential Commonweal Catholic, a brand of liberal American Catholicism that flowered in the darkness of the McCarthy era. He had dabbled in politics—running unsuccessfully for Congress on Long Island in the 1950s—but his thoughtful magazine writing garnered the most attention. His critique of Kennedy's *Look* magazine comments prompted a friendly response from the senator himself. Soon Cogley became convinced that Kennedy was the Catholic best suited to challenge the old prejudices. "I had had some experience with the suspicion of Catholicism which was around at the time, so I wasn't exactly optimistic," he remembered. "But I felt that his particular style and his particular background made him a kind of ideal first candidate." Kennedy knew that one more slip might mean a significant loss of support for his candidacy. "It is hard for a Harvard man to answer questions in theology," he whined to Cogley in a self-deprecating way. "I imagine my answers will cause heartburn at Fordham and B.C. [Boston College]." More than anyone, John Courtney Murray—a Jesuit scholar who studied the clash between the American and Roman Catholic traditions—seemed to have trained his whole lifetime for this moment. Since the 1940s, Murray had argued the American experience showed that the marriage of Catholicism with democracy required a separation of church and state—a view that at first got him censured by his Jesuit superiors. In his voluminous writings, Murray suggested the church became mired in affairs of state as a historical accident, made necessary in the Middle Ages because of the vacuum created by the Roman Empire's collapse. Today's church, he said, now needed to make the transition from the medieval to the modern. Murray pointed out that Catholics in the United States lived as a minority group and that such a separation had allowed the church to flourish in America.

Aware of the immigrant culture of their church, Cogley, Murray and fellow Jesuit Weigel were committed to seeing Catholics finally take a full part in American society. They not only admired Kennedy personally but shared a collective hope that his election to the presidency might forever shatter a significant cultural barrier. Initially, Joe Kennedy had suggested that his son consult with these religious experts informally. But as the campaign developed, their help and guidance was needed constantly and proved of crucial assistance to Kennedy in the days to come.

Chapter Twenty-Four

West Virginia

ON JANUARY 2, 1960, the entire extended family filled the U.S. Senate Caucus Room for John Fitzgerald Kennedy's announcement. Brothers, sisters, parents and other relatives mixed in among some three hundred friends, supporters and journalists. Jackie Kennedy, appearing radiant, stood beside her husband as he outlined his vision for the presidency.

In his speech, Kennedy, only forty-two years old, spoke of his military experience, his fourteen years in Congress and of the "real issues" facing the American electorate. *End the arms race with the Soviets. Rebuild American science and education. Prevent the collapse of the farm economy and the decay of cities. Expand the economy for all Americans.* All these issues, as Kennedy recited them with his staccato speaking style, generated strong applause from the friendly crowd. It had the air of a political rally, just as designed. Afterward, Kennedy agreed to answer reporters' questions. He was asked about the campaign's biggest issue—religion—which his speech hadn't addressed at all.

"I would think that there is really only one issue involved in the whole question of a candidate's religion—that is, does a candidate believe in the Constitution, does he believe in the First Amendment, does he believe in the separation of church and state?" Kennedy said, pausing for the crowd's enthusiastic response. When the applause died down, Kennedy added another hopeful note: "When the candidate gives his views on that question—and I think that I have given my views fully—I think the subject is exhausted."

Despite his wishful thinking, the religious issue was far from exhausted. No one understood this better than the Kennedys themselves. In their private plans, Kennedy's camp acted strategically to maximize the benefits of being the first Catholic in a generation to run for the presidency and to minimize its obvious liabilities. From their polling research, Kennedy's advisers knew that a Catholic on the national ticket would be a magnet for votes in several key industrial states in the Northeast and the Midwest. A certain level of public anti-Catholic prejudice rallied Catholics to their cause and made Kennedy a sympathetic figure among Protestants who might have otherwise rejected him. Yet, this course was treacherous. If religion became too dominant in the presidential debate, Kennedy would surely lose. In May 1959, *Time* magazine published a public opinion poll that found evidence of a more tolerant America; voters were generally more moderate about religion, certainly compared to the anti-Catholic sentiments of 1940. However, the poll still underlined the difficulty JFK faced since one of every four respondents wouldn't vote for a presidential candidate who was Catholic. Even more disquieting, half of those polled by *Time* didn't even know that Kennedy was a Catholic. As the 1960 campaign began to heat up—and Kennedy's religion was repeatedly discussed by the press—the public became more aware of his heritage. Some politicians predicted that polls showing tolerance for Kennedy's religion might be misleading. Virginia's junior senator, A. Willis Robertson (whose son, Pat, later built his own evangelical empire on television and ran for president himself), said that some falsely gave the impression of "no prejudice in the South against a Catholic for the presidency," but he conceded this goodwill might fade away "in the secrecy of the ballot box."

In the hardball tactics of a presidential campaign, Kennedy also used the "religious issue" as leverage. His announcement made clear his refusal to take second place on a national ticket "under any condition" if he failed to win the presidential nomination. This bold move carried an implied threat. As columnist James Reston wrote, Kennedy's ultimatum was regarded by many political leaders "as something far more ominous: as a warning to the Democratic leaders not to think they can reject his bid for the Presidency on religious grounds and still retain the backing of his supporters by giving him the Vice-Presidential nomination." In Reston's analysis, JFK's front-runner status had spawned two movements in the Democratic Party. "One is to block the New Englander lest the anti-Catholic vote hurt the Democratic chances of victory," he wrote, "and the other is to keep the

votes of his supporters by giving him the Vice-Presidential nomination."
Kennedy's all-or-nothing gambit upped the ante "obliquely and skillfully,"
Reston noted. The Democrats risked the defection of a large bloc of
Catholic voters if Kennedy was denied the nomination simply because of
his religion. In this sense, Kennedy's flat-out rejection of the vice presidency was not the move of a traditional frontrunner jockeying about
within mainstream politics, but rather of a politician from a politically disenfranchised minority group who recognized the often hidden obstacles
before him and was attempting a bold stratagem to the top. "Nobody is
going to hand me the nomination," he insisted before the campaign began.
"If I were governor of a large state, Protestant and fifty-five, I could sit back
and let it come to me."

Some liberal Democrats also objected to Kennedy's candidacy, often for
reasons that smacked of religious bias. Some issues were quite legitimately
in the public realm, including Kennedy's views on birth control, the
appointment of an ambassador to the Vatican and the use of public funds
for parochial schools. But most doubts seemed based on fear and stereotypes of the nation's then 36 million Catholics—what *Time* magazine
wondered aloud about a looming "Catholic America"—and whether
Kennedy could resist pressure from the church's hierarchy. New York's
Liberal Party was so worried that they assigned Protestant theologian
Reinhold Niebuhr to question Senator Kennedy "in depth." Niebuhr
reported back that Kennedy's answers were sufficient to quell fears, at least
about this Catholic. "Much of it was open, some of it intelligent, but the
bulk of it and the worst of it was an unreasoning, unanswerable bigotry just
below the surface," campaign strategist Ted Sorensen observed. "His religion had played at least a subconscious role in the initial opposition to his
candidacy from many liberals and intellectuals." A classic example of this
subtle bigotry appeared in *Life* magazine under the byline of Archibald
MacLeish, one of the nation's best-known writers. He suggested that Irish
Catholics ("who are among the most persistent and politically powerful
advocates of increasing censorship in the U.S. and who are brought up to
submit to clerical authority in matters which the American tradition
reserves to the individual conscience") didn't properly understand such
American notions as liberty and freedom. He also implied that Catholic
schools perpetuated a "historical ignorance and moral obtuseness" that
kept students from sharing in the American dream. Such poisonous stylings
from a self-professed progressive intellectual left open the door for more
crude expressions of the same idea.

On a personal level, Jack Kennedy was stunned to find that such rank prejudice still existed. As Sorensen wrote, Kennedy was "at first startled to learn that many well-meaning, unbigoted Protestants and Jews genuinely feared that his church might tell him how to act on matters of state and might excommunicate him if he refused." These views were not just shared by over-the-top bigots but by articulate and thoughtful people, those who might otherwise vote for him without reservation. For Kennedy, the continual focus on his religion was often exasperating. Long afterward, Gore Vidal recalled standing beside the senator at a 1959 party when a beautiful young woman began an idle chat with the candidate:

"You're in politics, aren't you?"

"Uh . . . well, yes, I am. I'm . . . uh, running for president."

"That's so fascinating!" gushed the young woman. "Will you win?"

"Well, it won't be so easy."

"Why not?"

"Well, you see, I'm Catholic . . ." Kennedy began.

"But what's that got to do with anything?"

The candidate turned to Vidal and said, "Oh, Gore, you tell her."

During the first several weeks of the 1960 presidential campaign, Kennedy's problem with the "religious issue" only became more difficult. The subtle, whispered comments of the past were now becoming public utterances made from the pulpit and carried in the next day's newspaper headlines. Kennedy realized he could no longer just dispel the fears with broad assurances, but that he had to confront the issue head-on. And nowhere was this uneasiness about his Catholicism more apparent than in West Virginia.

WHEN JACK KENNEDY arrived in Cabin Creek in late April 1960, he hopped off his chartered bus and was mobbed immediately by hundreds of school students, many of them bobby-soxers who squealed with delight. Kennedy appeared touched by the youngsters' warmth in this small coal-mining town in West Virginia. During this campaign swing, Kennedy was genuinely distressed by the misery he witnessed in the nation's poorest state. In various speeches, he vowed to do something to improve their lives if elected president. Yet a single question continued to nag at Kennedy—his religion. At one stop, Kennedy acknowledged with an ambivalent smile that his Catholicism was becoming "very well known—fortunately or unfortunately." On this issue, the disparity between young and old in West Virginia was striking. "The anti-Catholicism that is prevalent among adults in this area had obviously not rubbed off on their children," the *New York Times* observed. "They applauded Senator Kennedy's every reference to his membership in the Roman Catholic Church as no inhibition on his ability to serve as President."

As the May 10 primary neared, West Virginia, with its high percentage of Protestants and few Catholics, would be the pivotal testing ground for John F. Kennedy and his chances to gain the Democratic nomination for president. In Wisconsin the month before, Kennedy had won the primary election against Minnesota Senator Hubert Humphrey by a wide margin, but in a way that drew more doubts about his viability as a national candidate. While in Wisconsin, Jack had studiously avoided any hint of ethnic politics. Campaigning through Eau Claire on St. Patrick's Day, a street-corner drunk came up to the candidate and, good-naturedly, invited him to have a drink from his bottle. Kennedy politely declined. "That might play well in certain parts of Boston," he turned and laughed to press aide Pierre Salinger, "but *The New York Times* wouldn't like it." In winning Wisconsin, however, Kennedy's results were skewed along religious lines. Numerous Catholics voted as a virtual bloc for him, but political experts noted that he lost to Humphrey in three so-called Protestant districts. After the Wisconsin primary, commentator Walter Lippmann worried that national politics in the future would divide along Protestant-Catholic lines.

Celebrating victory at their Milwaukee hotel campaign headquarters, Kennedy's sister, Eunice Shriver, inquired why he seemed so glum.

"What does it all mean, Johnny?" she asked.

Jack knew exactly. "It means that we've got to go to West Virginia in the morning and do it all over again," he replied.

IN HEAVILY PROTESTANT West Virginia, analysts predicted that Kennedy wouldn't fare well and might indeed show an inability to attract voters worried about his religion. Almost each day, the newspapers carried accounts of religious objections concerning Kennedy's candidacy. Soon after the senator announced his candidacy in January, nearly half of all Presbyterian ministers who responded to a church magazine poll said they wouldn't vote for a Roman Catholic who ran for president under any circumstances. "I'm sorry," wrote one of the respondents, "But this is the way it is."

In the same poll, many Presbyterian ministers agreed that "since the end justifies the means for Roman Catholics, a member of that church could not be believed even if he gave assurances that he would maintain a separation between church and state." The following month, Dr. Ramsey Pollard, president of the nine-million-member Southern Baptist Convention—the second largest Protestant group in the United States— vowed not to "stand by and keep my mouth shut when a man under the control of the Roman Catholic Church runs for the Presidency of the United States." In Kansas City, the American Council of Christian Churches passed a resolution disapproving of a Roman Catholic for president. The National Association of Evangelicals—representing thirty-five Protestant denominations in the conservative tradition—expressed "doubt" that a Roman Catholic president "could or would resist fully the pressures of the ecclesiastical hierarchy." In a national magazine, two leading Protestant churchmen—the Reverend Dr. Eugene Carson Blake of the Presbyterian Church and Bishop G. Bromley Oxnam of the Methodist Church—both said they'd feel "uneasy" with a Catholic in the White House. Dr. Franklin Clark Fry, president of the United Lutheran Church in America who officiated at the 1956 Democratic Convention, advised congregates to follow their own consciences, but added there was no question as to "the stand of the Catholic church favoring state-church relations." In Indiana, a group of picketers—identifying themselves as "Christian Patriots of America, Indianapolis"—challenged the candidate to debate his fitness, as a Roman Catholic, to be president. Most times, Kennedy ignored the hecklers, protestors, the people who stood with homemade signs insulting his religion, by trying to stay on course with his overall message.

Before the Wisconsin primary, Joe Kennedy predicted this state would be pivotal to his son's chances. "If we do not do very well there, I would say that we should get out of the fight," he told Galeazzi. "If we cannot make a showing and if the religious thing becomes very acute, then I am for stepping out and letting the boys fight it out amongst themselves." To another family friend that same month, however, Joe showed his family's steely determination to overcome the old cultural barriers. "I really have no patience with the Catholics who want to duck a fight," he explained. "When you said to me that you hated to see these bigoted ideas arise, I asked you what we were supposed to do, just duck this question for the rest of our lives. If Jack's heart is broken because he may be beaten on the religious question, then so be it."

As they did throughout the 1960 campaign, the Kennedys called in every chit they possessed in the world of American Catholicism, no matter how remote to politics. In a letter to Mother O'Byrne of Manhattanville, Rose asked for the list of alumnae whom she might contact in Wisconsin in anticipation of the primary there. Rose underlined that "the results will be carefully evaluated and they will have a strong psychological effect on the voters." O'Byrne wrote back to say she'd send the book of alumnae names, but the tone of her letter suggested that she was uncomfortable with the request. Some Catholics didn't want a repeat of the 1928 campaign, afraid of being disappointed again. While campaigning in Eau Claire, Wisconsin, Kennedy met a kindly, older woman who held his hand in hers for a moment and said, "Not now young man, it's too soon, too soon." Kennedy just smiled. "No Mother, this is it," he replied. "The time is *now.*"

Even Kennedy's seventy-year-old mother, who proved a popular campaigner in Wisconsin with a series of teas and receptions, faced anti-Catholic criticism. After one luncheon in Eau Claire, Rose Kennedy chatted amiably with three Protestant clergymen who explained their reasons for opposing her son. "It is based on the fear of the predominantly Protestant population of America that the Roman Church will use, through pressure and coercion, the office of the Presidency to achieve ends which are not in keeping with Protestant beliefs," said one of the ministers, the Reverend Forrest W. York of Eau Claire's First Congregationalist Church. Although Rose was among the family's best campaigners, she didn't repeat her familiar round of teas and receptions for the West Virginia primary, mainly because of concern about anti-Catholic bias. Her honorific as a "papal countess," conferred by Pope Pius XII, was a great source of family pride, mentioned at various church ceremonies and special events when she traveled in predominantly Catholic countries in Europe. But with religion dominating the debate in West Virginia, the Kennedy campaign decided Rose shouldn't appear at all. Instead, she spent the campaign at the family's Florida vacation home. Bobby Kennedy, the campaign manager, tried to break the news gently to her.

"Mother, after you worked so hard in Wisconsin, go on back to Palm Beach and get some rest for a few days," he advised. But Rose understood the real reasons for her absence. "In West Virginia, with 'Popery' suddenly the big issue, the media there surely would bring it up in interviews and feature articles if I came into the state to campaign," she later wrote. "I would have been, to say the least, 'counterproductive.'" Rose, the daughter of Honey Fitz, didn't need any more reminders of the lingering ghosts from Al Smith's 1928 campaign.

BOBBY KENNEDY, more so than his brother, appeared aghast at the degree of religious prejudice they faced. Early in the West Virginia campaign, Bobby, and two top Kennedy aides, Larry O'Brien and Kenny O'Donnell, began a meeting of local campaign workers by asking what problems they might face.

A man stood up from the crowd. "There's only one problem," he shouted. "He's a Catholic. That's our goddamned problem!"

The room erupted in a litany of complaints about Kennedy's religion, which wasn't well known by most West Virginians until the newspaper and TV coverage of the previous Wisconsin primary. One after another, these campaign workers complained of suffering abuse from friends and neighbors for supporting Kennedy. By the end of the meeting, Bobby Kennedy appeared stunned. "He seemed to be in a state of shock," remembered O'Donnell. "His face was as pale as ashes."

Right after the meeting, Bobby Kennedy rushed to a telephone booth to call his brother in Washington and tell him the bad news.

"It can't be that bad," Jack said after listening for a few minutes. He reminded Bobby that the pre-campaign poll in West Virginia had showed substantial support.

Bobby, his voice sour with dismay, was unmoved. "The people who voted for you in that poll have just found out that you're a Catholic."

At another point, an exhausted Bobby Kennedy, at a campaign appearance on behalf of his brother, defended his family on the charge that their religion made their allegiance to the United States suspect. During this talk, Bobby recalled his family's commitment to serving their country, and mentioned the death of his oldest brother, Joe Jr., shot down in battle during World War II. At the mention of his fallen brother, Bobby stopped and sat down, too overcome by emotion to continue. When news of this appearance reached Jack, he shook his head. "Bobby must be getting tired," he said.

As primary day neared in West Virginia, the religious issue took center stage. The state's largest newspaper, the *Charleston Gazette,* published an advertisement that, in the guise of a private "poll," was a direct attack on Kennedy's religion. The newspaper ad asked the question:

Who is the bigot? A candidate for the Presidency believes it is a mortal sin for him to worship with a faith other than his own. A voter votes against him on account of this belief. Who is the bigot?

The ad was paid for by a Joseph I. Arnold of Cambridge, Massachusetts, who let reporters know he'd published a similar ad aimed at "non-Catholics" in nineteen religious publications in the South. Informal surveys of West Virginia voters "made it clear that anti-Catholicism would be their primary reason for voting against Senator Kennedy and for Senator Humphrey in the primary," the *New York Times* said in a story about the "bigot" ad. "The issue has made Senator Humphrey the favorite." A study by the Anti-Defamation League of B'nai B'rith found a "distressing amount of bigoted expression about a Catholic in the White House" and reported that "anti-Catholic extremists today are circulating petitions on a large scale, demanding of both Republican and Democratic National Conventions that they nominate no Catholics for President or Vice-President."

Humphrey, as a Congregationalist, was the beneficiary of the anti-Catholic vote against Kennedy, though no evidence existed of prejudice on his part. Nevertheless, the Humphrey campaign did little to disavow the religious bias efforts against Kennedy, and even suggested these reports of bigotry were exaggerated. During one television interview, Humphrey implied that Kennedy was "crying" about anti-Catholicism among West Virginia voters. In turn, the Kennedy camp issued a blistering statement, calling Humphrey guilty of conducting a "gutter campaign" to win the nomination. "Why is he letting himself be used as a tool by the strangest collection of political bedfellows that has ever joined to gang up on one candidate?" Kennedy asked in the statement.

To overcome the uneasiness of some Protestants, the Kennedys enlisted another Protestant with a beloved Democratic name in West Virginia, Franklin Delano Roosevelt Jr., to work on their behalf. Earlier in the year, Joe Kennedy had arranged for young Roosevelt to pay a visit to the family's Palm Beach compound, where he agreed to campaign in West Virginia for Jack. In this coal-mining region, the name of Roosevelt was revered because of New Deal legislation that gave miners the right to unionize and earn decent living wages. To these voters, young Frank Jr. had the same looks and charm as his sainted father. A former war hero himself, Roosevelt stressed Kennedy's military record, regaling crowds with the heroism Jack displayed in saving crew members from his destroyed PT-109 ship in the South Pacific. Around the state, the campaign emphasized the Kennedy-Roosevelt connection, even though Joe Kennedy's alliance with FDR had ended in alienation and Eleanor Roosevelt, a preeminent liberal Democrat in the postwar years, initially preferred Stevenson in 1960. She thought JFK a coward for not standing up to the witch hunt of Senator Joseph McCarthy.

Given this history, getting young FDR Jr. on the Kennedy bandwagon was a major coup. At numerous rallies, Roosevelt held up two fingers tightly pressed together. "My daddy and Jack Kennedy's daddy were just like that!" he exclaimed. To drive home the point, Joe Kennedy arranged for endorsement letters signed by Roosevelt to be shipped to Hyde Park, New York, where they were postmarked and mailed to West Virginia voters. Roosevelt's impact in West Virginia proved significant, author Richard Reeves observed, "as if the son of God had come to give the Protestants permission to vote for this Catholic."

Over the objections of both his father and brother Bobby, Jack Kennedy decided on his own to confront the Catholic question directly in West Virginia. During the primaries, most of his advisors preferred to wait, hoping the religion issue would fade. But as Sorensen recalled, Kennedy decided "to combat it out in the open then and there instead of permitting it to fester until fall or prevent his candidacy from surviving until fall." In his speeches, he pointed out that religion wasn't a factor when he joined the navy to fight in the war, and that "nobody asked my brother if he was a Catholic or a Protestant before he climbed into an American bomber plane to fly his last mission." Adroitly, Jack made religious bias appear anti-American rather than an act of nativism. In a paid statewide television program with FDR Jr., Kennedy reiterated the same theme.

"When any man stands on the steps of the Capitol and takes the oath of office of president, he is swearing to support the separation of church and state," he avowed. "He puts one hand on the Bible and raises the other hand to God as he takes the oath. And if he breaks his oath, he is not only committing a crime against the Constitution, for which the Constitution can impeach him—and should impeach him—but he is committing a sin against God."

His high-risk strategy worked remarkably well. Kennedy pulled off a surprise victory in West Virginia, upsetting Humphrey by such a large majority that the Minnesotan withdrew from the remaining primaries. Once the challenger, Kennedy now became the frontrunner, his nomination inevitable unless something untoward stopped him. "If Senator Kennedy is to be turned down, those in control of the convention will be under heavy pressure to make a convincing demonstration that his religion was not officially responsible," observed the *New York Times,* correctly recognizing the significance of the moment.

With the size of this victory, Kennedy declared the controversy surrounding his Catholic faith had been put to rest—an assertion far removed
from reality. As he remarked, it was "buried eight feet deep in West Virginia;
now if we can get the Catholics to stop talking about it." Some commentators expressed hope that the country had turned a corner. In the most
unlikely place, particularly given West Virginia's history of anti-Catholicism,
Kennedy's victory suggested that the religious barrier to the presidency
finally could be overcome.

IN LOS ANGELES, at the Democratic National Convention that July, John
F. Kennedy became his party's presidential nominee. At his father's insistence, he rounded out the ticket by asking Lyndon Baines Johnson to be
his vice-presidential running mate—believing the Texas senator would
bring enough votes from traditional Democrats in the South to offset those
lost on the religious issue. To Jack's surprise and the dismay of Bobby,
Johnson accepted. Despite his sons' gloomy ambivalence, Joe Kennedy
declared the Johnson selection a masterstroke. He believed Johnson's presence on the ticket might help avoid some of the ugliness and difficulties
ahead for Jack as a Catholic running for president. Already problems existed in the Democratic ranks.

At a luncheon for Adlai Stevenson shortly before the convention began,
Eleanor Roosevelt tried to swamp Kennedy's candidacy by casting doubts
about his religion, contending that she "did not believe Senator Kennedy
could win the election, nor could he win the Negro vote." When reporters
inquired further about her inflammatory statement, the former first lady reiterated her concerns about whether America was ready for a Catholic in
the White House. "I felt that there would be less chance for a ticket headed
by Senator Kennedy," she explained. "I doubted he could carry the Negro
vote, and also, while I am extremely gratified not to find any real prejudice
from the religious point of view, I couldn't be sure, from the trends I have
seen, that this situation would continue through the November election."
To be sure, many Negro Baptist churchmen said they'd never vote for a
Roman Catholic. If Kennedy's candidacy carried some symbolism about
their own fate—as members of another minority group in America—these
ministers were blind to it. Their denouncements were every bit as loud and
determined as those of other Protestant churches opposed to Kennedy. For
her own reasons, Eleanor Roosevelt felt this sentiment was enough to deny
Kennedy his chance. By that point, he already had enough delegate support
to secure the nomination. But Mrs. Roosevelt insisted the best ticket in

1960 would be "Stevenson-Kennedy"—the young Catholic taking second place. Jack found such a notion distasteful. Eventually, he met with the former first lady to alleviate her concerns, even if she was motivated, as the Kennedy family suspected, by less than fair-minded principles. Yet if liberal Democrats with the name Roosevelt harbored such fears, how could he expect to win?

ARRIVING BACK in Hyannis Port after the convention, Kennedy was swarmed by at least fifteen thousand people, mostly from Boston, who heard him give a short speech of thanksgiving. Elated by his nomination, Kennedy reminded this crowd of many immigrant descendants how his own family had struggled for this moment. He mentioned his great-grandparents from Ireland, how they had sought the freedoms and opportunities America had to offer and what it meant to him. Some Catholics were so consumed with pride by Kennedy's candidacy that their words spilled into hyperbole. The editor of *America*, the Jesuit magazine, predicted the United States was entering a "post-Protestant era" and claimed Kennedy's candidacy was "filled with immense sociological and cultural meaning," partly because JFK "makes no secret of the fact that he is a Catholic of Irish descent."

With his keen historical sense, Kennedy recognized that his campaign had become a quest for the rights and dignity denied his predecessors, for an end to the restrictions that kept minorities from achieving America's greatest honors. "The nomination of the second Roman Catholic ever to run for President of the United States brought appeals from Catholic, Protestant and Jewish clergymen yesterday for a campaign without reference to religion," the United Press International reported on the day of Kennedy's acceptance speech. But that same week, the cover of *Time* magazine featured a profile of Kennedy and his "clan" replete with patronizing references to his faith and ethnicity. "The Kennedy clan is as handsome and spirited as a meadow full of Irish thoroughbreds, as tough as a blackthorn shillelagh, as ruthless as Cuchulain, the mythical hero who cast up the hills of Ireland with his sword," the magazine reported. The article highlighted father Joe Kennedy, "whose shrewd Irish instincts were first and foremost focused on making a name and a fortune." When FDR appointed him ambassador to Britain, he became "the first Irish-American to hold the job—the clan moved into the embassy residence on Prince's Gate." Readers learned how neighbors in Hyannis Port once looked down their noses at the Kennedys as "moneyed Boston Irish," and how grandfather Honey Fitz represented "the old, colorful and rascally breed of Boston Irish politics." It even suggested that Jack was keeping his father out of sight during the 1960 campaign "because of the Catholic issue."

The *Time* profile was only one of many such examples. Much had changed in America since 1928, but the old ghosts continued to appear: how would Jack Kennedy break through this historic barrier and not become just another painful failure, Al Smith all over again?

The Fall, 1960

FROM THE START, Richard Nixon insisted that he wouldn't make religion an issue in the 1960 campaign. The Republican vice president had grown up as a Quaker, a Protestant domination that had historically endured its own persecution, and he vowed that "under no circumstance" would he raise the subject. In an inter-office memo to his staff, he forbade everyone connected with his campaign from discussing religion, even informally or casually. By the general election campaign, however, it was clear that Nixon's promise, regardless of his intent, would be impossible to keep.

At a White House press conference in late August, President Eisenhower, who studiously avoided the controversy surrounding Kennedy's religion, was prodded for a response about the growing number of anti-Catholic statements around the nation. Publicly, Eisenhower agreed with Nixon that religion should not be an issue, but he was asked about the increasing role of Protestant clergymen in this debate.

"A man whom you have publicly esteemed, Evangelist Billy Graham, now says it is a legitimate issue and could be a decisive one in this election. Do you have any comment?" queried Edward P. Morgan, an ABC television correspondent. Three months earlier, Graham was present when the annual Southern Baptist Convention unanimously passed a resolution expressing doubts about electing Kennedy or any Roman Catholic to the presidency. Graham also gave a thinly veiled endorsement of Nixon at that conclave.

Eisenhower's discomfort with this mix of politics and religion was apparent in his pained expression and his rambling response. He restated his hands-off position, alluding to the Constitution and its promise of religious liberty. "But I—on the other hand—I am not so naïve that I think that in some areas it will not be," the president added. "It is just almost certain, because as long as you have got strong emotional convictions and reactions in this areas, there is going to be some of it—you can't help it. But I certainly never encouraged it."

Within a week, John Kennedy's Catholicism became the central issue of the presidential campaign. "We think at this point there is a substantial danger that the campaign of 1960 will be dirtier on the religious issue than it was in 1928," warned Bruce L. Felknor of the Fair Campaign Practices Committee, citing the widespread circulation of "rabidly anti-Catholic material." In the Senate, Estes Kefauver said religious hate literature aimed at Kennedy's defeat was being sent by the Ku Klux Klan and other such groups. Similarly, Roy Wilkins of the National Association for the Advancement of Colored People (NAACP) blamed a "hideous apparatus of hate" for injecting religious bigotry into the presidential campaign and charged that "the same scurrilous, filthy type of literature being passed around against Negroes is now being passed out against Catholics." Wilkins reminded that "most of the Protestant churches that pictured the Negro as virtually a chimpanzee now picture the Roman Catholic Church as an evil octopus." Though little evidence existed of an active role by the Republican Party, nearly all those expressing anti-Catholic statements were Nixon supporters. For example, the Reverend Dr. W. O. Vaught, an Arkansas minister and vice president of the Southern Baptist Convention, delivered the invocation at one of the sessions of the Republican National Convention that nominated Nixon for president in July. Two months later, Reverend Vaught was announcing "religious freedom rallies" in Little Rock to combat Kennedy. "We cannot turn our Government over to a Catholic president who could be influenced by the Pope and by the power of the Catholic hierarchy," he declared.

Bobby Kennedy admitted that his brother faced an uphill struggle in six traditionally Democratic Southern states, including Florida and Texas, because of his Catholicism. "I think that's the major problem at the present time, at least from what I've heard," he told reporters. "Right now, religion is the biggest issue in the South, and in the country." Despite his initial preference to avoid the topic, Bobby had come around to his brother's view that the best political course was to deal directly with the religious issue and assert their unequivocal belief in a separation of church and state. To help overcome prejudice, the Kennedys enlisted a lay Protestant leader, James W.

Wine of the National Council of Churches, to interpret the senator's position on religious questions and allay fears. Nevertheless, the issue of religion continued to intensify.

ON LABOR DAY, former President Harry Truman accused the Republicans of fostering religious bigotry against Kennedy, and he held Nixon personally accountable. "While he stands at the front door proclaiming charity and tolerance, his supporters are herding the forces of racial, religious and anti-union bigotry in by way of the back door," Truman said in an Indiana speech. "And no one will ever make me believe he is not smart enough to know what is going on." (Earlier in the primary campaign, Truman had opposed Kennedy, indicating to reporters that his reasons had more to do with the candidate's father than his religion: "I'm not against the Pope," said Truman, "I'm against the Pop.") Later on, Truman backed away from his personal accusation of Nixon, but he still blamed the GOP for fanning the flames of intolerance. "In my home town, the Republicans are sending out all the dirty pamphlets they can find on the religious issue," said the man from Independence, Missouri. He described the hate literature as "long sheets resembling the dirty sheets which they used against Al Smith in the Twenties."

Truman's comments prompted Eisenhower to respond publicly to the religious issue for the second time in less than a month, once again creating front-page headlines. "I not only don't believe in voicing prejudice—I want to assure you that I feel none, and I am sure that Mr. Nixon feels the same," Eisenhower said at a White House press conference. Eisenhower also came to the defense of his party. "I know of no one, certainly no Republican has come to me and said: 'I believe we should use religion as an issue,' or intimate that he intends to use it either locally or nationally." Eisenhower's frustration was evident when he alluded to the general defensiveness Republicans felt about charges linking them to anti-Catholic hate mongers. "The very need, apparently, for protesting innocence in this regard now, in itself, seems to exacerbate rather than to quiet it," the president said, expressing hope that a candidate's religion could be "laid on the shelf and forgotten until after the election."

On the same day, however, the most explosive episode of religious bias in the campaign took place. Eisenhower's comments were undermined with a statement unveiled by the National Conference of Citizens for Religious Freedom, headed by the Reverend Dr. Norman Vincent Peale, a prominent Protestant minister, author of the best-selling book *The Power of*

Positive Thinking and, most significantly, a close supporter of Nixon. The group charged that a Roman Catholic president would be under "extreme pressure from the hierarchy of his church" to align the foreign policy of the United States with that of the Vatican. The statement by the group of 150 ministers and laymen—including Billy Graham's father-in-law, Dr. L. Nelson Bell, an editor of *Christianity Today*—disputed Kennedy's promise of independence from his church. He loudly proclaimed that freedom from "Romish influences" would be a major issue in the "momentous decision" of the 1960 election, and he urged the Protestant faithful to "question claims of freedom from domination" by a Roman Catholic candidate. Bell also outlined grievances against Catholics in general: "In various areas where they predominate, Catholics have seized control of the public schools, staffed them with nun teachers wearing their church garb, and introduced the catechism and practices of their church." At a news conference, Peale denied bigotry by his group which, he said, engaged in "an intelligent approach to the religious issue on a high philosophical level." The statement charged that Kennedy, as a Catholic, was bound by his church's belief that "Protestant faiths are heretical and counterfeit and that they have no theoretical right to exist."

POLITICALLY, THE GROUP'S statement drew attention because of Peale's allegiance to Nixon. Peale served as pastor of New York's Marble Collegiate Church, which Nixon occasionally attended. At the group's press conference, Peale said he had not discussed the statement with Nixon who, he admitted, "probably would have disapproved of it had he known." The statements by Peale and his group were roundly criticized (the *Philadelphia Inquirer* even dropped his weekly column because of the furor). Eventually, Peale felt compelled to renounce his part in the movement he had helped create. "I was not duped," he told the *New York Herald Tribune,* "I was just stupid."

But the Kennedys seized on Peale's comments as evidence of the Republicans' part in a religious smear campaign. "Their close relationship with Mr. Nixon and the Republican party in the election leads me to question the sincerity of their statement and their judgment in issuing it," campaign manager Robert Kennedy said of the ministers. On its own, the Democratic National Committee compiled a memorandum of "questions frequently asked by fair-minded persons" about such issues as parochial schools and birth control, along with answers taken from Kennedy's past statements, and sent it to party workers and private citizens inquiring about the senator's position. When asked during a Los Angeles appearance about the Peale group's statement, Kennedy bristled at the attacks on his religion. "I do not accept the view that my church would place pressures on me," he declared. During an earlier stop in Modesto, California, the candidate encountered a heckler who demanded to know whether he considered Protestants to be heretics. "No, and I hope you don't believe all Catholics are," Kennedy replied briskly. The crowd of several hundred onlookers burst into applause, a response that emboldened him to continue. "May I say that it seems that the great struggle today is between those who believe in no God and those who believe in God. I really don't see why we should engage in close debate over what you may believe and what I may believe. That is my privilege and your privilege."

Nixon kept his distance from the Peale group's statement. During a television appearance on NBC's *Meet the Press,* Nixon kept firmly to his position of not discussing religion, and he called upon Kennedy to agree to a "cut-off date" from talking about it in the campaign. Nixon said he had no doubt Kennedy would place the Constitution above his faith and added that it would be "tragic" if his opponent lost simply because he was a Catholic. "I don't believe there is a religious issue as far as Senator Kennedy is concerned," Nixon said. "I have no doubt whatever about Senator Kennedy's loyalty to his country." Nixon's high-mindedness in this situation is remarkable, particularly given his penchant for dirty tricks and political infighting. Kennedy said that he, too, wished for an end to the religious debate, but his campaign had already accepted an invitation to address these concerns formally at a meeting of conservative Protestant ministers in Houston.

JACK KENNEDY was unchactertistically nervous. He rubbed his fists, sipped water several times and pushed his thumbs back and forth as he waited through the perfunctory introductions and opening prayers of the Greater Houston Ministerial Association. Inside the Rice Hotel ballroom on a sultry afternoon in September 1960, Kennedy turned anxiously to his press aide, Pierre Salinger.

"What's the mood of the ministers?" the candidate asked.

Salinger gave him the news bluntly. "They're tired of being called bigots," he growled.

Kennedy could only muster a wan smile. For days, he had been preparing a five-page speech on "the religious issue." In most campaign speeches, he'd vary from the prepared script with some impromptu humor or relaxed comments. In this one, though, he resolved to stay strictly to his text, but promised to entertain questions from the floor when he had finished his speech.

The stakes were extraordinarily high. Kennedy knew he could lose it all: not only his bid for president in 1960 but also any realistic chance for a Catholic to aspire to the nation's most powerful office anytime in the near future. "We can win or lose the election right there in Houston on Monday," Sorensen confided to a friend before the speech.

Kennedy had prepared his Houston speech with a battery of tests. Sorensen read its contents over the telephone to Father John Courtney Murray to avoid "any loose wording this time that would unnecessarily stir up the Catholic press." James Wine, the candidate's liaison with the Protestant community, and *Commonweal's* John Cogley, who took a leave from the magazine to assist the senator, also reviewed each word, each phrase. Some lines were lifted almost verbatim from Cogley's *Commonweal* columns on the issue. Sitting next to Sorensen in Houston, the air thick with tension, Cogley quipped: "This is one time that we need those types that pray for Notre Dame before each football game!" Kennedy's appearance that day in Houston—in the heart of the nation's Bible Belt—reflected his intent to confront prejudices directly in a polite and respectful manner. If these wary Texans could only see him talking politics sensibly on television, see that he didn't have horns or wear a Roman collar, perhaps they could be convinced to pull the Democratic lever in the ballot box. Kennedy did everything he could to set aside their fears. He came to this meeting of Protestant ministers "looking something like a parson himself," as *Time* magazine observed, dressed as he was in a somber black suit with a black tie. After the initial remarks, he strode purposefully to the microphone and took command.

"I believe in an America," Kennedy began with his clipped New England accent, "where the separation of church and state is absolute— where no Catholic prelate would tell the president, should he be a Catholic, how to act, and no Protestant minister would tell his parishioners for whom to vote."

AS BIG AND BROAD as the state itself, Texas overflowed with passion about John Kennedy's candidacy in 1960. Early in the primary season, its favorite son, Lyndon Johnson, had lost to Kennedy; but once he was chosen as a running mate, Johnson spoke out forcefully about the "hate campaign" surrounding Kennedy's religion. He predicted that most Southerners would judge Kennedy on his political qualifications, not his religion. "I believe that most people think that if a man is good enough to fight for his country and die for his country, he ought to be allowed to serve his country without a test of his race, religion or regional status," Johnson proclaimed.

Nonetheless, Texas was home to much of the anti-Catholic allegations against Kennedy, particularly Dallas. A group called Texans for Nixon was headed by Carr B. Collins, a member of the First Baptist Church in Dallas, where congregates were instructed not to vote for Kennedy. Collins had his own anti-papist pedigree. As investigative columnist Jack Anderson reported, "Collins sparked the drive in Texas against Catholic candidate Al Smith in 1928 and is now organizing the campaign against Catholic candidate Jack Kennedy." On a Sunday morning sermon the day before Independence Day, Dallas radio listeners could hear Collins's pastor, the Reverend Dr. W. A. Criswell, preach against the threat of a Catholic in the White House. "Roman Catholicism is not only a religion, it is a political tyranny," the reverend declared. The *New York Times* identified Criswell as pastor of "the nation's largest all-white Baptist congregation" with twelve thousand members. Criswell's radio sermons were so clearly political in overtone that the Democrats demanded and received equal time from the radio station for a response by the Reverend F. Braxton Bryant, a Methodist minister and Kennedy backer. "Leaders of the Nixon forces, not Nixon himself, are using the religion issue against Mr. Kennedy," said Bryant. "Even Billy Graham—he's for Nixon—is being political every time he says, 'Religion is a major issue, but I'll wait till I enter the voting booth to express my convictions.'"

Throughout Texas, preachers and churchgoing people received leaflets in the mail with such titles as "Can We Afford to Elect a Catholic President?" The letter was sent by a group called Christians United for a Free America, located outside of Dallas and devoted to opposing Kennedy on religious grounds. In the words of its founder, the Reverend Tom Landers, an independent Baptist, the massive mail campaign aimed to convince all Protestants and right-thinking Americans to reject the Massachusetts Democrat because "he owes allegiance to a sovereign power over and above that of the United States." The sheer expense of this large-scale anti-Catholic propaganda campaign by the local churches led many political observers to wonder where these churches were finding the money. Eventually, some wealthy Texan businessmen, among them oil billionaire H. L. Hunt, were identified as the behind-the-scene sponsors for this tax-free bigotry. "It is not only that the majority of Protestant churches are openly opposing him [Kennedy], but equally important that influential economic interests are supporting the anti-Catholic preachers," wrote columnist James Reston. "The flood of this kind of material is now running into the millions, and clearly this kind of money is not normally available to individual churches or their central organizations."

In an attempt to defeat Kennedy, religious opponents announced that the biggest distribution of anti-Catholic material would be aimed at the last ten days of the campaign, with sermons and rallies planned for Reformation Sunday, October 30, when Protestant sentiment would be at its height. The Justice Department disclosed a total of 144 producers of anti-Catholic "hate" literature sent through the mails. "I would oppose any Roman Catholic for President—the name doesn't make a difference," said Harvey H. Springer, the "cowboy evangelist" based in Colorado, remarkably unabashed in his venom. "Let the Romanists move out of America. . . . Did you see the coronation of Big John [Pope John XXIII]? Let's hope we never see the coronation of Little John. How many Catholics came over on the Mayflower? Not one. . . . The Constitution is a Protestant Constitution." Springer extended his warnings about Catholics to Jews and blacks as well. "I'm perfectly willing to admit I'm a bigot," he boasted.

THE KENNEDYS met this sheer hate with a composed, often courageous stance. "I don't believe we should have any candidate running, Catholic or Protestant, who doesn't believe in separation," insisted Robert Kennedy. "If we did, I would campaign against him." But this message, honed in West Virginia, wouldn't receive a full national airing until Jack Kennedy accepted the invitation in Houston.

Before the group of conservative Protestant ministers, Kennedy promised to remain always independent of church pressures. "No power or threat of punishment could cause me" to deviate from the national interest, Kennedy promised during the question period. "But if the time should ever come—I do not concede any conflict to be even remotely possible—when my office would require me to either violate my conscience or violate the national interest, then I would resign the office, and hope any conscientious public servant would do the same." His aides worried about mentioning a possible resignation over conscience, but most of Kennedy's brain trust felt it necessary to "unscramble" the public's doubts, as Cogley put it.

Kennedy said his political affiliation should never be confused with his religious identity. "Contrary to common newspaper usage, I am not the

Catholic candidate for President," he said, with an undertone of annoyance. "I am the Democratic Party's candidate for President who happens also to be a Catholic." During another moment in his speech, Kennedy invoked the memory of his dead brother and expropriated some of the same phrases from the Peale group's statement. "I believe in an America where religious intolerance will someday end," Kennedy declared. "This is the kind of America I believe in, and this is the kind of America I fought for in the South Pacific, and the kind my brother died for in Europe. No one suggested that we might have a 'divided loyalty,' that we did 'not believe in liberty' or that we belonged to a disloyal group that threatened the 'freedoms for which our forefathers died.'"

To many, the Massachusetts senator seemed like a modern-day Sir Thomas More, victimized by his religion but willing to stand up for principle in a composed and reasoned manner. Kennedy's confrontation with the Houston clergymen convinced doubters that Kennedy had the stuff to be president. Even Kennedy himself conceded that the "controversy" nevertheless had given him unparalleled national attention as well as the admiration and sympathy of many voters. "The curious fact remains that Senator Kennedy has got so far as he has simply because he is a Catholic. It has been his special 'gimmick,'" observed one London newspaper. "Kennedy's skillful and aggressive answers satisfied many people or at least induced in them the sort of guilt that made it squalid to bring these questions up."

KENNEDY'S TRIAL by fire in Texas resonated with the historic struggle of Catholics for acceptance in America. During one question, posed by a clergyman who identified himself as V. E. Howard, a minister of the Church of Christ in Houston, Kennedy was asked for his response to obscure quotations from the *Catholic Encyclopedia,* an article from the Vatican periodical *L'Osservatore Romano* and from papal statements about the church's role in guiding its flock. Kennedy ducked most of the question by professing theological ignorance, yet reasserted his political autonomy from the church.

"Then you do not agree with the Pope on that statement?" Howard interjected.

Kennedy didn't take the bait. "Gentlemen, now that's why I wanted to be careful because that statement it seems to me is taken out of context," the candidate said. "I could not tell you what the Pope meant unless I had the entire article."

Many of the ministers, at least publicly, approved of Kennedy's answers. In one sense, they felt they had won by securing an unequivocal promise from Kennedy of no interference from his church. If elected, Kennedy would become America's "first anti-clerical President," teased columnist Murray Kempton. But Kempton and other observers also detected that the tide was turning for Kennedy because he was now picking up the support of many Americans who felt "widespread disgust" for the sheer bigotry faced by the Democratic candidate. The Kennedy campaign recognized the dramatic success of the Houston speech and used snippets of it in campaign television commercials. Though he arrived nervous and slightly hoarse, Jack Kennedy had found his "voice" in Houston, with an authoritative, indeed presidential style, that would carry him for the rest of the campaign.

In New York, the Catholic Church honors the memory of Al Smith each year with a gala dinner in his name at the Waldorf Astoria, an event held close enough to Election Day so that no mayor, governor or political aspirant would dare not to attend. But in 1960, Jack Kennedy didn't want to go. He and his aides felt they had sewn up New York politically and didn't need to remind the rest of the nation of the last fateful time a Catholic had tried to run for the White House. In a campaign where he promised a strict separation of church and state policy, Kennedy didn't need to be seen at a church fundraiser in the company of Cardinal Spellman and photographed with a bevy of Catholic clergymen. Besides, the family was upset with Spellman for his perceived lack of loyalty. Joe Kennedy's disappointment in Spellman was so deep that he now sounded like a lifelong anticleric. "As you know, I've never been anxious to have anything to do with priests, nuns or any of the hierarchy," Joe insisted to Galeazzi in Rome, who clearly knew better. "This was driven into me by my father and mother, who always believed that the clergy had their place and the family had their own." Initially, Galeazzi defended the cardinal, his closest ally in the American hierarchy, and insisted that Spellman's fondness for the Kennedys hadn't changed. "Jack is confronted with the tremendous responsibility of being a champion of a fight that goes beyond the borders of his own country," responded the familiar voice from Rome. Galeazzi's words, meant to soothe, only added to the sense of betrayal. Things had indeed changed, not only with a new Pope but among the Kennedys themselves.

Politically, Spellman proved an apostate. Though the cardinal had presided over the marriages of some of Kennedy's siblings (Jack preferred Cushing), the New York potentate adopted a position in 1960 that he considered best for the church rather than for the interests of one family.

Spellman believed Richard Nixon would be more flexible to the church's needs than Jack Kennedy, who was now handcuffed by his own words on the separation of church and state. All the issues pressed by the Catholic hierarchy—funding for parochial schools, a U.S. ambassador at the Vatican, tough stands on communism and sexual morality—would be likely pushed by Nixon. Most American bishops were sympathetic to Kennedy. But as a Vatican official told the *New York Times,* the view from Rome was that "a Roman Catholic in the White House at this moment might do more harm than good to the Church."

For Jack Kennedy, the lack of support from his own institutional church was "ironically, the cruelest blow" of the campaign, Sorensen recalled. The cardinal knew that if Kennedy was installed in the American presidency, he would no longer be the most powerful Catholic in the country. By the time of the Al Smith dinner, Spellman had tipped his hand, indicating his preference for Nixon. Jack's invitation seemed almost perfunctory. "I was shocked by his [Spellman's] attitude in the presidential campaign," Joe Kennedy later seethed to Galeazzi. "I was shocked at the reception Jack got at the Al Smith dinner, and with many other incidents about which I have written you." Of all the Kennedys, Jack probably had the least regard for Spellman. The cardinal's duplicity was most transparent to him, even though Spellman appeared to behave like a loyal family friend when he wrote Kennedy a note during the Democratic Convention that summer:

Dear Jack,

Congratulations on your wonderful victory. I remained up until four fifteen this morning watching the proceedings and shall hear your acceptance speech tomorrow.

I hope you will arrange your speaking program so as to be with us at the Al Smith dinner at the Waldorf the evening of October 19. Vice President Nixon will also speak. I know how happy are your mother and father and brothers and sisters.

Devotedly and prayerfully,

The cardinal's ruse, the friendly affectations while acting busily behind the scenes to undermine his candidacy, appalled Jack Kennedy. "He never liked Cardinal Spellman," Bobby later recalled. "All of the conversations that we got back from Spellman were strongly against my brother, and the person who was strongly against Spellman, of course, was Cushing, who was far more liberal."

After considerable internal debate, however, Kennedy decided to attend the Al Smith dinner, even though he would be surrounded by the cardinal's courtesans and partisans. He was slated as the last speaker, but threw out half his speech because he was not scheduled to speak until after 11:00 P.M. He was determined not to let his emotions show; his only armament of the evening was his sense of humor, arguably his best weapon.

"Now that Cardinal Spellman has demonstrated the proper spirit, I assume that shortly I will be invited to a Quaker dinner honoring Herbert Hoover," he began, drawing a titter from the crowd. With a wry smile, Kennedy gazed upon the assembled politicians, including the governor of New York, Nelson Rockefeller. "Cardinal Spellman is the only man so widely respected in American politics that he could bring together amicably, at the same banquet table, for the first time in this campaign, two political leaders who are increasingly apprehensive about the November election—who have eyed each other suspiciously and who have disagreed so strongly, both publicly and privately—Vice President Nixon and Governor Rockefeller," he quipped, which brought about a healthy round of laughter. To this crowd of twenty-five hundred people, it seemed that Kennedy surely wouldn't make this jest unless he was in the cardinal's good graces.

With the same light touch, Kennedy poked fun at Nixon, at the various charges leveled during the campaign and even at himself. When confronted with the inanity and hypocrisies of political life, Jack Kennedy could signal to the crowd, without condescension or undue cynicism, that he was in on the joke. "On this matter of experience," he added, referring to a Republican criticism of himself, "I had announced earlier this year that if successful I would not consider campaign contributions as a substitute for experience in appointing ambassadors. Ever since I made that statement, I have not received one single cent from my father."

Looming over the whole evening was the religious issue—the great unknown wild card of the 1960 campaign—which he handled gracefully, ever aware of the historical ironies in appearing at this dinner. During his speech, Kennedy spoke somberly of a presidential candidate who suffered a humiliating defeat, carried only a few states and lost even his own.

"You all know his name and his religion," Kennedy said, pausing properly for effect, "Alfred M. Landon, *Protestant.*"

The crowd erupted in laughter. For his closer, Kennedy made a gentle reference to the attacks on President Truman, who, in salty language, had condemned Republicans by saying they should go to hell for stirring up emotions over religion. Then Jack looked down at a slip of paper, a note that he told the crowd he had sent to Truman. "Dear Mr. President," he read, "I have noted with interest your suggestion as to where those who vote for my opponent should go. While I understand and sympathize with your deep motivation, I think it is important that our side try to refrain from raising the religious issue."

Kennedy sat down at the dais to laughter and applause. The night crackled with energy and tension. Even though the religious issue could explode in front of him, Kennedy employed his wit and a cool, breezy delivery that allowed him to emerge a winner that night. When he left the building, he still marveled at Spellman's duplicity. "It undoubtedly goes to show that, when the chips are down, money counts more than religion," he later commented to Arthur Schlesinger. Publicly, Kennedy didn't appear to let crude snubs and subtle insults about his religion bother him. Each question had to be carefully considered, each answer weighed and either replied to with precision or defused with a humorous comment. In Los Angeles, when a reporter slipped and asked whether a Protestant could be elected president, Jack jumped like a big cat with his punch line. "If this Protestant candidate is willing to submit to questions on his views concerning the separation of church and state, I don't see why we should discriminate against him," Kennedy replied.

While being driven through Manhattan, Kennedy was chatting with *Time* reporter Hugh Sidey when their limousine passed St. Patrick's Cathedral. As Sidey recalled decades later, Kennedy was "suddenly seized by the inner imp," and, grinning widely, saluted the massive gothic spires of the Catholic church. Then with mock horror, realizing how he'd just confirmed the nightmares of so many, he yelled at the reporter: "That's off the record!" And one Sunday morning, at a parish in Anchorage, Alaska, aide Dave Powers reminded the candidate of the old Irish tradition that three wishes are granted to those who visit a church for the first time.

"New York, Pennsylvania and Texas," Kennedy whispered.

FOR ALL HIS HUMOR and charm, Jack Kennedy could be quite threatening to much of America. His candidacy marked a dividing line between where the country had been and where it was headed. On television during the campaign, Kennedy made a conscientious effort to be as comforting and commonsensical as possible. Yet there was no denying his separate status in the eyes of Protestant America. Kennedy represented change—a switch in stewardship from those whose forebears founded the republic and into the hands of those immigrants who ar-rived generations later to take advantage of the liberties and opportuni-ties of America. The nation would no longer be just theirs if he won. Some Protestant churches, notably the Presbyterian Church, took no official position in the election, as did so many Lutheran and Methodist congregations. But the Southern Baptist Convention, the nation's second largest Protestant denomination, declared that "when a public official is inescapably bound by the dogma and the demands of his church, he can-not consistently separate himself from these." Kennedy's challenge to this land of old-time religion was more than a test of whether he could keep the pontiff at bay. His candidacy suggested a decline in the WASP hege-mony, a loss of grip in their society. As Arthur Moore, an editor of a Methodist monthly, observed: "Southern Baptists feel beleaguered—integration, mechanization, urbanization are destroying the world they knew and, since it was an intensely Protestant world, it is quite easy to tie anti-Catholicism in with their bewilderment and fear." Moore noted that far more alarm bells and apocalyptic warnings were issued by the evangelical side of American Protestantism than from its more historic "mainstream" churches.

Kennedy's run for the presidency revived anti-Catholicism in the United States to an extent that many found startling and profoundly disturbing. "Anti-Catholicism, whether of 'the educated' or without the B.A., receives its major thrust today because it answers an acute need in American Protestantism," wrote Franklin H. Littell of the Chicago Theological Seminary during the campaign. "And many otherwise decent and genuinely good men—pastors, college presidents, superintendents and bishops, men among whom an anti-Semite is virtually unknown—will unabashedly lend their names to anti-Catholic programs of the most vicious and depraved sort." Kennedy's challenge also forced many fair-minded Protestants to recognize that their dominance over America's culture—what some sociologists called the civil religion or the national faith—would be no longer exclusive or absolute. Spiritual themes and con-ventions evoked by the Founding Fathers in creating the political institu-tions of the country were unmistakably Protestant. After decades of immi-gration, however, the country was far more diverse. Kennedy's money, edu-cation and aspiration for power underlined how much things had changed for mainstream Protestants. In a sense, the Irish Catholic from Boston rep-resented every minority group in the country looking for a share in the American pantheon of fame and legitimacy.

As ELECTION DAY NEARED, some Catholics still resented Kennedy's effort to explain himself and his religion. The Jesuit magazine, *America,* said it was humiliating to watch Kennedy "appease" anti-Catholic bigots. After spending late summer in the South of France, Joe Kennedy couldn't believe how much the religion issue still held center stage. "I came home to find the campaign not between a Democrat and a Republican but between a Catholic and a Protestant," he wrote to his friend, Lord Max Beaverbrook, the British press baron. "We can lick it now. But with the Baptist ministers working in every pulpit every Sunday, it is going to be tough."

To be sure, the Catholic Church's inconsistent stance on the separation of church and state also created havoc for Kennedy. "Caught as he sometimes was between the criticism of Catholics and the criticism of Protestants, he must frequently have felt as if he were being offered to the gods of history," sympathized *Commonweal.* During the primaries, Kennedy was quizzed about an unsigned editorial in *L'Osservatore Romano,* the Vatican newspaper, insisting that the church hierarchy has the "right and duty to intervene" in politics when necessary. Though the piece was intended to fend off the Marxists in Italy, reporters questioned its universal application in America. In a widely publicized statement, Father Gustave Weigel—one of the theological experts originally suggested to the Kennedys—provided strong moral support for Kennedy's stand when he unequivocally endorsed the church-state separation principle.

Such pronouncements became vital when, late in the fall campaign, the bishops of Puerto Rico wrote a lengthy pastoral letter forbidding Catholics to vote for the island's popular local governor. The overt directive by the Puerto Rico church, violating the traditional sense of church and state in the United States, startled the Kennedys; indeed, campaign advisers feared the directive could be a death knell to Jack's chances. "The day the bishops' statements came out, everybody thought this was the end of the line, and I must say I felt that way somewhat, too," John Cogley recalled. Tactically, the Kennedy camp decided to hold its breath and say nothing.

American church leaders, led by Cardinal Cushing, quickly distanced themselves from the Puerto Rican fiasco. "It is totally out of step with the American tradition for the ecclesiastical authority here to dictate the political voting of citizens," Cushing stated. He endorsed church and state separation without ruling out the influence of moral and religious considerations in the thinking of each Catholic. "We must repeat that, whatever may be the custom elsewhere, the American tradition, of which Catholics form so loyal a part, is satisfied simply to call to public attention moral questions with their implications and leave to the conscience of the people the specific political decision which comes in the act of voting."

Once again, like some political guardian angel, Cardinal Cushing came to Jack Kennedy's rescue. The Puerto Rican storm cloud quickly blew past.

Overall, the political impact of the "religious issue" galvanized support for Kennedy among Catholics, many of whom might have voted otherwise for the more conservative Republican candidate. In the last presidential election, Eisenhower garnered more than 60 percent of the Catholic vote. Nixon's pollsters warned him that he hovered in the mid–20s among Catholics. Despite his earlier pledge, Nixon's campaign reversed its hands-off position concerning religion. "The Kennedy camp is attempting to exploit the religion issue to solidify what they regard as a 'Catholic vote,'" complained Nixon's press spokesman, Herbert Klein. Nixon's counterpunch was too late. In a preelection analysis, political correspondents from the *New York Times* rated "religion" as the number one issue of the campaign—ahead of the Cold War, national defense and the economy, and noted that "Kennedy gains more than he is losing" because of the dispute.

On the night before the election, John Kennedy appeared on the ABC television network in a paid thirty-minute telecast in which he sat at a table and fielded questions posed by his three sisters, Jean, Eunice and Pat (Jackie Kennedy, only three weeks away from giving birth, didn't attend). A day earlier, Nixon had held his own telecast, the questions being primarily about foreign policy. But Kennedy's inquiries were most notably about religion. "When I take that oath—if I take it—to God to defend the Constitution, that's the highest oath," he explained during the broadcast. "I don't think any fellow Americans have cause for the slightest concern. You may want to elect a Republican, but not for that reason—religion should not be your concern." Looking into the eye of the camera, Kennedy assured voters that his own family was as "devoted as any fellow Americans to defending the Constitution and separation of church and state." He noted that two Chief Justices of the Supreme Court had been Catholics, and that world leaders such as Konrad Adenauer in West Germany and France's Charles de Gaulle didn't let religion mix with their politics.

From beginning to end, Kennedy was forced to address his religion in a battery of tests that the Constitution once promised no American would have to endure. Survey analysis belied the hopeful claim of many Democrats, including Kennedy himself, that America had changed dramatically since Smith's era and that religion wouldn't be a serious obstacle in 1960. In fact, America was still a very bigoted country, not only for a Catholic but virtually for any minority member who dared reach for society's highest positions. The assurances Kennedy gave on this final telecast of the campaign were the same as those he had offered in his announcement speech in the Senate Caucus Room, in his televised debate in West Virginia and in his inquisition before the Houston ministers. What he had repeatedly answered and put to rest throughout the campaign remained a nagging question until its very last day.

ON NOVEMBER 8, 1960, Election Day, a strong Catholic turnout in such key states as Illinois and Pennsylvania provided Kennedy's tiny margin of victory in one of the closest presidential contests in American history. As the Bailey Report had predicted four years earlier, a Catholic on the ticket had its greatest impact in key electoral states. The 1960 electoral college vote was far wider for Kennedy, 303 to 219, than the razor-thin popular vote percentage (49.72 percent to Nixon's 49.55). The religion issue played a deciding role, nearly causing Kennedy's defeat. Nixon won five Southern states, usually in the Democratic camp, where anti-Catholic sentiment festered among fundamentalist groups and conservative Protestant denominations. By one estimate, as many as 4.5 million Protestants who voted for Stevenson in 1956 switched to Nixon in 1960. "American Protestants were remarkably preoccupied by the fact that Kennedy was a Catholic," concluded the University of Michigan Survey Research Center. A careful analysis by the Fair Campaign Practices Committee found that John F. Kennedy had faced more hateful material than Al Smith in his infamous 1928 race.

Many journalists and contemporary historians didn't recognize the true significance of Kennedy's achievement until years later. In his otherwise masterly account, *The Making of the President 1960,* author Theodore H. White, like many other political commentators, downplayed the significance of Kennedy's religion on the race—an error that White had the grace to acknowledge and correct in a later memoir:

> For all the many words and pages I wrote about [the 1960 election], it was a passage that clarified itself only as time went by. The election of 1960 was devoid of cause only if one failed to recognize that the man himself, John F. Kennedy, embodied the cause; and the cause was not borne by his tongue, his grace, his proposals. The cause lay in his birth: he was a Catholic, and ethnic from outside the mainstream of American leadership. To elect John F. Kennedy president was to make

clear that this was a different kind of country from what history taught of it, that it was rapidly becoming, and would become in the next twenty years, so much more different in its racial and ethnic patterns as to make life in some of America's greatest cities completely unrecognizable.

Kennedy's election victory represented far more than a momentary triumph. For more than a century, the Irish in America had suffered from religious intolerance, and now one of their kind had broken the most significant barrier to power in this land of immigrants. He had faced an extraordinary crucible of insult, derision and pure hatred of the kind that had crushed Al Smith's soul. Yet, in 1960, the press suggested, as if giving a compliment, that Jack was somehow cleansed and purified, freed of the ethnic baggage of such Irish-American politicians as Smith and his own grandfather, Honey Fitz. On its front page, the *New York Times* quoted political observers who, trading off the old stereotypes, saw Kennedy as a president "not in the ordinary mold of Irish-American politicians." For most of his life, Kennedy, like his father Joe, had avoided being identified as either too Irish or too Catholic. In making history, however, he was forever identified with his religion, still in patronizing tones.

The sweetness of his victory was tempered by over-the-top hate and prejudice during the campaign. It forced John Kennedy to confront these undeniable aspects of his Irish Catholic identity and subtly transformed his outlook. Somehow, the politician who avoided controversies now seemed more sensitive to the devastating consequences of bigotry and was determined to act upon it. Both father and son were affected deeply by the outcome of this race. As Joe later explained to his Vatican friend Galeazzi: "I was asked for reasons why I did not expect the race to be so close and I answered (1) I was wrong in expecting that we would get a bigger Catholic vote than we did and (2) bigotry played a much larger part in the campaign than we thought it would." By confronting prejudice, John Kennedy and his brother Robert had developed a far different perspective from the average white Protestant politician. Whether they had the courage to act upon these beliefs in the White House remained to be seen.

Across the Atlantic, no one needed time to understand its historic significance. Along the stone quay in New Ross, Ireland, the place the itinerant farmer and cooper named Patrick Kennedy had once called home, five thousand people lit bonfires and danced and sang through the night to celebrate this great-grandson's swearing in as president. "Fourteen years ago this summer I visited New Ross and saw the home from which over 110 years ago my grandfather had journeyed on his long voyage from Ireland to America," the new president messaged. "Three generations have passed since then but across this long time and across the seas I send to all of you my best wishes. New Ross and Washington DC are tied together today."

John Fitzgerald Kennedy and his family were now the exemplars for the Irish Catholic experience in America and, in doing so, they'd change their country forever.

Part IV

The Rites of Power

"There was perhaps something very Irish
about it all—the loyalty to family, the irony
and self-mockery, the mingling of romantic
defiance with a deep sadness; something
very Irish American too, for the Irish legacy
in its Kennedy form had to accommodate
itself to the puritan ethic, the belief in discipline, work and achievement. Being an
Irish American, as Henry James might have
said, was a complex fate."

—ARTHUR M. SCHLESINGER JR.

"...There's an element of poetry in it, and
then the element of tragedy enters into it—
that the hero is slain and becomes a kind of
Christ figure. All of this is important. So it's
part sociological, part psychological, and
part mythical. Put it all together and you
can see the tremendous influence J.F.K. has
had on American Catholicism."

—JOHN COGLEY

Chapter Twenty-Six

A Catholic in the White House

JOHN FITZGERALD KENNEDY JUNIOR, swaddled in a white-laced christening robe, came to the world's attention on the cover of *Life*—the first but certainly not the last time he'd adorn the cover of a popular magazine. A series of photographs, spread over several pages inside this issue, showed the youngest Kennedy being baptized into the Catholic faith. The *Life* article turned this private Kennedy family affair into a very public catechism lesson. Like some *National Geographic* sojourn into some strange and distant land, it also provided an explanation into the mysterious rituals of the Roman Catholic Church, a religion that for most Americans was alien and decidedly unfamiliar.

"Expel from him all blindness of heart . . . "

In the chapel of Washington's Georgetown University Hospital, the Reverend Martin J. Casey, pastor of Holy Trinity Church, where the Kennedys worshipped, recited a prayer. Casey opened the child's robes—once worn by the baby's father—and anointed his chest with sacred oil. Then the gray-haired priest in sacramental garb began "the ancient exorcism against demons," as *Life* described it, speaking in a Latin tongue that the magazine conveniently translated for its readers in Middle America.

"Receive the salt of wisdom, May it win for you mercy and the everlasting life."

The infant Kennedy arrived on November 25, 1960, just two weeks after one of the most acrimonious elections in U. S. history. "Isn't he sweet, Jack," murmured the baby's mother. "Look at those pretty eyes." His father, the new president-elect, beamed for the camera; while Jackie, dressed in a black wool broadcloth suit and black tulle toque, peered down almost Madonna-like at their first-born son.

"Enter into the temple of God . . . "

The 1960 presidential election unleashed its own demons, ugly spirits of intolerance that many hoped America had outgrown. Kennedy avoided being photographed with priests and nuns, careful not to stoke the fires of anti-Catholicism scattered across the land. Yet critics still wondered whether America's first Catholic president would be able to keep his own religion at bay. In this sense, Kennedy's decision to allow a reporter and a photographer to record his son's baptism—one of his first events since his election as the thirty-fifth president of the United States—seemed curious indeed, almost provocative.

"I exorcise you in the name of the Father and of the Son and of the Holy Ghost."

The godparents stepped forward to the baptism font, and the priest made the sign of the cross over the baby's forehead. The rest of the Kennedys watched in respectful silence. Ceremonies such as baptisms and confirmations and weddings were sacraments that brought the family together and bound them as one. For the Kennedys, the powerful hold of family and religion reached back to their Irish ancestors.

"Will you be baptized, John Fitzgerald Kennedy Junior?"

In unison, the godparents and family answered on the infant's behalf—"I will."

THIS MUCH-PUBLICIZED baptism proved one of the few overt and unabashed displays of Catholicism during John F. Kennedy's presidency. After he entered the White House, there were many displays of religion—with the president only too happy to be seen greeting evangelist Billy Graham, for instance—so long as the religion was not his own. His most fixated critics worried that a Catholic Mass would be said inside the White House, a barrier Kennedy never crossed. Instead, on the morning of his inaugural, Kennedy went to Mass at the Holy Trinity Church to pray for his country and to pray for himself. Despite his all-American appearance and rhetoric, Kennedy knew from his own sense of history that he must walk a tightrope as the nation's first chief executive from a minority group. His presidency would test the degree to which any chief executive could influence the broader majority culture without denying their own heritage. Just as in the campaign, there were no history books to explain what to do, how far he could go, before he was rejected by the majority. In the first several months, Kennedy instinctually proceeded with caution. "I know that the primary concern in the mind of Jack Kennedy was what kind of image he would leave for history as the first Catholic President of the United States," Cardinal Cushing later recalled about their talks together. Kennedy assumed this challenge as his singular burden, as perhaps the most significant test of his presidency, the one by which he would be most remembered. When a reporter congratulated him after the election for breaking the religious barrier, Kennedy quickly corrected. "No, I have not broken it," he insisted. "I have only been given the opportunity to break it. If I am not a successful President, the barrier will be back higher than ever."

IN THE BRILLIANT SUN and starkly frigid temperatures of Inauguration Day 1961, Cushing gave a long and windy invocation (Cardinal Spellman wasn't invited to an inauguration for the first time in years) that was briefly interrupted when the sound system began to smoke, nearly causing a panic until it stopped. A poem was read by one of America's great poets, Robert Frost, whose age and inability to read in the blinding light prevented him from finishing his recitation. Perhaps Frost's greatest insight that day could be found inscribed in the book of poems he gave Kennedy as a gift. *"Be more Irish than Harvard,"* Frost beseeched. Over time, the inscription became subject to wide interpretation by historians, who often viewed Kennedy from their own distinct vantages.

Frost's intent is fairly easy to trace. He liked and admired the Massachusetts senator. During the campaign, Jack incorporated verse from the poet into his speeches. In Frost's lexicon, the Irish were the proverbial outsiders, the historically embattled minority, a stark contrast to the old WASP culture epitomized by Harvard. On the day Kennedy won the election, Frost declared it "a triumph of Protestantism—over itself." As a native Protestant New Englander aware of the old Brahmin prejudices, Frost was thrilled by this victory, particularly when Kennedy chose a mutual friend, Stewart Udall, as his new interior secretary. "Great day for Boston, Democracy, the Puritans and the Irish," said Frost's telegram to the new president. "Your appointment of Stewart Udall of an old Vermont religion reconciles me once and for all to the party I was born into."

Not all Kennedy chroniclers interpreted Frost's words in the same way. For example, David Halberstam, author of *The Best and the Brightest*—which showed how Kennedy's New Frontier, Ivy League–trained technocrats and academics could lead a nation into the morass of Vietnam—later cited Frost's words as a call for aggression. Halberstam's rather curious interpretation seemed to rely on its own cultural stereotype. Along with several other American historians, Halberstam perceived Kennedy as an ideal end product of the assimilation process, far more a Harvard man than an Irishman, so good that he could fool the unblinking eye of the television camera. "He was catapulted forward in his career by his capacity to handle the new medium, thus to be projected into millions of Protestant homes without looking like a Catholic," Halberstam wrote in his acclaimed 1972 book, which specifically mentioned Frost's inscription. The *Times* of London, noting the Brahmin history of Harvard as the high temple of Anglo-Americanism, later suggested that Frost's words were a mild admonishment to JFK for being such an apparent Anglophile himself. The newspaper called it "a little sad" and "strange that the first President to emerge from a minority group should ignore the rich potential of the later immigrant groups."

But other interpretations of Frost's advice suggested just the opposite. The Jesuit magazine *America* described the poet's comment as "one of the most perceptive and titillating observations that anyone has made about our new President." The magazine perceived the president as performing an elaborate balancing act, fully engaged in this pinnacle of American society without self-denial. "He is an Irishman descended from a long line of Irish politicians," the magazine editorialized. "He is an Irishman from New England. And when you've that kind of Irish in you, it doesn't and shouldn't readily rub off."

Now that Kennedy was president, it appeared the Establishment was trying to adopt him, to perform a makeover in their own image, that his finer qualities of intelligence and style couldn't possibly fit their idea of an Irish Catholic politician. But in its essay, *America* said that Kennedy was no "stage Irishman" and that his patrician style was similar to that of "many of today's offshoots of ancient Hibernian stock." In taking stock of the nation and its new president, the magazine lamented that "some people—to their discredit—will never forgive or forget the fact of Mr. Kennedy's origins." By *America*'s estimate, Frost's words were a reminder to Kennedy of his strengths rather than his weaknesses. "Harvard hasn't hurt his career, but it did not and could not make him over into a Yankee, or into anything other than what he is in his deepest marrow—an Irish-American from Boston." One historian pointed out that a reading by a poet was virtually unprecedented at presidential inaugurals and was more in line with "the ancient Irish tradition that demanded the presence of the poet at the coronation of the High King." In his own 1977 tribute to his brother, *Words Jack Loved,* Teddy Kennedy offered a distinctly one-sided quotation from Frost that was probably more than the poet ever said. "You're something of Irish, and I suppose something of Harvard. My advice to you as President is to be Irish," said Frost, according to the youngest brother in a section of his small book marked "Irish Heritage."

The vastly divergent interpretations of the poet's words were testament to the elliptical nature of John Kennedy's character and personality—an image of splendor and high calling in whom many Americans could claim to see themselves, in whom so many willingly filled in the blanks. To the Establishment insiders of the early 1960s, Kennedy was the perfect specimen of America's melting pot, polished and shined at Choate and Harvard. To those on the outside, he was one of their own, forever Irish, beloved for succeeding in places once believed out of reach, beyond their dreams. Each formed their own part of the broad Kennedy constituency, just as the new president mingled artists, writers and scientists among the big-city politicos and party hacks at his inaugural gala. As Gore Vidal observed: "It is a tribute to Kennedy's gift for compartmentalizing the people in his life that none knew to what extent he saw the others."

Close observers noticed the ethnic strains in their boss. Though JFK "departed considerably from the Irish-American stereotype," Harvard professor, historian and White House aide Arthur M. Schlesinger Jr. wrote, the "Irishness remained a vital element in his constitution. It came out in so many ways—in the quizzical wit, the eruptions of boisterous humor, the relish for politics, the love of language, the romantic sense of history, the admiration for physical daring, the toughness, the joy in living, the view of life as comedy and as tragedy." Perhaps Frost's insights were exaggerated, but clearly the words were contemplated by their recipient. When Arthur Goldberg recalled the inscription to him later in 1961, Kennedy smiled. "As President," he explained, "I have to be both Harvard and Irish."

A STERLING EXAMPLE of that intended mix was Kennedy's inaugural address. His words were filled with Yankee idealism, Cold War rhetoric, a pronounced faith in God and the righteousness of his cause against communism. They underscored the threat of nuclear annihilation, both perceived and real. The bomb—with its sheer terror and randomness of sudden extinction—lent a fatefulness to decisionmaking that now seemed beyond human grasp. "The world is very different now, for man holds in his mortal hands the power to abolish all forms of human poverty and all forms of human life," Kennedy proclaimed. "And yet the same revolutionary beliefs for which our forebears fought are still at issue around the globe— the belief that the rights of man come not from the generosity of the state, but from the hand of God." Kennedy suggested that certain beliefs were still immutable, worth fighting for, perhaps even dying for. "Let every nation know, whether it wishes us well or ill, that we shall pay any price, bear any burden, meet any hardship, support any friend, oppose any foe to assure the survival and the success of liberty," Kennedy declared in an often-quoted line that served as a philosophical underpinning for his "long twilight struggle" against Soviet tyranny.

The fervent, almost apocalyptic anti-communism in the president's inaugural address was balanced by his liberal idealism for the world. He emphasized his support for "human rights to which this nation has always been committed," to the United Nations ("our last best hope in an age where the instruments of war have far outpaced the instruments of peace") and to eradicating poverty, famine and disease through U.S. assistance. "To those people in the huts and villages of half the globe struggling to break the bonds of mass misery, we pledge our best efforts to help them help themselves . . . because it is right," Kennedy declared. In his ending, calling for "high standards of strength and sacrifice," the new president asked for divine guidance "but knowing that here on earth God's work must truly be our own."

An immediate outcome of this speech was the creation of the Peace Corps, headed by Sargent Shriver, Kennedy's brother-in-law. Over the next quarter century, the Peace Corps would send more than 120,000 volunteers to "help others help themselves" in underdeveloped nations around the world—perhaps the most vivid demonstration of the idealism expressed in Kennedy's inaugural. Its philosophic origins could be traced to a 1951 speech that Kennedy gave in Massachusetts in which he advocated a federal program whereby "young college graduates would find a full life in bringing technical advice and assistance to the underprivileged and backward Middle East." As this speech suggests, his family's experience with Catholic charities and his own observations around the world formed the prototype for what would become the Peace Corps. "In that calling," Congressman Kennedy explained, "these men would follow the constructive work done by the religious missionaries in these countries over the past 100 years." Kennedy determined that his Peace Corps would be the West's answer to the atheism and socialism extoled by Soviet apparatchiks in the countryside. His movement would inspire a generation of "young Americans [to] serve the cause of freedom as servants of peace around the world." He didn't want the new international effort to become a "nest of spies" for the CIA, as the Communists accused it of being, nor a tool for U.S. corporate interests. His selection of Shriver, a devout Catholic married to Jack's equally devoted sister, guaranteed that the Peace Corps would live up to its high moral principles in the way Kennedy intended. Yet the Peace Corps honored Kennedy's vow of a firm wall between state and religion. Shriver made sure the agency stayed separate from the missionary enterprises of all churches, including his own—a move resented by some in the Catholic hierarchy. Another early Kennedy program, the Alliance for Progress, though not as successful in the long term, reflected much of the same idealism, promoting democracy and development in the poor nations of Latin America.

THE BALANCE OF competing interests in Jack Kennedy's own mind, the mix of insider and outsider influences, was reflected in the composition of his staff and how the new commander in chief relied upon them. As a minority president elected with the slimmest of margins—as what his civil rights adviser Louis Martin called "the first really ethnic President"— Kennedy deliberately cultivated the counsel of the Establishment's wise men, venerated figures such as Robert Lovett, W. Averell Harriman and banker John McCloy, to help guide his way through the corridors of power. From academia, Kennedy recruited many talented administrators and advisers, so much that some joked a Phi Beta Kappa key was needed to enter the White House gates.

Early in the administration, the press noticed a schism between the intellectuals, or "eggheads"—such as Harvard dean McGeorge Bundy appointed to the National Security Council and Ford Motors chief Robert McNamara to the Defense Department—and the political aides in a separate group dubbed the "Irish Mafia" ("a newspaper designation bitterly resented by its designees when first published," recalled Sorensen) that included congressional liaison Larry F. O'Brien, Ken O'Donnell and the ever amiable Dave Powers. Some even counted the attorney general in that crowd. At his father's insistence, Bobby had joined the government despite the old-style feel of political nepotism behind it. Jack used wit to defuse the critics' howl. "I'll open the front door of the Georgetown house some morning about 2:00 A.M., look up and down the street, and, if there's no one there, I'll whisper, 'It's Bobby,'" he quipped. Later, he claimed that he selected his brother as the nation's top law-enforcement official to give him "a little legal experience before he goes out to practice law."

President Kennedy looked for key aides who were experienced and yet open to new ways of solving problems. (Sargent Shriver, acting as a headhunter for his brother-in-law, was impressed that McNamara, a Protestant, was reading a book on contemporary Catholic theology. "How many other automobile executives or cabinet members read Teihard de Chardin?"

asked Shriver, referring to the French Jesuit theologian whose book, *The Phenomenon of Man,* he too had studied.) As the first Irish-Catholic president, Kennedy opened the door to the first Italian-American in the cabinet, the first of Polish ancestry and the first Negro in a major domestic post, Robert Weaver, as housing administrator. "In many ways, Jack still felt something of an upstart, an Irish Catholic who looked to the Brahmins for a model of how to act," recalled his friend Lem Billings. One astute observer of the Kennedys, columnist Murray Kempton, originally claimed in 1960 that there was no Irishness to JFK who, he said, wanted to "purge the Boston Irish off his trouser cuff." Upon reflection, though, Kempton arrived at a more nuanced view. As he wrote in 1965: "The President seems to us now to have been born for command. He was not. He was a Catholic politician in a country so Protestant as to have turned many of its Catholics dourly Presbyterian in its atmosphere."

Publicly, Kennedy's attractive air of sophistication and wit—exemplified by his often entertaining press conferences, his ability on television to handle deftly any pointed question or barb thrown his way—conveyed a charismatic impression that he very much wanted for himself. He was fascinated by Richard Neustadt's rumination on presidential power and the importance of heroic image making. When asked by the media for his favorite books, the list seemed taken from the musty library of a British aristocrat: *The Young Melbourne* by Lord David Cecil, *Pilgrim's Way* by John Buchan, the future Lord Tweedsmuir, and one or two Ian Fleming novels about the fictional British secret agent James Bond. "He was an Anglophile and delighted in the romantic accounts of the British Empire," declared Hugh Sidey, whose aggrandizing accounts in *Time* magazine helped weave this image around JFK. (Interestingly enough, Sidey's comments are contained in an introduction to JFK's European diaries from the summer of 1945, which actually show a far different reading list. His handwritten journal notes show Kennedy devoured such books as *The Irish in America* by Thomas Dowd, *Irish in America* by James Farley, and *Ireland's Contribution to the Law* by Hugh Carney—all presumably in preparation for running for Congress in Boston the following year.) For those inclined to project Anglophilic imagery to their new president, Kennedy appeared only too happy to oblige.

Throughout America, there seemed a need to ignore the psychic consequences of the nation's first election of a president from a minority group, with its devastating suggestion that this land founded by Puritans might no longer be theirs exclusively. Few journalists and historians at that time examined its cultural significance and instead dressed up this non-WASP president in familiar cultural garb, as if the impact of his election might somehow be diluted or mitigated if America could be convinced that Kennedy was not really ethnic at all. In *The Kennedy Imprisonment,* author Garry Wills shares this Anglophile interpretation to Kennedy's character and devotes a chapter to exploring JFK's British mannerisms and affiliations. As others do, Wills suggests that the Kennedys were not a progression of the Irish-American experience in America but rather "a miniature aristocracy he [Joseph Kennedy] created, hovering above the Irish-American scene." Yet Kennedy's own diary notes and family letters suggest something quite different. In a 1945 visit to see Kathleen in England, for instance, Jack was far from enthralled with what he witnessed of real-life British nobility. "The Duke of Devonshire is an eighteenth-century story book Duke in his beliefs—if not his appearance," Jack wrote about the father of Kick's dead husband, the same father-in-law who hosted his visit. "He believes in the Divine Rights of Dukes, and in fairness, he is fully conscious of his obligations—most of which consist of furnishing the people of England with a statesman of mediocre ability but outstanding integrity." Hardly a ringing endorsement.

Journalists noted Kennedy's long-time friendship with David Ormsby-Gore, Billy Hartington's cousin and the future Lord Harlech, and how the president convinced British Prime Minister Harold Macmillan to appoint Ormsby-Gore the British ambassador to the United States. Ormsby-Gore was a trusted international adviser who shared much of the same view about the postwar world as Kennedy, particularly on how to deal with the Soviets. Many suggested that Kennedy emulated Ormsby-Gore's cool, elegant style as part of some innate desire to be like the British. A simpler and more direct reason for their closeness, however, lies in their early history together and their sentimental link to the president's beloved sister, Kathleen. Unlike the Hartingtons, Ormsby-Gore never showed religious bigotry or rank prejudice when he married his Catholic wife, Sissy. The couple were quite supportive to Kathleen in the 1940s, during this very difficult time in the Kennedy family's life. Ormsby-Gore showed understanding and respect for Catholics in Britain. More important, he demonstrated personal loyalty to the Kennedys, a trait highly prized by the family.

Ormsby-Gore was the only foreign diplomat with whom the president "really had a close relationship at all," explained Robert Kennedy. "He was part of the family, really. . . . You see Kick was the godmother to their oldest child and they were married into the same family. His mother's sister was Kick's mother-in-law." Indeed, Bobby recalled how his brother worried that he might not get along with Macmillan at all "because of his youth—

the kind of person he was—Irish—Joe Kennedy's son—'How can I possibly get along with this boy when I had such a nice relationship with Eisenhower?'" Ormsby-Gore helped ease the way between his boss and the young president, and was instrumental in the creation of the Test Ban Treaty. As with most things Kennedy, Bobby's explanation suggested Ormsby-Gore's good graces with the president lay not in his British mannerisms or political acumen but in his relation to the clan.

Kennedy's friendship with the Ormsby-Gores was evident in their ease together. At a White House cocktail party, another old London friend, William Douglas Home, recalled that Sissy went up to Jack as she was leaving and said, in front of several journalists, "I don't know whether to kiss you or say 'Good-bye Mr. President.'"

Without hesitancy, Kennedy replied teasingly: "You're a good Catholic, Sissy—you can kiss my ring."

For all of JFK's perceived British stylings, the president privately still retained much of the cultural heritage of his Irish Catholic background, often in surprising ways. Instead of classical music or the opera among the highbrows, he preferred in the company of friends those Irish roundabouts or tearjerkers such as "Danny Boy." Around his neck, he "possessed with pride" a set of dog tags engraved with the identification: *Kennedy— Commander in Chief—Blood Type O—Roman Catholic*. In chats with Tip O'Neill, he liked to reminisce about the old crowd of Irish pols from the 11th Congressional District ("he still had a feeling in his heart for those old friends that started with him," O'Neill recalled). To Red Fay, his Irish Catholic pal from the navy, Kennedy complained that the Irish still couldn't get into the Somerset Club in Boston, including himself as president. Part of the delight of hiring Brahmins such as McGeorge Bundy was the ability to tease them about their own biases. (Bundy once called Paul Blanshard's book attacking American Catholics a "very useful thing" during a 1950 Unitarian panel discussion.) When a scandal broke out exposing the restrictive policies of Washington's Metropolitan Club, prompting Bobby Kennedy and several other administration officials to quit the place, Bundy defiantly kept his membership. After much ribbing by the president, Bundy became annoyed and pointed out that Kennedy had belonged to clubs in New York, such as The Links, that didn't have many Jews or Negroes. "Jews and Negroes," responded Kennedy. "Hell, they don't even allow Catholics!"

Without much provocation, the Kennedys could revert back easily to their family's immigrant roots. When India's Nehru met JFK in November 1961, he recounted the indignities suffered by his people at the hands of the

British. Kennedy replied that what they did to the Irish was far worse. Not to be outdone, Bobby engaged a British official in a heated conversation about Ireland during an embassy dinner. "Why are we, the Kennedys, here in America? Why are we here at all?" Bobby demanded, ready with his own reply. "It is because you, the British, drove us out of Ireland."

Among the Kennedys, the clannish nature of the Irish could be found in references to being "brothers," not only among themselves—Jack, Bobby, Teddy as flesh-and-blood siblings—but to those who worked and acted on their behalf. The idea of brotherly fidelity, particularly in the face of adversity, seemed to strike a chord in President Kennedy. In many ways, he had entered politics as a way of redeeming his brother, realizing the goal that dead Joe Jr. aspired to at his father's behest. If Jack fell, just as in ancient Irish folklore or the songs depicted about the Boys of Wexford in a long-ago battle, another brother would expect to take his place. His administration was a particularly male-dominated social dynamic, not unlike the customs in rural Ireland or those practiced by the Boston machine pols. Much of the Kennedy legacy was promulgated by "the men who came to spend their lives with them, who came to envy them their brotherhood, who came to want the love they had for each other, a love they expressed shyly, as men seem to, as Irish men particularly seem to, in banter and bravado, their fierce tenderness camouflaged in semigenial competition," author Anne Taylor Fleming observed. To aides and associates, Jack fondly recalled "St. Crispin's Day" from Shakespeare with lines spoken by a prince before going into battle: "We few, we happy few, we band of brothers; / For he today that sheds his blood with me, / Shall be my brother." On one campaign swing, Francis X. Morrissey recalled, his boss suddenly turned green with nostalgia for their early days on the hustings. "Frankie, remember you with me on St. Crispin's Day," he implored.

Rather than imitating the British of old or the Brahmins of his youth, Kennedy forged his own style in public. He didn't revert to the Irish Catholic rituals or rhetoric that some critics expected immediately upon his arrival in the White House. "John Kennedy was the more secure, the freer, of the two—freer of his father, freer of his family, of his faith, of the entire Irish-American predicament," Schlesinger stated in his biography of Robert Kennedy. Yet there was far more to Kennedy's actions than some liberation from the "Irish-American predicament," as Schlesinger put it. Though he steered clear of the Catholic hierarchy's interests in the first years of his administration, Kennedy never intended to detach himself from his religion or ethnic roots. He was clearly more of a "traditional Catholic" during his presidency than a "nominal Catholic," as so many later portrayed him. In 1962—the only full year of his presidency—the *New York Times* recorded that Kennedy attended Sunday Mass thirty-three times, not counting several private Masses at Camp David and elsewhere that undoubtedly accounted for an attendance record to rival any faithful communicant. At St. Stephen's Church in Washington, as well as parishes in Palm Beach, Hyannis Port and Los Angeles during that year, photographers and reporters noted Kennedy's attendance at Mass. As one typical *Times* account summarized: "Kennedy attends mass, swims, cruises on [the presidential yacht] Honey Fitz with [long-time Kennedy friends] Ormsby-Gores, Fays, Reeds, Auchinclosses." Before leaving Mexico, he went to Mass at Basilica de Guadalupe—not exactly the kind of religious service designed to win him votes back home among some bigoted Americans. Of course, no one is sure whether Kennedy spent the usual hour-long Mass in prayer or penance, atoning for the sins of the world or his own actions—or simply looking out the glass-stained windows as the priest droned on. But as such evidence suggests, the basic signposts of Kennedy's Catholicism were often ignored by contemporary journalists and subsequent historians, just as the impact of his family's cultural history went unmeasured.

When chroniclers did look beyond the immediate, they found patterns to Kennedy's behavior that went beyond the pop psychology of labeling him a sexual compulsive or of giving him some Freudian diagnosis. Historian William V. Shannon, who covered Kennedy as a journalist, contended that this American president possessed a particularly Catholic approach to government. Kennedy's view of human nature and politics, he said, reflected the philosophy of St. Thomas Aquinas. From his own Irish Catholic perspective, Kennedy didn't talk in moral absolutes, as some intellectuals with their own ideological orthodoxies were wont to do. John Cogley, the 1960 adviser who returned to *Commonweal* and later became a religion writer for the *New York Times,* said JFK's most "Catholic" contribution to American life was his attitude toward the use of power which, he said, was distinctly Thomistic, "learned not in the classroom but absorbed from his Irish forebears." Unlike the Puritans of his native Massachusetts, he didn't see its exercise as intrinsically evil. Kennedy's utilitarian approach to power was, Cogley believed, "a kind of cultural overflow of Catholicism which was very deeply reflected in Kennedy." In particular, Kennedy's culturally influenced social concerns were reflected in his campaign against hunger and poverty (he was shocked by conditions he found in West Virginia during the 1960 primary), as well as his administration's embrace of Michael Harrington's book *The Other America* exposing this national problem. "Kennedy was a liberal, an Irish Catholic liberal," explained

Shannon. "He could easily have been a conservative, but again history and circumstances made it more likely and more fitting that he go to the White House as the protagonist of those most in need of a champion: the old in need of medical care, the slum child in need of a better home, and, beyond America's shores, all those who hunger and wait."

In style, if not substance, Kennedy became a new kind of Irish Catholic politician. He was wary of the stereotypes of old—particularly those inner-city machine hacks such as Curley in Boston and Mayor Richard Daley in Chicago, who were analyzed with disdain by the liberal reformers. But he was still uncertain about the emerging conventions of the new. As president, his Harvard side was clearly in view, while the "Irish" side remained opaque, often imperceptible to the public at large. To be reelected in 1964, Kennedy knew he'd have to keep his political equilibrium, to build his own majority as a minority president, to master the art of coalition politics. Perhaps with this in mind, Kennedy once asked his long-time aide Kenny O'Donnell for his opinion of who were the best politicians in America. O'Donnell mentioned Daley and Senator Mike Mansfield of Montana, the orphaned son of Irish Catholic immigrants.

The president considered the names for a moment and nodded. "The Irish do seem to have an art for government," Kennedy agreed. Then with a conspiratorial grin, he said to O'Donnell: "Perhaps we are both prejudiced."

Holy Wars

STEPPING OFF A PLANE at Tokyo's airport in early 1962, Robert Kennedy appeared determined to take Japan by storm. During his five-day goodwill tour, the attorney general and his wife, Ethel, would travel throughout the island nation, absorbing the culture of Japan and exuding a distinctly American brand of their own. Like some foreign evangelist, Robert carried a gospel extolling the virtues of democracy and a warning about the evils of communism. With his boyish charm and toothy smile, he announced in awkward Japanese: "My brother, who is the President, wishes me to convey to you all his very best regards."

At one stop, hundreds of Tokyo schoolchildren pushed forward with raised arms and yelled, "*Kennedy-san,* shake hands!" After meeting with local politicians and business leaders, the Kennedys were serenaded with a Japanese folk song called "The Coal Miner's Song." It prompted Bobby to reciprocate with a folk song of his own—"When Irish Eyes Are Smiling."

At Tokyo's Waseda University, a large crowd of students greeted them. When Bobby tried to give a speech, however, members of *Zengakuren,* the Communist-leaning Japanese student organization, confronted him and mercilessly booed. They attempted to drown him out with their noise. Finally, Bobby pointed to his loudest critic.

"You sir, have you something to tell us?" he asked, his finger jabbing into the air, his Irish tough face set firmly. Kennedy invited his critic up to the platform. He held the microphone while the Japanese student lashed into America and the abuses of capitalism.

Bobby tried to respond, but he was heckled again by the screaming students, especially by the one that he had invited to the platform. Adding to the mayhem, half the stage lights in the auditorium were knocked out by a power failure, along with the public address system. Kennedy was handed a police megaphone so that he could address the crowd, but that didn't work, either. The boos and catcalls worsened. Whatever hope Kennedy had of converting the crowd, of convincing them of his message, was lost. His appearance at the school turned into a small disaster.

Recalling the incident two years later for an oral history, Bobby offered a simple reason for his failure with these Japanese students. "If they're Communists," he explained, "you can't get through to them."

THE KENNEDYS SHARED a strong opposition to communism. Though guarded about his religion on the domestic front, President Kennedy's Catholicism considerably influenced his view on international communism. Over the next few years, both the president and his brother Robert brought these values to bear during their deliberations on the nuclear threat posed by Soviet Russia, the escalating guerilla war in Vietnam and threats in Latin America. In one sense, their campaign against communism was only a slight variation on America's prevailing foreign policy of containment following World War II. But in an unprecedented way for an American president, Kennedy's behavior often involved the Roman Catholic Church, his actions justified and actively encouraged by its religious leaders, including his own priests. In its words and provocative deeds, the Kennedy administration conducted a vigorous worldwide campaign against Communist nations—what Soviet leader Nikita Khrushchev complained were U.S. "holy wars."

Goodwill tours around the globe for Robert Kennedy took on the tone of missionary zeal against communism. When he flew down to Brazil, Bobby informed local leaders dutifully that within their ranks there were a "number of Communists in important positions—in the labor unions, in the military, and in the government generally." Bobby, who had authored a book called *The Enemy Within* a few years earlier about labor corruption, brought the same fierceness to rooting out international Communists. He became fascinated with the idea of indoctrination, proposing an international school "to teach insurgency and teach about communism." Despite President Kennedy's rhetoric about freedom and self-determination, his government generally preferred dictators to elected officials who showed Communist leanings. Stopping communism justified almost any action. Even the assassinations of international leaders—such as Rafael Trujillo in the Dominican Republic, Ngo Dinh Diem in Vietnam and the CIA effort to poison Fidel Castro in Cuba—seemed secondary to this overriding concern. The domino theory—the belief perpetuated by U.S. analysts that one country's fall to the Communists might lead to the collapse of other neighbors and eventually entire regions—became an article of faith, the building block of Kennedy's foreign policy. As Robert Kennedy plainly stated: "It doesn't matter what kind of system you have in another country as long as it's anti-Communist."

IN THE BATTLE against the godless Communists, the Roman Catholic Church became intertwined with the policies of the new American administration. For decades, the Kennedys had worked with priests, cardinals and a long line of church officials leading all the way to Rome in an effort to curb communism. None were more vigorous than Cardinal Spellman, the church's most prominent cold warrior. During the 1950s, American authorities consulted regularly with Spellman, still military vicar of the U.S. Armed Forces, a title he had held since World War II. President Eisenhower felt compelled to assure Spellman that he wasn't getting soft on communism when the United States made initiatives toward bilateral talks with the Soviets. After the 1960 election, however, John Kennedy wanted nothing to do with Spellman. In his own Cold War against communism, Kennedy turned instead to Cardinal Cushing when he needed a point man between the church and government, and Cushing proved as anti-Communist as any Catholic leader. More important, Kennedy knew he could trust Cushing as a close friend and confessor. In the international arena, outside the purview of his domestic critics, Kennedy could relax his wall between church and state without fear of complaint. When brother Ted went to Peru and throughout much of Latin America in 1961, for example, Cushing arranged for him to meet with several priests and religious leaders who helped rally support for America's campaign against communism. In this fight against communism, the interests of the church and Kennedy's government were often the same.

By far, Cushing's most extraordinary intervention in U.S. foreign affairs came after the disastrous April 1961 Bay of Pigs invasion in Cuba. Urged by the CIA and his military aides, President Kennedy went ahead with a plan—hatched in the waning days of the Eisenhower administration—that launched a sneak attack on Cuba by 1,400 exiles forced from their homeland by Fidel Castro's Communist takeover. Despite strong evidence that Castro enjoyed wide popular support, Kennedy became convinced that the Cuban people—many of whom were Roman Catholic—were just waiting to be liberated from the Communists. (Unaware of the personal differences between the two men, Castro charged that Kennedy and Spellman were working together to overthrow him.) When the Cuban exiles landed, they were overwhelmed by Castro's vastly outnumbering armed forces. Kennedy canceled the expected U.S. air assault, fearing it would look like a direct attack by the United States. When the short-lived invasion was over, Castro had captured and jailed 1,113 exiles. They were released after twenty months in exchange for $53 million worth of medicine and other supplies.

During negotiations with Castro, the church became a behind-the-scenes force and Cardinal Cushing, who emerged as a key player, both helped the Kennedy administration and was aided by it. The cardinal served as an important adviser to the Cuban Families Committee, made up of friends and relatives of those who'd been taken prisoner at the Bay of Pigs. He vowed to prevent three prisoners who were Catholic priests from dying in a Communist prison. He also arranged for a hundred Cuban refugee children to be transported to Massachusetts, where they were taught English by Spanish-speaking nuns in a Framingham convent. But the cardinal's greatest gift to the Kennedy administration came on the day before Christmas, 1962, when he received an anxious call from the attorney general, who was putting together the final ransom package for the Cuban Communist leader.

"Castro wants an extra $2,900,000 and everybody wants to get the prisoners home to Miami by Christmas," Bobby explained in his 5:00 A.M. call, and then told the cardinal he needed the money by three o'clock that afternoon.

Neither were involved in the Bay of Pigs fiasco, but both tried desperately to extricate the president from its aftermath. JFK felt his blunder had cost brave men their lives. A man with the crusty exterior of a longshoreman but a soft heart, Cushing was genuinely moved by Kennedy's sense of culpability for his actions. "I remembered a talk I had with Jack about the Bay of Pigs prisoners," Cushing recalled. "It was the first time I ever saw tears in his eyes."

Bobby trusted Cushing to keep his ransom plea private. The cardinal acted quickly and quietly to raise $1 million in needed money, which, according to Cushing, came from friends and church patrons in the Latin American community. (The rest of the money was put up by General Lucius Clay, who solicited funds from various U.S. corporations.) Though he didn't like the idea of being blackmailed by a Communist leader, Cushing rationalized the money payment for these imprisoned fighters.

"The payment saved the prisoners from languishing in prison and possible death," he later explained. "I wouldn't call it ransom, just an exchange."

On his own, Cushing already raised some $200,000 for a tractors-for-prisoner deal, never consummated because Castro kept raising his overall ransom demand. A network of Latin American contributors were assembled by Cushing to underwrite the Missionary Society of St. James the Apostle, which carried on its own aggressive anti-Communist campaign. Founded in 1958, the society recruited priests from the United States and Ireland to serve among the poor in Peru, Bolivia and Ecuador. By sending $1 million each year to Latin American bishops for the construction of schools, churches and seminaries, Cushing intended for the society to "help missionaries be zealous apostles of Christ and ambassadors of good will for the United States." The cardinal certainly felt no need to keep his religion out of his nation's fight against communism: "It is appropriate and fitting . . . for a Catholic prelate of the United States to have a part in the liberation of the 'Cuban Freedom Fighters' who love their country and the 'Faith of their Fathers,'" he wrote.

When the cardinal finally gathered the $1 million at Bobby's request, Francis X. Morrissey handled the money, bringing it down to Washington to give to the attorney general. Morrissey claimed he didn't know exactly where the money had come from, but he later contended that the cardinal's last-minute financial assistance was justified given how much help the Kennedys had provided in the past to the Boston archdiocese. When rumors circulated that Joe Kennedy or the Kennedy Foundation or some other source was responsible for the ransom money, the cardinal denied it in the diocesan newspaper. "I alone am responsible for the collection of this extraordinary sum," he insisted.

THE RANSOM MONEY and the release of the prisoners didn't prevent Jack Kennedy from being roundly criticized for the Bay of Pigs fiasco. Several commentators called him weak and indecisive; others dismissed him as too young and too inexperienced for the job. Within the American foreign policy establishment, the new president was still perceived as the ambitious son of an amoral social climber and bootlegger devoid of principle and integrity. Some who opposed the invasion even believed, as Undersecretary of State Chester Bowles wrote in his private diary, that the new chief executive lacked "a genuine sense of conviction about what is right and what is wrong . . . [and] a basic moral reference point." But few analyzed how Kennedy's religion and its antipathy toward communism—an important reference point throughout his political career— played a significant role in the Bay of Pigs, underlined by Cardinal Cushing's very prominent role in the messy aftermath.

Church support for Kennedy's actions never wavered, even when the Bay of Pigs' failures were fully realized and its moral implications questioned. Soon after their release, the invaders were honored by their fellow Cuban exiles with a rally at Miami's Orange Bowl. Both President Kennedy and Cardinal Cushing were invited. Although several Kennedy aides advised the president not to go, Bobby urged him to appear at the rally in order, as aide Kenny O'Donnell later put it, to "ease the President's sense of guilt." Defiantly and unrepentant at the rally, Kennedy spontaneously promised the crowd that someday Cuba would be free of communism.

Publicly, Kennedy accepted the blame for the Bay of Pigs failure. Privately, he resolved never again to depend solely on the military establishment's small circle of advisors. Jack couldn't hide his disappointment in CIA director Allen Dulles, who had overseen the ill-fated invasion plans and soon resigned. "The advice of every member of the executive branch brought into advise was unanimous—and the advice was wrong!" Kennedy fumed. The Bay of Pigs reminded Jack Kennedy to trust his own instincts, no matter how much he listened to the State Department and CIA. To ensure that his interests would always be represented in discussions about national security, he placed his brother, the attorney general, into the inner circle. "Now he realized how right the old man had been," explained Lem Billings, "family were the only ones you could count on." By the time of the next crisis over Cuba, Bobby Kennedy, the most virulent anti-Communist in the family, would be fully in place.

AFTER THE 1960 campaign, some Catholics were openly skeptical about John Kennedy's promise that his presidency would adhere to a strict separation of church and state. These assurances to a predominately Protestant nation were necessary for obviously political reasons, but did the American people really want a leader whose conscience in time of crisis would be so purposefully divorced from his religious principles? As *Ave Maria,* a journal published by the University of Notre Dame, presciently asked: "It is not beyond the realm of possibility that the President elected in 1960 may well have to decide whether or not to instruct our Air Force to engage in obliteration bombing of a foe which has delivered a sneak attack on us. Can we realistically say that this decision may be reached apart from a President's 'private' religious beliefs?" This hypothetical quickly turned into reality during the 1962 Cuban missile crisis, which raised all these ethical concerns and more.

The Kennedy administration's obsession with Cuba after the Bay of Pigs became a personal crusade to eliminate communism in the Western Hemisphere, an overall goal given the blessing of American church leaders. (When Cardinal Spellman sent out a letter, seeking jobs and homes for 60,000 Cuban exiles in Miami, Moscow warned that "Spellman is trying to arm the criminals who fled from Cuba.") To the Kennedys and the church hierarchy, Cuba's embrace of Castro appeared unholy. During the twenty-month confinement of the Bay of Pigs invaders, Bobby took a personal interest in their plight and worked to clean this black mark against the political record of his brother. Cubans exiled in Miami had kept their faith in the church, but the rest of their country was imprisoned by a Communist tyrant—exactly the kind of ideological battle that Bobby, the Cold War warrior, relished. With his tough-minded arrogance and lack of historical irony, Bobby had little sympathy for a small island's trying to exert its own independence over a large neighboring power. Communism was far too serious a threat.

Dissatisfied with Dulles, Bobby pushed his brother to appoint a new CIA director, John McCone, a wealthy Republican who had served in both the Truman and Eisenhower administrations and shared their unbending view of communism. A convert to Catholicism, McCone went to Rome as Eisenhower's representative, along with Claire Boothe Luce, for the funeral of Pope Pius XII. Similar to Robert Kennedy's, McCone's hard-line worldview against the Communists was deeply influenced by his religion. But even McCone was surprised by the degree to which the anti-Communist frenzy had grown in the Kennedy administration.

By then, President Kennedy's anti-communism rhetoric was carried out in the covert actions of his brother, the attorney general, who was given wide and unprecedented latitude on national security matters. After the Bay of Pigs, Robert Kennedy pushed the CIA to develop a secret plan, a bag of dirty tricks called "Operation Mongoose," that would destabilize Castro's government and be a way of declaring war without actually having to do so. "Do not know if we will be successful in overthrowing Castro but we have nothing to lose in my estimate," Bobby concluded in one memo. In some plans, the CIA conspired with Cuban exiles who had ties to organized crime—the same entity Robert Kennedy was attempting to defeat as attorney general. One dubious notion of "Operation Mongoose" called for the CIA to promote the idea among Cubans that a second coming of Christ would soon occur. A U.S. submarine would shoot star shells into the night sky as a supposed sign to Cuba's faithful, who then would throw off the godless yoke of Castro's tyranny. Bobby's bloodlust to get Castro led to a fascination with "counter-insurgency" programs and special forces units designed to fight these undeclared wars. During vacations at Hyannis Port, Bobby invited the Green Berets to show the young Kennedy kids how to swing from trees and overcome barricades, to become little warriors themselves. Sargent Shriver, chief of JFK's "peace" army and a liberal Catholic, disliked the idea. When Eunice called for him to come outside and look at the paramilitary soldiers, Shriver said he "did not like the children watching—it was not a good influence."

By far, the most controversial CIA plot featured the proposed assassination of Fidel Castro. A variety of guerilla methods—poisoning, explosives—were discussed and known to the attorney general. Some loyal Kennedy aides later minimized Bobby's involvement in the Castro assassination plot, or didn't mention it at all in their memoirs. But the evidence revealed by the 1975 Senate Select Committee investigating U.S. intelligence activities pointed directly to the attorney general. "Robert Kennedy ran with it, ran those operations, and I dealt with him almost every day," Richard Helms, a key CIA figure involved in the plans, told biographer Richard Reeves two decades later. At the time, when McCone found out about the plot to kill Castro during an August 1962 meeting, he made it clear that he would not abide by such a murderous conspiracy and that assassination should never be discussed or condoned by American officials. "I think it is highly improper," McCone declared. He said the very mention of assassination should be expunged from the meeting's record. Unlike Bobby, McCone's abhorrence of communism did have its limits, based on the same profession of faith. By his own understanding of Catholic doctrine, McCone concluded, "I could get excommunicated for something like this."

Historians would debate whether President Kennedy ever approved such plans, though documents suggest he was aware that such murderous ideas were being considered by subordinates. As a matter of general policy, particularly after the CIA provided weapons to rebels who killed Trujillo in the Dominican Republic, Kennedy issued directions prohibiting American involvement in the assassination of foreign leaders. But Cuba, only ninety miles away from Miami, was different. Castro was a millstone around Kennedy's neck and the president was under intense pressure to do something. At social events, Jackie Kennedy warned friends and family that her husband didn't want to discuss the subject at all. One former CIA official later claimed to have overheard Kennedy liken his dilemma with Castro to the question posed by Henry II about Thomas à Becket: "Who will free me from this turbulent priest?"

This covert war convinced Castro to avail himself of the Soviet offer to place nuclear missiles on his tropical island. When missiles were discovered by American spy planes in October 1962, the Cuban crisis escalated into an unprecedented threat of nuclear war. Kennedy demanded the Cuban missiles be removed and, when refused, he ordered a blockade around the island by U.S. Navy vessels. For several days, Americans and people around the world held their breath as they visualized the dark mushroom cloud of atomic devastation. Religious leaders around the world, including those at the Vatican, decried its awful moral consequences. "Today, while 'experts' calmly discuss the possibility of the United States being able to survive a war if *'only fifty millions'* (!) of the population are killed; when the Chinese speak of being able to *'spare'* three hundred million and 'still get along,' it is obvious that we are no longer in the realm where moral truth is conceivable," warned well-known Catholic writer Thomas Merton, author of *The Seven Storey Mountain.* In the White House, there was little indication that President Kennedy heeded church teachings that uncontrolled annihilation of human life was "not lawful under any title," or that Catholics were obliged to strive for peace "with all means at their disposal." Yet several cultural and religious references by Kennedy and his brother during the Cuban missile crisis suggest that their own brand of morality came into play.

As he prepared a nationwide television speech on the crisis, John Kennedy's mind seemed to veer between the clinical tactician and a metaphysical philosopher. At times, he was coldly calculating the odds of nuclear war with the Soviets as one out of three; at other times, he sat on the back porch of the White House talking "not of his possible death," as Sorensen recalled, "but of all the innocent children of the world who had never had a chance or a voice." The almost incomprehensible number of deaths caused by a nuclear war—"very bloodcurdling" as Bobby recalled the projection of the U.S. death toll—seemed most vivid, to hit home most forcefully, only when illustrated in terms of the family, the most important social unit for the Kennedys.

With Dave Powers, his old friend and aide, Kennedy worried about the deadly consequences of his decisions. "Dave, we have had a full life," confided the president, saying he had no fear of dying but dreaded the possible impact for his own children. When U-2 surveillance plane commander Major Rudolph Anderson Jr. was shot down by a Soviet-operated jet over Cuba, Kennedy was trying to relax in the heated White House pool.

Grimly, he accepted the news, swam a few laps in silence and then looked up at Powers. "I wonder if the pilot had a wife and family," Kennedy thought aloud. Before Kennedy could dry off and dress for another meeting on the crisis, Powers recalled, he learned that the missing and presumed-dead pilot had two sons, including one "the same age as John-John." At one point during the missile crisis, Kennedy asked his wife, Jackie, whether she wanted to bring their children to an assigned evacuation center, just in case the worst happened. Jackie refused. If an attack came, she wanted them all to be together. Late one night, after dropping off some papers, Powers came upon the president reading a book to his young daughter, Caroline, and wondered to himself whether "it would be the last one he would read to her." Trying to maintain a calm appearance during the crisis, Kennedy slipped into St. Matthew's Cathedral and instructed his press spokesman, Pierre Salinger, to say he was merely observing the National Day of Prayer, though in fact it provided a few moments of prayer and reflection. At the darkest moments, Kennedy's fatalistic sense of humor lightened the burden. Powers recalled how Bobby Kennedy, after meeting secretly with Anatoly Dobrynin, the Soviet ambassador, rushed back to the White House and debriefed the president with his gloomy assessments about avoiding nuclear war. As the two brothers conferred in an anteroom, Bobby ate a sandwich and Powers munched away on a bucket of chicken left behind by the chef.

"God, Dave, you are eating like it is 'The Last Supper,'" the president suddenly told his aide.

"After listening to Bobby and you," replied Powers, "I am not too sure it isn't."

The Cuban missiles became a crucible for the Kennedys, transforming their abrupt, action-oriented political style into a slower, more deliberative process, lest their hastiness result in mass destruction. Their strident and bellicose anti-communism became more conciliatory. As a result of this 1962 crisis, they were more willing to search for peace, as the Pope encouraged. Indeed, some tried to negotiate through Kennedy's church as a back-channel means of finding peace. Father Felix P. Morlion, president of Pro Deo University in Rome and a close ally of Pope John XXIII, enlisted a friendly acquaintance, Norman Cousins, an American journalist close to the Kennedys, in a secret attempt by the pontiff to intervene with both sides to avoid a nuclear cataclysm. Cousins eventually became an intermediary for the Pope, the American president, and the Soviet leader, Nikita Khrushchev, in their private negotiations. John Cogley, a Kennedy adviser during the 1960 campaign on the religious issue, also called the White House to suggest the Vatican be involved with a statement calling for calm.

Surprisingly, the most important ethical concerns expressed during the missile crisis came from Robert Kennedy, arguably one of the men most responsible for this confrontation in the first place. Some generals and White House top advisers urged an immediate, all-out invasion of Cuba— a move virtually certain to incite a war with the Soviets. During meetings of top presidential advisers, however, Bobby showed none of his old brashness and anti-Communist zeal that bordered on recklessness. Against the prevailing wisdom, he argued that an unannounced attack on Cuba would differ very little morally from the insidious Japanese attack on Pearl Harbor, the most defining moment of their generation.

"My brother's got to be able to live with himself," Bobby insisted. "If we did this, I don't think America could, and I don't think my brother could."

President Kennedy heeded his brother's advice. A ring of U.S. Navy destroyers—including the USS *Joseph P. Kennedy Jr.*—was sent to "quarantine" the island until the Soviets agreed to return their offensive missiles to Russia. Rather than a full-scale war, the more limited and measured American response of a naval blockage afforded the Soviets enough time of their own to reconsider and retreat, saving face by declaring they had rescued Cuba from invasion. The world, aware of its closeness to the atomic abyss, never dared venture to those extremes again during the Cold War. President Kennedy understood "the terror and fear implanted in the human spirit by the constant threat of holocaustal atomic war," Cardinal Cushing later explained. "JFK knew, in the words of Isaiah, that all too many members of the human family walked in darkness and 'in the shadow of death' because of the dread of the H-Bomb."

On Sunday morning after the Russians backed down, Kennedy stepped out of St. Stephen's Church and seemed to have an epiphany himself. "I feel like a new man," he exclaimed to Dave Powers. "Do you realize that we had an air strike all arranged for Tuesday?"

More starkly than his brother, Bobby Kennedy viewed this struggle against communism as a morality tale, good versus bad, those who believed in God and those who didn't. To him, Khrushchev and the Russians were like Jimmy Hoffa and the crooked union officials that the Kennedy brothers had pursued years earlier on the Senate Rackets Committee. During the Cuban crisis, Bobby Kennedy recalled, the president reminded him that their Russian adversaries "were like the gangsters that both of us had dealt with, that Khrushchev's kind of action—what he did, and how he acted— was as an immoral gangster who acts not as statesman, and not as a person with a sense of responsibility." Years later, Murray Kempton wrote that the attorney general's "Catholic conscience," which served as "his zenith," a clarion call for morality at a most perilous time, was in full force during these tense deliberations. "Thank God for Bobby," the president told Dave Powers, out of earshot.

With the public approval rating soaring after staring down the Soviet threat, Jack indicated to his brother that the Cuban missile might be the greatest moment of his presidency.

"This is the night I should go to the theater," the president quipped. It was a familiar reference to President Abraham Lincoln, who, after winning the Civil War and saving the Republic, was shot at Ford's Theater by an assassin.

Bobby laughed along. "If you go," he chimed in, "I want to go with you."

Conversion and Subversion

"It matters not how small a nation is that
seeks world peace and freedom, for, to
paraphrase a citizen of my country: The
humblest nation of all the world, when
clad in the armor of a righteous cause, is
stronger than all the hosts of error."

—JOHN F. KENNEDY, IN A 1963 SPEECH TO THE
DAIL, THE IRISH PARLIAMENT

ON THE OPPOSITE END of the world, far away from Cuba, Vietnan
burned with gunfire and napalm, another hot spot in America's Cold War
on communism during the early 1960s. As with Latin America, the confluence of Catholic and anti-Communist influences played a significant role
in Kennedy's commitment to South Vietnam, its embattled leader, Ngo
Dinh Diem, and the direction of U.S. foreign policy.

The Kennedys had taken sides long ago. At a June 1956 Washington conference sponsored by the American Friends of Vietnam, one of Diem's
greatest friends in the Senate—John F. Kennedy—gave a lengthy speech
titled "America's Stake in Vietnam" praising the "amazing success" of Diem
in running South Vietnam. The senator's speech was pure domino theory,
identifying the weakest link against the Communist "kind of revolution,
glittering and seductive in its superficial appeal." The speech would be a
blueprint for future Kennedy administration policy.

"Vietnam presents the cornerstone of the Free World in Southeast Asia,
the keystone to the arch, the finger in the dike," Senator Kennedy
explained. "Burma, Thailand, India, Japan, the Philippines and obviously

Laos and Cambodia are among those whose security would be threatened if the Red Tide of Communism overflowed into Vietnam."

During this time, both Senator Kennedy and fellow Democrat, Senator Mike Mansfield, pushed the Eisenhower administration to support the new Diem regime. "If we are not the parents of little Vietnam, then surely we are the godparents," Kennedy declared in his 1956 speech. "We presided at its birth, we gave assistance to its life, we have helped to shape its future. . . . This is our offspring—we cannot abandon it, we cannot ignore its needs."

JOHN KENNEDY didn't always feel this way about Vietnam. In 1951, then-Congressman Kennedy, accompanied by his brother Bobby, spent a day in Saigon during a round-the-world junket. He listened to a French military commander confidently tell him how his troops would defeat the local Viet Minh guerilas in the countryside. Later that night, however, Kennedy chatted at the Caravelle Hotel with a young American consular officer, Edmund Gullion, who, when asked warned the future president about the quagmire of a Vietnam engagement. Gullion was apparently convincing enough so that Kennedy, when he returned to the States, openly questioned the $50 million in U.S. aid to the French in their jungle war. "I am frankly of the belief that no amount of American military assistance in Indochina can conquer an enemy which is everywhere and at the same time nowhere," Kennedy declared.

Equally elusive, however, was Kennedy's own change of heart about Vietnam. By the mid–1950s, the Massachusetts senator no longer had doubts. His support for Diem's new regime was strong and unequivocal. Fears of Communist subversion spreading throughout Southeast Asia convinced Kennedy to become Diem's outspoken ally in Washington. Decades later, Roger Hilsman, assistant undersecretary of state for Far Eastern affairs, suggested that Kennedy's religion had played a major role in this turnabout. "The long answer is that Kennedy was a Catholic, Ngo Dinh Diem was a Catholic, and when Diem became president of Vietnam, American Catholics generally thought that this was a wonderful hero and should be backed," recalled Hilsman.

Diem was an unlikely hero. He became the first president of South Vietnam, a nation formed by international arrangement, after the colonial French were defeated in 1954 by Communist revolutionaries led by Ho Chi Minh. The partition of Vietnam left the Communists in the north, and Diem in the south. A devout Catholic and lay celibate, Diem spent much of the early 1950s in exile in the United States to protest the French occupation. The church became a not-so-hidden factor in Diem's rise to power. During this time, his brother, Ngo Dinh Thuc, who was a Catholic bishop, arranged for Diem to stay at the Maryknoll Seminary in Ossining, New York. Diem soon came to the attention of Cardinal Spellman and other Americans looking for a strong Vietnamese leader to fend off the Red advance of Ho Chi Minh. As it turned out, the pontiff in Rome didn't want Vietnam to turn Communist any more than those policy-makers in Washington.

Diem's rise began when Dean Rusk, then heading the State Department's Asian section in the early 1950s, suggested through an intermediary priest that Cardinal Spellman confer with the visiting Bishop Thuc. A meeting eventually took place at the cardinal's New York residence that was also attended by the bishop's exiled brother, Diem. Spellman was impressed by Diem's ardent anti-communism and religious faith. At the same time, Bishop Ngo Dinh Thuc's influence with the Vatican had its own effect. After receiving a papal directive, Spellman promoted Diem as a viable leader to the Eisenhower administration. In the church's secret campaign to prop up Diem, the American cardinal also turned to the Kennedys for help. Spellman directed one of Diem's key supporters in the United States to approach Joe Kennedy about gaining publicity for their cause in newspapers and magazines. Joe Kennedy and his cardinal lobbied hard for Diem among U.S. foreign policymaking experts, stressing his ardent Catholicism as a sure cure for socialism in the region. The two also helped create a private committee to promote Vietnam, with a list of prominent members that included Joe Kennedy's eldest son. Jack Kennedy's 1956 speech to the American Friends of Vietnam was one by-product of this alliance.

BY THE TIME Kennedy became president, Diem's troubles were very apparent in South Vietnam. Catholics accounted for only 10 percent of his country's population, and Diem's ties to both the church and the United States were resented by his countrymen, particularly the majority Buddhists. Many Vietnamese remembered how Catholic priests had helped perpetuate the oppressive French colonial rule. Ho Chi Minh's own writings popularized the charge that church authorities had massacred farmers and grabbed their land. Although he turned increasingly nationalist and resentful of U.S. interference, Diem was perceived as an American puppet.

When Cardinal Spellman, dressed in his army khakis, visited Vietnam in the mid–1950s at the Pope's instruction, he praised Diem and presented a $100,000 relief check to aid the refugees, many of them Catholic, fleeing from the north. Rather than rally the country against the Communists,

Spellman's visit provoked more bitterness toward Diem's dictatorial government. "It is Catholicism which has helped ruin the government of Mr. Diem, for his genuine piety . . . has been exploited by his American advisers until the Church is in danger of sharing the unpopularity of the United States," wrote Graham Greene, himself a Catholic, in London's *Sunday Times*. To Greene, the Vietnamese leader appeared "obstinate, ill-advised, going to his weekly confessions, bolstered up by his belief that God is always on the Catholic side, waiting for a miracle."

American foreign aid greased the corruption seeping throughout the country. The political problems encircling Diem—a religious mystic who was exquisitely ill-equipped to run his own government and who often remained oblivious to his surroundings—only became worse. As historian and former war correspondent Neil Sheehan later observed, Diem "lived in a mental cocoon spun out of nostalgic reveries for Vietnam's imperial past." Diem embraced Catholicism as, in effect, the state religion. It became another instrument used to maintain political control and brutally repress Buddhists and other religious groups. Conversion to Catholicism became, at least in Diem's mind, a remedy to subversion by the Communists. In early 1963, when his older brother, Thuc, celebrated his twenty-fifth anniversary as bishop, Catholics placed blue-and-white Vatican flags all around Thuc's home city of Hue, once the capital of a united Vietnam. Yet the same Diem government soon afterward deeply offended many Vietnamese when it prohibited the Buddhist flag to fly on the 2,587th birthday celebration of Buddha. On May 8, 1963, a crowd of Buddhists protesting that ban were fired upon by Diem's Civil Guards. Led by a Catholic officer, they killed nine people, including several children, and injured more than a dozen.

In response, Diem's government cracked down harder, prompting even more unrest. The following month, to protest the outrages against his religion, a seventy-three-year-old Buddhist monk, sitting in a lotus position on a Saigon street corner, was immersed in gasoline, and then set himself aflame. A photograph of the Buddhist monk's self-immolation was printed around the world. The incident shocked and embarrassed the Kennedy administration, underlining the desperation within a divided Vietnam. Diem's abuses were so stark that a Buddhist delegation went to Rome and, against the advice of Spellman, received an audience with the new pontiff, Pope John XXIII. Soon the Catholic Church took steps to distance itself from Diem's government, including the decision to recall Archbishop Thuc to Rome. (Thuc was later excommunicated in the 1980s by Pope John Paul II for his extremely unorthodox views.) Even the hard-liner Spellman backed away reluctantly from Diem's government.

The Kennedys never seemed to recognize the historical ironies for them in Vietnam. Here was a nation of Buddhists who suffered abuse and faced religious discrimination by a government leader of a different faith, imposed upon them by a foreign power, a situation that split their nation into partitions in the north and south. America became as resented in this Vietnamese civil war as much as the British once occupying Eire were resented. Yet their own anti-Communist faith seemed to prevent the Kennedy brothers from accurately recognizing Diem's weaknesses and understanding the reasons for Ho Chi Minh's appeal in the countryside. Instead, Jack Kennedy maintained his support for Diem's despotic regime. He appeared inspired by such tales as that of a Catholic priest named Father Hoa who managed to flee the Communists in China and round up enough followers in Vietnam to fight the Communist guerillas there. Though focused on other matters such as civil rights and Cuba, Bobby Kennedy clearly agreed with his older brother who "felt that he had a strong, over-whelming reason for being in Vietnam and that we should win the war in Vietnam. . . . If you lost Vietnam, I think everybody was quite clear that the rest of Southeast Asia would fall." The domino theory became a sacred tenet of U.S. foreign policy, not to be violated. The Kennedys, as executors of American power, sided with the tyrants.

Another tragic irony was in the men Kennedy entrusted to enact his Southeast Asia policy. As his eyes and ears in Vietnam, Kennedy dispatched Henry Cabot Lodge Jr.—the old-school Brahmin Republican whom JFK beat in the 1952 Senate race and who ran as Nixon's vice-presidential choice in 1960—to serve as U.S. ambassador. During his time in Saigon, Lodge did little to solve the underlying problems of that small poor nation, and quite arguably made them worse. His selection was a curious choice. Given the Kennedy family's history with Brahmins, and specifically with Lodge himself, the presidential appointment seemed destined for failure. Lodge appeared ill-suited for dealing with the intricacies of an embattled and increasingly despotic Catholic ruler of a Buddhist nation in the midst of a civil war.

There was more than a little irony that foreign policy experts such as Lodge and special assistant McGeorge Bundy, complete with their Harvard connections and Brahmin-like pedigrees, became architects and prosecutors of this disastrous war. (Bundy, a former Harvard dean, was related to A. Lawrence Lowell, the former Harvard president who once preached that the duty of the Brahmins was to "Americanize" the incoming Irish immigrants.) Bobby Kennedy, who thought Lodge was terribly lazy, opposed his selection, but Jack felt it would be good to have a Republican in this troubled spot. In Vietnam, Lodge accurately assessed Diem's ineptitude and held him in disdain. "As U.S. ambassador, Lodge showed almost as much disrespect for Diem as his grandfather had for Kennedy's grandfather," wrote Ken Hughes in the *Boston Globe* after reviewing the White House documents and tape recordings made by Kennedy (declassified in 1999) and documents that captured much of these deliberations. Lodge's actions opened the door for a coup and the eventual murder of Diem at the behest of his own generals.

Kennedy's vacillation about Diem, including whether to support a coup, sealed his fate. On November 1, 1963, Kennedy appeared vexed about the issue as he left the Cabinet Room during the middle of a meeting so that he could celebrate Mass for All Saints' Day, a holy day of obligation in the Roman Catholic Church. "I think we have to make it clear this is not an American coup," he insisted on the way out. Meanwhile, in South Vietnam—where All Saints' Day was celebrated officially by the government—the generals staged their revolt. Assassins pulled Diem from a Catholic church in Cholon, where he'd taken refuge, and put him in an armored passenger vehicle alongside his brother, Ngo Dinh Nhu. Both brothers were shot in the back of the head.

Inside the White House, when he heard the news of Diem's death, Kennedy appeared visibly shaken. The initial reports about Diem suggested suicide.

"It's hard to believe he'd commit suicide given his strong religious career," exclaimed Kennedy, who had helped project Diem's image as a trustworthy, devout Catholic leader capable of resisting the Communist onslaught from the north.

"He's Catholic, but he's an Asian Catholic," said Hilsman, the assistant undersecretary of state for Far Eastern affairs, who was strongly for the coup against Diem's regime.

"What?" Kennedy asked, not sure what he meant.

"He's an *Asian* Catholic," Hilsman repeated. "And not only that, he's a mandarin. It seems to me not at all inconsistent with Armageddon."

Hilsman's odd comments hung in the air while Jack Kennedy seemed lost in thought about what had happened in Vietnam. As the evidence became clear concerning Diem's assassination, Kennedy expressed "shock" and private remorse that he might have been responsible for Diem's assassination. Another senior aide, Mike Forrestal, later described Kennedy's reaction as "both personal and religious," and indicated to historian Herbert S. Parmet that Kennedy was, in Parmet's words, "especially troubled by the implication that a Catholic President had participated in a plot to assassinate a co-religionist." Some Kennedy-era historians have repeated Cardinal Spellman's claim that the president knew in advance Diem was going to be removed, probably by assassination, but was powerless to do anything about it. Given the estrangement between the cardinal and Jack Kennedy, the veracity of this supposed candid confession seems far-fetched. A more likely scenario is that Spellman made such a claim only after Kennedy's death for what appears the cardinal's own hawkish political purposes in support of America's escalating war in Vietnam. Although there is no evidence suggesting that Kennedy personally approved Diem's killing, the available records show he did little to stop it.

IN THE LAST MONTHS of his presidency, Kennedy began privately reconsidering America's commitment to the Vietnam conflict, even though his public rhetoric remained vintage New Frontier, ready to fight the Communists at any turn. After several aides expressed their dismay about the war's outcome, the president sent a trusted Senate ally, Mike Mansfield, to Vietnam on his own fact-finding trip. Mansfield, himself a Catholic, had supported Diem's government since the early 1950s. In his 1956 speech about Vietnam, Kennedy quoted a letter that Diem wrote to Mansfield, his long-time supporter: "It is only in winter that you can tell which trees are evergreen." When Mansfield returned from his mission, however, he advised Kennedy to stop increasing the number of U.S. military advisers to Vietnam and think about a gradual pullout. The president seemed angry as he listened to Mansfield's pessimistic assessment. "If I tried to pull out completely from Vietnam, we would have another Joe McCarthy Red scare on our hands, but I can do it after I'm re-elected," Kennedy told Kenny O'Donnell after Mansfield left. "So we better make damn sure that I am re-elected."

The president's partisans—O'Donnell, Mansfield and others such as historian Arthur M. Schlesinger Jr.—later suggested that Kennedy planned to leave Vietnam after the 1964 election. Hilsman said Kennedy became convinced after the Buddhist protests that Diem's regime was doomed to fail and was beginning to prepare for American withdrawal. "He [Diem] surrounded himself with Catholics, but also they happened to be northerners who had fled the north when the Communists took over," Hilsman explained. "So he was surrounding himself with zealots, you see, anti-Communist Catholic zealots. . . . So it was a hopeless situation and Kennedy came to this conclusion."

Nevertheless, Kennedy provided the philosophical framework for what was to become America's disastrous war in Vietnam. The elements of geopolitical containment often came wrapped in the rhetoric of a crusade, a distinctly religious one, in which the enemies were godless socialists and the heroes were blessed by their priests. During the Kennedy years, the moral consequences of this crusade went largely ignored. The legitimacy of America's role in Vietnam's civil war, the conspiracies of torture, suppression and, ultimately, government-sanctioned assassination that surrounded the Diem regime were not examined fully until many years later.

In their words and actions, Jack and Bobby Kennedy's holy war reflected the Catholic Church's own obsessive battle against the Communist threat growing out of the post–World War II era. On their watch, they insisted that neither Cuba nor Vietnam would be "lost," spoken in the same way the church might refer to an apostate soul. The Kennedys came to modify their position as hard-line anti-Communists with great reluctance, and only when the realities of these jungle conflicts forced them to reexamine their policies and perhaps their own consciences. They were unflinching supporters of the church's struggles against international communism throughout the 1950s and early 1960s. But by 1963, a new Pope had changed the course of many church policies, including its often confrontational approach with the Soviets. The new Pope would want peace and world harmony, not a human race nearing nuclear destruction. And once again, the Kennedys proved an integral part of this new era.

The Two Johns

ACCOMPANIED BY THE PAPARAZZI and worldwide attention, Jacqueline Kennedy arrived at the Vatican in March 1962 with a distinct air of apprehension. Little more than a year had transpired since her husband had won the American presidency in an election overflowing with anti-Catholic bigotry and talks of papist conspiracies. In his first year in the White House, John Kennedy bent over backwards to appear neither parochial nor deferential to the church. His wife's official visit to the Throne of St. Peter threatened to enflame these passions once again.

When the young and beautiful first lady walked through the second-floor library entrance for a papal audience, no one was sure how Pope John XXIII would greet her. His coterie of advisers suggested calling her "Mrs. Kennedy," or thought "Madame" might be appropriate since they would both speak fluent French to each other. Instead, the eighty-year-old Pope welcomed her with the first name that popped into his head.

"*Jac-que-line!*" he exclaimed, *très familiar.*

Photographs sent around the world pictured the rotund pontiff, resplendent in white and gold and smiling gregariously, standing next to a bevy of red-robed cardinals and the thin, elegant first lady, whose sense of style made her reverential black dress and black lace mantilla seem chic. In thoughts and deeds, this Pope acted very differently from his predecessor, the austere diplomat Pius XII. He made small talk with Jackie and gave her rosaries for herself, her two children and the president. The son of Italian peasants, John XXIII didn't stand on formality.

During his brief four-and-a-half-year reign, "Papa John," as his admirers called him, would open up the Roman Catholic Church to unprecedented changes. He advocated a new age of "ecumenicalism" to end the narrow-minded prejudices of the past, and urged Catholics to embrace other religions in a spirit of Christ's love, unity and peace. After the Cuban missile crisis, Pope John XXIII spoke forcefully to a world on the brink, with an encyclical teaching about humankind's responsibility for ending the nuclear threat. His most profound changes came from a convocation of the Vatican Council II. American Catholics no longer spent Mass looking at the back of a priest speaking Latin; instead, they faced a priest praying in their own tongue. In the United States, this new progressive reputation of the Roman church helped Kennedy's political efforts in America.

After the election, Rose, Bobby and Ted Kennedy all paid separate visits to the Pope, though none garnered the public attention of the first lady's stop in Rome on her way to India. ("The President is a wonderful man," the aging pontiff told Norman Cousins. "I have met some of his family. They're all very fine people. The President is a splendid representative of the American people.") Jackie Kennedy's visit to the Vatican was hailed as a success. "Notably absent, back home, was the chorus of complaint that might have been expected from certain quarters, professing scandal at the sight of the wife of the President of the United States forced for protocol reasons to garb herself in medieval black and to genuflect three times before the Holy Father," wrote one commentator. It was a small but significant sign of a more tolerant America.

During the early 1960s, Pope John XXIII and President John F. Kennedy personified a period of unprecedented hope and reform in the American Catholic Church. It became an all-too-brief epoch inspired by the actions of these two men and what they represented to millions around the world. In many homes, they became symbols of pride, icons whose framed portraits would be venerated beside pictures of Jesus and the Virgin Mary. Ironically, they would never meet, in part because of Kennedy's lingering concerns about the religion issue, a bittersweet consequence of his election. Nonetheless, the two men, whose most prominent times coincided and complemented each other, would have a profound and lasting impact on American Catholics. Both struggled with reactionary forces within the church and eventually helped to redefine what it meant to be Catholic in the late twentieth century. Similarly, America—with a long-standing view of itself as a WASP nation and its slow acceptance of any kind of minorities, including Catholics—began to transform, dramatically and unalterably. This was the era of "The Two Johns," as many later called it.

WHEN KENNEDY took office, the rumors spread quickly. Talk of an "Irish Mafia" in the administration, of Catholics being given top-ranking White House jobs, of friends and co-religionists being secreted into the government in disproportionate numbers by a papist president, stirred Protestants and Other Americans United for Separation of Church and State (POAU) to do its own investigation. During the 1960 election, POAU had been a fountainhead of bigotry, openly questioning whether *any* Roman Catholic could rightly serve as an American president. If their suspicions could be confirmed by Kennedy's subsequent pattern of hiring and appointments, POAU believed their fears about a Catholic president would be grounded in fact.

By early 1962, an investigation published by C. Stanley Lowell, editor of POAU's *Church and State Review,* underlined the deep religious aversions still surrounding Kennedy. The group examined more than a thousand appointments to federal offices and judicial nominations. But the hard facts dispelled suspicions about Kennedy. His cabinet included only one Roman Catholic, the group reported, and his first U.S. Supreme Court appointment was an Episcopalian. POAU's investigation found Kennedy's federal appointments were 80 percent Protestant, 15 percent Roman Catholic and 5 percent Jewish—roughly mirroring the religious make-up of the United States. If anything, the Catholic population was slightly underrepresented. Nominations to the federal bench followed a similar pattern. "President Kennedy has been impeccably indifferent to the religious affiliation of his appointees to the highest levels of government," declared *Christian Century,* which had voiced much anti-Catholic advocacy during the presidential campaign. The rumors accusing Kennedy of "showing a preference for members of his own faith," reported the magazine, "are false and are based on groundless speculation."

In the White House, Kennedy went to great lengths not to appear partial or parochial on religious matters. Despite his own father's long-time campaign for a U.S. representative at the Vatican, JFK never sent an ambassador, just as he had promised. He attended prayer breakfasts with the Reverend Billy Graham and attended funeral services in Protestant churches. Kennedy aides, such as Deputy Attorney General Nicholas De B. Katzenbach, noticed the president was very concerned with possible criticism by Paul Blanshard and others who might charge he'd reneged on his assurance of church and state separation. This was one vow he didn't intend to break. As Bobby Kennedy later explained, "He'd taken a position during the course of the campaign, and he wasn't going to take a position that was different from that." When Kennedy proposed an education bill with federal funding for private colleges, he invited Blanshard, that avatar of anti-Catholicism for many Americans, to the White House to explain his carefully modulated position. Blanshard's visit was kept secret, Sorensen later wrote, "so that even visitors in the White House could not know."

Kennedy wisely kept his Blanshard rendezvous away from the scrutiny of fellow Catholics. Awareness of such a meeting would confirm the murmurs that America's first Catholic president was a sell-out who ignored his own people—the same Irish Catholics who had voted for his grandfather and supported him throughout his career. None of the issues championed by Cardinal Spellman and the U.S. bishops were taken up by the new president during his first year. Many Catholics expected that, for all his campaign promises, Kennedy would still be more understanding of their concerns than conservative WASP politicians, the kind that traditionally kept minority groups at bay. But Kennedy didn't abide any of that. Even his admirers and defenders were surprised by how little Kennedy accommodated Catholics in his first several months in office. In January 1962, the editors of *America,* the Jesuit weekly, observed:

> As the first American President to profess the Catholic faith, he was, is and will remain a marked man. . . . How has this first Catholic President conducted himself with respect to his Church? The answer: more or less as almost any Catholic President might have been expected to conduct himself in a land largely dominated, in the cultural sense, by a strong residual Protestant tradition. Thus, for understandable political reasons, Mr. Kennedy has not been inclined to parade or in any way make much of his Irish or his Catholic background.

Put most charitably, the magazine posted a mixed score on Kennedy's conflicting loyalties: "Harvard 6, Irish 6." By the second year of Kennedy's presidency, the expectations had turned sour. Some were just proud and grateful to have a Catholic in the White House, but many in the church hierarchy resented the political handcuffs they perceived Kennedy wore because of his religion. "I thought he was bending over backwards to a certain extent," recalled Monsignor Francis Hurley, of the U.S. Catholic

Conference. "The President assessed that he could count on the Catholic vote because of the over-riding consideration among Catholics for the first time to be able to put a Catholic in office and break down the pattern of antipathy that has existed in the past. . . . But I don't think it buried the issue by a long shot." Politically, Kennedy not only felt the American Catholic clergy were no help to him, but at times were out to aid his opponents. And nowhere were these differences more intense and more personal than on the matter of federal aid to parochial schools.

FOR MUCH OF THE twentieth century, successive waves of Catholic immigrants—the Irish, Germans, Italians, Poles—sent their children to parochial schools. In these modest settings, immigrants barely conversant in English learned the language and the more sophisticated aspects of becoming an American citizen. By 1961, during the height of America's baby boom, these schools were overseen by parish priests but effectively run by nuns and lay teachers. The cost of tuition was modest. In Boston and New York, Catholic parochial schools often served as the neighborhood center of cultural, political and social life. Their gyms and cafeterias were filled at night with Catholic Youth Organization (CYO) basketball, bingo games and Knights of Columbus get-togethers. By day, children learned grammar and math and were inculcated in the spiritual truths of their religion.

Historically, Catholic schools proved to be a vehicle for remarkable social and economic ascendancy for generations of immigrants, many of whom faced discrimination almost immediately upon arriving on these shores. By the time of Kennedy's election, half of the American Catholic population was still composed of immigrants and their children. But many other Catholics had become college graduates, eager to assume top positions in American society. As author and sociologist Reverend Andrew M. Greeley noted, "Almost without warning, and largely unnoticed by the hierarchy, Roman Catholicism was becoming a religion of the well-educated suburban professional-class American."

For Cardinal Spellman, Catholic schools were sacrosanct, the jewels of each archdiocese. In the Boston diocese of the 1930s, Catholic parents sent their children to these schools as surely as they dutifully attended Mass each Sunday. Spellman fully expected a Catholic elected as U.S. president to understand these bonds of loyalty. But John Kennedy, the nation's prominent Catholic, took a different path. Catholics noted that Kennedy's education took place at Choate and Harvard, his year at Canterbury all but forgotten, sometimes obliterated, from his official biographies. However, as a politician from Boston, Kennedy was well aware of the nexus between politics and church-related organizations. He had attended numerous events and ceremonies in parochial schools. While in Congress, John F. Kennedy sponsored a $300 million federal aid-to-education bill that included a provision for bus service to parochial schools. In those days, Kennedy, as a member of the House labor committee, had championed the cause of church leaders and won the approval of parishioners in his district who sought his help for federal school aid. "He had a different view then," recalled Monsignor Frederick G. Hochwalt, education chief for the National Catholic Welfare Conference. "Two priests from this office helped prepare the school bus provision, and they visited Congressman Kennedy's office at least six times."

But with Kennedy's transformation from local congressman to national political leader, his view on federal aid to parochial schools changed. In 1960, Kennedy adopted a position in accord with that of the U.S. Supreme Court, which ruled out direct payment of public funds to sectarian schools. Though Spellman and other bishops expressed misgivings, their resentment didn't boil over until President Kennedy proposed a large increase in federal aid for education that didn't include them. His bill would forego assistance to parochial schools—a position similar to Eisenhower's. Spellman didn't wait to attack. The cardinal launched his caustic remarks a few days before Kennedy's inauguration, determined to show who really was the most powerful Catholic in the land. Despite the advice of Hochwalt and others, Spellman sharply criticized Kennedy's task force on education, saying it was "unthinkable that any American child be denied" this aid because parents selected a "God-centered education." Kennedy realized he faced a battle with his own church's elders. "The bishops never took that position during Eisenhower's eight years," the president remarked angrily to his aides, "and now they do it to me."

Ironically, Kennedy's nuanced view didn't entirely oppose federal aid for religiously affiliated schools. In addition to his previous support for funding auxiliary services such as buses, Kennedy supported a higher-education bill, eventually passed in 1963, that provided federal aid to colleges, whether public or private. A legal analysis by Kennedy's Justice Department concluded that such funding was constitutional because none of these college students were required by state law to attend as they were in the secondary and elementary grades overseen by the government. (Years later, scholars would debate whether the secular criteria needed to qualify for these federal dollars offered in the 1960s had robbed Catholic colleges of their identity.) But Kennedy concluded that his main proposal—his Federal Aid to Education Bill in 1961—could not include parochial schools without violating his promise on separation of church and state. When he indicated the bill would apply only to public schools, he sparked one of the most bitterly divisive debates in the nation. Kennedy tried to defuse the hard feelings with self-depreciating wit. "Speaking of the religious issue, I asked the Chief Justice whether he thought our new educational bill was constitutional," Kennedy quipped. "He said it was constitutional—it hasn't got a prayer."

Spellman and the bishops condemned as "discriminatory" any education bill that didn't cover their schools. Cushing tried to talk them out of it, but the church hierarchy voted to oppose Kennedy's bill, regardless of its benefits for millions of children, including many Catholics, in public schools. Within a few months, the U.S. Senate passed the measure. By the time it arrived in the House of Representatives, the bishops found a way to stop it. Congressman Jim Delaney, a Democrat on the House Rules Committee, joined several Republicans in defeating the measure. To Kennedy's embarrassment, the religious bigots who had renounced him in 1960 now supported him in this fight. "We hope that the American people will support President Kennedy against the Bishops of his church," announced POAU, which applauded the president for his stand. But the school-aid bill was dead.

The Kennedys were livid with Cardinal Spellman for the mischief he wrought so early in Jack's first year. Watching from a not-too-distant sideline, Joe Kennedy sent an embittered note to Galeazzi at the Vatican about the cardinal's behavior and his lack of personal loyalty. "During all these times, I continued my friendship with our friend [Spellman], and I like to think that I contributed just as much to that friendship as he did," Joe wrote, before citing a litany of Spellman slights against his son, including this latest salvo on education. "I consider it another exhibition of the judgment of a man who should know better. As far as I am concerned, I am disgusted, and I prefer not to have any further contacts [with Spellman]." Galeazzi tried to ease Kennedy's hurt feelings about Spellman. He suggested their old threesome might still act productively as behind-the-scene forces between the White House and Vatican, just as they had done in 1936 with Pacelli's trip to FDR's home in upstate New York. As Galeazzi beseeched, "I should accept gladly any personal penalty or suffering to see you two agree again as it was ever since the happy beginning when you were the master of the railway historical trip to Hyde Park. Remember?" But Joe would have none of it.

At a 1961 Gridiron Club dinner, President Kennedy made light of the situation with Spellman and the Catholic hierarchy. With tongue firmly in cheek, he recalled an old joke about Al Smith who, after losing the 1928 presidential campaign because of fears of "a Catholic takeover," sent a one-word note afterward to the Pope: "UNPACK!"

Then, without missing a beat, Kennedy added, "Well, after my stand on the school bill, I received a one-word wire from the Pope myself. It said, 'PACK!'"

IN ROME, the old Pope was far more simpatico with the young American president than his cardinal in New York. John Kennedy and John XXIII both favored innovative new approaches, not those bound simply by tradition. Of the two, the aging pontiff proved far more radical. Chosen for the Holy See as a caretaker expected to do nothing, John XXIII transformed his church with a historian's eye and an ambitious teacher's sense of vision. By proverbially throwing open the church's windows, he provided much needed "fresh air" to the stuffy, Machiavellian atmosphere of his predecessor, Pius XII. (He dismissed many of Pius XII's aides, including the controversial Mother Pasqualina, leaving Count Galeazzi's powers diminished and Cardinal Spellman without a friendly patron in Rome for the first time in decades.)

As a young priest, John XXIII had witnessed the sins of religious bigotry and mass violence first hand. During the Nazi pogroms of World War II, the future Pope, Angelo Roncalli, then a Vatican diplomat in Greece and Turkey, arranged for unsigned baptismal certificates for thousands of Jews to avoid persecution without asking for vows of conversion. He believed innocent suffering from war was unconscionable and that the threat of nuclear annihilation posed a profound moral challenge almost beyond human measure. Pope John realized that the nearly two-thousand-year-old Roman Catholic Church was often cold and too distant from its flock. "Pope John was a phenomenon, one sent by God to bring a little glimpse of Heaven," said Kennedy's former adviser, John Cogley. "In the last four years of his life, he would do for our world what Francis of Assisi did for the infinitely less complicated society of medieval Christendom."

After the Cuban missile crisis, when Krushchev and Kennedy stared down one another with atomic weapons, John XXIII initiated a different approach with the Soviets and their satellite nations called *Ostpolitik,* "Opening to the East," that served as an olive branch to Khrushchev. Through intermediaries, Vatican diplomatic relations were opened up with the Kremlin. The Russian leader, who, like Roncalli, had grown up on a farm, cautiously praised the pontiff in *Pravda,* the state newspaper. At the same time, Pope John moved to safeguard the religious rights of Catholics in the Soviet bloc nations— many already martyred, tortured or imprisoned for their beliefs—and to secure the departure of Hungarian Cardinal Josef Mindszenty from his refuge in the U.S. legation in Budapest. His concerns were raised to another level after the U.S. showdown with the Russians in October 1962. A grateful Kennedy thanked the Pope for his help in resolving the crisis, but the pontiff, a spiritual leader for the world's 558 million Catholics, set out to address the broader implications of this unacceptable confrontation.

In his masterwork, *Pacem in Terris,* "Peace on Earth," which he addressed not to just Catholics but to "all men of good will," John XXIII issued an eloquent plea. Having witnessed the cruelties and anti-Semitism of his own church, the Pope's encyclical instructed that every human being has the right "to worship God in accordance with the right dictates of his own conscience, and to profess his religion both in private and in public." Such words repudiated the old doctrines of Catholic exceptionalism—the insistent cry by armies, crusaders and inquisitioners throughout history that the Mother Church was the one and only true religion. Though he called communism a "false philosophy," the Pope recognized the capability of socialism in some countries to raise living standards and ease the pain of the poor. Unlike his predecessor, he supported the United Nations, not as a secular threat but as a legitimate forum for seeking international peace and justice. Most notably, he warned about the evils of thermonuclear war, an indiscriminate plague on humankind that only leaders with moral conscience and with God's help could prevent.

John XXIII's remarkable teachings were published around the world, often quoted at length in the Western media and printed selectively in the Soviet press. No longer could a Western leader such as Kennedy look to the Vatican to justify the continuation of the Cold War. The old theories of "a just war"—first espoused by Saint Augustine and later expanded by St. Thomas Aquinas—demanded that such conflict be morally justified. Under these old rules, a "just war" was declared by a nation for a righteous cause as a last resort, usually for self-defense, and waged with limited means. Atomic warfare clearly violated these traditional concerns by indiscriminately killing thousands of innocent civilians along with armed combatants. The former concerns about "proportion" were now outdated, for the evil caused by the Bomb's destruction outstripped any claims of righteousness over a competing political ideology such as communism.

After a brush with nuclear catastrophe, the world was ready for Pope John XXIII's wisdom and counsel. "In a dark and chilly epoch, the short reign of Pope John XXIII was memorable for light and warmth, qualities generated by his own personality," writer Evelyn Waugh later explained. "Under Pope Pius XII, the church had inspired resistance to the Communist world with the result that many naïve Catholics had assumed that any government that opposed Communists had a holy cause." The Kennedys were among these hard-line Catholics; but now, President Kennedy seemed ready for a change.

At the White House, Kennedy teased the press corps for its adoring embrace of the Pope's encyclical. "You Protestants are always building him up," he said dryly. Aware of the political consequences of appearing soft on communism, Kennedy didn't immediately give up the old rhetoric. When the Pope received Khrushchev's daughter and son-in-law during an April 1963 trip to Rome, the president expressed his concern by sending CIA director John McCone to the Holy See. But Kennedy let the world know that he'd read *Pacem in Terris* and contemplated it carefully. "As a Catholic, I am proud of it," said Kennedy about the Pope's encyclical, "and as an American I have learned from it."

Indeed, two months afterward, in a commencement address at American University, Kennedy echoed much of the same spirit as John XXIII concerning the nuclear arms race. He ordered his aides to come up with the landmark speech about two weeks after the Pope's encyclical. As a tangible sign of his good faith, Kennedy announced an immediate unilateral moratorium on the testing of nuclear weapons in the atmosphere. Rather than pursue a headstrong campaign against the Communists, Kennedy offered to end the Cold War and be more conciliatory toward the Soviet Union. The Pope's encyclical, as well as the Vatican's entente with Russia, eased the way for Kennedy's overtures of peace. The lofty, spiritual words from one John's message in Rome seemed to inspire another's in Washington. Many called it John Kennedy's finest speech. "If we cannot end now all our differences, at least we can help make the world safe for diversity," the president urged. "For, in the final analysis, our most common basic link is that we all inhabit this small planet. We all breathe the same air. We all cherish our children's future. And we are all mortal."

POPE JOHN XXIII's actions helped other progressive measures pushed by the Kennedy administration—not so much by direct contact or coordination, but rather by the Vatican's setting the stage in America, both spiritually and eventually politically, for Kennedy's initiatives. American Catholics, particularly conservatives who might have previously attacked conciliatory gestures to the Soviets, were tempered by the Pope's teachings. The Pope's 1961 encyclical, *Mater et Magistra,* took Catholic social thought expressed earlier in Pope Leo's *Rerum Novarum* and brought it up-to-date by suggesting that government had the moral duty to provide a social safety net for the disadvantaged. Improving education and medical services for the poor and physically and mentally handicapped was also a moral imperative, the new Pope instructed. John XXIII recognized democracy as likely the best governmental system to bring about social justice.

By far, the greatest changes emanated from John XXIII's Vatican II ecumenical council, which not only altered church policies but reached into the life of the local parish. Seeking Christian unity, Pope John taught that centuries-old animosities with Protestants must end, even when faced with anti-Catholic bigotry, and that any hint of anti-Semitism must be removed from the church's teachings. Vatican II opened dialogue on church-state relations, religious freedom and an increased role of the laity in the church. The Pope spoke of "aggiornamento"—the Italian term for updating—while rediscovering the basic roots and meaning of church traditions. There was even serious talk of the church's modifying its stance on birth control and its barriers for women. At the first session of the council, the Pope encouraged bishops from around the world to speak their minds, though the Roman Curia fought him every step of the way. "We can't possibly get a council ready by 1963," one Curia member said to the Pope's original request. "All right," he replied, "We'll have it in 1962."

The world—Catholics and non-Catholics alike—rejoiced in a wave of good feeling about this Pope and his long-awaited changes. "For if Vatican II was about anything, it was about optimism," journalist E. J. Dionne wrote from Rome two decades later. "Its documents ring out with the words 'freedom' and 'liberty.' More than anything, Vatican II shattered a tradition within Catholicism that saw the modern world as an enemy to be fought and resisted. The message many drew from Vatican II was that modernity had a lot to be said for it; at the very least, it had to be assimilated."

IN AMERICA, Kennedy's social programs mirrored the same spirit as the Pope's teachings. Spellman and other conservatives in the American church hierarchy, who might have been even bolder in their challenge to Kennedy, were eclipsed by this new vision of the church's role in the world. For liberal voices within the church—many of whom had helped John Kennedy in his 1960 campaign—this era was a golden moment, perhaps the only time during the twentieth century that they felt fully in tune with the Holy See. Jesuit theologian John Courtney Murray, whose writings argued convincingly for a modern separation of church and state rather than a medieval theocracy, became one of the most prominent churchmen of this era. Immediately after Kennedy's election, *Time* magazine devoted a cover story to Murray and these dramatic changes in the church and its effect on America. "In his view, Catholics can make a decisive contribution—perhaps the decisive contribution—to an American society in spiritual crisis," the magazine reported. "Whether or not the Catholics have been the true custodians of the American consensus, as Murray would have it, there is no denying that a new era has begun for Catholics in America."

Murray, and a few progressive Catholic theologians who came into prominence during the Kennedy era, had previously endured estrangement from their conservative brethren in the Catholic clergy. During the 1950s, Murray was instructed by the Roman Curia not to express his view on church and state matters—his academic specialty—just as Rome had earlier forbidden Jesuit paleontologist Teihard de Chardin from publishing anything but works on scientifically technical matters while he was alive. Most of de Chardin's profound theological insights about the role of God in the evolutionary process and other earthly matters were published after his death. "In the Catholic Church of the 20th Century," one priest told *Time,* "the grace of martyrdom has been given to the intellectual."

John XXIII's spiritual protection allowed critics, some of whom might have been called heretics by a different pontiff, to express their concerns and suggest reforms. The young Swiss-born priest, Hans Küng, wrote a best-selling book that argued the highly centralized church should allow more freedom and decisionmaking to regional bishops and laity. "Even today the spirit of the Inquisition and unfreedom has not died out," Küng declared to packed auditoriums as he toured America. Küng was selected to add intellectual heft to the Pope's reforms by serving as a *peritus,* "theological expert," for Vatican II. Pope John XXIII was well aware of the curia's opposition to his reforms, and their condemnations of him as "the Red

Pope" for supposedly favoring socialism. "They are men of zeal, I am sure, but they are not running the church," he confided to a friend. "I am in charge, and I won't have anyone else trying to stop the momentum of the council's first session." Both Küng and Murray embodied a more truly catholic kind of church, one not obsessed with secrecy and subversion, but that preached a gospel of Christian love and tolerance. To the delight and surprise of many in this era, the powers in Rome and Washington did not resist these changes. As Küng recalled years later, "Pope John XXIII and John Kennedy—together, they embodied our hope."

AN INTERMEDIARY between the two leaders was Cardinal Richard Cushing—Kennedy's favorite priest—a guileless man with a good heart, much like the Pope himself. Cushing became a vocal supporter of both men, calling them the "two great Johns." During the Vatican II sessions, Cushing pushed for a declaration on religious liberty and ecumenicalism, including a specific statement in support of Jews. "More changes have been made in the church since the Second Vatican Council than in all the years since the Protestant Reformation," Cushing declared, a bit of hyperbole not far from the truth. He contended that the peaceful measures of meetings and negotiations to ease the threat of nuclear war, as spelled in John XXIII's *Pacem in Terris* encyclical, had been put into practice by John Kennedy during the Cuban missile crisis.

In Boston, Cushing lived up to his public rhetoric, helping the old Irish and Italian neighborhoods adapt to this new ecumenical era. Protestants and Jews were embraced by Catholics rather than shunned, resented or beaten. He visited synagogues and huddled with Protestant ministers about such thorny issues as interfaith marriages. As Thomas H. Connor observed in his history of Boston's Irish, Cardinal Cushing "helped define a new level of human relations in an archdiocese theretofore noted for bitter and some-times violent conflicts among people of different religious, ethnic, and racial backgrounds." With Spellman and other conservative bishops kept at a dis-tance by the Pope, Cardinal Cushing stepped forward as the most outspo-ken and visible spokesman of this newly revitalized American Catholic Church. "If there is a bit of the Last Hurrah in Boston's crusty and contrary Cardinal Cushing, there is also a generous measure of the new spirit of Pope John XXIII," observed *Time,* which devoted another cover story to this Kennedy-affiliated prelate. "He personally illustrates the stirring of that placid giant of Roman Catholicism, the church in the U.S."

To be sure, Cushing, the son of Irish immigrants, could make a defensive statement or two about their treatment. "Forty years ago, the only places for an Irishman in Boston were in the Church or in politics; as far as banking was concerned 'Irish need not apply,'" he begrudged. Like Cardinal O'Connell, he once suggested that Catholics lose their faith in secular institutions such as Harvard. But his admiration for the new Pope and his friend Jack Kennedy was boundless, a sentiment returned by the White House. "The president felt closer to him than any other clergyman," Robert Kennedy observed. Cushing later said that Kennedy dedicated himself to two major goals: to avoid war in a nuclear age and "to create a lasting image as the first Catholic President."

WHEN JOHN XXIII DIED in 1963, the whole world mourned. America's view of Catholics, once so intolerant and pedantic, was somehow different because of this pontiff and the new president. The papacy of John XXIII and the policies of John Kennedy had, as historian William V. Shannon wrote, "substantially affected the reputation and cultural environment of the American Irish." No longer perceived as defensive or parochial, the immigrant's church in America was finally accepted, even if some stereotypes still lingered. Because of Kennedy's actions as president, aide Ted Sorensen wrote, "the Catholic Church in this country became less subject to recriminations from without and more subject to reform from within."

With Pope John's passing, the White House issued its official condolences. Kennedy agreed to meet soon with the newly elected Pope Paul VI. When the president arrived at the North American College in Rome shortly afterward, a somber group of cardinals met him, including the one from Boston. With a broad smile emerging on his face, Cushing, a large, grappling man, approached the president and gave him a mock punch in the solar plexus. "Hi, Jack!" he proclaimed.

The assemblage of cardinals and bishops were shocked by Cushing's behavior. His jocular gesture, like a boxer in the ring, underscored the friendliness between the two. "It was getting awful formal there so I wanted to shake him up a bit," Cushing explained sheepishly.

During his audience with the new Pope, Kennedy didn't kneel and kiss the pontiff's ring—a gesture made by Al Smith that had incited his anti-Catholic critics. Instead, Jack Kennedy bowed and simply shook hands. White House officials carefully underlined it was an "unofficial" visit for Kennedy, so as not to stir fears of some papal conspiracy. A

Vatican newspaper, *L'Osservatore Romano,* hinted that the United States might want to reestablish diplomatic relations with the Holy See, particularly given the central role the Vatican played in Cold War negotiations with the Soviets. Aware of the sentiments back home, however, JFK kept his vow not to name a Vatican ambassador. On this trip to Rome, Kennedy felt confident enough to suggest something that had never been done before, something that would have certainly caused a nativist riot earlier in his nation's history: he invited the new Pope to visit America.

Chapter Thirty

Doing the Right Thing

JAMES BALDWIN WASN'T buying any of Robert Kennedy's jive. His heavy hooded eyelids could barely conceal his contemptuous glare.

"Your family has been here for three generations," Baldwin scolded. "My family has been here far longer than that. Why is your brother at the top while we are still so far away?" The rhetorical question lingered in the air for all to contemplate.

Only a day earlier, the attorney general had asked Baldwin to set up a meeting in New York with his friends—artists, writers and entertainers—to talk about race. Baldwin, the celebrated author of *The Fire Next Time,* had been recently featured on the cover of *Time* magazine and portrayed as the angry but brilliant voice of America's restless Negro population. Kennedy said he wanted to know what Baldwin and his friends were thinking.

Their meeting in May 1963 took place at Joseph P. Kennedy's spacious Central Park South apartment. To these invitees, the Kennedy place, with its trappings of a self-made millionaire many times over, exuded American wealth and privilege—the forces of white supremacy that had once enslaved African-Americans and blatantly discriminated against them with Jim Crow laws, lynching and constant indignities. Attorney General Robert Kennedy certainly didn't view his father's New York residence in this same way. In Bobby's estimate, this apartment reflected his father's achievements, the triumph of one hardworking Irish Catholic in an often hostile world, an example for other minorities to emulate, not abhor.

At one point, Kennedy suggested to Baldwin and his guests—a distinguished group that included social psychologist Kenneth B. Clark, Lorraine

Hansberry, author of *A Raisin in the Sun,* singers Lena Horne and Harry Belafonte, and a few whites such as actor Rip Torn—that Negroes must be patient, that they should consider the example of his own family. Kennedy then proceeded to lecture about his family's roots and how Irish Catholics were able to overcome discrimination in this country. Somehow, Kennedy seemed to view Negroes as just another immigrant group on its way to acceptance. Not too long ago, "the Irish were not wanted" in Boston, Bobby reminded them, yet his brother, the great-grandson of an immigrant, made it to the White House. "You should understand that this is possible— that in the next fifty years or so, a Negro can be President," he insisted.

The assembled guests, no matter how sympathetic to the attorney general, listened in utter disbelief. Baldwin's dressing down expressed their frustration with Kennedy's analogy to the Irish. "As a group, we were hardly impressed by Bobby's assertion that he understood black suffering because of the discrimination his own family had endured as the result of being Irish," Clark later said. "After all, they were white." As Belafonte recalled decades later, "White, Irish-Catholic, anti-Communist, wealthy— all of these were, for us, obstacles."

In the cauldron of American racial politics, there was little wiggle room for historical analogies about religious and racial bigotry. As immigrants, the Irish had experienced discrimination and attacks from the very same white Anglo-Saxon Protestants who had enslaved African-Americans, and they, too, erupted occasionally in their own violent riots and protests. In Boston, several historians noted that Irish Catholics were treated worse than blacks, and some called the Irish "the white Negro" by means of comparison. Yet by most contemporary American standards, the previous suffering of white immigrant groups generally did not compare in size or scope to the experience of blacks in America, the descendants of those who arrived in chains on slave ships. Racism and slavery were America's original sin, a moral calamity not yet fully absolved. The social and economic progress of other minority groups—indeed the success of men such as Joseph P. Kennedy— only served to highlight the raw inequities faced by African-Americans, and the feeling that bigotry would fade in America only if your skin color was white.

For nearly four hours, the group assembled before the attorney general told them of their deep frustration. In the South, school children were blocked from public schools, and the Northern cities seemed ready to boil over in violence. Bobby Kennedy still viewed civil rights for Negroes in the same polite vein as progressive reforms of immigration laws that discriminated. Both defensive and at times clueless, Kennedy's performance was maddening to his guests. "My brother is President of the United States, the grandson of immigrants," he insisted. "You should understand this is possible."

Baldwin scoffed at this contention. They lived in a world where a black man was "still required to supplicate and beg you for justice," he intoned. Baldwin and other guests said the president and the nation's chief law-enforcement officer should treat civil rights as a "moral issue" rather than a vexing political demand by another interest group who appeared, in Bobby Kennedy's term, "insatiable." They suggested that President Kennedy, as a sign of his commitment, escort a black child into a school in the Deep South, a request that Bobby dismissed out of hand as an empty gesture.

During the meeting, one young invitee, Jerome Smith—who had been beaten and jailed during the Freedom Ride protests in Mississippi—bitterly surveyed the racially motivated confrontations around the nation and suggested that he could not conceive of "fighting for my country" under such conditions. Bobby Kennedy was outraged, his face turning redder by the moment, as if he didn't understand the young man's estrangement at all. One of the Kennedy brothers had been killed in World War II, and the president nearly lost his own life. Whatever their resentments about bigotry or institutional barriers in Boston, Irish Catholic immigrant families never expressed such brazen anti-American feelings. As newcomers, the Irish were determined to appear as superpatriots, eager to fight for the cause of their adopted homeland. Kennedy attacked the young man's audacity, bringing the others to Smith's defense. They were disappointed that Bobby just didn't get it.

Eventually, in deep frustration, the guests, led by Lorraine Hansberry, stood up, coolly thanked the attorney general and walked out the door.

"Bobby Kennedy was a little surprised at the depth of Negro feeling," Baldwin explained afterward. "We were all a bit shocked at the extent of his naïveté."

DURING THEIR FORMATIVE years, John and Robert Kennedy had spent little time wondering about the plight of African-Americans. They knew only a handful of Negroes, the common term during their youth, usually people working for the family as valets or in other menial jobs. In many ways, the Kennedy brothers' lack of interaction with Negroes reflected the experience of fellow Catholics from the Boston area. While growing up, as Bobby later admitted, he "didn't lie awake at nights worrying about the Negro in this country." The Kennedys were too engrossed in their own tribal struggles, particularly the Irish grab for power and social acceptance from the Brahmins, to consider a population found predominantly in the Deep South. "As far as separating the Negroes for having a more difficult time than the white people, that was not a particular issue in our house," Bobby later acknowledged in the mid-1960s. Joe Kennedy didn't throw around epithets about Negroes as he did about the Jews, but one suspects he might have done so if he had known more. Because Negroes in Boston were few and were predominantly Protestants, many Irish Catholics paid them little attention until after World War II. As more Negroes moved north, however, the racial dynamic changed dramatically in Boston. Thousands of whites, regardless of religion or ethnicity, fled their old neighborhoods, a pattern that was mirrored in cities such as New York and Chicago.

The Irish, once confined to the ghetto, were now found solidly within the ranks of the middle class. Because many Irish now perpetrated bigotry, several violent white-black confrontations occurred in the 1960s. Cardinal Cushing, in the ecumenical spirit of Vatican II, warned that the church would not tolerate racism and segregation. Despite the ugliness of some Irish, national opinion polls showed that Irish Catholics were among the most liberal-minded whites in America on the matter of race. Nationally, the Roman Catholic Church advocated the desegregation of schools and public facilities throughout the 1940s and early 1950s—well before the U.S. Supreme Court cases striking down Jim Crow laws and racially segregated schools. In some dioceses in the South, local Catholics were threatened with excommunication for bigoted actions against blacks. Despite the uneasiness of its flock on racial matters, many members of the Catholic clergy often proved to be among the most progressive voices for civil rights around the nation.

The Kennedys, however, were slow to understand or embrace the political causes of African-Americans. In the Senate, Jack Kennedy appeared to be a feckless supporter of civil rights when he forged an uneasy alliance with Southern conservative Democratic senators such as James Eastland of Mississippi and the Texan, Lyndon Johnson, solely for his own political gain. JFK's willingness to compromise on a watered-down 1957 Civil Rights Bill, which many Northern Democrats such as Hubert Humphrey opposed on principle as too weak, was described by one critic as "a profile in cowardice." The first time Kennedy met the nation's most prominent civil rights leader, the Reverend Martin Luther King, he failed to impress. "He didn't know too many Negroes personally," King recalled. On civil rights issues, there seemed little difference between Kennedy and his likely Republican rival, Richard Nixon. King worried about Kennedy's lackluster civil rights voting record and his family's previous alliance with Joe McCarthy. Jack Kennedy, like his brother, seemed to view Negroes through the prism of his family's own immigrant experience. In *A Nation of Immigrants,* John Kennedy cast Negroes as an unassimilated immigrant group rather than a subjugated people who had arrived on these shores against their will. "Only in the case of the Negro has the melting pot failed to bring a minority into the full stream of American life," he contended. "Today we are belatedly, but resolutely, engaged in ending this condition of national exclusion and shame and abolishing forever the concept of second-class citizenship in the United States."

Blacks were not without their own stereotypes of Kennedy. In his 1960 presidential run, Kennedy courted several African-American leaders but failed to engender much support, at least initially. Many in the predominantly Protestant Negro religious community expressed severe reservations about voting for a Catholic, often showing overt religious bias. Negro leaders showed little sympathy or identification with Kennedy as a minority facing bigotry in America. Rather, Kennedy appeared as a wealthy white man with a strange and unfamiliar religion, perhaps more unlikely to help their cause than a white politician from their own denomination. A *Jet* magazine survey in 1959 showed that "many Negro ministers opposed his candidacy on the religious basis alone." Several Southern Baptists favored Nixon over Kennedy, a sentiment shared by King's father, the Reverend Martin Luther King Sr., the pastor of the Ebenezer Baptist Church in Atlanta. As his son remembered, the senior King and other Negro ministers were wary of Kennedy, sharing "this holdback, a feeling that a Catholic should not be president for religious reasons." When word reached him about King's father, Kennedy seemed shocked.

"That was a hell of an intolerant statement wasn't it?" he exclaimed to his aides. "Who could have thought Martin Luther King could have a bigot for a father?"

Then, Kennedy paused and smiled at the rich irony of the moment.

"Oh well," he sighed, "we all have our fathers, don't we?"

FOR MUCH OF THE campaign, Kennedy tried to attract black voters without alienating more Southern white voters. At times, this strategy appeared to fail at both ends. Kennedy's overtures to well-known black politicians, such as New York's Representative Adam Clayton Powell, were rebuffed. Two months before the 1960 Democratic Convention, Kennedy gave a speech before some African diplomats at a Washington luncheon in which he likened America's race problem to a scene in a popular movie called

The Defiant Ones in which a white man and a black man—bound to-gether—get out of a pit only by helping each other. "The movie's theme had a personal meaning for the late President," Simeon Booker later wrote in *Ebony.* "As a member of a minority, both in heritage and religion, he knew and had felt the sting of discrimination." Yet fearful of losing crucial support in traditionally Democratic Southern states already inflamed by the religion issue, Kennedy's commitment to civil rights often seemed thin and insincere.

Aware of his difficult balancing act, Kennedy asked Sargent Shriver to put his own budding political career in Chicago on hold to work full time for his presidential campaign. Shriver soon became the chief contact with liberals and Negro leaders. His own liberal Catholicism served Shriver well in this new role. As a founder of the national Catholic interracial move-ment, Shriver was the first to introduce Martin Luther King Jr. to a public audience in Chicago. During the campaign, Shriver worked closely with civil rights expert Harris Wofford, recruited from Notre Dame Law School by Joe Kennedy with the help of his old friend, former university president Father John Cavanaugh. Wofford remembers the skepticism at Notre Dame about Kennedy's chances, and the resentment about his strict promise to keep religion out of constitutional duties. "I found only one Catholic mem-ber of the faculty who was openly and actively for the Senator," Wofford said. "The priests were particularly dubious." But the Kennedys persuaded Wofford to join their effort, and as a former counsel to the National Civil Rights Commission, he brought along many close alliances with key Negro leaders, including Dr. King. For weeks, Wofford and Shriver pushed hard to gain some public signal, if not an outright endorsement, from the nation's best-known and most revered Negro leader. "We thought it [King's approval] would add important momentum to the campaign, and help counteract the anti-Catholic mood of many deeply Protestant Negro cler-gymen," Wofford wrote in a memoir of the era.

The turning point was Martin Luther King Jr.'s arrest in Atlanta that October. Police took the civil rights leader into custody along with dozens of others during a sit-in protest. They objected to the blatant discrimina-tion at one of the South's largest department stores, which routinely refused luncheon service to Negroes. King sat in jail for four days, refusing on prin-ciple to post bail, while his pregnant wife, Coretta Scott King, remained at home worried about his safety. In the streets, the Ku Klux Klan made threatening noises. During the middle of the night, King was shackled and transported from the county jail to a state prison more than two hundred miles from Atlanta—raising even greater concerns for his safety.

Behind the scenes, Wofford helped arrange for King's release on the tres-pass charge. At the last moment, though, a local judge declared that King had violated his probation from an earlier incident and sentenced him to four months of hard labor. Southern Democrats already resented the Kennedy camp's efforts to free King. Conversely, many Negroes worried that the Democratic presidential candidate would do nothing. At a crucial point, Wofford suggested to Shriver that he convince Kennedy to call Coretta King, simply as a sign of his personal concern for her husband. Shriver rushed to the Chicago airport hotel where Kennedy and his aides were staying that night. He waited until he was alone for a moment with his brother-in-law to broach the idea. "Negroes don't expect everything will change tomorrow, no matter who's elected," Shriver argued. "But they do want to know that you care." Kennedy thought about it briefly. "What the hell," he replied, almost reflexively, "That's a decent thing to do. Why not?" Kennedy placed the call without telling any of his chief political aides, including his brother Bobby, the campaign manager.

In conversation with Mrs. King that night, Kennedy offered any help his family could provide. News of the late-night telephone call soon leaked out. When Bobby discovered what had gone on behind his back, he was furious. He inflicted a vigorous tongue lashing to Wofford, swearing that his politically dangerous advice to Jack had probably cost them the election. As he stewed about King's plight in jail, however, Bobby Kennedy took it upon himself to call the local judge. He argued strenuously over the telephone until the judge agreed to allow King to post bond. In the middle of the night, Bobby called Louis Martin, another Kennedy aide admonished that day along with Wofford. Martin heard Bobby describe what he'd accom-plished. "*You* are now an honorary Brother," joked Martin, a Negro, in irreverent delight.

Within the next few days, the Kennedys' intervention rallied Negroes around the country. On Election Day, African-Americans would vote by a margin of about 80 percent for Kennedy, a pivotal margin in several large states around the nation. The senior King immediately dropped his support for Nixon and promised a swell of Negro votes for the Democrats. "I had expected to vote against Senator Kennedy because of his religion," admit-ted Daddy King. "But now he can be my President, Catholic or whatever he is." As Martin Luther King Jr. later observed, Kennedy's telephone call required some courage—"a risk because he was already grappling with the religious issue in the South." Returning home to Atlanta, King gave a rous-ing sermon, praising Kennedy's actions and speaking out against any who might shun the candidate as a Catholic. "I never intend to be a religious bigot," King preached to his many followers. "I never intend to reject a man running for President of the United States just because he is a Catholic. Religious bigotry is as immoral, undemocratic, un-American and un-Christian as racial bigotry."

King's healing, spiritual words suggested a common thread in the struggles of all minority groups in America. Even if their origins were very different, King suggested the shared pain of discrimination could be ultimately unifying for minority groups. Jail became for him another test of this faith. "We must master the art of creative suffering," King implored. To the Kennedy brothers, however, Negroes remained another minority group striving for their place in the American establishment. The Kennedys were learning, but still quite defensive about race. It would take many months, and several more crises, for them to realize how intractable problems were for black Americans.

THE WHITE HOUSE became considerably less white under the new president. Without any fanfare, several Negroes, including Louis Martin, were appointed to high-ranking positions, and all-white bastions in the government were integrated for the first time. At the inaugural, for example, Kennedy was perturbed to find that the Coast Guard unit assigned to the celebration was without any Negroes, a point he later mentioned to his wife. As first lady, Jacqueline Kennedy changed the social dynamic of the White House so that blacks were not merely entertainers for invited white politicians, but distinguished guests themselves. In her conversations and gestures, Jackie never appeared phony or patronizing.

On the subject of race, however, the most surprising Kennedy proved to be Bobby, who became the nation's top law-enforcement officer at his father's urging. Bobby had favored Abraham Ribicoff of Connecticut, who turned down the job. "He [Ribicoff] didn't think a Jew should be putting Negro children in white Protestant schools in the South—that wasn't the way to handle it—at the instructions of a Catholic," RFK later recalled. In retrospect, Bobby would insist that the religious discrimination of the 1960 election—the barrage of hate mail and threats from the Klan—made it inevitable that civil rights would be a priority in his brother's administration. "If the campaign meant anything, if what Jack Kennedy had always stood for meant anything, it meant doing something in this field," Bobby said about civil rights. "It was never a question of sitting around and thinking, 'Well, should we do it or should we not do it' because it was always quite clear that we would do it. And *had* to do it."

Not everyone was convinced. Notre Dame University president, the Reverend Theodore Hesburgh—who did not hold the same unabashed admiration for the Kennedys as his predecessor, Father Cavanaugh—felt that JFK acted slowly to alleviate racism in the South. As an Eisenhower appointee to the national Civil Rights Commission, Hesburgh met Kennedy twice in private and was heartened by his words and intended actions. But then nothing happened, certainly not enough for Hesburgh's liking. "During the Kennedy Administration, the civil rights issue really imposed itself upon them, rather than they imposing themselves on civil rights," he observed. Initially, Kennedy issued executive decisions to prevent discrimination in housing and other areas, but his major goals had yet to be addressed by the third year of his presidency. Frustrated with the pace, Wofford asked to work with Shriver at the Peace Corps.

Before leaving, Wofford urged Kennedy to replace him with Louis Martin as special assistant for civil rights "for we are heading into stormy weather with Negro leadership in view of the rising disappointment over our current slower strategy." Martin, a former executive with the Chicago Defender Publications, emerged as an important bridge between the Kennedys and the Negro community. Shriver, who liked and trusted Martin, invited him to join the transition team after the election. Martin pushed for progress, carefully and steadily, with clear objectives in mind. When Kennedy selected Robert Weaver as the first black to a cabinet-level post, some Negroes grumbled that Weaver was too deferential to whites. Without hurting his own credibility, Martin took the long view. "This guy, whatever you think of his militancy or whether you call him an Uncle Tom or whatnot, has a chance to make history," Martin urged. "Let's make some history." On the matter of civil rights, his overall message to Kennedy remained a moral argument, logically and persuasively put.

EARLY IN THE ADMINISTRATION, Hesburgh remembered a telephone chat with Bobby in which he offered "free advice," as a good pastor might tug at the conscience of a parishioner. The priest told him that civil rights was "the greatest moral problem facing our country" and that Kennedy, as the nation's top law-enforcement official, could provide the necessary leadership. "Bob is for something, or he's against it," Hesburgh observed. "And normally, I think he's on the side of the angels, and this is good." Privately, Bobby complained about "second-guessing" from Hesburgh and the Civil Rights Commission, as if they were unaware of the political realities of dealing with the South. Over time, though, a succession of dramatic, often violent, events in the South transformed Kennedy himself. Once a zealous and often callous protector of his brother's political fortune, the young attorney general became the administration's catalyst for change. Bobby's headstrong, almost pugnacious morality, now applied to civil rights in the same way he once tackled the Mafia and union corruption. This epiphany amused his older brother as it moved him. "Don't worry about Bobby," Jack teased as an old friend wondered about the attorney general's dour mood. "He's probably all choked up over Martin Luther King and his Negroes today."

Within the administration, Robert Kennedy increasingly advocated the strongest case against discrimination, the toughest measures for ensuring liberties to all Americans of color. When James Meredith was denied entry as the first Negro to attend the University of Mississippi, he dispatched federal marshals in 1962 to ensure that a U.S. appeals court order opening the door was enforced. After a bloody confrontation that left two dead and many injured, President Kennedy was forced to send in the military to restore calm at the Ole Miss campus. "We could just visualize another great disaster, like the Bay of Pigs, and a lot of marshals being killed or James Meredith being strung up," Bobby recalled. For all of their teasing and talk of toughness ("Go get 'em, Johnny boy," Bobby cried mockingly before the president got on the phone with the recalcitrant Mississippi governor), the Kennedy brothers were shocked by the bloodshed in the South. They seemed taken aback, as if their own background had not prepared them for the severity of America's race problem.

These battles disturbed Robert Kennedy's restless soul, his fierce inner voice that had once prompted Alice Roosevelt Longworth to remark that "Bobby could have been a revolutionary priest." By his own measure, Bobby, the devout Catholic, found his church wanting in racial matters. When he resigned from Washington's Metropolitan Club because of its restrictive membership, critics pointed out that the attorney general's kids attended a still all-white Catholic private school in Virginia. To the Vatican's Apostolic Delegate to the United States, Kennedy complained that some priests and Catholic laity were fostering discrimination as much as white Protestants, even though their immigrant forebears had been once so targeted. Kennedy told the Pope's representative that the "most racist institution in the South is my own church." With no sense of irony, the Apostolic Delegate claimed that he didn't get involved in politics.

Though the history of Negroes in America was vastly different than the Irish, the attorney general continued to rely on analogies to better understand the injustice of their situation. Such an occasion arose during a tense situation in Montgomery, Alabama, when Martin Luther King and several hundred Freedom Riders found sanctuary in a Baptist church, away from an angry white mob twice their number. On the telephone to Washington, King pleaded with Kennedy to increase the small band of U.S. marshals protecting the Freedom Riders inside the church. During their conversation, as he assured King that he'd do everything possible to protect him, the attorney general seemed to find parallels between the Negro and Irish immigrant experiences, just as he had done with James Baldwin and his group. As the civil rights leader listened, Kennedy recalled stories his grandfather, Honey Fitz, had once told him about anti-Catholic mobs surrounding Boston in the nineteenth century, threatening immigrants' lives and burning a convent outside of Boston. "As long as you're in church, Reverend King, and our men are down there, you might as well say a prayer for us," Bobby joked. Just like Baldwin, King wasn't amused and didn't appreciate the analogy. Peeved by King's lack of appreciation, Kennedy reminded the civil rights leader that if he hadn't called in the federal marshals to provide protection, King might have been "as dead as Kelsey's nuts"—a Kennedy variation of an old Irish phrase.

POLITICS AND RELIGION were deeply woven into the civil rights debates of the Kennedy years. Although the administration's decisions were essentially legal and tactical, King's movement for racial equality was shaped by his own religiosity—a blend of Christianity with the nonviolent idealism of Gandhi. Robert Kennedy became a behind-the-scenes advocate for King's efforts, despite reservations of his own. As the nation's top cop, he disagreed with massive demonstrations of civil disobedience. FBI director J. Edgar Hoover convinced the attorney general that one of King's top lieutenants was a secret Communist and put a wiretap on King's phones. These transcripts also revealed that King was less than saintly in sexual matters. Bobby passed along this compromising information to his brother, who warned King that he was under surveillance and should be careful about Communists in his own ranks. Nevertheless, King's words and actions had their effect on the Kennedys. His appeal to conscience was heeded by Bobby, who compelled his brother to act more resolutely on civil rights. If JFK felt he could ignore his civil rights promises until a second term, Bobby convinced him that they could no longer wait. As Martin Luther King Jr. noted, there were "two JFKs" during the thousand days of Kennedy's tenure. As a candidate and early occupant in the White House, King thought "he [Kennedy] would compromise basic principles" and renege on his promises in order to maintain power. But over time, a second JFK emerged, the one who developed "a great understanding of the moral issues" surrounding civil rights. It would take another set of tragedies in the South to place both Kennedy brothers firmly in King's camp.

IN SPRING 1963, national television showed black Americans engaged in peaceful protest against discrimination in Birmingham being blasted by water hoses, chased by K-9 police dogs and beaten by police. Scenes of pandemonium illustrated the evils of Jim Crow laws and institutional racism in the South far better than any speech or sermon. The Birmingham house of King's brother, the Reverend A. D. King, was bombed, and so was the motel that King himself used as a temporary headquarters. Weeks later, four black girls were killed when a bomb ripped through a Baptist church, which brought unbearable sorrow to their families and horrified the nation. The events in Birmingham forced President Kennedy to place civil rights at the top of his political agenda, with a moral conviction evident in his words and actions. Kennedy's television address in June 1963 condemned the violence and bigotry in the South and proposed a sweeping new civil rights bill. He spoke to the nation on the same day that Alabama Governor George Wallace blocked the doorway of the University of Alabama to incoming black students. Though one of the most historic addresses of the Kennedy era, the speech was put together so quickly and under such a short deadline that the president ad-libbed some parts and read some lines from the back of an envelope.

"We are confronted primarily with a moral issue," Kennedy proclaimed. "It is as old as the Scriptures and is as clear as the American Constitution. The heart of the question is whether all Americans are to be afforded equal rights and equal opportunities, whether we are going to treat our fellow Americans as we want to be treated." He outlined some of the fundamental inequities facing Negroes in America—lower wages, less education, a shorter life expectancy than whites. He emphasized that the federal government wouldn't tolerate the racial mayhem tearing apart Birmingham or any other place in the nation. "I hope that every American, regardless of where he lives, will stop and examine his conscience about this and other related incidents," Kennedy said. "When Americans are sent to Viet Nam or West Berlin, we do not ask for whites only." This phrase echoed the reply Kennedy had made in the 1960 campaign about anti-Catholic bigotry in which he noted that no one had asked his religion when he served in the Pacific during World War II. His words about the second-class status of Negroes also carried a certain resonance with a president whose parents and grandparents had once told him about the "Irish Need Not Apply" signs in old Boston. As he asked, "Are we to say to the world—and much more importantly to each other—that this is the land of the free, except for Negroes, that we have no second-class citizens, except for Negroes, that we have no class or caste system, no ghettos, no master race, except with respect to Negroes?" In response, Kennedy sent to Congress new legislation to ensure that public facilities—hotels, restaurants, theaters and stores—would be open to all Americans, regardless of race. He also promised that the federal government would seek more power to bring lawsuits against public school districts that segregated children according to skin color, and eliminate all Jim Crow barriers and obstacles to voting for Negroes.

"Therefore, let it be clear," Kennedy concluded, "that it is not merely because of the Cold War, not merely because of the economic waste of discrimination, that we are committed to achieving true equality of opportunity. The basic reason is because it is right."

If America, wracked by civil unrest throughout the South, needed any more convincing about Kennedy's appeal to the nation's collective conscience, it came that same night, shortly past midnight, when an assassin shot civil rights leader Medgar Evers outside his home. Evers was coming from a late-night NAACP meeting with a stack of T-shirts bearing the slogan "Jim Crow Must Go." His three children, who had waited up to hear his opinion of Kennedy's speech, instead saw their father bleed to death.

PLENTY OF DOUBTS lingered among Kennedy aides. Ranking members of the Irish Mafia—Kenny O'Donnell and Larry O'Brien—felt the president's speech went too far, that their boss could not afford to lose any more Southern votes. White voters in the North, many of them Catholics and from ethnic immigrant backgrounds, were uneasy with the civil rights marches, the violence and the protests. Few saw parallels with their own experiences as minorities in American society, particularly as they became ensconced in the middle class. "This could cost me the election," Kennedy conceded to one Negro leader, "but we're not turning back." By that summer, Kennedy's civil rights proposals were "threatening to generate a large-scale revolt in the South," warned *U.S. News and World Report,* and predicted that JFK "cannot draw enough votes alone from the big-city States to win" in 1964.

Within the White House, the president gauged the vehement reaction of Southern senators and congressmen and wondered whether he'd made a colossal mistake. "Do you think we did the right thing by sending the legislation up?" Kennedy asked his brother, as though he needed reassurance. "Look at the trouble it's got us in."

Robert Kennedy instinctually knew the president's actions were correct and showed the moral courage that John Kennedy extolled in his writings. As the prodding force behind the president's embrace of civil rights, Bobby was vilified in the South. He became his brother's biggest political liability, and seriously considered resigning from his job before the 1964 reelection campaign. Yet Bobby never lost his faith in the civil rights movement. He also saw to it that money went to King's Southern Christian Leadership Conference (SCLC) rather than more radical black leaders who would inflame white opposition.

For the massive March on Washington that summer, Robert Kennedy acted like an organizer for King. Initially, President Kennedy tried to discourage the event, worried that it could threaten his civil rights success in Congress. But when King's march became inevitable, Bobby directed a Kennedy advance man, Jerry Bruno, to oversee the public address system for the ceremony at the Lincoln Memorial. When Cardinal Patrick O'Boyle, the archbishop of Washington, D.C.—who had desegregated Catholic schools in the late 1940s—balked at giving the invocation because of what he considered a violence-provoking line in the prepared text of another speaker, Bobby Kennedy fixed the problem and convinced the archbishop to stay. He was well aware of the need to keep Catholics, especially those who might remember the discrimination against their own families, from leaving the civil rights movement or being alienated by it. As Bobby later acknowledged, "It would have been very bad if the Catholic Church . . . I mean the Archbishop was pulling out of the civil rights movement." Instead, the Kennedy brothers' help set the stage for one of the most eloquent moments in American history— King's "I have a dream" speech in front of thousands before him and an anxious nation watching on television. That night, King visited the White House. A visibly impressed President Kennedy reached out to shake his hand and told him, "*I* have a dream."

THE CHANGES IN THE Kennedy brothers were remarkable to behold. Once indifferent to race, almost callously so, Bobby's experiences in 1963— including the raucous meeting with writer James Baldwin and friends— had taught him that there was no turning back, that America must change, and without a bloody revolution. "As an authentic disaster, the Baldwin meeting made Robert Kennedy a pioneer in the raw, interracial encounters of the 1960s," historian Taylor Branch observed. "What was intensely personal no longer seemed so distinct from policy, nor public from private."

John Kennedy's transformation was more enigmatic, far more difficult to trace than his brother's emotional route. Some suggest Kennedy made the link between racial and religious prejudice well before he became president. In an oral history for the Kennedy library, Belford Lawson, an African-American political supporter from Washington, D.C., recalled his introduction to Kennedy during the 1956 Democratic Convention. He later suggested how the black vote might help Kennedy become the first Catholic elected to the presidency. "Being a member of a minority, I knew what his problems might be," Lawson recalled. "He went on to tell me, as he had said several times since, about the problems the Irish have." When Lawson asked Kennedy for a recommendation for his son's entry to Groton, the New England prep school, Kennedy "went on to spell out how he couldn't get into Groton" because of prejudice and instead went to Choate. Lawson wasn't sure how seriously to take Kennedy's comment, but he said the story "was indicative of our consensus regarding the problems of minorities."

As president, Kennedy seemed to welcome comparisons to Abraham Lincoln's dilemma over the Emancipation Proclamation, how that revered president had wavered for months in office until he took a strong stance for racial equality. Some biographers suggest that Kennedy's enlightenment on race came from his innate faculties, nurtured in progressive citadels such as Harvard, and came shining through in splendid form during his televised civil rights speech, the product of a refined and detached intellect. "Contrary to some reports, Kennedy was not converted to this cause by the eloquence of some persuasive preacher or motivated by his own membership in a minority group," contended Sorensen. "John Kennedy's convictions on equal rights—like his convictions on nearly all subjects—were reached gradually, logically and coolly, ultimately involving a dedication of the heart even stronger than that of the mind." As eloquent a Boswell as Sorensen could be to his boss's memory, there was clearly more at play in this transformation than Kennedy revealed. This development, this moral struggle seemed better appreciated from a distance, especially by those who had once feared Kennedy's commitment to civil rights would be merely rhetorical. "Historians will record that he vacillated like Lincoln, but he lifted the cause far above the political level," Martin Luther King Jr. later said of the president with whom he'd cajoled and struggled. "You could see emerging a new Kennedy who had come to see the moral issues involved in the civil rights struggle and who not only came to see them but who was now willing to stand up in a courageous manner for them. . . . He came to see in a way that he had probably never seen—and in a way that many other people finally came to see—that segregation was morally wrong and it did something to the souls of both the segregator and the segregated."

By appealing to America's collective conscience, with actions and imagery that struck a chord with millions, Kennedy finally asserted himself to heal the wound of America's racial divisions. He began to understand the unique difficulties of the black experience in America in a way he had never done before. Those who doubted his sincerity about civil rights realized that Kennedy's background probably made it easier for him to relate to the black experience. "He had an Irish sense about the comedy of life and a tragic view of the human condition, but he had a remarkable belief that reason can be brought to bear to solve these problems," Harris Wofford recalled. Jack Kennedy could see parallels with other minorities who landed in America. "Mr. Kennedy's whole life gave him an understanding of discrimination and bigotry, because he came from a religion and a nationality which had known persecution," observed Harry Golden, author of *Only in America,* who was one of the few white commentators to make the connection between Kennedy's long-held views on immigration and his emerging advocacy of civil rights. "When Mr. Kennedy publicly applauded the unorganized street demonstrations and approved the March on Washington, he may have related this vitality of the American Negro to the determination with which the Irish immigrant went about the task of making a better world for his children."

Within a few weeks of the Birmingham television speech, the president announced his intent to fight racism in another part of government—the nation's immigration system—a topic far less heralded in the press but one even closer to his own history.

IMMIGRATION NEVER left his mind. At the time he announced his new immigration plan, Jack Kennedy was preparing an update of his little-known book, *A Nation of Immigrants.* He now planned to use a newly revised version of his 1958 booklet to help push his legislation for immigration reform. As Bobby later pointed out, his brother intended the updated book "as a weapon of enlightenment" in the battle to get his legislation passed.

President Kennedy's strong commitment to immigration reform, motivated by more than politics, was engrained in family lore. Nearly a century earlier, Honey Fitz had opposed the arbitrary and often racist restrictions that Know-Nothings would have placed on the flow of immigrants into the country, many of them ethnic Catholics like the Kennedys. In *A Nation of Immigrants,* Kennedy railed against the "national origins" restrictions in immigration law since 1924 that favored Northern Europeans (including the Irish) but shut down immigration from Italy, Greece and Southern Europe and virtually barred any immigration from Asia and Latin America. His new program, unveiled in July 1963, called upon Congress to eliminate this quota system. In his announcement, Kennedy said "a compelling need" existed for a new immigration system "that serves the national interest and reflects in every detail the principles of equality and human dignity to which our nation subscribes."

Under Kennedy's plan, immigration would not be based on race or ethnicity implicit in the national origins system, but upon three criteria: skills, family reunification and priority of those applying. Kennedy knew the odds for his immigration reform were long, not unlike his civil rights program. As Tom Wicker of the *New York Times* calculated: "Congressional approval of these changes, most of them controversial, is not believed likely this year and promises to be difficult at any time in the House of Representatives." Indeed, many of the same white Southern legislators, such as Democratic Senator Sam Ervin of North Carolina, who opposed Kennedy's civil rights program also planned to block his reform on immigration. By abolishing the "national origins" system of immigrants, Kennedy opened the door particularly for Chinese immigrants, blocked since the first racial-restrictive law, aimed specifically at them, was passed in 1882. "The so-called 'yellow peril' caused an emotional reaction not unlike the prejudice against Negroes that resulted in the racial segregation laws of the eighteen-nineties," the *Times* reminded its readers. Kennedy's proposed change, upping the total immigrant entry by less than 10 percent, sounded relatively modest. "Such legislation does not seek to make over the face of America," he assured. Yet inherently, like Kennedy's civil rights program, the results of these proposals would become transforming to the nation.

America's long history of racial discrimination, epitomized by the shame of slavery and Jim Crow, was also found in its immigration laws. Rather than persecuting those already here, this form of racism ostracized those who wished to share in the American dream of opportunity for all, denying the promise inscribed on the Statue of Liberty to "huddled masses yearning to breathe free." In finding a common bond between the two, the Kennedys made plain their intent to address both injustices. As Robert Kennedy later explained, "It doesn't make any sense that we discriminate against people because of the color of their skin and it doesn't make any sense when we discriminate because of the place of their birth."

Unlike the civil rights struggle, John Kennedy had a much lengthier involvement in this effort. His brother later claimed that "every step in immigration legislation since World War II bore the John F. Kennedy imprint." As much as the cool and detached president was willing to reveal anything publicly, this feeling about immigration reflected something deep inside him, part of his own history. So much of the Kennedy family's experience in America—the deep resentments of his father against Boston's Brahmins, the history of Irish Catholic struggles on both continents mindfully taught by his grandfather and mother—seemed wrapped up in this effort for reform.

JOHN ROCHE, a former JFK advisor and historian, agreed in a 1986 preface to *A Nation of Immigrants* that Kennedy's impetus for immigration reform could be found within his own family's experience. Rather than resort to resentment or defensiveness, however, Jack Kennedy, an Irish Catholic on his own terms, turned his familial desire for reform, perhaps even payback, into a national initiative. "John and his siblings grew up in an environment where the plight of the Irish, at the hands of the British and of the Americans whom they encountered in emigration, was a vibrant cause," Roche contended. "The great jump between Joseph P. Kennedy and his son was that the Ambassador's concern was purely for the Irish-Americans and their woes, while the Senator who prepared this primer had broadened his vista to include all immigrant groups—including a number his father would have surely kept outside the pale!" Though JFK was cautious in many realms of political life, Roche noted there was one area where "Kennedy, despite himself, went over the line between political cost/benefit analysis and crusading: immigration."

In 1963, immigration reform didn't burn with the ferocity of the civil rights movement, nor were there Know-Nothings to oppose Kennedy directly. Newspaper editorials and religious leaders suggested the newest immigrants must be treated fairly and with dignity, just like all Americans. Before his passing, Pope John XXIII reminded Catholics that governments have the moral obligation to accept immigrants, other peoples arriving on their shores. But rather than a directive from his church or political pressure, Kennedy's commitment to immigration came from the heart, from his own sense of family—the best reason, as his proposals suggested, to let someone into the country. In his bones, this president understood why so many came to America. "If he failed to achieve the dream for himself,"

A Minority President. JFK's election in 1960 shattered the long-held maxim that a Catholic couldn't win the White House. But without fanfare, it also began a new era of political empowerment by minority groups in America. As author Theodore H. White later said: "To elect John F. Kennedy President was to make clear that this was a different kind of country from what history taught of it, that it was rapidly becoming, and would become in the next twenty years, so much more different in its racial and ethnic patterns as to make life in some of America's greatest cities completely unrecognizable." *Library of Congress*

The Irish Brahmin. Unlike many Irish Catholic politicians in the past, John F. Kennedy didn't act, talk or look like a big-city ward boss. His Harvard education and his 1956 Pulitzer Prize-winning book, *Profiles in Courage,* gave him the appearance of an "Irish Brahmin," said another Massachusetts politican. As he assumed the American presidency, many wondered if Kennedy would live up to his promise of church and state separation. *Kennedy Library*

We Band of Brothers. Kennedy defused accusations of nepotism and dynasty-building by using wit. When asked about how he'd announce his brother's appointment as U.S. Attorney General, Jack said: "I'll open the front door of the Georgetown house some morning about 2 A.M., look up and down the street, and, if there's no one there, I'll whisper, 'It's Bobby.'" *Wide World Photo*

Catholic Culture. Whether a sinner or a saint, Jack Kennedy's religious practice remained traditionally Catholic throughout his life (seen here attending Easter mass with wife Jackie and their two children). Shortly after his 1960 election, Kennedy's namesake son, John Jr., was baptized in a ceremony that made front pages nationally. *Wide World and United Press International*

Texas. Texas produced some of the most hateful screeds of the 1960 campaign but was vital to Kennedy's victory. Joe Kennedy pushed Lyndon Johnson on the ticket, much to the chagrin of Bobby Kennedy and purportedly JFK himself. After Jack's 1963 assassination in Dallas, Bobby privately accused LBJ of saying "divine retribution" was responsible for his brother's killing. *United Press International*

West Virginia. During the 1960 campaign, both Robert Kennedy and his brother were genuinely distressed by the poverty they witnessed in the nation's poorest state and, in various speeches, vowed to do something to improve their lives while in the White House. *Kennedy Library*

Kennedys and King. As Irish Catholics, the Kennedys viewed blacks as another immigrant group among America's minorities. Rev. Martin Luther King, Jr. (seen on left) later said there were "two JFKs" during his thousand days. Initially, King thought JFK would compromise his basic principles regarding civil rights in order to maintain power. In time, King said a second JFK emerged who developed "a great understanding of the moral issues" surrounding civil rights. *Kennedy Library*

The Two Johns. The early 1960s witnessed an extraordinary but short-lived period of liberalism for American Catholics, personified in Rome with Pope John XXIII (seen here with Rose Kennedy and Count Enrico Galeazzi) and Kennedy in the White House. When both died in 1963, Hannah Arendt said, "The whole world changed and darkened when their voices fell silent. And yet the world will never be as it was before they spoke and acted in it." *Kennedy Family Private Collection*

Homecoming. During his 1963 trip, President Kennedy was embraced by the Irish people, including those pictured here in New Ross, where his great-grandfather left for America more than a century earlier. *Wide World*

Tea Beside the Fire. On a sentimental journey to his family's ancestral homestead, "Cousin Jack" recalled his earlier 1947 visit and shared a sip of tea with Mary Kennedy Ryan and his other Irish cousins. "We want to drink a cup of tea to all the Kennedys who went and to all those who stayed," he toasted. *Wide World*

Eire. Decades afterward, Mary Ann Ryan fondly recalled President Kennedy's visit but said she doubted her American cousin knew much about their family's Irish Republican past. While speaking of her father's memory, she pulled out his old IRA medal inscribed with the words "Eire" and "Cogadh na Saorise" (The Fight for Freedom) with a crest of the four provinces and a soldier standing at attention. On the back, her father's name is etched along with his Wexford outfit. *Joyce P. McGurrin*

"King of Ireland." Out near the barn where Jack Kennedy once took their picture, Mary Kennedy Ryan and her daughter, Mary Ann, flanked the American President at a brief ceremony, also attended by his two sisters, Eunice Kennedy Shriver and Jean Kennedy Smith. "John Fitzgerald Kennedy barely squeaked to election as President of the United States, but it seemed Thursday that he was King of Ireland by popular demand," the *Boston Globe* reported on its front page. *Wide World*

Why, God, Why? His brother's death left Robert Kennedy shattered, trying to rectify his faith with such a tragedy. In his first public speech after Jack's death, Bobby addressed a St. Patrick's Day crowd in Pennsylvania, invoking his brother's words about "the emerald thread" running through Irish immigrant history. *United Press International*

"They Cried the Rain Down." In Ireland, John Kennedy's death was met with the same shock and sadness, the image of this fallen hero venerated like some icon. Both Prime Minister Eamon DeValera and Kennedy cousin, Mary Ann Ryan, flew to Washington to attend JFK's funeral. In his tears, DeValera realized his hope of seeing the reunification of partitioned Ireland, at least in his lifetime, was now probably gone. *Library of Congress*

Father McSorley. After the death of her baby and the shooting of her husband, Jacqueline Kennedy confided her sorrows and suicidal feelings to Georgetown priest, Rev. Richard McSorley. "Do you think God would separate me from my husband if I killed myself?" she asked. When Jackie moved to New York, McSorley visited and took three-year-old John Jr. to the World's Fair (seen here). *Georgetown University Library*

A Friend in the Church. At her husband's funeral, Jackie Kennedy was genuinely touched when Cardinal Cushing referred to his departed friend as "dear Jack." Cushing's loyal friendship to the Kennedys proved itself when the Vatican threatened Jackie with excommunication for marrying Greek tycoon Aristotle Onassis. Cushing said he'd resign as cardinal unless the criticism of Kennedy's widow stopped. *Kennedy Library*

Coming Back in the Springtime.
When JFK left Ireland in 1963, he promised to return in the springtime. In 1967, Jacqueline Kennedy returned with their children, riding horses in Waterford and going for a ride along the sea. They also visited the Kennedy cousins in Dunganstown. *United Press International*

"Huelga." Robert Kennedy's strong support for the striking United Farm Workers earned him the loyalty of its union leader, Cesar Chavez, and thousands of Latin American immigrants in California. "With Senator Kennedy, it was like he was one of ours," said Chavez (seen here next to Kennedy at a mass to mark the end of a hunger strike). *Kennedy Library*

The 1968 Campaign.
On St. Patrick's Day, Robert Kennedy announced his presidential candidacy in Washington and then traveled to New York to march in the annual parade honoring the Irish in America. Along Manhattan's Fifth Avenue, Bobby turned and recognized Jackie and John Kennedy Jr., waving from their apartment window. *Wide World Photo*

Sen. Eugene McCarthy. Long before they faced each other in the 1968 Democratic primaries, Bobby Kennedy disliked McCarthy, a feeling mutual with the liberal Minnesotan. "Gene McCarthy felt he should have been the first Catholic President just because he knew more St. Thomas Aquinas than my brother," said Bobby (both seen here attending the funeral services for slain civil rights leader, Rev. Martin Luther King, Jr.). *Wide World Photo*

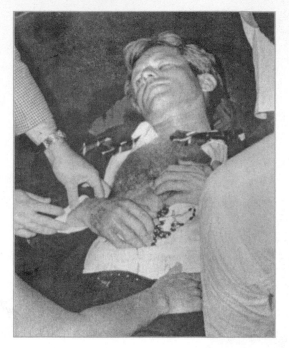

Tragedy Again. Bobby Kennedy's maverick campaign, built on votes from minorities as much as traditional white Democrats, came to a tragic end when he was shot after winning the California primary. A busboy placed a small crucifix and rosary beads in his hand while Kennedy lay bleeding on the floor. "Is everybody safe, OK?" Bobby asked, before he passed out, never to regain consciousness. *United Press International*

Stoic Faith. Rose Kennedy sat alone in silent prayer in a Hyannis Port church after a mass for the recovery of her son, Bobby Kennedy, fighting in vain for his life in a Los Angeles hospital. When asked by Cardinal Cushing, Rose confirmed her belief in God's love despite all the tragedies that befell the Kennedys. Besides, she added, "If I collapsed, the morale of the family would be lowered." *United Press International*

Family in Mourning. At his funeral, the awful consequences of Bobby Kennedy's assassination were evident in the faces of his pregnant wife, Ethel, and their children. "I remember, after my father died, the desolation I felt, the endless ache of missing him," later recalled Rep. Joseph P. Kennedy II, Bobby's oldest son, elected to the same Congressional seat once occupied by JFK and Honey Fitz. *Library of Congress*

A Third Generation. The grandchildren of Rose and Joseph Kennedy carried on the family's legacy of public service, despite some much-publicized instances of destructive behavior. Kathleen Kennedy Townsend (seen here as a teenager with her grandmother) was one of several Kennedys who took to heart Rose's reminder from the Bible: "To whom much is given, much will be expected." *Wide World Photo*

Busing in White and Black. In the 1970s, Boston's Irish objected strenuously to court ordered busing of blacks and other minorities into their schools, and sharply attacked Sen. Edward Kennedy's support of the plan. "We can't express one rule for Birmingham, Alabama, and another rule for Boston, Massachusetts," Ted explained at a news conference before being shouted down by an angry crowd at City Hall. *Wide World Photo*

Solidarity Forever. After a disappointing run for president in 1980, Sen. Kennedy remained one of the most effective legislators for improving health care, human rights and immigration reforms. "You do not have to be Irish to appreciate the Polish," he said during a 1980s visit to Communist-ruled Poland where he met with Solidarity's Lech Walesa, "but it helps, because our two proud people share. . . a role as victims in world history." *World World Photo*

IRA Violence. A 1975 terrorist bomb planted by the IRA in the car of an old JFK friend in London nearly killed Caroline Kennedy and took the life of an innocent passerby. On St. Patrick's Day two years later, Ted Kennedy and three other well-known Irish-Americans — Speaker of the House Tip O'Neill, New York Gov. Hugh Carey and soon-to-be Sen. Daniel Patrick Moynihan of New York—denounced the money and armaments sent to the IRA by private American organizations. *Wide World Photo*

In the Name of the Father. The Kennedys used their famous name to heighten public awareness to the legal injustice against Paul Hill (pictured here flanked by his wife, Courtney Kennedy Hill, and brother in-law, Rep. Joseph Kennedy II). Hill's conviction in Northern Ireland as an accused IRA murderer was later overturned after he spent years in prison. *Wide World Photo*

Golden Handshake. President Bill Clinton, who as a teenager once shook JFK's hand at the White House, was very friendly during his administration with the Kennedys, including John Jr., pictured here in 1998. At the urging of the Kennedys, Clinton's administration became actively involved in Northern Ireland's "troubles." *Wide World Photo*

Kennedy Women. With the same chieftain-like qualities as the Kennedy men of an earlier generation, women in the family emerged as leaders during the 1990s, including U.S. Ambassador to Ireland Jean Kennedy Smith (seen here with Ted Kennedy and his second wife, Victoria). In appointing Smith, Clinton proclaimed her "as Irish as Americans can be. I can think of no one who better captures the bonds between Ireland and the United States." *Corbis*

Peace for Ireland. The Kennedy family's intervention on behalf of Sinn Fein's Gerry Adams led to the successful 1998 peace negotiations in Northern Ireland. At an award ceremony hosted by Caroline Kennedy at the JFK Library in Boston that year, key participants in bringing about peace were honored, including Adams (at left), Northern Irish leader John Hume and U.S. envoy George Mitchell (right). *Kennedy Library*

Kennedy said of the striving immigrant in his book, "he could still retain it for his children."

John Kennedy didn't see his own dream come to fruition. His proposals eventually led to the passage of the 1964 Civil Rights Act as well as the Immigration and Nationality Act of 1965, largely as a tribute to his memory. The two pieces of legislation dramatically changed life in America for millions of people of color—"non-Caucasians" under the old system— whether their ancestors had been sharecroppers or boat people or migrants from across the Rio Grande. As president, Kennedy sought to ensure that all minorities were given the same opportunities that his own family enjoyed, a sentiment repeated again and again by other Kennedys. A few months before the immigration bill passed, the reissued edition of *A Nation of Immigrants* was published. In its front, Robert Kennedy, mindful of his roots, dedicated the new book—"To those committed to the battle for immigration reform."

Chapter Thirty-One

In the Springtime

DOROTHY TUBRIDY HAUNTED her old friend Jack. She reminded him that no American president—despite all the Irish emigrants who became productive and distinguished U.S. citizens—had ever traveled while in office to Ireland. As the first Irish-Catholic president, Jack could visit his family's ancestral homeland and surely be welcomed as a native son. With a wink and smile, Tubridy pestered him as only a family friend could. She vowed "to persecute him until he did come."

Tubridy was like an Irish cousin to the Kennedys. Her husband, an Irish riding champion, met Ethel Kennedy in the early 1950s at a horse show in New York and the two young newlywed couples hit it off as friends. When Dot's husband was killed in an accident, Ethel and Bobby invited their grief-stricken friend for an extended getaway in America, where she met all the Kennedys, including a week or two spent with Jack and Jackie at the family's summer place in Palm Beach. When they breezed through Dublin in 1956, Jack and Jackie stopped by to see Tubridy as well. Usually when Dot came to call, Jack and the other Kennedys spent the night by the piano, singing and playing the Irish tunes.

During the 1960 West Virginia primary, she knocked on doors with the Kennedy sisters and asked in her Dublin accent for a vote for her friend Jack. Some flatly told her they weren't for the "Catholic candidate," but others invited her in for tea and a chat about the old country. "I thought West Virginia was rather like Ireland," she remembered, "because it's quite a poor state compared with the other states in America, and the people there are very reserved and very quiet and noncommittal." Dot rejoiced with the other Kennedys on primary night at Jean's house. When Jack became president, she reminded him about visiting Ireland.

Finally in early 1963, Dot received a telephone call from the White House, saying the president wanted to see her. At that time, she was living in the States, working for the Waterford crystal company. When she arrived, Jack could barely contain his grin.

"I want you to be the first to know," he began, "I'm coming to Ireland."

Nearly forty years later, Tubridy still recalls her excitement at the news. "I felt he would immediately identify with the Irish people, and he did," she said at her home near Dublin. "Here was the most powerful person in the world, that he was Irish Catholic, and I knew it would be a great uplift for the country. There were a lot of people in the White House who said he shouldn't go, but he was determined. He said, 'I *want* to go.'"

With America entangled in a bloody and protracted battle over civil rights, several in the press wondered aloud whether the trip to Ireland was nothing more than a joyride. Even the Irish Mafia within the White House questioned Kennedy about it. "It would be a waste of time," argued aide Kenny O'Donnell, when he first heard of the president's plans. "You've got all the Irish votes in this country that you'll ever get. If you go to Ireland, people will say it's just a pleasure trip."

Amused at the thought, Kennedy replied, "That's exactly what I want—a pleasure trip to Ireland."

The next day, after conferring with McGeorge Bundy, the president's foreign policy expert, who agreed the Irish stay was unnecessary, O'Donnell persisted. Finally, Kennedy looked up from the newspaper he'd been reading and cut him off.

"Kenny . . . let me remind you of something," he said. "I am the President of the United States, not you. When I say I want to go to Ireland, it means that I'm going to Ireland. Make the arrangements."

OVER THE NEXT several weeks, Kennedy brushed up on his Irish history, adding to the tales he had learned at home and deepening his understanding of the troubles that plagued this land. He read of ancient Irish kings, their brave fights to be free of England and of the cruelties endured by the Irish. He gravitated to the story of Owen Roe O'Neill (Eoghan Ruadh O'Neill) and the Thomas Davis poem that expressed the pain of the Irish at their leader's sudden death, particularly the refrain that cries out: "Oh, why did you leave us, Owen, why did you die?" Around the White House, he recited the poem so often that it stuck in other people's heads. Kennedy studied Irish émigrés who fled their homeland as "wild geese" and played a part in American history. He absorbed the writings of John Boyle O'Reilly, who, after he fled Ireland, became a writer in Boston and a favorite of Honey Fitz. The Irish Brigade's exploits during the American Civil War became a point of pride. Few knew of Kennedy's long-held interest in Irish history, which dated back to the mid–1940s when he had visited Ireland on his own. Dave Powers was duly impressed. "He's getting so Irish," said the president's crony, "the next thing we know he'll be speaking with a brogue."

Kennedy's sojourn to Ireland in late June 1963 came on the back end of a long European trip, highlighted by his stirring speech in Berlin in defense of liberty against the Soviet threat. All free people were Berliners at heart, resisting communism, and he proudly declared "*Ich bin ein Berliner.*" Later that same day, he flew to Ireland, exhilarated but physically drained from the intensity of Berlin. A throng of joyful Dubliners lined O'Connell Street, the city's main thoroughfare, to catch a glimpse of Kennedy as he waved from an open limousine.

When Kennedy entered the U.S. embassy at Phoenix Park, Dot Tubridy could see the fatigue in her friend's face. "He was very tired, I thought, and he seemed in a very thoughtful mood," Tubridy recalled. Ireland rejuvenated his spirits and "as each day went on, he became happier and more relaxed." For a time, they talked of staying only in Dublin, but Kennedy was persuaded by Tubridy and others to travel the countryside during his three days in Ireland—an idea that didn't require much arm-twisting. On the plane ride from Germany, Kennedy had regaled Powers and O'Donnell with stories from his earlier trips to Ireland, including his 1947 visit to Lismore Castle, and about his own search for the Kennedy ancestral home in Dunganstown. He was particularly enthusiastic about seeing his Irish relatives again.

At the embassy that night, the president chatted with guests. "To what do you attribute your success?" one asked him offhandedly. Kennedy paused but for a moment in reflection.

"To my family," he asserted, then added, as if with a tip of the hat to his audience, "*and my Irish heritage.*"

As he gazed out at the lush landscape of Phoenix Park, Kennedy vowed to endorse the first Democratic presidential candidate in 1968 who'd appoint him ambassador to Ireland and send him back to live in the embassy.

THE NEXT MORNING, Kennedy rose early. Though Jacqueline Kennedy, seven months pregnant, had stayed home, the president's entourage resembled a small army, including White House aides Dave Powers and Larry

O'Brien, as well as his two sisters, Eunice Kennedy Shriver and Jean Kennedy Smith, and Jackie's sister, Lee Radziwill. After his helicopter touched down at New Ross, where he engaged in the humorous encounter with Mayor Minihan and his troublesome dung heap, Kennedy moved on to Dunganstown and similar misadventures.

For the arrival of their world-renowned relation, Mary Kennedy Ryan and the other Kennedys of Dunganstown scrubbed their modest homestead from head to toe. They cleaned up the yard and slapped a new coat of whitewash on the farmhouse. But their efforts weren't enough to please Matt McCloskey, the rather brusque U.S. ambassador to Ireland. McCloskey, a Philadelphia contractor appointed to his post more for his mastery of fundraising back home than his international diplomacy, insisted that Mrs. Ryan do something about the unrelieved muck in front of her barn. After all, the president was expected to stand there and perhaps say a few words without sinking in ankle-deep.

Mrs. Ryan, a plump, full-bosomed woman whose gentle blue eyes had seen their share of sorrows, didn't like to be pushed around. She and the American ambassador argued for days about the plans. Finally, three weeks before the presidential visit, Mrs. Ryan relented. The concrete was poured across her backyard. Mrs. Ryan, a widow who lived with her daughter Josie at the homestead, endured a number of other changes. The Secret Service drilled through the walls of her parlor and set up a special red "hotline" telephone for the president's use in an emergency. Indoor plumbing was installed to create what some wags called "John's john." A small souvenir shop selling hand-painted pictures, rosary beads and mementos of her famous relative popped up on Mrs. Ryan's farm, now dubbed "The Kennedy Homestead." Out in the barley and wheat fields, a landing field for the president's helicopter was prepared. It wasn't far from the large beer tent erected by Smithwick's, makers of the popular ale in Ireland, to entertain guests and members of the press. In scouting out the trip, presidential aide Kenny O'Donnell remembered how he witnessed several distant relatives haggling Mrs. Ryan for an invitation.

"You haven't shown your face at this door in twenty years and now you're horning in here because President Kennedy is coming!" she shouted at one startled man, her finger pointing at his face.

O'Donnell later asked this estranged cousin for his name. "John Kennedy," the man replied sheepishly.

WHEN PRESIDENT KENNEDY arrived in Dunganstown, he spotted the winding, crooked road leading to the Kennedy Homestead—the same dirt pathway with maze-like hedgerows he remembered from 1947. He thought of the stranger he had encountered while driving around lost. "See if you can find that fellow Burrell," the president instructed, still amused by Burrell's highly entertaining methods of giving directions. When the Secret Service finally found him, Robert Burrell didn't want to be bothered with Kennedy again. "I met him sixteen years ago," Burrell replied obstinately. Kennedy's aides fibbed a bit and told the president that Burrell, the man he wanted to thank, was not feeling up to par. No matter. Plenty of well-wishers gathered around the farm, pushed back from its rock walls and metal gate by police. Security agents remained alert to all sorts of potential dangers (including monks who might be assassins in disguise). Kennedy ignored them and embraced the crowds, shaking as many hands as he could. At Mrs. Ryan's doorstep, the president kissed his hostess on the cheek. She wore a simple flowered frock and had tied her hair in a bun. Kennedy then grasped the hands of her two daughters, Josephine and Mary Ann, and began asking the names of all the cousins. "He was regarded as an Irishman coming home," recalls Mary Ann Ryan, who stood next to her mother as their famous cousin reintroduced himself.

The president entered the modest farmhouse and was ushered into the living room, where turf simmered in the fireplace. "The fire feels good," he told Mrs. Ryan. She sat in a chair beside him and smiled for a photograph of them sipping tea that was carried around the world the next day. "Cousin Jimmy, meet Cousin Jack," Mrs. Ryan motioned to one of the older men in the house. James Kennedy, a gaunt, ruddy-faced man who ran the other Kennedy farm in town, offered their guest something else to warm his bones. A healthy amount of Jameson's whiskey was poured into a glass with the expectation that the president would slowly imbibe its pleasures. Instead, when no one was looking, Kennedy slipped the whiskey glass to Dave Powers, who dutifully downed its contents in a few gulps. Kennedy recognized the rascal inside this cousin. Eating cold salmon spread on wheat bread, served from a silver tray atop a white-linen tablecloth, the president motioned to James Kennedy and inquired about his meal. "Was this one poached?" the president asked his cousin, an impish remark that delighted his Irish relatives.

Outside in the back, the Ryans and Kennedys and dozens of other Irish kin and neighbors from Dunganstown, including the local parish priest, helped prepare for a formal ceremony and served cakes and tea to the crowd of dignitaries. Some wore aprons over their Sunday best. Mary Ann, a blonde-haired twenty-three-year-old, poured the tea for the president. Milk and two lumps of sugar, she was told. A local baker produced a mammoth sheet-cake fashioned in JFK's likeness. With a proud, beaming smile, Mrs. Ryan gave him a knife to do the honors. Kennedy gently kidded his relatives, staring at his frosted image in the cake, and asked them teasingly, "Cut myself?" After more small talk and good humor, the president turned to all those assembled, lifted his cup and offered a toast. "We want to drink a cup of tea to all the Kennedys who went and to all those who stayed," he declared.

As his sisters and closest aides noticed, President Kennedy enjoyed himself immensely. Jack was genuinely affected by the beautiful land and the warmth of the Irish people. "John Fitzgerald Kennedy barely squeaked to election as President of the United States, but it seemed Thursday that he was King of Ireland by popular demand," the *Boston Globe* reported on its front page. The Irish newspapers, with a more historical perspective, stressed Kennedy's visit as the grand ending for a long and hard journey reaching back to the famine deaths and diaspora of the 1840s. "John F. Kennedy is the symbol of the closing of a chapter of our history," declared the *Irish Independent* in Dublin. "After three generations a young man of fully Irish stock has reached the last point of integration into American life—the chief executive post of the nation. The great emigrations to America have come intimately into the lives of most Irish families." The *Cork Examiner* wrote that "when President John Fitzgerald Kennedy set foot on Irish soil he made a mark on the history of this country that can never be effaced."

In his brief remarks at the old family homestead, Kennedy recognized the moment's import. "When my great-grandfather came to America and my grandfather was growing up, the Irish-Americans had a song about the familiar sign which went: 'No Irish Need Apply,'" Kennedy recalled to his extended family and the assemblage. "In 1960, the American people took the sign down from the last place it was still hanging—the door of the White House." In the United States, Kennedy rarely characterized his election as a barrier-breaker. Among the immigrants of Boston, Grandpa Honey Fitz once luxuriated in such resentments, his stock-in-trade as a politician. But that wasn't Jack Kennedy's style. In a predominantly Protestant nation, he knew there was still too much to lose politically by pointing out such things. Yet here in Dunganstown, Kennedy felt at home enough to make these connections, to savor his Irish roots and acknowledge his own achievement.

The allotted hour for their visit was almost over. Frank Aiken, the Irish minister of external affairs, busily suggested to the president that they should move along to the next stop in Wexford. Mrs. Ryan would have none of it. "You won't be hurrying him out of here," she scolded Aiken.

Like some older aunt, she instructed the president to ignore the highest-ranking Irish official in their presence. "Don't mind that fellow—you don't have to go yet," she counseled. No one dared suggest the contrary. Mrs. Ryan wanted the president to plant a juniper tree in her yard, a living reminder of the day, before she'd let him go.

Family relations, more than foreign relations, carried the day in Dunganstown. Some American reporters asked Mrs. Ryan a few perfunctory questions, but the Kennedy family's vast and troubled history in Ireland remained largely ignored. No one seemed to realize that the U.S. president was visiting the home of a woman who had been active for years with the old IRA's women's auxiliary, had once carried weapons underneath her garments to supply IRA soldiers and whose husband had received an IRA memorial when he died. If President Kennedy was aware of Mrs. Ryan's republican past, he gave no hint of it. But it was very much part of the history of those Kennedys who stayed.

In departing, Kennedy thanked Mrs. Ryan and his cousins for their hospitality and invited them to visit him in Washington. Before he flew off in his presidential helicopter, Kennedy apologized for any hardships his visit may have caused. "We promise to come only every ten years," he joked.

From this remote farm, the party journeyed to the bustling port town of Wexford, where the English conquest of Ireland first took hold and where Oliver Cromwell once massacred civilians in an arena near the River Slaney. In Crescent Quay, Kennedy laid a wreath at the memorial to John Barry, an Irish émigré who had fought valiantly in the American Revolutionary War, and paid homage to the Irish Brigade, the band of "wild geese" immigrant soldiers, led by Thomas Meagher, who fought at Gettysburg and then Fredericksburg during the U.S. Civil War. This was the same Meagher who led the 1848 uprising in Wexford against the British. "They went into battle wearing a sprig of green in their hats and it was said of them what was said about Irishmen in other countries: '*War battered dogs are we, gnawing a naked bone, fighting in every land and clime, for every cause but our own,*'" Kennedy reminded the crowd at Redmond Place in Wexford.

Before taking off for Dublin, Kennedy went on a mission for his mother's Fitzgerald side of the family. Outside of Wexford, his motorcade stopped at the Loretto Convent, where Mother Superior Clement Ward, a nun who was Rose's third cousin, greeted him at the gate along with twenty-seven other nuns. Mother Clement described herself as "the relation nobody knows about." Mother Clement's quip was rather clever for, in the days prior to the trip, dozens of Irish people claimed to be long-lost relatives of President Kennedy, the most bitter disputes coming from those with the

Fitzgerald surname. In all, the newspapers estimated that Ireland contained eighteen thousand Kennedys and some twelve thousand Fitzgeralds. The president seemed intent on shaking hands with each one.

"There is an impression in Washington that there are no Kennedys left in Ireland, that they are all in Washington, so I wonder if there are any Kennedys in this audience," he wondered to a crowd in Wexford.

A few hands stretched into the air.

"Well," the president said with a grin, "I am glad to see a few cousins who didn't catch the boat."

KENNEDY'S OWN sensitivities to Ireland's history, its divided status between the north and the south, were displayed discreetly but consistently throughout his three-day visit, never more so than with the Irish president, Eamon De Valera. Now eighty and nearly blind, De Valera remained the heart and soul of the Irish Republic. His job was largely ceremonial, having given up his powerful post as Taoseich a few years earlier, yet he was the first to shake President Kennedy's hand when he arrived under gray damp skies in Dublin. For nearly three decades, the Kennedys had known De Valera and, in their own way, remained as fascinated by this charismatic leader as the Irish people themselves. Even in his salutations, De Valera never stopped reminding the world that Ireland was still a divided nation.

"*Céad Míle Fáilte,*" said De Valera, a Gaelic phrase meaning "a hundred thousand welcomes." It was more than an exercise in nostalgia. For years, DeValera's messianic campaign to bring about one united Ireland also relied, unsuccessfully, upon a return to their native tongue. In his greeting, he invoked the ancient memory of long-lost kings on the emerald isle. "I have thought it fitting that my first words of welcome to you should be in our native language, the language that was spoken by the great Kennedy clan of the *Dal gCais,* when nine and a half centuries ago, and almost on the spot on which we are now standing, under their mighty King Brian Boru, they smashed the invader and broke decisively the power of the Norsemen," recounted De Valera, straining to read from his notes. "That language, Mr. President, which has never ceased to be spoken, will, please God, one day soon again become the everyday language of our people."

For the Irish people, there could be no more disparate image of their fate than these two men together. JFK, the robust Irish-American with his free-flowing brown hair, suntanned face and handsomely tailored business suit, was the very picture of modernity; indeed, he personified a direction that so many young Irish people admired and wanted to emulate. The aged and austere face of De Valera, with his thick eyeglasses and thin wisps of hair, recalled an older time of desperate violent resistance, an unresolved splitting of their country, and a backward, defensive approach to the future. Though gifted in revolution, De Valera proved poor at governance. He insisted on keeping Ireland an agrarian nation without much modern industry. He maintained a dogged indifference to his country's economic plight, prompting some six hundred thousand people to emigrate from Ireland in 1956 alone, the highest number since the "black 1880s."

Nevertheless, both men knew and respected what each meant for the Irish. In almost mythic terms, De Valera portrayed Kennedy "as the distinguished scion of our race," whose election as U.S. president seemed to embody the dreams of every Irish family who saw their loved ones float away on a ship bound for America. As if fulfilling some ancient prophesy, Kennedy represented "that great country" in the New World where "our people sought refuge when the misery of tyrant laws drove them from the motherland, and found a home in which they and their descendants prospered," the older man said. "We are proud of you, Mr. President," he added, as if speaking to a son. During the Dublin Airport welcoming ceremony, Kennedy equally praised De Valera, treasuring him as "an old and valued friend of my father." He echoed themes of Irish immigration to America mentioned by the New York City–born De Valera, whose own mother was an immigrant. Kennedy suggested that many Irish-Americans "kept a special place in their memories, in many cases their ancestral memory, of this green and misty island, so, in a sense, all of them who visit Ireland come home."

FOLLOWING HIS TRIP to County Wexford, Kennedy once again joined De Valera and his wife, Sinead, for a garden party at *Aras an Uachtarian,* the presidential residence in Dublin, similar in appearance to the White House. Kennedy was a bit anxious about what to expect. Before leaving America, he had conferred with Thomas J. Kiernan, the Irish ambassador to the United States, and asked whether he'd be expected to wear a formal morning suit to this event. "My father wore striped pants, I know, at a Garden Party in Dublin, but a dark suit is . . ." Kennedy began to explain, hesitantly. Kiernan immediately assured him that a business suit would suffice. The ambassador recognized the significance of this trip to the Irish people and was determined to ensure its success. After witnessing the population drop by millions with the mass emigration, his country was searching for such a hero, such a symbolic ending to the diaspora. "Here was a fellow who came from famine stock on both paternal and maternal sides and who had reached the very top in the United States—

that was felt throughout the country," Kiernan recalled. "I think in that sense you could say he wasn't coming as the king, he was coming as an ending to a bad epoch, a bad century."

During the early 1960s, Kiernan developed a friendliness with the young American president (they were "on the same wavelength," in Kiernan's words) that allowed him to gain a sense of Kennedy's personality, to view this Irish-American as a combination of forces. Kennedy teasingly described Kiernan, a short wry man, as having "sort of an elfish look about him, but he is very, very good." In the ambassador's estimation, the president was clearly an Irishman. "Kennedy was in his blood reactions—which after all were completely Irish on both sides—was Irish in his speed of communication, in his wit, in his debunking—his self-debunking, which is part of the Irish attitude," he observed. But Kiernan also detected "the Harvard attitude," more outwardly dominant in his demeanor, part of "those with Irish names in America [who] are still wanting to be accepted as part of the establishment, or at any rate not to be regarded as outsiders." Borrowing from Carl Jung's theories of a collective unconscious, Kiernan, with his own brand of analysis, suggested that Kennedy's reactions as president often reflected this split cultural background. "One could apply that to Kennedy himself, this racial unconsciousness and the reaction coming from it," the ambassador contended. "The culture superimposed upon it is a hard culture, a culture of living up to Boston's Harvard, which for an Irish person treated as they were [made it difficult]. . . . Kennedy couldn't divide that Irish heritage, but what was superimposed upon it made him often wish, as I think it makes many Americans often wish, that they could avoid it. He couldn't avoid it because it was there in his blood."

In his dealings with the president, Kiernan continually stressed the Kennedy ties to the old country, even if they were a few generations removed. The ambassador arranged for the Office of Heraldry in Dublin to trace the lineage of the Kennedys and the Fitzgeralds and their well-developed roots in Ireland. During one St. Patrick's Day in Washington, he presented a Kennedy coat of arms to him. For the 1963 trip, the two governments worked together to create an Irish-American Foundation to counter criticism that Kennedy's journey was merely frivolous. But in their talks, Kiernan mentioned that the issue of Irish partition would arise during his visit, a topic he knew De Valera was bound to bring up.

"The President looked as if another headache had struck him and asked me was he expected to say anything in public," Kiernan recounted in a memo marked "secret" and sent back to the Irish government. The ambassador told Kennedy that no public statement condemning partition would be necessary but that De Valera and the *Taoseich,* "prime minister," Sean Lemass, probably wanted to discuss it privately. Kiernan knew American officials didn't want to upset their Cold War alliance with the British. Kennedy had turned down an offer from Northern Ireland to visit during his stay, mainly because he didn't want to raise the partition issue. The president said he viewed partition as an internal Irish problem.

"Well, that is the British line very good," Kiernan remarked to Kennedy. "But partition was enforced against the wishes of both parts of Ireland by the British. No country cuts itself in two."

Kennedy seemed taken by the logic of this statement, as if he were suddenly reminded of his own past written observations on the issue. "That is true, of course, it is a British issue," Kennedy responded.

As they discussed the matter, Kiernan pointed out how the British provided more than $100 million a year to the six counties in Northern Ireland, perpetuating the divisions between the Irish, and that a stronghold in Ireland was no longer needed for Britain's defense in this new age of atomic warfare. If England were to end its financial assistance and express support for a united Ireland, Kiernan said, the moral support for "the junta" in the six counties would soon collapse. "Well, you know it's very hard," Kennedy responded. "I can see the British difficulty. It's very hard to say that on account of the past history."

Kiernan reminded Kennedy that, as a U.S. senator, he had sponsored a legislative call for the end of partition in Ireland. "You know, you're one of those who put forward a bill in the Senate," Kiernan said. "You got 17 votes, I think."

Kennedy burst out laughing, enjoying the moment at his own expense. "That's right," he said.

As both men realized, Kennedy could no longer appease the Irish loyalists back in Boston without regard to the far broader interests of American foreign policy. As president, he was far more cautious, less willing to be seen offending such a close American ally as the British. During his trip to the Free State, Kennedy indicated that he'd be agreeable to listen to a practical, step-by-step plan to reunify Ireland, but only in private. Before Kiernan left the White House, where they discussed other details of the trip, Kennedy reasserted his position.

"Is it understood that I am not to refer publicly to partition?" Kennedy asked the ambassador in a somber, earnest tone. As Kiernan recalled to his bosses back home, "I assured him, to his relief I think, that this was so."

After the garden party and a state dinner that followed, De Valera talked about Irish reunification while Kennedy listened respectfully. At another private meeting with Taoseich Sean Lemass, Kennedy brought up the partition issue himself and asked whether progress had been made recently. "I said I believed that this is a question which, in the ultimate, must be settled in Ireland, that any form of international pressure would not alter the basic situation," Lemass recorded in his notes of their meeting. Kennedy suggested that a new Labour Party government at Downing Street might improve the chances of reunification. Though avoiding public discussion of partition, Kennedy repeatedly hinted at his own personal feelings about Ireland's struggles. "To the extent that the peace is disturbed by conflict between the former colonial powers and the new and developing nations, Ireland's role is unique," Kennedy declared in a nationally televised speech to the Dail, the Irish Parliament. "For every nation knows that Ireland was the first of the small countries in the twentieth century to win its struggle for independence. . . . For knowing the meaning of foreign domination, Ireland is the example and the inspiration to those enduring endless years of oppression." At a memorial service at Arbour Hill, where the executed leaders of the 1916 Easter uprising are buried, Kennedy appeared particularly moved. He stood at attention with Lemass as Irish military cadets performed a drill ceremony, impressive enough so that Kennedy mentioned it repeatedly to his family. "As Kennedy watched the funeral drill of the army cadets when he laid a wreath on the heroes' graves, he seemed more the deeply moved patriot in his homeland than the powerful President of another country," Irish writer Joseph Roddy recounted in *Look* magazine. "In the close-ups on television, he was a man being confronted with the proof of how Irish he really was."

Kennedy was enthralled by the Irish fight for freedom. In private, he quizzed De Valera about his part in the rebellion and asked why he wasn't shot along with the other prisoners. Back in 1945, young John Kennedy had written about De Valera's daring escape from the British jails, but this question lingered in his curious mind. De Valera explained that the British knew he'd been born in New York, and therefore were reluctant about executing an American citizen. "But there were many times when the key in my jail cell was turned and I thought my turn had come," the old man added. Just as he had done two decades earlier, Kennedy listened with fascination to De Valera's stories about the civil war and the guerilla-like tactics in the struggles for independence against the British Black and Tans. "If you are weak in your dealing with the British, they will pressure you," De Valera told him. "If you are subject to flattery, they will cajole you. Only if you are reasonable, will they reason with you, and being reasonable with the British means letting them know that you are willing to throw an occasional bomb into one of their lorries." As he later told his biographer, De Valera walked away from their meetings believing that Kennedy, if elected to a second term, would act to end the partition and help unify Ireland.

FAR MORE THAN a matter of politics, Kennedy's visit celebrated what it meant to be Irish, both for those living in Eire and in far-flung places such as the United States. Before the Dail, he reminded listeners of Ireland's ancient history, its arts, its writers and philosophers. He quoted John Boyle O'Reilly ("The world is large when its weary leagues two loving hearts divide / But the world is small when your enemy is loose on the other side") and James Joyce—still banned as scandalous by most of Ireland's politicians and Catholic priests—who described the Atlantic filled with famine ships as a "bowl of bitter tears." He summoned memories of Ben Franklin's trip to Ireland in 1772 to seek a joint alliance with the Irish in a quest for "more equitable treatment" by the British. He reminded how Daniel O'Connell, Ireland's fabled liberator, was influenced by George Washington. "No larger nation did more to keep Christianity and Western culture alive in their darkest centuries," Kennedy declared. "No larger nation did more to spark the cause of independence in America, indeed, around the world. And no larger nation has ever provided the world with more literary and artistic genius." As proof, he quoted George Bernard Shaw, who, speaking as an Irishman summing up his view of life, said other people "see things and say: Why? . . . But I dream things that never were—and I say: Why not?" Shaw's encapsulation of the Irish spirit—what Kennedy called "that remarkable combination of hope, confidence, and imagination"—would become a familiar refrain associated with his own family.

For a small nation feeling bruised and inconsequential, his words were a boost to their collective morale. As he journeyed from place to place, Kennedy's enthusiasm and good humor became infectious. "I don't want to give the impression that every member of this administration in Washington is Irish—it just seems that way," Kennedy jested before a crowd at City Hall in Cork. He introduced them to "the pastor at the church which I go to, who is also from Cork—Monsignor O'Mahoney. He is the pastor of a poor, humble flock in Palm Beach, Florida!" The president's entourage, well aware of the affluent, suntanned parishioners in Palm Beach, laughed heartily at that insider's joke.

Kennedy seemed to enjoy each stop on his whirlwind tour. Before an academic reception at St. Patrick's Hall, Dublin Castle, he teased about the difference between Trinity College, the Harvard-like institution in Ireland favored by Protestants, and National University, the one attended historically by Catholics. "I now feel equally part of both and if they ever have a game of Gaelic football or hurling, I shall cheer for Trinity and pray for National," he vowed. As a special favor, he jumped out of his official car to greet the mayor of Galway's eighty-two-year-old mother, and signed his name to an old American history book for her. When 320 schoolchildren of the Convent of Mercy, dressed in green, white or gold, formed the Irish flag in a nearby field, Kennedy came over to them in thanks, and at his request, they sang "Galway Bay." In Limerick, a gray industrial town along the River Shannon, he asked some Fitzgeralds, who claimed to be related, to stand up and be recognized by the crowd. "One of them looks just like Grandpa," he said with astonishment to his sisters about a white-haired man in the audience, "and that *is* a compliment." To Dubliners as he departed, Kennedy bid farewell almost lyrically: "I can imagine nothing more pleasant than continuing day after day to drive through the streets of Dublin and wave, and I may come back and do it."

The warm reception by throngs of people, stretching their arms and hands to touch his own, left an indelible mark on this Irish-American president. He seemed to savor each Celtic song, each step dance performed for him and occasionally could be seen joining in himself by humming or tapping his feet. In Limerick, he recalled the verses of a song—"*Come back to Erin, Mavourneen, Mavourneen, come back aroun' to the land of thy birth. / Come with the Shamrock in the springtime, Mavourneen.*" Someday, he promised, he, too, would "come back in the springtime."

Whatever magic Kennedy hoped for in Ireland had taken its effect. On his last day, Kennedy admitted "it is strange that so many years could pass and so many generations pass and still some of us who came on this trip could come home and—here to Ireland—and feel ourselves as home and not feel ourselves in a strange country, but feel ourselves among neighbors, even though we are separated by generations, by time, and by thousands of miles." At Shannon Airport, the presidential jetliner ready to take him back to America, Kennedy pulled out a piece of paper and recited lines he had scribbled down from a poem that De Valera's wife had shared with him:

> 'Tis it is the Shannon's brightly glancing stream,
> Brightly gleaming, silent in the morning beam,
> Oh, the sight entrancing,
> Thus returns from travels long,
> Years of exile, years of pain,
> To see old Shannon's face again,
> O'er the waters dancing.

Upon his return home, Kennedy couldn't stop talking to friends and family about his experiences in Ireland, sometimes staying up past midnight. He wrote a formal note of thanks to Lemass, and, to De Valera, he called the trip "one of the most moving experiences of my life." He told Jackie about his visit to the Kennedys' ancestral home and urged her to go to Ireland with him some day soon. He practiced speaking Gaelic with Ted's Irish-speaking nanny and he decided to give his family's new vacation home in Virginia the name "Wexford." Eunice, aware of her brother's delight, planned to give him a recording of "The Boys of Wexford" for that Christmas, 1963. Repeatedly, he showed films of his trip to Jackie, Bobby and some of his oldest pals. "All we are getting here still is his Irish visit," moaned Red Fay to another of their friends. "Every time we call at the White House, Jack brings the conversation back round to it and invariably shows the film which I have now seen for the sixth time."

Bobby recalled that his brother seemed to show these films "every night when he got home. Everyone had to go in and watch the movie." Later, upon reflection, Bobby agreed that the Irish trip was "I suppose the happiest time of his administration." Nearly forty years afterward, Ted could still remember its emotional resonance for his brother. "He appreciated Ireland even more," recalled Ted. "He loved the time he spent there and the people he met. He was deeply touched by the warmth of his reception. He had always valued Irish traditions, and their love of poetry and literature and music, but now he felt a very special bond." Ted also spoke of his brother's insistence on showing the film of his trip. "Jack enjoyed it so much he invited everyone to gather with him the next night to see it again," he recalled. "But by the third night, when he still wanted to see it one more time, he and I were the only two people sitting down to watch."

The Kennedy family crest that De Valera presented to him was engraved on a Waterford crystal bowl with the help of Dot Tubridy, who worked for the glass company. In a note accompanying the bowl, she inscribed, "Don't forget—this is where it all began." That bowl sat on the president's desk, Tubridy recalled four decades later, as "a reminder of his Irishness—he took it for what it meant." Jackie took the "O'Kennedy" crest and made a seal ring, which her husband later told her he had used mischievously—in sealing a letter to the Queen of England.

In Ireland, Jack Kennedy seemed to rediscover something in himself. For a president who got elected by proving himself more American than the next and avoiding ethnic or religious entanglements as much as he could, the trip to Ireland was like a coming out party. As his sister Jean remembered four decades later, "It was a wonderful trip for the President, obviously it would be a high point of anyone's life, especially his. Coming back, the first Catholic, so young, the first Irish Catholic—it was obviously very moving." What so many bigoted Americans shunned in John Kennedy and found repulsive—his Irish Catholicism—he now embraced with remarkable ease, gracefully displaying his affections to the world in a three-day extravaganza. Journalist Pete Hamill, who vividly remembered JFK's 1963 visit to Ireland, described Kennedy "often more Harvard than Irish, but he was more Irish than even he ever thought." Most of the American press misconstrued the whole venture. The *New Yorker* magazine dismissed the Irish sojourn as a "psuedo-event" and other correspondents suggested that it was nothing more than a public relations stunt. In observing the enigmatic JFK—that media creature who usually revealed little about himself—the press failed to recognize the significance of what Kennedy's friends and family later recalled as his most treasured moment of the presidency. The long "emerald thread" of Irish emigration to America, as Kennedy once called it, had been tied together symbolically with this president's visit to his ancestral homeland. In a sense, the wild geese had come home.

When Lemass visited Washington in mid-October, Kennedy rolled out the red carpet, intent on returning the courtesies paid to him in Ireland. At a state dinner, one of his last in the White House, Kennedy arranged for a night of Irish music played by the U.S. Air Force bagpipe band followed by a private party upstairs, where Gene Kelly sang and danced for the guests. With little inducement, Teddy Kennedy got up and carried a tune. That night, the band made sure to play the president's favorites from his trip—"The Wearin' o' the Green" and especially "The Boys of Wexford."

Chapter Thirty-Two

The Ritual of Mourning

"Many times man lives and dies
Between his two eternities,
That of race and that of soul,
And ancient Ireland knew it all.
Whether man die in his bed
Or the rifle knocks him dead,
A brief parting from those dear
Is the worst man has to fear."

—WILLIAM BUTLER YEATS

JOE KENNEDY'S SPIRIT seemed imprisoned. In his wheelchair and rolled out by a nurse onto the open porch of his Hyannis Port home, the old man sat silently in a red bathrobe and watched his son's presidential helicopter arrive and ascend into the distance from the same green fields where his family once played.

In December 1961, months after that sine qua non moment of his son's inauguration, the aging patriarch suffered a devastating stroke that sapped the strength from his arms and legs. The fulsome, cocksure smile of the former ambassador to the Court of St. James was now atrophied and empty-looking. He had made millions on Wall Street and talked of running for the White House himself as Roosevelt's successor; he had been a patron of bishops and the Pope's confidant, the most influential American Catholic of his era. Yet now Joe Kennedy existed in his own form of purgatory, an active mind trapped inside a broken body, patronized and pitied more than feared. Only his blue eyes still seemed alive.

When the president came home for a visit, he tried to cheer up his father. But Jack's own pained eyes sometimes gave him away. "It was distressing to him, as it was to everybody, to see my father in that condition when he'd been so active and able," recalled Bobby Kennedy about his brother's reaction. "He [Jack] was almost the best with my father because he really made him laugh and said outrageous things to him. My father used to just sit out there Friday afternoon waiting for the helicopter to arrive, and so he used to get excited and then Jack used to come over and spend some time with him."

Before leaving on Sundays, the president kissed his father gently on the forehead and bid him goodbye. Then Joe Kennedy watched from the porch as his son flew away. "He's the one who made all this possible, and look at him now," Jack commented to an aide, on what turned out to be his last visit to Hyannis Port in October 1963.

AN AWARENESS of life and death never left Jack Kennedy. Unlike most young men, he had carried with him, certainly since World War II, a sense of mortality, both of his own and of those closest to him. The biblical adage from St. Luke that his mother had so often pointed to in their youth—"To whom much is given, much will be expected"—seemed almost Faustian in its divine administration. The Kennedy family, seemingly so blessed by God, endured the tragedies of Joe Jr. and Kathleen during the 1940s in a way that Jack never forgot. Kathleen's vibrant personality remained transfixed in his memory. After his triumphant presidential trip to Ireland, Jack made sure to stop briefly, privately, at Kathleen's grave at Chatsworth, England, where he knelt and prayed. He watched as Jean, with a bouquet of red and white roses picked in Ireland, placed them by her sister's headstone. Death at a young age, he once wrote, gave his older brother's life "a completeness . . . the completeness of perfection." During the PT-109 accident, he'd witnessed death and barely escaped his own. During his 1947 trip to Ireland, Jack appeared sickly and soon collapsed in a London hospital, gravely ill from Addison's disease—what appeared to be his own death sentence. Before his risky 1954 spinal fusion operation, a priest administered the last rites of the church, yet once again he won his life-and-death gamble. Over the next decade, his illnesses and pain were covered over in Florida tans, a masking wit, and public talk of vigor, courage and physical fitness. In private, though, an air of fatalism pervaded Kennedy's outlook about his own future. He didn't indulge himself in Irish melancholy or a cursing of the fates. Instead, he steeled his soul for what he felt was to come.

"Frank, I want you to make sure that they close the coffin when I die," he instructed Morrissey, morbidly and out of the blue. Morrissey, the family lackey slightly older than Jack, didn't know how to respond to talk about death, especially from someone who seemed so full of life and passion. But the request came up again, repeatedly, as if Kennedy sensed something in the air. "He seemed to have a premonition about it," Morrissey remembered, "and he asked that eight or nine times." The thought that an assassin could be lurking always worried Dave Powers whenever Kennedy appeared in public. Powers particularly feared such at attack when Kennedy went to church— perhaps a gunman in the choir loft or killer waiting in line for Communion at the altar. Kennedy, with his gallows humor, made light of small incidents— false alarms such as firecrackers going off or strangers who came too close— that reminded them all of his vulnerability. "What would you have done if that fellow had a grenade in his hand instead of a mike?" Kennedy asked Powers, after a microphone-wielding broadcaster got past his Secret Service protection. Powers quipped that he'd say a quick Act of Contrition, the Catholic prayer of penance and forgiveness, perhaps the church's greatest sacrament. Kennedy immediately understood and laughed at his aide's joke.

For his staff and loved ones, the most disconcerting aspect of Kennedy's demeanor was that he viewed an early death not as matter of if, but when— an inescapable proposition. "The President took a fatalistic attitude about the possibility of being assassinated by a fanatic, regarding such a danger as being part of his job, and often talked about how easy it would be for somebody to shoot at him with a rifle from a high building," O'Donnell recalled. In his own memoir about Kennedy, Sorensen claimed that his boss "had no morbid fascination with the subject of death" but accepted the dangers of being pres- ident without complaint, "with an almost fatalistic unconcern for danger" as part of the presidency's risk and as part of his overall embrace of life. "Occasionally he would read one of the dozens of written threats on his life he received almost every week in the White House," Sorensen recalled. Kennedy shared these premonitions and perceived inevitabilities about death not only with the men around him but with his young wife, Jacqueline, already a mother of two children and pregnant with a third. "The poignancy of men dying young always moved my husband, possibly because of his brother Joe," Jacqueline Kennedy later recalled. When they were alone together, he often asked Jackie to recite Alan Seeger's poem, "I Have a Rendezvous with Death"—made more poignant by the knowledge of the poet's own early death. The verse had an applicability, a resonance, to his own life:

> *I have a rendezvous with Death*
> *On some scarred slope of battered hill,*
> *When Spring comes round again this year*

And the first meadow-flowers appear. . . .
But I've a rendezvous with Death
At midnight in some flaming town,
When Spring trips north again this year,
And I to my pledged word am true,
I shall not fail that rendezvous.

If his Irish wit served as a kind of illuminating full moon, leaving all about him in his effervescent glow, John Kennedy's fatalism existed as its darker side. Fatalism was a birthright of the Irish in America, certainly shared by Kennedy's ancestors, and by generations of other Irish émigrés who died in transport on famine ships, or suffered an early death from disease, poverty and relentless work in America. Such a dreadful *moira* was in his bones. Kennedy's experiences with death only seemed to heighten this consciousness of life's limits, his determination to squeeze every bit of what earthly existence he may have, an approach expressed in the Latin as *carpe diem*.

Kennedy's energies, ambitions and passions—including his extramarital activities, known initially to his intimates and later to the world—seemed part of this complex mix. Sex and death have a curious linkage in Irish Catholic tradition. The Reverend Andrew Greeley, in his prolific writings about Irish-Americans, suggests a strong "duality" in their character, the "strange propensity" to laugh at death and defy it with raucous Irish wakes filled with laughter and sometimes even "life-affirming" sexual activity. "The Irish reaction to death is perhaps the most intricate combination of our pagan past and our Christian past," Greeley explains. "The corpse is in the house, the mourners are singing and dancing and drinking and telling stories, and out in the fields lovers are having intercourse. 'Fuck death,' says the Celtic comic." Among Catholic believers, the finality of death is overcome by a faith in eternal life—in Christ's promise of redemption for one's earthly sins bringing about an everlasting communion with God and one's loved ones in Heaven. After the deaths of Joe Jr. and Kathleen Kennedy, many of the memoriam cards and handwritten letters to the Kennedys, including Jack, embraced and clung to such Catholic beliefs. Perhaps someday in an afterlife, they suggested, all the Kennedys would be back together again, reunited as one happy family, just like those glossy idealized pictures from the 1930s. Without Greeley's eye for ethnography, several biographers have speculated that Kennedy's carnality was somehow linked to an impending sense of doom. The closer he came to his Irish roots, the more Kennedy seemed wistfully aware of his perceived fate. At a White House ceremony attended by Irish Ambassador Thomas Kiernan in 1961, Kennedy received a Wexford cup to honor the christening of the president's namesake son, John Jr., and then listened to the ambassador read a poem for the occasion:

> *When the storms break for him*
> *May the trees shake for him*
> *Their blossoms down;*
> *And in the night that he is troubled*
> *May a friend wake for him*
> *So that his time may be doubled;*
> *And at the end of all loving and love*
> *May the Man above*
> *Give him a crown.*

The poem served as a prayer of safekeeping for Kennedy's newborn son, a prayer that he would be spared from an untimely death. After Kiernan finished his lines, Kennedy stepped up to the microphone and motioned toward him.

"I wish that was for me," he whispered.

Years later, Sorensen wrote that Kennedy's exchange with the Irish ambassador was indicative of the sense of awaiting tragedy in his soul, when "perhaps he came closest to revealing his inner thoughts" about his fate. Though he was accepting of the possibility of his own death, Kennedy was unprepared for the tragedy that befell his family in August 1963.

Images of the young president smiling and playing with his young children are timeless reminders of the Kennedy emphasis on family and its allure to the American public. One particularly memorable set of photographs show Caroline, at age five, and her two-year-old brother, dubbed "John-John" by the press, romping in the Oval Office to their father's delight. Journalists lionized Kennedy as a family man. "I sensed a tribal quality about him that wasn't evident when I first met him," recalled Laura Bergquist Knebel, who wrote several pieces about the Kennedys for *Look* magazine. "Once he had kids of his own, he became a patriarch, he was fascinated by not only his own children but other kids." In reality, though, Kennedy's marriage had suffered considerably from his long absences, the persistent rumors of his infidelities and at times his callous insensitivity to his wife. In the mid–1950s, when Jackie suffered a miscarriage followed a year later by a stillborn baby by cesarian section, Jack barely stopped his whirlwind schedule to comfort her. At times, her husband's constant political campaigning made her feel more like a constituent than a participant in his life. For Jackie Kennedy, like so many Catholic women of her generation—and like her mother-in-law before her—divorce seemed out of the question. The obligations of church law and family life took precedence over any unhappiness she might feel, regardless of wealth or social status. "The most important thing for a successful marriage is for a husband to do what he likes best and does well," she advised readers of *Redbook* magazine during the 1960 campaign. "The wife's satisfactions will follow." To a friendly journalist, Fletcher Knebel, Jackie conceded that she and her husband were like two icebergs, "the public life above the water—the private life is submerged." Sometimes, their two lives converged. In April 1963, the news of her fifth pregnancy was greeted with a special press briefing. When a reporter asked whether the news conference was being called to announce Kennedy's plans to go to Ireland, Teddy Kennedy shook his head. "No," he replied, with a vulpine grin. "It's sexier than that."

Not since the days of Grover Cleveland had a baby been born to a president living in the White House. Under a headline "Big Year for the Clan," *Time* magazine proclaimed: "Every year is family year in the Kennedy clan, but 1963 figures to be really outstanding." Not only was Jackie Kennedy pregnant, but so were her sisters-in-law, Ethel (expecting her eighth child), and Teddy's wife, Joan (carrying her third). As if keeping track of stock prices or electoral college votes, the press pointed out the new presidential baby would be the twenty-third grandchild for Joe and Rose Kennedy. The first lady's doctors, aware of her past history of troubled pregnancies, advised that she give up all official duties until her baby was born late that summer.

Up at a horse farm in Cape Cod with her children, five weeks before her intended due date, Jackie felt premature cramps and slipped into labor. At the time, she was in a car driven by a Secret Service agent. Her two children, on their way to a Wednesday morning horse ride, had already dashed out the door. Jackie never left the vehicle. The driver called her doctor and then sped to the Kennedys' rented summer house on Squaw Island, not far from Joe and Rose's home in Hyannis Port. A helicopter flew the first lady to Otis Air Force Base's hospital twenty miles away while the president was notified. Jack flew immediately from Washington in a small airplane. He was still in the air when his wife gave birth to a tiny, premature baby boy. He weighed only four pounds, ten ounces—barely enough to sustain himself. Jackie's obstetrician, Dr. John Walsh, called for a Catholic priest and Father

John Cahill, an air force chaplain, baptized the infant shortly after birth. His parents decided there would be another Patrick added to the Kennedy lineage—Patrick Bouvier Kennedy. He would spend the rest of his life in a glass-enclosed incubator.

Later that afternoon, President Kennedy viewed his brown-haired infant son for the first time, lying in a special private nursery set up for the occasion. By evening, he wheeled the incubator up to Jackie's bed. Outside, reporters were informed that mother and child were doing fine, but inside the hospital, doctors feared the newest Kennedy might not survive. He suffered from hyaline membrane disease, an often fatal ailment common among premature babies. In an ambulance, they rushed the infant, wrapped in a blue blanket, to Children's Medical Center in Boston. Little Patrick was accompanied by his worried father while Jackie convalesced at the Otis Air Force Base hospital. At one point, the president flew to Cape Cod to visit his wife, and then returned promptly to the Boston hospital. Over the next day and a half, the president hoped for a miracle, willing to try anything to save his dying son. As a desperate measure, the doctors recommended putting Patrick into a huge hyperbaric pressure chamber to force-feed oxygen to his starving lungs—a radical move that had not been tried before for such an ailment. By Thursday afternoon, the weary president called his wife at Otis and let her know of the serious turn in their baby's condition. He dined alone that evening, lost in a reverie of thoughts. When he returned to the hospital once more, Bobby and Dave Powers were there at his side to buoy his spirits. The baby's frail body wasn't responding to treatment. Jack decided to spend the night near his son. He napped in a doctor's lounge until early Friday morning, around 2:00 A.M., when he awoke with word that his son's breathing was nearly at collapse. He hurried again to his son's bedside and watched a team of five doctors, a nurse and a technician tend to his son; at four o'clock that morning, Patrick Bouvier Kennedy's short life slipped away.

Against the glass wall of the oxygen chamber, Kennedy slammed his fist in anguish. "He put up quite a fight," the president said, remorsefully. "He was a beautiful baby."

Then Kennedy returned to the doctor's lounge and wept.

THE SACRAMENT of baptism for young Patrick was soon followed by his burial Mass. The service was held at Cardinal Cushing's residence, in a tiny, private chapel with just eighteen seats. Only the Kennedy family members were invited, Jackie's sister and mother and a small circle of family intimates. Jackie remained in the hospital, not to be released for another four days. Surprisingly, Frank Morrissey accompanied Cardinal Spellman, whose presence at the service was accepted as a gracious gesture to the grief-stricken family. Spellman knelt in the back. Wearing white vestments rather than the customary black for the requiem, Cushing sprinkled the baby's flower-filled coffin with holy water and began the Mass of the Angels. "As soon as they leave this world, You give everlasting life to all little children reborn in the font of baptism, and we believe You have given it today to the soul of this little child," Cushing prayed in his croaking voice. Kennedy could be seen weeping in the front row.

After the Mass, family members slowly exited in silence, broken only by muffled sobs on their way to the cemetery. The president, visibly upset, stayed inside the chapel until nearly everyone had left but the cardinal. Cushing watched as his friend stretched his arm across the white coffin and then placed inside it a gold St. Christopher's medal Jackie once gave him as a gift. Kennedy, wracked with tears, appeared as though he couldn't bear to leave his lost son.

"My dear Jack, let's go," Cushing finally urged him. "Let's go, nothing more can be done."

Cushing assured him that "God is good," though the pain of the moment surely blunted his ability to envision it. The cardinal had presided over the marriage of Jack and Jackie, and now he was being called to bury their baby. "At the end of the Mass, I read a prayer I wrote that I thought would be a source of consolation to the mother, for she had now lost three children," he later recalled. As they left the chapel, Cushing could not help weeping with his friend.

After the funeral, Kennedy returned to Squaw Island to care for Caroline and John while Jackie recuperated. The fragility of life, the strains on a marriage, and the sometimes brutal, inexplicable twists determined by a supposedly loving God were all exposed in this child's death. "The loss of Patrick affected the President and Jackie more deeply than anybody but their closest friends realized," Dave Powers recalled. Sorensen commented that the president "seemed even more broken than Jacqueline" by the infant's death. For several weeks, Jackie stayed away from the White House, deciding to accept her sister's arrangement of a Greek cruise aboard the giant yacht *Christina,* owned by shipping tycoon Aristotle Onassis. Though Jack disliked Onassis, he didn't stand in his wife's way. "Jackie has my blessing to go anywhere that will make her feel better," he explained. Jackie later told author Theodore H. White that, in their shared grief following the baby's death, she and Jack were never closer, realizing their love for each other and commitment to their family.

Throughout the fall, Kennedy's fatalistic apparitions persisted. When they chatted in October 1963, author Jim Bishop said Kennedy "seemed fascinated, in a melancholy way" about his book on Lincoln's assassination. He confided to a friend that he, too, preferred to die by gunshot. Friendly historians such as Arthur Schlesinger Jr. dressed up Kennedy's darker moments by saying the president was "possessed by a fatalism which drove him against the odds to meet his destiny," just as others ignored his philandering. Less charitable chroniclers noted that the cortisone shots Kennedy injected to combat his Addison's disease had invigorated his body, perhaps fueling his various trysts with women other than his wife. Kennedy's Irish Catholicism didn't hinder this behavior and may have been as much responsible for it as any part of his character. Let the Puritans and the ascetic priests be damned, his actions seemed to say, with all their dry restrictions. As Garry Wills observed about the Kennedys, "There was no hint of Jansenist views on sex." His Irish fatalism and illicit sex were two parts of the same psyche, far from the one that Americans ever saw. The urges of life and death seemed to consume him like some Celtic king of old who knew he was not long for this world. With his own ironic, bittersweet humor, Jack Kennedy understood how quickly everything fades, how life is gone in a flicker, as he witnessed with his own son.

Several weeks after Patrick was buried inside a family plot at Holyhood Cemetery in Brookline, the president returned to Boston for a Harvard football game. During the game he appeared lost in his own private thoughts. Near halftime, the president's gaze suddenly snapped to attention. He instructed his aides to bring him to the cemetery for an unannounced visit. "I want to go to Patrick's grave," he told them. At the gravesite, he looked at the stone face he had designed for his son, and the large "KENNEDY" inscribed in its granite. "He seems so alone here," Kennedy sighed.

SINCE HIS ELECTION to the American presidency, the city of Dallas's hatred for Kennedy remained thick and oppressive—just like the midday atmosphere of November 22, 1963, as Jackie Kennedy remembered it. ("Hot, wild. . . . The sun was so strong in our faces," she recalled of their open-air limousine ride from Love Field airport.) Throughout the 1960 campaign, Dallas was an epicenter of hate, the home of numerous anti-Catholic bigots where pastors preached on the radio against Kennedy and Roman Catholicism in general.

Three years of John Kennedy in the White House had transformed so much of American life, had altered the flow of some of its deepest undercurrents. The country's long-time nativist view toward Catholics, pervasive for most of the twentieth century, was beginning to dissipate. A Gallup poll taken in the early fall of 1963 showed that Kennedy's conduct in office had significantly reduced the old stereotypes and biases. The percentage of Americans who agreed they'd vote for a qualified Catholic running for president had moved up from 70 percent in 1960 to 84 percent. Only 13 percent of the national sample said they refused to vote for a Catholic under any circumstance, and most of these were older voters and living in the South.

Over time, Kennedy gained credit for living up to his promise on church and state. By the fall of 1963, JFK accepted an invitation to appear that December as the main speaker before a once largely hostile Protestant group, the General Assemblies of God. The Reverend Eugene Carson Blake of the United Presbyterian Church would later say the invitation "clearly symbolized the beginning of a new era of hope for Christian cooperation in the United States." Though Kennedy's tenure was short, Blake added, "it was long enough to make abundantly clear that those who had feared, for any reason, a Roman Catholic President had misunderstood both the man and his church." During this era, ecumenical actions between Protestants, Catholics and Jews emerged to support Kennedy's nuclear test ban treaty, discuss birth control in impoverished lands and combat racism in the South. Kennedy's tenure not only helped ease religious tensions but expanded the national dialogue to include immigrant and minority groups.

But his presidency didn't seem to do much to change things in Dallas. On the morning of his arrival in 1963, a full-page ad in the *Morning News,* paid for by H. L. Hunt and other right-wing businessmen who abhorred Kennedy's election, greeted the president with a frontal attack accusing him of all sorts of alleged misdeeds. "Why have you ordered . . . the Attorney General to go soft on Communism?" it screamed, in one of its more coherent charges. The ad was given a funereal black border, like a death announcement. Plastered around the city were placards with pictures of Kennedy and the slogan "Wanted for Treason." A *Morning News* sports columnist instructed Kennedy to make sure his speech in Dallas was about something other than politics, such as sailing. "If it is about Cuber, civil rights, taxes or Vietnam," the columnist lectured, "there will sure as shootin' be some who heave to and let go with a broadside of grape shot in the presidential rigging." When he saw the newspaper ad, Kennedy acted with revulsion and informed his wife, "We're really in 'nut country' now."

On the brief plane ride from an earlier stop in Fort Worth, Kennedy discussed the problem of political fanaticism in Dallas with the state's Democratic U.S. senator, Ralph Yarborough, a liberal Democrat like himself. Texas was expected to be a key state in his 1964 reelection effort, and there were many fences to mend in the state's Democratic Party. Rather than shy away, Kennedy hoped to bring the factions together. In Dallas, there seemed something in the air, the kinetic energy of impending violence that everyone in the presidential party seemed to sense, including his wife. "Jackie, if somebody wants to shoot me from a window with a rifle, nobody can stop it, so why worry about it?" he said to his wife before leaving that morning.

THE KENNEDYS were nearing their downtown destination, delighted by the long lines of friendly crowds along the motorcade route, when a cry rang out in the limousine. "Oh, no, no. . . . Oh my God, they have shot my husband!" Jackie screamed, as her husband clutched his throat and then, with another shot, his shattered head slumped toward her. Jack's blood and bits of brain matter rushed into her lap, smearing her elegant pink suit. For years to come, the kaleidoscope of Zapruder film images and conspiracy theories surrounding Kennedy's assassination would haunt America, as though some great truth might be revealed by its constant repetition. No one was ever sure why Kennedy was killed. The Warren Commission examining his death for an aggrieved nation concluded that Lee Harvey Oswald, with his own murky allegiance to communism, was a lone assassin—a contention thoroughly disputed for the next several decades. (The Warren report noted, in a small aside, that a Dallas police detective asked Lee Harvey Oswald whether some form of anti-Catholicism might be at play in his actions. Oswald denied any animus toward Catholics.)

In her own agony and grief, Jackie Kennedy made sure that concerns about her husband's eternal soul were addressed. At Parkland Memorial Hospital, a Catholic priest, the Reverend Oscar Huber, administered the last rites to the president, who was lying on an emergency table, his face covered with a white sheet. Father Huber had been eating lunch at a nearby parish, heard the news and rushed to the hospital. When he gained entrance into the emergency room, Huber anointed the president's body and began his prayers. Jackie stood beside her husband, sometimes kneeling on the bloody floor. She was dazed by all she'd witnessed, but joined in the prayers. The priest gave Kennedy conditional absolution in the belief that the president was sorry for his sins and was ready for death. "I see no reason why he wouldn't be of the mind that death would probably come every time he entered into a large room of people," Huber later explained. "In fact, it seems to me someone stated that he said, 'If they want to get you, they can get you no matter how many Secret Service men you might have surrounding you.' That would show he must have felt that death could come at anytime."

Over the next three days, the rituals, both sacred and secular, continued for the dead president, his family and a stunned nation. In Dallas, a group of fourth-grade children at a local public school reportedly clapped and cheered when their teacher told them of the assassination, but most adults were thunderstruck by the tragedy and sought out religious leaders to help them make sense of it. "In the name of God, what kind of city have we become?" asked the Reverend William Holmes, pastor of the city's Northaven Methodist Church, before a national television audience. In grim black-and-white images, television brought home Kennedy's death to millions watching around the world; there was a shared communal feeling of grief not felt in America since FDR's death. But this felt far worse. Kennedy's youth and robust appearance, the memories of him frolicking with his children and escorting his beautiful wife only made his death more agonizing for the country, as if someone they had barely gotten to know had been stolen away.

While the nation mourned publicly, the Kennedys dealt with the tragedy in their own private, distinctly Catholic ways. Hearing the news at the Peace Corps office, Eunice and Sargent Shriver both took to their knees, praying Hail Marys—a simple, almost childlike prayer that ends by beseeching Christ's mother to "pray for us, sinners, now and at the hour of our death, Amen." Then they headed to the White House to comfort other family members. In California, a priest, two nuns and other friends helped Patricia Lawford with her grief. In Hyannis Port, the last Kennedy to learn of the assassination was the man who made Jack's rise to the presidency possible, who had envisioned an Irish Catholic breaking such a cultural barrier long before his son had. Ted and Eunice flew up to tell their father, who had never recovered from his stroke and spent most of his time convalescing in his second-floor room. "Jack was in an accident, Daddy," Eunice cried. "Oh Daddy, Jack's dead. He's dead. But he's up in heaven. He's in heaven." Rose Kennedy had learned already in a telephone call from Bobby that Jack's wounds were fatal. Stoically, she went for a wistful walk along the cold beach with her nephew, Joe Gargan, telling him how they "must go on living," to be strong for others who needed them.

In these dark days, the most singular profile in courage—what Kennedy defined as grace under pressure—was his widow. As Air Force One carried JFK's body back to Washington, Jackie sat near his casket, still wearing her pink suit stained with her husband's blood. She witnessed Lyndon Johnson's impromptu swearing in aboard the plane. On the plane ride, Jackie reminisced with Dave Powers and Kenny O'Donnell, who had been with her husband so often when she was not. "How I envied you being in Ireland with him," she admitted, recalling how much Jack was moved by the drill performance at Arbour Hill in Dublin. Then turning to the business at hand, she added, "I must have the Irish cadets at his funeral."

On the night before the funeral, the Kennedys of Jack's generation and his dearest friends told stories spiked with laughter at the impromptu wake they held for him. "It's a very Irish thing," explained Jack's old friend, Chuck Spalding, who recalled Jackie's brave attempt to participate. "Jackie was a completely different type, but she understood the whole Irish thing and tried to be part of it." At one point, Teddy began to sing "When Irish Eyes Are Smiling," joined by much of the crowd, while Bobby wept in the hallway. The legendary Kennedy stoicism—the admonition to keep moving forward despite adversity and tragedies—was so much in keeping with the Irish relationship with death. Maybe an Irish wake, if not to revive the dead, could at least ease their pain by savoring the best times of John Kennedy's life. "Not being Irish, I tried to get into the swing of things, but I was thoroughly destroyed," recalled the president's brother-in-law, Peter Lawford. "But it really was the best way to handle it."

Once more, the Kennedys relied on their priests for advice. At the White House, on the night when she returned with her husband's body, Jackie Kennedy consulted Father Cavanaugh, the Kennedy family's old friend from Notre Dame, about the funeral service. "I wish you would make the Mass as fast as you can," she requested. Despite her overwhelming grief, Jacqueline Kennedy tried to oversee nearly every aspect of the public and private tributes as a final gift to her husband. Bobby asked Sargent Shriver to ensure that each of her requests happened as planned. Cardinal Cushing, sensitive to Jackie's wishes, presided over a Low Mass spoken aloud, rather than a High Mass with its chants and longer prayers, which would be more befitting for the occasion but take nearly twice as long. When the Apostolic Delegate, the Pope's representative in Washington, insisted on five absolutions at the end of the Mass, Cushing brushed aside the idea as too much of a "hassle" that would only further burden the Kennedy family. The hierarchy also wanted the Capitol's huge Romanesque Shrine of the

Immaculate Conception used for the Mass to the fallen president. But Cushing sided with Jackie's wishes for the smaller St. Matthew's Cathedral, where she had fond memories of attending Mass with her husband and children. "I don't care—they can all stand in the streets," Jackie said when Bobby tried to broach the issue. "I just know that's the right place for it." Cushing prevailed over one of the Kennedy family wishes. They had wanted the late president buried in Brookline, next to the body of his son Patrick. The cardinal dissuaded them, underlining that the Boston neighborhood cemetery was far too small for what would become a national shrine. Instead, Arlington National Cemetery was chosen, visible across the Potomac River from Washington.

On that terrible first night after arriving home from Dallas, Bobby tried to calm Jackie, his mother, Rose, Jackie's mother, Janet Auchincloss, and other distraught family members gathered upstairs at the White House. Though physically and emotionally drained, they could not bring themselves to sleep. Because of the lateness of the hour, Bobby gently urged them to get some rest. After everybody went off to their rooms, he still appeared tense but under control and lingered for a few minutes with Jack's old friend, Chuck Spalding, who suggested that he take a sleeping pill. When Spalding returned with one, Bobby appeared calm and under control and began talking. "It's such an awful shame," he said with fatigue, as if he'd had the stuffing knocked out. "The country was going so well. We really had it going."

Spalding listened, bid him goodnight and closed the door to Bobby's room. As he started to walk down the hall, Spalding could hear the attorney general cry out in pain. "He just gave way completely, and he was just racked with sobs and the only person he could address himself to was 'Why, God, why? What possible reason could there be in this?'" Spalding recalled. "I mean just the terrible injustice of it, the senselessness of it all hit him, and he just collapsed. . . . He sobbed by himself in the night and slept."

By Monday, November 25, three days after the assassination, a solemn pilgrimage of 220 world leaders—including France's Charles de Gaulle, Ethiopia's Haile Selassie and Ireland's Eamon De Valera—arrived for Kennedy's funeral, an expression of the worldwide grief for the dead president. Over the weekend, his body rested in state inside the Capitol's Rotunda, where thousands of mourners waited in line for hours to pay their last respects, a procession lasting throughout the night. For three days, the entire nation came to a halt, transfixed by images on television, each of the networks devoted exclusively to bearing witness to the president's funeral and the investigation of the assassination. The networks aired the running commentary of the Reverend Leonard Hurley, director of communications for the New York archdiocese, who explained each part of the president's funeral Mass, as if to share the religious experience with a polite but unfamiliar audience at home. Many newspapers, including the *New York Times,* also published a transcript of Hurley's comments. Aware of the symbolism of American history as well as the rituals of her church, Jackie asked Kennedy aides Arthur M. Schlesinger Jr. and Richard Goodwin to research the rites for Abraham Lincoln, with instructions to make her husband's funeral "as Lincolnesque as possible." She'd always found a sense of solace and strength in the Lincoln bedroom of the White House, and the similarities between the two assassinations resonated with her. (Apotheosizing presidents has a long history in America. Because Lincoln was killed on a Good Friday, symbolically the same day of Christ's death on a cross, many Americans in 1865 agreed with a minister that Easter Sunday who proclaimed, "Jesus Christ died for the world; Abraham Lincoln died for his country.") Jackie asked an artist friend to pull another book inside the White House library—she knew exactly where it was—about Lincoln's White House lying-in-state, and made sure everything was replicated down to the dark draping. At Arlington Cemetery, the president's widow stopped by to review her husband's gravesite. She asked that his remains be placed on a direct line between the flagpole at the Robert E. Lee mansion and the august Lincoln Memorial.

On the morning of the funeral, nine soldiers placed Kennedy's flag-draped coffin upon the same caisson that had carried FDR's body and, as with Lincoln's affair, the president's casket was led away by a caparisoned, riderless horse. The skittish chestnut-haired gelding, named Black Jack, carried a sword and a pair of shiny black boots, reversed in the stirrups, to signify the loss of its commander. In another act of symbolism, Jackie saw to it that the Irish military cadets performed their drills at his funeral; she also invited Mrs. Ryan's daughter, Mary Ann, to represent the Dunganstown Kennedys at the funeral.

As the caisson left the White House, several of Kennedy's favorites were played, including "Come Back to Erin" and "The Boys of Wexford." Another subtle reminder of the Kennedy family's history was a hymn played during the funeral procession called "The Cross and the Flag," written by the late Cardinal William O'Connell. The song was an Irish Catholic answer to the nativism of the 1920s, a proud and insistent statement that these immigrants and their children loved their country as much as any

American. So much of Honey Fitz's politics—and even his own father's career—seemed intent on proving the worthiness of Irish Catholics in the eyes of their fellow Americans, of removing the second-class status they felt in society. During Jack's youth, the newspapers reported, he'd probably sung its defiant verses, familiar to many Catholics in Massachusetts. His family's inclusion of Cardinal O'Connell's hymn with its martial air was an intriguing, almost provocative, selection to be played with his death:

> All o'er the land, the hearts of men are crying,
> Chilled by the storms of grief and strife.
> All o'ver the land, the rebellion's flag is flying,
> Threatening our altars—and the nation's life . . .

As mourners entered the cathedral, they received memorial cards composed by Jackie with the inscription: "Dear God—Please take care of your servant—John Fitzgerald Kennedy." In another personal touch, Jackie asked Luigi Vena to sing "Ave Maria" at the funeral Mass, just as Vena had sung the same sonorous hymn on their wedding day. Aware of her husband's own preferences in the church, she asked that Auxiliary Bishop Philip N. Hannan—"sort of a Jack in the church"—read five passages she'd selected from Scriptures along with an excerpt from his inaugural address, rather than Archbishop Patrick A. O'Boyle, the ranking churchman in Washington. *"There is an appointed time for everything . . . a time to be born, a time to die,"* Hannan read from the third chapter of Ecclesiastes, one of Jack's favorite Bible passages, *"a time to love, and a time to hate; a time of war, and a time of peace."*

During the Communion, several other priests assisted Cushing at the altar, including the Reverend John F. Fitzgerald, who left his Massachusetts parish to attend his cousin's funeral. The Kennedys first came to the altar rail, Jackie raising her black veil to receive the thin pale-white wafer representing the risen Christ. At the end of the Mass, Cushing walked toward the coffin placed in the heart of the church, circled three times while sprinkling holy water and intoned words of prayer in Latin. The day before, at a memorial Mass telecast by the Boston diocese, Cushing gave an emotional eulogy that, in almost Christ-like imagery, painted his friend as one who had been killed trying to help others. There was no formal eulogy at the president's funeral Mass, but in the final prayer at the end, Cushing suddenly broke out in his own impromptu prayer. "May God, dear Jack, lead you into Paradise," Cushing suddenly declared in English, his words coming directly from within. "May the martyrs receive you at your coming. May the spirit of God increase and mayest thou, for all who made the supreme sacrifice of dying for others, receive eternal rest in peace. Amen."

Then he slowly made his way toward the Kennedys and gave Caroline a kiss on the cheek. Fighting back tears, Jackie whispered, "Thanks for calling him dear Jack." She'd later give the cardinal, as a lasting memento, Jack's metal navy dog tags, inscribed with his name, his "Commander in Chief" title, his "O" blood type and his religion—"Roman Catholic."

Outside the church, Jackie and her two children stood with the rest of the Kennedy family on the cathedral steps while the presidential funeral procession began its trek to Arlington Cemetery. As the casket moved away, she leaned down to her young son and instructed, "John, you can salute Daddy now and say good-bye to him." Some of his father's friends had shown him how to salute like a soldier. And now, he made good use of it, leaving an indelible image in the minds of millions of a little boy bidding farewell to his father. This sad day happened to mark John Jr.'s third birthday, and later, not to disappoint him, the family held a small party for him. "It must have been the saddest 'Happy Birthday' ever sung," Powers remembered. "We all put on an act."

At the cemetery, Kennedy was laid to rest. The Irish Guards and a U.S. Marines detachment performed a military salute, and the presidential plane, Air Force One, flew overhead with a roar. Bagpipes wailed another Kennedy favorite, "The Mist Covered the Mountain," and then a bugler played taps. The stars and stripes draped over Kennedy's coffin was lifted, tightly folded into a triangle and presented to his widow. Unlike the honor guard at Kennedy's inaugural, this one included African-Americans, a quiet reminder of the changes Kennedy had brought about during his presidency. With television cameras parked at a respectful distance, the whole nation watched as Jackie and the president's two brothers, Bobby and Ted, took a taper and ignited a blue flame—"an eternal flame"—at his gravesite. Before leaving, Cushing embraced Rose Kennedy, the only equal to her daughter-in-law in dealing with tragedy with such grace. "Good-bye my dear," the cardinal whispered. "God be with you."

In the struggle to make sense of John Kennedy's death, the majesty of the Catholic requiem Mass—as well as a nation's secular rituals for honoring its most venerated dead—were combined in potent union. Quite deliberately, the Kennedys melded the rites of their Irish Catholic culture almost seamlessly into the traditions of the broader American society. The power of these rituals, from the martyr images to the allusions of Lincoln's funeral, were powerfully drawn by Jacqueline Kennedy, enough to touch the soul of a nation. "Mrs. John F. Kennedy and the White House staff who had served the President so well in life were determined that his spirit would be served in death," *Newsweek* observed. "She chose to make the ritual a consummate gesture of adoration—up to the ultimate touch (unprecedented in the U.S., except at the Gettysburg battlefield): the eternal light she lit at his grave."

Kennedy's loss was felt in a remarkably personal way by the public. After three years in Washington, many of the Kennedys were known on a first-name basis to Americans—not only Jack the president, but his brothers, Bobby and Teddy, his wife, Jackie, mother Rose, and children Caroline and John-John. Their private grief was transformed into a communal agony, beyond the constitutional replacement of one elected official with another. The Kennedys were treated like extended family members by every American deeply affected by the president's death.

To many minority citizens—those who believed Kennedy could make a significant improvement in American life—the assassination was a cutting blow. "His last speech on race relations was the most earnest, human and profound appeal for understanding and justice that any President has uttered since the first days of the Republic," expressed the Reverend Martin Luther King Jr. after Kennedy's death. "The unmistakable cause of the sincere grief expressed by so many millions was more than simple emotion. It revealed that President Kennedy had become a symbol of people's yearnings for justice, economic well-being and peace."

The Irish felt his loss most keenly. After attending the funeral, Eamon De Valera met briefly with Jacqueline Kennedy, paying his respects in the upstairs private chambers of the White House. Then he came down to the Cabinet Room, tears filling the old warrior's eyes. With poetic license, De Valera likened the killing of Kennedy in Dallas to another assassination in Irish history, the fall of a king-like leader who had resisted Cromwell centuries earlier. "He said, in Ireland, historians would compare the tragic death of John Kennedy to one of Ireland's own great liberators, Owen Roe O'Neill, and he quoted a poem that Thomas Davis wrote, something about a sheep without a shepherd, 'why did you leave us, why did you die?'" recalled Powers. "And he sobbed." In his grief, De Valera realized that any hope of seeing the reunification of his partitioned nation, at least in his lifetime, was now probably gone.

In Ireland, the entire nation collapsed into remorse at the news of Kennedy's death. "Ah, they cried the rain down that night," said a Fitzgerald relative to an American magazine journalist, who described how "the wakes lasted three days all over the country, with the mourners falling silent every time the television people showed scenes from the other three days in June." Kennedy's visit had raised hopes of a new future, and now his death reminded them once again of the past, of having so many Irish dreams dashed.

A similar sad refrain could be heard in the United States among Irish-Americans, particularly those who recognized Kennedy's fatalism in their own outlook. "I don't think there's any point in being Irish if you don't know that the world is going to break your heart eventually," said Daniel Patrick Moynihan, Kennedy's assistant secretary of labor, who had his own keen eye for the Irish experience in America. "I guess that we thought we had a little more time. . . . [Newspaper columnist] Mary McGrory said to me that we'll never laugh again. And I said, 'Heavens Mary. We'll laugh again. It's just that we'll never be young again.'"

Such romantic pathos, though, obscures the genuine significance of Kennedy's presidency. Because he was the first and only minority president, John Kennedy came to symbolize, regardless of his Brahmin erudition or Harvard pedigree, the long struggle for acceptance—not only for generations of Irish Catholic immigrants and their descendants but for all those considered estranged in American society. Only from a distance, viewing America with its hot-boiled brew of bigotry and violence from a continent away, could his achievement be appreciated fully. "John Fitzgerald Kennedy was a miracle," writer Frank O'Connor declared in the *Sunday Independent* of Dublin, two days after JFK's death. "In three different ways, he broke through age-old American prejudices against Catholics, against Irishmen and against intellectuals, and you have to have lived in America to realize how strong these prejudices are."

In life, President Kennedy managed to remain true to his promise of keeping a separation between church and state; and he changed the old stereotypes about big-city Irish politicians while still remaining true to himself and his own family background. He didn't preach or display much about his religion or his ethnicity, yet the difference between his cultural identity and that of the thirty-four presidents before him was repeatedly made clear for all those who took notice. At the very end, Kennedy broke one last barrier with the rites and rituals surrounding his death. On the day after the president's battered body was brought back to Washington, a Catholic Mass was said in his memory—as Sorensen noted, the first time a Catholic service was ever celebrated inside the White House. "To me, the least explicable religious objection encountered during the entire campaign was the fear that a Roman Catholic Mass might be held in the White House," Sorensen noted. "To those who expressed this worry, I can give assurance that it happened only once—on November 23, 1963."

It was fittingly symbolic. Kennedy's presence in the White House altered the nation for Catholics and non-Catholics alike. During the campaign, Kennedy "had for the first time more fully and explicitly than any other thinker of his faith defined the personal doctrine of a modern Catholic in a democratic society," as Theodore H. White put it. Because of Kennedy, Irish Catholics would no longer consider themselves outsiders again. For those millions of Americans who remained on the periphery of American society, his example remained a lasting inspiration. Even his critics sensed that Kennedy had opened doors for minorities that could no longer be shut again. "The Kennedy years saw great forces in America and in the world take on new impetus, new directions. We can still only dimly perceive the full import of these changes; it is all the harder, therefore, to estimate how accurately John F. Kennedy appraised them, to what extent he guided events and to what degree they governed him," eulogized the *New York Herald Tribune,* the eloquent but fading voice of New York Republicanism. "His attitudes during the campaign of 1960 and after assured that the tradition against a Catholic in the White House need never again trouble the conscience and the politics of the United States."

Forty years after his death, that achievement—a member of a minority group elected to the White House—has yet to be matched.

Part V

The Emerald Thread

"To whom much is given, much will be expected, and to whom more dignity is ascribed, more service will be exacted."

—ST. LUKE, 12:48

"Our mother taught us we should never forget where we came from."

—JEAN KENNEDY SMITH

Chapter Thirty-Three

A Living Wound

ON A MILD SPRING DAY in April 1964, Richard McSorley, a Jesuit theology teacher at Georgetown University, sauntered out to the tennis court on Bobby Kennedy's Hickory Hill estate, his new tennis partner, Jacqueline Kennedy, following close behind. As they neared the nets, three-year-old John Kennedy Jr., his unruly brown hair messed, ran up to them.

"Father, I cut my lip—*look*," the little boy insisted. He'd been playing in the backyard, near the slate patio and white garden furniture, and now he stuck out his bruised lip for inspection.

McSorley, a friendly middle-aged priest with grayish hair and a backhand respectable enough to become Georgetown's tennis coach, feigned great concern as he eyed John's wound.

"You must have kissed the ground," McSorley teased him.

Little John Kennedy gave a quizzical look. "Did I kiss the ground, Mommy?" he asked.

Jackie Kennedy, dressed in tennis whites and holding a racket, smiled at her son's innocent question. "Father is so nice to you," she replied, wistfully.

As the priest and the president's widow continued toward the tennis court, McSorley reminded Jackie that since the assassination, on the twenty-second of each month, inside a small chapel on the Georgetown campus, he offered a Mass for her husband's eternal soul. Jackie seemed surprised.

"Do you think that does any good?" she asked.

"Of course it does," the priest insisted. "It does him good and it does good for us."

Wracked by her own pain and doubts, Jackie's pace slowed to a halt, as if weighed down by her own disbelief. "I don't know how God could take him away," she sighed. "It's so hard to believe."

With these words, Jackie's dark expressive eyes filled with emotion and she began to cry, as McSorley later recorded in his personal diary. After providing such a brave front in public for her family and the nation, the long, lonely months since her husband's death had left Jacqueline Kennedy feeling isolated and deeply depressed.

"When I awoke this morning, I thought he was still there," Jackie explained to the priest, who would become her confessor and her confidant. "You know how it is before you know where you are when you wake up? I thought he was in the room with me. It's just so hard to believe."

IN THE WAKE of her husband's death, Jacqueline Kennedy's struggle to believe in anything, including herself, caused alarm among her family and friends. Six months after the assassination, she remained despondent, far more so than an admiring public realized. During the daytime, she tended her children and worked on the initial plans for a Kennedy presidential library; at night, though, like a lost soul, she often stayed up well past midnight, reading about her husband and sorting through his effects. "I am a living wound," she told one journalist friend. "Nearly every religion teaches there's an afterlife, and I cling to that hope."

During this difficult period, Jackie often relied on Bobby Kennedy for help and counsel, and his advice was characteristically sympathetic but stoic. "Sorrow is a form of self-pity," Bobby said. "We have to go on." Concerned with her mental health, Bobby decided his brother's grieving widow should see McSorley, one of the Kennedy family's favorite priests, for counseling under the guise of giving her tennis lessons. Catholics of their generation, regardless of their social strata, were far more inclined to seek out priests than psychiatrists to help with their problems. As McSorley recalls, there was even talk that the obsessions and loss of mental stability that afflicted Mary Todd Lincoln after her husband's assassination could hold the same fate for Kennedy's widow. "She was advised by Ethel and Bob to get out of the doldrums," McSorley remembered decades afterward. "She really struggled with the death of her husband. The newspapers were making remarks of how well she was getting along. She didn't need the tennis. She knew more than I showed her. It was an excuse not to mope around and get out of the house."

Father McSorley was a fixture in the Kennedys' lives. Often during their White House years, Bobby attended 7:30 A.M. Mass with McSorley at the

Georgetown chapel, sometimes assisting the priest as a server, before going off to work at the Justice Department. A Jesuit with his own liberal bent, McSorley sometimes talked about racism with Bobby. Each agreed the Catholic Church needed to do more to ease tensions and promote integration in the South. McSorley was different from the conservative Jesuits who, before Vatican II, had espoused defensive, often reactionary views. As a young priest in a Maryland parish, McSorley tried to end the segregated dispensing of Communion, where whites came up to the altar before blacks. During the civil rights movement, he drove a carload of Georgetown students to march with Martin Luther King in Selma and Montgomery, Alabama, and helped in voter registration drives in Mississippi. McSorley's students remember that he wore a protest sign asking, "Would you want your sister to marry Gov. Wallace?" Years later, during the Vietnam years, he joined in an antiwar protest in London with a recent Georgetown alumnus, Bill Clinton, who recognized McSorley and asked him to say a prayer at an interdenominational service. McSorley, a thin, nimble man with gentle eyes and smile, had seen the brutality of war up close. As a seminarian, he spent three years in a Japanese prison of war camp where he ate worms to keep from starving. *Washington Post* columnist Colman McCarthy, a friend of many years, later called McSorley "a priest of courage and one of the most loved professors at Georgetown in the past 30 years."

With the Kennedys, McSorley tended to the family's private needs. He understood the deeply engrained concept of family among Irish Catholics. McSorley himself grew up as one of fifteen children, several of whom became priests and nuns. In 1963, he sent Rose Kennedy a copy of his book about growing up in such a large clan, aptly titled, *The More the Merrier.* In a thank-you note, Rose wrote that she was particularly interested in a section called "Family Philosophy" and made a fleeting comparison to their families. "How blessed were your parents to have given so many sons and daughters to the Church," wrote Rose, "I always hoped that at least one of our children might have had a vocation for the religious life, but God had other designs." Rose signed her letter "your respectful child" as she, a Child of Mary, sometimes addressed clergy.

During 1963, McSorley came often to Hickory Hill to tutor Bobby and Ethel's oldest sons, Joseph II and Robert Kennedy Jr., whose school performances were lacking. Like most Catholic parents, Robert and Ethel Kennedy were deferential to clergymen such as McSorley; yet, at other times, they treated him as an unpaid servant in their employ. As a kind of reward, Ethel invited him once to the White House where he met the president. When Bobby Kennedy thanked him for his sons' tutorials,

McSorley—who believed strongly in the progressive politics of the New Frontier—replied that the favor was returned with all the good work Bobby did for the nation. Bobby knew that Father McSorley, who had been to his house so many times, could be trusted. The family secrets would be safe with him, especially the little-known cracks in the former first lady's shattered psyche.

When Jackie called to ask about tennis lessons, McSorley immediately grasped the subtext of her request. A beautiful young woman in her mid-thirties, Jackie desperately needed a lifeline, a place of solace she could find within her religion. She needed someone whom she could trust like a family member but was not part of the Kennedy clan—someone like Father McSorley, the teacher who could use his theological skills to help her sort out the inexplicable tragedies in her life. In the coming days, their talks on the tennis court became a dialogue about fate, God, belief in an afterlife—the essence of Catholicism. McSorley found their exchanges so remarkable that he kept a diary of their conversations, which he later preserved in the Georgetown University Library along with some of Jackie's letters.

"DO YOU THINK God would separate me from my husband if I killed myself?"

Jackie's question, lobbed over the net like one of her casual volleys, left McSorley dumbfounded. He just stared as the former first lady poured out her feelings.

"It is so hard to bear," Jackie exclaimed, in her little girl voice. "I feel as though I am going out of my mind at times. Wouldn't God understand that I just want to be with him?"

McSorley didn't realize the full depths of Jackie Kennedy's despair until their second tennis session together at Bobby's house. The previous afternoon, they had talked about the assassination and Jackie's regrets at not being able to save her husband with some last-minute heroics before the bullets struck him. "I would have been able to pull him down, or throw myself in front of him, or do something, if I had only known," she said, full of remorse. McSorley ended their initial round together by comparing Jack's death to Christ's death on the cross—a comparison that McSorley acknowledged was "almost blasphemous," but it seemed to please his widow.

The following day on the tennis court, Jackie showed an even greater sense of trust in McSorley. She eventually shared her thoughts about suicide.

"Do you think I will ever see him again?" she asked.

McSorley proceeded gingerly. The priest, well aware that for Catholics committing suicide meant God's eternal damnation, immediately turned to the canons of faith. "Yes, the resurrection of the body is part of our faith," he replied.

Jackie shook her head. "Oh, that's just one of those myths," she retorted. "It never really happened. Nobody ever really came back from the dead."

They slapped the tennis ball back and forth.

"Yes, Our Lord came back from the dead," McSorley maintained. "It's no myth—it's part of our faith."

"You mean it's part of our faith that the body will come alive again?" she asked, half incredulously, half longing that it was true.

McSorley explained that the Catholic Church viewed death as a separation of the body from the soul but that God would eventually bring them together again someday. He felt the Catholic beliefs in the transformation of the soul could give hope to a bereaved first lady, particularly the vision of being reunited someday with her dead husband. Yet the priest's explanations did little to ease the pain of the current moment.

"But it's so lonely," Jackie said after McSorley's explanation of Catholic doctrine. "I don't want to marry. I don't want to live with some of these old men friends some ten or fifteen years from now. It'll be so lonely when the children go away to school in about ten years."

McSorley gently chastised her for worrying about things so far into the future. It was too much of a burden. "It's the devil's work," as he called it, to concern herself with fifteen years of problems. "Today's problem is just to live through today, and to do the best you can today." After all, McSorley added, she might not even be alive in fifteen years.

Jackie, in her white tennis outfit, seemed intent on her decision.

"Will you pray that I die?" she asked.

By now, the tennis playing had stopped. Father McSorley looked Jackie in the eyes with total honesty. He felt compelled to dissuade her from thoughts of suicide, but he would not try to stop her from wishing for death itself.

"Yes, if you want that," McSorley said. "It's not wrong to pray to die."

Jackie, such a radiant presence in the White House, was now, in her brother-in-law's backyard, a picture of dejection and near hopelessness. She no longer felt adequate even as a mother to Caroline and John Jr. "The children would be better off here anyhow," she stated. "I'm no good to them. I'm so bleeding inside."

Jackie's pain was etched in her face and impossible to hide in her tender, widely spaced eyes. It was so overwhelming that others might have left her alone in her sorrow. But McSorley, having spent many hours in the busy, sometimes frenetic Hickory Hill homestead, knew that Jackie's suggestion was untenable. He argued against the logic of her plan. "They wouldn't be better off here," McSorley scolded. "Ethel Kennedy can't give the personal attention to the children—to her own children—she has so much pressure from public life and so many children. Nobody can do for them except you."

Their conversation wandered off onto a comparison of Jack with FDR, and how Eleanor Roosevelt had treated her husband during their White House years. McSorley emphasized the need for Jackie to keep on moving ahead, to get on with her life and to look forward to a day when she might be reunited with her husband in eternity. The Irish priest even suggested that someone might write a novel in which God brought President Kennedy back to life, and he wondered aloud what would happen if Jack walked into the White House.

"They'd never let him in the gate," Jackie interjected, sounding almost like Bobby.

"They wouldn't be able to keep him out," McSorley insisted. "I wonder what Johnson would say?" McSorley, ever a Kennedy partisan, was already appalled by Johnson's actions as president.

Jackie smiled, briefly.

OVER THE NEXT several weeks, McSorley met regularly on the hard court at Hickory Hill with Jackie. Sometimes, Ethel joined her sister-in-law as a doubles partner against McSorley, and together they made an earnest attempt at carefree moments. But most of the time, Jackie and the priest played alone, sharing a conversation over the netting so that Jackie could alleviate herself of the terrible pain inside. The loss of a baby and her husband in less than a year was more than she thought she could bear.

"Does God know everything?" she inquired one afternoon. "Why did He take my son Patrick if He knew my husband was going to die?"

In these moments, Jackie gave a glimpse of her anger and frustration, what writer Murray Kempton called "the rage at God" in her ordeal. "Rage moved Mrs. Kennedy to her grandest gestures—the refusal to change her suit with her husband's blood on it ('Let them see what they have done'), her insistence against all suggestions that she and the coffin make their exit at Andrews Field from the starboard side ('I want them to see what they have done!'),'' wrote Kempton.

More often than not, however, Jackie seemed curious with McSorley. She posed thoughtful questions about her Catholic faith rather than express some existential anger or estrangement from God. If there was a divine plan in this bloody mess, she was determined to try to understand it. When McSorley further explained the Catholic belief of general resurrection, of uniting the body with the soul for eternity, she wanted to know whether Jack would be the same age—forty-six—as when he had died. She wondered "how old will I be if I see him again" in heaven? She fretted over whether Jack had gone to Communion before he died, and whether the church considered him to be in a state of grace. "If he isn't in heaven or in the state of grace or whatever you call it," she vowed at one point, "then I would never go back inside a church." She ruminated aloud about getting married again. "Would it be looked on as adultery if I married someone else?" she asked McSorley, without mentioning names. "I don't really want to get married. It would be awful to be with someone else. But yet it's so lonely."

These exercises in apologetics were accompanied by McSorley's uplifting words, his urging her to focus on her children and live up to the hopeful ideals set forth in Jack's inaugural address. "It is not disloyal to look forward to grief being lessened by time," McSorley insisted. "Holding on to grief will not help the children, it will not help the friends of President Kennedy."

After several weeks, Jackie appeared better, as if she had turned a corner, only to fall further into an abyss of despondency and gloom. In May 1964, a few days before what would have been Jack's forty-seventh birthday, she again brought up the idea of killing herself. Jackie even suggested she'd be glad if her death, as she told McSorley, "set off a wave of suicides because she was glad to see people get out of their misery." The priest was startled to hear her say that "death is great" and talk about other suicides. "I was glad that Marilyn Monroe got out of her misery," she told the priest. "If God is going to make such a to-do about judging people because they take their own lives, than someone ought to punish Him." Jackie's adamancy left McSorley deeply disturbed, so much so that he worried throughout the night about what she might do next. "Yesterday she had me scared that she was really thinking of suicide," McSorley recorded in his notes.

The following afternoon, McSorley came prepared with an argument against suicide. In his best Jesuitical manner, he pointed to her previous day's contention that those who committed suicide were "off their head so they weren't responsible" for their actions in God's judgment. Perhaps so, he conceded, but the opposite might be equally true. "Suicide is taking one's own life, so let's compare it to a person who takes someone else's life for a moment—consider Oswald taking President Kennedy's life," he began, in an audacious comparison. "Are you willing to say that he was so completely off his head that he was innocent of doing anything wrong? Are you willing to say that he was not responsible for all the previous acts, the previous decisions he made that brought him to this state of mind where he might have been crazy enough to shoot the President? Well, a person who commits suicide may be off their head at the moment of it, but there is a long train of things leading up to it, and they're responsible for not doing something about those decisions."

Jackie had listened to enough. She interrupted McSorley's monologue with an assurance that she wasn't serious about committing suicide.

"I know I'll never do it," she conceded. "I know it's wrong. It's just a way out. It's so hard to think about facing every day, the many days ahead."

As she spoke, Jackie blamed herself for a litany of things. Caught in a fog of depression, she found getting up in the morning difficult; often an hour and a half would pass before she was fully awake and able to rise. None of the Kennedy fires burned in her, none of their Irish Catholic stoicism in confronting the world's harsh realities. She was not a fighter, certainly not in her current state. "I guess I'm lazy," she brooded. "I'm too lazy even to play tennis. I just can't get excited about it. I don't have any competitive spirit. I can't be like Bob and Ethel, trying to win. . . . I just don't want to exert myself." She didn't possess the Kennedy clannishness, their outward-looking spirit and ability to find redemption in numbers. "I'm not the kind of person that can work with children or with the poor or with a crowd," she explained. She preferred to be by herself. "That's why I like horseback riding and the solo sports," she said simply. "I always like to be alone."

Her rambling self-recriminations extended to what she admitted were her own failures in her marriage to Jack. According to McSorley's notes, she consistently blamed herself for their problems together, never hinting at her husband's constant absences, the rumors of adultery or the obsessive commitment to politics and public life. Unlike her husband, she confessed that she wasn't a very diligent Catholic, either. "He never complained about me not getting up and going to Mass, but he always went," she recalled. "I could have gone and made things so much better for him." Their last few months together left her with so many regrets. "I was melancholy after the death of our baby and I stayed away last fall longer than I needed to," she explained. "And then when I came back he was trying to get me out of my grief and maybe I was a bit snappish; but I could have made his life so much happier, especially for the last few weeks. I could have tried harder to get over my melancholy."

After several tumultuous years together, she and Jack finally arrived at a mutual understanding, a greater love for each other. Whatever thoughts there may have been about divorce were forbidden by the church, which taught that the bonds of marriage lasted forever. Jackie made so many sacrifices for her husband's career and desires that his sudden loss left an awful void in her existence. "I had worked so hard at the marriage," she explained. "I had made an effort and succeeded and he had really come to love me and to congratulate me on what I did for him. And, then, just when we had it all settled, I had the rug pulled out from under me without any power to do anything about it."

These matters were all discussed while McSorley and his partner battered tennis balls around the court, emptying one bucket after another. Before their several sessions ended that spring, the priest prepared a list of questions for her to contemplate, to help her overcome her grief. Jackie assured him that she would think about each one. After an hour's session on the court, they were usually interrupted when John Jr. sought his mother's attention, or when the normal exuberance of life overflowing on the Hickory Hill estate, filled with Kennedy nieces and nephews, encroached upon them. As they packed up, readying to leave, the former first lady thanked McSorley and often left him with a lingering thought or two.

"If I only had a minute to say good-bye," Jackie sighed after one session, thinking aloud about her lost husband. "It was so hard not to say good-bye, not to be *able* to say good-bye. But I guess he knew that I loved him."

By summer 1964, Jackie decided that she could no longer stay in Washington. The elegant house she rented from family friend Averell Harriman immediately after the assassination had become like a prison. Hordes of passersby, some well-meaning and others morbidly curious, had turned her home into a tourist attraction, a roadside freak show, forcing her to keep all the shades drawn to maintain her privacy. Washington had become too painful, filled with people and places that reminded her of Jack. She needed a new beginning, just as she had discussed with Father McSorley. She decided to move to New York City and stay temporarily at the Carlyle Hotel on Manhattan's Upper East Side. Before she left town in July 1964, Jackie wrote to McSorley and told him that she'd never forget all his kindness and compassion. "A priest gives so much to other people, and sometimes you must wonder if you do truly help them," her letter stated. "Well, I just want to tell you that you did to me when I needed it the most. To be able to come out to Ethel's to make an attempt at getting strong again—to bring John and Caroline and see how much you meant to them—and then to talk to you, helped me through an awful time."

Her correspondence with the priest continued through the summer; on light blue stationary she dashed off heartfelt letters in her distinctive hand-writing, her sentences punctuated with her customary dash marks. "You are right," she wrote in July, "it is so much the best thing for all of us to move to New York—Just the effort of adapting to a new place and creating new lives for my children there—will be good for me and stop brooding—But we will miss you so much—especially John and I." She urged McSorley to come to Manhattan for a visit; he could stay either at her apartment or per-haps at the rectory near Caroline's new school, the Sacred Heart Convent on 91st Street, run by the same order of nuns who taught and trained three generations of Kennedy women. Toward the end of this note, Jackie addressed her frame of mind. She assured McSorley that she was following his advice.

"I am trying to make all the efforts you said I should make—It doesn't get one bit easier—If you want to know what my religious convictions are now—they are = [sic] to keep busy and to keep healthy—so that you can do all you should for your children—and to get to bed very early at night so that you don't have time to think," she wrote. Jackie had no intention of misleading her priest-confessor and sympathetic tennis partner by denying the hurt and pain she still harbored. "You wrote me that list of things to think about—'Do I feel guilty about getting over my grief?'—Well, I wish I had that problem, because I know now I won't ever get over it—but I am getting better at hiding it from my children—I am able to do more things with them now," she ended.

After Labor Day, McSorley wrote back to Jackie, applauding her inten-tions of keeping busy and healthy with her children. Her efforts at getting better, he suggested, were "certainly what God wants you to do." McSorley urged her not to give up her tennis exercise which, he wrote, seemed "a successful part of your struggle to fight your way through sorrow." McSorley's advice, deeply rooted as it was in the Catholic theological view of transformation, was given in the hope that with enough love and for-giveness she could convert her grief into a transcendent commitment to help others. As he explained in the letter:

"I agree that you will never get over it in the sense that the grief will disappear. But you may be able to transform your grief into a source of energy which will be beneficial to you, your children, and to many others. Transformation does not mean that grief will disappear but that it can have new and even beneficial aspects in it that you did not see at first. This has happened with human grief before and it can happen with you."

EARLIER THAT SUMMER, McSorley bestowed similar advice on Bobby Kennedy, very much a victim himself of the same spiritual agonies that Jackie was suffering. Though he felt protective of his sister-in-law, Bobby nursed his own wounds, coped with his own vulnerabilities after his brother's death. Immediately after the assassination, Bobby seemed determined to appear strong, to keep others from the same deep anguish he undoubtedly masked. "Cheer up, Cheer UP," he repeatedly told his young associates at the Justice Department, though no one believed him. The Georgetown priest recognized Bobby's pain through his tough demeanor. McSorley knew how much he missed Jack, and his letter addressed the overwhelming grief felt by Bobby. "I look at you as his twin spirit," wrote the priest. "Your grief goes as deep as your love. But that is only half the picture. Because you were close to him, you received the impact of his rare personality more fully than others. Yours was the inspiration of constant, daily, personal contact. God knew that you would need this as a counter-balance against your grief. The very weight of grief is a measure of the treasure which God gave to you in the close friendship of a brother gifted with so many rare qualities."

Father McSorley urged Bobby, then considering a run for the U.S. Senate from New York, to remain in public life as a tribute to his fallen brother. The priest was well aware of the thousands of young people— many of them Catholics he knew at Georgetown—whose idealism was inspired by President Kennedy, who came of age imbibing his lofty words of public commitment. McSorley didn't want to see that spirit die. Instead of wondering whether Bobby should tend to the private needs of his family after such a crisis—a problem that McSorley was well aware of—he urged him to assume an even greater public role. He quoted JFK's inaugural address and suggested that Bobby carry out its mission. "When he [Jack] said, 'In your hands, my fellow citizens, more than in mine, will rest the final success or failure of our course,' the words have special significance for you," McSorley implored. "No one is in a better position to lead those whose hearts have caught fire from his flame than you." In his pastoral pep talks with both Jackie and Bobby, McSorley reminded them that Jack would not want them to languish in grief over his passing. Appealing to Bobby's strong Catholicism, McSorley cast this duty to his brother's memory in distinctly religious terms. "Just as the believers in Christ looked to

His close companions for leadership in making those beatitudes known to the world, so the world that believes in President Kennedy's ideals looks to you, as his brother and chief associate in public life, to help us understand and put into practice the ideals contained in that address."

In McSorley's view, Bobby needed to transform his grief into action. How much the attorney general listened and put into the practice the old priest's advice is uncertain. But there is no doubt of the gift of comfort and confession he provided to Jackie Kennedy at an excruciating time in her life. That fall in New York, she and her children were delighted when McSorley came to visit again.

As he entered Jackie's apartment, Father McSorley was greeted by John Jr., who almost immediately asked the priest to take him to the recently opened World's Fair. His sister, Caroline, had left already for class at the nearby Sacred Heart school. Jackie came into the living room dressed in black, and provided a list of places that she thought might interest little John. She was anxious for her son to have some male role models in his life now that Jack was gone. As had often happened at Hickory Hill, McSorley acted as a surrogate guardian for the day, escorted in this case by two Secret Service agents.

McSorley departed with little Kennedy, off to the fair in the outlying borough of Queens. At lunch and while taking in the various attractions, John made sure to address the priest always as "Father McSorley." He thoroughly enjoyed their adventure together. All the newspapers the next day carried stories about their escapades. In photos, a smiling, mop-topped little John Kennedy held McSorley's hand while playing with a toy. McSorley was pictured in his black priestly suit and white Roman collar, a slight, gentle grin on the handsome Jesuit's face. During his short stay in New York, McSorley also went with John to the Central Park playground to look at the animals. When they returned late that day, Jackie asked the priest to say a few prayers with her son. They both knelt beside his bed. McSorley watched the little boy bless himself correctly before saying a prayer for his father, mother and other family members. Jackie came inside the room as they finished. She lifted up John and tucked him into bed.

"Maybe Father will sing you a song," Jackie told her son, while she looked at McSorley. "His daddy used to sing him 'Danny Boy.' Could you sing that, Father?"

McSorley did his Irish best with the song, though he forgot the words to a few verses. He knew the familiar melody well enough, however, to touch some of the former first lady's emotions. "As I sang through it, John listened with complete attention and Mrs. Kennedy's eyes filled with tears," McSorley recalled in his diary. Tenderly, Jackie kissed her son on the forehead and said good-night. But the little boy wasn't ready, and insisted that his mother also sing him a song.

"Well, I don't have a very good voice John," Jackie explained. "What do you want me to sing?"

"'America the Beautiful,'" the little boy replied.

McSorley watched as the former first lady sang for her son; he noticed that Caroline was standing in the bedroom's doorway, seemingly amazed at the sight.

"America, America, God shed his grace on thee / And crown thy good with brotherhood / From sea to shining sea," Jackie sang as best she could. McSorley smiled and would never forget the sadness and poignancy of this family trying to mend.

AFTER THE CHRISTMAS holiday, McSorley returned to New York in January 1965 and visited Jackie and her children at their new apartment on Fifth Avenue. It was agreed that McSorley would take John to the New York City Museum on 103rd Street. Then Jackie asked her priest friend for a particularly difficult favor. Jackie's face was somber. It was a request involving her four-year-old son, something that she could probably ask only of Father McSorley.

"Maybe, sometime, you will get the chance to answer the question that comes to John—'Why did they kill him?'" Jackie suggested.

McSorley stared and just listened without reply. He could see Jackie's eyes filling with tears as she offered a further explanation. "This question comes from television or hearing about it," she explained. "I don't know what to say. I don't know what's a good answer and I feel inadequate about saying anything." Her futility and grief rose to the surface together, overwhelming her. She began to weep. McSorley waited in silence, patiently, until Jackie composed herself. "Just a word of explanation," she added, "and then moving on to some other subject will be enough."

The opportunity for such a discussion soon presented itself. As they traveled through Manhattan with their Secret Service escort, McSorley and the little boy passed Grant's Tomb, prompting John's curiosity.

"Who lives it?" he asked.

"Grant" came the reply.

"Can we visit him?" John asked.

"No, because only his body is there. His spirit went to meet God."

"Does everybody here go to meet God when they die?"

"No," said the priest, "only those who are good meet God." He didn't use the word "hell" but explained to John that people who are bad are in pain after they die, sort of like stubbing his toe.

John seemed satisfied with the exchange for a few minutes, and McSorley went on to talk about the virtues of Ulysses Grant.

"Did General Grant see Daddy?" the little boy interrupted.

McSorley said he didn't know.

"If we visit Daddy's grave, can we see him?" John persisted.

"No, only his body is there and his body has turned to dust," McSorley explained. He proceeded to answer further questions about where God could be found, and all the people with Him. What adult Catholics believed as a matter of faith—that the body and spirit would someday be united by God in a general resurrection—was far beyond the little boy's comprehension. At one point, he asked innocently, "How can you go to the bathroom if you don't have a body?"

McSorley realized that Jackie, too, was puzzled by the church's belief in resurrection. When McSorley recounted his conversations with her son, she asked some more specifics—wondering if the body would shrink back to its youthfulness when reunited with the soul. As any loving widow would, Jackie seemed to hope beyond measure that someday she might see her husband again. McSorley admitted his own shortcomings in providing a definitive theological answer. "All these thoughts are speculative and seem quite out of place in the context of grief and tragedy in which the Kennedys talk about the question," McSorley later explained. A simpler effort to stay connected with the spirit of Jack Kennedy could be found in the children's bedrooms, in the photographs on their walls. Images of them playing with their father—out on the White House lawn bending over to pick up John, with Caroline seated on her daddy's lap—were captured and framed in these pictures, some bearing their father's inscriptions to them. "By these family pictures right above their beds," McSorley observed, "it is clear that their mother wants the children to understand something about their father."

JACKIE'S EFFORTS for her children to understand more about their father extended to Ireland as well. She found that her husband's joyous Irish trip, shortly before his death, was remembered again and again by his friends and associates in her conversations with them. As Jack had wanted, she renamed their "Atoka" country home near the Blue Ridge Mountains in western Virginia, the place of many pleasant family memories, and instead called it

"Wexford," to commemorate the county where the Kennedys had origi-
nated and honor the place where her husband found such delight. She kept
many gifts and mementos of Jack's trip to Ireland inside Wexford's airy cabins. Outside on the grounds, the pony that Sean Lemass, the Irish prime
minister, had given to little John was stabled there. Jackie was far too sophisticated to revel in ethnic customs during her White House years, certainly
not the sentimental warbling of Irish songs enjoyed in private by some
Kennedys, including her husband. But in her grief and suffering, Jackie
seemed better to understand the Irish side of her lost husband's nature.
Echoing a favorite line of poetry from Yeats, she wrote that "I should have
known that it was asking too much to dream that I might have grown old
with him."

In preparing selections of her husband's favorite readings for a ceremonial opening of the Kennedy library, she made sure to include the Irish
poets among selections from Shakespeare, American history and the Greeks.
"President Kennedy was of Irish heritage and Irish poetry was close to his
heart," Jackie wrote as an aside to these offerings. "Not the sentimental
verse people often think of as Irish, but the poetry of their struggle for freedom, full of bitterness and despair." She recalled how her husband, long
before his election to the presidency, had quoted lines from the Thomas
Davis poem about Irish patriot Owen Roe O'Neill, especially the last two
lines about sheep without a shepherd. "Now, that is the way we all feel
about him," Jackie added. In her own attempts to use imagery and poetry
to fashion a lasting memorial to her husband's memory, she wrote her own
verse about Jack that underlined his roots.

> *Jack Kennedy heard the wind in the skies*
> *And the look of eagles was in his eyes.*
> *He could call New England his place and his creed*
> *But part he was of alien breed*
> *Of a breed that had laughed on Irish hills*
> *And heard the voices in Irish rills*
> *The lilt of that green land danced in his blood*
> *Tara, Killarney, a magical flood*
> *Surged in the depths of his too proud heart*
> *And spiked the punch of New England so tart.*

Eventually, Jackie determined that she must go to Ireland with her children to retrace many of the steps taken by President Kennedy. They left in
the summer of 1967 and spent several weeks on holiday, staying mostly at a

rented twenty-room mansion near Waterford, a bit west of County Wexford. One night with friends, she dropped in at an Irish pub in a tiny fishing village about four miles away. The startled fishermen sang "The Boys of Wexford" for her, and she requested that they sing "Danny Boy" as well. She began most mornings riding on horseback, her long black hair flowing in the breezes, or walking alone on the rocky beaches. Because the widowed first lady's visit initially drew a rush of press attention, she waited for things to settle down before visiting the Kennedy Homestead in Dunganstown. In a note to her husband's relative, Jackie attempted to arrange a convenient time for all. "Dear Mrs. Ryan—At last we really are in Ireland—and the children and I are looking forward so much to coming over to see you and to meeting all our cousins," she wrote. "I would have asked to come much sooner but there have been so many newspapermen and television cameras around—I did not want them all to follow us and spoil a happy family meeting. The children have been looking forward to Dunganstown for such a long time—they both have pictures of your house in their room at home—and I thought for little children, all the impressions at seeing the place their family came from, might be ruined if we were surrounded by photographers."

None of the hoopla, none of the crowds that marked her husband's visit followed Jackie's quiet, unassuming arrival in a rented car with her two children. The old Kennedy Homestead, stretched across the hillside and its cows and chickens and horses milling about in the fields, evoked the raw and simple quietude of rural life. The stone buildings and artifacts of another time, such as the coopering tools and wooden barrels in the barn, were reminders of what the farm must have looked like more than a hundred years earlier, before Patrick Kennedy left for America. Though they had never met, Mrs. Ryan embraced Jackie like a long-lost relative. "It was an easier visit because there weren't any crowds," recalled her daughter, Mary Ann Ryan, in 2001. "It was all family. We had tea and she walked around the garden and the yard. The children played around the yard and found a pair of kittens and wanted to take them home."

Nevertheless, there was a sense of melancholy about Jackie Kennedy's trip, nearly four years after her husband's assassination. In her chats with these Kennedy cousins, she recalled her husband's enthusiasm for Ireland, the tremendous response he received from its people and the small but grand discoveries from the 1963 trip. "She talked a lot about his [JFK's] visit and she wanted to go over everything again," remembered Mary Ann. "She seemed to know more about that visit than we did, because he had told her so much about it. She said she wanted her kids to get the sense of farm life, to absorb the atmosphere." It was agreed that while Jackie took care of some business in Waterford, Caroline and John would be allowed to return the next day to the Kennedy Homestead simply to play and frolic on this ancestral land, still very much a working farm. Mrs. Ryan's other daughter, Josie, by then married and living on the farm with her own family, tended to the two Kennedy cousins from the United States. "They played with the baby pigs and she [Josie] had to wash them up before they left," recalls Mary Ann. "She didn't treat them any differently." Jumping around in the high grass of the farm, John swore there was electricity in the sting of the net-tles from the underbrush. Everyone had a good laugh at the little boy's expense. He was a living reminder of the delight that his father brought them during his own visit. Jackie's appreciativeness and regard toward these Irish cousins only served to underline the intrinsic sadness surrounding her visit. Mrs. Ryan was deeply touched by the widowed first lady. "My mother loved her," recalls Mary Ann. "She really hit the spot in everyone's heart."

The trip to Ireland was all part of the healing process for Jackie, a woman who a few years before had described herself as a living wound. In the dark-est moments after her husband's death, she found that the church's sacra-ments and the Kennedy family's sense of Irish Catholic identity could be of comfort to her, perhaps more than she ever realized while Jack was alive. Though Father McSorley didn't have all the answers to eternity, he did lend a kindly ear within the trust of the confessional in allowing a very private person to sort out her problems. More so, the poetry and prayers—such as the sad laments for brave men killed in their prime—gave a poignant voice to her grief and became part of the legacy left to her children. The Kennedy children were acutely aware of their father's absence. They mentioned him in holiday cards written to their grandmother Rose and other relatives, and his memory was sometimes reflected in their school work and small per-sonal decisions. As a student enrolled with the same order of nuns that had taught her grandmother, Caroline chose the confirmation name of Joan, after seeing a portrait of Joan of Arc, the valiant French girl burned at the stake and eventually canonized. "I took her name in confirmation because she was killed like my father," Caroline explained.

These icons of faith, these rituals of belief seemed to bolster Jackie Kennedy's courage when she most needed it, such as on the rainy day in March 1967, shortly before her trip to Ireland, when she again went to Arlington National Cemetery. There in prayerful silence, she witnessed her husband's body being reinterred with the tiny bodies of Patrick Kennedy and her previously stillborn daughter. Both their remains had been trans-ferred from Holyhood Cemetery in Brookline. Cardinal Cushing flew down from Boston to oversee the short, private service at the gravesite. In the drizzle, Cushing watched Bobby staring into the open grave at his brother's coffin, and the cardinal felt sure that Bobby "relived every moment of his past life, the tragedy of the assassination and the years since." During the brief prayers, Jackie stood in the downpour, somberly and with great composure, just as she had acted with so much silent dignity at Jack's funeral. Only a few knew how much she truly suffered.

Watching Jackie and the rest of the Kennedys slowly walk back to their cars from the graves, Cushing later described the scene as one of the saddest moments of his life. As he admitted, "I don't know how they can stand it."

The Awful Grace of God

In the mirror, Robert Kennedy practiced, time and again, until he felt confident he could recite the poem without crying. He didn't want to be seen as weak or maudlin in public. As his father had always told him, Kennedys don't cry. Yet each time he read from Thomas Davis's poem about Owen Roe O'Neill, he couldn't help but lose his composure. The lines that cried, "Oh! why did you leave us, Owen? Why did you die?" were like a stab to the heart. This same verse stuck in the mind of writer William Manchester, who once confided to Bobby, while relaxing at poolside, how often he had thought of the poem since Dallas. Bobby gave "one of his upward, swift looks," Manchester remembered, "said he had the same problem, and quickly changed the subject."

For his first public speech since his brother's death, Kennedy accepted the invitation of the Friendly Sons of Ireland in Scranton, Pennsylvania, to be their featured speaker at the annual St. Patrick's Day celebration. An early version of his speech, resembling the same talks Jack had dispensed on past St. Patrick's Days, included the sad poem about Owen Roe O'Neill. But these lines were edited out of the final draft given to Bobby for his approval. When Kennedy spotted the cut, he turned to Ed Guthman, his press aide. "Why did you do that?" he demanded.

"You'll never get through it," Guthman replied. "You don't have to put yourself through that."

The omission seemed merciful. Caught in his own remorse and painful memories, Bobby still wasn't sure that he wanted to stay in public life. He was not only the father of a large brood, but his father's stroke and his brother's assassination mandated that Bobby effectively become the head of the Kennedy clan; with those responsibilities, he had taken on the great duty of helping Jackie and her two children recover from their tragedy. Bobby wore these burdens visibly. His face no longer had the shiny, youthful tone of his early years in Washington but was now weathered and puffy with lines of fatigue around his blue eyes.

"I've been practicing," he said of the poem. Though he appreciated Guthman's kindness, he couldn't relieve himself of this self-imposed duty. "I can't get through it yet . . . but I will."

Bobby Kennedy would need every ounce of will to get through this St. Patrick's Day 1964. In the brilliant daylight of a chilly morning, he escorted Jackie to Arlington National Cemetery, where she pulled a sprig of shamrock from her coat's pocket and placed it on Jack's grave. Jackie was dressed in black and her mood was even darker. She stared down at the ground intently where Jack's body was buried, lost in her own thoughts. Next to them Thomas Kiernan, the Irish ambassador to the United States, whose joyous White House visit for St. Patrick's Day 1963 was relished by President Kennedy, knelt down and planted a cross of shamrock and a green clump of sod from Ireland.

Afterward, Bobby went with journalist Mary McGrory to Jackie's temporary residence, where McGrory remembered an "excruciating" conversation took place, two Kennedy spirits crushed by gloom. As they left, McGrory tried to assure Bobby that things in his own life would soon get better. Instead, he sobbed.

DESPITE SOME misgivings, Kennedy flew that afternoon to Scranton-Wilkes-Barre Airport, where a crowd of two thousand well-wishers greeted him. Most were young people who jumped through the police lines to sneak a peek and perhaps touch him—the living Kennedy who most reminded them of his brother. Yet there was some cause to wonder whether President Kennedy's legacy was still alive.

That same evening in New York, Lyndon Johnson, who considered himself Kennedy's political inheritor as well as his successor, addressed a wealthy, influential and conservative crowd of Irish-Americans at the Waldorf-Astoria. The new chief executive rattled off the names of half a dozen persons of Irish descent who had served Kennedy and who were still in his administration. With his huge grin, Johnson declared himself "an Irishman by osmosis." In Massachusetts, more ominous repudiations of Kennedy's legacy were on display. During the St. Patrick Day parade in South Boston, the city's schism between whites and blacks erupted in racist violence. A float sponsored by the NAACP was bombarded with beer bot-tles, rocks, cherry bombs and garbage. The float bore a large-sized picture of President Kennedy and a sign urging the crowd to remember: *"From the fight for Irish freedom, we must fight for American equality."* Walking in the same parade, about ten minutes ahead of the float, Ted Kennedy was unaware of the crowd's response, which quickly became ugly. At some points in the parade, men leapt into the street to shout, "Nigger go home."

Miles away, and increasingly distant from the center of power in the White House, Bobby Kennedy sloshed through the snow in Scranton. He stopped at a ground-breaking ceremony for a new elementary school named for his brother. He shook hands with hundreds of ordinary folk, who stood with umbrellas in the downpour. Irish immigrants first came to Lackawanna County in the mid-1800s, mostly to work in the coal mines, and their children wound up slowly rising to prominence in politics, local business, law, medicine and religion. Seeing Robert Kennedy reminded them a little bit of their own heritage. The overwhelmingly emotional response from the crowds, as Guthman later wrote, helped convince Bobby to remain in public life.

At the Hotel Casey, before the Friendly Sons, Bobby gave a rousing tour of Irish history that would have done Honey Fitz proud. He reminded them of the British indifference to the Great Famine and its haunting epi-taph in the words of Joyce. "As the first of the racial minorities, our forefa-thers were subject to every discrimination found wherever discrimination is known," Kennedy declared. "The Irish have survived persecution in their own land and discrimination in ours." He recalled President Kennedy's trip the previous summer to Ireland and likened the Irish struggle for basic lib-erties during the time of the penal laws to the struggles for civil rights by African-Americans in modern-day America. The Irish were an inspiration in the fight against the "tyranny of communism" in Vietnam. The entire speech, like its presenter, was still very much beholden to John Kennedy's memory.

"I like to think—as did President Kennedy—that the emerald thread runs in the cloth we weave today, that these policies in which he believed so strongly and which President Johnson is advancing, are the current flow-ering of the Irish tradition," Bobby declared. "And I like to think that these policies will survive and continue as the cause of Irish freedom survived the death of . . . Owen Roe O'Neill." With this introduction, Bobby Kennedy began to read the closing lines of the poem. The audience in the grand ball-room watched as this man vilified as ruthless, a tough Irish mick like his father nearly melted into tears. Among this generation of Irish-Americans, the loss of their young president was every bit as rueful as the fallen hero in the old poem.

As he promised, Bobby made it through the poem—"just barely," as Guthman wrote years later. "Among the stalwart sons of Erin in the audience," said Guthman, "many a man wept openly." That night with the Friendly Sons of Ireland marked "a turning point" for Bobby Kennedy, a night that rekindled those intense, inner fires that had seemed extinguished with his brother's death.

THE SIZEABLE BROOD of Robert and Ethel Kennedy assembled for breakfast at Hickory Hill on a sad quiet morning soon after the president's killing. At the family table, the Kennedy children were sometimes quizzed at dinner by their parents about current events, just as Rose Kennedy conducted examinations at meals when her children were growing up. But on this moribund morning, Bobby decided that a different conversation was in order. "At this breakfast, not long after my uncle's death, my father had the discipline to tell the older children to write down the significance of Jack's death to the United States," recalled his sixth son, Michael Kennedy, years later. "I remember that incident very, very well. I remember thinking, 'Oh, I'm glad I don't have to do that yet.'"

Bobby's request to his children underlined his own search for answers to find any meaning in his brother's senseless death. His struggle took on many forms, from the silent to the frenetic. "Anyone who has gone to the President's grave at Arlington with Robert Kennedy—although never a word is spoken—gets the sense that he feels that something great was broken here, and that as his brother's brother he has an obligation to continue it," said one of his advisers, William vanden Heuval. After the funeral, Bobby retreated to Florida, where he played a vicious game of touch football with other grieving Kennedy aides. But action could only fill part of the void. "People were smashing into each other to try and forget that John Kennedy was dead," recalled Pierre Salinger, "and Bobby was one of the toughest guys in the game."

The most obvious target of Robert Kennedy's wrath in this world was the man who took his brother's place, Lyndon Johnson. After the Scranton speech and other public appearances, political talk obsessed on whether Johnson might ask Bobby to be his vice-presidential running mate in 1964. The idea appealed briefly to Kennedy as a way to ensure that Jack's promises were fulfilled. But Johnson quickly scratched that plan for more than ample reason. In the past, there were many disagreements between the two, often petty and egotistical, accompanied with the sparks that fly when opposites clash. Although hagiographers embellish Bobby's finer nature as he matured, his relationship with Johnson reminds us of his raw, competitive, sometimes vindictive side. This aspect of his personality—the side that Jack Newfield described as "too Catholic, too physical, too combative"— repelled liberals; it had even nearly landed him in a fistfight with lawyer Roy Cohn during their days as aides to Joe McCarthy. This hard-edged side forced even colleagues such as Adam Walinsky to admit that Bobby could be "a nasty little prick" when provoked. But no one irked Bobby more than Lyndon Johnson. Within close circles, Bobby constantly said that Johnson was "incapable of telling the truth"—an assessment he claimed his brother made to Jackie Kennedy the day before he was killed in Dallas. After Jack's death, one particular rumor, passed along by Salinger, infuriated Bobby: Johnson had suggested the hand of God might have struck down President Kennedy as some biblical punishment for the deaths of Diem in Vietnam and Trujillo in the Dominican Republic. In a lengthy oral history given later for the John F. Kennedy Library, Bobby repeated Johnson's homey Texas allegory to his interviewer, John Bartlow Martin, with vintage disdain:

> MARTIN: Did he [Johnson] mean divine retribution? Or was he suggesting conspiracy?
>
> KENNEDY: No, divine—divine retribution. He [Johnson] said that, and then he went on, I think, and talked and he said that when he was growing up somebody that he knew who had misbehaved ran down a tree—no, was on a sled or something and ran into a tree and hit his head and became cross-eyed. And he said that was God's retribution for people who were bad and so you should be careful of cross-eyed people because God puts his mark on them, and that this might very well be God's retribution to President Kennedy for his participation in the assassination of these two people.

Martin laughed nervously at this tale, and then there was a long pause. "But otherwise," Kennedy added, his sarcasm dripping, "it's a friendly relationship."

AT THE 1964 DEMOCRATIC Convention, Robert Kennedy made a dramatic appearance, interrupted by a wave of emotion and sustained applause, before he could introduce a filmed tribute to his brother. As he tried sheepishly to begin ("Mr. Chairman . . . Mr. Chairman . . . "), there was no doubt in anyone's mind for whom they were clapping. Many thought his political career would be forever dependent on his brother's memory. Two days earlier, Bobby had announced his candidacy for the U.S. Senate in New York, a race in which he faced an incumbent moderate Republican, Kenneth Keating, whose upstate patrician style resembled that of his brother's 1952 opponent, Henry Cabot Lodge Jr. Saddled with the charge of "carpetbagger," Kennedy found that many liberals opposed his bid (and some even called him "the Irish Roy Cohn"); certainly there was a long list of detractors, including Gore Vidal, I. F. Stone and James Baldwin, as well as the editorial page of the *New York Times*. After watching him on the stump, columnist Jimmy Breslin predicted that Bobby Kennedy "will always be confused with his brother." Congressman John V. Lindsay, soon to become mayor of New York City, observed, "I feel sorry for Keating—he's running against a ghost."

Lacking the help of his immobilized father, his fallen older brother, and his younger brother, Edward, who was running for reelection in Massachusetts, Bobby relied on assistance from further down the family totem pole—his sister Jean's husband, Stephen Smith, who had served ably for JFK in 1960. Smith became Bobby's campaign manager. For most of the race, Keating remained close to Kennedy, partly because the traditional Democratic Party coalition was falling apart in New York. The old machine bosses such as Congressman Charles Buckley of the Bronx (one of the first and strongest of Catholic politicians to support Jack's 1960 presidential candidacy at a time when many Catholics were wary of his chances) were losing ground to a new ethnic coalition. At the same time, many reform Democrats showed a distinct ambivalence toward the former attorney general. Even some of Jack's former aides wondered about Bobby. "I was less attracted by what I then perceived as a kind of moral righteousness, rooted in a primitive Catholicism," remembered speechwriter Richard Goodwin, who took a job with the Johnson administration that year.

At times, the strain of Bobby's new life in politics showed. "This great doom which so many of the Irish live by and have in their faces made him look gaunt," Breslin described, after watching Kennedy at a lively, sometime prickly exchange with students at Columbia University. When one undergraduate pushed him about the findings of the Warren Commission, and mentioned other conspiracy theories suggesting that perhaps Oswald was not a lone assassin, Bobby became visibly upset. "I've made my statement, is this one yours?" he snapped. Then, his head bowed and the gaggle of television cameras with their klieg lights continued to roll as Kennedy's eyes moistened with tears.

That November, Robert Kennedy was swept into office largely on the strength of Lyndon Johnson's landslide presidential victory, an irony that no one missed. In his relatively short campaign, Kennedy managed to find his own extemporaneous voice. He began to form a political coalition—not only the ethnic Catholics, who responded to his familiar, culturally conservative image—but also the new minorities in New York, the thousands of Puerto Ricans who moved from the island, and the many African-Americans who came up from the South to live in the city's urban neighborhoods, often replacing whites who had fled to the suburbs. The machine bosses and local leaders, afraid of losing their fiefdoms, were slow to register these minority voters. So Kennedy's campaign ran their own special registration drive, picking up thousands of new and previously disenfranchised voters, particularly in black and Puerto Rican neighborhoods. "John Kennedy had the bearing of a patrician, but seeing Bobby, you wouldn't know he came from a wealthy background," recalled Herman Badillo, then a Democrat, who was elected Bronx borough president the following year. "He looked like he was from any Irish family in New York. He related to Puerto Ricans as if he were one of them, and that's why he got such firm support."

This hybrid Democratic coalition, probably the most remarkable aspect of Kennedy's otherwise lackluster 1964 Senate campaign, seemed a minor miracle to those familiar with the internecine, tribal warfare of New York politics. Manfred Ohrenstein, a Manhattan Democratic politician and avid supporter, recognized the Kennedy appeal in bringing disparate and virtually powerless groups together. "They brought with them the ethos of the Catholic Church," Ohrenstein explained about the Kennedy effect. "This whole group of blue-collar people—Irish and Italians—felt comfortable that this was one of theirs, that the Kennedys understood where they came from, these people who had pulled themselves up by their bootstraps, people to whom religion was an important means of elevating themselves and of keeping their families together. . . . The Kennedys had this ability to communicate to blue-collar Catholics that they understand their concerns, just as they could communicate with poor blacks. They represented a successful immigrant family."

In his last days as attorney general in July 1964, Bobby testified in support of his brother's proposed overhaul of the nation's restrictive immigration laws, which he called "cruel" and a "source of embarrassment to us around the world." As a Democratic candidate for the Senate, he turned immigration into a campaign issue in his race against Keating. He pointed out that President Kennedy's bill, introduced in July 1963, remained stalled in the Senate Judiciary Committee, where Keating was a prominent member. "The truth is that [Keating] does not have enough influence in his own committee to secure a hearing on immigration reform," Kennedy charged. Keating, who actually favored the bill, said that Bobby's newfound interest in immigration was simply a matter of election-time expediency. Nevertheless, in immigrant–filled New York, Kennedy's accusation carried weight.

Discrimination and the reuniting of families were the two reasons for immigration reform that Kennedy emphasized. Ironically, the flow of Irish immigrants had slowed to a trickle by the mid-1960s. But thousands of applicants from southern and central European nations still waited for years under this system. Those from Latin America, Asia and Africa were often denied. The last effort by Congress to deal with this system—the 1952 McCarran-Walter Immigration Act, passed over President Truman's veto— only confirmed these racial quotas. "Everywhere else in our national life, we have eliminated discrimination based on one's place of birth," Bobby stated. "Yet this system is still the foundation of our immigration law."

Kennedy's efforts in New York were aided inadvertently by Republicans who injected their campaign with some old-fashioned nativism. Vice-presidential nominee William E. Miller denounced the proposed Kennedy changes to the nation's immigration laws, and the party's presidential candidate, Senator Barry Goldwater of Arizona, declared that "Americans are sick and tired" of having "minority groups run the country." The furor over Goldwater's remarks forced his aides to claim he meant "pressure groups," not "minority groups." But the old battle lines on immigration were drawn. The mayor of New York City, Robert Wagner, chairman of the All Americans Council of the Democratic National Committee, a group representing immigrants and minorities in the party, blasted Goldwater for his "woeful ignorance of the role of immigrants in the history of America." To emphasize his point, Wagner told the press of his plans to send Goldwater a copy of President Kennedy's book, *A Nation of Immigrants*.

More than any family member before him, Robert Kennedy learned to embrace as part of his constituency those immigrants, farm hands and factory workers earning less than minimum wage, those who worked in the most dangerous jobs or were given the least desirable tasks outside the purview of government or labor unions. He became, in Schlesinger's term, a "tribune for the underclass." Kennedy's politics were slowly transformed, starting almost imperceptibly with the 1964 campaign. He was no longer an insider, no longer a confidant to the president, but rather an irritant in Lyndon Johnson's White House, deliberately kept at bay. Physically, Bobby

Kennedy looked, spoke and acted like an outsider, regardless of his vaunted status as a United States senator. No longer would he rail against things in the same defensive, sometimes reactionary, conservative mode as he had in the 1950s and early 1960s, when he operated under the protective wing of both his brother and father. Only in retrospect would those closest to him realize how far he had traveled.

ROBERT KENNEDY'S spiritual odyssey after his brother's death is difficult to trace. Friends, relatives and former colleagues recall Kennedy from their own particular experiences or vantage, but their memories provide only limited insight. Kennedy's public comments are recorded in more than a dozen books and biographies, yet the private struggles of his soul remain largely *ignis fatuus,* a metaphysical will-o'-the-wisp difficult to grasp. As Anthony Lewis, a *New York Times* columnist and Harvard classmate, remarked of him: "Most people acquire certainties as they grow older; he lost his."

Bobby Kennedy must be understood against the backdrop of the 1960s, a period of tremendous social changes within the United States, when the Vietnam War and the civil rights movement unleashed a torrent of moral unrest. Nearly every institution seemed under scrutiny or, in some way, under siege, to the extent that some even wondered, as *Time* magazine posed on its front cover, "Is God Dead?" President Kennedy's death seemed to leave America unhinged, suspicious that the old verities provided by church and state no longer held true. Bobby's individual agonies, his search for answers, became part of this larger national drama. These changes in Kennedy—from the zealous 1950s McCarthyite engaged in anti-Communist crusades to the reflective, ecumenical progressive of the mid–1960s—also embodied the remarkable changes in the mindset of the American Catholic Church. The almost reactionary hierarchy personified by Cardinal Spellman gave way to the reforms of Vatican II. In this respect, Robert Kennedy's journey reflected the experiences of thousands of Irish-Americans. "In this era, the Catholic Kennedys traced the same narrative arc as their church," James Carroll later observed, "from the worship of aris-tocracy to a liberating preference for the poor."

Some former aides tend to cast Kennedy as an existential hero and downplay whatever role his Catholic culture played in his decisionmaking. "While he [Kennedy] remained a good Catholic, he was freshly infused with a skepticism that loosened the rigidities of his belief and the personal moral code that had ruled his conduct," Richard Goodwin wrote. "Painful experience had drawn him closer to the Greek wisdom that a man's destiny was governed by an arbitrary, often whimsical fate; led him away from the loving protective God of his earlier, literal Catholic belief." But these assessments are at odds with many closest to the Kennedy family, and, ironically, with Robert Kennedy's own words.

Family intimates, such as cousin Joseph Gargan, say Bobby's sense of being a Catholic was "a very important influence on what he did," such as his efforts to improve civil rights and his championing of migrant workers. His eldest daughter, Kathleen Kennedy Townsend, said the family's Irish Catholic heritage played a significant role in his public actions and in dealing with personal tragedies. When asked about her father's most identifiable Irish trait, she replied, "I think the stoicism, the sense that you have to work, and go forward, even in the toughest of times. Clearly, there was a sense that religion was a very strong part of our life, in the sense that we would never miss Mass on Sunday. We had prayers at every meal. And of course, nightly prayers. . . . We would quote St. Luke's admonition—'To those who have been given much, much will be expected.' So there really was a sense of duty and responsibility . . . as well as an empathy for those who are less fortunate."

Many aspects of Irish Catholic life in America—the devotion to large extended families, the deference to clergy and church, the allegiance to Democratic politics—were a part of Robert Kennedy. "Because he was so pure Irish, he seemed part of a company," wrote Murray Kempton in 1964, predicting that Bobby Kennedy would "begin again down, one suspects, a road entirely unexpected, unconventional, intimate and Irish." Kempton, a more astute observer than most, was unique in his perception of the deeper currents in Bobby Kennedy's psyche. "There are persons so constituted that they can go nowhere without some piece of faith to serve as light," he wrote. "Robert Kennedy is a Catholic; and naturally he sought his faith there."

The evidence of Robert Kennedy's beliefs, the remnants of his private and public search, abound. On a yellow sheet, shortly after his brother's death, he scribbled: "The innocent suffer—how can that be possible and God be just." In politics, he learned that church and state could not be antiseptically separated, as his brother had been compelled to promise in the 1960 election. Rather, the lessons of the 1960s reaffirmed for him that the most effective struggles against war, poverty and racism often require the actions of those motivated by religion. In the personal postscript to his last book, *To Seek a Newer World,* Kennedy underlined the power of religion and faith in his work in the U.S. Senate and, presumably, as a future president. "It is not realistic or hard-headed to solve problems and take action unguided by ultimate moral aims and values. It is thoughtless folly," he declared. "For it ignores the realities of human faith and passion and belief, forces ultimately more powerful than all the calculations of economists or generals."

Because religion, like money and sex, was generally a private matter, the Kennedys were often portrayed solely in secular terms by journalists and historians who could not become acquainted with an Irish-Catholic culture that made them uncomfortable. "Many liberals could not understand him," Schlesinger wrote in his 1978 biography. "They found him hard to understand because he was a Catholic. Not many liberals believed in original sin."

AS A SENATOR from New York, Kennedy sometimes felt estranged from Democrats who espoused liberal causes for what he deemed all the wrong reasons. Too often, liberals had no idea of the everyday indignities faced by working-class and poor people. They viewed these people with mild distaste or, worse, patronizingly from their town house windows. "Robert Kennedy, who, while espousing liberal ideas, hated to be thought of as a liberal (since there was something quite deep in him which viewed liberals as being soft)," noted David Halberstam. Among intellectuals and media types in Manhattan, Kennedy also sensed a deep strain of anti-Catholicism. He privately repeated a familiar complaint that "anti-Catholicism is the anti-Semitism of the intellectuals." Some wondered whether Kennedy's cultural unease with New York liberals might contain some latent anti-Semitism of his own, inherited as the son of Joseph P. Kennedy, reviled for his attitude toward Nazi Germany.

Bobby harbored grudges against particular targets. Liberals on Manhattan's West Side didn't like him, he claimed, "because I'm a Roman Catholic with ten children." Although the *New York Times* had boldly exposed the religious bigotry plaguing his brother's historic 1960 campaign, certainly as much as any newspaper in the country, Bobby remained irked by their coverage of himself. In private, he complained that the paper of record never noted Mayor Lindsay's Protestant religion as it did with his own. To columnist Jimmy Breslin, a fellow Irish Catholic, he expressed surety that the *Times* was prejudiced. "Their idea of a good story is—'More nuns leave convents than ever before,'" he told Breslin.

One of the most influential portrayals of Robert Kennedy during this time is contained in journalist Jack Newfield's 1969 biography, *Robert Kennedy: A Memoir*. A genuine cri de coeur written in memorial, Newfield's book recognized the strong Irish Catholic cultural influences on Kennedy, but presented them with distinct ambivalence. "Kennedy's Catholicism reinforced other parts of his personality," Newfield contended. "His sense of service, sacrifice and responsibility. His loyalty to his family, with its hierarchical structure. His strong sense of Good and Evil." Kennedy maintained a sentimental bond to his church, almost as much as his family. As Newfield observed, "In the oddest of places—rural Kansas, the heart of Watts [the scene of a deadly 1965 urban riot in Los Angeles]—nuns would appear in the middle of crowds, and Kennedy's face would brighten." Ultimately, Newfield blamed "Kennedy's cultural condition as a Boston Catholic" for his early admiration of Senator Joseph McCarthy, and for a side of his personality that was more "emotionally sympathetic to policemen" than the American Civil Liberties Union (ACLU). Newfield and subsequent biographers make much of Kennedy's reading of Albert Camus, the French existentialist writer, and the ancient Greek philosophers, and credit it with more transforming power than anything Kennedy found in his religion. Before his 1969 book, Newfield mentioned Camus in a 1966 article in the *Nation,* in which he suggested Kennedy's "complex liberalism . . . has a philosophical base to it," reflected in Camus's *Myth of Sisyphus,* where "fate is cruel and often absurd, but vulnerable man must make the effort to push his heavy burden up the slope of history." Was Robert Kennedy an "existential hero," as Newfield termed him, or a Christian believer whose faith was sorely tested by the randomness and cruelty of life?

Family members suggest these existential interpretations of Kennedy were overdrawn and underestimate his faith. "I think he was always a spiritual human being," said Kathleen Kennedy Townsend, in a lengthy conversation about her father's beliefs. "With every tragedy, it deepens one's understanding, and being open to learning from it. And that's what he was able to do. . . . I think that Jack Newfield story—and he wrote a wonderful book—is sort of exaggerated, because one can always grow, but I think the depths of his spirituality were always there." Instead, Townsend suggested that much of her father's stoicism and fatalism, often attributed to French existentialists or ancient Greeks, more accurately finds its roots in his Irish Catholic background. "The Irish have seen lots of cruelty, so there wasn't a sense that there was a disjunction between God and what happened on Earth," she explained. "That's been part of the Irish tradition for centuries, that life is tough. And so, what God gives you is the strength to deal with the toughness. I think with the (Irish) stoicism, you go forward. Those kind of questions [about existentialism] are more modern questions. I don't think that is part of the Irish tradition, and it was not part of our tradition."

During a November 2000 conference at the John F. Kennedy Library, Townsend spoke of "one aspect of my father's legacy that often gets overlooked," which she described as the "profound link between my father's religious principles and his political principles." She said these convictions, moored by his Catholic faith, revealed themselves in everything from outrage at poverty and racism to a need to reform the welfare system so that human beings are not denied a sense of purpose and self-respect. "There was a spiritual grounding to his life, which offered him a sharp lens through which he viewed the nation and the world," she explained, offering several examples. "It gave him a sense of urgency and passion with which he approached the political realm." Undoubtedly, this loving assessment by Kennedy's daughter, more than thirty years after his death, hardly accounts for some of the vitriol and arrogance of her father's character, particularly in his earlier years as his brother's enforcer or as an unapologetic wiretapper of Dr. King. But in understanding Kennedy's politics in the 1960s, Townsend highlighted a major aspect of her father's development left largely unexplored.

As THE WHOLE WORLD witnessed, Robert Kennedy knew what it was like to be humbled in the deepest sense. On the campaign trail and as a public servant, he referred to a fragility in life born of his own family tragedy. He often mentioned human suffering. He spoke of it with great empathy, enhancing his appeal to those alienated from American society. "I always felt that Bobby had an aura of fatalism around him after his brother's death," remembered speechwriter Michael Novak. "He would do his best and do what he had to do, and the rest would be left in the hands of God. He seemed the most vulnerable of the Kennedys."

In various speeches after November 1963, Robert Kennedy turned his own pain into a greater understanding of the afflicted and found a shared comfort in suffering. Never were these sensibilities more on display than the night Martin Luther King was assassinated in April 1968. Once again, Kennedy's face showed the struggle to rectify, somehow make sense of a world where a proponent of nonviolence and Christ's love—a winner of the Nobel Peace Prize—could be struck down by an assassin's bullet. Before a group of one thousand mostly African-American people in Indianapolis, Kennedy announced the horrifying news and then, extemporaneously, he spoke from the heart.

For those of you who are black and are tempted to be filled with hatred and distrust at the injustice of such an act, against all white people, I can only say that I feel in my own heart the same kind of feeling. I had a member of my family killed, but he was killed by a white man. But we have to make an effort in the United States, we have to make an effort to understand, to go beyond these rather difficult times.

My favorite poet was Aeschylus. He wrote: "In our sleep, pain which cannot forget falls drop by drop upon the heart until, in our own despair, against our will, comes wisdom through the awful grace of God."

What we need in the United States is not division; what we need in the United States is not hatred; what we need in the United States is not violence or lawlessness, but love and wisdom, and compassion toward one another, and a feeling that justice toward those who still suffer within our country, whether they be white or they be black.

Riots and looting erupted that night across America, though not in Indianapolis. We don't know whether Kennedy's speech helped soothe the anguish and righteous anger of African-Americans in that city, nor do we know whether any of his words helped at all. No one could dispute, though, that Kennedy's pain was real, for he, too, had experienced the "awful grace of God."

The Politics of Outsiders

AFTER A CONTROVERSIAL TOUR of South Africa in June 1966, Robert Kennedy's entourage flew to Rome, where the senator from New York confronted Pope Paul VI with all he had heard and seen of apartheid. "I told him how important it was the church take a clear position . . . how cruel the system was," Kennedy recorded in his notes. He even warned that many Africans believed, as one informed him, that "the Christian God hates Negroes."

The pontiff's response was polite but tepid, while Kennedy's soul remained inflamed. Throughout South Africa, he had witnessed the devastating impact of racism in the name of religion. Whites justified their system of apartheid by arguing that blacks, after centuries of tribalism, couldn't be trusted with such a Western refinement as democracy. "Suppose God is black?" Kennedy replied at a South African university to a questioner defending the state's white supremacy. "What if we go to Heaven and we, all of our lives, have treated the Negro as inferior, and God is there, and we look up and He is not white? What then is our response?"

South Africa struck a chord in Robert Kennedy, as did similar trips abroad in the mid-1960s to Communist-dominated Poland and poverty–ridden Latin America, where minorities suffered from bigotry and oppression. For all his power, fame and money, Kennedy still could identify with those beaten down by the system. In his own personal mythology, the Kennedy family had suffered such a fate. "My father left Boston . . . because of the signs on the wall that said 'No Irish Need Apply,'" he told the crowds in South Africa. When a writer back in the United States questioned him about his recollection of his father's departure ("the Irishman who left Boston . . . in his own Railway car," as the dubious letter writer put it), Kennedy good-humoredly acknowledged a bit of blarney in his facts. In reply, he argued that his Irish anecdote about his family was "symbolic . . . at least that was what I was told at a very young age . . . both my parents felt very strongly about the discrimination." Family history became a parable, if not gospel truth.

ROBERT KENNEDY'S heritage was so infused in his being that he generally didn't need to parade his ethnicity or religion as other politicians might. Yet his family's Irish Catholic cultural sensibility often surfaced in issues where Kennedy showed his greatest passion, like his rooting out of organized crime figures in the 1950s Payoffs, beatings and other forms of corruption became morality tales where the sides of good and evil were often sharp and distinct. Murray Kempton later said that RFK had never felt so "at home with sister and brother Catholics" as when he mingled with those without power, particularly those involved in the labor union struggle for decent wages and health safeguards. Kennedy strongly endorsed unionizing efforts among immigrants and minorities, and he praised the Association of Catholic Trade Unionists as "the brightest spot" in the movement. Robert Kennedy became what Kempton called "a Catholic radical" who interpreted President Kennedy's words and policies into a bolder and much more progressive ideology. "From the need to identify at once with his triumphant brother and with the great company of losers in life to which he had fallen, he invented a John F. Kennedy that never was, the buried spirit of radical discontent," wrote Kempton.

As a senator, Robert Kennedy's concerns revealed him to be a socially conservative Catholic as much as a disciple of liberal orthodoxy. He questioned the role of the federal welfare system and its impact on poor families, and he stressed the need for neighborhood control in running schools and antipoverty programs. His appeals to the conscience rather than to convenience seemed to assume that every citizen was able to feel responsibility as well as pleasure. He implored a materialistic American society to be more charitable, yet he believed that government handouts were ultimately corrupting. These infusions of spirituality into his down-to-earth politics were captured in an oft-quoted speech in South Africa, where Kennedy beseeched: "Each time a man stands up for an ideal, or acts to improve the lot of others, or strikes out against injustice, he sends a tiny ripple of hope, and crossing each other from a million different centers of energy and daring those ripples build a current which can sweep down the mightiest walls of oppression and resistance." Increasingly, his politics, like his religion, became visionary rather than dogmatic.

In 1966, the plight of California's migrant workers roused Kennedy's moral outrage. Kennedy was persuaded by friends to fly to Delano, California, for a hearing of the Senate's Subcommittee on Migratory Labor. In the vineyards of Delano, located in the San Joaquin Valley, grape pickers earned below minimum wages, were sprayed like produce with harmful insecticides and were fired or threatened when they tried to unionize. Eventually, they declared a strike and marched with signs warning *Huelga,* "Strike." Some Mexican workers were imported as scabs to help break the union's effort. Cesar Chavez, an earnest, unschooled Mexican-American whose heroes included St. Francis and Gandhi, led the farm workers. Some called him a Communist for trying to extend basic government labor protections afforded most Americans, such as minimum wage, to his members toiling in the fields. Though some were sympathetic, many white Southern California farm owners reacted with angry nativist-tinged bigotry toward these Hispanic immigrant workers and the Catholic clergy who supported their cause. A handful of young, idealistic priests set up a Migrant Ministry to aid striking workers, some of whom were beaten by thugs. These priests spoke up for the workers at public hearings and helped them pay for food, lodging and other essentials. For these embattled migrant workers, the church was a refuge, a source of strength. "All the Mexicans are Catholic," Chavez explained. "The church is the one group that isn't expecting anything from us. All the others, the unions, the civil-rights groups, they all want something in return for their support. Not the church."

Kennedy's appearance at the Senate subcommittee hearing put a national spotlight on the problems facing migrant workers. His outrage was so intense that he grilled the local sheriff after he had explained how striking workers were arrested for unlawful assembly when they were simply protesting. "Can I suggest that the sheriff read the Constitution of the United States," Kennedy said dryly. A gaggle of reporters followed Kennedy to the hearing and one asked whether Chavez and his union organizers were Communists. "No, they're not Communists," Kennedy replied with authority. "They're struggling for their rights."

Chavez was surprised by Kennedy's peppery, hard-nosed questioning at the hearing and "at how quickly he [Kennedy] grasped the whole picture." The farm workers strike dragged on for months. "Boycott grapes" signs were placed in groceries and liquor stores across the country. In early 1968, Chavez went on a hunger strike. During the fast, Senator Kennedy sent him a telegram saying: "I fully and unswervingly support the principles which led you to undertake your fast." When it ended twenty-five days later on a Sunday, Kennedy joined Chavez for a Mass and a bread-breaking ceremony attended by more than four thousand people. Chavez was so weak that he had to be helped to the local park where a flatbed truck was used as an outside altar. Though some liberal supporters of the union were uncomfortable with it, Kennedy marveled at the grassroots role of the Catholic Church in helping these workers, and appreciated Chavez's use of religious symbolism in his struggle. That day, the large gathering of immigrant laborers treated Kennedy as something more than a visiting politician. They waved their tattered union flags and soiled baseball caps in salute. Some blessed themselves as he passed.

"*Hool-ga!*" Bobby shouted, in fractured Spanish meant to sound like *Huelga*. "Am I murdering the language?" he turned and asked, laughing with the crowd at his poor Spanish. But Bobby felt a sodality, a cultural connection, that wasn't readily apparent. "He was a hardscrabble liberal who clearly sympathized with the plight of migrant workers and the poor," explained historian Douglas Brinkley. "But perhaps most importantly, like all of them, he was a Catholic in America run largely by Protestants."

In these California vineyards, among immigrant laborers and the radicalized clergy who supported them, Bobby Kennedy found himself closer to his faith than he ever had in Rome. "God, those priests—Communists," he said mockingly, in a way that probably wouldn't have occurred to him a decade earlier. Chavez and his union of Latino immigrants looked at Kennedy "as sort of a minority kind of person himself," Chavez attested, "with Senator Kennedy, it was like he was one of ours." Though the bigotry faced by Jack Kennedy eight years earlier had abated, Chavez noted that when Bobby "was put down for being a Catholic, this made points with the Mexicans." In time, a photo of Bobby would hang in Chavez's union office in Delano, part of a trinity of 1960s memorials on the wall to the Kennedy brothers and Martin Luther King.

IMMIGRANTS BECAME, once again, an important part of the family's constituency. In early 1965, the Kennedy brothers in the United States Senate, Robert of New York and Edward of Massachusetts, continued to push for the immigration reform legislation first proposed by JFK. "It doesn't make any sense that we discriminate against people because of the color of their skin and its doesn't make any sense when we discriminate because of their place of birth," Bobby said, reprising his brother's language from 1963. Looking back decades later, Ted Kennedy is even more blunt in his assessment. "At the time, our immigration policies supported legally sanctioned race discrimination," he said.

The racial aspect of the immigration issue became clear when President Johnson reintroduced the bill in 1965. Ted Kennedy, as floor manager of the bill, encountered problems from several Southern Democratic senators, some of whom had opposed the 1964 Civil Rights Act. Savvy to the Senate's ways, Ted Kennedy convinced Senator James O. Eastland, a Democrat from Mississippi, to hold Judiciary Subcommittee hearings despite his own opposition to the bill. During the hearings, the president of the Daughters of the American Revolution (DAR), a woman who identified herself as Mrs. William H. Sullivan Jr., said that getting rid of the national origins quota system would destroy the country's "first-line of defense" against a tide of "potentially unassimilable aliens." Eastland seconded the DAR's view. Ted Kennedy disagreed but didn't quiz Mrs. Sullivan until she claimed that elimination of the existing national origins system was a major goal of the Communists.

"You don't suggest that anyone who opposes the [existing 1952 McCarran-Walter Immigration] act or wants to change it is a Communist, do you?" Kennedy pressed.

Mrs. Sullivan seemed momentarily flustered. "No, indeed," she replied. Then in the code words of the DAR, a long-time opponent of immigrants, she went on to explain her support for the existing system which, she said, would preserve the nation's "cultural heritage, its free institutions and its historic population mixture."

During the hearings, Senator Sam Ervin, the avuncular, white-haired Democrat from North Carolina, wanted to clamp down on the flow of immigrants from Mexico and other Latin American nations. With great alarm, Ervin predicted the new law could bring a flood of new Hispanics into the United States. "He [Ervin] does not make clear just why this would be so terrible, contenting himself with arguing that many potential immigrants from Great Britain ('our great ally') would be cut off in favor of Latin Americans," *Commonweal* complained. Others were more direct in their interpretation of the Southern Democrats' motives. "Nativism is far from dead in the United States," warned *America,* the Jesuit magazine, "and the militant bands of Anglo-Saxon breast-beaters have already begun—and will no doubt continue—to predict the dire consequences of disturbing the long entrenched nativist triangular base of anti-Catholic, anti-radical, and anti-foreign sentiment." At the Senate hearings, Ervin pounced on Attorney General Nicholas De B. Katzenbach when he testified for the bill. The Johnson administration argued the new law would hold the number of new entrants from the Western Hemisphere to 120,000 annually and give priority to skilled and educated émigrés overall.

"Do you think, Senator, that a maid from Ireland really will contribute more to the United States than a trained doctor from an Asian country?" Katzenbach asked rhetorically during a heated exchange.

The senator, who preferred that the world know him as a simple country lawyer rather than a studied segregationist, looked over at his colleague Ted Kennedy, who was presiding over the hearing. Ervin seemed to remember enough of the Kennedy family history, even if he couldn't recall Bridget Kennedy by name.

"Oh, I don't know," Ervin replied wryly, to knowing laughs.

Despite these minor contretemps in the Senate, only a handful of politicians and commentators opposed the 1965 Immigration Reform Act. Ted Kennedy assured his Senate colleagues that "our cities won't be flooded with a million immigrants annually." He said the new law wouldn't change "the ethnic mix" of the country, and wouldn't displace Americans from their jobs.

On the Senate floor before the vote, Robert Kennedy echoed the words of historian Oscar Handlin, who proclaimed in an article reprinted in *Reader's Digest* that the new immigration law "will have tremendous symbolic significance, and it will remedy wrongs of 40 years standing." The House passed the new immigration law by a lopsided margin, and the Senate voted 76 to 18 in favor. "After 40 years, we have returned to first principles," Teddy declared in victory. "Immigration, more than anything else, has supplied America with the human strength that is the core of its greatness."

The press dutifully covered the 1965 Immigration Act without any hint of its impact on America in the decades to come, nor did the early Kennedy histories, including those written by Sorensen and Schlesinger, give it much weight. But in her own memoir, Rose Kennedy emphasized the importance of the immigration issue to her family. "Jack had proposed abolishing the discriminatory parts of our immigration laws," she said. "It was Ted who guided the bill through the Senate."

On a sunny October day, beneath the Statue of Liberty, President Johnson signed into law the new bill eliminating the national origins system. "We can now believe it will never shadow the gate to the American nation with the twin barriers of prejudice and privilege," Johnson declared. Both Ted and Bobby stayed in the background even though they had been prime movers of this legislation. In his speech, Johnson made no mention of them, though the day was a triumph for the Kennedys.

AT THE FUNERAL for Cardinal Spellman in December 1967, Bobby Kennedy fidgeted impatiently in St. Patrick's Cathedral, a majestic building on Fifth Avenue in the heart of Manhattan. In many ways, the cathedral stood as a defiant, unofficial monument to the rise of Irish Catholics in America. Nearly all Roman Catholic bishops and cardinals in New York City's formative years were of Irish descent, including Spellman himself.

The cardinal's passing held personal and public significance for Kennedy. Fifteen years earlier, Spellman had offered a private consecration before Bobby and Ethel's marriage, a courtesy as a family friend and favor to Joseph Kennedy. At that time, Bobby shared not only the same religion with Spellman but similar views about international communism, the FBI's J. Edgar Hoover, and Bobby's future boss, Senator Joseph McCarthy. In his waning days, Spellman resisted—or reluctantly acceded—to nearly every reform brought about by Vatican II. His politics turned increasingly conservative and he even socialized with Bobby's old nemesis, Roy Cohn. The cardinal referred to the escalating conflict in Vietnam as "Christ's war"—a mortifying allusion to the bad old days of the Crusades. Long ago, Bobby Kennedy had distanced himself from the cardinal, and not just because Spellman had committed the unforgivable sin of favoring Nixon in the 1960 presidential campaign.

American Catholicism was headed in a far more progressive direction than the moral stasis of the septuagenarian cardinal would have permitted, and no one represented this shift in the 1960s more than the Kennedys. Their idealism and high-minded rhetoric exuded the brimming confidence of American Catholics, as church attendance soared and seminaries and religious vocations thrived. Shortly after President Kennedy's death, the Second Vatican Council approved its "Declaration on Religious Liberty"—largely shaped by Jesuit John Courtney Murray and the experience of the 1960 presidential election—which gave Catholic politicians around the world the freedom to voice their political decisions without interference from the church. In the same vein, twenty-six Catholic university educators met in 1967 to formulate a "declaration of independence" for their institutions from the American church hierarchy—a determined answer to the

Blanshard-like criticism of the 1950s that the church, encumbered by religious orthodoxy, fostered anti-intellectualism and a lack of inquiry. Though many still looked to Spellman and the hierarchy as the only voice of the church, some of the era's most significant actions were being taken by socially active priests and nuns, such as the Berrigan brothers, the antiwar activists far more liberal than Kennedy himself.

Kennedy was now a different kind of Catholic, no longer the authoritarian-minded former altar boy. At this stage, he had enough confidence in his faith (or possessed enough sheer guts or audacity) to lecture the Pope about why the American church should do more for Latin and Asian immigrants. During a stop in Rome in February 1967, Kennedy told Paul VI that the Vatican must become "the foremost champion for changing this kind of difficult, poverty-stricken life." Bobby's experiences in California with Chavez and immigrant workers had made him realize how alienated the official church could be from its flock. Kennedy said that the hierarchy in Los Angeles was "a reactionary force and in New York it was not particularly helpful"—an indirect swipe at Spellman. Although the Pope's reaction was less than inspiring, their conversation underscored the remarkable transformation between the Vatican and its American laity. Unlike his father, Bobby didn't curry favor with cardinals or whisper in the ear of Galeazzi to get his point across with the Holy See. Though reverential and courteous, Kennedy spoke to the Pope like an equal, something Joe Kennedy would never have dreamed of doing. For Bobby, Spellman's funeral marked the end of an era. At the funeral Mass, he dreaded sitting in a pew near President Johnson. Instead, he thumbed through a copy of the Old Testament. "All the way up to Absalom, Absalom," he delighted in telling a friend, referring to the story of King David and his son, Absalom, in the second book of Samuel. "Test me, and I'll prove it."

BOBBY'S APOSTASY from Lyndon Johnson was largely of his own making. Although he was never a key architect of his brother's Vietnam policy, he remained a staunch anti-Communist who supported the official U.S. position well into the early portion of Johnson's presidency. As his doubts multiplied, Kennedy kept dutifully silent, loyal to men such as McNamara and Bundy, aides to his brother who were still serving Johnson, even if he was ambivalent about that. ("I thought that they felt the king was dead, long live the king," Bobby lamented.) Well into 1967, long after other liberals came out publicly against the war, Bobby finally spoke his mind. "I can testify that if fault is to be found or responsibility assessed, there is enough to go around for all, including myself," he admitted to his Senate colleagues. His delays cost him considerably. Some critics chalked up his change of heart to calculated ambition, a heartless reading of public opinion polls rather than a profile in moral courage. While he fiddled, the war in Vietnam raged; 350,000 Americans were committed there, 10,000 were already dead and more than 60,000 had been wounded. The thousands of civilians killed, particularly the murdered and maimed children, haunted him.

For the first time in his public life, Bobby Kennedy appeared weak. In trying to find some middle ground, trying to straddle the narrow gap between the antiwar protestors and the more conservative ethnic voters in the Democratic Party who supported Johnson's effort, Bobby lost his greatest political strength—the millions of Americans who admired the Kennedys and yearned for a restoration of the Camelot era. In his own gut, he knew that many Catholics, with a long history of showing their patriotism in times of war, still backed the administration's position. At Marymount College in Tarrytown, New York, he talked about the war and found, in an informal survey, that students at this all-girls school favored more bombing of North Vietnam, not less. Kennedy chastised them with the zeal of a recent convert. "Do you understand what that means, when you ask for more bombing?" he cajoled. "Don't you understand that what we are doing to the Vietnamese is not very different than what Hitler did to the Jews?"

He no longer viewed Vietnam as a moral battle against the atheistic forces of international communism, the Red guerillas intent on disassembling the regime run by Catholics, but rather as a regional civil war where the presence of a large imperial power was deeply resented. Drawing upon biblical imagery, he appealed to Senate colleagues to rethink their Vietnam commitment:

Few of us are directly involved while the rest of us continue our lives and pursue our ambitions undisturbed by the sounds and fears of battle. To the Vietnamese, however, it must often seem the fulfillment of the prophecy of Saint John the Divine: *"And I looked and beheld a pale horse: and his name that sat on him was Death, and hell followed him. And power was given unto them over the fourth part of the earth, to kill with sword, and with hunger, and with death."* All we say and all we do must be informed by our awareness that this horror is partly our responsibility; not just a nation's responsibility, but yours and mine. It is we who live in abundance and send our young men out to die. It is our chemicals that scorch the children and our bombs that level the villages. We are all participants.

Invoking this apocalyptic vision, Kennedy portrayed an America so absorbed in its materialism, so caught up in its own political hubris, that the consequences of its actions were ignored, its collective conscience inured to the suffering it caused. His speech addressed diplomacy and public opinion, but there was no doubt that its impetus, its driving force, was his own conscience. As he asked in that same Senate speech, "Are we like the God of the Old Testament that we can decide in Washington, D.C., what cities, what towns, what hamlets in Vietnam are going to be destroyed?"

Bobby Kennedy remained a paradox. Unlike most liberal politicians, Kennedy didn't placate the young. He grew his hair longer, shaggier, like the 1960s generation, yet scolded students he caught smoking and thought ill of those who engaged in sex outside the bonds of marriage. Although he became one of the most forceful advocates for peace, Kennedy's critics didn't think of him as part of the New Left found in intellectual circles and on college campuses. His own Catholic sense of obligation, his own conservative, almost prudish ethos, looked askance at the hippie generation of free love, acid trips and dropping out of the system. Was this what his brother's New Frontier and its call to youthful idealism had come to? Bobby didn't consider himself a "dove" demanding an immediate withdrawal, but instead favored a negotiated settlement. He particularly objected to the selective service system as a way of evading military duty. Despite his increasing doubts about Vietnam, he still lectured college audiences about the inherent unfairness of the draft, a system that sent poor minorities to war but allowed deferments for university students. In his eyes, those who fled to Canada to avoid the war were cowards, but those who paid the price and went to jail as conscientious objectors somehow earned his begrudging respect. He supported his brother Ted's proposal in 1965 to replace the draft system with a no-exemption lottery. "It's the poor who carry the major burden of the struggle in Vietnam," Kennedy lectured to an audience at the Indiana University Medical Center in a talk interrupted by boos and catcalls. "You sit here as white medical students, while black people carry the burden of the fighting in Vietnam."

When not throwing out invectives about the war, he looked inward, almost in disgust at his own equivocation about Johnson. His rancorous private confrontations with the president made it easier to disagree with Vietnam policy, but he still found it quite difficult not to support his brother's successor for reelection. Even if Johnson's administration was engulfed in Vietnam, his domestic agenda accomplished many of the New Frontier's goals and provided a far better direction than where either Nixon or Goldwater would lead the nation. For months, Kennedy seemed unable to find a resolution, his own answer for the country's troubles, which, he later said, "flow from the fact that for almost the first time the national leadership is calling upon the darker impulses of the American spirit." In his private notebook, Kennedy wrote down a quotation from Camus that seemed to address his own dilemma: "We are faced with evil. I feel rather like Augustine did before becoming a Christian when he said, 'I tried to find the source of evil and I got nowhere.' But it is also true that I and a few others know what must be done."

Kennedy equivocated and waited so long that another Democrat, Senator Eugene McCarthy, launched his own bold challenge to Johnson in 1968. McCarthy's strong second-place showing in the early New Hampshire primary rallied the antiwar Democrats to his banner. The professorial Minnesotan emerged as a giant killer, the rightful claimant as the peace candidate. Some old-time Kennedy aides such as Richard Goodwin, thinking Bobby wouldn't run, committed themselves to McCarthy's campaign. Goodwin found McCarthy, who had once thought of becoming a priest, to be different from any Irish politician he had met in Boston. "He was a reverential Catholic but not in the way most Irish are Catholic," Goodwin wrote. "He responded to priestly authority not in dread of eternal damnation, but in the more intellectual, ideological—not less fierce in belief—manner of the educated European. . . . Committed to the moral ambiguities of politics, something in him longed for the purifying possibilities of religious life, which, later, he would seek in its only secular counterpart—the austere discipline of poetry." When issuing words of praise, Goodwin recalled, McCarthy quoted St. Augustine to him.

Kennedy disliked McCarthy's highbrow loquaciousness and his attitude of moral and intellectual superiority. His antipathy dated back to 1960, when McCarthy supported Lyndon Johnson at the convention after Minnesota's favorite son, Humphrey, lost in the primaries. "Gene McCarthy felt he should have been the first Catholic President just because he knew more St. Thomas Aquinas than my brother," Bobby ridiculed. Despite their similar ethnic heritage and political outlooks, neither man could abide the other. As a politician, Kennedy's approach was more visceral, more from the gut, than McCarthy's cerebral, somewhat aloof manner. Speechwriter Michael Novak, observing the differences between the two men, said that "it's a mixture of lower-class-Catholicism-become-wealthy against middle-class Midwestern Catholicism, which is rather comfortable and easy going. They don't understand one another too much." Jack had begrudgingly admired McCarthy, even if they differed politically at times. His youngest brother, Ted Kennedy, once had McCarthy campaign for him in his 1962 Senate race. "He was all Irish, making all the Irish rounds in Boston," McCarthy recalled of the jocular, thirty-year-old Teddy. Decades later in an interview, McCarthy expressed affection for President Kennedy and nothing but disdain for Robert Kennedy. "Bobby had an inferiority complex, but Jack never did," McCarthy insisted.

ON ST. PATRICK'S DAY in March 1968, Robert Kennedy announced his candidacy for the presidency in the same Senate Caucus Room in which his brother had launched his 1960 bid. Bobby's speech contained both the soaring rhetoric of the New Frontier and some seemingly necessary fabrications. He claimed his challenge "reflects no personal animosity or disrespect toward President Johnson," and that his campaign against McCarthy would "not be in opposition to his, but in harmony." (McCarthy's response was incredulous: "An Irishman who announces the day before St. Patrick's Day that he's going to run against another Irishman shouldn't say it's going to be a peaceful relationship.") There might be more than a little truth to this judgment on Robert Kennedy, who offered an insightful political self-assessment after the victorious 1968 Indiana primary. When asked why, given his controversial support for civil rights for Negroes, the more conservative, somewhat bigoted ethnic working class voted for him, Bobby could offer only a depreciating reply. "I think part of it is that Gene [McCarthy] comes across as Lace Curtain to those people," he jested to Jack Newfield. "They can tell I'm pure Shanty Irish."

After his announcement, Bobby marched down Manhattan's Fifth Avenue in the annual parade celebrating the Irish in America. On this chilly, misty day when everyone wore overcoats, Bobby walked briskly in only a blue suit. With a green carnation on his lapel, he waved to the crowds and flashed his crooked, wide grin. Along the city's main boulevard, Bobby peered up at a specific building and waved in recognition to Jackie and John Jr. sticking their heads out from a window. Many onlookers dressed in green cheered and reached out their hands for Kennedy, but some along the parade route—those with a few bucks in their pockets who came in from the suburbs—roundly booed him as a coward and opportunist. As the *New York Times* observed, Kennedy "heard and saw enough to realize there was strong resentment to his candidacy, even among the Irish."

To these second– and third–generation Irish Catholics, Kennedy's anti-war position smacked of indecency when American boys were getting killed. They were too proud of their country not to support the president's effort. Kennedy had become too liberal for these Irish Catholics who had moved out of the old ethnic neighborhoods for the ranches, Cape Cods and split-levels in Westchester, Rockland and Long Island. At the same time, Kennedy's late entry into the presidential race appeared to many liberals as a cynical attempt to snatch away what McCarthy had earned. These feelings intensified after Johnson announced he wouldn't seek reelection, leaving the Democratic field wide open. "Sorry I can't join you," Murray Kempton, a McCarthy sympathizer, telegrammed back to an invitation for a party hosted by Ted Kennedy. "Your brother's announcement makes clear that St. Patrick did not drive out all the snakes from Ireland."

For all his troubles, one old problem never emerged. Religion did not become a divisive issue in Kennedy's 1968 campaign. Perhaps America had matured on the religion issue, or the crisis of Vietnam was too pressing that year. Or perhaps because Kennedy didn't have the Democratic nomination in hand, it was only delaying the inevitable hatred he'd face in a general election. After all, Robert Kennedy certainly wasn't a beloved figure in the South, not after his civil rights actions as attorney general. Many liberals were uncomfortable with Kennedy's purported authoritarian streak and with his Catholicism, a religiosity clearly more overt and devout than his brother's. As a sign of the potential difficulty ahead, the group called Protestants and Other Americans United for Separation of Church and State (POAU)—his brother's 1960 nemesis—expressed concern about both Robert Kennedy and Eugene McCarthy, the two Roman Catholics in the race. The group claimed these two candidates failed to take an "unequivocal" stand on separation of church and state, as JFK had promised in the past. "If there is any 'religious problem' in the coming political campaign, it lies with these men and they alone can resolve it," POAU warned. Although the traditional barrier against a Catholic in the White House had been broken, some national surveys showed the old prejudices lingered. Against Richard Nixon in a proposed 1968 presidential race, the Harris poll found Robert Kennedy would receive only 42 percent of the Protestant vote, a huge handicap for any candidate to face in a nation nearly three-quarters Protestant. Eventually, Nixon's campaign developed a strategy designed to capitalize on underlying fears and resentment among white Protestants in the South, particularly their disenfranchisement from the Democratic Party over civil rights, the war and "law and order" in riot-torn cities.

To succeed in a time when the political ground was shifting, Kennedy realized he needed to build a coalition beyond the traditional Democratic base of white ethnics, liberals and Southern Democrats, one that would embrace minorities and recent immigrants in a way they'd never been courted before. These recent newcomers perceived the Kennedys as the quintessential immigrant success story. Bobby Kennedy's politics mirrored their emphasis on family concerns as well as a progressive outlook on social issues affecting the future. "The poorer people like me—Negroes and Puerto Ricans, for instance," Kennedy explained. "The Deprived, if you like, they are for me."

Bobby was forging a new democratic coalition—a politics of outsiders—that he could only hope would be enough to gain the nomination. Kennedy emerged as "our first politician for the pariahs, our great national outsider, our lonely reproach, the natural standard held out to all rebels," Kempton observed. "That is the wound about him which speaks to children he has never seen. He will always speak to children, and he will probably always be out of power." Once the hard-charging realist of his brother's campaign, Bobby Kennedy turned into an almost quixotic candidate who jumped into the murky waters of 1968 on impulse rather than by calculated design. Teddy Kennedy and other seasoned advisers doubted the wisdom of being drawn into this campaign. They argued that 1972 was a better choice and would allow him to attend to the needs of his family. Jackie Kennedy feared that if Bobby entered the race "they'll do to him what they did to Jack." But once he made up his mind, after months of vacillation, Bobby wouldn't hear of not running. What he said about the lessons of Vietnam now seemed to apply to himself and his country: "Tragedy is a tool for the living to gain wisdom, not a guide by which to live."

BACK IN NEW YORK, the hour was late, well after midnight. On television from Los Angeles, those who stayed up saw the image of a victorious Bobby Kennedy, smiling sheepishly, squeezed between his family and supporters gathered on the podium, as he thanked everyone for helping him win the California primary.

Kennedy's appeal to the disenfranchised worked. The turnout in the minority communities of Southern California proved tremendous, nearly 90 percent of some precincts casting their votes for this white millionaire's son. Mexican-Americans, at the urging of Chavez and the United Farm Workers, voted for Kennedy by wide margins and pushed his overall statewide lead over McCarthy by nearly 5 percent. Overall, seven of every eight Mexican-Americans who voted were for Kennedy. Blacks also favored Kennedy in such large numbers that McCarthy complained about "bloc" voting among minorities and immigrants. Among high-income predominantly white Democratic voters in California, McCarthy won two of every three votes statewide.

Without his band of immigrants and minorities, Kennedy would have lost. His victory marked the first time Hispanic voters played such a prominent role in presidential politics, a harbinger of their growing power in large states around the nation. Kennedy's win was, in a sense, a more significant milestone for them. In his brief remarks that night, Bobby mentioned Chavez and the United Farm Workers, expressing his gratitude for support "in the agricultural areas of the state, as well as in the cities" of California. He promised to bring all Americans together to end "the divisions, the violence, the disenchantment in our society." Ethel, dressed in a silk green outfit and pregnant with their eleventh child, stood beside her husband as he stuck up two fingers in a victory sign to the crowd of well-wishers. Then she followed him as he made his way toward a back exit in the kitchen of the Ambassador Hotel.

BOBBY SHARED his dead brother's fatalism. "I know that there will be an attempt on my life sooner or later," he told French writer Romain Gary in Los Angeles shortly before the primary. "There is no way to protect a candidate during the electoral campaign. You must give yourself to the crowd and from then on you must take your chances." Schlesinger, his biographer, said Kennedy didn't court death but he possessed "an almost insolent fatalism about life. No one understood better the terrible fortuity of existence."

In the final hours of the California race, Kennedy's words seemed heavy with foreboding, of a man ready, if not willing, for death. "It is less important what happens to me than what happens to the cause I have tried to represent," he assured. After Martin Luther King's assassination in April, friends and allies worried about Kennedy's safety more than ever. "There was just about nobody else left but Bobby Kennedy," recalled Hosea Williams, an aide to King, who, like many blacks, looked to Bobby for answers following King's death. "I remember telling him he had a chance to be a prophet. But prophets get shot." Late on the night of King's death, Kennedy seemed lost in thought as he mumbled to an aide "that fellow Harvey Lee . . . Lee Harvey; he set something loose in this country."

Inside the Ambassador Hotel's kitchen, a Jordanian nationalist named Sirhan Sirhan, a thin young man with curly dark hair, waited with a .22-caliber revolver while Kennedy shook the hands of nearby cooks, waitresses and busboys. According to a notebook later found by police in his apartment, Sirhan burned with an "unshakeable obsession" to kill Kennedy, to become a hero in the Arab world, or so he believed, for eliminating such a prominent friend of Israel. As a New York senator, Kennedy proved a consistent ally of the Jewish state and a close friend of many Jews—a far cry from the anti-Semitism in the Kennedys' private letters years earlier. In the bustle of the kitchen, Sirhan suddenly shrieked Kennedy's name and a volley of gunshots went off. The rapid popping noises sounded like firecrackers. Screams and panic poured out from the kitchen doors. Television cameras, still beaming their signals nationwide, recorded the mayhem. Friends wrestled Kennedy's assailant to the ground and disarmed him. Newfield remembered a young woman in a bright red party dress sobbing, "No, God, no. It's happened again."

On the concrete floor, Bobby lay dying in a pool of blood, his arms stretched out limply and his face looking up with almost a tranquil expression. A busboy named Juan Romero placed a small crucifix and rosary beads in his hand. "Is everybody safe, OK?" Bobby asked, before he passed out, never to regain consciousness. Later at the hospital, Ethel made sure, like her sister-in-law before her, that her husband received last rites from a priest. A bullet had shattered Bobby's brain, though his body kept functioning for several more hours, as his family, friends and the whole world learned of his fate. In the end, his heart was the last to fail.

THE SOUNDS OF LATIN and smell of incense—the residue of church rituals for the dead—were no longer foreign nor peculiar for America. Even the television network cameramen in the back of St. Patrick's Cathedral seemed to know where to station themselves. The second funeral for a Kennedy in less than five years carried a haunting familiarity, a shared national trauma in which the Catholic Mass became part of a larger civic remembrance. So much of that day's oratory about Robert Kennedy placed his death in the context of America's destiny, as a martyr for his country. On this day, the Catholic liturgy seemed to transcend itself, providing comfort, solace and spiritual reflection to Americans regardless of their denomination. In death, if not always in life, the Kennedys, as Catholics, finally appeared accepted on their own terms.

The personal toll of Robert Kennedy's assassination didn't become fully apparent until his children mournfully walked up the aisle, past their father's casket, as their mother, clad in black, followed them into a stiff wooden pew.

Somehow the lofty goals and soaring rhetoric of the campaign trail seemed to pale at the painful reality of ten children left without a father. "This was the terrible culminating hour of all the dreaded apprehensions of almost five years," Norman Cousins observed about Kennedy's widow. "One would never know which was greater, the grief or the courage, for her face revealed both."

Ethel Kennedy made sure the priests for Bobby's Mass wore purple robes, a color signifying hope, instead of funereal black. "If there's one thing about our faith, it's our belief that this is the beginning of eternal life and not the end of life," she insisted. "And I want this Mass to be as joyous as it possibly can be." Bobby's funeral, far more than his brother's, reminded Americans that the Kennedys were more than just one notable individual, but rather an extended family of considerable talents and sizeable ambitions, including in-laws such as Sargent Shriver, who was then U.S. ambassador to France. The Kennedys' sense of being a clan, devoted as much by shared loyalties as by blood, emerged in death as in life as one of their most resonant qualities. "Family was clearly the leit-motif," said one editorialist of the RFK funeral. "Not family in the sense of the glamorous qualities that have, at times, made the Kennedys a political or social prodigy, but of the homely ability to band together for strength in adversity."

There were words and songs that reminded the gathering of the Kennedys' Irish Catholic background, of the sense of tragic fate so much a part of the family's history and the Irish-American experience. Yet nothing at the Mass struck the soul as much as his remaining brother's tortured voice as he delivered the eulogy. Teddy had been up for most of the night, working with aide Adam Walinsky to make sure his words captured his brother's spirit. By dawn, he was seen sitting alone in the eleventh pew, just staring at the plain mahogany casket flanked by six tall candles, their flames flickering. In his eulogy, Teddy quoted from a speech that Bobby had given to a group of students in South Africa in 1966. After that, he gave his own summary of Bobby. "My brother need not be idealized or enlarged in death beyond what he was in life," Ted reminded. "He should be remembered as a good and decent man who saw wrong and tried to right it, saw suffering and tried to heal it, saw war and tried to stop it." In closing, Ted Kennedy used the same words of Irish-born writer George Bernard Shaw that Bobby had borrowed so often on the presidential campaign trail, just as Jack had done before him. "Some men see things as they are and say, why," Teddy repeated, his voice cracking. "I dream things that never were and say, why not."

FROM NEW YORK, a train carried Robert Kennedy's body on a long slow pilgrimage headed toward Washington. The senator would be buried not far from his brother's grave at Arlington National Cemetery, the same site that Bobby and Jackie approved in 1963. When Jackie heard that Bobby had been shot, she flew immediately from New York to Los Angeles and offered her help in the family's preparations for the funeral. Despite her own moments of doubt, Jackie had developed a profound respect for the Catholic faith and what it meant to the Irish. "The Church is . . . at its best only at the time of death," she explained in Los Angeles to Frank Mankiewicz, Bobby's campaign spokesman. "The rest of the time it's often rather silly little men running around in their black suits. But the Catholic Church understands death. I'll tell you who else understands death are the black churches. I remember at the funeral of Martin Luther King. I was looking at those faces, and I realized that they know death. They see it all the time and they are ready for it . . . in the way in which a good Catholic is." The Kennedys knew the ritual and emotions all too well. "We know death," Jackie added. "If it weren't for the children, we'd welcome it."

The train ride with Bobby's casket became a traveling Irish wake. So many friends and family members tried hard to remember the good times of the past rather than dwell on the agonizing moment. "One particular aspect of the train ride that stood out was its Irishness," recalled author Michael Harrington, as the drinking, jokes and storytelling conveyed an "affirmation of life in the presence of death." Down the aisles of the train, Ethel ushered her eldest son, Joseph Kennedy II, who shook hands and embraced all those assembled like a politician working a crowd. The press later recounted this long pilgrimage as an odd, inebriated, almost eccentric event rather than a deeply felt celebration of Bobby's ascent into an eternal life, as so many of the Kennedys and their Catholic friends believed. They tried to be brave for each other and emphasize with their actions that somehow life would still go on. "You could look around and absolutely *see* which of those people were strong Catholics," remarked Geraldine Brooks, who was married to writer Budd Schulberg, an old RFK pal. Dave Powers, part of Jack's "Irish Mafia," entertained Kennedy family members and friends with his humorous tales of Wakes O'Shaughnessey, a legendary old Boston pol who scouted out obituaries from the newspapers. He'd curry favor from survivors by attending the wakes of their beloved dead, even though he never knew them. Eventually, O'Shaughnessey became a connoisseur of the Boston Irish's most macabre but uplifting observance.

"Wakes, what do you think of this one? Are you enjoying it?" one widow asked, as Powers told it.

"This is one of the greatest wakes of all time, Mrs. Murphy," says Wakes. "In fact, I think you ought to put him on ice and keep it going for another two days."

The uninitiated were told, somewhat to their amazement, how much President Kennedy enjoyed Dave's audacious stories, providing a small glimpse into the unexplored ethnic side of Camelot. This wistful humor became part of the atmosphere on the eight-hour funeral train ride for Jack's dead brother. Mankiewicz later noted the differing "religious culture" among those on the train. "The Irish were having a wake, the Protestants were at a funeral, and the Jews were weeping and carrying on," he said. Columnist Joseph Alsop, who had observed the Kennedy clan for decades, described the funeral as "medieval," something tribal and Celtic in root. "It was the funeral of the Irish chieftain," said Alsop. "One had the feeling that the clan had lost its chieftain and was going to bury him."

All the talk of succession, of the next in line to take charge of the Kennedy mantle, of hopeful speculation by usually sober voices suggesting Bobby's surviving brother run for president in 1968, seemed like the old days of the chieftains when the sept leader fell. "The Kennedy forces are for the moment leaderless," wailed the *Nation,* a usually sober publication. It urged Ted Kennedy to enter the race, assuring that "his policies are sound and . . . his heart is stout." Christ-like allusions and Catholic imagery were invoked by others to recall Bobby. "The last time I shook hands with him, I remember thinking of the stigmata," said radical Tom Hayden, who had watched Kennedy's frenzied crowds stretch out their arms, striving for a glimpse, a touch of him. "His hands reminded me of someone who had been crucified." Alsop said he received a dozen "supremely silly letters from outwardly perfectly intelligent people, saying that now that Bobby's gone, the only thing we can do is run Teddy for President. It was exactly as though now that O'Neill is gone, O'Neill's son is the only possible chieftain for the clan. It is not at all the normal thing in America, let me tell you."

For all the remembrances inside the train, the most remarkable scene, the most lasting testament to Robert Kennedy's politics existed *outside* the procession—in the faces of people gathered on the street corners, along the guardrails and standing in grassy fields near the tracks, white and black, young and old, filled with an empty forlornness, as though a friend had died. Thousands lined the route that carried Kennedy's body, paying their respects to his memory and what might have been. Whether Kennedy's long-shot bid to win the White House could have succeeded was far from certain, despite the inevitability suggested in so many accounts of his campaign. Vice President Hubert Humphrey, the eventual 1968 Democratic presidential nominee, was busily gathering all the delegates loyal to Johnson, and McCarthy still threatened a major show of support among liberals. If Kennedy had been elected, as some historians contend, the nostalgic haze surrounding him might have soon disappeared and given way to sharp criticism from the left as well as the right.

But at the moment of his death, Robert Kennedy held the potential of bringing so many different factions, so many new minorities into America's presidential politics. The most tantalizing aspect of his star-crossed campaign was how he managed to broaden the Kennedy legacy beyond the Irish and other white ethnics to include Latinos, blacks, Asians, women and other minorities. His cultural conservatism—what some observers called his Catholic side—blended with his social progressiveness to form a new inclusive political alliance. His candidacy represented a potent plan for the Democrats to build their old New Deal coalition rather than see it chipped away by the Republicans' Southern strategies and appeals to race. It was a prescription for the future, if only they would listen. With Bobby Kennedy, the tent was getting bigger, not being divided into small competing factions. In his final efforts, Kennedy died trying to incorporate these new faces into the party's base, to bring these "outsiders" in.

The Ghosts of Camelot

> "I don't think my books could have been
> written in the world that existed before
> the Kennedy assassination. And I think
> that some of the darkness in my work is a
> direct result of the confusion and psychic
> chaos and the sense of randomness that
> ensued from that moment in Dallas. It's
> conceivable that this made me the writer
> I am—for better or for worse."
>
> —DON DELILLO

AFTER THEIR QUICK-HIT sexual encounters, the president usually found enough time to converse postcoitally with his paramour, Judith Campbell Exner. A "slam-bam-thank-you ma'am" kind of lover, Jack Kennedy didn't like to linger for chitchat. Various women with whom he engaged in extramarital conviviality provided similar accounts of his businesslike approach, his single-minded intent and his amiable but not particularly engaged conversation during these interludes. Rarely did the president reveal what breezed through his mind as he relieved himself of all that pent-up Kennedy testosterone. But with Judith Exner, a strikingly beautiful brunette first introduced to him by singer Frank Sinatra, he discovered one particular commonality.

"He was very interested in the fact that I was from a large family and that I was a Catholic," Exner informed Seymour M. Hersh, whose 1997 compilation of Camelot's "dark side" obsessed on Kennedy's sexual peccadilloes with the zeal of a Comstocker. As a matter of fact, Exner's other married boyfriend, Chicago mobster Sam Giancana, was also a Catholic.

Adultery, though, was the least of their sins.

The sexual nexus between the president and the Mafia wasn't revealed publicly until more than a decade after Kennedy's assassination—long after the romantic but highly misleading Camelot legend had taken root firmly in the American psyche. The truth about the president's perfidy read like one of Kennedy's favorite spy novels. A lengthy November 1975 report by a U.S. Senate subcommittee investigating the CIA and its alleged assassination plots on foreign leaders mentioned, in a tiny footnote on the bottom of page 129, that Exner (identified only as "the President's friend") had been in contact with Kennedy's White House no less than seventy times from her home telephone. Her sexual relationship with Kennedy began shortly after his 1960 election and lasted until March 1962, when FBI director J. Edgar Hoover apparently informed the president during a private luncheon that his sexual liaisons with Exner were turning up in FBI field agents' case reports on Giancana. The Senate committee also discovered that Giancana, a "prominent Chicago underworld figure," was a central figure in the CIA's plan against Cuba during the Kennedy administration and boasted of a government-approved assassination plot against Fidel Castro.

The Senate revelations were, in the parlance of tabloidese, a bombshell. Coming on the heels of Richard Nixon's agonizing Watergate resignation, the nation's devastating retreat from Vietnam and a general disillusionment with America's imperial presidency, the Senate report had a profound impact on the public's view of the martyred president. "The Exner account was a sort of triple whammy laid on Kennedy's once golden memory—not only an illicit love affair in the White House, but a link to the Mafia, through a woman who was in turn linked to participants in an assassination plot," wrote *New York Times* columnist Tom Wicker, who seemed embarrassed about how little he had known of Kennedy's "dark side" while covering the White House. The Senate's rather sanctimonious-sounding "Church report"—named after Senator Frank Church, the committee's chair—startled a nation that was still fundamentally Puritanical. It disappointed many of Kennedy's admirers, particularly Catholics. Jack's sexual licentiousness left them with feelings of moral revulsion and betrayal.

Before this report, there were plenty of critiques of the Kennedy years, usually written by conservatives who could be dismissed easily as crackpots or reactionaries. After the Senate report, a flood of media documentation about Kennedy's sex life, including a 1977 ghostwritten book by Exner herself, seemed to sully and overwhelm his carefully nurtured legacy. The nation's largest news magazine, *Time,* which had once jockeyed for intimate family photos of John-John and Caroline, now informed their readers about "Fiddle" and "Faddle," the Secret Service code names for two young women traveling with Kennedy who had "no discernable duties." In this revisionist version of the Kennedy presidency, plots to blow up Castro with exploding cigars or to poison him with the help of gangsters were given moral equivalency with sexual threesomes played out in the pool behind the Oval Office. Ultimately, his critics relied on sex to tear at the Camelot legend, partly because Kennedy was no longer alive to cover it up. Camelot seemed like a long-lost fairy tale. And all the hagiographies and all the Kennedy men couldn't put this image together again.

From the very beginning, the Camelot imagery seemed an odd and determined attempt to cast the Kennedy story in decidedly Anglophile terms. This family of Irish Catholic immigrants who, at best, had an ambivalent relationship with Great Britain, now saw their dead beloved Jack portrayed as an English king. His brothers, Bobby and Ted, and other key administration officials became knights of the round table, and Jacqueline Kennedy was depicted as his regal widowed queen. Earlier attempts to portray the Kennedys as pioneers for American equality, for the ascendancy of immigrants into the mainstream of society, gave way to this storybook parable of British royalty and entitlement.

In an emotional interview days after her husband's murder, Jackie Kennedy mentioned the Broadway musical called "Camelot," how Jack liked to play its songs on their Victrola to relax at night, and how she felt the image of Camelot was so emblematic of her husband's presidency. Alone with the grief-filled widow, journalist Theodore H. White immediately grabbed on to the Camelot metaphor and milked it in a way that gave his own editors at *Life* magazine pause before printing it. Nevertheless, the allegory resonated with a nation still searching for answers to Kennedy's senseless killing and moved by the graceful majesty of his funeral. Fifteen years later, White acknowledged that "the magic Camelot of John F. Kennedy never existed." Like so many other journalists of his generation, White was mesmerized by Kennedy's charisma—a word so identified with JFK that it now seems dated. In hindsight, he identified a more significant aspect of Kennedy's presidency, far less Anglo-Saxon in orientation, as his lasting legacy. "It is quite obvious now, of course, that he was the man who broke up the old pattern of American politics," White wrote.

He was the man who ruptured the silent understanding that had governed American politics for two centuries—that this was a country of
white Protestant gentry and yeomen who offered newer Americans a
choice for leadership only within their clashing rivalries. . . .
Historically, he was a gate-keeper. He unlatched the door, and
through the door marched not only Catholics, but blacks, and Jews,
and ethnics, women, youth, academics, newspersons and an entirely
new breed of young politicians who did not think of themselves as
politicians—all demanding their share of the action and the power in
what is now called participatory democracy.

At the time of its invention, however, Camelot played to the Anglo-
Saxon inclinations of America's opinion makers. These top columnists and
television commentators, mostly white Protestant men themselves, generally subscribed to the "melting pot" school of American assimilation, where
ethnicity was left behind in the name of progress. Jack Kennedy appeared
the perfect graduate of this school of assimilation, an Anglophilic creation, like some modern-day Pygmalion, who had been scrubbed clean of
any hint of his Irish Catholic heritage. "He was a story-book President,
younger and more handsome than mortal politicians, remote even from his
friends, graceful, almost elegant, with poetry on his tongue and a radiant
young woman at his side," recalled James Reston of the *New York Times,*
then perhaps the nation's most admired columnist, a year after JFK's passing. In this nostalgic haze, they remembered Kennedy's princely handling
of press conference questions. They rewound and replayed the film clips
and photos of his interrupted presidency, sometimes accompanied by the
Camelot theme music, until the image became embedded in the minds of
Americans. Anniversaries of his death became cause for remembering the
Camelot myth. Even the press had a difficult time remaining objective. "It
is hard to think of another politician into whose life so many people read
themselves with such indulgence," observed Henry Fairlie in a 1973
Harper's essay revisiting the Camelot legend. At a Washington luncheon
sometime after JFK's murder, Wicker discussed Kennedy's legacy with a
group of political wise men, including Richard Scammon, the president's
Census Bureau director. "He'll be remembered for just one thing," declared
Scammon. "He was the first Roman Catholic elected President. Period."
Scammon had seen the numbers, counted the heads and knew a historical
ground shift when he saw one. But faced with a challenge to the accepted
boundaries of the Camelot legend, Wicker says, he was "scandalized by this
first hint of revisionism," and never explored the comment's significance.

Any detailed suggestion that John Kennedy's presidency might be influenced by his cultural background—or that his election signified not only a historic advance for Irish Catholics but for America's immigrants and minorities at large—wouldn't be welcome here. As historical analysis goes, the Camelot myth was more comfortable, a lot less ethnic and had its own secular catechism. As Gore Vidal noted mockingly, books by Kennedy's devotees were "not so much political in approach as religious." In retelling, Vidal said "the thousand days unfold in familiar sequence and, though the details differ from gospel to gospel, the story already possesses the quality of a passion play." These Camelot versions presented Jackie, Bobby and other key players in the drama as "demigods, larger than life," Vidal explained, and always included its "ritual" ending with Jack's death (sometimes featured in the first chapter). Unflattering facts were ignored by these authors; there were hints that bad things—such as the nation's quagmire in Vietnam—never would have happened if their lost king had lived.

"The sources of the holy family's power is the legend of the dead brother, who did not much resemble the hero of the books under review," attested Vidal. "The myth that JFK was a philosopher-king will continue as long as the Kennedys are in politics. And much of the power that they exert over the national imagination is a direct result of the ghastliness of what happened in Dallas." Interestingly enough, Vidal suggested the Kennedys' Irish Catholic background had more to do with their motives than many understood. "In a way, the whole Kennedy episode is a fascinating throwback to an earlier phase of civilization," Vidal observed. "Because the Irish maintained the ancient village sense of the family longer than most places in the West and to the extent that the sons of Joe Kennedy reflect those values and prejudices, they are an anachronism in an urbanized non-family-minded society."

SEX BECAME A STAPLE of the Kennedy bestseller for the next quarter century. In some books, Kennedy's promiscuity was used as a weapon to explain away legitimate political achievement (such as the Cuban missile stare down with the Soviets) as nothing more than unabated recklessness. Tales of who-was-doing-what-to-whom in Camelot was merely a fan dance to attract attention to other books, the musky lubricant for more sales. Numerous exposés speculated on Marilyn Monroe's alleged affairs with Jack and Bobby Kennedy, the Boswells ranging from the machismo Norman Mailer to the feminist Gloria Steinem. The 1960s Rat Pack friendships with Sinatra and presidential brother-in-law Peter Lawford, the Hollywood and Las Vegas–based atmosphere of starlets and wise guys, brought a

Runyonesque "Guys and Dolls" tone to these stagings of Camelot. Former girl friends, including Judith Exner and Gloria Swanson, cashed in with tell-alls that featured breathless re-creations of their sexual exploits with the Kennedys. In successive tomes, various Kennedy brothers, sisters, cousins, in-laws, and their hired help were all caught with their pants down. Each book touted its own new indiscretion, its own sneak peek behind into the Kennedy boudoir or White House bacchanalia. Whether real or imagined, sex acts among the long-ago dead seemed all that was left to rouse the living. Religion made Kennedy lust seem more enticing. The marital infidelities and the tales of unbridled urges seemed more sinful, more like a bite from the biblical forbidden fruit, because of their Roman Catholic faith and the church's taboos. Indeed, the Kennedys' obsessions underlined the sexual duplicity in their ancient church and in modern American society.

During this sexually permissive age of the 1970s—awash in media stories of free love on campus, spouse-swapping in the suburbs and other excesses of the flesh—similar disclosures about other former politicians merited only a ho-hum reaction, sort of like learning rumply old Eisenhower had a mistress. To many Americans, however, the adultery and carnal sins of the Kennedys confirmed their own prejudices about Catholic dogma and hypocritical edicts from Rome regarding sex. The clean, wholesome family image projected by the president's handlers contrasted with his satyr-like behavior in private. John Kennedy was voted into office in part because of his physical attractiveness, his magnetism in crowds and his appeal for women, and yet Americans appeared shocked when they learned he had acted out their adulterous fantasies.

Sexual hypocrisy pervaded the Kennedys' own actions. During 1960s, Attorney General Robert Kennedy brought a criminal pornography case against Ralph Ginsburg, publisher of a well-regarded art journal, *Eros,* because it printed nude photographs, including some of black men suggestively touching white women at a time when television wouldn't even show them kissing. "I ought to prosecute him, but it'll hurt me politically," Bobby told a top Justice Department aide. "They will blame it on my Catholicism." Sure enough, when the indictment came, Ginsburg blamed Kennedy's religious prudery for bringing such an affront to the First Amendment and eventually forcing him to jail. "He may not have thought I was ruining the country's morality, but the Catholics whispering in his ear thought so," Ginsburg said. If Bobby was a bloodhound in public on sexual immorality, he learned to keep his mouth shut on private matters close to home. He knew about the improper dossiers kept by FBI director J. Edgar Hoover containing information on the alleged extramarital affairs of his brother, but he remained quiet. In his oral history for the Kennedy library, Bobby indicated he knew about other sexual escapades of Washington politicians, shuttled to him by Hoover, including an FBI probe into call girls and at least "one Senator from the South who had a Negro mistress." But Bobby, because of what he knew, was in no position to throw stones.

In its own way, the sordid disclosures of the Kennedys' sexuality highlighted the pretense confronting American Catholics on sexual matters in general, a rank hypocrisy often staring at them in the mirror. As the nation's best known Catholics, the Kennedys, like millions of their co-religionists, professed an allegiance to a church run by an abstinent clergy and a distant papacy that inundated their flock with restrictions on sex, birth control, divorce and threats of condemnation if these rules weren't followed. Yet the complexity and sheer messiness of the Kennedys' adult lives underlined the difficulties for many American Catholics living with these strictures.

Tensions in the Kennedy family also reflected another dramatic change in the realm of sex—the role of women. Despite the considerable reforms already afoot, from Vatican II to the rising tide of feminism, most American Catholic women were still relegated to secondary status and often treated as either mother-Madonna figures or as male playthings. Kennedy women were no exception. Camelot was a near-exclusive male domain. None of the president's inner circle of advisers was female. In many respects, the all-male Irish Mafia of Kennedy's White House reflected the old Irish Catholic delineation between the sexes in public settings. The church's attempt to exert control over the lives and independence of Catholic women was particularly illustrated when Camelot's widowed queen announced she wanted to remarry.

In October 1968, Jackie made her intentions known regarding Aristotle Onassis, the Greek shipping tycoon, an older, gnarly multimillionaire, two inches shorter than Jackie and nearly twice her age. For several months, she discreetly dated Onassis but deferred to Bobby Kennedy's request that she not make any nuptial plans during the 1968 presidential campaign. He realized the impact this marriage would have on American public opinion and didn't want it to hurt his chances. After Bobby's assassination, Jackie determined that America, with its random violence that had shattered her life, was no place fit for her children ("If they're killing Kennedys, my kids are number-one targets") and announced her intent to marry Onassis and live in Greece. She seemed to be pulling the curtain down on the Camelot era, a myth she had created but no longer appeared willing to maintain. Summing up the view from the United States, the *New York Times* headlined: "The Reaction Here Is Anger, Shock and Dismay." The news shook Rome as well. The Vatican's press spokesman, Monsignor Fausto Vallainc, said the church had determined that Jackie "knowingly violated the laws of the church" with her marriage to Onassis and had thereby become ineligible to receive the sacraments, including Holy Communion. Rumors spread that Jackie now faced excommunication.

Appalled by the furor, Cardinal Cushing defended the former first lady as an act of conscience and out of loyalty to her dead husband. Before her wedding, Jackie sought Cushing's advice in Boston. During a highly emotional two-hour session at the cardinal's residence, he assured her that Caroline and John Jr. would remain Catholics and expressed confidence that some arrangement could be made for her to remarry. It sounded like something Joe Kennedy might say if he could. To comply with the church's rules, Onassis, a non-Catholic, sought his own annulment from a previous marriage. He contacted the Vatican's Sacred Rota, the church's supreme board deciding on such marital matters, but to no avail. The Vatican was clearly displeased. Cushing, the most high-profile progressive within the American hierarchy, discounted Rome's concerns. In a talk before his fellow Boston Catholics, the cardinal strongly supported Jackie's decision to marry. "This idea of saying that she's excommunicated, that she's a public sinner—what a lot of rubbish," he scoffed. "Only God knows who is a sinner and who is not. Why can't she marry whomever she wants?"

But a few days later, a church spokesman in Rome insisted that Jackie remained "in an irregular position" with the church and, with a swipe at Cushing, replied that "the cardinal certainly must have advised her of this." The Vatican City weekly, *L'Osservatore della Domenica,* again condemned her as a public sinner who had effectively walked away from the Catholic Church. Cushing was so embittered by the angry response against the former first lady—not only from the Vatican but in letters and remarks from many fellow Catholics—that he announced his resignation as Boston's cardinal. "There are a lot of people who hate the Kennedys," Cushing said. "They hated the grandfather, they hated the father, they hated the son, they hate the girls, and now they're picking on me." His resignation lasted for two weeks until he reconsidered.

THIS HIGH-PROFILE dispute illustrated the deeper divisions within the American church, particularly on matters relating to sex. The liberalism of Pope John XXIII was proving to be short-lived. The windows of change he once threw open were being closed again by the Curia and his more conservative successors in the papacy. Nowhere were these schisms more stark, more apparent than on the subject of birth control. For his part, Cushing indicated his willingness to help the church reconsider some of its teachings on this vexing issue, just as he'd done himself. During the 1940s, Cushing staunchly opposed the repeal of an 1879 Massachusetts law prohibiting birth control information. He railed against "birth controllers, abortioners and mercy killers." But by the 1960s, various factors prompted Cushing to modify his position.

At Harvard Medical School, a Catholic physician named Dr. John Rock, a fertility and birth control expert, wrote an influential book on the newly developed birth control pill and the morality of using artificial contraception. Cushing cautioned that the book didn't bear the church's imprimatur, but it clearly affected his thinking. His friendship with the liberal-minded Kennedys, and the prevailing view of theologians advocating a separation of church and state, convinced him that preventing birth control in a pluralistic society was wrong, even if Catholics were against it. This time, Boston's archdiocese didn't stand in the way when Massachusetts repealed its law preventing birth control information. Cushing expressed confidence that scientists and doctors like Rock might find a way for Catholics to use a reliable method of birth control acceptable to the Vatican. "The church's idea is that birth control through artificial means is contrary to nature . . . but I am convinced that through more and more research, especially along the lines of the rhythm theory, they will come up with a non-artificial way of controlling births," he predicted. "My sympathy does go out to those people who are having problems with large families and who are worried sick about the church's teaching." In the mid-1960s, Cushing expressed hope that another session of Vatican II and a papal commission studying birth control would more accurately reflect the everyday sexual life of married Catholic couples, he said.

But Cushing remained in the minority, as the church conservatives asserted themselves. Pope Paul VI's 1968 encyclical on birth control, *Humanae Vitae,* caused an uproar in the United States and left many faithful adherents embittered. After years of American wishful thinking that the hierarchy might change its position, Paul firmly rejected an advisory committee's recommendation to loosen the constraints on artificial birth control. Only the natural, almost primitive rhythm method of birth control— what critics called "Vatican roulette"—would be tolerated by Rome. In the confessional, ascetic priests faced their own moral crises as they commiserated with married working-class Catholic couples who didn't want to lose their eternal souls but cried out that they couldn't afford any more children.

The number of ordinations, which climbed after World War II, fell precip-itously after this encyclical and has yet to recover.

After generations of faithful compliance to the church's teaching, many Catholics found themselves directly at odds with the Pope on perhaps the most important decision of their lives—the creation of a family. Though not a central tenet of the faith, the church's ban on artificial birth control underlined the Pope's authority, establishing a certain cynicism within the flock. A Harris poll taken in 1967 showed that one in every three Catholics relied on birth control pills, condoms or other artificial devices. Rather than create honest dialogue, however, the Pope's decree compounded the church's sexual duplicity. The opposition thundered loudly in the United States. "The subsequent attack of over six-hundred American theologians on the papal position represented a coup de grace not only to the rationale for the 'Church's teaching' on contraception but for the clarity of faith in infallibility," observed sociologist William A. Osborne two years later in a book published by Notre Dame.

Regarding sexual concerns, the Kennedy brothers usually acted as social moderates, at least compared to their fellow Democrats. Before the 1960 presidential campaign, Jack Kennedy endured a gauntlet of questions about the birth control issue and whether he could live up to his responsibilities as president and a practicing Catholic. Columnist James Reston conducted a thorough vetting in print of the candidate on this issue. Kennedy's early stance—against linking birth control programs to U.S. foreign aid—was dis-missed by the *New Republic* and other critics as a sign of the church's sway over his thinking. Well aware of the Catholic vote and its importance to his electoral success, Jack Kennedy remained careful not to offend the church's hierarchy. As president, however, Kennedy "quietly but extensively" in-creased government support for birth control to other nations if they requested it, Sorensen later pointed out. A presidential commission on the status of women, initiated by Kennedy, eventually called in 1968 for repeal of restrictive abortion laws. Yet in his own lifetime, Jack didn't face the far more divisive issue of abortion as his brothers would.

IN EARLY 1967, Robert Kennedy was evasive and noncommittal about whether to liberalize New York State's abortion laws. Some liberal Catholic lay leaders pushed the junior senator to endorse the pending abortion bill in the state legislature, just as they had done successfully in overhauling the state's divorce laws. But that year, Bobby struggled and dodged the moral questions surrounding abortion. In January, a Kennedy spokesman told the press that Bobby wanted to study the proposed abortion legislation and "that even then he might not make a public statement." A month later, inside the gymnasium at Syosset High School in suburban Long Island, Kennedy blurted out his view in front of a group of inquiring students.

"Being a Catholic, what are your feelings on the current proposals to liberalize and update the abortion laws?" asked Martin Friedlander, a senior at Syosset High.

Kennedy appeared perplexed. "Being a Catholic?" he repeated.

"Well, being a Senator," the student amended.

The question clearly hit a vulnerable spot.

"Being a Senator or being a Catholic?" Kennedy mused.

"Being a Senator—a Senator who is Catholic," Friedlander replied persistently.

Playing to the crowd, Kennedy drew a laugh when he echoed aloud "a Senator who is Catholic," as if he needed to mull it over. Then he repeated the same separation of church and state position articulated by his brother in 1960, adding that "I try to make my judgment in these matters not based upon religion but upon how I believe as a Senator." Finally, after weeks of evasion, he decided the question was worthy of a response.

"I think there are obvious changes that have to be made," Kennedy said, claiming he hadn't yet studied the details of the state bill, which was outside his realm as a U.S. senator. "But I think changes could certainly be made." He said nothing more on the subject. When another Syosset student tried again to raise the issue, he said he'd already given his answer.

ABORTION HAD BEEN a crime in New York since 1883, permitted only if necessary to save a pregnant woman's life. The new bill proposed by state Assemblyman Al Blumenthal, a Kennedy supporter, extended the ability of a doctor to terminate a pregnancy when it posed a substantial risk to a woman's physical or mental health or of the birth of a "defective" child. The new law also would allow any unwed girl under age fifteen to get an abortion as well as victims of rape or incest. The original version of this bill wound up sidetracked in committee, but another version of the legislation passed in 1970. Two years later, under pressure from the Catholic Church and other abortion opponents, the state legislature voted to repeal the abortion reform. It was kept in place with a veto from Governor Nelson Rockefeller, a liberal Republican. But abortion continued to loom as a political minefield for decades.

In 1967, Bobby Kennedy wasn't alone in his chariness. Politicians who were Roman Catholics remained wary of taking the lead on an emotionally charged issue so clearly opposed by their church hierarchy. When the state legislature first considered it, a pastoral letter condemning the bill as "a new slaughter of the innocents" was read at Sunday Masses. A statewide group called the Right to Life committee, composed of many members recruited from Catholic churches and organizations, was formed to fight the bill. It became a precursor of the National Right to Life effort, which expanded greatly in coming years as the abortion debate spread across the nation.

For American Catholics, the abortion debate marked a political turning point. Cardinal Spellman's era of dominating New York politics was nearing its end, and increasing numbers of college-educated Catholics were demanding changes in all walks of life, including human sexuality. At the same time, many culturally conservative Catholics felt uneasy about legislating away the consequences of sex. They genuinely believed abortion to be murder. As this debate intensified, new political alliances would be formed and the broad bloc of Catholic voters that Democrat Jack Kennedy enjoyed in his 1960 march toward the presidency would be slowly, inexorably pulled apart.

The moral uncertainty could be found in the public opinion surveys of that time. Often, the abortion debate illustrated the dichotomy, the sexual artifice inherent in Catholic life. Despite the church's condemnation of abortions and their being largely illegal in the United States, medical experts estimated that about a million abortions were performed each year nationwide. Of the one hundred thousand in New York State, women were Catholic in equal proportion to other religious groups. Yet not all Catholic women, including those in the Kennedy family, were in favor of abortion reform. Early in the debate, Eunice Shriver expressed her concerns about the New York proposal. A long-time advocate for handicapped children, Eunice argued that legalizing abortion to prevent mental retardation would give medicine an unwarranted license to decide who should live or die in a "hard society." In the tradition of many Catholic social institutions, she felt society would be better served by encouraging unwed mothers to deliver their babies and perhaps give them to adoptive parents. Privately, Ethel Kennedy shared similar qualms about abortion and later described herself as a "friend of the fetus."

For Bobby, the need to articulate a public position on abortion became unavoidable. After his brief comments on Long Island, he expounded on his views at Skidmore College in Sarasota Springs, only to be confronted by a priest. In answering a female student's question, Kennedy said he wanted to see the current statute changed. "For example, if a lady is attacked and doesn't want to have a child, she should not have to have a child," he said.

Father Joseph F. DiMaggio had brought along sixty students from his moral ethics class at nearby St. Peter's Academy. Standing on the side of the college auditorium, he listened intently and then raised his hand to challenge the senator.

"To me, it seems you believe in some kind of doctrine wherein the end justifies the means," decried DiMaggio. "Wouldn't we lose respect for human life?"

Kennedy wouldn't have it. "If the question is—'Does the end justify the means?'—the answer is no," he insisted.

An uneasy ripple moved across the crowd of more than eight hundred, with sighs of exasperation and discontent directed toward the priest. Yet he persisted in making his point.

"True, we have sympathy for the woman attacked," the priest said, "but isn't there some question whether human life might be involved and whether the ends justifies the means?"

There was no point pursuing things further. "I think I answered your question, Father," Kennedy replied, politely and without contempt. "I don't think there is anything to be gained by continuing this discussion."

Outside the auditorium, DiMaggio said he liked Kennedy personally but, like many Catholics, didn't agree with his stand on abortion. "To favor abortion means you are willing to kill life," DiMaggio said. "It's definitely not the teaching of the church."

IN THE FAIRY-TALE world of Camelot politics—not even in the "psychobiographies" of his detractors—Jack Kennedy rarely appeared to worry about the truth or consequences of sex. The Roman Catholic Church was often an unabashed, albeit unofficial, ally for his ambitions and a compliant keeper of his secrets. To many established Catholics, Camelot was encased in fond memories, part of the climb out of the old ethnic neighborhoods of the past. "It may be hard to remember the impetus that Kennedy gave to a sense of Catholic 'arrival' in America," observed theologian Richard John Neuhaus after so many of JFK's transgressions were exposed. "Despite subsequent revelations about his private life (news photographers at the time, for example, agreed not to publish pictures of him smoking cigarettes), the Kennedy myth remains the forceful statement of Catholics having made it in America."

But by the 1970s, the Roman Catholic hierarchy was no longer enamoured with the Kennedy family or its politics. Many practicing Catholics felt increasingly alienated by the Kennedys, and they, too, seemed disillusioned by the rightward drift of their onetime followers. The Camelot myth remained strong in the minds of Americans, but it became a strangely secular one, no longer endorsed by churchmen such as Cushing but propagated by the media. For Jack's survivors, particularly his youngest brother, American society's obsessions with sex cast Camelot in an uncomfortable light, and gradually changed its meaning. Camelot came to signify the glories of a lost era, the blinding light of celebrity and having sex with other celebrities or sycophants. Rather than a high-minded call to public service, as Jacqueline Kennedy said she had intended, Camelot became a parable about excess and its consequences.

Slowly, Camelot transformed into a morality tale about cruel fate, repeated over and over, for a family affixed with a supposed curse. Untimely death and tragedy, rather than inappropriate sex, became the media's driving narrative, its new focus of attention. Even though their religion rejected such notions, "the Kennedy curse" became a popular refrain—a theme mentioned so often that even some family members seemed to believe it. In early family histories, the deaths of Joseph Kennedy Jr. and Kathleen Kennedy were usually described as unfortunate accidents, caused by war or weather; the assassinations of Jack and Bobby as the deeds of madmen rather than the vengeful acts of God. Yet the sense of a tragic fate brewing, the looming presence of a Kennedy curse, could be found as early as 1964, when a plane carrying Ted crashed, leaving him severely injured and killing others, including the aircraft's pilot. "I guess the only reason we've survived is that there are more of us than there is trouble," Bobby remarked. Rather than being the luckiest family in Boston, they seemed like the most unfortunate, as if they were being punished for something. After too many funerals, Cardinal Cushing admitted "the Kennedy family has had more tragic deaths and more family troubles than any family of my acquaintance."

Camelot's proponents took pains to deny any such competing myth. "There is no curse upon the Kennedys," Ted Sorensen insisted right after RFK's 1968 assassination. "They have more than their fair share of ill fate because they had more than their share of the courage and conviction required to dare and to try and to tempt fate." Soon, however, the true ending of the Camelot legend came when Ted Kennedy's Oldsmobile 88 slipped into the darkened Chappaquiddick in the summer of 1969. He had been drinking that night, sharing laughs and memories with those from Bobby's presidential campaign. He got in the car and left with a young blonde volunteer named Mary Jo Kopechne. When the car tipped off the bridge, Ted managed to save himself, but Kopechne drowned. The deadly accident and the senator's failure to alert authorities until hours later ended all realistic hopes that he might someday become president.

Days after, Kennedy went on television to explain the inexplicable. In an otherwise carefully prepared speech crafted by the old Camelot circle of advisers, the last Kennedy brother wondered aloud "whether some awful curse did actually hang over all the Kennedys." His dismissal of such a notion in the same speech seemed too late. The die was cast, the idea indelibly imprinted in the American psyche.

Probably the most difficult explanation that night was to his frail and infirm father, upstairs in a bedroom of the same Hyannis Port house where Ted gave his televised speech. "Dad, I've done the best I can," he apologized, "I'm sorry." The pale, contorted face of Joe Kennedy stared at his son without reply. Since his stroke in 1961, the once all-powerful patriarch had faded from public view altogether. He could no longer help his children, encourage their ambitious climbs, save them from their falls or make a call to a friend on their behalf. In his room, Joe had become a political afterthought, muffled voices outside his door deciding whether he should be disturbed by news from the outside world. With tears in their eyes, they came to tell him of Jack's death, and then Bobby's, and he could do nothing but stare. If he still had hopes for Teddy to take his brother's place in the White House, they were now gone. For even if he could utter a response, there were no words adequate for this sense of loss.

After Ted's Chappaquiddick disaster, Joe Kennedy's body and spirit withered. In November 1969, the doctors alerted the family that their patriarch was dying. When the end came, at his bedside were Rose and all his surviving children—Ted, Eunice, Jean and Pat (Rosemary was still institutionalized)—along with the rest of the extended family. Jackie flew in from Greece and spent a night comforting him. The Kennedys all clutched their rosaries and prayed the familiar prayers of their church. At age eighty-one, Joe lay unconscious, a life of frenetic striving now in total repose. When his family had finished murmuring the "Our Father" together, he was dead.

ONCE MORE, CARDINAL CUSHING tended to the Kennedys. Presiding over the funeral Mass, the family's favorite priest avoided black vestments and instead dressed in the white robes as Rose asked, underlining their belief in Christ's resurrection and an eternal afterlife. Only the family and close friends were invited, including Frank Morrissey and the other old cronies. "Brethren, we have become a spectacle to the whole world, to angels as well as men," the cardinal began. In death, the old controversies surrounding Joe Kennedy arose once more. The *Chicago Tribune* remembered him for backing Senator Joe McCarthy; the *New York Times* paid half-hearted homage to Ambassador Kennedy, reminding readers that "his pleas for appeasing Hitler, his repeated advice that Great Britain was finished, were appallingly wrong diplomatically and historically." Among those in public life, a sincere condolence came from Irish leader, Eamon De Valera, who knew very well how much the Kennedys meant to his country as well as their own.

The most meaningful tributes, however, were from the family itself. Several family members acted as honorary pallbearers and readers of prayers, and grandson Robert Kennedy Jr. served as an altar boy. During the funeral Mass, eight-year-old John Kennedy Jr. repeated by heart the twenty-third Psalm ("The Lord is my shepherd, I shall not want . . . "); Ted gave his own eulogy. "This is not as much a final prayer to Dad as a reminder to those of us he left behind of his deep love for us and our obligation and responsibility to lead the kind of lives he would want us to lead," the youngest son explained. Then he read from a memorial to their father written by Bobby a few years earlier for *The Fruitful Bough,* a small privately printed book of recollections gathered by Ted. No matter how painful, it seemed fitting that Bobby—the Kennedy son most like their father—should provide a posthumous eulogy. Most of all, Bobby remembered his father's drive, his ambitiousness for his sons without overwhelming or eclipsing them. "He loved all of us—the boys in a very special way," Bobby wrote. "I can say that, except for his influence and encouragement, my brother Jack might not have run for the Senate in 1952, there would have been much less likelihood that he would have received the Presidential nomination in 1960, I would not have become Attorney General, and my brother Teddy would not have run for the Senate in 1962."

In the rain, they drove from Hyannis back toward Boston, to the Holyhood Cemetery in Brookline, not far from where Joe and Rose had once lived and where the future president was born. Though others fashioned the Camelot myths around the Kennedy legacy, it was Joe who fashioned the reality, was the architect of their lives. They would never be the same without him. Cushing said a few last prayers before they all left. From then on, like some old Celtic myth where the flock is left without its leader, the Kennedy family awaited their next turn of fate.

Chapter Thirty-Seven

Last Hurrahs

"YOU'RE A DISGRACE TO THE IRISH!" a woman screamed as Senator Edward Kennedy walked away from Boston City Hall, the same place where his grandfather once ruled as champion of the city's Irish immigrants.

On the plaza that September morning in 1974, Kennedy wanted to explain his support of a controversial federal court order calling for busing to achieve school desegregation. Instead he got booed off the stage, unable to say anything. Under the court's plan, hundreds of black students from Roxbury and other minority communities would be transported into white neighborhood schools, while Irish and other white kids would be shipped into Roxbury High, infuriating their parents into a near riot. "Let your daughter get bused there so she can be raped!" the angry crowd shouted at Kennedy. They turned their backs to him and sang "God Bless America" to drown out his attempts to speak. As he left in frustration, the senator found himself surrounded by a sea of angry Irish faces screaming obscenities. Some threw eggs and tomatoes. One woman tried taking a punch at him.

No one wanted to listen.

THE IRISH IN BOSTON were always diehard Kennedy people, the core constituency of so many family political campaigns in the past. In spite of their vast differences in wealth and education, these working-class residents shared with the Kennedys an identifiably Irish Catholic ethos, a sense of obligation to family, church and country. During the post–World War II era, the conservative side of the Kennedys' politics appealed to these voters as much as the progressive—from the anti-Communist rhetoric of Senator Joseph McCarthy to the close affinity with the church and Cardinal Cushing. From the days of Honey Fitz, the Kennedy family always seemed to know what it was like to be Irish in Boston. They understood from experience the prejudice of the Brahmins, and the embittered feelings of being an outsider. These people viewed JFK as the embodiment of the American dream, the one among them who had made good. They cried when Jack was assassinated and Bobby was buried, and they kept a remarkable fidelity to Ted after the Chappaquiddick debacle. As they proved with James Michael Curley, the Boston Irish were willing to embrace a colorful rogue so long as they knew he was on their side. "Let them say what they want about our people—and we have many faults—they cannot say we are not loyal to our chieftain," Ted once declared in 1964, at a St. Patrick's Day ceremony to celebrate his brother's old "Irish Mafia."

Busing proved different, a distinct parting of the ways. A few days after Kennedy's confrontation, thousands of people from the old white ethnic neighborhoods such as Charlestown—the same area of Boston that John Kennedy once represented in Congress—were shouting again. On this first day of school, as buses filled with black children arrived, they cried "Niggers, go home!" They were not going to listen to a Kennedy, nor were they going to listen to the highest-ranking voice of Roman Catholicism in Boston. Cushing's successor, Humberto Medeiros, the Portguese-born, first non-Irish cardinal in Boston in more than a century, vaguely endorsed the government's busing edict and deliberately kept his distance from his enraged Irish parishioners. "The poor Irish, lacking the mighty church-state institutional edifice that had protected and guided them in years past, were left to sink into racism," writer Nicholas Lemann later observed.

The Catholic Church became complicit in this brand of urban Northern racism. Boston's parochial schools, once a haven for the children of Catholic immigrants when they were victims of prejudice, were now benefiting from racism. White students fled to these private Catholic academies as a fortress against the increased enrollment of black kids bused to their local public school. In 1973, before the court-ordered desegregation plan, white students made up about 60 percent of the public school enrollment in Boston; by the mid-1980s, after years of bickering and protest, the number of white students dropped to 26 percent. Although Medeiros discouraged white flight, most estimates indicate that about two thousand more white students each year were sent by their parents from public to parochial schools. Over the coming decade, black support for busing also fell dramatically, from about half favoring it in 1974 to a favorable rating of only 14 percent by 1982, according to a *Boston Globe* poll.

In jumping into the local busing imbroglio, Ted broke a fundamental rule of Kennedy politics. For years, both his father and his brothers had studiously avoided intramural disputes in Massachusetts politics. They tended to keep their distance from the Purple Shamrock and the corrupt practices of Honey Fitz's old cronies. With millions of their own, Joe Kennedy and sons didn't have to accept someone else's bribes to make their fortune. Despite calls to reform the state party, Ted steadfastly resisted. "Like Prince Hamlet, Ted is at the moment conducting a desultory dialogue with himself, undecided whether to plunge body and soul into the tangled issues of his state and party, or, like his late brother, withdraw from them," observed the *Saturday Evening Post* in 1965 during one Massachusetts squabble.

But in the 1970s, Ted Kennedy felt compelled to enter the local dispute on school desegregation, mostly because of the ideological commitments already made by his family. During the 1960s, his brothers enforced (and became vilified) for federal desegregation orders carried out in the South. When Federal Judge W. Arthur Garrity Jr.'s decision to desegregate became law in Boston, Ted responded to the call of the *Boston Globe* and other city liberals to get involved in Boston's debate. "We can't express one rule for Birmingham, Alabama and another rule for Boston, Massachusetts," Ted explained at a news conference on same day he was hooted down at City Hall.

IN THIS DISPUTE, Kennedy was pulled by conflicting loyalties. Judge Garrity, a soft-spoken thoughtful man who happened to be an Irish Catholic himself, had been appointed to the federal bench on Kennedy's recommendation. He was Ted's second choice when his first became a public fiasco. Back in the mid–1960s, Ted sought to fulfill his father's wish that the old family crony, Francis X. Morrissey, be placed on the federal bench. For years, Morrissey worked for the Kennedys as an all-purpose political fix-it man. Morrissey knew and kept the family secrets. As his reward, Morrissey became a local judge and badgered the Kennedys for a federal appointment—so much so that he became a pest. Joe Kennedy scolded Morrissey in 1960 for presuming that a federal judgeship would be "marked" for him. "I cannot imagine that I ever said that to you," he wrote, perhaps to cover his own tracks. The senior Kennedy's debilitating stroke in 1961 certainly didn't help Morrissey's chances. While their father was still alive, however, the Kennedy brothers wanted to make good on the old man's wish. "It's the only thing my father ever asked me," Ted reportedly told a friend.

Soon after Ted convinced President Johnson to nominate Morrissey, the truth about their crony's suspect legal credentials was exposed in the *Boston Globe* (the articles about Morrissey won a Pulitzer Prize). As it turned out, Morrissey's law degree came from a "diploma mill" in Georgia. He claimed he was practicing law there at the same time that he was running for the Massachusetts legislature and registering to vote as a Boston resident. The Kennedys and Cardinal Cushing tried to come to Morrissey's rescue, but his nomination was soon withdrawn. In his place, Garrity—who once worked in JFK's campaigns—was nominated successfully for the federal bench. His opinion in the school busing case, which stressed equal opportunities for all minorities in America, reflected the best of the Kennedy civil rights philosophy. Previously, Ted Kennedy had voiced doubts about the effectiveness of long-distance busing, but Garrity's ruling left little choice. He seemed honor-bound to speak out and support the judge's decision. As Kennedy once told a federal task force in Boston examining civil rights abuses, "For so long as we live in separate societies, one rich, one poor, one black, one white, one complacent, one despairing, we will not be the city we could be."

What Ted properly saw as noble, many angry Irish, Italian and other ethnic residents of South Boston perceived as arrogant. In particular, the Boston Irish, who had still viewed themselves as a minority long after their numbers became dominant, were often blind to their similarities with others. There seemed always a tension between the generous impulses of an embattled minority and the defensive posture of those feeling left behind in society. Historically, Kennedys and Fitzgeralds shared the view of that great Irish immigrant, John Boyle O'Reilly, who recognized the similar plight of Negroes and the Irish in the 1880s. "So long as American citizens and their children are excluded from schools, theaters, hotels and common conveyances, there ought not to be any question of race, creed or color— every heart that beats for humanity beats with the oppressed," he wrote. But by the 1970s, not all Irish Catholics were as magnanimous. Many lived in Boston's aging neighborhoods and had enjoyed little success in life. Working–class Irish Catholic residents of South Boston hadn't the money to move out to tony suburbs or to send their children to private academies. Their dreams were still blunted by low-paying, dead-end jobs; indeed, they were not unlike the black families they called names. They certainly didn't want the church or some rich Kennedy telling them what was right for their children. "The rage against Kennedy reached such a torrent because of the feeling, especially among Irish Catholics, that Kennedy, one of theirs, had betrayed them," wrote historian Ronald P. Formisano, nearly two decades later.

Once his core constituency, Kennedy's Boston Irish retreated for a time into a misplaced anger and resentment at blacks. One night in 1975, some extremists attempted to firebomb John Kennedy's birthplace and scrawled "Bus Teddy" on its sidewalk. In another incident, a militant group from Restore Our Alienated Rights (ROAR) jumped at Kennedy as he left a Quincy high school. They jabbed him with American flags and slashed his tires, forcing him to leave by subway with a police escort. Though heckled and jeered, Kennedy never attacked the Irish—what he called "my people"—for their behavior. He refused to call them bigots. He seemed to understand what their objections were, even if they didn't agree with him on the proposed remedy. Oddly enough, the Irish criticism of Ted's alleged betrayal occurred about the same time the senator experienced an awakening of his own Irish Catholic roots.

WHEN THE RIGHT moment arose, friends knew they could count on Teddy to sing the old Irish songs, to tell the stories carried down from the old days. "He could, when the mood stirred him, make any party come alive," recalled Theodore H. White, "as when he attended the wedding of Kenneth O'Donnell, John Kennedy's aide, and, lifting his tenor voice, led all the guests in Irish songs so that the wedding became a blessing in the memory of all there."

After his brothers' deaths, many family obligations became Ted's responsibility, a burden he managed well. The summer after President Kennedy's assassination, he traveled to Ireland, retracing many of his brother's steps in Dunganstown and elsewhere. He thanked the Irish for all that their hospitality meant to Jack. His Irish Catholic background seemed a crucial component in his makeup, an important cultural factor in deciphering Ted Kennedy as a public figure. Part of his pleasing victory for the Senate in 1962 against Republican George Lodge—son of Jack's 1952 opponent Henry Cabot Lodge and great-grandson of Honey Fitz's old Brahmin opponent—was his family's awareness of how the Irish in Boston overcame their detractors. "The identification of the Kennedy family with the Catholic Church is so great that really Ted is a Prince of the Church in this state," a Lodge aide complained, "You can't lay a glove on him." Ted Kennedy's dutiful nature carried over in religion as well as politics. Whatever his own difficulties with the church, he remained deferential to its rites and rituals. In the Senate, part of his great effectiveness stemmed from his willingness to work collegially within the high chamber's rules and honor its traditions and decorum. "There is a great deal that is very Catholic about Edward Kennedy: the almost instinctive respect for institutions (Congress and unions, for example) that makes him more conservative than many people would like to believe, and the separation between public and private morality that the church's rigid regulations forces on its children very early on in life," a Kennedy friend told Richard Reeves in 1974. "Whatever you think of Teddy's personal morality, he is a publicly moral man."

Although he was drawn to things Irish, Ted didn't demonstrate a public interest in the political affairs of his family's ancestral homeland until 1971, the year he spoke out in the U.S. Senate against the actions of British troops in Northern Ireland. "The Troubles," as the crisis in Northern Ireland became known, bothered Kennedy deeply. Catholics in the six partitioned counties of Northern Ireland began to object in the late 1960s against the prejudice and discriminatory practices of the dominant Protestant-controlled government. Their peaceful civil rights rallies gave way to a steadily growing anger that revived the old Irish Republican Army (IRA) with a new generation of young militants committed to violence against a recalcitrant government. In response, the British sent in more than thirteen thousand troops to occupy these six counties. Violence against protesting Catholics erupted in Ulster, leaving scores of innocent people dead in the streets.

As with most historic injustices in Eire, the international community was slow to respond. By fall 1971, John Lynch, prime minister of the Republic of Ireland, threatened to ask the United Nations to intervene after the British blew up roads leading into Ulster in an effort to stop IRA gunrunning. But the most stinging criticism that year came from Ted Kennedy, who introduced a U.S. Senate resolution calling for the ouster of British troops from Northern Ireland. Reviving De Valera's old demand, Senator Kennedy insisted on new talks toward unifying all of Ireland into one nation again. The measure was submitted jointly with Democrat Abraham Ribicoff of Connecticut, an old Kennedy ally, but it was Ted's words that particularly upset the English.

"Ulster is becoming Britain's Vietnam," Kennedy proclaimed, a particularly galling statement for Whitehall, England's foreign ministry, given the international unpopularity of the U.S. war at the time. "The conscience of America cannot keep silent when men and women of Ireland are dying. Britain has lost its way, and the innocent people of Northern Ireland are the ones who now must suffer." He recalled President Kennedy's description of America as a nation of immigrants and how many were wild geese forced from Ireland, "where millions have been driven from their homes, forced to leave the land they love, obliged to see a new life in nations where the yoke of repression could not reach." His words sounded like something Honey Fitz said decades earlier, a pungent renunciation of British cruelties against the Irish by a proud Irish-American.

Kennedy's analogy of the Irish troubles to Vietnam implied that both were unwanted imperialistic forays into essentially local civil wars—a lesson that his brothers never fully grasped in their handling of Vietnam. "Britain has seen it all before, for the tragedy of Ulster is yet another chapter in the unfolding larger tragedy of the empire," he said. "Indeed, it is fair to say that Britain stands toward peace in Northern Ireland today where America stood in Southeast Asia in the early 1960s." He pointed out that the people of Ireland voted 81 percent in favor of a united independent republic in 1918 and had been denied ever since by the British. "If only the cruel and constant irritation of the British military presence is withdrawn, Ireland can be whole again," Kennedy asserted. "To those who say that the inevitable result of a troop withdrawal will be a blood bath in Northern Ireland, I reply that the blood is upon us now, and that the bath is growing more bloody every week."

Ted's words were a distinct departure from his family's previous public positions. His ambassador father, eager to be accepted in a world of Yankees, generally avoided the Irish question whenever possible. During his 1963 visit, President Kennedy cannily dodged the issue of Ireland's partition and De Valera's insistence on an end to it. Even if he privately agreed, Jack Kennedy intended to do nothing right way. But in the America of the 1970s, humbled by its Vietnam and Watergate experiences, Ted Kennedy had absorbed the lessons of unbridled imperialism. He felt free enough to look backward, to comment on Ireland and his Irish heritage, without incurring bigotry at home. He first commented on the Northern Ireland troubles in 1969 when he sent an encouraging telegram to John Hume, leader of the protesting Catholics. "*Today, the Irish struggle again, but not alone,*" Kennedy cabled. "*Your cause is a just cause. The reforms you seek are basic to all democracies worthy of the name. My hopes and prayers go with you.*" Two years later, Kennedy's Senate proposal was downright radical. He insisted that British troops leave Northern Ireland and that local law enforcement be returned to civilian control. He asked that all IRA and Catholic protestors—"imprisoned under that brutal and arbitrary" system—be released by the British from their jails. He called for the dissolution of Northern

Ireland's parliament as "one of the overriding symbols of oppression of the Ulster minority," and insisted that many promised reforms in housing, employment and voting rights be put into place. A united Ireland of Catholics and Protestants could learn to live together peacefully, he suggested, just as the Protestants who formed 10 percent of the Irish Republic to the south had resided for years without incident. Without these changes, Kennedy warned, only more bloodshed would result. "No one doubts that Ireland stands today on the brink of a massive civil war," he concluded. "The specter we face is nothing less than the senseless destruction of Ireland herself. No American who loves Ireland or who remembers her proud and noble history can stand silent in the face of the tragedy and horror now unfolding in Ulster."

Politicians in London, threatened by IRA terrorism, reacted with outrage. They seemed mystified that Kennedy, an heir to America's Camelot legend, could speak like an heir to De Valera, and call for a reunited Ireland. A Conservative member of Parliament introduced his own motion criticizing the Massachusetts senator "for expressing moral judgments on anything"—a none-too-subtle reference to Chappaquiddick as a way of defusing Kennedy's remarks. "Looks like Kennedy's driven in at the deep end again," sniffed a sarcastic cartoon in London's *Evening Standard*. In Northern Ireland, Prime Minister Brian Faulker's comments were less personal but more direct. He said Kennedy "has shown himself willing to swallow hook, line and sinker the hoary old propaganda that IRA atrocities are carried out as part of a freedom fight on behalf of the Northern Irish people."

Ironically, this most recent Irish struggle could be traced to America. As they watched the 1960s civil rights movement, many Catholics in Northern Ireland identified with the plight of Negroes in the American South. They were inspired by the efforts of Martin Luther King Jr. and the Kennedy brothers. John Hume and other leaders of the Catholic cause in Northern Ireland later acknowledged their debt. "The people of Ireland took great pride in President Kennedy, and, having listened carefully to what he had to say, I found his words to be of supreme relevance to our own problems in Northern Ireland," Hume wrote in his memoir. "I am certain that it was no accident that the civil rights movement began here in the sixties, directly inspired, I believe by the American movement." At peaceful rallies against government discrimination in Northern Ireland, Catholics sang the old spiritual "We Shall Overcome" before being broken up by troops. A generation of young people became radicalized by the IRA when the British began a policy of internment without trial and alleged torture of Irish Catholic prisoners. "The random midnight roundup of suspects . . . the knock on the door, the violent entry, the arrest in the dark of night—rank as yet another flagrant example of the repression of the Ulster minority," Kennedy complained in his Senate resolution. In January 1972, Kennedy was incensed over the massacre of fourteen innocent Catholic civil rights marchers in Derry (the name for Londonderry often used by Catholics)—what became known as "Bloody Sunday"—and he compared the slaughter with another Vietnam analogy. He called it "Britain's My Lai."

Despite the bitter British response, Kennedy kept up his criticism, though his comments became more nuanced. He learned that despite De Valera's almost messianic desire for a united Ireland, many Irish in the republic were now content to keep things as they were, especially since partition kept out "the troubles" of the North. The Irish in Boston might still call for a united Ireland, but the cooler heads in Dublin weren't so sure. Increasingly, Kennedy asked Hume, a former teacher and founder of the opposition Social Democratic and Labour Party, for his insights into the problems of Northern Ireland. It turned into a close friendship that would last for the next three decades.

Regardless of his Irish cousins' Republican sympathies in the past, Kennedy purposefully kept his distance from the modern-day IRA, especially as their terror bombs murdered innocent civilians in Great Britain. The Kennedys were shocked when Caroline Kennedy, the only daughter of the late president, nearly got killed by an IRA bomb in October 1975. The blast was intended for Conservative Parliament member Hugh Fraser, an old British friend of the Kennedys who had spoken against terrorism. Seventeen-year-old Caroline was staying as a guest at Fraser's home when the attack occurred. It took the life of a local doctor—an innocent stranger walking by when the bomb went off too early. Caroline was moments away from getting into the sabotaged red Jaguar, to be driven by Fraser that morning to Sotheby's, where Caroline was taking an art course. The bomb planted beneath the car's front wheel ripped through the quiet, tree-lined street, shattering windows and leaving Caroline "very shaken." Jackie convinced Scotland Yard to assign an undercover officer to her daughter. IRA opponents pointed to the incident as an example of the terrorism receiving financial and moral support from the United States. "Irish Americans who don't want to be part of this shabby act should resist whatever temptation there is to contribute to Irish organizations that may be fronts for the terrorists," the *Chicago Tribune* warned after Caroline Kennedy was nearly killed. In America, little tolerance existed for terrorists who called themselves freedom fighters.

On St. Patrick's Day in 1977, Ted Kennedy and three other well-known Irish-Americans—Speaker of the House Tip O'Neill, New York Governor Hugh Carey and Senator Daniel Patrick Moynihan of New York—renounced the money and armaments sent to the IRA by private American organizations such as the Irish Northern Aid Committee (NORAID), which had a storefront in the Bronx. The pull of ethnic ties for these Irish-Americans remained as strong as the days of the Fenians. One estimate in July 1972 put the number of NORAID chapters at more than a hundred, with eighty thousand members, many of them third- and fourth-generation Irish-Americans who seemed to yearn for an ethnic identity in an increasingly diverse United States. Though many who sent cash to NORAID were conservative in their politics at home, they voiced approval for the IRA in Northern Ireland, whose official wing endorsed Marxism. The "Four Horsemen," as Kennedy called his colleagues (a humorous reference to the legendary Notre Dame football linemen with the same nickname), underlined that prominent Irish-Americans would not stand for terrorism. Hume, an advocate of peaceful methods, advised Kennedy in putting together their statement. When President Carter issued a similar statement in 1977, along with an offer of American foreign aid for job development in Northern Ireland, the British were incensed, but Kennedy was overjoyed. "No other President in history has done as well by Ireland," he penned in a note to Carter. Unlike the secret societies of his grandfather's era, Kennedy's group, as *Newsweek* magazine later noted, "helped make support for the IRA less fashionable—and have forced Irish-Americans to consider the bloody uses of their guns and money."

Critics of Kennedy's outspokenness on Northern Ireland suggest that he merely pandered to his Boston Irish constituents back home at a time when they were upset about school busing, abortion and his other liberal views that gave them pause. Others say Kennedy wanted to maintain his own national image during a time when his presidential chances seemed in eclipse. (After much speculation in 1972 and 1976, Kennedy declined to run both times for the Democratic nomination.) Yet consistently, Kennedy kept in touch with Hume and other Irish leaders. He held frequent meetings on the status of peace in Northern Ireland. "Were I neither Catholic nor of Irish heritage," he answered back, "I would feel compelled as a member of the Senate to protest against the killing and the violence in Northern Ireland." Awareness of his Irish background became part of Ted Kennedy's way of relating to people in other foreign lands who suffered oppression. "You do not have to be Irish to appreciate the Polish," he said during a

1980s visit to Communist-ruled Poland where he met with Solidarity's Lech Walesa, "but it helps, because our two proud people share . . . a role as victims in world history."

ONCE, THE PRESIDENCY had seemed inevitable. After the assassinations of his two brothers, however, Cardinal Cushing advised that "the smart thing for Ted Kennedy to do is to get out of politics and take care of the kids." A sense of impending doom—a repeat of Dallas and memories of the bloody floor in the Ambassador Hotel—stalked his potential candidacy. "We all know he might be assassinated, but it's never discussed," Rose Kennedy told the *Ladies Home Journal* in 1972.

By the late 1970s, Ted's family obligations seemed to preclude any challenge against the incumbent Democratic president, Jimmy Carter. Journalists noted Kennedy's established reputation as one of the Senate's most effective leaders, and that the Oval Office didn't seem as appealing to him as it had to his brothers. As the head of an extended clan, Ted's many nieces and nephews, particularly Bobby's children, looked up and depended on him as a steadying force in the turbulence of their young lives. His own son, Teddy Jr., at age twelve, suffered a leg amputation for a cancer that eventually went into remission. The senator's marital problems were compounded by his own rumored affairs and bouts of drinking. He separated from his wife Joan, who moved to Boston and sought treatment for her alcoholism and depression. With the 1980 presidential campaign approaching, even his mother agreed he shouldn't run. "The temptation to be the one who kills the third Kennedy brother is just too great," Rose said. "It's ironic, the polls indicate that he could be President . . . but then there is *that.*"

Assassination became an acknowledged risk factor calculated into his decisionmaking with almost the same matter-of-factness that other politicians worried about endorsements or campaign donations. Ted Kennedy didn't have his brothers or father to rely on should he make a run for the White House. None of his aides was willing to render judgment on the potential life-and-death gamble, lending a certain solitude to his decision about whether to run. "Because of, uh, what, uh, happened to my brothers," Ted explained, "nobody close to you will advise you."

His political instincts told him the time was right. Carter's abysmal ratings in the national polls, exacerbated by the taking of American hostages at the U.S. embassy in Iran, prompted Kennedy to challenge the incumbent president, whom he'd grown to dislike immensely. Pre-primary surveys underscored Kennedy's ability to beat Carter and potentially any

Republican in the fall. Regardless of the risks, Ted was willing to answer the public's call, to rescue the nation from its White House occupant, a man of genial ineptitude in a cardigan sweater. As journalist Richard Reeves wrote in *Esquire:* "Americans aren't quite ready to roll over and play dead yet, and Kennedy . . . seems at the moment to be the only politician capable of tapping America's most traditional trait, optimism."

Kennedy's campaign differed markedly from his methodical nature in the Senate. It possessed little of the machine-like quality of Jack's 1960 campaign. Ted's presidential effort had a slapdash feel to it, rather like Bobby's sudden jump into the 1968 race. His announcement speech in Boston failed to inspire, and his television interview with Roger Mudd of CBS News proved that he'd given little thought to his reasons for pursuing the presidency. "Nostalgia appeared to be his most important campaign issue," concluded political writer Joe Klein, who quoted a White House aide who once worked with Kennedy as saying, "'I feel sorry for Ted. He just hasn't figured out why he's running for president, other than the fact that he's a Kennedy and that's what Kennedys are supposed to do.'" Ted's organizers seemed to assume that once they sounded the clarion call, the vaunted throngs of Kennedy supporters—particularly the white ethnic Catholics who provided the swing vote in several key states—would rally to his cause. Some friends, among them Tip O'Neill, advised him not to run because they were trying to avoid internecine warfare among the Democrats. O'Neill even brought up the "moral issue," his polite euphemism for Chappaquiddick. But neither Ted nor his aides could see how much this last of the Kennedy brothers had alienated his family's bedrock of support.

For many Irish-Americans, Ted no longer represented the 1960s idealism of his brothers, but rather the aimless, indulgent libertinism of the 1970s; a Kennedy no longer pushing his church in a progressive direction but repeatedly at odds with its clergy and teachings. Ted repelled many culturally conservative Catholics with his public persona as a playboy and his liberal positions on public policy. Though he had inherited the luster of Camelot, Kennedy also reaped the consequences of all the revisionist exposés of his brothers' actions. In the Senate, Ted masterfully helped enact many pieces of important legislation close to the heart of working-class America—improving health care, education, minimum wages—as well as expanding civil rights for women, the disabled and other minorities. Yet as a campaigner, his reputation remained muddled and his rhetoric appeared off-putting to traditional Catholic voters. Though the Soviet empire was still intact, he rarely spoke of communism's threat with the same urgency that Jack once expressed. Whereas an unorthodox Bobby had wanted to expand the Democratic tent, managing to condemn the culture of welfare while calling for compassion, Ted seemed content to stand on his reputation as an orthodox liberal.

In Illinois, this perception became painfully clear. In 1960, Catholics in Chicago watched the overt religious bigotry confronting Jack Kennedy, saw themselves in his situation and jolted themselves into action. Kennedy was "young, Catholic, had been discriminated against—that brought us together," remembered Dan Rostenkowski, the city's most powerful congressman. "Goddammit, we had people coming out to vote we thought were dead." Twenty years later, many in the Chicago Democratic machine—which boasted several Irish-Americans among its powerful elite—endorsed Kennedy over Carter. But the recently elected mayor, Jane Byrne, was already so divisive that her enthusiasm for Kennedy wound up alienating many blacks, Hispanics and other minorities. Several Catholic politicians committed themselves to Carter or simply didn't like the idea of undermining a Democrat in the White House. Ted's image remained the most insurmountable problem. "There's not a strong identification of Ted Kennedy as a Catholic, even among traditionalist Catholics," said an Illinois congressional aide to the *Washington Post*. "He's seen as a guy who has taken positions opposed by the bishops, who is separated from his wife. . . . He's seen as a guy who is trying to usurp something that's not really his, riding his brother's coattails."

Within a generation, many Irish and other Catholic ethnics had moved from the South Side city neighborhoods and purchased homes in the distant suburbs. They were far more independent-minded than in the days when the machine's precinct captains came knocking on their doors on Election Day to see whether they'd yet voted. Priests and nuns no longer rallied to the Kennedy name. "Catholics are much more cosmopolitan than they were in 1960," explained Father Dennis Sanders, the principal of a Catholic high school for boys in Rostenkowski's district. "We are an accepted people. Once you're accepted, you don't have to fight for it."

The Land of Lincoln stopped any chance Kennedy might have had of overtaking Carter for the nomination. There were signs of his demise all over. On St. Patrick's Day, the day before the primary, Kennedy marched along a green-covered State Street and experienced the same kind of heckling that Bobby Kennedy met from the Irish during the New York parade in 1968. When somebody threw a pack of lit firecrackers nearby, the Secret Service lunged toward Kennedy and seemed momentarily to unnerve the candidate. The next day, Carter won the popular vote 65 to 30 percent. The president walked away with more than three-quarters of the delegates and an unassailable clinch on renomination. One preelection Illinois poll indicated that Catholics favored Carter by 51 to 33 percent. There were no miracle wins for Ted that spring, but rather a pattern of losses in several key states and narrow wins in races that should have been easy. When the campaign reached New York, Ted appeared almost relieved to know he wouldn't be winning. Several journalists noticed that his stride was almost jaunty, and humor flowed freely at each campaign stop. In the New York primary, Democrats gave Kennedy a surprise victory—as they might give an ovation to an aging star on Broadway, not so much for the performance that day but for the fond memories of yesteryear. The effort against Carter was repeated with Kennedy wins in Pennsylvania, New Jersey and California, but not with a total enough to overcome the president.

THAT SUMMER, at the Democratic National Convention inside New York's Madison Square Garden, Ted gave his most memorable speech of the 1980 campaign. He gracefully conceded to Carter so that the president could be nominated with a rousing voice vote. Then, Kennedy reminded them of what might have been, articulating a vision of his family's politics in a way he'd never before done so well. "It is surely correct that we cannot solve problems by throwing money at them—but it is also correct that we dare not throw our national problems onto a scrap heap of inattention and indifference," Kennedy declared. "The poor may be out of political fashion, but they are not without human needs. The middle class may be angry, but they have not lost the dream that all Americans can advance together."

As if sensing the end of an era, Kennedy addressed himself not just to the crowd, but to history. "Someday, long after this convention, long after the signs come down and the bands stop playing, may it be said of our campaign that we kept the faith," he said, his voice possessed of a bellowy, singsong quality. After building to a crescendo, Kennedy concluded: "For me, a few hours ago, this campaign came to an end. For all those whose cares have been our concern, the work goes on, the cause endures, the hope still lives, and the dream shall never die."

The Garden overflowed with emotion as Teddy waved his good-byes, his last hurrah, to presidential politics. In the end, neither a Kennedy nor the incumbent Carter were returned to the White House. Instead, a California Republican named Ronald Reagan, who claimed his own distant Irish roots, was elected. The gradual shift of white Catholics toward the

Republicans, temporarily halted during the Kennedy years, was now even more pronounced. Nationwide, Irish-Americans voted for Reagan in remarkable numbers, as did other white ethnics. With his Hollywood smile, Reagan wrapped his archconservatism in amiable, telegenic moral bromides that made sense to these ethnic groups who no longer felt like outsiders. With a Cold War passion that JFK had once expressed, Reagan and a new Pope from Poland began their own crusade against the Communists.

Chapter Thirty-Eight

A Matter of Faith

"If you have faith, it is a wonderful thing.
Try to encourage it, nurture it, transmit it.
But faith isn't given to everybody, unfortunately. And some people lose it for one
reason or another."

—ROSE KENNEDY

INSIDE THE ANCIENT ST. STEPHEN'S CHURCH in the North End of
Boston, hundreds of mourners huddled on a cold January morning in 1995
to pay their last respects to Rose Kennedy. At age 104, Rose's tiny, frail body
succumbed to pneumonia at her Hyannis Port home alongside Cape Cod.
The old Boston setting for this funeral Mass, celebrating the life of the
Kennedy family matriarch, seemed fitting.

St. Stephen's, originally built by the Brahmins but later bought and converted by the city's Irish Catholic immigrants, symbolized the ascendancy
of a people. This grand old church was the same place where Rose's father
was baptized in 1863, born to parents who fled famine-stricken Ireland.
Outside its doors, Honey Fitz introduced parishioners in 1946 to his grandson Jack Kennedy, who was running for his grandfather's old seat in
Congress. As with the church itself, Rose Kennedy's funeral was full of
memories, a reminder of all that had transpired.

"She sustained us in the saddest times by her faith in God, which was the
greatest gift she gave us, and by the strength of her character, which was a
combination of the sweetest gentleness and the most tempered steel," eulogized Ted Kennedy, her only remaining son. "She was ambitious not only
for our success but for our souls." To the amusement of all, he recalled a let-

ter his elderly mother had sent him soon after his failed 1980 bid for the presidency. "Dear Teddy," Ted read to the congregation, "I just saw a story in which you said: 'If I *was* President . . .' You should have said, 'If I *were* President' which is correct because it is a condition contrary to fact."

Nearly all the mourners, particularly her family, made mention of Rose Kennedy's faith. For her daughter Eunice, her mother's religiosity had inspired her own tireless volunteer work and acts of charity on behalf of others less fortunate. Others marveled at Rose's devotion to her church and how her abiding belief in God had carried her through so many tragedies. One obituary quoted Monsignor Jeremiah O'Mahoney, the late pastor of her church in Palm Beach and a family friend who once said that Rose was the most religious woman he had ever met. "She wasn't a crank, she was practical in her application of the teachings of God," said O'Mahoney. "After Jack was killed, I phoned her and said how sorry I was. She said she wanted no sympathy, only prayers that God would sustain her." Before he passed away in 1970, Cardinal Cushing declared that Rose "has more confidence in Almighty God than any priest or religious I have known." Cushing own's assuredness in God was shaken by Bobby's cruel fate. "We all have our troubles, but why should the Kennedy family have all these troubles—why, why, why?" Cushing asked her. With unwavering serenity, Rose confirmed God's love despite all that had happened. Besides, she added, "If I collapsed, the morale of the family would be lowered."

Family was the most visible expression of Rose Kennedy's faith. Her children often thought she might have gone into teaching if she'd not become a mother of nine. With almost evangelical resolve, she instructed each of her sons and daughters to strive for higher goals, and her spirit seemed reflected in their rhetoric. Throughout the 1970s until she suffered a stroke in 1984, Rose remained equally "zealous," as Ted said, in trying to influence her twenty-eight grandchildren and forty-one great-grandchildren. Seven of these children were given Rose as their first or middle names, underscoring her subtle impact on their lives. She offered suggestions and challenges on virtually everything—historical quizzes, poetry recitations (she asked each grandchild to memorize a stanza from "The Midnight Ride of Paul Revere" as an eighty-fifth birthday present), spiritual discussions on such topics as the meaning of Lent and even secrets of good posture. ("Caroline, keep your arms away from your sides; it makes you look thinner.") Though she didn't dwell morbidly on the past, she guarded her dead children's memory like a lioness. In late 1976, when *Times* columnist James Reston suggested that JFK wasn't much of an adherent to Catholicism, he received a swift rebuke from Rose. "President Kennedy did believe in and practiced his religion," Rose wrote back to the newspaper. "He attended church regularly, was a frequent communicant at Mass, and understood the meaning and value of daily prayer."

Despite her vaunted status as a papal countess, Rose Kennedy was very much like thousands of other Irish-Americans who turned to their parish priests for insight. "When I told my grandmother that we read the Bible, she was horrified," recalled Kathleen Kennedy Townsend. "She said Catholics didn't read the Bible. Priests did that." Although the one-dimensional portraits of her faith portrayed her as reflexive or unthinking, Rose sometimes revealed her doubts. After Jack's assassination, Rose "spent much time in our front yard or on our beach, and walked and walked and walked, and prayed and prayed, and wondered why it happened to Jack," she recalled in her memoir. "Everything was gone and I wondered why." Faith in God became her salve for a wounded heart. Her emphasis on family and religion were the constants in her life, stretching to the days of Irish immigrants at St. Stephen's Church. As her youngest son once explained, "Whatever contributions the Kennedys have made are very much tied into the incredible importance and power of that force in our lives—the family."

BY THE TIME of Rose Kennedy's death, the Kennedys were touted as America's family by the mass media. In many ways, the coverage of this Irish Catholic clan from Boston resembled the way the British followed the royal family, with no hint of irony or history. Along with Ted in the Senate, two of Rose's grandsons served in Congress and a granddaughter was elected as Maryland's lieutenant governor, but it was John F. Kennedy Jr. who won the greatest media honor—appearing on *People* magazine's cover as "The Sexiest Man Alive." Celebrity begat celebrity as one granddaughter, Maria Shriver, a network television newscaster, married Hollywood superstar Arnold Schwarzenegger, and another granddaughter, Kerry, married Andrew Cuomo, the son of New York's Democratic governor. The Kennedys became a soap opera drama with whom millions of strangers identified and followed in the news. The year before Rose's death, the funeral of Jacqueline Kennedy Onassis was treated like the death of a head of state with constant television remembrances of "The Camelot years." President Bill Clinton understood the prominence of the Kennedys as a national saga. Upon Rose's death as the family's matriarch, Clinton declared, "She played an extraordinary role in the life of an extraordinary family."

Along with the public acclaim came a certain amount of schadenfreude at their self-inflicted injuries and excesses. In the years after the assassinations, stories about the Kennedy family's private demons surfaced in the news with disturbing regularity. The Kennedys, originally touted in superlatives, now seemed like any other dysfunctional American family, awash in drugs, alcohol and sex. Whatever moral restraints that Rose Kennedy once counseled to her family seemed lost or forgotten. Despite the Chappaquiddick tragedy and its devastating impact on his presidential hopes, Ted Kennedy seemed confoundingly inured to its lessons. He fanned the tabloid flames with his private adolescent sexual antics. The next generation also appeared to suffer from its own weaknesses. Robert Kennedy Jr. scuttled any hopes of a political career when he was arrested in 1983 for heroin possession. The whole family grieved over the cocaine overdose death of another RFK son, David, who, intimates said, never recovered from his father's assassination.

The sexual behavior of the Kennedy men came into public cross-examination when police charged William Kennedy Smith, a son of Steve and Jean Kennedy Smith, with sexual assault against a young woman in 1991 while at the Kennedy winter home in Palm Beach, Florida. At trial, a jury eventually acquitted Smith, but not until Ted Kennedy went through an agonizing cross-examination by a local prosecutor about his own drinking earlier that night, accompanied by his son Patrick and Smith at a local bar. The trial tarnished Ted's reputation so much that a fellow senator warned him about his drinking. His usual effectiveness appeared diminished, quite evident during the Senate investigation of sexual harassment allegations against Supreme Court nominee Clarence Thomas. At the confirmation hearings, Kennedy barely said anything.

To be sure, some of the Kennedy family's difficulties were an aftermath of the extraordinary violence they suffered. Many friends noted, for example, the emotional strains that Ethel Kennedy displayed in trying to run a fatherless household. This third generation of Kennedys, many of whom gained significant achievements in their own right, occasionally spoke of their pain. "I remember, after my father died, the desolation I felt, the endless ache of missing him," recalled Joseph P. Kennedy II, Bobby's oldest son, elected to the same congressional seat once occupied by JFK and Honey Fitz. "I discussed it one night with my sister, Kathleen who said: 'When times get really tough, or I'm unsure what to do, I still talk to Daddy—and he's there.'" Young Joe made these candid admissions at the January 1998 funeral of his brother, Michael Kennedy, whose senseless death at age thirty-nine seemed to illustrate all the American public's ambivalence toward the remaining Kennedys.

Though he thought of running for public office, Michael Kennedy preferred to live out his family's legacy of public-spiritedness in his own manner. For years, Michael served as chairman of a nonprofit organization supplying heating oil to poor people. Previously, he helped coordinate relief missions to Africa, helped set up a Roman Catholic university in Angola and organized an anti-handguns advocacy group. His personal life also appeared ideal; he married Vicki Gifford, the daughter of sports broadcaster and football legend Frank Gifford, and the couple had three children. Yet Michael, too, was afflicted with this latter-day Kennedy curse of poor judgment and tragic outcomes. In 1997, law-enforcement authorities exposed his affair with his teenage babysitter and contemplated criminal charges. The embarrassing publicity that resulted forced his resignation as an adviser to his brother's campaign for Massachusetts governor.

Alarmed by how the family's reputation was being sullied and frittered away, Michael's cousin John Kennedy Jr. wrote a thinly veiled disclaimer about "poster boys for bad behavior," which rankled but accurately put a finger on his generation's penchant for self-destructiveness. "Perhaps they deserved it," JFK Jr. wrote about the public's disapproval for his cousins' behavior. "Perhaps they knew better. To whom much is given, much will be required, right?" That last line was a reminder of Grandma Rose's constant invocation of St. Luke to her young. Michael's tawdry behavior turned to tragedy a few months later when he was killed while recklessly playing football on skis. His head smacked into a tree and he died in his sister's arms. Once again, the press revisited their ruminations on a so-called "Kennedy curse" and ran the long list of tragedies haunting the family.

THIS NEW GENERATION of Kennedys often mirrored the complexity of many Catholics in America as they tried to sort out their own personal lives within the changing moral dictates of the church. The reforms of Vatican II were in the past. The forgotten era of "The Two Johns" faded under Pope John Paul II, whose reign began in 1978 and lasted for the rest of the century.

In his greatest triumph, this pontiff helped end the atheist threat of communism in Eastern Europe. Totalitarianism dominated his native Poland where Karol Wojtyla spent most of his life, actively resisting the Nazis and then the Soviets. With the same rigid determination of his embattled Polish church, Pope John Paul II looked upon Western culture as spiritually weak, hedonistic and sex-obsessed. In place of liberal reformers such as Cushing and Medeiros, this Pope placed Cardinal Bernard Law into the archdiocese of Boston and appointed other conservatives into top American positions, typified by Cardinal John O'Connor in New York, whose generous nature did not extend to Irish gay and lesbians wishing to march in the St. Patrick's Day parade. These conservative cardinals became bastions of the Pope's Cold War orthodoxy, stalwarts of the faith but often blind to its faults and unbending in its rules.

The Kennedys no longer shared a close relationship with the Vatican, certainly not as in the days when Galeazzi showed them around St. Peter's. Nevertheless, after his successful trip to Poland in 1987, Ted Kennedy journeyed to Rome; he was welcomed by a grateful Pope who bestowed a blessing on the Kennedys as one of the "great Catholic families of America." But back in America, the pontiff's cardinals were not always pleased with the Kennedys and their stance on personal and public matters. These differences often reflected just how much everyday life had changed for American Catholics.

The senator's philandering did not cause Boston's cardinal to intervene, as Cardinal William O'Connell had decades earlier when he warned Gloria Swanson to break off her affair with the family patriarch. (Despite his own adulterous behavior, Joe Kennedy Sr. repeatedly called on the church's teachings and let his children know that "marriage is a contract for life.") Instead in 1981, when Ted and Joan Kennedy announced their divorce shortly after Ted's failed presidential bid, the Boston archdiocese issued a conciliatory rather than condemning statement: "Few American families today are free from the unfortunate experience of divorce. No one should make a rash judgment about a family tragedy which is surely marked by personal pain." But as a divorced Catholic, Ted could not receive Communion, the most common sacrament shared by Catholics and the spiritual centerpiece of each Mass. Friends and colleagues knew that this estrangement from his church deeply bothered Rose Kennedy's youngest son. For years, many American Catholics hoped the Vatican would liberalize its rules on divorce, though the hierarchy resisted change. The preferred route for dissolution of a Catholic marriage became annulment—technically the declaration that a marriage had never existed in the eyes of church but in practice. Annulments, like paid indulgences from a distant era, became the most tangible representation of the church's internal contradictions. It put on display the church's torturous view of modern sexuality, particularly concerning the role of women, and the humiliations and the stretching of truths inflicted upon its practitioners like an emotional rack. In effect, annulments allowed Catholics who had once married in good faith to claim that they hadn't done so, to deny these marriages—despite their vows and often the existence of several children—rather than admit their error honestly and make a clean break.

When Ted Kennedy married Victoria Reggie in 1992, a divorced lawyer with two children, the modest private ceremony took place before a judge, not a priest. His new thirty-seven-year-old wife, Vickie, managed to get her first marriage annulled, but the senator had more difficulty in getting such an agreement from the church. His biographer, Adam Clymer, later reported that Joan Kennedy told him she hadn't contested it, and that the senator received the church's annulment only after admitting that "his marriage vow to be faithful had not been honestly made." Not until shortly before Rose Kennedy's funeral was Kennedy again in the good graces of the church and given permission to take Communion.

Joseph Kennedy II, by then the family's most likely candidate for the White House someday, wasn't as fortunate when his marriage ended in divorce. His wife, Sheila Rauch, bitterly contested his attempt to gain a church annulment, even though she wasn't Catholic herself. Rather than settle privately, as other aggrieved women had done in the past with Kennedy men, Rauch went public with her outrage and wrote a tell-all book, *Shattered Faith,* about her marriage to a Kennedy that sharply questioned the church's policy on annulments. The rancorous breakup of his marriage, along with the death of his brother Michael, proved more than Joe Kennedy II could bear. He dropped out of the race for governor in Massachusetts—once seen as a sure steppingstone to the White House— and apparently put an end to his career in politics.

ALONG WITH their private difficulties, the Kennedys increasingly became spokesmen for the loyal opposition in their church—the liberals who had once hoped for great things from Vatican II but now found themselves in public disagreement. For America's most prominent Catholic family, this proved to be an uneasy position. In September 1994, during the middle of his most troublesome reelection campaign, Ted Kennedy distanced himself from the Pope's decree that an all-male priesthood was an intrinsic part of the church and couldn't be changed. "I count myself among the growing number of Catholics who support the ordination of women as priests," Kennedy told the press. "I respect the fact that, as a matter of faith, others may not share my view on this issue." Conservatives attacked Kennedy as a virtual anti-Christ of the left, as a man devoid of faith. "This completes the journey of Ted Kennedy," fumed William Donohue, president of the Catholic League, a group sponsored by ever-defensive Cardinal O'Connor in New York to root out anti-Catholic bigotry in the media. "He's a man who's been engaged in fighting the Catholic Church's positions on a whole host of moral issues for the past couple of decades."

Slowly and more deliberately, Ted Kennedy agonized over the abortion issue, far more than his brothers. Before the U.S. Supreme Court's 1973 *Roe vs. Wade* decision legalizing abortion, Kennedy voiced his objection to any modifications of the existing antiabortion laws. "Legalization of abortion on demand is not in accordance with the value which our civilization places on human life," he said. Kennedy seemed culturally ill at ease with the women's movement and balked at their legislative agenda, which counted reproductive rights at the top of the list. If Ted agreed with any woman on this issue, it was his older sister, Eunice, who feared euthanasia of the unwanted. "I don't believe in abortion on demand," he said while campaigning for Senate reelection in 1970. "The day that we can solve the world's population problem, the problem of browns in Central America, the problems of blacks in the ghetto, by aborting them, that's unacceptable to me. How about the kids in the mental hospitals: they're parasites on the environment. How about the old people in institutions: they're cluttering up the landscape. Do you want to exterminate them, too?"

After the Supreme Court's decision, however, Ted Kennedy altered his stance on abortion. He began to support federal funding for abortions and resisted any attempts by the Catholic Church and other opponents to overturn the *Roe vs. Wade* decision. The rationale for his changed position was couched in the same separation of church and state language that his brother had used when faced with anti-Catholic prejudice in 1960. Ted's nuanced position sounded like sophistry to many Catholics. To them, it was disingenuous to support abortion in the public arena when he supposedly didn't believe in it privately.

Over the next decade, Kennedy's camp explained to reporters how the senator's position had "evolved" after the *Roe vs. Wade* decision; in 1994, a spokesman declared that "no one has been a stronger voice on a woman's right to choose than Kennedy." Once the favored son of the Catholic hierarchy in Massachusetts, Ted Kennedy now provoked their wrath with what one local bishop called "the weakening of your personal convictions." In 1998, the U.S. Catholic bishops issued a document that contended Catholics could not hide behind the rhetoric of church and state separation on the abortion issue. "Catholic public officials who disregard church teaching on the inviolability of the human person indirectly collude in the taking of life," it charged.

As a chief architect of the abortion statement, Boston's Cardinal Bernard Law pointed a finger at Kennedy and his Senate colleague John Kerry. "Both senators in my state are Catholic and wrong in the way they approach abortion," the cardinal pronounced, ". . . only I am right." His words carried a moral certainty that would have doomed earlier Irish Catholic politicians in Boston but now could be essentially shrugged off. "Senator Kennedy has great respect for Cardinal Law and the Catholic conference (of bishops), but he continues to support a woman's right to choose," said a Kennedy spokesperson, rolling out the boilerplate. Many pro-choice Roman Catholic politicians in America who followed Kennedy's example faced condemnation at the Sunday lectern. At the same time, because of the abortion issue, traditional Democrats who were Catholic became, as religion writer Peter Steinfels noted, "pariahs in their own party's ranks."

After having switched sides in this national debate on abortion, Ted Kennedy became a prominent, sometimes courageous pro-choice advocate. During the 1984 campaign, he went out of his way to join Governor Mario Cuomo of New York in defending vice-presidential candidate Geraldine Ferraro, who was attacked by Archbishop John O'Connor for her pro-choice position. As the first woman on a national ticket, Ferraro said that although she didn't personally approve of abortion as an Italian-American Catholic, she believed Americans should have the right to decide for themselves whether to terminate an unwanted pregnancy. At a fundraiser for a group called Coalition of Conscience, Kennedy insisted that a line could be drawn between private morality and public policy, adding that not "every moral command should be written into law." The senator seemed offended by O'Connor's thinly veiled support of the Republican president, Ronald Reagan. Though defending O'Connor's right to speak out against abortion, Kennedy cautioned that "we cannot be a tolerant country if churches bless some candidates as God's candidates—and brand others as ungodly or immoral."

At this conclave, Ted Kennedy once again became a disciple of his brother's 1960 Houston speech, invoking its teachings on the separation of church and state. He affirmed his belief in an America envisioned by John Kennedy "where no religious body seeks to impose its will on the general populace and where religious liberty is so indivisible that an act against one church is treated as an attack against all." The following year, Ted Kennedy expanded on these views before conservative evangelists at a religious broadcasters convention hosted by the Reverend Jerry Falwell. "Virtually no one now maintains that religious values have no place in public life," Kennedy said in agreement with the television preacher. But without a firm civic standard separating government from religion, Kennedy added, no one's faith would be safe. "Depth of feeling or clarity of scriptural command cannot be the determining factor," Kennedy proclaimed. "The Bible cannot be the balance wheel of our social compact."

AS SO OFTEN in their history, the Kennedys embodied the transformations among Catholics in America, even if now the church's hierarchy was not in accord. A 1993 Gallup poll showed Catholics supported many practices related to sexuality that the church opposed or regarded as sinful. Large percentages of Catholics believed birth control was acceptable (84 percent), agreed that divorced Catholics should be permitted to remarry (78 percent), favored the ordination of female priests (63 percent), that abortion should be tolerated (58 percent), and half of all respondents agreed that premarital sex or homosexuality was not always wrong. The church's sexual constrictions also were eroding the immigrant church in America, which had provided a means of social ascendancy for each wave of newcomers and was a traditional bedrock of political support for the Kennedys. As late as the mid–1960s, before the Pope's *Humanae Vitae* encyclical, Bobby Kennedy found a common bond in the Catholic symbolism of bread-breaking at Mass with Cesar Chavez and the Mexican immigrant farm workers on strike against the grape-growers. By the end of the century, however, some historians of the church noted how many Hispanic immigrants to the United States were leaving their Catholic faith for evangelical Protestant religions, often citing birth control as a reason. "Those willing to risk the dangers of immigration are predisposed toward modern values in the first place," wrote Alan Wolfe, director of the Center for Religion and American Public Life at Boston College, "and when faced with a choice between limiting family size to escape poverty and remaining with the church, they opt for a new religion."

The Kennedys themselves seemed caught in the widespread divisions within American Catholicism. Though some older relatives privately agreed with the church's hierarchy, the Kennedys in public office came to represent those Catholics favoring reforms on these sexual concerns. For example, Kathleen Kennedy Townsend, as a political candidate, quietly supported a woman's right to choose on abortion, though her mother, Ethel, adamantly opposed it. "I'm clearly Catholic and the church is not in favor of abortion," Kathleen explained. "But it's not something that I want to speak about loudly." In trying to find some elusive middle ground on abortion in the mid-1990s, Patrick J. Kennedy, the senator's son elected to Congress in Rhode Island, voted to ban the second- and third-trimester surgical procedure called partial birth abortions by opponents. His press spokesman said Kennedy felt the procedure "too extreme"—though he still considered himself a pro-choice supporter. More than ever, the Kennedys were allied solely with the liberal wing of the Democratic Party in a way that appeared to be abandoning the ethnic Catholics, including many Irish-Americans, who abided by the Pope's moral instruction. Increasingly, these old John Kennedy Democrats of the 1960s flocked to the "family values" rhetoric of the Republicans.

Like so many Catholics with a sentimental, cultural kinship to the church, Ted Kennedy and his family still considered themselves practitioners in good stead. On occasion, they looked back at the past, at a time when the Kennedys and their fellow Irish Catholic immigrants were still pariahs in American society. They were proud about how JFK overcame anti-Catholic bigotry in the 1960 election and, as Robert F. Kennedy Jr. later wrote, fondly remembered "the droves of nuns and priests and lay brothers who marched from the rectories, convents and priories to campaign for Uncle Jack with the fervor of the Crusades." This third generation of Kennedys was made mostly of "traditional" Catholics who attended Mass weekly and asked for God's grace before dinner. Their commitment to so many different forms of public service—from human rights advocacy to journalism to environmental causes—seemed to be an effort to live up to the family's legacy and, at times, a form of penance for failing it. "What it's all about is carrying out service to others, primarily God, than to family and country, but that doesn't always mean that we live up to those principles," explained Robert Jr. "I went through a long period where I was knowingly living against conscience."

Whether a Catholic in name only or by true devotion, Ted Kennedy attended Mass, received Communion and knew all the prayers. And he could say to his Jesuit friend, the Reverend Robert Drinan, with evident sincerity, that he regretted there were no priests in his family.

Chapter Thirty-Nine

Looking Backward and Forward

FOR DECADES, IRISH-AMERICANS had focused so much on being absorbed into American society and proving their commitment to their adopted country that they did not concern themselves much with the tiny island nation on the other side of the Atlantic. "When the Irish came to America, [politics] was the only way they could get jobs," Kathleen Kennedy Townsend recalled learning from her grandmother, Rose, as an article of faith. "There was terrific discrimination against the Irish."

To many, the Kennedys were the apotheosis of that struggle. By the end of the twentieth century, Irish-Americans had melded into every facet of American society without restriction—virtually eradicating any hyphenated ethnic reference from their identity. Their religion, if still a target for subtle bigotry, no longer barred them from the corridors of power or social status. The Kennedys even had their name on a building at Harvard, an unthinkable proposition for an Irish Catholic in the 1920s. Yet, as with all immigrant families, the Kennedys' actions begged a broader question: Does being accepted in America ultimately mean a loss of faith and one's own culture?

Now that the long Irish struggle for acceptance was won in America, their descendants seemed willing to look back in a way that their forebears never dared. In the United States, where some forty million people claimed Irish heritage, a surge of popular culture dedicated to Irish themes emerged over the next decade—from Frank McCourt's bittersweet memoir *Angela's Ashes* to the step-dancing Broadway revue of *Riverdance* to melodramatic Hollywood films about Ireland's recent history. This homogenized generation of Irish-Americans, the lightest possible shade of green, turned to Ireland for a bit of self-discovery. The Kennedy grandchildren journeyed to Ireland as teenagers and young adults, first as a curious idyll to see the sights and perhaps the old Kennedy Homestead in Dunganstown. Over time, though, their interest developed as impassioned advocates of the emerald isle's causes.

"I am delighted so much of the Irish legacy has percolated down through my bloodlines and family culture," wrote Robert F. Kennedy Jr. for a book called *May the Road Rise to Meet You*, its title referring to the traditional Irish blessing. He and other young Kennedys talked about how their family's experiences in America mirrored the Irish hatred of oppression, their admiration of moral and physical courage. In a 1998 speech in Dublin about racism, Representative Patrick Kennedy of Rhode Island said the Irish "more than anyone, should be able to identify with those who have been downtrodden and struggled and spat upon and stepped upon and who are the outcasts of society because that's the history of Ireland."

Although gossip columns followed every move of the Kennedys in the United States, few of their actions in Ireland rated attention by the American media. The same tabloids that kept singing the Camelot tune, presenting the Kennedys as American royalty, seemed to have no idea how many Britons despised this family for their views on Ireland. The Irish connection among the Kennedys was much stronger than perceived generally, and certain historical events that were downplayed or ignored, such as JFK's 1963 trip to Ireland, were given elevated status in family lore. "The fact that the president went to Ireland was very significant," explained Kathleen Kennedy Townsend. "All my brothers and sisters have gone over, and my mother's sister married an Irish man. So my particular family has spent a lot of time in Ireland. My sister Courtney married an Irish man. The Smith family clearly, because their mother was the ambassador to Ireland. So I'd say there's a fairly strong connection."

Despite their quintessentially American demeanors, Joe and Rose Kennedy's children heard the stories of Ireland from Honey Fitz, their mother and their father's host of Irish cronies. "They grew up with all the talk of Ireland," explained Dorothy Tubridy. "The grandchildren are very staunchly Catholic and in their sense of being Irish—and that influence stays with you no matter how far you wander."

After the early 1970s Bloody Sunday riots in Northern Ireland, the Kennedy family's commitment became more serious, more intensely political. Congressman Joseph Kennedy II visited Ireland in 1988 and expressed outrage at the "tremendous oppression" that existed in the northern six counties and at the "intimidation of Irish Catholics" by the Protestant majority. After visiting Northern Ireland, he traveled to the steps of Wexford Muncipal Hall and drew loud cheers when he called for a British ouster. "The British have no right to occupy the north of Ireland," insisted this Kennedy named for the former U.S. ambassador to the Court of St. James. "The occupying forces are telling us what to do, what to eat, who to pray to, how to think." It was the kind of speech that De Valera wished the congressman's uncle might have given in 1963. The eldest son of RFK said he couldn't be like Americans who observed the Irish troubles from an emotional distance. "You wouldn't be satisfied with me if I came here simply as a tourist," he explained. "We all have brothers in the north and they need our help and support."

The British were not pleased. On the BBC television, one of Prime Minister Margaret Thatcher's top aides chastised Kennedy. "He should get back to Massachusetts as quickly as possible," Energy Secretary Cecil Parkinson retorted, "and I hope we never set eyes on him again."

WHILE IN NORTHERN IRELAND, Joe Kennedy II championed the cause of several young Irish Catholics jailed by the British as suspected IRA members. The inmates were found guilty of alleged terrorist bombing attacks, but supporters claimed their convictions were based on false charges. Joe Kennedy's commitment went far beyond that of most contemporary Massachusetts politicians, beyond the token gesture and press release to please the Irish vote back home. He called on Thatcher's government "to change its attitude to the Irish Catholics of this nation."

Americans were no longer as concerned about Ireland as they were at the beginning of the century. In 1920, when three Irish nationalists starved themselves to death, more than a hundred thousand outraged Irish-Americans marched in protest to Boston Common. They provided a steady stream of money and weapons to their Irish cousins back home in their struggle for independence. Now, the flame of Fenian spirit barely flickered. The south of Ireland was its own Republic and Irish-Americans didn't seem bothered by the troubles of the minority Catholics in the north. Indeed, when IRA suspect Bobby Sands died in 1981 during a hunger strike in prison, barely a hundred people protested outside the home of the

British consul general in Boston. Some said that Representative Joe Kennedy's motivations in Ulster's dispute were an exercise in ethnic cheerleading. But his actions seemed compelled by family history as he became more outspoken on Irish issues than his Uncle Teddy.

Joe Kennedy visited in prison the so-called Guildford Four, including Gerry Conlon and Paul Hill, whose conviction on trumped-up charges for a 1974 bombing later became the inspiration for an Oscar-nominated film (*In the Name of the Father,* starring Daniel Day-Lewis and Emma Thompson). Kennedy urged both Conlon and Hill to come to America after their impending release on bail and testify before a congressional hearing on human rights. At the April 1990 hearing in Washington, Hill recounted his story of spending fifteen years in prison for a crime he didn't commit. Hill emphasized that he never joined the IRA, but was simply another Irish Catholic from Belfast whose life had been torn apart by the religious strife in the north. That same year, Hill published an autobiography about his experience, titled *Stolen Years,* describing IRA members in friendly terms. "To us, these men were not terrorist gangsters," he wrote. "They were our neighbors, the brothers of our friends, the sons of respected people in the district."

Hill's hardscrabble existence in West Belfast was spent mostly on the streets. He was the long-haired disaffected son of parents, one Catholic and the other Protestant, who couldn't get along at home. Paul wound up living with his grandparents, and had scant hope for the future. When the troubles started, Hill and the other Catholic youths rebelled against the British soldiers who invaded their community. "Every kid in West Belfast threw stones at the British army. Every kid in West Belfast sees themselves as the defenders of their neighborhood," he said. "I engaged in political protest, but if you ask me if I lifted a gun, certainly not." He and Gerry Conlon were petty thieves, not political terrorists. Yet when they were caught breaking into a hooker's apartment, the two young Irish Catholics became suddenly entrapped in the political tragedy of Northern Ireland.

The October 1974 bombing of two crowded neighborhood pubs in the town of Guildford, outside London, killed five people, injured sixty-five more and left Britain in a revenge-seeking frenzy against the IRA's campaign of terrorism. Until then, though the crucial decisions about Ulster's fate were made in London, most of the resulting violence occurred in Northern Ireland. The Guildford attack was among more than thirty bombs planted in England. The four-month reign of terror prompted the British public and police to respond with outrage. Into this wide dragnet fell Hill and Conlon. Over the next two days, Hill faced an endless interrogation by police determined to make an arrest for the pub bombing. "I was beaten, slapped around," Hill recalled. "I was threatened with firearms. Members of my family were threatened. I was denied sleep for long periods. I was denied food for long periods, completely disoriented, just—just utterly terrified. Sheer complete terror."

In the panic over the IRA attacks, England passed the Prevention of Terrorism Act. It allowed suspects to be detained without the traditional civil liberties of Her Majesty's other subjects, including rights to a defense lawyer. Hill became the first detainee under the new terrorism law, questioned on the same day the law went into effect. Pointing at him, the British police demanded and eventually got a confession for the bombing. "They said they were going to fucking kill me," Hill recalled. Similar confessions, with no other evidence, were collected from Conlon and two other Irish hippies, Carol Richardson and Paddy Armstrong, whom the British press dubbed "the Guildford Four." Conlon's father and five other members of Conlon's Irish Catholic family living in London were rounded up as accomplices. At a non-jury trial, Hill found himself convicted, along with the others, and sentenced to life imprisonment. The judge's only regret, as he passed judgment on Hill, was that the defendant wasn't charged with treason so he could impose the death penalty.

Over the next fifteen years, Hill languished in a prison cell even though British police soon obtained evidence of his wrongful conviction. After Hill's trial, the police arrested a group of IRA bombers who confessed to the Guildford crime and provided enough specific details for authorities to realize they had condemned four innocent people. Yet, the fears and prejudices surrounding the British conflict in Northern Ireland prevented any action being taken for years. Journalists, human rights organizations and politicians such as the Kennedys brought enough international attention to these cases that an independent inquiry was eventually ordered by the British government. In 1989, the panel ruled that Hill and the other Guildford Four had been framed by the police. Their convictions were overturned.

When he appeared before Kennedy's congressional hearing, Paul Hill was temporarily free pending an appeal for another alleged crime—the murder of an ex-soldier in Belfast named Brian Shaw—the charges based on the same confession fabricated by police. In the audience, Ethel Kennedy listened and was deeply moved by Hill's tale. "What he said, and how he said it, was very powerful," she remembered. Ethel Kennedy walked up to Hill when the hearing ended, introduced herself and began talking about her daughter Courtney and her interest in Northern Ireland. She said she wished Courtney had been able to attend, but her daughter had suffered a neck injury while skiing and was recovering inside her Manhattan apartment. By any chance, Ethel asked, would Hill be going to New York and possibly be able to stop by and say hello?

"Well, as a matter of fact . . ." replied Hill, and soon received Courtney's New York address.

When Hill arrived at her Fifth Avenue apartment, the fifth child of Ethel and Bobby Kennedy was feeling low; her decade-long marriage to a television producer had fallen apart and her broken body was trying to mend. Ethel called ahead to alert her daughter of Hill's visit. Courtney quickly agreed with her assessment of Hill's rough-hewn, long-haired handsomeness. As they conversed, she could barely understand Paul's thick working-class Belfast accent, though she'd been to Eire plenty of times. As a young adult, she became fascinated with Irish culture after a visit abroad with her sister, Kerry, and later decided to study at Trinity College in Dublin. Paul teased her about all the get-well flowers in her apartment. The couple realized they shared a similar sense of humor and began seeing each other regularly.

Mary Courtney Kennedy, her given name, remained one of the most taciturn Kennedys. She was rather a reclusive thirty-five-year-old woman who had been an undistinguished student. She had developed an ulcer by age twelve—the year after her father was shot to death in Los Angeles. "I did not react well," she later described. "I wasn't rebellious like the boys, I just kept things in. I was unhappy." Paul Hill's suffering in Northern Ireland struck a chord in her, as though they were both victims of political violence. "I think there was some empathy and understanding that we had with each other that other people would not have," Courtney said. "Our histories had some kind of similarities in that we both had sufferance in loss." They recognized how many thought they were an odd match—the rich American girl of Camelot and the accused IRA terrorist—yet their relationship only became closer. "Our love has grown because we are concerned about the same things," Hill explained. "It was important that her family had such a caring and moral stand. They too have suffered from political violence. Courtney is a supremely caring person, which is very hard to find in people who are established in life."

By the time they became engaged, Hill was living off the proceeds of his best-selling autobiography and working as a volunteer for Amnesty International, Helsinki Watch and other human rights groups. Although authorities in Northern Ireland offered him a deal—an agreement to plead guilty to the Shaw murder in return for time already spent in prison—he adamantly refused. Before returning to fight his case on appeal, Hill married Courtney in July 1993 aboard a ship on the Aegean Sea. Ethel Kennedy attended along with several relatives, including a smattering of distant Kennedy cousins from Ireland. One of those in attendance was an Irish priest named Michael Kennedy from the coastal town of Dungarvan, who said he was a fourth cousin of the assassinated president, and was embraced by his American kin. Father Kennedy said Mass at the Hill-Kennedy wedding celebration and later that November served as chief celebrant of a memorial Mass in Dublin to mark the thirtieth anniversary of President Kennedy's death, attended by the Irish prime minister, Albert Reynolds. In a profile, the *Times* of London suspiciously described the popular priest as "closely identified with the republican cause" and a friend of Hill's. When Rose Kennedy was dying, the family asked Father Kennedy to fly over to lead the family's final prayers. "He has got a lovely, kind, warm face," Courtney described. "The whole feeling about him is, I suppose, very holy."

Hill knew how lucky he was to marry into the Kennedy family and recognized what they had meant historically. "The Kennedys were kind of the epitome of what Irish people could do in America," he explained. "They were the American dream for Irish people."

ON A SNOWY DAY in Belfast, a limousine pulled up to the High Court. Paul Hill and his new American family stepped out briskly past cameras and reporters and took their seats in the front rows of the justice chamber. The Kennedys were out in force—Ethel Kennedy, her daughters, documentary maker Rory, Kerry Kennedy Cuomo, Kathleen Kennedy Townsend, her son, Michael, and another Kennedy on his way in a jet, Joe Kennedy II. "We're here to support my brother-in-law in his struggle for justice in Northern Ireland," the Massachusetts congressman declared, arriving in time for the session after lunch.

The British were appalled. Never before in their relationship as allies with the United States had they witnessed such prominent American figures coming to their shores to raise such ugly issues as political torture and gross violations of human rights in Northern Ireland. Before his return, Hill and his in-laws had appeared on American television shows to tell his side of the story. Some television shows intermingled film clips from *In the Name of the Father* and treated Paul and Courtney as the latest rising stars in the Kennedy constellation. As if to highlight the inequity in the case, the Kennedys invited sixteen international observers to attend Hill's appeal hearing. "The Meddling Kennedys," decried a *Times* of London editorial writer, who equated the family's support for Hill with their alleged sexual misdeeds in Palm Beach and their "pro-German grandfather" when he was ambassador to Britain. "For Irish-Americans in general, and the Kennedys in particular, the grim and grey political situation in Northern Ireland is black and white, an opportunity for moral and nationalist posturing, but little serious contemplation," said a *Times* columnist. In London, the *Evening Standard*'s headline of the proceeding ("Scum As Kennedy Clan Fly In To Aid Terror Case Man") was hardly contemplative of the miscarriage of justice that might have occurred with Hill. The *Daily Mail* aimed much of its wrath at Joe Kennedy. "He is a loud, hate-filled voice against Britain on Capitol Hill, but his real knowledge of the Irish problem is only as deep as a plate of water," opined columnist John Edwards, who reminded his readers that the Kennedys were "the nearest America ever got to its own royalty."

Hill won his appeal, though there was little sense of justice. Sir Brian Hutton, the Lord Chief Justice, tossed out the conviction. He ruled the police's use of a gun to coerce Hill's confession was a "disgraceful and grossly improper action, which clearly constituted inhuman treatment." Yet the halfhearted attempts by Ulster authorities to prosecute the police for their criminal actions eventually collapsed. Even Hill didn't have the stomach for pursuing it. The family of murdered Brian Shaw—pistol-whipped to death by IRA interrogators—remained convinced the authorities had convicted the right man. They were outraged and saddened to see Hill go free. The IRA men in jail who confessed to the crime were never charged. And Hill himself, who received two hundred thousand pounds as an interim compensation payment, felt little vindication. "No one knows the monetary value you can put on fifteen years," he explained. "I don't think there is anyone alive who can come out of that experience and not be scarred. . . . To those who say, oh, he's livin' well, you have no idea."

Over the next several years, Courtney and Paul Hill lived permanently in America, though they maintained their ties to Eire through repeated visits. A reminder of this Irish connection arrived in 1997 when Courtney gave birth, at age forty, to a baby girl they named Saoirse Roisin, Gaelic for "Freedom Rose." Grandma Ethel Kennedy nicknamed her "Rebel." Through the Kennedy family's involvement, Hill's case came to the attention of President Clinton. Eventually, Great Britain changed its view, realizing the injustice to the Guildford Four. Six years after Hill's successful appeal, Prime Minister Tony Blair issued a formal apology; he addressed it, tellingly, to Courtney Kennedy Hill. "I believe that it is an indictment of our system of justice and a matter for the greatest regret when anyone suffers punishment as a result of a miscarriage of justice," Blair wrote. "There were miscarriages of justice in your husband's case, and the cases of those convicted with him. I am very sorry indeed that this should have happened."

The false charges against Hill and the other Guildford defendants underlined the rush to judgment by a nation feeling itself in the grip of terrorist attacks. England's concession was extraordinary, something considered impossible only a few years earlier—and it happened mostly because of the Kennedy connection. "They're behind me solidly, as any Irish family would be," Hill said of his new in-laws. "And that's perhaps indicative of their Irishness, that—that they are prepared to stand with me right to the end of the road."

Hill began a new life in America, yet like so many émigrés from political strife in Ireland, he maintained a long-held view about his homeland. "I believe Ireland is a separate country," he insisted. "I believe that, in my lifetime, I will see a unification of Ireland. A political solution is the only solution to the current troubles."

WHILE THE PAUL HILL legal saga played out in a Northern Ireland courtroom, another Kennedy turned her sights on Ireland to fulfill a family promise and eventually became fully immersed in the process of a political solution for the Irish troubles.

On a long trip in summer 1992, Jean Kennedy Smith, the youngest of Joe and Rose Kennedy's daughters, visited Dublin and other parts of Ireland. She traveled about in the same way that other family members and so many Irish-Americans each year returned to see the sights of their ancestral homeland. Her vacation proved almost therapeutic after one of the most difficult periods of her life—following the 1990 death of her husband, Stephen, and the sexual assault trial of her son, William Kennedy Smith. For Jean, the trip kindled an intense interest in Ireland. There were her memories of accompanying President Kennedy on his triumphant trip three decades earlier. She visited the beautiful surroundings of the U.S. ambassador's residence at Phoenix Park, where Jack joked about supporting any presidential candidate who'd send him back as the new Irish ambassador. And she remembered how Jack had promised to "come back in the springtime" as he departed Ireland.

Upon her return to America, Jean shared her memories with brother Ted. She floated the idea of becoming the Clinton administration's new ambassador to Ireland. "It sort of developed as a wisp of a thought," Ted recalled. "We had all been to Ireland and we talked about that house [at Phoenix Park] and how wonderful it would be to live there. We were chatting about it as if we were dreaming." Ted Kennedy set out to ensure his sister's appointment. Though there were other candidates for the post, including some who were friendly with the Massachusetts senator, Kennedy convinced the president to nominate Jean. Clinton's announcement took place on St. Patrick's Day, 1993. With a bowl of shamrocks before him at the White House, Clinton introduced Jean, noticeably nervous, as his new ambassador-designate. The president touted her "as Irish as Americans can be. I can think of no one who better captures the bonds between Ireland and the United States."

That same week, there was another subtle sign of how much life in America had changed for Irish Catholics. The day before the St. Patrick's Day announcement, Clinton appointed Ray Flynn, the Irish Catholic mayor of Boston, to serve as U.S. ambassador to the Vatican—a position created in 1984 by President Ronald Reagan after decades of rancorous, often bigoted, debate. (In 1969, Nixon broke an eighteen-year hiatus since Myron Taylor's departure by sending Henry Cabot Lodge as his personal representative to the Holy See.) Before Reagan made his decision, several Protestant denominations expressed their opposition to a U.S. ambassador in Rome, particularly Baptists and conservative Evangelicals, as well as liberal civil libertarians. The Reverend Jerry Falwell opposed it and the Reverend Billy Graham was reportedly cool to the idea. Ironically, the proposal that Joe Kennedy and Count Galeazzi had pushed for years was brought to realization by Republicans such as Senator Richard Lugar, who oversaw the repeal of the 1867 law prohibiting any funding for a Vatican embassy. Lugar said the repeal ended "a discriminatory law against Catholics." More important, the move eliminated an old sore point at a critical time of U.S.–Vatican Cold War cooperation in squeezing communism out of the Soviet bloc nations.

Irish Catholics felt similarly slighted in their government's treatment of Ireland. For many decades, American presidents sent U.S. ambassadors to Dublin who shared Britain's view of Ireland's future, certainly not those who were sympathetic to the Irish Republican cause. Jean Kennedy Smith's selection threatened to change these old alliances and upset many in Northern Ireland and Britain. Conor Cruise O'Brien, a distinguished Irish historian and diplomat, worried that the Kennedys would bring only a simplistic Irish-American viewpoint to efforts for peace in Northern Ireland. "She has nothing to contribute to reconciliation," said O'Brien. "She's wholly aligned with one side. The idea that you can get peace in Northern Ireland by catering to the IRA is wrong, and I'm afraid that's what the Kennedys are after."

Ted Kennedy shepherded his sister's nomination through the Senate and ensured that a political neophyte would not be grilled on her qualifications to head an embassy. When she left America in late spring 1993 as the new U.S. ambassador to Ireland, Jean carried with her a photo from the day of her nomination; it was signed by her brother with the inscription: "For Jean, who is going back in the springtime." The *Boston Globe* dourly predicted that Kennedy Smith was "not likely to stir much enthusiasm in Dublin although she is, after all, a Kennedy."

On her first day, she traveled to Dunganstown. Although Mrs. Ryan had passed away long ago, her daughter Mary Ann, now near sixty, still lived in the old homestead. So did her young nephew, Patrick Grennan, a tall, handsome young man with auburn hair and a Kennedy-like smile who continued as a farmer and ran a small museum about the American Kennedys in the family's old barn. "Jean came back here quite a few times, and unveiled a plaque on the wall of the little house, where the original Kennedys lived," recalled Mary Ann, of the whitewashed stone and mortar edifice where Patrick Kennedy once lived. "I think she feels a link along with her brother, Teddy."

With her actions that day, Jean let all of Ireland know a Kennedy had returned in the springtime.

Chapter Forty

Principles of Peace

"There are those who regard this history of past strife and exile as better forgotten. But, to use the phrase of Yeats, let us not casually reduce "that great past to a trouble of fools," for we need not feel the bitterness of the past to discover its meaning for the present and the future."

—JOHN F. KENNEDY, 1963

GERRY ADAMS NEVER ATE chocolate chip cookies so good, nor had he ever tasted political success so sweet. Over time, the Sinn Fein leader's relationship with Jean Kennedy Smith became cordial enough to tease the new American ambassador about those delicious morsels she offered guests. "She claimed to have made them herself—and I have no reason to doubt that—though I have to say I never actually saw her make them," Adams remembers with a smile. But he held no doubts about her abilities in the corridors of power. After all, it was Jean Kennedy Smith, with her tenaciousness, who had spearheaded the effort to get Adams a visa for his highly controversial trip to America in 1994.

The Kennedys were determined to help bring about peace in Northern Ireland. When Adams arrived in Boston, Ted Kennedy greeted him publicly, and pushed the Clinton administration for a formal conciliatory gesture toward Sinn Fein—officially banned for years by the American government. Courtney Kennedy Hill took Adams to visit the graves of her father and JFK at Arlington National Cemetery. And Courtney invited the Sinn Fein delegation to her mother's house in Virginia so that Adams could stay overnight and be ready early the next morning for an all-important telephone call.

At around 8:30 A.M. on October 3, 1994, Vice President Al Gore called Hickory Hill and spoke with Adams, sitting in Bobby Kennedy's old office at a desk with his photograph on it. The conversation between Gore and Adams was cordial but brief. The Clinton administration—bombarded by opponents of Sinn Fein, the political arm of the IRA—worried about the British response to giving recognition to an organization linked to terrorism. Politically, Adams was still so radioactive that the White House refused to let him meet President Clinton. After much wrangling, it was decided that Gore would make a courtesy call, but not in person. During their telephone conversation, Adams stayed close to the responses he had practiced the night before. Gore informed him that Sinn Fein was no longer a banned organization in the eyes of the American government, and a subsequent cable sent by the White House that day invited Adams to begin a "process of engagement" toward peace. But the Clinton administration remained wary of Adams.

Over the next four years, the peace effort in Northern Ireland would become one of the highlights of Bill Clinton's presidency. The bitter struggle had its deep roots in the splitting of Ireland after the 1920s war for independence. Since 1969, "the troubles" had claimed more than 3,200 lives, injured thousands more and tore apart neighborhoods along religious lines. Previous American presidents, including John F. Kennedy, had considered Ulster's woes as mostly an internal domestic dispute. That view changed dramatically during the Clinton presidency, urged on by the Kennedys, who held considerable sway with this Democratic president. Other politicians and diplomats helped set the terms for peace in Northern Ireland but, as Adams recalled, few were more willing to take the risks for peace than the slim, almost frail sixty-seven-year-old ambassador with virtually no diplomatic experience.

"Jean Kennedy Smith was exactly in the right place at the right time," said Adams. "She brought a personal touch, a very progressive openness to the position of ambassador, and she also brought her own influence and the considerable influence of the Kennedy clan. She wasn't at all reticent when she thought she needed to use that influence to speak directly to President Clinton, the State Department and others as well as the Irish Taoiseach or to us. Her influence was quite considerable, particularly in getting the process started in 1994."

WHILE GROWING UP, Jean Kennedy didn't think much about Ireland. After marrying in St. Patrick's Cathedral in 1956 before Cardinal Spellman, Jean worked on behalf of the church and other charitable organizations. After nearly a lifetime behind a private veneer, part of the traditional secondary status accepted by Kennedy women and so many women of her era, Jean slowly emerged with her own distinct impassioned voice, ready to express a controversial view if she felt it right.

She was no longer the demure, almost girlish sister who had accompanied her brother, the president, on his memorable 1963 journey to Ireland. Her personal tragedies made her more aware of the sorrows in life. "Despite having grown up rich and privileged, there was always a hint of melancholy about her," observed *Boston Globe* journalist Kevin Cullen. Some who met her said Jean's wit could at times appear arrogant and flip. "She's full of ideas, and she imparts them on anyone within hearing distance," Ted once explained diplomatically. Her generation didn't wave the Hibernian flags as their grandparents had; they were too busy looking ahead as full-blooded Americans. For Jean, JFK's 1963 trip was more like a vacation than some personal mission. She doesn't think the current crop of Kennedys have any particularly avid interest in Ireland beyond that of most Irish-Americans. "We took vacations but there was no burning thing in my family about Ireland—except for the senator and myself," she insisted. Nevertheless, those who worked with her on the peace process during the 1990s say the ambassador was motivated by her heritage, a personal affinity for Ireland, that she sometimes acknowledged was rooted in her family. "When I looked at my mother, I always saw a bit of Ireland," she said during her tenure in Dublin. "And I suppose when I look to Ireland, I see a bit of my mother—her faith, her wit, her endurance." Jean Kennedy Smith's interest deepened in 1974 when she visited Derry, which was in the throes of violence and protests. She stayed as a guest at the home of John Hume, the leading Catholic politician in Northern Ireland, who advocated nonviolent resistance. The everyday aspects of violence in this scarred city made a strong impression on her. Two years earlier, when British soldiers started firing in his hometown and killed thirteen people, Hume protested by laying down in front of a tank. A ruddy-faced, beefy man with a wave of dark flowing hair, Hume always impressed the Kennedys as sincere and dedicated to peace. He often repeated Martin Luther King Jr.'s adage that "an eye for an eye leaves everyone blind." Over the years, Ted Kennedy relied on Hume for advice, and Jean kept in contact when she visited Ireland, almost every year, as part of her Very Special Arts program for children suffering from mental retardation and other disabilities. Hume's friendship with the Kennedys would prove crucial in the days to come.

Hume was the leader of the Catholic Social Democratic and Labour Party (SDLP), composed mostly of the middle class. Before Jean's arrival as ambassador in 1993, he began meeting privately in talks with Adams, whose Sinn Fein party was favored mainly by working-class Catholics. These discussions were suggested by a Belfast priest, the Reverend Alec Reid, part of a grassroots movement of Roman Catholic clergy determined to stop Ulster's violence and end discrimination against their people. Back in 1988, the two had also met briefly without results. This time, though, Hume was more than ever convinced of Adams's intentions toward peace, especially his willingness to overcome the militant factions within the IRA who insisted on total British capitulation.

Shortly after moving to Dublin, Ambassador Kennedy Smith ventured north to learn about the situation firsthand. During her initial trip, she met the mother of a teenage boy, one of several imprisoned without trial on suspicions that they were IRA lookouts. "I saw the suffering this woman was experiencing for her son and as a mother I responded," Jean later explained. The new U.S. ambassador infuriated London by attending a court hearing the following day for the boy. She talked with another woman in Belfast whose husband had been shot recently. "When the men who killed her husband ran out of the house, her two children ran out after them, screaming, 'You bastards!' She was so afraid that they'd shoot her kids too," Kennedy recalled. "She was extremely brave and I was very moved. She opened up to me because I think she saw me as someone who's been through it. I think she felt that we had some bond there."

Because of the ongoing violence, she couldn't contact Sinn Fein directly, but a close friend, Irish author and journalist Tim Pat Coogan, arranged for a lunch with Father Reid, who put the suffering into a religious context. Too often, Father Reid had prayed over the remains of those lost souls shot and blown to bits by terror.

"I'm only interested in stopping the violence," the priest told her. "I feel the Church should get involved. Even as we're talking here at this moment, there's probably someone being killed."

Jean was visibly moved. As the priest described each atrocity, she murmured repeatedly, "Awful, Awful."

After discussions with Hume, she became convinced she should take a chance on Adams as well. "He [Adams] had been talking with John Hume when I came up there and he is a great friend of our family," Jean recalled.

"I knew John was talking to him and I didn't see any downside to it, frankly. I didn't see any point to him stringing me along. So it was very logical to say he was attempting to find some kind of peaceful solution to the conflict there. I just felt that he [Adams] was sincere in his efforts because there was no point in him being otherwise. Misleading me or misleading John would lead him nowhere."

GERRY ADAMS'S LINKS to terrorism would give any prudent politician pause. A bearded man with gentle eyes, the eldest of ten from a Catholic family in West Belfast, Adams claimed that he'd never been a member of the Provisional IRA—the organization responsible for much of the bombings and killings—though few believed him. His uncle had been a prominent member of the IRA and political violence became a way of life for his friends and family. As a young man, he was sent by the British to a prison boat off the coast of Belfast, where he was interrogated and beaten, and he wound up spending four years in prison without a trial. It was enough to embitter anyone, part of the rage that kept the gunfire and strife in Northern Ireland going for years. But Adams soon focused his attention on republican politics rather than acts of terror. He realized that much of the discrimination aimed at Catholics was economic, not just political and social. Catholics were often deprived of the stable, well-paying jobs in the region's strained local economy. With his earnest, professorial style, Adams helped take control of Sinn Fein from an older generation who ran it from the south. In 1983, he was elected as a member of Parliament, but in keeping with his group's boycott, he refused to serve in Westminster, the home of Parliament.

Although he was often blamed for the IRA's murders, Adams was a target of repeated violence himself. His wife and son were once nearly killed when a grenade went off by their home. In 1984, Adams managed to survive after being shot five times. Only his bulletproof flak jacket prevented a fatal wound to the heart. His would-be assassins were linked to the Ulster Defense Association (UDA), the major Protestant paramilitary organization and, in many ways, the Orange counterpart to the IRA. During this time, the UDA was purportedly linked to the Democratic Unionist Party, led by the Reverend Ian Paisley, who had his own long history of anti-Catholicism. A fundamentalist Free Presbyterian with a doctorate from Bob Jones University in the United States, Paisley once referred to the Pope as "the Antichrist." Within Northern Ireland, Paisley had a larger following than Adams, and perhaps even Hume. Though Protestants comprised two-thirds of Ulster's population, they felt themselves threatened. The long-standing call for a unified Ireland would sever their historic links to the British crown and probably leave the Catholics in charge. With demagogic fervor, Paisley incited Unionist anger against the Irish Catholic minority by appealing to their prejudices and fear. He remained a fierce critic of Adams and Sinn Fein. The year after Adams's shooting, an assassination plot against Paisley failed.

Throughout the 1980s and early 1990s, while the violence in Northern Ireland continued, Adams increasingly distanced himself from the IRA's bloody campaign. After one errant IRA bomb killed ten innocent people in Enniskillen, Adams admitted that such an atrocity couldn't be justified. "Military solutions by either of the two main protagonists only mean more tragedies," he said in news reports in Ireland. (For years, Adams had been banned from appearing on news programs in Northern Ireland.) Hume took note of Adams's bold conciliatory words and eventually became convinced that the Sinn Fein leader might hold an important key to peace.

By fall 1993, Jean Kennedy Smith became convinced that Adams wasn't anything like her view of the fanatical masked IRA gunmen—as she told one friend, "the kind of people who killed my brothers." She asked Ireland's new Taoiseach, Albert Reynolds, whether the United States could trust Adams, and he endorsed the notion. Although she wasn't supposed to go officially to Northern Ireland—diplomatically under the jurisdiction of the U.S. ambassador in London, not Dublin—Smith says Clinton instructed her to seek out possibilities for peace. During the 1992 presidential campaign, Clinton promised to appoint a special peace envoy for Northern Ireland, but so far in his presidency, he'd been convinced by political advisors that the idea was too premature. Clinton wanted Jean to take another look. "President Clinton had thought of sending over a peace envoy to Ireland, so that had been discussed in my briefings," she recalled. "I knew that was in the air—whether that was a good idea or not—and it was to be looked at when I was over there, to see whether it was something that could be worked out."

FOR HER FIRST Christmas season in Ireland, Jean invited her brother Ted Kennedy and his new wife, Vicki, for a visit. The senator had barely unpacked when his sister floated her notion of getting a U.S. visa for Gerry Adams. The Sinn Fein leader's eight earlier requests had been rejected. But perhaps, she suggested, Teddy could prevail on the president. "He's a terrorist," the senator replied.

On that holiday vacation together, the Kennedy siblings debated the idea some more during a meal at the home of Tim Pat Coogan. During his distinguished career, Coogan wrote biographies of the two most influential Irish figures in the twentieth-century conflict—Eamon De Valera and Michael Collins. (Smith later appeared in a cameo role in the film based on Collins's life, directed by Neil Jordan, a frequent guest at the ambassador's dinner parties.) The writer presented Collins as a brave man who fought for independence and died trying to forge peace; he portrayed De Valera scathingly as an insular, almost fanatical ascetic whose leadership of Ireland kept the nation poor, myopic and doomed to self-destructiveness. During their chat, Coogan suggested that a visit by Gerry Adams to America would place him on an international stage, rehabilitate his demonized image and add enough to his prestige to compel the British to deal more constructively with Sinn Fein. Ted Kennedy remained doubtful.

At another dinner arranged by Jean, Prime Minister Reynolds argued to Ted that getting the Adams visa could reinvigorate the stagnant peace talks in Northern Ireland. Reynolds knew the senator possessed enough clout with Clinton to end his nation's ban on Adams and Sinn Fein. Earlier that month, Reynolds had persuaded Clinton to call the British prime minister, John Major, to ask him to agree to what became known as the Downing Street Declaration—a significant agreement in which the English conceded they had no economic or strategic interest in Ulster and would only seek peace. Reynolds had been present in the White House when Clinton announced Jean Kennedy Smith as the new ambassador. That day, Reynolds said warmly to Smith, "Welcome home." He admired the Kennedys' mythic status in Ireland, and he knew this chieftain-like quality could extend to women members of the clan. "The Kennedy men were regarded as the politicians," Reynolds later said. "She has shown herself to be as strong a leader, if not more so." Though the Irish leader was limited in what he could say publicly, Reynolds became an ally in the ambassador's sub-rosa peace efforts. "He was very instrumental, and he was always in touch," Jean said of Reynolds. "He encouraged me and encouraged the process."

Everyone knew that Ted Kennedy's endorsement mattered the most. Before he returned to Washington, the senator listened carefully to Hume and the experts his sister had assembled to argue Adams's case. In the end, though, he looked to the opinion of his older sister, just as other Kennedy siblings had relied on each other with earlier political questions. Even as children, the two youngest children of Rose and Joe Kennedy were always close—"they were a pair," their mother later wrote. Ted knew that Jean was not one to be bowled over by sentiment or naïveté. "What impressed me was Jean's observation of the strong commitment that Adams had to ending violence," the senator later told the *Boston Globe*. Now that his thinking about Gerry Adams was substantially different, Ted returned to Washington in early 1994 determined to do what he could.

BILL CLINTON savored his own favorite image of JFK. The 1963 photograph of young Clinton—then an Arkansas high school student visiting the White House with his service group, Boy's Nation, beaming as he shook hands with President Kennedy—was reprinted ubiquitously during his 1992 presidential campaign. For years, Clinton had pointed with pride to his JFK handshake. Clinton biographer David Maraniss later suggested the photo symbolized "a transference of politics" for the future president. Another Irish journalist quipped that it appeared "like a laying on of hands by JFK"—from one American chieftain to another. On Inauguration Day in 1993, Clinton visited President Kennedy's grave and stood in the cold before the eternal flame to pay homage to his hero.

During his White House years, Clinton and his wife, Hillary, became friendly with several Kennedy family members, including Jackie Kennedy, with whom they went on a leisurely sailboat ride along Martha's Vineyard the first summer Clinton was in office. "We may have had [Democratic] nominees who talked about him, but none who acknowledged as directly and as almost emotionally his kinship with President Kennedy," noted Frank Mankiewicz, Bobby Kennedy's former press spokesman. Clinton relied on Ted steadily for advice. In leaving office years later, Clinton said, "Whatever I have accomplished as President, so much of it would never have been possible if Ted Kennedy wasn't there every single step of the way."

Though Clinton's political kinship with the Kennedys seemed natural, his affinity with the Irish Catholic community was more of an acquired taste. A Baptist comfortable with his own religion, Clinton had attended Georgetown University, the renowned Jesuit-run school in Washington, D.C., where the young undergraduate student was introduced to various aspects of Catholic cultural life. At Oxford, as a Rhodes scholar in the late 1960s, he followed the initial civil rights disputes in Northern Ireland. Several friends say Clinton, as governor of Arkansas, possessed an impressive knowledge of Irish politics. "I saw the (beginning) of a lot of what the people there had lived through for the last twenty-five years," Clinton explained as president, "and I thought if there was anything we could do to make a positive difference we ought to try."

Clinton didn't give much mind to Irish-Americans as a political force until the bruising 1992 New York primary, when he courted them as an important swing vote. During a forum in New York set up by prominent

Irish-Americans, candidate Clinton promised that if he got elected he would appoint a special envoy to help broker a peace in Northern Ireland. After his election, genealogists traced a small portion of Clinton's lineage to Ulster Protestants, through the Cassidy family on his mother's side. Clinton embraced this finding with a bit of his own blarney. "I've always been conscious of being Irish," he said. "I mean, I'm sort of—I look Irish; I am Irish . . . it means a lot to me." Events would suggest that Clinton's statement might be true, at least figuratively speaking.

Upon returning in January 1994 from his trip to see his sister, Senator Kennedy urged the White House to grant a visa to Gerry Adams, who'd been invited the following month to a forum hosted in New York by many of Clinton's top 1992 supporters in the Irish-American community. For much of the post–World War II era, while the "special relationship" between the United States and Great Britain prospered, the Irish government appeared to do little effective lobbying with the American government, or with the many Irish-Americans who could affect U.S. foreign policy. This New York–based group wanted the American government to pay more attention to the troubles in Northern Ireland. At first, Clinton demurred on the Adams visa because he wanted to consult other Irish experts. Speaker of the House Tom Foley and others in Washington advised against the idea. But Nancy Soderberg, a former aide on Ted Kennedy's staff who was now overseeing Irish strategy for Clinton's National Security Council, counseled the president to go forward cautiously.

Within a short time, at the urging of both Kennedys, the White House signaled the State Department to approve a two-day visa for Adams. Instead of applying in Belfast for a visa through the U.S. embassy in London—as he had previously in his failed attempts—Adams asked for his visiting pass through Ambassador Jean Kennedy Smith's office in Dublin. "There was huge protestation, there was hysteria from the British about the possibility of me getting a visa," Adams recalled "There was advice from the FBI, the State Department and Justice Departments that I should not be given the visa. So President Clinton had a decision to make which meant effectively going against his own system." Ultimately, Clinton decided the political risks were worth the chance for peace.

GRANTING A VISA to Gerry Adams stunned and angered the British. Prime Minister John Major visibly cooled toward the White House. Only months before, Major and several top advisers had nearly been killed by an IRA bomber. In this post–Cold War atmosphere, though, Clinton realized he could be more flexible than past presidents—certainly more so than

John Kennedy during the early 1960s nuclear stare down with the Soviet Union, when a British alliance with America was crucial. During the Reagan and Bush years, U.S. policy had remained decidedly tilted in the British favor, particularly while Margaret Thatcher was prime minister. Clinton realized that America didn't have to keep blinders on regarding Northern Ireland any longer. The voices of Irish Catholics in America could now be heeded by a friendly American president.

During spring 1994, the visa for Adams set in motion a series of negotiations, including some carried out privately and unofficially by Clinton's Irish-American supporters. In August, Niall O'Dowd, an energetic, Irish-born founder of the *Irish Voice* in New York, and former Congressman Bruce Morrison, a classmate of Clinton's, flew to Belfast to meet with Adams and other Sinn Fein leaders. They hoped to work out a potential cease-fire agreement. But there remained one sticking point. Sinn Fein insisted that an American visa first be granted to Joe Cahill, an elderly IRA member with a notorious history. In return, Cahill would talk with his Irish-American friends in Irish Northern Aid Committee (NORAID) about the benefits of such a settlement. Adams knew that hard-liners in America would be nearly as important to success as those in Ulster. After years of conflict in Ireland, peace could easily be undermined by political feuds and breakaway splinter groups unwilling to compromise. But under a long-standing U.S-British agreement on terror aimed specifically at the IRA, Cahill could not be granted a visa to New York. His past appeared to doom his chances. Years earlier, Cahill had barely escaped the hangman's noose for the killing of a Royal Ulster police official, for which another IRA member, Tom Williams, was executed. British authorities urged Clinton to refuse Cahill a visa and make no further accommodations to a terrorist organization responsible for so many killings. Meanwhile, Dublin urged the president to go ahead with a visa for Cahill. When Reynolds called, Clinton referred to the rather extensive government dossier on Cahill's alleged IRA terrorism connections.

"Have you seen this man's record?" the president asked.

"Well, we didn't suggest for a moment he was a saint or a parish priest," replied Reynolds.

Perhaps the most persuasive calls and cables came from Jean Kennedy Smith, who urged the president to take one more step. Finally, in a telephone call at five in the morning, she learned that Cahill's visa would be granted. In America, Ted Kennedy's behind-the-scenes efforts pushed toward a cease-fire. "He eventually became the single most important U.S. politician on this issue, the one that the American presidents would consult," said Niall O'Dowd. "It [Ireland] is one of the dearest things to him—I know from talking with him."

Shortly after Cahill's entry to the United States, the IRA declared a cease-fire. The stunning announcement was hailed by many Irish and condemned by some diehards. Perhaps most important, it opened the way for further contacts with the United States. In September, Gerry Adams received another visa for a two-week visit that turned into a cross-country celebration and fundraiser around the possibilities of peace. The American media interviewed him extensively and gave a great public airing to Sinn Fein's side of the Northern Ireland dispute. Editorialists and policymakers discovered that Adams did not fit their stereotype about this organization. Though he'd never visited the United States before 1994, Adams emphasized that his views on the Northern Ireland struggle were affected greatly by two transcending American movements of the 1960s—civil rights and the tradition of church and state separation, an ideal that had played such a prominent role in John F. Kennedy's election. "I think that [separation of church and state] is an important dimension in the U.S.A. that could usefully be duplicated here in Ireland, with the need to protect civil and religious liberties, but at the same time to ensure that politics and religion are not mixed," Adams explained.

At Boston's airport, Ted Kennedy met Adams for the first time and assured him of Clinton's commitment for lasting peace. During a press conference, Kennedy praised Adams as "a voice for setting aside the violence." The senator stressed to reporters that he wouldn't have met Adams unless Sinn Fein had renounced political violence, and then not until there were signs the cease-fire was holding. "We're interested in the future," said Kennedy. "The violence has halted. It's difficult for many of us to understand why people are carping on the past."

In the middle of his own tight Senate reelection campaign, Ted Kennedy's involvement in Irish affairs abroad appeared to some Massachusetts Republicans as a ploy. "With the polls showing Irish Catholics are deserting Kennedy in droves, it's obvious why he did this," complained Ron Kaufman, state representative for the Republican National Committee. The same day of his arrival, Adams was escorted by Kennedy to a private reception hosted by prominent Irish-Americans in Boston; among the guests were the senator's niece, Courtney Kennedy Hill, and her husband, Paul. Adams was grateful to his Kennedy patrons. "I know that Teddy Kennedy talked to President Clinton about my visa, and I know at other times, Teddy Kennedy had intervened directly with the president," he said. "The Kennedys were there to say [that] the right thing to do was to give me the visa." The October 1994 trip's most significant moment—his telephone conversation at Hickory Hill with Vice President Gore, which opened the door to diplomacy with Sinn Fein—was one more contribution by the Kennedys to the cause of peace.

IN IRELAND, Jean Kennedy Smith stirred controversy beyond her attempts at peacemaking. She received criticism from Dublin's archbishop when she and the Irish Republic's president, in an ecumenical gesture, received Communion at a Protestant service. A curate in County Cork declared that Smith had committed a mortal sin, infuriating his congregates enough for many to storm out of their church. Smith refused to recant. "Religion, after all, is about bringing people together," she replied. "We all have our own way of going to God."

As part of her job, Smith kept up contacts with many sides in the north. She made a concerted effort to reach out to the Unionist community, where she made many Protestant friends. Nevertheless, she was branded a "nationalist" by her British critics, who claimed that her only intent was unifying Northern Ireland into one country with the south. State Department detractors sneered privately that Smith had overstepped her authority as ambassador. They accused her of "clientitis"—the diplomatic jargon for letting oneself become too identified with the host nation and forgetting American interests.

Within the Dublin embassy, some objected to the ambassador's personal, action-oriented style that often ignored or trampled diplomatic niceties. Two embassy staffers disagreed with her Sinn Fein efforts and filed angry protests with the U.S. State Department. Months later, the department's inspector general reprimanded Smith formally for punishing the two staffers who had voiced objections. British newspapers floated stories of Smith's being recalled or blamed for setbacks in the peace efforts, only to be denied firmly by Clinton officials. But her most severe critic was Raymond Seitz, the U.S. ambassador to Great Britain. He objected to Smith's initiatives and wrote a memoir after leaving office that sharply attacked her actions. Seitz called her shallow, naïve and "an ardent IRA apologist." Seitz claimed she routinely leaked American and British intelligence to Adams, which then wound up in IRA hands. "America, which had suffered so often at the hands of terrorists around the world, should have been the last place to offer a platform to Gerry Adams," Seitz contended.

When the book appeared, the ambassador's nephew, Congressman Patrick Kennedy of Rhode Island and Ted's youngest son, rebuked Seitz, warning that his comments were "destructive" to the ongoing peace process. Young Patrick defended his aunt's work by underlining its impact. And the White House denied all the allegations and expressed "full confidence in Ambassador Smith." When the London correspondent for the *New York Times* called for comment, Smith replied, "History will be the judge."

BY 1995, THE CLINTON administration had committed fully to achieving a lasting peace settlement. British officials and Ulster Protestants continued to raise skepticism about the IRA, especially as sporadic acts of violence occurred. In November, Clinton went to Ireland; he invited seven Irish-Americans along for the trip, including Maryland's lieutenant governor, Kathleen Kennedy Townsend, and Mayor Richard Daley of Chicago. "I think he (Clinton) was influenced a great deal both by her work and by what Senator Kennedy has been pushing for over many, many years," Townsend said of her aunt. "He appointed her ambassador which was his tribute to my family; and the fact that he stood up for her when it was not popular with the State Department, that he supported her when many others criticized the peace process, is a real tribute to him."

In a style reminiscent of JFK's 1963 visit, the Irish energized Clinton, who later called his visit "the best days of my presidency." In Dublin, Ambassador Jean Kennedy Smith appeared delighted as she rubbed her hands with sheer nervous energy and watched the large crowds pour out their good wishes for the president. The Clintons visited Derry and stayed in the Europa Hotel in Belfast, the target of repeated IRA bombings in the past. The president appointed former U.S. Senator George Mitchell to act as an international mediator and seek a method by which the IRA and its Orange counterparts in Ulster could surrender their arms in a permanent peace. Ian Paisley complained that Mitchell could not be an honest broker because he was "an Irish Catholic from the Kennedy stable."

Prime Minister John Major, realizing the fundamental change in America's position, worked with the Clinton administration begrudgingly. A few months later in New York, O'Dowd's magazine, *Irish America,* bestowed its annual award to Clinton at a February 1996 reception attended by dozens of Irish-American politicians and business people, including Ted Kennedy and his sister, Jean, the ambassador. During the ceremony, Ted Kennedy, wearing a green tie that nearly glowed, lionized Clinton's bold and courageous efforts. As the senator recalled his brother's promise to return to Ireland, his voice choked. Clinton could be seen with tears in his eyes. In his own remarks, President Clinton said that Northern Ireland's people "do not deserve to have a small group choose bloodshed and violence, shattering their dreams. We must not allow those who have been hardened by the past to hijack the future."

Despite these intentions, the peace efforts in Northern Ireland stumbled and nearly fell apart. In 1996, not long after Clinton's visit, an IRA bombing broke apart the first cease-fire. White House officials blamed Adams and Sinn Fein and didn't return to the bargaining table until 1997. During this time, Mitchell expanded his role as special envoy, mending fences and negotiating toward a compromise package that everyone could live by. While still dealing openly with Hume and Adams, Mitchell carefully avoided alienating the British government of newly elected Prime Minister Tony Blair of the Labour Party, nor David Trimble of the Ulster Unionists. Blair, far more liberal-minded than John Major, aided the American peace negotiations considerably; indeed, he increasingly put his own political capital at stake in seeking a peace agreement.

By April 1998, all sides had agreed to what became known as the Good Friday Agreement. It called for a new Northern Ireland Assembly that would be composed of Protestants and Catholics, and for "exclusively democratic and peaceful means" of resolving future disputes. The agreement outlined ways for the IRA and Orange extremists to get rid of their terrorist weapons, methods for the release of political prisoners and the administering of police and justice. The Irish Republic would also drop its territorial claim on Ulster—the call for a unified Ireland contained in its constitution, one of the last vestiges of De Valera's rule.

The violence didn't end. Weeks after the signing, twenty-eight people died in a bomb blast in Omagh, Northern Ireland, perpetrated by dissident republican militants. Yet the fragile settlement survived even this outrage and provided a realistic framework for peace.

As THE GOOD FRIDAY Agreement neared its conclusion, Jean Kennedy Smith announced her plans to retire and return home to America. Many of the same sectarian hatreds in Northern Ireland still existed, but her presence had made a significant difference in a hopeful pact that could end the suffering, a peace that might last.

At *Aras an Uachtarain* in Dublin in July 1998, the Irish president, Mary McAleese, and the Taoiseach, Bertie Ahern, conferred honorary Irish citizenship on Jean Kennedy Smith at a ceremony that reflected her family's historic link between the two countries. It was the same place where De Valera had given a garden party in 1963 for her brother, the first American president to visit Ireland. The nation that her Kennedy and Fitzgerald ancestors felt compelled to leave, an Ireland suffering from famine and oppression, was now a land enjoying prosperity to an extent not seen before in modern times. The role of the Kennedys—and by extension the role of all Irish-Americans who cared about the fate of their ancestral homeland—played a significant part in these improvements.

Though this ceremony paid tribute to the departing ambassador, McAleese noted that it was, in a sense, a recognition of the Kennedy family's contributions to the Irish-American saga. It was fitting that "we should complete the circle begun almost 150 years ago when Patrick Kennedy of New Ross sailed for the United States," McAleese said. "To his children and grand-children he handed a baton of love for Ireland. Today we are proud to hand his outstanding and distinguished descendant the highest accolade we can offer." Jean, who for much of her life had stayed in the background while the family's men took the limelight, appeared deeply moved. Without her, the visa for Adams probably would never have been issued, and the peace process would surely have been delayed for several more years, if not for another generation. She thanked them and, unassumingly, said she felt fortunate to have played a "small part" in this pivotal era in Irish history.

Before she left, the seventy-year-old ambassador stopped by the family's ancestral homestead in Dunganstown once again to pause and reflect on all that had happened. "My great-grandfather's brother never left," she explained. "And his great-grandson, Pat Kennedy, is a farmer in Wexford. I visit him and we talk. We always have a chuckle about what would have happened if his great-grandfather had gone over, and how life would have been so different."

Jean paid tribute to other parts of the Kennedy story in Ireland. In County Wexford, she attended the bicentenary anniversary of the 1798 Wexford uprising, another dramatic episode in the struggle of Irish Catholics for religious and civil liberties and their freedom from Britain. Kennedy ancestors were among those pikemen who fought at Vinegar Hill with the United Irishmen. At a memorial parade, Jean saluted those who marched in memory of the dead. She was presented with a bronze pikeman for her prominent role in the peace process. To the crowd, she recalled how Jack had always sprung to life whenever the rousing "Boys of Wexford" song was played. "Jean Kennedy Smith, so bright, so alive, so evidently enjoying the celebration, talked of her brother and his affection for the Boulavogue song and its memories," wrote an attending reporter for the local republican newspaper. "History coalesced." That same year, other Kennedys honored Ireland's past and the promise of its future. In Boston, the family awarded a special "Profile in Courage Award" to the Irish peacemakers in a ceremony held at the John F. Kennedy Presidential Library. Hume, Adams,

Trimble, David Ervine, leader of the Protestant paramilitary force, Monica McWilliams of the Northern Ireland Womens' Coalition representing women of Catholic and Protestant faiths, and Mitchell were all praised for their tireless work toward the Good Friday pact. The late president's daughter, Caroline Kennedy, said the award recognized "the fear they overcame in reaching out to their historic enemies in the spirit of peace."

When speaking of Ireland, the Kennedys usually framed their message in the context of their own family experience. Ted Kennedy said their personal history was "certainly a factor" in efforts by Jean and himself to bring about peace, despite the considerable political risks. "It made us want to think big and dare to try new things that might cause a breakthrough, such as encouraging President Clinton to grant Gerry Adams a visa," he noted in comments for this book.

At the University of Ulster in Derry in early 1998, Ted started a speech in similar personal terms, by calling attention to two sets of parents—one Catholic and the other Protestant—whose sons were killed in the conflict but were now working for some resolution. Kennedy noted the "apt coincidence" of the peace accord's occurring on the two-hundredth anniversary of the United Irishmen Rebellion, and praised all those who had "taken risks for peace." Mentioning various threads of history interwoven between the Irish and the United States, Kennedy said many of the estimated forty-four million Americans of some Irish ancestry were Protestant, not Catholic, yet they all learned to live together and prosper in America's diversity. He warned of those "who seek to wreck the peace process" by political violence. "Like so many of you here, my family has been touched by tragedy," the senator said, his Irish audience surely knowing its cause. "I know that the feelings of grief and loss are immediate—and they are enduring. The best way to ease these feelings is to forgive, and to carry on—not to lash out in fury, but to reach out in trust and hope."

In closing, Ted read from a recently discovered letter his father wrote privately in 1958 to a friend whose son had died. Joe Kennedy was long gone but he was still a presence in the Kennedys' lives. To his Ulster audience, Ted reminded them of his eldest brother, Joe, who died in World War II, and his eldest sister, Kathleen, killed a few years later in an air crash. They needed no reminders of Jack and Bobby. Then Ted shared his father's words about dealing with such sorrow:

There are no words to dispel your feelings at this time and there is no time that will ever dispel them. Nor is it any easier the second time than it was the first. And yet, I cannot share your grief because no one could share mine. When one of your children goes out of your life, you think of what he might have done with a few more years and you wonder what you are going to do with the rest of yours. Then one day, because there is a world to be lived in, you find yourself a part of it again, trying to accomplish something—something that he did not have enough time to do. And, perhaps, that is the reason for it all. I hope so.

Too many sons and daughters of Eire had been lost in the troubles. Now, the American senator urged, was the time for them to seek a lasting peace in Northern Ireland.

Chapter Forty-One

Legacies

AN AIR OF ANTICIPATION always surrounded John F. Kennedy Jr., as if he were the long-awaited heir to some fabled legacy or the son of a fallen chieftain. Countless media stories and interviews suggested, without fail, that he, too, might rise to power and lead a grateful nation. In fin-de-siècle America, pop culture transformed the Kennedys into a brand name, marketed by the media as a family drama with endless sequels. John-John was the little boy who had grown into a handsome, amiable young man while a nation watched. His full story, though, had yet to be written.

Upon graduating from Brown University in Rhode Island, he traveled around, volunteering for a short time with Mother Teresa's organization serving the poor in India. "The three days I spent in her presence was the strongest evidence this struggling Catholic has ever had that God exists," he later said. When John dabbled in theater in the 1980s, he took a part in Irish playwright Brian Fiel's *Winners*—a drama in which Kennedy's character remains lost at sea with his female companion until their dead bodies are found. Instead of show business, however, Jackie Kennedy encouraged a career in the law for her son. John eventually landed a job in the Manhattan district attorney's office, prosecuting run-of-the-mill crimes. At the 1988 Democratic Convention, John excited the crowd with a speech about his father's legacy. His appearance set off rumors that he'd soon follow in his father's political footsteps. "He said he was interested but still too young," recalled Pierre Salinger, his father's old spokesman. "He told me that he had an idea that he should go into politics in the next century."

After his mother's death, John entered another career that his father had once pursued—journalism. With backing from the Hearst organization, he founded a magazine called *George,* dedicated to chronicling the confluence of politics and culture. As his father had done in the 1940s, John used his role as a journalist to learn about the world and converse with important leaders. Politics flowed in his blood but he was determined to express his interest in creative, often ironic ways. In June 1997, John ventured across the Atlantic for a difficult interview with Sinn Fein leader Gerry Adams—then the bête noire of the peace talks. Several months before Kennedy's visit, Sinn Fein had been ousted from the negotiations after a February 1996 IRA bomb ripped through London's crowded Canary Wharf, killing two and injuring several others. The Clinton administration placed the responsibility for this deadly blast at Adams's doorstep. Hoping to be invited again into the talks, Adams undoubtedly realized the value that a high-profile media interview with JFK's son and the Irish ambassador's nephew would have in Washington.

John checked in at the Shelbourne Hotel, where his parents had once stayed, rather than stay with his aunt at the ambassadorial residence in Phoenix Park. John had visited Ireland only once before—the 1967 trip as a child with his mother and sister, Caroline—though he seemed conversant in Irish history and gripped by the ongoing struggle in the north. To the British government's dismay, this son of Camelot attended the funeral of Patrick Kelly, an IRA solider convicted in England of involvement in a bomb plot against Princess Anne. Kelly died in a British prison after his skin cancer was diagnosed too late and authorities refused his request to be transferred to Ireland. Kennedy made no comment at the funeral, but his presence raised many eyebrows.

The next day, John boarded a train to Belfast, where two Sinn Fein officials, Richard and Chrissie McAuley, met Kennedy at the station and showed him the city. "We were his tour guides for the day," remembered Richard McAuley, Adams's press spokesman. They walked through the downtown markets area, where extensive numbers of British troops were patrolling, giving the visiting American the impression of Ulster as an occupied nation. Kennedy learned that the military were nervous about the possibility of another summer of sectarian rioting during the "marching season"—when Protestants paraded in the streets to mark William of Orange's 1690 victory over King James II, the exiled English Catholic monarch, at the battle of Boyne. As Kennedy later explained in his *George* article: "Catholics are deeply offended by these triumphant displays, especially when the processions pass through their neighborhoods. The marches are a reminder of more than 800 years of English persecution." Later during his Belfast tour, Kennedy went over to Milltown Cemetery for a look at the graves of the Irish hunger strikers who died in 1981 protesting their treatment as political prisoners. "I remember Kennedy remarking how young they were when they died, and how tragic the loss of so many men had been," McAuley said. By day's end, they wandered into the Felons Club, a pub in West Belfast often frequented by Sinn Fein and former IRA members. John raised a pint with his escorts.

The soft-spoken magazine editor absorbed the sights, sounds and emotions of embattled Northern Ireland as though he were a native. Back home, like most Irish-Americans of his generation, John showed only faint glimmers of interest in Ireland. He rarely alluded to himself in ethnic terms, and most considered him a true-blue New Yorker, if not the all-American male. Yet months earlier in New York, Richard McAuley had accompanied Adams when they were first introduced to young Kennedy, who showed a distinct receptivity to the republican view. During their discussions, John compared the discrimination facing Catholics in Northern Ireland to the 1960s plight of blacks during the civil rights struggle in the American South. Perhaps Kennedy's words were a bit of overstatement to convince Adams to sit for an interview, but the Sinn Fein leader, whose own life sometimes depended on his judgments of men, thought he was sincere. The Kennedys he'd met all shared a similar interest in their family's heritage. "Like many Irish-Americans, they have a very strong sense of their Irishness," Adams explained. "Not only do I think politically conscious Irish-Americans have a sense of discrimination—because, after all, that's why they are in the States in the first place—but they are also motivated by public service, and feel a need to do something about it."

When Adams attempted similar rhetorical flourishes during his magazine interview, John Kennedy challenged him. "Though his charm is disarming, it is difficult to unfasten his thinking much beyond the rigid nationalist dogma that underlies so much of Sinn Fein's politics," Kennedy described skeptically. "His answers, while lengthy, are hardly ever personally revealing." As a thoughtful questioner, John asked about Sinn Fein's links to the IRA and quizzed Adams about "allegations of shake-downs in order to force people to tow the Republican line." Near the end of their interview, Kennedy asked Adams why, outside the Irish community in the United States, any American should care about Northern Ireland. Adams referred to the kind of political violence with which his interviewer was painfully familiar.

"The U.S. can be a very progressive force in this situation," Adams replied. "I was moved when Martin Luther King Jr. was killed, when your father was killed. . . . You know, if it isn't right to be discriminated against in the United States, well, then it shouldn't be right here."

THE BUZZ OF FUTURE political office, perhaps even the presidency some-day, remained with John Kennedy as he settled down and married at age thirty-five, about the same time in life that his father wed. Carolyn Bessette, his elegantly beautiful, blonde-haired wife with high-fashion friends and tastes, appeared the perfect companion. The couple lived in New York, where rumors speculated that John might run in 2000 for the U.S. Senate seat being vacated by Daniel Patrick Moynihan in New York (a post later won by first lady Hillary Rodham Clinton) or perhaps some high office at a later date.

In July 1999, John Kennedy still spent much of his time on *George,* his fledgling enterprise. He worked until late one Friday summer evening when, near dusk, he took off in a private plane with his thirty-three-year-old wife and her sister, Lauren. In the twilight, they headed towards Hyannis Port, where the next day they planned to attend the wedding of John's cousin, Rory, the last of Bobby and Ethel Kennedy's children. A large white tent was set in place on the grounds of the Kennedy compound and most of the guests had already arrived for the celebration. Family was important to this generation of Kennedys, just as it was for their parents and grand-parents; indeed, family was perhaps the most consistent ideal among them.

After a certain point, John's absence became worrisome. A few inquiries revealed the awful truth—his plane was missing. Coast Guard boats and hel-icopters combed the Cape Cod shoreline, past the beaches where Jack and Jackie Kennedy had once strolled with their son. As the hours stretched into days, a potential rescue mission for survivors turned into a recovery effort for remains of the aircraft. President Clinton ordered the federal search to continue beyond any hope of a miracle. It was a personal gesture to the Kennedys as well as an appropriate response by a nation horrified that their slain president's son was dead. On the third day, all three bodies were found submerged in the plane, located at the bottom of the ocean. Dreams of restoring a lost Kennedy presidency were gone.

DAN RATHER STARED somberly into the camera. "The Kennedy name has attracted the spotlight in this country," Rather announced, "but this family, which has often basked in fame, had also felt the glare of the spotlight at moments of tragedy . . . "

As the vintage film clips of Camelot flashed on the screen, the CBS anchorman narrated the familiar melodrama. Rather made his name in network news during the 1963 tragedy in Dallas. Now, he played master of ceremonies to a network news program devoted to the death of the president's son. Once more, the Kennedy deathwatch had begun for the American public, a ritual once stately and reverential, now macabre and almost prurient. Celebrity—once so avidly sought by Joe Kennedy's publicity men—had long ago stripped this family of their privacy. The outpouring of public emotion confirmed the degree to which so many Americans, often with little or no family of their own, identified with this large clan.

Outside the Manhattan couple's apartment, bouquets of flowers and cards were placed at its entrance as if it were a shrine. Strangers congregated and lit candles in memory of a man they had never met. "We've become a rather lonely nation in spite of our communicative skills," observed Mike Barnicle, a Boston columnist, during a nationally televised show outside the funeral services. "We don't know our neighbors, we don't know the people upstairs. But we know the Kennedys. And whether you like them politically or not, they are a universal bond that extends across this country and, I think, perhaps the world."

In Hyannis Port, members of the family, their heads bowed, wept as they silently entered the Kennedy summer house. Each Kennedy was recorded by cameras providing around-the-clock mourning on cable television. From far away, a telephoto lens spotted Ted and Ethel in the large white party tent once meant for a joyous family wedding. They could be seen receiving and holding chalices as Communion was given out at a Mass said privately for the benefit of Kennedy's loved ones. Father Michael Kennedy, the distant Irish cousin from Waterford who had come for the nuptials, now attended to their grief. In the voracious maw of celebrity, this intensely private family moment became a candid video image surreptitiously commandeered into the homes of millions. At the White House, President Clinton spoke for a nation when he issued a statement of heartfelt sorrow. Even in Ireland, the news came hard. The Taoiseach expressed "the great distress felt by Irish people around the word." The Kennedy Homestead in Dunganstown closed its doors in tribute, reminiscent of the same sorrow felt on the day John's father had died.

Once more, supposedly serious commentators on the news wondered aloud about a so-called Kennedy curse. Though ample evidence existed of poor judgment by Kennedy in trying to fly into that evening's hazy dusk, the fatal outcome was often attributed to a long litany of tragedies bedeviling the family. The circumstances of this plane crash were so heartbreaking that some assumed a Kennedy curse must exist. "He seemed to be a Kennedy without falling under the Kennedy curse," bemoaned *USA Today*. "We provide our own interpretations and questions—are these wounds self-inflicted or divine punishment, or coincidence?—because the saga's bare facts offer no suggestion of a rational universe or a benevolent deity." Various journalists noted that John Jr.'s plane crash came at about the same time as the thirtieth anniversary of Chappaquiddick and the *Apollo 11* moon landing—arguably the low point and the high point of the Kennedy epoch. Even the sober-minded Doris Kearns Goodwin advised that "the curse cannot be seen as something they've brought on themselves."

Although Roman Catholicism comprised the nation's largest denomination, the American media seemed unable, or unwilling, to explore this tragedy in the religious context that the Kennedy family used to deal with their loss. How does a family that professes to believe in God deal with such repeated instances of tragedy? The answers offered to the American public were mostly trite sound bites or sentimental greeting-card explanations. Only a few offered any insight. "They are people of strong Catholic faith—this is the core of their existence," explained Orrin Hatch, a Republican senator who counted Ted Kennedy as a friend. "There's a special hurt that comes from seeing his brother's only son die."

Ted Kennedy scoffed at the notion of a Kennedy curse, a divine execration, something he had raised three decades earlier, after Chappaquiddick. "No, that's not the way we've been," he said, when asked about the Kennedys' fate, "I've been very, very fortunate, and very lucky." At his nephew's funeral, he remained a source of strength for his family, no longer jaunty and young but a jowly, older man with white hair, encumbered by age and girth, who bore an increasing resemblance to Honey Fitz, his grandfather. Dutifully, he was there when the bodies were recovered. And he stood aboard the naval destroyer that took John's cremated remains out to sea. Ted Kennedy seemed destined to attend to the living while burying the dead. At the memorial service held at the Church of St. Thomas More, the small century-old stone church where Jackie had often worshipped, he gave a warm and heartfelt tribute to his nephew. The 350 mourners, gathered by invitation only, included President Clinton, first lady Hillary Rodham Clinton and numerous friends and associates from the Camelot era. About a third of the guests were Kennedy relatives. In the church, full of tears and memories, the senator began by humorously recalling what

John once said he'd do if he ever ran for president and got elected—"I guess the first thing is call up Uncle Teddy and gloat."

The assembled guests laughed through their pain. "I loved that," Ted added, as if telling a yarn at a large Irish wake. "It was so like his father."

The senator recalled John's wit and energy, his creative ambition. He remembered how he suggested that instead of model Cindy Crawford posing as George Washington on *George's* first cover, John should have used his Uncle Ted. "Without missing a beat, John told me he stood by his original editorial decision," he said.

Despite the remembrances of wit to ease the moment, there remained an unbearable sense of loss, a yearning for what once was and an inclination of what might have been. "From the first day of his life, John seemed to belong not only to our family, but to the American family—the whole world knew his name before he did," the senator said. "He had a legacy, and he learned to treasure it. He was part of a legend, and he learned to live with it. . . . He had only just begun. There was in him a great promise of things to come."

Then Ted recalled the poem written by Thomas Kiernan, the Irish ambassador, shortly after John's birth and presented to his parents at the White House in 1961. The verses, once a hopeful wish, now seemed almost prophetic ("If the storms break for him, May the trees shake for him / Their blossoms down / In the night that he is troubled / May a friend wake for him / So that his time be doubled . . . "). Teddy's eloquent good-bye ended with his own reference to another poem. "We dared to think, in that other Irish phrase, that this John Kennedy would live to comb gray hair, with his beloved Carolyn by his side," he lamented, his voice cracking. "But like his father, he had every gift but length of years."

When he had finished, Caroline Kennedy stood up, walked over to her uncle and hugged him.

THE DAY BEFORE this ceremony for John, a memorial Mass placed the Kennedy legacy in greater historical context. Sponsored by the Emerald Isle Immigration Center—a group helping the current wave of Irish immigrants, some here illegally without immigration green cards—this event wasn't so much to mark a singular death as to recognize and give thanks for what an Irish Catholic family had achieved in America.

At the old St. Patrick's in downtown Manhattan, the cathedral where generations of newly arrived immigrants once attended Mass and received the sacraments, they held their own poignant commemoration. The pews were filled not only with Irish faces, the first immigrant wave, but those succeeding groups of racial, ethnic and religious minorities who arrived from Latin America, Asia, the Caribbean and Eastern Europe. Seated inside was Sargent Shriver, as a family representative, but most of those at this remarkable "people's Mass" were the unknown laborers of the city. In a different time and a different city, one might have seen Patrick Kennedy from Dunganstown sitting out there among the immigrant faces. Three thousand more stood in the nearby streets, lined five and ten rows deep on that humid night. "If the Kennedy family is America's royalty, then John Jr. was the people's prince," declared Carolyn Ryan of the Emerald Isle Immigration Center, who helped bring the event together.

The influence of the Kennedys as chieftains, as rallying points for the disparate groups of underprivileged and underrepresented people in American society, was never so evident. If the service uptown illustrated what the Kennedys had become with their power and celebrity, this Mass gave a true sense of where they had come from, the long journey of Irish-Americans struggling to succeed in a new and often hostile land. To these new Americans, the Kennedys represented the promise of opportunity, the chance that they could not only survive but someday thrive. There were tributes that recalled the contributions of the Kennedys to American life, along with Irish songs and bagpipes wailing and poems read, one of them about Owen Roe O'Neill. Even the priests were consumed by a distinct Irish fatalism. At the Mass, the church pastor, the Reverend Keith Fennessy, paraphrased Senator Moynihan's comment after President Kennedy was killed. "Part of being Irish is knowing that someday the world will break your heart," said the priest. "We all feel very Irish tonight."

DESPITE THE SORROW of the evening, the presence of this crowd underlined the family's longstanding commitment to immigration, the most hopeful and enduring part of its legacy. Indeed, many of these immigrants wouldn't be in these pews, wouldn't be living in America, if not for the intervention of the Kennedys in public life. Most probably could not recite the family's history chapter and verse. They just knew the Kennedys had been there for them—the immigrants of the city—when they were most vulnerable, most in need.

By the time of this old St. Patrick's memorial, the full impact of the 1965 Immigration Reform Act was evident throughout the United States. Over the previous thirty years, millions of new immigrants from places such as Mexico, China, Vietnam, Haiti, Poland and El Salvador had transformed the nation in the same way the large influx of Irish, Italians, Germans and Eastern European Jews had invigorated the nation a century before. Just as they did then, some politicians demanded protective barriers. They railed suspiciously against these newcomers, and some blamed the Kennedys. "Seldom has a bill had such unintended consequences. In fact, the 1965 Act opened the floodgates," complained James Goldsborough in a 2000 issue of *Foreign Affairs.* "By the early 1980s, the United States had a full-blown immigration crisis." In response, Ted Kennedy noted the 1965 act was intended to end discriminatory policies and not increase the nation's immigration numbers. "At that time, no one could have predicted the economic trends that would shape U.S. immigration in the years to come," he added. Since 1965, Kennedy has helped to pass several measures designed to fix problems in America's immigration system; but he believes the current system still is ripe with abuse, having "created an underground labor economy that encourages smuggling, document fraud, exploitation, and low wages."

The historical parallels are not lost on Kennedy. Today's unwashed immigrant workers who barely speak English are often willing to take virtually any job, regardless of risk. The hovels they live in, the dangerous jobs and below-minimum wages, the poor sanitation and the marginal health care are often analogous to the conditions Patrick and Bridget Kennedy found along the Boston waterfront 150 years ago. Arguably, given the tenuous legal status of more than eight million undocumented newcomers in states such as California, Texas, Florida and New York, their plight is even worse. Though his own family is now far removed from the customs gate, Ted Kennedy, as a leader of the Senate's Health, Education, Labor and Pensions Committee, has done as much to help today's immigrants as any other legislator. In this sense, he's been quite true to his family legacy. "There are similarities between the early Irish immigrants and today's immigrants, particularly undocumented workers," said Kennedy. "As with the early Irish immigrants, the undocumented community has been blamed for all sorts of societal ills such as high crime and high unemployment. In many ways, it is not fairer today than it was when my great grandparents arrived."

Nationally, the challenge of giving voice to this recent generation of newcomers may fall to some other immigrant family—perhaps a Latino "Kennedy" somewhere—who might recognize their own version of the "emerald thread" of which President Kennedy once spoke. Today, the path to power is likely to be as difficult as ever. Since JFK's groundbreaking 1960 election, minorities and newcomers have won many notable races for state and city offices. But in the intervening years, the reform measures designed to eliminate the old inner-city political machines has, in effect, reduced the chance of today's immigrants to use local politics as a way to bring about meaningful changes. Many "illegals" cannot vote, and other immigrants are too afraid or too overworked to exercise their electoral franchise. Without the clubhouse, without outspoken leaders to rally them, these immigrants depend on the social, charitable and advocacy groups that, for all their good intentions, lack the political acuity to produce a city mayor like Honey Fitz, or even a local chieftain like P. J. Kennedy. For today's immigrants, the path contains far more obstacles than the Kennedys ever faced in marching from ward healer to City Hall and, perhaps, someday to the White House.

In a similar way, the Catholic Church is unlikely to provide the kind of symbiotic aid that enabled John F. Fitzgerald to build an organization from Boston's immigrant church, nor for his grandson Jack Kennedy to succeed after World War II, when he recruited hundreds of new voters at Communion breakfasts and Knights of Columbus meetings, and doled out foundation checks to Catholic-run orphanages and old-age homes. Today's newcomers to America don't turn to the immigrant church in quite the same way as those immigrants from County Wexford or Limerick. A sizeable number who crossed the border as Catholics have since joined evangelical or other Protestant denominations. In the Catholic Church, prelates such as Boston's former Cardinal Bernard Law appeared to abandon the outreaching spirit of Vatican II and that short-lived era of "the two Johns." The scandal of priest sex abuse, originating in the Boston diocese and spreading across the nation, highlighted the sexual duplicity in the church's own ranks. More so, it undermined the singular and hard-won moral authority of the church in a society that prizes the secular and homogenous. The hierarchy's cover-up eventually forced Law to resign, but left a generation of Catholics staggered by their actions. In Rome, Pope John Paul II—for all his effectiveness in combating the evils of international communism— seems constantly at odds with American Catholics on issues of sex, family planning and the role of women. That the Kennedys, once venerated as the leading Catholic family in America, should so often be in public disagreement with Rome speaks volumes about the state of the church itself, estranged from so many of its faithful. The Irish, as research studies show, still believe in the old verities of God, eternal life and the sanctity of the family. But they are at a loss, like so many of their co-religionists, to explain the behavior of their priests.

WHATEVER THEIR human failings, the idealism surrounding the Kennedy legacy endures, particularly as a personal beacon of hope for America's minorities. Sophisticates such as television commentator Tim Russert still remember how the Irish Catholics in his old Buffalo neighborhood, the morning after the 1960 election, bounded out of their houses and yelled, *"We won! We won!"* "He was Irish Catholic and one of us," Russert recalled. "For me it was so important because I now realized we could do anything. There were no more obstacles, no more limits." Senator Joseph Lieberman of Connecticut, the first Jewish person nominated on a major national ticket, recalled how much Kennedy's victory meant to him: "When JFK broke the barrier, I felt—as I'm sure so many other Americans who seemed outside the full mainstream of American life—that President Kennedy was bringing us in with him, that he was opening the doors of opportunity not only for Catholics, but for everybody in America."

During his vice-presidential run in 2000, Lieberman didn't confront the KKK and organized hate groups that plagued Al Smith. He didn't have to face the repeated questioning about church and state that Kennedy endured. Because of JFK's victory, Lieberman's Jewishness didn't become the prime issue in the campaign, nor did any sizeable portion of the electorate vote against him simply because of his ethnicity or beliefs. Perhaps only those who had lived long enough, someone like Lieberman, could appreciate the changes since 1960, the remarkable transformation in the United States so thorough, so complete that it became ubiquitous, nearly taken for granted. "You can see how far America has come, how much America has changed for the better," he said at the Kennedy library in May 2001 at a symposium touching on the family's legacy. "I faced no bigotry, and had to explain nothing more than the perfectly understandable questions about what I could or do not do on the Sabbath, with the dispatch of my public responsibilities."

IT SHOULD NOT be said that more cannot be done, as Bobby Kennedy often insisted and as this generation of Kennedys repeatedly point out. Four decades after John Kennedy's election, America has yet to elect another president from a minority group, and the White House is still a bastion of white Protestant men. Perhaps the grossest omission involves women, whose numbers would make it a misnomer to call them a minority except for their continued secondary treatment in American society. Although a host of nations—Ireland, Israel and Great Britain among them—have have selected female national leaders, no woman has occupied the Oval Office, nor does the possibility appear on the horizon. Within the Kennedy family, women have played a significant, arguably preeminent role in public life during the past decade, far from their supportive but subservient role in the past. Jean Kennedy Smith helped bring a semblance of peace to Northern Ireland, and Kathleen Kennedy Townsend sought the governorship in

Maryland in 2002. Maria Shriver became a distinguished national news anchor, and Caroline Kennedy continued writing books, running the family's "Profile in Courage Awards" and, in the fall of 2002, accepted a non-paying role as chief fundraiser for the New York City school system.

Like many Irish Catholic women who once felt constrained by the demands of their culture or church, these women emerged with a public-minded independence in American society that Rose Kennedy could only have imagined. During this decade, the Kennedy women have acted as chieftains, leaders of the clan, like the emerald kings of old, willing to step forward even when the men in their family stumbled or failed. They were mindful of their heritage, which informed so much of their work, yet they were not afraid to differ with male authority figures. "I figure they were wrong about Galileo, and it took them a couple of centuries to figure that out—and they'll figure this out, too," said Townsend of the current difficulties in the American Catholic Church. "It is an institution . . . and they have done a lot of good. But that doesn't mean they are going to change immediately. You can still love the Mother Church with an understanding that it may take a little longer to learn modern science—and using Galileo is a good example."

During the past century and a half, this remarkable family, like so many other Irish Catholics, ascended from beleaguered famine survivors to affluent, fully assimilated citizens. They not only reflected the changes in political, social and cultural life for Irish Catholics but often proved instrumental in their transformation. Today, the Kennedys still retain their appeal in the public's imagination—though no longer out of loyalty to one candidate, a particular ethnic group or even to the Democratic Party itself, as Kathleen Kennedy Townsend found in her failed bid for governor. Their family's history speaks to a broad egalitarian ideal about government and the positive impact it can make in people's lives, the role of family and faith in sustaining individuals in turbulent times, and the promise of opportunity regardless of one's status in society.

In August 2000, at the Democratic National Convention in Los Angeles, the Kennedys brought this message with them when they appeared on the podium together, as a family, demonstrating their strength in numbers. In this city, they had experienced great triumph and shattering loss. Senator Ted Kennedy mentioned how proud President Kennedy would be that a "new barrier of bigotry" was broken by Lieberman's nomination. Television viewers saw Ted's son, Congressman Patrick Kennedy, the environmentalist Robert F. Kennedy Jr., and his sister, Lieutenant Governor Kathleen Kennedy Townsend, all speak of their family legacy during the convention.

But a year after her brother's death, Caroline Kennedy Schlossberg's appearance drew the most attention.

As she walked to the microphone, the band played the strains of Camelot. The packed auditorium seemed collectively to recall the memory of her father—though many delegates were children or not even born when John Kennedy was nominated in this same city forty years earlier. Caroline was now a dignified forty-two-year-old woman, an author in her own right. In a nervous, heartfelt voice, she reminded the national audience of abiding lessons from her parents' generation.

"They taught us the importance of faith and family, and how these values must be woven together into lives of purpose and meaning," said Caroline, amid blue signs all around her emblazoned with just her first name. "Now it is our turn to prove that the New Frontier was not a place in time but a timeless call. Now, when many of us are doing so well, it is time once again to ask more of ourselves."

It was the kind of speech, with echoes of St. Luke and her father's inaugural, that would have made her ancestors smile.

A Note on Sources

At its heart, this book relies on the personal and public documents of the Kennedy family as well as research and interviews conducted by the author in Ireland, Italy and the United States.

In August 2000, the voluminous private papers of Joseph P. Kennedy, housed at the John F. Kennedy Presidential Library in Boston, were made available to historical researchers granted permission to review them by the family foundation's screening committee. These Joseph P. Kennedy (JPK) papers cover a period of five decades and served as an important primary source for much of the documentation and context in this narrative. In gaining access to these papers, the author was asked for a general description of this book, but no restrictions were placed on the use or interpretation of these documents. Much of the material quoted from the JPK papers appears for the first time in this work. Similarly, the author was granted full access to the Kennedy Family Collection of private photographs, some of which have never been published. In addition, the Kennedy Homestead in Dunganstown Ireland granted access to the privately held 1947 photograph taken by young John F. Kennedy on his visit to meet his Irish cousins, which also appears here for the first time.

Other documents and research materials were provided from the Boston Public Library, the Library of Congress, the National Library of Ireland in Dublin, the County Wexford Library, the County Cork Library, Biblioteca Apostolica Vaticana in Vatican City, the Vatican Secret Archives, Biblioteca Nazionale Centrale Di Roma, the Boston College Library, the Archdiocese of Boston archives, the Fordham University Library archives, the Boston Police Department archives, the New York City Public Library, the University of Massachusetts–Boston Library, the New York City Historical Society, the Queensborough Public Library, the Lyndon B. Johnson Library and Museum, the Franklin D. Roosevelt Presidential Library and the unprocessed personal papers of Rev. Richard McSorley in the archives of the Georgetown University Library. The author's local library, the Commack Public Library in Commack, N.Y., provided assistance in securing numerous books, research papers and oral histories, for which Susanne McGovern and Joanne Kelleher deserve my gratitude. At the JFK Library, Stephen Plotkin, Megan Desnoyers, Allan Goodrich, James Hill, Michael Desmond and several other staff members were unflaggingly gracious and helpful. Kia Campbell at the Library of Congress helped secure several photos and drawings used in this book.

In Ireland, a great deal of the material and interviews cited below were obtained with the help of Patrick Grennan at the Kennedy Homestead. He runs the family farm, a museum dedicated to the history of JFK's 1963 visit, an informative website (www.kennedy.homestead.com)

about the Kennedy's Irish history and provided great insight and hospitality to the author. Others who shared their comments include: Sen. Edward M. Kennedy, former U.S. Ambassador to Ireland Jean Kennedy Smith, former Maryland Lieutenant Governor Kathleen Kennedy Townsend, Joseph Gargan, Amanda Smith, Theodore Sorensen, former U.S. Sen. Harris Wofford, former U.S. Sen. Eugene McCarthy, Gerry Adams, Niall O'Dowd, Edwin Guthman, Rev. Richard McSorley, Rev. Andrew Greeley, William Haddad, Melody Miller, Dorothy Tubridy, Mary Ann Ryan, Patrick Kennedy (JFK's third cousin in Dunganstown), Thomas Grennan, John W. Pierce, Richard Macauley, Elizabeth Shannon, James M. O'Toole and Ruth-Ann Harris. In addition, this work relied on the more contemporaneous recollections of several people who granted oral history interviews for the JFK Library, including John M. Bailey, Rev. John Cavanaugh, Cesar Chavez, Lucius D. Clay, John Cogley, Cardinal Richard J. Cushing, Mark J. Dalton, William Douglas Home, Allen Dulles, Hugh Fraser, Josephine Grennan, David L. Hackett, Lord Harlech (William David Ormsby-Gore), Rev. Theodore Hesburgh, Robert F. Kennedy, Thomas J. Kiernan, Martin Luther King Jr., Belford V. Lawson, Marjorie McKenzie Lawson, Sean Lemass, Henry Cabot Lodge, Louis Martin, Andrew Minihan, Francis X. Morrissey, Patrick J. "Patsy" Mulkern, Fletcher Knebel, Thomas P. "Tip" O'Neill, Frank M. O'Ferrall, David F. Powers, Eunice Kennedy Shriver, Charles Spaulding, William J. "Billy" Sutton, Dorothy Tubridy, James W. Wine and Harris Wofford.

Part I: From Ireland to Irish-American

The quotation from George Bernard Shaw can be found in Michael Holroyd, *Bernard Shaw: The One-Volume Definitive Biography.*

Chapter One: The Boys of Wexford

Various published accounts, oral histories and interviews described JFK's visit to New Ross in 1963, along with several files at the John F. Kennedy Presidential Library that deal directly or indirectly with this trip. This reportage was also supplemented with firsthand observations and research by the author in New Ross, Ireland. Kennedy's statements during his Ireland trip are contained in public documents available in *Public Papers of the Presidents*, and in JFK Library folders relating to presidential aide David Powers. Other lively accounts of JFK's trip used in this chapter are included in Joseph Roddy, "Ireland: The Kennedy Cult—They Cried the Rain Down That Night," *Look,* November 17, 1964; Richard Rovere, "Journal of a Psuedo-Event," *New Yorker,* July 13, 1963; Tom Wicker, "Ireland Prepares for Kennedy Visit Thursday," *New York Times,* June 23, 1963; Tom Wicker, "Kennedy Sees the Cousin Who Didn't Catch the Boat," *The New York Times,* June 28, 1963; "When Kennedy Went 'Home' to Ireland," *U.S. News and World Report,* July 8, 1963. JFK's conversations in New Ross were supplemented with the oral histories of New Ross Mayor Andrew Minihan, Dorothy Tubridy at the JFK Library; Jean Kennedy Smith's recollections of the trip are from the author's conversation with her and in Laurence Leamer, *The Kennedy Women.* Other details of the trip can be found in Kenneth P. O'Donnell and David Powers, *Johnny, We Hardly Knew Ye,* and the National Archives of Ireland file marked "President Kennedy Visits Ireland."

Firsthand descriptions of the River Barrow valley, the Kennedy Homestead where Patrick Kennedy once lived, the homes of other Kennedy relatives in the community and an examination of Kennedy headstones at the local cemetery were obtained by the author in Dunganstown and surrounding area. More detailed renderings of life on the Kennedy farm during the 1840s were provided by Patrick Grennan and Mary Ann Ryan, who run the Kennedy Homestead today. They pointed out to the author various artifacts discovered over the years on the premises, including cooping tools and "Cherry Bros." barrels. Grennan also compiled a family tree of the Irish Kennedys dating before Patrick Kennedy. These accounts were verified or added to by others, including Kennedy relatives Thomas Grennan and James Kennedy, as well as local historian John Pierce. The description of New Ross during these famine years comes from accounts in bound volumes of the *Wexford Independent* reviewed by the author in the County Wexford Library as well as in Anna Kinsella, *County Wexford in the Famine Years;* and John Pierce, *The Kennedys Who Left and the Kennedys Who Stayed*. Pierce's privately published account was sponsored by the Kennedy Homestead and the Irish Kennedys generally credit him with the most thorough generational research of their family. Further insights of 1848 farm life were in Tim Pat Coogan, "Sure and It's County Kennedy Now," *New York Times Magazine,* June 23, 1963.

Chapter Two: The Heirs of Brian Boru

For the 1963 presidential visit, the Library of Congress prepared a genealogical report tracing the Kennedy family's lineage back to the chieftains in Ormond and, at one time, the ancient kings of Ireland, which can be found in files relating to this trip at the JFK Library. The reliability of this historic account may be debatable, though similar accounts about the "O'Cinneide" clan and its relation to Brian Boru can be found in several published Irish histories, notably by The Irish Family History Foundation and in Dermot Gleeson, *The Last Lords of Ormond*. Similar accounts also appeared in Maurice N. Hennessy, *I'll Come Back in the Springtime: John F. Kennedy and the Irish;* and in Rev. J.F. Brennan, *The Evolution of Everyman*.

The British involvement in Ireland, including the Cromwell suppression of uprisings in Wexford and the resulting penal law against Catholics, is discussed in numerous histories, including Robert Kee, *Ireland: A History;* Antonia Fraser, *Cromwell, The Lord Protector;* and Terry Golway, *For the Cause of Liberty: A Thousand Years of Ireland's Heroes*. In the National Library of Ireland, additional details about the 1798 Wexford uprising were found in Kevin Whelan, *The Catholic Community in 18th Century Wexford;* and Fr. Fintan Morris, *A Time of Change and Consolidation—Ferns in the 19th Century*, both of which were contained in *Memory and Mission,* Walter Forde, ed. The impact of O'Neill's death on the Irish people is captured in "Lament for the Death of Eoghan Ruadh O'Neill," by Thomas Davis, 1814–1845, reprinted in numerous anthologies of Irish poetry as is the popular verse "The Wearin O'The Green." The involvement of Kennedy family members in the political battles of 1798 are mentioned in various published accounts, though none with great specificity due to the largely unrecorded circumstances of the time. These versions vary from accounts found in the County Wexford Library, to interviews with local historians John Pierce and Thomas Grennan, to such published accounts as Edward Laxton, *The Famine Ships: The Irish Exodus to America*, as well as Brennan's *The Evolution of Everyman*, and Pierce's *The Kennedys Who Left and the Kennedys Who Stayed*. The Kennedys affected by the 1798 uprising in Wexford were those who were contemporaries of James Kennedy, the father of Patrick Kennedy who emigrated to America.

Chapter Three: The Starvation

The opening quotation is from John Stuart Mill, *John Stuart Mill on Ireland*. The author's review of land records, grave headstones and other documentation, including a detailed family tree prepared by the Kennedy Homestead—which dates back to the birth of Kennedy forebearer, John Kennedy, in 1738—informed this account of Patrick Kennedy's beginnings. In Richard Griffith's "General Valuation of Rateable Property—1850," it lists "Patrick Kennedy" instead of "James Kennedy" on the land where James Kennedy eventually runs his farm, even though Patrick Kennedy was living by then in Boston. The reasons are lost to history. Though Pierce isn't convinced, some family members, such as the Grennans, suggest it is likely that Patrick Kennedy was sympathetic to the popular political cause of Irish freedom, though no definitive proof exists. (One claim said Patrick Kennedy had been an active rebel, probably a sworn United Irishman, before he left for America, and was published in a local newspaper article entitled "Our Golden Haired Bit of Graduer," Biatas—The Tillage Farmer, October 1988, contained in the Dave Powers files at the JFK Library.)

The political brilliance of Daniel O'Connell is recalled in Cecil Woodham-Smith, *The Great Hunger: Ireland 1845–1849;* and Kee's *Ireland: A History*. O'Connell writings about the power of nonviolent agitation in overcoming prejudice appeared in the *Wexford Independent,* April 10, 1847. Deaths and other suffering from the Famine's impact in Wexford were outlined in considerable detail in Kinsella's *County Wexford in the Famine Years*, as well as Mary Gwinnell, "The Famine Years in County Wexford," *Journal of Wexford Historical Society*, and Liam Kennedy et al., *Mapping the Great Irish Famine: A Survey of the Famine Decades*. Specific details about the Famine in Wexford, and its likely impact on the Kennedys, were derived from newspaper accounts appearing in the *Wexford Independent,* on January 20, 1847, February 27, 1847, and an April 10, 1847, dispatch from a *Waterford Freeman* correspondent that was reprinted in *The Wexford Independent.* All these accounts were reviewed by the author from existing bounded volumes at the Wexford County Public Library or the National Library of Ireland in Dublin. In addition, further insights about the role of the nineteenth-century Irish church were in Charles Morris, *American Catholic;* Mon. Patrick J. Corish, "Irish Catholics Before the Famine: Patterns and Questions," *Journal of Wexford Historical Society* and previously mentioned texts.

Chapter Four: American Wake

The opening verse by Ethna Carbery appears in "The Passing of the Gael," taken from Seumas MacManus, ed., *The Four Winds of Eirinn: Poems by Ethna Carbery.* The "American Wake" and other aspects of Patrick Kennedy's departure from Dunganstown is derived from several sources, mostly from interviews with Patrick and Thomas Grennan, Mary Ann Ryan, local historian John W. Pierce, along with several published accounts, including Laxton's *The Famine Ships: The Irish Exodus to America,* Kee's *Ireland: A History,* Kinsella's *County Wexford in the Famine Years* and Brennan's *The Evolution of Everyman.* Further context was provided by Hasia R. Diner, *Erin's Daughters in America: Irish Immigrant Women in the Nineteenth Century;* Thomas Gallagher, *Paddy's Lament;* and Kerby A. Miller, *Emigrants and Exiles.* Numerous books and articles dating to the present contend that Patrick Kennedy left directly from Ireland for Boston, and that aboard ship he met Bridget Murphy. However, the limited evidence suggests something quite different. A manifest of the passengers aboard the *Washington Irving*—a microfilmed copy of which was examined by the author in the special collections section of the Boston Public Library—shows Kennedy left from Liverpool, England, before arriving in the U.S. on April 28, 1849. Kennedy cousins and local accounts in Ireland contend Patrick left Wexford in the fall of 1848, crossed the Irish sea and stayed for several months in Liverpool before saving enough for the fare to Boston. They also contend it is likely that Patrick and Bridget, though traveling separately, met earlier in Ireland where they made their plans to marry once they were united in America. This version appears the most accurate and conforms with the limited available documentation of their journey and the historical accounts of Irish émigrés from this region at that time. Details about the famine ships and life for the transigent and often desititute Irish staying in Liverpool could be found in Pol O'Conghaile, "Chasing the Famine Ships," and accounts of the Irish emigration reported in the *Wexford Independent* and the *Waterford Freeman,* found in the archives of the National Library of Ireland. In addittion to specific details about this ship, a general awareness of the Liverpool-American route for Irish coffin ships is mentioned in John F. Kennedy's *A Nation of Immigrants* and in John Henry Cutler, *Honey Fitz,* the biography of Kennedy's grandfather, former Boston Mayor John F. Fitzgerald. Views about the Irish situation from the *Times of London* are quoted in Gallagher's *Paddy's Lament,* and also in actual news accounts from the *Times* of London, dated March 8, September 17, 1847 and October 4, 1848, and the *Dublin University Magazine,* April 1847. What it was like to leave Ireland during the Famine is recalled in Robert Whyte, *Journey of an Irish Coffin Ship;* Ruth-Ann M. Harris, *The Search for Missing Friends.* Census and local government documents, including the assessor's report for Ward Two, provide a sketchy account of the humble, hardscrabble life shared by Patrick and Bridget Kennedy in East Boston. Further details come from various published accounts, including Peter Collier and David Horowitz, *The Kennedys: An American Drama.*

Chapter Five: Brahmins and Bigotry

Information about "the foreign element" and other aspects of Irish immigrant life in Boston was found in the 1855 Boston census, a bound volume available at the Boston Public Library research section. Similar statitistical information and analysis of Boston's Irish appeared in Ruth-Ann Harris, *The Search for Missing Friends,* as well as additional insights provided by Harris in conversations with the author. More detailed historical analysis of the Irish in Boston can be found in Oscar Handlin, *Boston's Immigrants: A Study of Acculturation;* Dennis P. Ryan, *Beyond the Ballot Box;* Hasia R. Diner, *Erin's Daughters in America: Irish Immigrant Women in the Nineteenth Century;* Kerby

A. Miller, *Emigrants and Exiles;* Thomas H. O'Connor, *The Boston Irish: A Political History;* Noel Ignatiev, *How the Irish Became White;* and Oscar Handlin, *The Uprooted.* Various accounts of early Kennedy family life in East Boston were found in Richard J. Whalen, *The Founding Father: The Story of Joseph P. Kennedy,* Leamer's *The Kennedy Women,* Cutler's *Honey Fitz,* as well as an obituary of Bridget Kennedy in *East Boston Argus Advocate* on December 29, 1888, found in the microfiche collection of the Boston Public Library. DuBois comments are from his book *Dusk of Dawn* (Harcourt Brace, 1940).

The Catholic Church's history in Massachusetts and its experience with bigotry is mentioned in several of the texts above, including JFK's *A Nation of Immigrants,* and thoroughly examined in Thomas H. O'Connor, *Boston Catholics: A History of the Church and Its People;* John Henry Cutler, *Cardinal Cushing of Boston;* and John Higham, *Strangers in the Land: Patterns of American Nativism 1860–1925.* Also see, Lance Morrow, "The Rise and Fall of Anti-Catholicism," *Time,* October 15, 1979. Details about the Know-Nothings and Lincoln's response is mentioned in Arthur M. Schlesinger Jr., *The Disuniting of America,* Lincoln's *Speeches and Writings, 1832–58;* and Chilton Williamson Jr., *The Immigration Mystique.* Details about P.J. Kennedy's early life and political career come from Whalen's *The Founding Father;* David E. Koskoff, *Joseph P. Kennedy: A Life and Times;* Michael R. Beschloss, *Kennedy and Roosevelt,* as well as newspaper reports about Kennedy appearing in the January 12, 1896, edition of *Boston Post* and his obituary in *The Boston Transcript* of May 21, 1929. Details about P.J. Kennedy's continuing interest in the lives and welfare of his Irish cousins comes from interviews with Mary Ann Ryan, John Pierce and is mentioned briefly in Peter Collier and David Horowitz, *The Kennedys: An American Drama* and in Pierce's *The Kennedys Who Left and the Kennedys Who Stayed.*

Chapter Six: The Long Climb to Acceptance

The rise of John F. Fitzgerald and Boston's Irish Catholics is detailed in John Henry Cutler, *Honey Fitz;* and Doris Kearns Goodwin, *The Fitzgeralds and the Kennedys.* More generalized information about Fitzgerald and the Irish in Boston was obtained from Thomas H. O'Connor, *The Boston Irish: A Political History;* Jack Beatty, *The Rascal King;* Oscar Handlin, *The Uprooted;* Thomas J. Curran, *Xenophobia and Immigration, 1820–1930;* John Higham, *Strangers in the Land: Patterns of American Nativism 1860–1925;* and Barbara Miller Solomon, *Ancestors and Immigrants.* Additional biographical information about Fitzgerald was derived from "Origins," *New Yorker,* June 15, 1963; George Kibbe Turner, "Honey Fitz," *Collier's,* November 9, 1907, and from Fitzgerald's obituary in "Former Hub Mayor Dead," *Boston Post,* October 3, 1950.

Historical information about Cardinal William O'Connell and his impact on Boston's Catholics appeared in James M. O'Toole, *Militant and Triumphant;* John Henry Cutler, *Cardinal Cushing of Boston;* Dennis P. Ryan, *Beyond the Ballot Box;* William O'Connell, *Recollections of Seventy Years;* Thomas H. O'Connor, *Boston Catholics: A History of the Church and Its People;* as well as Shaun O'Connell, "Goodbye to All That: The Rise and Demise of Irish America," *New England Journal of Public Policy,* Spring/Summer 1993; "Massachusetts on Trial," *Saturday Evening Post,* June 5, 1965; and Francis Russell, "Why Massachussetts Loves the Kennedys," *National Review,* August 11, 1970.

Chapter Seven: The Family Enterprise

The scene of young Rose Fitzgerald and her beau, Joe Kennedy, at Old Orchard Beach, Maine, is captured in a photograph contained in the Kennedy Family Private Collection, which has appeared in several publications. Rose's recollections come from her memoir, *Times to Remember,* as well as from interviews she granted prior to her death with Doris Kearns Goodwin for *The Fitzgeralds and The Kennedys* and several magazine and newspaper profiles. Cardinal O'Connell's sizeable influence with Irish Catholics in Boston, including the Fitzgeralds and Kennedys, is also discussed in William Shannon, *The American Irish;* "Brahmins and Bullyboys: William Henry Cardinal O'Connell and Massachusetts Politics," *Historical Journal of Massachusetts,* January 1982; Louise Callan, *The Society of the Sacred Heart in North America;* Charles Morris, *American Catholic;* Thomas H. O'Connor, *The Boston Irish: A Political History;* John Henry Cutler, *Honey Fitz;* David E.

Koskoff, *Joseph P. Kennedy: A Life and Times*; James M. O'Toole, *Militiant and Triumphant*. Joe Kennedy's views about ethnicity come from several aforementioned texts, including Michael Beschloss, *Kennedy and Roosevelt*; as well as Laurence Leamer, *The Kennedy Women*; and Peter Collier and David Horowitz, *The Kennedys: An American Drama*. The Kennedys' distinctly Irish concept of family and the clan is discussed in Gore Vidal, "The Holy Family," *Esquire*, April 1967; as well as Lawrence H. Fuchs, *John F. Kennedy and American Catholicism*, reviewed by Msgr. John Tracy Ellis, *America*, April 1, 1967. Joe Kennedy's check to the Guild of St. Apollonia in thanksgiving after Jack's illness is detailed in the Joseph P. Kennedy papers, granted special access to the author at the John F. Kennedy Library. Rose's comments about the family "enterprise" is from her memoir.

Chapter Eight: Hard Lessons

Rose Kennedy's view about Catholic schools and the indelible imprint of religion she wanted in her children's lives was discussed extensively in her memoir, from which these quotations are taken. Joe Kennedy Jr.'s first taste of romance and anti-Catholic bigotry is recalled in Hank Searls, *The Lost Prince*.

Jack's early days in the Catholic school, Canterbury, is mentioned in Herbert Parmet, *Jack*; John Henry Cutler, *Honey Fitz*; as well as from the JFK Personal Papers at the John F. Kennedy Presidential Library. JFK's letters home about going to Communion at the Canterbury School and "practicing the singing of the Kyrie Santus [sic], Agnus Dei and so on" are contained in his letters in the Joseph P. Kennedy papers (JPK papers) at the John F. Kennedy Library. Details of the Kennedy siblings growing up in the 1920s and 1930s comes from Richard Whalen, *The Founding Father*; Garry Wills, *Kennedy Imprisonment*; and Amanda Smith, *Hostage to Fortune*. Rose's observation about Joe Jr. as Cadet Club president as "probably the only Catholic in the country to hold that honor" and Rose's sense of religion and her family life is mentioned in "Rose-Colored Glasses," *Time*, April 22, 1974, and "Rose Kennedy at 76," *America*, November 18, 1967. Additional insights were gained in interview with Joseph Gargan.

The relationship between Joe Kennedy and his two oldest sons is captured in many of their letters, found in both the JFK papers and the JPK collection at the JFK Presidential Library. Joe Sr. gives young JFK a major pep talk in December 1934, evoking the divine strains of St. Luke's gospel that becomes a major part of the Kennedy's religious dynamic. "Now aren't you foolish not to get all there is out of what God has given you and what you can do with it yourself?" Joe asks in a letter found in his private papers. Further context was provided by Goodwin's *The Fitzgeralds and the Kennedys*, and Smith's *Hostage to Fortune*. Examples of the Kennedy's awareness of Irish bigotry is also detailed in Arthur Mitchell, *JFK and His Irish Heritage* ("Those aren't cobblestones . . . "); and John Henry Cutler, *Honey Fitz*; (Boston "was no place to bring up Catholic children"). Shannon's quote about the "glass ceiling of religious bigotry" is in William Shannon, *The American Irish*. Joe Kennedy as "a bundle of ancient hatreds and prejudices" is from Murray Kempton, "Ashes of the Kennedy Legend," *Newsday*, June 5, 1991.

Part II: The Family Faith

Joe Kennedy's comments about not being "completely assimilated, but all my ducks are swans" is taken from his letter dated February 12, 1959, part of the JPK papers at the JFK Library.

Chapter Nine: Happy Warriors

Details about Sen. George Norris's support of Gov. Alfred E. Smith were contained in John F. Kennedy, *Profiles in Courage*. JPK's actions in the 1924 presidential campaign appeared in David E. Koskoff, *Joseph P. Kennedy: A Life and Times*. Amanda Smith underlines her adoptive grandfather's interaction with Al Smith's 1928 campaign and his possible vote for Hoover, Amanda Smith, *Hostage to Fortune*. Oscar Handlin recalls the impact of Al Smith on JFK in the introduction to Handlin's updated 1987 book, *Al Smith and His America*. Other aspects of Smith's 1928 campaign and its impact on Irish Catholics in America are extensively detailed in Robert A. Slayton, *Empire*

Statesman. Also see Al Smith's essay prior to the 1928 race about the issue of religion, Alfred E. Smith, "American Catholic," *Atlantic Monthly*, May 1927. Smith's aside, "Will someone tell me what the hell a papal encyclical is?" is recalled in "Catholics and the State," *New Republic*, October 17, 1960. In 1928, John W. Davis blames anti-Catholicism, *Newsweek*, June 1, 1959. JPK's comments about the anti-Irish tone of a Fortune magazine profile of him are mentioned in Amanda Smith, *Hostage to Fortune.* In 1932, Honey Fitz sticks by Al Smith at the Democratic Convention, John Henry Cutler, *Honey Fitz.* A description of Eddie Moore as "Irish as a clay pipe" also comes from *Honey Fitz* though Moore's prediction about JFK is repeated in Michael Beschloss, *Kennedy and Roosevelt.* An account of Joe Sr.'s speech to Irish in Boston appeared in the *Boston Post*, Sunday, March 14, 1937.

The relationship of Boston Irish Catholics to faith and family were analyzed in Philip F. Lawler, "The End of the Irish Century," *Catholic World Report*, January 1996, and later reprinted in *National Catholic Reporter.* Cardinal O'Connell clout in Boston during Joe Kennedy's early years of money and power is discussed in David E. Koskoff, *Joseph P. Kennedy: A Life and Times.* The public uproar and the church's part in the Father Charles Coughlin controversy is mentioned in Alan Brinkley, *Voices of Protest;* Michael Beschloss, *Kennedy and Roosevelt;* and Thomas H. O'Connor, *The Boston Irish: A Political History.* Coughlin calling Joe Kennedy "the shining star among the dim 'knights' of the Administration,'" is based on a *Boston Post* article of August 16, 1936 cited in David E. Koskoff, *Joseph P. Kennedy: A Life and Times.* Felix Frankfurter's prescient description of the impact of Father Coughlin on FDR and whether the Vatican would "silence" him is in JPK papers at the JFK Presidential Library. Other Coughlin-related articles provided specific detail: "Coughlin Quits Air, Suspends His Union, Saying Farewell," Associated Press, *New York Times*, November 8, 1936.

The long-time association and friendship between Joe Kennedy, Count Enrico Galeazzi and Boston Auxiliary Bishop Francis Spellman (later New York cardinal) is pieced together mainly from Kennedy's own letters contained in the JPK papers granted access to the author and numerous other published accounts. Cardinal Pacelli's visit to America is mentioned Robert I. Gannon, SJ, *The Cardinal Spellman Story;* John Cooney, *The American Pope: The Life and Times of Francis Cardinal Spellman;* Charles R. Morris, *American Catholic;* Paul I. Murphy, *La Popessa;* and his visit to the Kennedy home in Bronxville is cited in Doris Kearns Goodwin, *The Fitzgeralds and The Kennedys.* A long-term view was provided by Jim Nicholson, "A Brief History of U.S-Holy See Relations," *30 Giorni Magazine*, November 2002. Specific details of Pacelli's trip are cited in Otto D. Tolischus, "Roosevelt Victory Foreseen in Reich," *New York Times*, Nov. 4, 1936; "Pacelli Lunches With Roosevelt," *New York Times*, November 6, 1936; "Cardinal Visits FDR," *New York Daily News*, November 6, 1936. In an interview, Joe Gargan confirms that the seat that Cardinal Pacelli sat in had a special place in the Hyannis Port house for years afterward and that no one was allowed to sit in it, an assertion confirmed by Sen. Edward Kennedy's office. Similarly, Kennedy's long and complex relationship with Cardinal Spellman was detailed in Gannon's *The Cardinal Spellman Story;* John Cooney, *The American Pope: The Life and Times of Francis Cardinal Spellman;* David E. Koskoff, *Joseph P. Kennedy: A Life and Times;* and in various correspondences between the two contained in the JPK papers at the Kennedy presidential library. Details about John J. Reynolds, Spellman's real estate adviser, was found in his obituary in the *New York Times*, May 27, 1981.

The early press descriptions of Count Enrico Galeazzi are sketchy, because he kept himself in the background of most Vatican-related events, including the 1936 Cardinal Pacelli-FDR meeting that he helped arrange in collaboration with Joe Kennedy and Spellman. But details about the relationship of Galeazzi and his half brother, Dr. Ricardo Galeazzi-Lisi, to Cardinal Pacelli/Pope Pius XII are later mentioned in "Vatican City Official Clipper Bound to U.S.," *New York Times*, September 4, 1943; Sam Pope Brewer, "Spellman Hailed at Rome Airport On His Arrival for Consistory," *New York Times*, January 15, 1946; "Pius Doctor Is Barred From Practice in Italy," Associated Press, *New York Times*, December 13, 1958; "Doctor Describes Illness of Pope," *New York Times*, October 12, 1958; "Pope's Strength Is Ebbing, Vatican Bulletin Indicates," *New York Times*, February 6, 1954; "Dr. Ricardo Galeazzi-Lisi Dies; Sold Deathbed Story of Pius XII," Associated Press, November 17, 1968; as well as in John Cornwell, *Hitler's Pope.*

Chapter Ten: An Irishman in the Court of St. James

Joe Kennedy's appearance at the St. Patrick's Day dinner of the Clover Club in Boston was recorded in a lengthy article and an editorial cartoon in the *Boston Sunday Post*, March 14, 1937. The prominent roles of several Irish Catholics, such as Joe Kennedy, in the New Deal under FDR is discussed in William Shannon, *The American Irish*, who sagely commented that "none of these figures became a real presidential possibility, but as a group they made possible the transition from Al Smith to John F. Kennedy." FDR's initial suggestion to Kennedy that he become ambassador to Ireland is mentioned in Rose Kennedy's memoir, James Roosevelt, *My Parents: A Differing View*; Amanda Smith, *Hostage to Fortune*, and reflected in the JPK papers reviewed by the author, including a May 4, 1934 letter to his son, Joe Jr. (The Kennedys' friendship with James Roosevelt would later prove crucial in the 1960 West Virginia primary.) FDR's appointment of Joe Kennedy to the Court of St. James was recalled in several books, including Michael Beschloss, *Kennedy and Roosevelt*; Richard J. Whalen, *The Founding Father: The Story of Joseph P. Kennedy;* Harold L. Ickes, *The Secret Diary of Harold L. Ickes;* and Arthur M. Schlesinger Jr., *The Age of Roosevelt*. Details of Amb. Kennedy's trip to Dublin are contained in various press accounts from July 1938, and mentioned in Hank Searls, *The Lost Prince*. De Valera's contacts with the Kennedys are detailed in Arthur Mitchell, *JFK and His Irish Heritage;* Rev. J.F. Brennan, *The Evolution of Everyman;* Maurice N. Hennessy, *I'll Come Back in the Springtime: John F. Kennedy and the Irish,* as well as JPK papers reviewed by author.

Chapter Eleven: The Vatican Go-Between

Joe Kennedy's detailed recollections of the Kennedy family's trip to Rome for the coronation of Pope Pius XII in 1939 are contained in diary notes and correspondences in the JPK papers provided by special access at the Kennedy Presidential Library. On Sunday, March 12, 1939, Joe Kennedy wrote a long, detailed diary entry about those he meets at the coronation, including Eamon DeValera who pushed the idea of ending partition by unifying Northern Ireland with the South. During private meeting, Pope says he "rejoices" that Kennedy is the US representative for the coronation, and he recalls meeting with FDR in Hyde Park and Kennedy puts in a good word for Spellman, based on author's review of JPK papers, as well as those cited in Amanda Smith, *Hostage to Fortune*. In the *New York Herald Tribune* edition of March 14, 1939, Kennedy tells the world that the new Pope "had a great admiration for President Roosevelt" because he always admired his stand for religion.

Joe Kennedy's difficult relations with President Roosevelt is explored in several biographies, but none of those examined mention Kennedy's belief that FDR harbored anti-Catholic bias. Diary and private letters from Kennedy in the private JPK collection make this clear, however. In his diary, Joe Kennedy expresses the belief that "deep down in his heart Roosevelt had a decidedly anti-Catholic feeling," he writes. He points out that FDR had not appointed a prominent Catholic lately and that FDR made pointed comments about Joe Patterson's conversion to Roman Catholicism in conversation with Lord Beaverbrook, a diary entry also cited in Amanda Smith, *Hostage to Fortune*. In other diary notes marked January 7, 1942, he indicated that Roosevelt looked upon him as a stubborn "Irishman." In a 1943 letter to his son, Jack, Kennedy objects to Roosevelt's public comments about the Allied attempts "that we were going to drive on Rome to save the Pope" which he angrily said "really struck a new low in political propaganda." Rose Kennedy's reminder to her husband that "The President sent you, a Roman Catholic, as Ambassador to London, which probably no other President would have done" is cited in Michael Beschloss, *Kennedy and Roosevelt*. FDR's trip to Boston where he refers to former Mayor John F. Fitzgerald as "Dulce Adeline" was found in John Henry Cutler, *Honey Fitz*. Further anecdotes about the political difficulties for Irish Catholics in the New Deal administration were found in Kenneth S. Davis, *FDR: Into the Storm 1937–1940;* Doris Kearns Goodwin, *The Fitzgeralds and The Kennedys;* and Ted Morgan, *FDR: A Biography*. In advance of the 1940 presidential campaign, FDR dismissed "the idea that Joe Kennedy could be elected President" as "absurd," Michael Beschloss, *Kennedy and Roosevelt*, also see, "Will Kennedy Run for President?" *Liberty*, May 21, 1938, and other press accounts. Instances of Joseph Kennedy's anti-Semitism is discussed in numerous books, including both Whalen and Koskoff biographies; Amanda Smith, *Hostage to Fortune;* Ronald Kessler, *The Sins of the Father;* and reflected in several letters and diary entries reviewed by the author in the JPK papers at the Kennedy library. In February 1939, *Social Justice* devoted its full cover page to a picture of the Kennedy family and designated the ambassador as its "Man of the Week," according to Herbert S. Parmet, *Jack: The Struggles of John F. Kennedy*.

Chapter Twelve: Tortured Souls

As its primary source, the heart of this chapter derives from the numerous, lengthy and often painful letters between Kathleen Kennedy, her parents, and her fiancé, Billy Hartington, which were reviewed by the author in several files of the JPK papers at the Kennedy library. Several details from these letters have not appeared before (such as the opening anecdote about her "persecuted Irish ancestors" and instances of her own anti-Semitic views), though this ill-fated romance has been discussed extensively in many Kennedy histories, particularly Lynne McTaggart, *Kathleen Kennedy: Her Life and Times*; Hank Searls, *The Lost Prince: Young Joe, the Forgotten Kennedy*; Doris Kearns Goodwin, *The Fitzgeralds and The Kennedys*; and Laurence Leamer *The Kennedy Women*. Several of the letters suggest the religious and cultural conflicts of the Kennedys concerning the prospect of Kathleen marrying into the Cavendish family with evidence of its own avid anti-Catholicism.

Kick's increasingly pro-British views, far different from the Irish perspective of Honey Fitz and her ancestors, is mentioned in her letter dated on Christmas, 1943, contained in the JPK papers. Hints of anti-Semitism in her letters, including the February 1943 comment ("the Hebes stick together even in death") were also found in the JPK papers. Her awareness of her own Irish Catholic background is reflected in a handful of letters, including the January 2, 1943, letter to her family that the English seemed intrigued by Catholicism. Her letters to her brother, Jack, are filled with humorous asides, such as her February 22, 1944, letter in which she says "am sure you'll get the wunderlüst or other kinds of lust before the passing of many moons."

More than a dozen letters in the JPK papers detail the difficulties involved with Kathleen Kennedy's relationship with Billy Hartington. One of the most common threads is the degree of anti-Catholicism in young Kathleen's life in London. In her August 1943 letter, Kick recounts how her Protestant friends and Billy's family tell her the nearest Catholic church is miles away and she couldn't possibly go. In the same letter, she mentions the arguments about Catholicism involving Lady Nancy Astor. In a February 1944, letter home, Kick tells how Billy's father, the Duke of Devonshire, gave her a surprise gift for her birthday— the *Book of Common Prayer* of the Church of England. It also talks about her own desperation to find some "loophole" that would allow her to marry without losing her Catholicism. Rose's letter, dated February 24, 1944, expresses concerns about Kick maintaining her religious faith and mentions that Joe Kennedy had consulted Count Galeazzi for possible help. Billy's heartfelt letter to Rose in April 1944, months before he's killed, is also included in the JPK papers. Even after the couple marry, Kick admits that Billy's father "has given in as the one thing he has always dreaded is that one of his sons should marry an R.C." and "he always sees within me a sort of evil influence," according to a May 1944, letter from Kick in the JPK papers. (Some of these letters do not bear exact dates, and the time period and estimated dates on these letters and used in this book were determined by the JFK presidential librarian researchers, based on the best available information.) The assassination of Lord Frederick Cavendish in Dublin was detailed in Robert Kee, *The Green Flag*, while Fitzgerald's characterization of the murder place as "a Catholic monument" was found in Peter Collier and David Horowitz, *The Kennedys: An American Drama*. Fitzgerald's membership in the Ancient Order of Hibernians is mentioned in John Henry Cutler, *Honey Fitz*. Further background about Hartington's family appeared in Lynne McTaggart, *Kathleen Kennedy*; Herbert S. Parmet, *Jack: The Struggles of John F. Kennedy*; and Amanda Smith, *Hostage to Fortune*.

The letters in the JPK papers also underscore the significant influence of the Briitsh Catholic intellectual circle on the Kennedys and their own associates in London. Background context about the Kennedy's circle of British friends and acquaintances who were Catholic, including Evelyn Waugh, Martin D'Arcy, SJ and others, comes from Selina Hastings, *Evelyn Waugh: A Biography*; Martin Stannard, *Evelyn Waugh*; Joseph Pearce, *Literary Converts: Spiritual Inspiration in An Age of Unbelief*; "Rev. Martin D'Arcy, A Jesuit Philosopher Dies in London at 88," *New York Times*, February 19, 1951; Joseph Epstein, "Maurice Baring & the Good High-Brow," *New Criterion*, October 1992. Kick's account of her conversation with Rev. D'Arcy is included in her

February 22, 1944, letter to her parents. Jack's past with Coleman at the Spee Club was reflected in Kick's letter to him contained in JPK papers, and supplemented with background from Ralph Martin, *Seeds of Destruction*; Nigel Hamilton, *JFK: Reckless Youth.*

Chapter Thirteen: Hero Worship

Honey Fitz's observation that "the Catholic element in New England is standing up admirably" in WWII was written in 1945 to Bobby, Jean and Pat Kennedy, contained in the JPK papers. John F. Kennedy's writing about the Irish bases appeared in the February 2, 1941, *New York Journal American* owned by Hearst, as cited in Herbert S. Parmet, *Jack: The Struggles of John F. Kennedy.* "Politics make strange bedfellows" comment by JFK is in a 1939 letter to his parents, contained in JPK papers. JFK's tease to his mother about "your latest chapter on the '9 little Kennedys and how they grew, by Rose of Old Boston'" is from a 1942 letter found in JPK papers. JFK's letters to Rose Kennedy in 1942 include his request for Rev. Bertrand L.Conway's *The Question Box*, contained in JPK papers. Rose's comment that Jack "also thinks it would be good for Joe's political career if he died for the grand old flag, although I don't believe he feels that is absolutely necessary" was found in the same collection. Though he prefered his comments light and breezy, young JFK makes several trenchant comments about death, fatalism and the afterlife reflected in letters sent during the war and contained in the pre-presidential papers at the JFK Library and also in the JPK collection. Other details about Jack's view of his background were found in Arthur Mitchell, *JFK and His Irish Heritage*; Amanda Smith, *Hostage to Fortune.* At least one Massachusetts parochial school class prayed on their knees for Jack's safe return, Ralph Martin, *A Hero for Our Times.* "Jesus Loves Me" is from James MacGregor Burns, *John Kennedy: A Political Profile.* The most well-known account of the incident is John Hersey, "Survival," *New Yorker*, June 17, 1944, though subsequent accounts have placed more blame for the fatal accident on Kennedy's poor nautical judgment. Jack's first letter after the PT-109 incident ("I can say that I am well and thanking my St. Christopher, my St. Elmo and my St. Clair. One of them was working overtime") is dated August 29, 1943, and is contained in the JPK papers. Johnny Iles comments are from Joan and Clay Blair Jr., *The Search for JFK.* The passing interest of JFK in the work of Dorothy Day is mentioned in William D. Miller, *A Harsh and Dreadful Love: Dorothy Day and the Catholic Worker Movement.* An example of Joe Sr.'s anti-Semitism passed along to his children is found in his letter to Joe Jr. in which he claims JFK has "become disgusted with the desk jobs and all the Jews," dated June 20, 1942, in the JPK papers. The scene of Jack returning home and being embraced by his grandfather at an honorary luncheon appears in John Henry Cutler, *Honey Fitz*, with Joe Jr.'s reaction recorded in Hank Searls, *The Lost Prince*; Joan and Clay Blair Jr., *The Search for JFK.*

Chapter Fourteen: Blood Brothers

Rev. Maurice S. Sheehy's friendship with the Kennedys is evident in several letters contained in JPK papers. The story of Joe's early morning antics toward Jewish servicemen and its undertones of anti-Semitism ("Don't they have souls?") is recalled in Hank Searls, *The Lost Prince*, probably the most thorough account of Joseph Kennedy Jr.'s life. Joe Sr.'s letter repeating the whispers about a Republican and his advise to his oldest son that "You better be sure to marry yourself a nice Irish Catholic girl" is from a July 18, 1942, letter in the JPK papers. Several letters between Joe Sr. and his eldest son implicitly reflect their intention for a future political career for Joe Jr., including his son's assessment of the 1940 Democratic Convention, and how the Irish would view things back home in Boston. For Joe Jr.'s birthday in 1942, Rose sends several packages including the *Catholic Digest*, found in Rose's letter dated July 23, 1942, in JPK papers. Rose writes to Jack and Joe Jr about the education of Teddy and Bobby in a "Dear Boys" letter dated September 10, 1942, in JPK papers. Rose's characterization of herself as "just an ordinary, staunch believing Irish Roman Catholic" is in Rose Kennedy, *Times to Remember.*

In August 1944, Joe's letter to Jack is keenly aware of the exploits of PT-109, and despite their rivalry, he says he won't "risk my fine neck in any crazy venture." In a letter dated July 26, 1944, Joe concedes he's going to do "something different for the next three weeks. It is secret, and I am not allowed to say what it is, but it isn't dangerous, so don't worry," contained in JPK papers. Details about the events leading up to young Kennedy's death and its aftermath are mentioned in numerous Kennedy histories, notably Hank Searls *The Lost Prince* as well as Joan and Clay Blair Jr., *The Search for JFK;* Doris Kearns Goodwin, *The Fitzgeralds and the Kennedys.* Details about Rosemary Kennedy's lobotomy were in Goodwin's book and Laurence Leamer, *The Kennedy Women.* Several letters, cards and comments in the JPK papers, however, document some of the family's attempt to deal religiously with the tragedy of Joe Jr.'s death, including those by Dick Flood, Mrs. John Pillsbury, Mike Grace, Max O'Rell Truitt, Harry Bagan, Margaret Prior, Gertrude and Joe Bateman and Jack's old teacher at Canterbury. Quotes from the small booklet prepared by John F. Kennedy, *As We Remember Joe,* includes those from Honey Fitz and Rev. Sheehy as well as his own comment that his brother "had a deep and abiding faith—he was never far from God—and so, I cannot help but feel that . . . 'death to him was less a setting forth than a returning.'" In a February 27, 1945, letter to her brother "dearest Jackie," contained in JPK papers, Kick suggests he quote from poet Maurice Baring in the memorial booklet.

After Billy's death, Rose's letter of condolence to Kick suggesting she turn to God is in JPK papers, as is Kick's own letter to Jack, dated October 31, 1945, talking of her difficulty getting over Billy's death. "Kick's apostasy" according to Evelyn Waugh, and the angry reaction of American Catholics to her marriage is cited in Amanda Smith, *Hostage to Fortune;* Doris Kearns Goodwin, *The Fitzgeralds and the Kennedys.* In December 1944, after Billy's death, Kathleen Kennedy details the depressing state of Belgium after the conflict in a December 19, 1944, letter. Joe tries to comfort his daughter in a December 20, 1944, letter, conceding that 1944 "has been a difficult year for all of us," he writes. "We still have lots for which to thank God." Both letters are in JPK papers. Arthur Krock's observation of Joe Kennedy's reaction after his son's death were in Arthur Krock, *Memoirs: Sixty Years On the Firing Line,* while his own written observations were in letters written by Joe Sr. contained in JPK papers. The senior Kennedy's emotional difficulty reading *As We Remember Joe* was mentioned in Bob Considine, *It's All News To Me.* Rose's attempts to keep up her family's spirits with cheery notes, such as the October 6, 1944, letter ("We are having some little prayer cards made out for Joe") was found in JPK papers. Rev. Sheehy's "dark Christmas" letter to Joe Kennedy was dated December 22, 1944, with Joe's reply dated January 6, 1945, both in the JPK papers.

Chapter Fifteen: A Lighter Shade of Green

The many changes for Boston's Irish Catholics in the post–World War II era were discussed in Charles Morris, *American Catholic;* Jack Beatty, *The Rascal King;* and Thomas H. O'Connor, *The Boston Irish: A Political History.* The political rise of JFK as a young congressman was traced in several books, including Herbert S. Parmet, *Jack;* James MacGregor Burns, *John Kennedy: A Political Profile;* Nigel Hamilton, *JFK: Reckless Youth;* and Joe McCarthy, *The Remarkable Kennedys.* JFK reciting the rosary on the radio with Cardinal Cushing in 1951 is from a December 12, 1955, letter to Joe Kennedy contained in his private papers. The gushing letter from reporter Leland Bickford is in the JFK personal papers at the JFK Library. Joe Kane, the architect of the 1946 run, was a JFK cousin, according to John Henry Cutler's *Honey Fitz,* which adds that Kane's mother was a sister of PJ Kennedy's father. The same book repeats Honey Fitz's prediction that Jack will be the President of the U.S. someday.

JFK's rather sympathetic account of DeValera's views, including the Irish leader's condolence call to the German upon the death of Adolf Hitler, has gone largely unexamined by Kennedy historians. The dispatch about DeValera and Ireland appeared in John F. Kennedy, "DeValera Aims to Unite Ireland," *New York Journal American,* July 29, 1945. JFK's speech before the Crosscup-Pishon American Legion Post on November 11, 1945, was found in the pre-presidential papers at the Kennedy library, which indicates it was JFK's first major address as a politician. A United Press account of DeValera's personal call at the German legation to pay condolences upon Adolf Hitler's death was carried on the front page of the *New York Times,* May 3, 1945, an action which was criticized in an editorial the following day. Winston Churchill's criticism of DeValera's neutrality in the war was mentioned in Clifton Daniel, "Totalitarian Rule Unwanted, Churchill Tells Free Europe," *New York Times,* May 14, 1945. DeValera's response to Churchill appeared in Hugh Smith, "DeValera Defends His Neutrality; Makes 'Allowances' for Churchill," *New York Times,* May 17, 1945. George Bernard Shaw's support for DeValera's action appeared in *New York Times,* May 19, 1945. DeValera's defense of his action before the Dail Eireann (the Irish Parliament) was recorded in Hugh Smith,

"DeValera Defends Honor for Hitler," *New York Times*, July 20, 1945, which also says the action was viewed by many as a "first-class blunder." The letter to Joe Kennedy, dated January 17, 1946, from the U.S. delegation in Dublin warning of DeValera's attempts to draw American Catholics into the partition debate after the war was found in the JFK Library. In addition, John Kennedy with Deirdre Henderson, ed., *Prelude to Leadership: The European Diary of John F. Kennedy*, also provided further context. "DeValera is quite content to sit happy and see us strangle," Churchill complaint to Roosevelt about DeValera is in Winston Churchill, *Their Finest Hour: The Second World War*.

The political scene surrounding JFK's 1946 congressional campaign is recounted in several books, though very little is mentioned about the relationship between Kennedy money and the church's direct and indirect support of Jack's political efforts. The description of the many immigrant groups in the 11th Congressional District, and some key Kennedy helpers, like Patsy Mulkern, come from the oral histories of Francis X. Morrissey, Thomas P. O'Neill and Mulkern at the JFK Library, as well as private memos sent to Joe Kennedy from Morrissey contained in the JPK papers. The connection between church donations and politics begin almost immediately after the war as Jack Kennedy prepares to run for Congress. A list of 1945 donations from the Kennedy's charity was found in JFK pre-presidential papers. But the correlation between the donations and their impact on building up support for Jack politically is spelled out in a handful of 1954 private memos from Morrissey to Joe Kennedy contained in the JPK papers, which includes the comment of the monsignor who says JFK is "in excellent shape as far as the Italian vote is concerned." Morrissey says in one memo dated May 26, 1954, that "I can build this up to a tremendous thing among the Italians in making sure that Jack gets a maximum amount of publicity on it." In another note that same month, Morrissey writes to JPK about the "negro" groups that are being "buttered" by Kennedy largesse. Morrissey relies on Knights of Columbus contacts to set up Jack in speeches in the 11th Congressional District, according to his oral history. Joe Kennedy becomes a Knight of Malta named by the Pope, according to a January 3, 1942, story in the *Boston Herald*, also cited in David E. Koskoff, *Joseph P. Kennedy: A Life and Times*. Further background information came from John Henry Cutler, *Cardinal Cushing of Boston*. In a December 28, 1954, letter, Joe Kennedy told Morrissey that he'd like to give money from the Kennedy Foundation to some non-Catholic groups "because 96 or 97 percent of what money we give goes to Catholic causes, but I really don't want to do anything for them unless they really help as they should." From Rome that previous summer, Joe Kennedy wrote to Morrissey about Galeazzi's behind-the-scenes help and that he's gained the highest honor bestowed by the Vatican. In 1955, Joe Kennedy's good words to the Pope about Cardinal Cushing makes a friend for life, and even more so a powerful ally for Jack's political ambitions; see Cardinal Cushing letters, dated July 6, 1955 and July 18, 1955, in the JPK papers.

Chapter Sixteen: Eire

Details of life at Lismore Castle were derived from Kathleen Kennedy's letters and postcards contained in the JPK papers, along with Lynne McTaggart, *Kathleen Kennedy*; and Doris Kearns Goodwin, *The Fitzgeralds and the Kennedys*. JFK's awareness of the anti-British feeling among Boston's Irish Catholic voters and that "I'm running for Congress and not Parliament," is in a 1946 letter contained in the JPK papers. Several letters from Kick in the JPK papers talk about her pleasure at Jack's congressional success, her lack of regard for Spellman and her complex friendship with Lady Astor and her negative views of Catholicism. After Billy's death, Kick visited Ireland in August 1945, staying at Lismore Castle in Wexford, and writes on postcard home about the "peaceful atmosphere which Mother would love," according to her correspondence in JPK papers. "I wish I knew where our ancestors came from." Kick's awareness of Lord Frederick Cavendish's assassination is reflected in her August 8, 1945, letter from Lismore Castle.

JFK's trip to Ireland in 1947 was recounted in James MacGregor Burns, *John Kennedy: A Political Profile*, including Kennedy's later written recollection of the trip to Burns available at the JFK Presidential Library. Various accounts of his drive with Pamela Churchill to the Kennedy anestral home were studied, including those by Dave Powers, Goodwin and Pamela Churchill Harriman herself. Mary Ryan's recollection of 1947 visit by JFK is from Tim Pat Coogan, "Sure and It's County Kennedy Now," *New York Times Magazine*, June 23, 1963. In 1947 trip to Ireland, JFK's visit to Mulligan's on Poolbeg Street, recognizing it from James Joyce's *The Dubliners*, was reported in Joseph Roddy, "They Cried the Rain Down That Night," *Look*, November 17, 1964. James Kennedy greets John Kennedy as "a nice slip of a lad, but he looked very young to be a Congressman" comes from Maurice N. Hennessy, *I'll Come Back in the Springtime: John F. Kennedy and the Irish*. Jack goes to New Ross with a letter of introduction from his Aunt Loretta, who'd visted Ireland with PJ Kennedy in the 1920s, is in Peter Collier and David Horowitz, *The Kennedys: An American Drama*.

The Irish Republican history of the Kennedys and Ryans from Dunganstown is based on the author's interviews with Mary Ann Ryan, Patrick Grennan, Thomas Grennan, Patrick Kennedy (Ryan's cousin), John Pierce, all conducted in Ireland. It is also alluded to briefly in Pierce's *The Kennedys Who Left and the Kennedys Who Stayed*, privately published by the Kennedy Homestead. Both in interviews and a follow-up note to the author, Patrick Grennan underlined that the old IRA of his grandfather "fought for Irish freedom and no control of an area" and was far different than the IRA of today. Other details are from John Henry Cutler, *Honey Fitz;* and Arthur Mitchell, *JFK and His Irish Heritage*. Additional historical background about the IRA and its women's auxiliary, Cumann na mBan, during the 1920s and 1930s (when Mary Kennedy Ryan and her family were active) was supplied by Robert Kee, *The Green Flag;* Tim Pat Coogan, *The IRA: A History;* Dan Breen, *My Fight for Irish Freedom;* and R. F. Foster, *Modern Ireland 1600–1972*. Details about Kathleen Kennedy's death were taken from Lynne McTaggart, *Kathleen Kennedy;* Doris Kearns Goodwin, *The Fitzgeralds and The Kennedys;* Rose Kennedy, *Times to Remember;* as well as letters from Enrico Galeazzi, dated June 18, 1948 and June 26, 1948, in JPK papers.

Part III: Rise to the Presidency

Archbishop John Ireland was quoted in John Tracy Ellis, *American Catholicism*.

Chapter Seventeen: The Irish Brahmin

The prominent family history of Henry Cabot Lodge was traced in "Case History Of a Senate Race," Cabell Phillips, *New York Times Magazine*, October 26, 1952; *Time* August 18, 1952; and Thomas Oliphant, "Revisiting JFK's '52 Race," *Boston Globe*, March 27, 2000. Joe Kennedy's support of his son's position about the possible release of James Michael Curley was reflected in a letter he wrote on July 30, 1947, contained in JPK papers. Joe tells Dave Powers how good Jack looks and to keep him healthy if they want to win in his letter dated February 14, 1952, in the JPK papers. A description of the formidable Kennedy publicity machine during the campign was explained in the Thomas P. O'Neill Oral History at the JFK Library, in which he also says Jack, like some Irish chieftain, "had a real yen for patronage—he wanted to take care of this one; take care of that one." Futher background information about the 1952 Senate race was found in Thomas J. Whalen, *Kennedy vs. Lodge;* Jack Beatty, *The Rascal King;* Herbert S. Parmet, *Jack;* James MacGregor Burns, *John Kennedy: A Political Profile;* John Henry Cutler, *Cardinal Cushing of Boston;* Doris Kearns Goodwin, *The Fitzgeralds and the Kennedys;* Kenneth P. O'Donnell and David Powers, *Johnny, We Hardly Knew Ye;* Jean Stein and George Plimpton, *American Journey: The Times of Robert Kennedy;* John Henry Cutler, *Honey Fitz;* William Shannon, *The American Irish;* Nigel Hamilton, *JFK: Reckless Youth;* and Joe McCarthy, *The Remarkable Kennedys*.

Robert Kennedy's sense of faith and family were mentioned in numerous works, including Evan Thomas, *Robert Kennedy: His Life;* and Arthur M. Schlesinger Jr., *Robert Kennedy and His Times*. Bobby talks about entering the navy in a letter (circa 1944) at the JFK Library. RFK's confrontation with Father Feeney is mentioned in Richard Goodwin, *Remembering America;* Evan Thomas, *Robert Kennedy: His Life;* and in interview with Joseph Gargan. "My God, he's unassimilated," says the Brahmin poet, Robert Lowell, in Peter Collier and David Horowitz, *The Kennedys: An American Drama;* and Michael Beschloss, *The Crisis Years*. Also see, "What Drives Bobby Kennedy," *New York Times Magazine*, April 7, 1963, and Hendrik Hertzberg, "Scaling Mt. Kennedy," *New Yorker*, November 20, 2000, RFK "came from some deeper Celtic root" is in Pete Hamill, "JFK: The Real Thing," *New Yorker*, November 28, 1988. RFK and JFK didn't always agree with Joe Kennedy because "he doesn't require it," based on author interview with Edwin Guthman. Joe Kane was interested in Bobby as a potential political candidate in 1952, but Joe

Kennedy dissuaded him saying "we have one good contest coming up this year," letter dated February 14, 1952, in JPK papers. During fall campaign, Joe solicits donation help from Bobby's father-in-law, George Skakel, asking him to line up twenty people who will give $5,000 each, from Kennedy letter dated September 6, 1952, in JPK papers. John McCormack's phony story to placate the Jewish voters in his district so they'd support JFK is told in the Thomas P. O'Neill Oral History, JFK Library. Joe Kennedy's prediction that Eisenhower would lose in 1952 was in a letter to Mark Dalton dated February 14, 1952, in JPK papers. In follow-up, he sees little worth to a James A. Farley presidential bid, according to February 26, 1952, letter in JPK papers. After 1952 Senate victory, Joe Kennedy predicts, "Jack will be president of the United States now, no doubt of it," in Francis X. Morrissey Oral History, JFK Library. Father Sheehy writes to Joe about Jack's success and says "how proud his brother Joe would have been of him! Jack is destined to do great things for his country and his Church," in Sheehy letter dated December 12, 1952, in JPK papers. Joe Kennedy comments that the press feels "Jack has commited the unpardonable social error of beating Lodge" in November 14, 1952, letter contained in JPK papers.

Chapter Eighteen: A Child of Fate

Robert Kennedy's letter to his father about a friend's marriage annulment ("As a Papal Count Married To a Countesss, I Am Sure You Will Have an Answer") was dated February 8, 1958, in JPK papers. The rancorous debate surrounding Catholic intellectual life, the cultural barriers remaining from the Irish immigrant experience and the sharp criticisms of Paul Blanshard are discussed in numerous books, notably Paul Blanshard, *American Freedom and Catholic Power*; Mark S. Massa, *Catholics and American Culture: Fulton Sheen, Dorothy Day and the Notre Dame Football Team*; John T. McGreevy, "Thinking on One's Own: Catholicism in the American Imagination —1928–1960," *Journal of American History*, June 1997; "Liberalism and Catholicism," *American Prospect*, March 13, 2000; Peter Steinfels, "Beliefs," *New York Times*, May 3, 1997; and Lance Morrow, "The Rise and Fall of Anti-Catholicism," *Time*, October 15, 1979.

Sargeant Shriver's December 21, 1956, letter in JPK papers thanks his father-in-law for all that he has done. A description of Shriver's Maryland family was in David E. Koskoff, *Joseph P. Kennedy: A Life and Times*. In undated letter, Eunice writes to Dad "Jack is right—We may all get our 'drive' from our mother but from whom better could we receive the gift of generousity than you," in JPK papers. In February 1957 speech to South Side Catholic Women's Club, Eunice underlines the religious underpinnings of the family's work with the Kennedy Foundation, a copy of which is in the JPK papers. Pat Lawford writes about the OB-GYN physician she's trying to select in Los Angeles, and whether the doctor is a Catholic is clearly a factor, in 1954 letter in JPK papers. Joe Kennedy offers career counseling to Peter Lawford but urges Pat to focus on her health in March 7, 1955, letter in JPK papers. Rose seemed uneasy with the Pat and Peter Lawford situation. In a letter to Ted, she recalls how Joe's conversation with Peter was overheard by Pat and two others listening in. "It seems to me that it is almost as bad as having your wire tapped," Rose says, in May 17, 1957, letter in JPK papers.

A portrait of Rose's spiritual interests is derived from several of her letters in the JPK papers. "If Rose had been a boy, she—not Jack—would have been the first Catholic president of the United States," says Marie Greene, an often-mentioned quote repeated in Randy Schultz, "Matriach of an American Dynasty," *Palm Beach Post*, January 23, 1995. Rose is 'thrilled' to have a large crowd at Manhattanville for her "speaking debut" and writes thanks to O'Byrne in January 4, 1953, letter in JPK papers. At Manhattanville in 1956, Rose gives address "so full of faith and the practical expression of devotion to the Sacred Heart." Rose also is "brave" as she talks about Kathleen Kennedy, in March 12, 1956, letter from Mother O'Byrne to Joe Kennedy in JPK papers. Rose writes to Jackie again in June 1958, about going on religious retreats. "I have spent a long, happy life with a few baffling as well as tragic moments, and I have found that these spiritual signposts along the way have helped me tremendously," in June 9, 1958, letter in JPK papers.

Rose's comments about Ted's new girlfriend and husband Joe's response in a July 25, 1949, letter in JPK papers. Rose's comment about Jack's trip to Jamaica ("After all, he's over 21 and he knows what he is doing") is in a letter to Eunice dated January 25, 1950, in JPK papers. Sexually tinged jokes and comments from Joe Sr. to Jack about "a very beautiful blond" who comes looking for a job on the stage, and says she know Jack, is in a November 16, 1943, letter in JPK papers.

Jack's Spring 1940, letter to father urging him "before resigning give my social career a bit of con-sideration" was in the JPK papers. In letter that spring, JFK also tells Dad that he's taking Kick's friend, Charlotte McDonnell, to the Princeton game, which he notes "will be my first taste of a Catholic girl so will be interested to see how it goes." Also, see Laurence Leamer, *The Kennedy Women,* for further background. JFK's comment to Red Fay about marriage and that "this means the end of a promising political career, as it has been based up to now almost completely on the old sex appeal," is retold in Gore Vidal, "The Holy Family," *Esquire,* April 1967. Some of the early frostiness between Rose and Jackie is reflected in some letters in JPK papers. In return letter to Rose, the mother of Jacqueline Bouvier tells her how happy she is they met and that "Jackie has chosen to marry a man whose mind and whose religion and whose great charm give them so much in common," in an undated letter from Janet Auchincloss in the JPK papers. Rose writes back in letter that she and Joe "could not be more thrilled to know that Jack had won such an out-standing bride who is so charming, so cultured and such a devout Catholic," also in JPK papers. The death of Jackie's father, John Bouvier, while she is pregnant is recalled in 1957 letter from Jackie to Rose and Joe in JPK papers. In heartfelt letter dated August 23, 1957, Joe advises Jackie not to let the political battles bother her. "Remember I've always said he's a child of fate, and if he fell in a puddle of mud in a white suit he'd come up ready for a Newport ball," Joe writes of his son in letter contained in JPK papers.

Chapter Nineteen: Articles of Faith

Msgr. Maurice S. Sheehy's view on communism and religion comes from *U.S. News and World Report,* April 6, 1956. More details about Sheehy and his views were in David J. O'Brien, *American Catholics and Social Reform: The New Deal Years.* Cushing's view on communism's impact were described in John Henry Cutler, *Cardinal Cushing of Boston.* JFK's 1958 talk about religion as "at the root of the struggle" against communism is from Russell W. Gibbons, "The Real Christianity of John F. Kennedy," *St. Joseph Magazine,* April 1965. JFK mentioned the Catholic War Veteran plan for films about Communist threat in a letter to his father dated April 13, 1948, in JPK papers. Cushing's meeting with J. Edgar Hoover was discussed in his letter dated November 12, 1956, in JPK papers. Kennedy's letter of praise to Hoover was dated March 11, 1953, in JPK papers. Further context was provided by an FBI memo describing Joe Kennedy as "a devout Catholic and is very well versed on Communism," reported by Edward A. Soucy, the FBI's special agent in charge in Boston. It was sent in a confidential memo to FBI chief J. Edgar Hoover, dated December 27, 1943, contained in the FBI file on Joseph P. Kennedy Sr. obtained from the agency's Freedom of Information office.

Details of Robert Kennedy's trip to Soviet Central Asia were found in Robert Kennedy, "The Soviet Brand of Colonialism," *New York Times Magazine,* April 8, 1956; Michael Beschloss, *The Crisis Years;* and *U.S. News and World Report* interview from October 21, 1955, also contained in the FBI's file on Robert Kennedy obtained through the agency's Freedom of Information office.

The Kennedy family's support of Sen. Joseph McCarthy is detailed in numerous biographies, including David Oshinsky, *A Conspiracy So Immense: The World of Joseph McCarthy;* David E. Koskoff, *Joseph P. Kennedy: A Life and Times* Donald F. Crosby, S.J., *God, Church and Flag: Senator Joseph R. McCarthy and the Catholic Church, 1950–1957;* Evan Thomas, *Robert Kennedy;* Arthur Herman, *Joseph McCarthy: Re-examining the Life and Legacy of America's Most Hated Senator;* Joseph Dever, *Cushing of Boston: A Candid Portrait;* and James MacGregor Burns, *John Kennedy: A Political Profile.* It is also mentioned in JFK letter to his father, dated August 19, 1954, in JPK papers. Further context provided by Hendrik Hertzberg, "Scaling Mt. Kennedy," *New Yorker,* November 20, 2000; and Marshall Frady, "The Transformation of Bobby Kennedy," *New York Review of Books,* October 12, 1978.

Chapter Twenty: A Nation of Immigrants

Details of JFK's trip to Dublin with his wife Jacqueline were derived from the oral history of Liam Cosgrave, conducted in Dublin in 1966 for the JFK Presidential Library. Further details about Father Leonard and the Kennedy trip were found in Maurice N. Hennessy, *I'll Come Back in the Springtime: John F. Kennedy and the Irish,* and the inscriptions on the Baring book and others featured by Jay Dixon Rare Books and Manuscripts, March 2001. Also see, Laura Lovat, *Maurice Baring: A Postscript.*

Joe Kennedy's concern about JFK considering the vice-presidential spot on the 1956 Stevenson ticket, fearing that Catholicsm might be blamed for the loss to Eisenhower was contained in James Reston, "Party's Debate on Kennedy Takes Note of Catholic Vote," *New York Times,* January 3, 1960. Also see, Francis X. Morrissey oral history, JFK Library. Agnes Meyer's warning about Roman Catholic prejuidice in 1956 was mentioned in Herbert S. Parmet, *Jack: The Struggles of John F. Kennedy.* JFK's claim that his brother Bobby "is the smartest politician I have ever met in my life" is quoted in the oral history of Thomas P. O'Neill at the JFK Presidential Library. JFK's assessment to Fletcher Knebel is quoted in Knebel's oral history at the JFK Presidential Library. Details about Sorensen, his background and the issue of religion were found in Theodore C. Sorensen, *Kennedy.* "Those poor little Catholics" comment allegedly made by Stevenson camp is repeated in Ralph Martin, *A Hero For Our Time.* Details about the 1956 Bailey Report were discussed in the September 7, 1959, and the August 1, 1960, editions of *U.S. News and World Report.* Joe Kennedy's comment that "this country is not a private preserve for Protestants" is from the recollection of Rose Kennedy in Doris Kearns Goodwin, *The Fitzgeralds and the Kennedys.* JFK's initial failure to become overseer at Harvard University is reflected in letter of Frank Morrissey to Joe Kennedy, dated June 21, 1955, in the JPK papers. Futher details and context were provided by John Henry Cutler, *Cardinal Cushing of Boston;* and Arthur Mitchell, *JFK and His Irish Heritage.* John P. Roche's comments are contained in the 1986 preface to reprinted edition of John F. Kennedy, *A Nation of Immigrants.* Sen. Edward Kennedy's recollections about *A Nation of Immigrants* are based on a written response to the author's questions.

Chapter Twenty-One: Matters of Church and State

Details of Joe Kennedy's 1950 meeting with President Truman come from Kennedy's own written account provided in Amanda Smith, *Hostage to Fortune,* an account in the Feb. 10, 1950, edition of *U.S. News and World Report,* and exchange of letters between Kennedy and Truman, including one dated Jan. 31, 1950, contained in the JPK papers. Another account about Truman and any US representation at the Vatican is outlined in July 3, 1950, letter from Kennedy to Galeazzi, in which Kennedy says "a Jewish minority group, well-organized, gets what it wants and we get nothing"—contained in the JPK papers. Kennedy's expressed fidelity to the Pope and top aide's wishes ("I don't know what I can continue to do to be of any assistance to him, but you know all you have to do is command me and, if it is humanly possible, I shall do it.") is in a March 2, 1949, letter from Kennedy to Galeazzi in the JPK papers.

Cooney's quote about Spellman's maneuvers is from John Cooney, *The American Pope: The Life and Times of Francis Cardinal Spellman,* which includes Rev. Carl McIntyre's comment about the threat of "Spellmanism" to America. Kennedy's "personal and confidential" correspondence to Spellman about his trip to Rome ("The Holy Father, as I have found out in my last four visits with Him, is still incensed that nothing is being done in America," including his comments about the lack of political power among Catholics and his comparison with Jews) is in a June 27, 1955, letter from Kennedy in the JPK papers.

Chapter Twenty-Two: A Friend in Rome

The letters between Count Enrico Galeazzi and Joseph Kennedy Sr. underscore their long-time confidence and friendship, all of which are contained in the JPK papers at the Kennedy Presidential Library. Prior to JFK's 1947 Vatican visit, his father's telegram of September 25, 1947, mentions that "Spellman arranging with Galeazzi in Rome your appointment." A returned favor by Joe Kennedy—helping Galeazzi's son-in-law get a job as a doctor in the United States—is outlined in two letters, one from Galeazzi dated May 20, 1948, and a reply from Joe Kennedy dated June 18, 1948. Joe Kennedy's letter asking Galeazzi to arrange a papal for Ed Sullivan, newspaper columnist and TV host, was dated July 3, 1950, in the JPK papers. A note from Ed Sullivan to Joe Kennedy offering tickets to his TV show was dated March 31, 1952. Other letters with Sullivan, dated February 8, 1960 and February 24, 1960, in the JPK papers indicate Sullivan offered private advice and help during the 1960 campaign. *New York Times* columnist James Reston's letter requesting to send some "confidential information" with Joe Kennedy's help to Galeazzi and Pope

Pius XII was dated November 11, 1955, and is contained in the JPK papers. Kennedy's observation "I think that the Irish in me has not been completely assimiliated, but all my ducks are swans," was written to Galeazzi and dated February 12, 1959, in the JPK papers. Jack's recovery in 1954 from "two very close calls with death" is mentioned in November 29, 1954, letter to Galeazzi, which also passes along thanks for Pope's special message and Joe's comment that Pius XII "is the only one who speaks for all civilization—all leaders of countries speak for their own." Joe's mention of Jacqueline Kennedy's miscarriage was contained in an August 1956, letter. After the 1956 Eisenhower landslide, Joe's comment to Galeazzi that he's happy JFK wasn't on the Democratic ticket ("It would have absolutely set back the possibility of a Catholic in the White House for another fifty years because the defeat would have been blamed on the Catholic") was in a Kennedy letter to Galeazzi dated November 9, 1956, in JPK papers. At Christmas 1957, Joe Kennedy tells family "what a wonderful gift it has been to have been so close to the Holy See during the past 20 years, a privilege not given to any other family in the world and it is all due to you" in February 7, 1958, letter to Galeazzi in JPK papers.

Joe Kennedy's monetary contributions to church-related activities is mentioned in several letters, including in 1957 financing for the Basilica of Saints John and Paul mentioned in May 10, 1957, letter from Galeazzi to Kennedy. Several letters in the JPK papers mention or allude to the Vatican's effort to procure U.S. reparations for damage to papal properties during World War II, including a detailed memo prepared from Galeazzi dated September 5, 1955, in JPK papers. A private letter from Sen. John F. Kennedy to his father about the passage of the "Vatican bill" was contained in a June 29, 1956, letter in the JPK papers. Spellman's letter for thanks to JFK for getting the federal money for the damaged church property was in a "Dear Jack" letter from Spellman dated July 30, 1956 in JPK papers.

JFK's role as "white knight" in support of certain federal aid for private and parochial schools was praised in a March 18, 1950, edition of the *Boston Pilot* contained in the JFK early years collection of papers at the JFK Presidential Library. The same newspaper is quoted in James MacGregor Burns, *John Kennedy: A Political Profile*. Details about the exchange of Rogers and Congressman Kennedy can be found in the Hearings before Subcommittee Number One of the Committee on Education and Labor, House of Representatives, 80th Congress, 1st Session, Vol. 1, p. 332–357, also cited in Burns's *John Kennedy*. Spellman's position on federal education aid was discussed in John Henry Cutler, *Cardinal Cushing of Boston*; John Cooney, *The American Pope*; and Robert I. Gannon, S.J., *The Cardinal Spellman Story*. Quotations from the written public exchanges between Spellman and Eleanor Roosevelt was documented in Gannon's book as well as Burns, Cooney and others cited in this chapter. When Spellman blasts the film, *Baby Doll,* in 1957, Kennedy bans it from his Kennedy-owned theaters without seeing it, David E. Koskoff, *Joseph P. Kennedy: A Life and Times.*

The discussions about JFK's own sense of Catholic faith and culture varies greatly. Jacqueline Kennedy's quip about her husband being "such a poor Catholic" and Bobby who "never misses mass and prays all the time" was repeated in several works, including Garry Wills, *The Kennedy Imprisonment.* The description of JFK's churchgoing to that of going to a club, and as a person who "avoided all forms of ethnic chauvinism" is from Richard D. Mahoney, *Sons & Brothers: the Days of Jack and Bobby Kennedy.* Lem Billings's recollection of JFK and religion were contained in Nigel Hamilton, *JFK: Reckless Youth.* Sorensen's comments about JFK and religion were from the author's two separate interviews with him, in 2000 and 2002, and from Sorensen's *Kennedy.* Schlesinger's brief assessment of the cultural impact of Catholicism on Kennedy was in Schlesinger's *A Thousand Days.* Gargan's comments are from an interview with the author.

Galeazzi's encouragement to Joe Kennedy "for the great goal which is ahead" was found in a letter dated February 6, 1959, in JPK papers. The secret meeting between CIA director Allen Dulles and Joe Kennedy at his Florida home is mentioned in his April 15, 1958, letter to Galeazzi in the JPK papers. In this letter, Kennedy tells the Vatican administrator of his willingness to act as a go-between with Dulles. There is no indication that this author could find, either in the histories of this period or in Allen Dulles's oral history at the JFK Library, that Galeazzi or any other Vatican official ever acted on Joe Kennedy's offer. Dulles remained with the CIA during the early days of the Kennedy administration, but left the agency shortly after the disasterous Bay of Pigs episode. Galeazzi's half brother who was barred from practicing medicine after he sold Pope's deathbed stories is detailed in the *New York Times,* December 13, 1958. The decline of Galeazzi's influence at the

Vatican (under Pius XII, he held nine separate posts within the Vatican, according to the 1958 Vatican yearbook) is discussed in a magazine profile about the new tenure of Pope John XXIII in Robert Neville, "The Pope and The Vatican," *Look,* March 17, 1959.

Joe Kennedy's bitterness toward Rev. Theodore Hesburgh of Notre Dame and about the American Catholic Church hierarchy's lack of support for Jack's presidential candidacy was discussed in his letter to Galeazzi, dated March 30, 1959, in the JPK papers. After Galeazzi's calming note, Joe Kennedy wrote back that Jack Kennedy is less affected than his father by the church's position "but he is definitely upset," according to a letter dated April 17, 1959, in JPK papers. Joe Kennedy's August 9, 1959, letter to Vatican Secretary of State Cardinal Tardini, invoking Galeazzi's name high up, recalled the 1928 Al Smith fiasco, asked for the church to keep quiet on the "religious issue" and suggested the difficulty that a future Catholic might face in running for president if Jack Kennedy lost in 1960.

Chapter Twenty-Three: Primary Lessons

Author's interview with former Sen. Eugene McCarthy of Minnesota (and later presidential candidate in the 1968 Democratic primaries) formed the basis for the opening scene at the Kennedy's Georgetown dinner. "All we have are Protestants and farmers" was taken from Theodore Sorensen, *Kennedy.* JFK's comment about McCarthy to Joseph Alsop ("Well, Joe, there's an old saying in Boston politics, never trust a Catholic politician who reads his missal in the trolley car") is from Joseph Alsop Oral History cited in Arthur M. Schlesinger Jr., *Robert Kennedy and His Times.* Photos and quotes from the Kennedy clan appeared in Laura Bergquist, "The Rise of the Brothers Kennedy," *Look,* August 6, 1957. JFK's quote that "all of us want a big family too," like his parents, was in "A Debut into a Burgeoning Family," *Life,* April 21, 1958. Joe Kennedy's quotes about the Kennedys' sense of family and their Irish heritage appeared in Harold H. Martin, "The Amazing Kennedys," *Saturday Evening Post,* September 7, 1957. Mention of JFK's "poor Irish immigrant stock" appeared in Cabell Phillips, "How to Be a Presidential Candidate," *New York Times Magazine,* July 13, 1958. JFK's conversation about religion with Rev. Henry Knox Sherrill was recalled by the candidate in Fletcher Knebel, "Democratic Forecast: A Catholic in 1960," *Look,* March 3, 1959. Kennedy's firm public stance on separation of church and state and disagreement with some church positions on public policy—including the appointment of a U.S. ambassador to the Vatican—made it one of the most controversial pieces of the campaign. In this same article, while talking about Kennedy, Knebel states that "some people believe Mrs. Roosevelt opposes Kennedy because he is a Catholic." Knebel never identified who "some people" might be by name, though the inference is clearly from the Kennedy camp, and Knebel quotes Mrs. Roosevelt's firm denial of holding such anti-Catholic sentiments. Knebel's anecdote about JFK's angry reaction to the Senate chaplain's anti-Catholic comments was recorded in the oral history of Fletcher Knebel at the JFK Presidential Library. The negative reaction to Kennedy's interview was reflected in "On Questioning Catholic Candidates," *America,* March 7, 1959; and "Senator Kennedy and His Critics," *Commonweal,* March 20, 1959, with examples of the negative reaction nationally in the Catholic press compiled in "Aftermath of the Kennedy Statement," *Commonweal,* March 20, 1959.

When Jack wins the Pulitzer Prize, Cardinal Cushing writes: "I don't know when a Catholic was awarded such an honor," in letter dated May 7, 1957, in JPK papers. Cushing's liberal Catholicism and his support for JFK's political effort was discussed in Jospeh Dever, *Cushing of Boston: A Candid Portrait;* John Henry Cutler, *Cardinal Cushing of Boston;* and Thomas H. O'Connor, *Boston Catholics: A History of the Church and Its People.* Bishop John Wright's relationship with the Kennedys involves seeking money in 1957 from the Kennedy Foundation, and offering political support the following year to Joe Kennedy ("Would not a dramatic action, like the election of a Catholic president all of a sudden, help to exorcise these demons?") in letters dated September 6, 1957, and May 7, 1958, in the JPK papers. In January 22, 1959, letter to Joe Kennedy, Cushing is boldly partisan for JFK ("I wish this Democratic National Convention was over. I dream about it. It is my opinion that if we can get by the Convention with a victory, we are 'in.'") By March 1959, Cardinal Cushing meets privately with David Lawrence, then governor of Pennsylvania who has expressed doubts about JFK or any Catholic presidential candidacy, but whose potential support, as Joe notes in a March 23, 1959, letter, is "very, very important." Cushing also gave a "courageous, generous speech on Jack's position" regarding church–state separation, which "gave me confidence that there was somebody left in high places in the Catholic Church who saw something in this battle that Jack is making," the senior Kennedy said in the same letter contained in the JPK papers. Joe Kennedy tells Cushing that "this letter really adds up to saying that if Jack stays in this fight, it will be you who has kept him in. If he wins, it will be you who has made it possible." In letter dated September 23, 1959, Cushing wrote to Joe Kennedy, promising to lobby on Jack's behalf and contact Wright (formerly a lower-ranking aide in Boston, who became bishop in Worchester and then Pittsburgh) "to the end that he [Wright] will start a little aggressive talk among the folks in his area that will reach the ear of the Governor of Pennsylvania." In a note to his son "Dear Jack," Joe Kennedy tells of his conversation with Father Cavanaugh of Notre Dame who suggests seeking advice on the religious question from Rev. John Courtney Murray and Rev. Gustave Weigel in seeking to "prepare some answers to the Protestant interrogation" on the church and state issue, in Joe Kennedy letter dated January 14, 1958, in JPK papers. John Cogley's experiences with JFK were recalled in John Cogley, *A Canterbury Tale: Experiences* and in Cogley's oral history for the JFK Presidential Library. JFK's quip to Cogley ("It is hard for a Harvard man to answer questions in theology. I imagine my answers will cause heartburn at Fordham and B.C.") was found in John Cogley, "Kennedy the Catholic," *Commonweal,* January 16, 1964.

Chapter Twenty-Four: West Virginia

The scene and circumstances of JFK's presidential candidacy announcement comes from several sources, including Theodore H. White, *The Making of the President, 1960*; James Reston, "Party's Debate on Kennedy Takes Note of Catholic Vote," *New York Times,* January 3, 1960; and Russell Baker, "Kennedy in Race," in the same issue. Kennedy's comment that he believed the religious issue was "exhausted" was in the July 4, 1960, edition of *Life* magazine. Speculation about what Protestant Americans might do "in the secrecy of the ballot box" was discussed in Herbert S. Parmet, *Jack: The Struggles of John F. Kennedy.* Criticism of Archibald MacLeish's comments in *Life* magazine about Irish Catholics appeared in "Reality and the American Dream," *Commonweal,* July 8, 1960. Gore Vidal's recollections were in Gore Vidal, "The Holy Family," *Esquire,* April 1967. Kennedy says his religion is becoming "very well known—fortunately or unfortunately" in "Kennedy Hailed by Bobby Soxers," *New York Times,* April 21, 1960. "That might play well in certain parts of Boston but *The New York Times* wouldn't like it" from Pierre Salinger, *P.S., A Memoir,* St. Martin's Press, 1995. Eunice Shriver's question to her brother "What does it all mean, Johnny?" came from Kenneth P. O'Donnell and David F. Powers, *Johnny, We Hardly Knew Ye; Memories of John Fitzgerald Kennedy,* and was cited in several other works. In the April 17, 1960, issue of the *New York Times,* political writer Leo Egan said "Kennedy's religion appears to be becoming the dominant issue" of the primary campaign. The resolution passed by Southern Baptists—the nation's second largest Protestant denomination—fearing a Catholic president was reported in the July 4, 1960, edition of *Life* magazine. The president of Southern Baptists vow that he wouldn't "stand by and keep my mouth shut when a man under the control of the Roman Catholic Church runs for the Presidency of the U.S." was reported in "Attack on Catholics," *New York Times,* February 11, 1960. The Missouri Baptist leader identified as "a Negro" who asked for "the Lord's blessing and assistance" in electing a Protestant to the White House in 1960 was reported in "Catholic Opposed," *New York Times,* April 9, 1960. Before the Wisconsin primary in 1960, Joe Kennedy confided to Galeazzi that "if we cannot make a showing and if the religious thing becomes very acute, then I am for stepping out," in letter dated March 31, 1960, in JPK papers. "If Jack's heart is broken because he may be beaten on the religious question, then so be it," was mentioned in JPK's April 8, 1960, letter to Michael Morrissey in JPK papers. Rose Kennedy's attempts to enlist the help of Mother O'Byrne of Manhattanville in obtaining names of alumnae who can be contacted in Wisconsin in anticipation of the primary was in Rose's letter dated January 19, 1960, in the JPK papers. O'Byrne's reply was dated January 25, 1960. Rose Kennedy's efforts in her son's primary campaign and the underlying reasons why she wasn't involved in West Virginia were recounted in Rose Fitzgerald Kennedy, *Times to Remember.* Bobby Kennedy's chagrined reaction to the religion problem in West Virginia ("There's only one problem. He's a Catholic. That's our goddamned problem!") was recounted in Kenneth P. O'Donnell and David F. Powers, *Johnny, We Hardly Knew Ye; Memories of John Fitzgerald Kennedy.* Bobby's emotional comments about his older brother's death and the religious issue prompts JFK to say "Bobby must be getting tired," in Theodore Sorensen, *Kennedy Legacy*. The *Charleston Gazette* advertisement aimed at Kennedy was reported on in April 30, 1960, edition of the *New York Times*. The survey by the Anti-Defamation League of B'nai B'rith finding large-scale amount of anti-Catholic circulars and other religious bias toward Kennedy was cited both in the June 5, 1960, edition of the *New York Times*, with a copy of report in the file marked "The Religion Issue in 1960 Campaign" at the JFK Presidential Library. The important role of Franklin D. Roosevelt Jr. for Kennedy in the West Virginia primary was detailed in several accounts, including Richard Reeves, *President Kennedy: Profile of Power*. After the West Virginia victory, JFK said religious issue was "buried eight feet deep" reported in July 4, 1960, edition of *Life*. The Kennedy clan "as handsome and spirited as a meadow full of Irish thoroughbreds, as tough as a blackthorn shillelagh, as ruthless as Cuchulain, the mythical hero who cast up the hills of Ireland with his sword," is from "Pride of the Clan," *Time*, July 11, 1960.

Chapter Twenty-Five: The Fall, 1960

Richard Nixon's public refusal to bring up the religious issue in the 1960 campaign was discussed in "Nixon Previews Campaign," January 28, 1960, *New York Times*; an updated look at Nixon's position appeared in August 23, 1960, *New York Times*, and the role of Nixon and other Republicans on the religious issue was discussed in Theodore H. White, *The Making of the President, 1960*. Eisenhower's comments about religion in the 1960 campaign were taken from published excerpts of a presidential press conference and an accompanying article in the August 25, 1960, edition of the *New York Times*. Robert Kennedy's statements identifying six Southern states where the religious issue was a problem for his brother's campaign appeared in "Kennedy Faces Southern Battle," September 8, 1960, the *New York Times*, and discussed further in Evan Thomas, *Robert Kennedy: His Life*. Kennedy's appointment of James Wine, Presbyterian minister, to "interpret church-state position" for his campaign was reported in the August 25, 1960, edition of the *New York Times*. Ex–President Harry S Truman's comments about religion in the campaign and the role of the Republicans was found in "Truman Accuses GOP of Bigotry," September 6, 1960, *New York Times*; later in "Truman Hails Nixon on Religious Issue," September 15, 1960, edition of the *New York Times* as well as the September 26, 1960, issue of *Time* magazine.

The critical role of Protestant ministers in the 1960 campaign, including Dr. L. Nelson Bell, Billy Graham's father-in-law, is in a *Washington Post* article of September 8, 1960, by John J. Lindsay, and an undated newspaper column entitled "Religious Issue: Nixon's Attitude," by Joseph Alsop, both of which were contained in the JFK Presidential Library archives, as well as "Protestants in Politics," *New Republic*, September 19, 1960, and "Protestant Unit Wary on Kennedy," *New York Times*, September 8, 1960. Bobby Kennedy's response to the Peale group's statement was contained in "Peale Criticized," *New York Times*, September 9, 1960. The impact of a Catholic priest, John F. Cronin, an anti-communism expert, was discussed in Christopher Matthews, *Kennedy and Nixon*; as well as Irwin F. Gellman, *The Contender*.

Kennedy's speech in Houston before the ministers and its aftermath were recounted in the September 26, 1960, edition of *U.S. News and World Report;* "Test of Religion," *Time,* September 26, 1960; "Kennedy Accepts Invitation," *New York Times*, September 9, 1960; "Kennedy Assures Texas Ministers of Independence," *New York Times*, September 13, 1960; and "Campaign Issues," *New York Times,* November 3, 1960; as well as David Burner, *John F. Kennedy and a New Generation*; Theodore Sorensen, *Kennedy*; William Shannon, *The American Irish*; and John Cogley, *A Canterbury Tale*. Cogley's oral history at the JFK Presidential Library also provided insight.

The anti-Catholic effort against Kennedy's campaign, including the comments of Rev. Springer, were reported in Jack Anderson, "Nixon Is Linked to Billy Graham," *Washington Post,* September 12, 1960; John W. Finney, "Democrats List 5 as Extremists," *New York Times*, September 17, 1960; John Wicklein, "Vast Anti-Catholic Drive Slated Before Election," *New York Times*, October 16, 1960; John Wicklein, "Anti-Catholic Groups Closely Cooperate in Mail Campaign to Defeat Kennedy," *New York Times*, October 17, 1960; Gladwin Hill, "Religion Remains Big Issue in Texas," *New York Times*, November 3, 1960; and "Morton Blames Rivals," *New York Times*, November 6, 1960; James Reston's comments were found in "Dallas," *New York Times,* September 14, 1960. Murray Kempton's quip that JFK would be America's "first anti-clerical President" was

repeated in Victory Lasky, *J.F.K.: The Man and The Myth*. Joe Kennedy's angry reaction to the oppo-
sition of Spellman and other Catholic prelates was reflected in his February 6, 1961, letter to
Galeazzi, also cited in Amanda Smith, *Hostage to Fortune*. The senior Kennedy's reaction to the
Catholic hierarchy was also discussed in David E. Koskoff, *Joseph P. Kennedy: A Life and Times*.
Robert Kennedy's recollection of his brother's antipathy for Cardinal Spellman was contained in
RFK's oral history at the JFK Presidential Library. JFK's joke to reporters about "the fate of the
free world" appeared in Hugh Sidey, "Back Door No Longer," *Time*, October 15, 1979; as did the
"That's off the record" anecdote about riding in a limosine outside St. Patrick's Cathedral in New
York. "Southern Baptists feel beleagured" quote was reported in "Before the Election,"
Commonweal, November 11, 1960. An analysis of Kennedy's religious obstacles in the fall campaign
appeared in "Protestants in Politics," *New Republic*, September 19, 1960. The editor of *America*
magazine talked about Kennedy and potential Catholic president in "Jesuit See Shift in Political
Era," *New York Times*, February 28, 1960, and the criticism that JFK had to "appease" anti-Catholic
bigots was in "Priest Sees Bias as Bad as 1928," *New York Times*, September 10, 1960. Joe Kennedy's
describing "the campaign not between a Democrate and a Republican, but betweeen a Catholic
and a Protestant" was in a letter to Lord Beaverbrook dated September 9, 1960, in JPK papers; also
cited in Amanda Smith, *Hostage to Fortune*. Weigel's comments and Kennedy's position were evaluated in Reinhold Niebuhr, "Catholics and the State," *New Republic*, October 17, 1960 and particularly in John W. Finney, "Jesuit Rules Out Church Control Over a President," *New York Times*,
September 28, 1960. Nixon spokesman Herb Klein's comment about a "Catholic vote" were contained in "Economy Slipping," *The New York Times*, October 31, 1960. Several political analysts
regard the "religious issue" as the number one issue of the 1960 campaign as reported in
"Campaign Issues," *New York Times*, November 3, 1960. JFK's televised assurance of separation of
church and state was contained in "3 Sisters Put Questions to Kennedy in Telecast," *Washington
Post*, November 8, 1960. The Fair Campaign Practices Committee report was quoted in "Striking
Changes in the Way Protestants and Catholics Feel about Each Other," Walter Goodman, *Redbook*,
March 1964. Impact of religion on the campaign was analyzed in John Wicklein, "Campaign
Issues: Effect of Anti-Catholic Sentiment Is Weighed as Factor at the Polls," *New York Times*,
November 3, 1960. *New York Times* comment that "the next president is not in the ordinary mold,
for example, of Irish-American politicians" appeared in its November 10, 1960, edition. Theodore
H. White's 1978 re-evaluation underlining belatedly the significance of JFK's election as a minority in 1960, was mentioned in Theodore H. White, *In Search of History: A Personal Adventure*. JFK's
note to New Ross upon his election was recalled in both Doris Kearns Goodwin, *The Fitzgeralds
and The Kennedys;* and Maurice N. Hennessy, *I'll Come Back in the Springtime: John F. Kennedy and
the Irish*.

As part of the research for this chapter, the author examined a large file at the JFK Library,
marked religious bigotry, containing several articles and pamphlets handed out during the
1960 campaign. Among those documents that provided information for this chapter were
"Kennedy Runs True to Form," *Dallas Morning News*, September 7, 1960; "Youth Writes Anti-
Catholic Pamphlet," *Minneapolis Sunday Tribune*, September 11, 1960; letters from Norman Vincent
Peale regarding his statements about Kennedy and a Catholic running for president; *The Religious
Issue in the 1960 Election Campaign*, A Report of the Anti-Defamation League of B'nai B'rith;
"Religion in the Campaign," *Des Moines Register*, September 17, 1960; "Religion and Politics,"
Time, August 22, 1960; "Who Keeps Religion in the Campaign?" *Chicago Daily Tribune*, undated;
Robert S. Bird and Jo-ann Price, "All-Out Religious Attack on Kennedy Planned by 38
Fundamentalist Sects," *Washington Post*, undated; Drew Pearson, "Texas Repeats 1928 Campaign,"
Nashville Tennessean, August 23, 1960; "Wanted to Stay in Office," *Dallas Morning News*, Octo-
ber 30, 1960.

Part IV: The Rites of Power

Arthur M. Schlesinger Jr.'s description of the Irish Catholic cultural influence on the Kennedys
came from Arthur M. Sclesinger Jr., *Robert Kennedy and His Times*. Cogley's comment is from an
oral history given for the JFK Presidential Library.

Chapter Twenty-Six: A Catholic in the White House

Details and dialogue from the baptism of John F. Kennedy Jr. came from "The Kennedys and Their Son at Christening," *Life*, December 19, 1960; and "John Jr.," *Time*, December 5, 1960. Kennedy's comment that "if I am not a successful President, the barrier will be back higher than ever" was cited in William Shannon, *The American Irish*, which also mentions the Robert Frost inscription to be "more Irish than Harvard." Other discussion of its meaning occured in Arthur Mitchell, *JFK and His Irish Heritage*; Shaun O'Connell, "Goodbye to All That: The Rise and Demise of Irish America," *New England Journal of Public Policy*; Jean Stein and George Plimpton, *American Journey: The Times of Robert Kennedy*; David Halberstam, *The Best and the Brightest*; "Harvard, 6; Irish, 6," *America*, December 9, 1961; and Edward M. Kennedy, *Words Jack Loved*. Cushing's statement about JFK as first Catholic U.S. President was derived from "Cardinal Cushing Remembers: 'Twice, I saw Jack Kennedy Cry,'" *Look*, November 17, 1964. Further background about Frost came from Lawrance Thompson and R.H. Winnick, *Robert Frost: The Later Years, 1938–1963*. A 1951 JFK speech as genesis of the Peace Corps was mentioned in Laurence Leamer, *The Kennedy Men*. Discussion of "Irish Mafia" and its surrounding sentiment was in Theodore Sorensen, *Kennedy*. JFK's "I'll open the front door." quip was cited in Irving Bernstein, *Promises Kept: John F. Kennedy's New Frontier*. Sargeant Shriver's influence on Kennedy decision-making was discussed in Harris Wofford, *Of Kennedys and Kings: Making Sense of the Sixties*. Lem Billings's assessment of JFK as "something of an upstart, an Irish Catholic who looked to the Brahmins for a model of how to act" was quoted in Collier and Horowitz, *The Kennedys*. Kempton's reassessment of the Catholic cultural influence on Kennedy was written in Murrary Kempton, "Sorensen's Kennedy," *Atlantic Monthly*, October 1965. Hugh Sidey's comment was from his introduction to *Prelude to Leadership: The European Diary of John F. Kennedy, Summer 1945*, which included JFK's observation about the Duke of Devonshire. JFK's long-time personal ties to David Ormsby-Gore/Lord Harlech were detailed in Lynne McTaggart, *Kathleen Kennedy: Her life and Times*, as well as in oral histories by Robert Kennedy, William Douglas Home and Ormsby-Gore for the JFK Presidential Library. Several works mention JFK's fondness for Irish songs, including the time he induced a Boston politician to sing "Danny Boy" on a visit to the Senate, as recounted in Theodore Sorensen, *Kennedy*. Tip O'Neill's recollection came from his oral history for the JFK Presidential Library, and Fay's view was in Paul B. Fay, *The Pleasure of His Company*. Bundy's comment about Paul Blanshard's book was cited in "Liberalism and Catholicism," *American Prospect*, March 13, 2000. Kennedy's "Hell, they don't even allow Catholics!" was from David Halberstam, *The Best and the Brightest*. RFK's remark to the British ambassador to the US: "Why are we, the Kennedys, here in America?" came from Michael Beschloss, *Kennedy and Roosevelt*. The staffers who want to be "brothers" were described in Anne Taylor Fleming, "The Kennedy Mystique," *New York Times Magazine*, June 17, 1979. Jack's "St. Crispin's Day" reference was recalled in the oral history of Francis X. Morrissey at the JFK Library. Schlesinger's view of John Kennedy "as the more secure, the freer, of the two—freer of his father, freer of his family, of his faith, of the entire Irish American predicament" came from Arthur M. Schlesinger Jr., *Robert Kennedy and His Times*. The number of times JFK reportedly went to Mass in 1962 was counted by the author from the published index to the *New York Times* for that year. Shannon's view of Kennedy came from William V. Shannon, *The American Irish*; and Cogley's view from his oral history for the JFK Presidential Library and from John Cogley, *A Canterbury Tale: Experiences*. O'Donell's recollection about the best politicians in America was from Kenneth P. O'Donnell and David F. Powers, with Joe McCarthy, *Johnny, We Hardly Knew Ye; Memories of John Fitzgerald Kennedy*.

Chapter Twenty-Seven: Holy Wars

RFK's trip to Japan was detailed in "More Than a Brother," *Time*, February 16, 1962, and his own recollection "If They're Communists, You Can't Get Through to Them" from oral history at JFK Presidential Library. Khrushchev's comment of "holy wars" was in Hugh Sidey, "What the Ks Really Told Each Other," *Life*, June 16, 1961. Bobby's proposal "to teach insurgency and teach about communism" and other comments about international communism were found in his oral history at JFK Library. Cushing's involvement with Ted Kennedy's trip to Peru and Latin America was detailed in a July 19, 1961, letter from him in the JPK papers. The cardinal's involvement in the money raised for the prisoners from the Bay of Pigs invasion was discussed in "Catholicism in the

U.S.," *Time*, August 21, 1964; John Henry Cutler, *Cardinal Cushing of Boston*; John H. Fenton, *Salt of the Earth: An Informal Portrait of Richard Cardinal Cushing*; and the oral history of Francis X. Morrissey at the JFK Presidential Library. Chester Bowles's diary note that JFK "lacks a genuine sense of conviction" was from David Halberstam, *The Best and Brightest*. Billings's comment about "how right the old man had been" was found in Collier and Horowitz, *The Kennedys*; and repeated with further context and background provided by Michael Beschloss, *The Crisis Years*. Shriver's reaction to his children being shown paramilitary techniques came from Harris Wofford, *Of Kennedys and Kings*. Richard Helms's quote was in Richard Reeves, *President Kennedy: Profile of Power*. Thomas Merton's view after the Cuban missile crisis was in "Nuclear War and Christian Responsibility, *Commonweal*, February 9, 1962. JFK's thoughts of "all the innocent children" came from Theodore C. Sorensen, *Kennedy*. RFK's "very bloodcurdling" comment of a nuclear death toll was mentioned in his oral history for the JFK Presidential Library. JFK's comment about "a full life," his reaction to the U-2 plane shot down and the "Last Supper" comment were found in the David Powers files at the JFK Library. Norman Cousins's actions during the crisis were detailed in Norman Cousins, "The Improbable Triumvirate," *Saturday Review*, October 30, 1971. Cogley's actions were recalled in Cogley's oral history at JFK Library. Bobby Kennedy's comment during crisis showdown that "my brother's got to be able to live with himself" is recalled by George Ball in Jean Stein and George Plimpton, *American Journey: The Times of Robert Kennedy*. Cushing's recollection of JFK's concerns about nuclear war were in Joseph Dever, *Cushing of Boston: A Candid Portrait*. The St. Stephen's exchange between JFK and Powers was recalled in Michael Beschloss, *The Crisis Years*. After the Cuban missile crisis, JFK's characterization of Khrushchev and Russian officials as "like the gangsters that both of us had dealt with" came from RFK's oral hsitory at the JFK Presidential Library. The attorney general's "Catholic conscience" during the Cuban missile crisis was remembered in Murray Kempton, "His Catholic Conscience," *Newsday*, June 3, 1993. The president's quip "This is the night I should go to the theater" was repeated in *Robert Kennedy, Thirteen Days*.

Chapter Twenty-Eight: Conversion and Subversion

The excerpt from JFK's June 28 address before the Irish Dail was recorded in *Public Papers of the Presidents*. JFK's 1956 speech about Vietnam was published in John F. Kennedy, "America's Stake in Vietnam," *Vital Speeches*, August 1, 1956. Edmund Gullion's recollection was in Richard Reeves, *President Kennedy: A Profile in Power*. Roger Hilsman's quote came from "The Cold War, Episode 11- Vietnam," CNN, December 1998. Cardinal Spellman's relationship with Diem and Vietnam was discussed in John Cooney, *The American Pope: The Life and Times of Francis Cardinal Spellman*; and to a lesser extent in Robert I. Gannon, S.J., *The Cardinal Spellman Story*. The first quote from Graham Greene was repeated in Cooney's book; the second comment came from David Halberstam, *The Best and the Brightest*. Neil Sheehan's description of Diem was from *A Bright Shining Lie: John Paul Vann and America in Vietnam*. Bobby Kennedy's recollection that his brother "felt that he had a strong, overwhelming reason for being in Vietnam" was in his oral history for the JFK Library. McGeorge Bundy's Brahmin heritage was detailed in Halberstam's book. The reaction of Kennedy and Hilsman to Diem's death was cited in Ken Hughes, "JFK and the Fall of Diem," *Boston Globe Magazine*, October 24, 1999. Bishop Thuc's later excommunication was reported in Nancy Frazier, "Viet Prelate Excommunicated," *Chicago Catholic*, April 15, 1983. Mike Forrestal's reaction was recorded in Herbert S. Parmet, *JFK: The Presidency of John F. Kennedy*. JFK's reaction to Mansfield's changed view of Vietnam was recalled in Kenneth P. O'Donnell and David F. Powers, with Joe McCarthy, *Johnny, We Hardly Knew Ye; Memories of John Fitzgerald Kennedy*.

Chapter Twenty-Nine: The Two Johns

The description of Jacqueline Kennedy's trip to the Vatican and Pope John XXIII's response was described in "Man of the Year," *Time*, January 4, 1963; "President's Wife Received by Pope," *New York Times*, March 11, 1962; with further context from "JFK to the Vatican," *America*, June 1, 1963. POAU's 1962 survey of Roman Catholics in new federal posts with Kennedy's presidency was reported in "POAU Defends Kennedy Against Bias Charges," *Christian Century*, May 16, 1962. Robert Kennedy's assessment of his brother's position on church and state issue was mentioned in RFK oral history for JFK Presidential Library. Blanshard's secret White House meeting was cited in Theodore C. Sorensen, *Kennedy*; during interview with author, however, Sorensen couldn't remember details of the meeting. The comment about Kennedy's difficulty with Catholic leaders on church and state issues was mentioned in "Church and President," *America*, January 18, 1962. Further context was provided by Fletcher Knebel, "The Bishops vs. Kennedy," *Look*, May 23, 1961. "He was bending over backwards" comment was from Francis Hurley oral history at JFK Presidential Library. Kennedy's efforts on church-related issues in the Senate was partly documented in James MacGregor Burns, *John Kennedy: A Political Profile*. Hochwalt's view was cited in Fletcher Knebel's article. JFK's quip "it hasn't got a prayer" repeated in Gerald Gardner, *All the Presidents' Wits: The Power of Presidential Humor*. JFK Gridiron Club dinner quip about the Pope's note: "Pack!" was mentioned in Theodore C. Sorensen, *Kennedy*, and provided further context in author's interview with Sorensen. John XXIII's sweeping out of Pope Pius XII's old guard was detailed in Paul I. Murphy, *La Popessa*; Paul Johnson, *Pope John XXIII*; and John Cooney, *The American Pope*. Cogley's assessment of John XXIII's tenure came from his signed July 12, 1963, *Commonweal* editorial. "You Protestants are always building him up" mentioned in John Henry Cutler, *Cardinal Cushing of Boston*. JFK's comment "As a Catholic, I am proud of it" was repeated in Joseph Roddy, "Pope John: The Astonishing Catholic Pontiff," *Look*, July 2, 1963. John Courtney Murray and his impact on the Catholic Church was disccused in a cover story in *Time*, Dec. 12, 1960; with further context provided by John Courtney Murray, S.J., *We Hold These Truths*; Russell Hittinger, "The Catholic Theology of John Courtney Murray," *Weekly Standard*, January 4, 1999; and Charles R. Morris, *American Catholic*. John XXIII's comment about the Roman Curia ("They are men of zeal, I am sure, but they are not running the church") was in "The Papacy—Vatican Revolutionary," *Time*, June 7, 1963. "The grace of martyrdom has been given to the intellectual" came from "Roman Catholics: Clear It with the Vatican," *Time*, September 20, 1963. Küng's comment that Pope John XXIII and John Kennedy "embodied our hope" was in James Carroll, "A Theologian Who Took Up the Torch in the Quest for World Peace," *Boston Globe*, February 23, 1999. Cushing's calling his pope and his president the "two great Johns" was repeated in John Henry Cutler, *Cardinal Cushing of Boston,* from which Cushing comment about Vatican II was also taken. Cushing's ecumenical impact on Boston was in Thomas H. O'Connor, *Boston Catholics*. Kennedy's response that Pope John's encyclical "makes me proud to be a Catholic" came from Joseph Dever, *Cushing of Boston: A Candid Portrait*. Cushing's embracing "the new spirit of Pope John XXIII" and his impact on the American church was analyzed in "Catholicism in the US," *Time*, August 21, 1964, which also detailed his friendship with Kennedy. Cushing's recollection of "Irish need not apply" signs was recalled in John H. Fenton, *Salt of the Earth: An Informal Portrait of Richard Cardinal Cushing*. Robert Kennedy's assessment of Cushing's closeness to JFK was in RFK's oral history at the Kennedy Library. JFK and Cushing in Rome was described in "Catholicism in the U.S.," *Time*, August 21, 1964. The impact of Kennedy and the Pope's time assessed by Hannah Arendt was quoted in Xavier Rynne, "Letter from Vatican City," *New Yorker*, January 18, 1964.

Chapter Thirty: Doing the Right Thing

The Bobby Kennedy–James Baldwin encounter was recounted in several sources, including "Kennedy and Baldwin: The Gulf," *Newsweek*, June 3, 1963; C. David Heymann, *RFK: A Candid Biography of Robert Kennedy*; James W. Hilty, *Robert Kennedy, Brother Protector*; Evan Thomas, *Robert Kennedy: His Life*; Jean Stein and George Plimpton, *American Journey: The Times of Robert Kennedy*; and "Mortalized," *New Yorker*, February 13, 1971. Robert Kennedy's own account, in his oral history for the JFK Presidential Library, interestingly doesn't include the Irish-Negro analogies mentioned in other versions. RFK's statement that in growing up the Kennedys "didn't lie awake at nights worrying about it (civil rights)" was taken from his oral history for the JFK Presidential Library. King's assessment of Kennedy's personal contact with Negroes came from his oral history for the JFK Library. The 1959 *Jet* survey was quoted in Simeon Booker, "How JFK Surpassed Abraham Lincoln," *Ebony*, February 1964. JFK's compromise on a 1957 civil rights bill described as "a profile in cowardice" cited in James MacGregor Burns, *John Kennedy: A Political Profile*. King's recollection of his father's "holdback" and other black ministers in the South in supporting a Catholic was also recalled in King's oral history. Slightly different versions of the same anecdote about Kennedy's reaction to King's father appeared in Murray Kempton, "Ashes of the Kennedy

Legend," *Newsday*, June 5, 1991; and Theodore C. Sorensen, *Kennedy*. Wofford's recollections come
from his 1980 book, *Of Kennedys and Kings,* and in an interview with the author. Further details
and context were provided by Wofford and John Seigenthaler's comments in Jean Stein and
George Plimpton, *American Journey: The Times of Robert Kennedy*; "The Competent American,"
Look, November 17, 1964; and the oral histories of Wofford, Rev. Theodore Hesburgh and Louis
Martin at the JFK Presidential Library. Bobby's recollection of Ribicoff's reasons for declining the
attorney general position came from his oral history. JFK's "Don't worry about Bobby" came from
Peter Collier and David Horowitz, *The Kennedys: An American Drama*. Alice Roosevelt
Longworth's full quote ("I see Jack in older years as the nice little rosy-faced old Irishman with the
clay pipe in his mouth, a rather nice broth of a boy. Not Bobby. Bobby could have been a revolu-
tionary priest') was in Jean Stein and George Plimpton, *American Journey: The Times of Robert
Kennedy*. RFK telling the Apostolic Delegate to the US that the "most racist institue in the South
is my own church" was recalled by Rev. Richard McSorley in an interview with author. The reac-
tion of white voters to Kennedy's civil rights program was documented in "Is Kennedy in Political
Trouble at Home?" *U.S. News and World Report*, July 8, 1963; "Politics: JFK's Lost Votes," *Newsweek*,
October 21, 1963; "Now a New Worry for Kennedy: The White Vote in '64," *U.S. News and World
Report*, September 9, 1963. RFK's conversations with his brother about whether their civil rights
actions were "the right thing to do" were recalled in his oral history for the JFK Presidential
Library. Further context was provided by Taylor Branch, *Parting The Waters: America in the King Years,
1954–63*. After King's speech, JFK tells him, "I have a dream" recounted in "The Competent
American," *Look*, November 17, 1964. Belford Lawson's recollection was from his oral history at
the JFK Library. Harry Golden's comments were in a 1964 article, "Mr. Kennedy and the
Negroes," contained in *The Kennedy Reader*, edited by Jay Davis. RFK's introductory comments
were in the 1964 re-edition of John F. Kennedy, *A Nation of Immigrants*, contained as well in 1986
edition with John Roche's introduction. Chilton Williamson Jr.'s comment were in Chilton
Williamson Jr., *The Immigration Mystique*.

Chapter Thirty-One: In the Springtime

Dorothy Tubridy's encounters with the Kennedys, and specifically learning of the 1963 presidential trip to Ireland, were recalled in an interview in Dublin with the author and in her earlier
oral history for the JFK Library. Kennedy's insistence on going to Ireland was recalled in Kenneth
P. O'Donnell and David F. Powers, with Joe McCarthy, *Johnny, We Hardly Knew Ye; Memories of
John Fitzgerald Kennedy*. Powers recollection of JFK's preparation for the trip were recalled in the
Dave Power papers on file at the JFK Library, while his comments about Kennedy ("he's getting
so Irish, pretty soon he'll be speaking with a brogue") appeared in Arthur Mitchell, *JFK and His
Irish Heritage*. "To what do you attribute your success?" recalled in author's interview with
Tubridy. McCloskey and his encounter with Mary Kennedy Ryan were recalled in Dave Powers
papers at JFK Presidential Library, in author's interview with Mary Ann Ryan, and the oral his-
tory of former New Ross Mayor Andrew Minihan at the Kennedy library. JFK's memories of
Robert Burrell and the effort to finding him in 1963 were recalled in Joseph Roddy,
"Ireland: The Kennedy Cult," *Look,* November 17, 1964. JFK's "Irish Need not Apply" comment
in Dunganstown recalled in Thomas Kiernan oral history for JFK Library. Further details of JFK
at New Ross and Dunganstown were recorded in "President Kennedy Visits Ireland" file at the
National Archives of Ireland in Dublin. Details about Mother Clement were from "Our Golden
Haired Bit of Graduer," *Biatas* – The Tillage Farmer, October 1988, contained in the Dave
Powers papers at the JFK Presidential Library; and in "Kennedy Visits Convent to See Cousin, a
Nun," *New York Times,* June 28, 1963. JFK visit with cousins came from Tom Wicker, "Kennedy
Sees the Cousin Who Didn't Catch the Boat," *New York Times*, June 28, 1963. De Valera's greeting
in Gaelic and his reference to JFK's ancenrtal ties to Brian Boru and the "great Cinneide Clans of
the Dal gChais" was repeated in J.F. Brennan, *The Evolution of Everyman*. Further details about De
Valera and JFK's visit were in Sydney Gruson, "Kennedy Praises Ireland as Model to Small
Nations," *New York Times*, June 29, 1963, "Ireland—Lifting the Green Curtain," *New York Times
Magazine*, July 12, 1963; and Sydney Gruson, "Dublin Acclaims Kennedy As One Returning
Home," *New York Times*, June 27, 1963. The oral histories of Amb. Thomas Kiernan and Sean
Lemass at the JFK Presidential Library, as well as their notes and letters in a file about JFK visit at

the National Archives of Ireland, provided many details about the various activities of the trip and the private conversations about Ireland's partition. JFK's reaction at Arbour Hill and other details of the trip were recalled in Joseph Roddy, "They Cried the Rain Down That Night," *Look*, November 17, 1964. Also see, "President Vows a Return to Erin," *New York Times*, June 30, 1963; "The Kennedy Homestead," *Newsweek*, July 1, 1963; and "Kennedy's Trip—The Mood and the Flavor," *New York Times*, June 30, 1963. Mary Ann Ryan and Patrick Kennedy also shared their rememberances of JFK's visit with the author. Further details and context were provided by Joseph Roddy, "Ireland: The Kennedy Cult," *Look*, November 17, 1964; an unbylined account of JFK's trip in the July 5, 1963, edition of *Time*; "Journal of a Psuedo-Event," *New Yorker*, July 13, 1963; Tom Wicker, "Ireland Prepares for Kennedy Visit Thursday," *New York Times*, June 23, 1963; "When Kennedy Went 'Home' to Ireland," *U.S. News and World Report*, July 8, 1963; JFK's remarks and speeches in Ireland recorded in *Public Papers of the Presidents*; Maurice N. Hennessy, *I'll Come Back in the Springtime: John F. Kennedy and the Irish*; Pete Hamill, "JFK: The Real Thing," *New Yorker*, November 28, 1988; Pete Hamill, "Book Review," *National Review*, August 2000; "Two Presidents Greet 2,000 Guests," *Irish Press*, June 28, 1963; "And President Kennedy Enjoys Every Minute," *Irish Press*, June 28, 1963; "Kennedy's Irish Kin," *Life* Magazine, July 1963; Theodore C. Sorensen, *Kennedy;* and the oral history of Robert Kennedy at the JFK Library. Sen. Edward Kennedy's recollection of his brother's reaction to the Ireland trip was contained in written response to questions posed by the author. Amb. Jean Kennedy Smith's recollection of her 1963 trip with JFK were recalled in a telephone conversation for this book.

Chapter Thirty-Two: The Ritual of Mourning

The opening verse came from William Butler Yeats' "Under Ben Bulben." JFK's visits with his infirmed father were recalled in Robert Kennedy's oral history for the JFK Presidential Library. "He's the one who made all this possible, and look at him now" was from Kenneth P. O'Donnell and David F. Powers, with Joe McCarthy, *Johnny, We Hardly Knew Ye; Memories of John Fitzgerald Kennedy*. JFK's comment about his older brother's death as "a completeness . . . the completeness of perfection" came from John F. Kennedy, *As We Remember Joe*. JFK's instruction to "close the coffin when I die" was recalled in Francis X. Morrissey oral history for the JFK Library. Seeger's poem was cited in Theodore C. Sorensen, *Kennedy*. Rev. Andrew Greeley's observations on Irish fatalism were described in Andrew Greeley, *The Irish Americans*, and further discussed in an interview with the author. Mass cards and other correspondence with religious references following the deaths of Joe Kennedy Jr. and Kathleen Kennedy were contained in several files of the JPK papers examined at the Kennedy library. Kiernan's gift and poem for the christening of JFK Jr. were recalled in Theodore C. Sorensen, *Kennedy*, and in Kiernan's oral history for the JFK Library. Laura Bergquist Knebel's remark about the "tribal" quality to JFK were in her oral history at the JFK Library. Details about Jackie's fifth pregnancy, including an earlier miscarriage and a baby stillborn by cesarian in 1956, were reported in "Big Year for the Clan," *Time*, April 26, 1963; also see, "JFK: Chipper at 46, Pointing to '64," *Newsweek*, June 3, 1963. The death of baby Patrick Bouvier Kennedy was detailed in *Time*, August 16, 1963; Joseph Dever, *Cushing of Boston: A Candid Portrait;* John H. Fenton, *Salt of the Earth: An Informal Portrait of Richard Cardinal Cushing;* Christopher P. Andersen, *Jackie after Jack;* "Cardinal Cushing Remembers: 'Twice, I saw Jack Kennedy Cry,'" *Look*, November 17, 1964; John Henry Cutler, *Cardinal Cushing of Boston*; Russell W. Gibbons, "The Real Christianity of John F. Kennedy," *St. Joseph Magazine*, April 1965; "The Family in Mourning," *Time*, December 6, 1963; and Francis X. Morrissey oral history for JFK Library. Jacqueline Kennedy's recollection of Dallas before ("Hot, wild. . . . The sun was so strong in our faces"), during and after the assassination were recalled in Theodore H. White, *In Search of History*. The actions of the *Dallas Morning News* were discussed in "May God Forgive Dallas," *Newsweek*, December 9, 1963. John Kennedy's election brings about a "thaw" in antagonism between Protestants and Catholics according to Gallup poll just before his death and detailed in *Redbook*, March 1964, including comment by Rev. Eugene Carson Blake. Rev. Oscar Huber's recollection of last rites at hospital were described in his oral history for the JFK Library. Numerous books described the Kennedy family's reaction to the assassination, including Arthur Schlesinger, *Robert Kennedy and His Times*; Laurence Leamer, *The Kennedy Women*; Peter Collier and David Horowitz, *The Kennedys: An American Drama*; and William Manchester, *Death of a President*. The Irish-wake atmosphere after JFK's death was described by Chuck Spalding in Christopher P. Andersen, *Jackie after Jack*, which included Lawford's comment. Jackie's plea ("I don't care. They can all stand in the streets") was recalled in John Henry Cutler, *Cardinal Cushing of Boston*. Bobby's cry, "Why, God, why?" was recalled in Charles Spalding's oral history for the JFK Library. Jackie's awarness of the Lincoln funeral was discussed in "The Family in Mourning," *Time*, December 6, 1963; the public's own connections between Lincoln and Kennedy's death was cited in "A Compendium of Curious Coincidences," *Time*, August 21, 1964. "His last speech on race relations" was from King quoted in Claybourne Carson, ed., *The Autobiography of Martin Luther King Jr.* Powers recollection of DeValera's reaction to JFK's death was recalled in the Dave Powers papers at the JFK Library. Frank O'Connor assessment of JFK appeared in Dublin's *Sunday Independent* and was repeated in Maurice N. Hennessy, *I'll Come Back in the Springtime: John F. Kennedy and the Irish*. Further details and context were provided by "In Her Time of Trial," *Newsweek*, December 9, 1963; and "In their Own Words," *Dallas Morning News*, November 21, 2000.

Part V: The Emerald Thread

St. Luke quotation is from the New Testament of the Bible. (Several slight variations of this verse can be found in different Bible translations.)

Jean Kennedy Smith's quote ("Our mother taught us . . . ") came from Laura Blumenfeld, "A Green Light at the White House," *Washington Post*, March 18, 1995.

Chapter Thirty-Three: A Living Wound

The scenes of tennis and conversation between Jacqueline Kennedy and Rev. Richard McSorley, S.J., are based primarily on the author's interviews with McSorley, Kennedy's correspondence with McSorley, and McSorley's own diary notes contained in his unprocessed papers at the Georgetown University Library, Special Collections Division. These papers were made available to the author with McSorley's expressed permission. Rose Kennedy's letter to McSorley is in the same personal McSorley papers. Other background material included Richard T. McSorley, *The More, the Merrier: The Story of a Mother of Fifteen Children*; Arthur Jones, "McSorley and His Famous Friend Go Way Back; Georgetown University's Richard McSorley," *National Catholic Reporter*, July 28, 1995; Colman McCarthy, "The McSorley Connection," *Washington Post*, October 16, 1992; James Di Liberto, "Civil Disobedience," *Hoya of Georgetown University*, Jnauary 21, 2000; Mary Jordan, "Minister Waging War for Peace and Justice," *Washington Post*, January 7, 1991. "I am a living wound" comes from Jacqueline Kennedy interview in Laura Bergquist, *Look*, November 17, 1964; also, Jacqueline Kennedy, "The Words JFK Loved Best," *Look*, November 17, 1964. Jackie's "rage at God" was described in Murray Kempton, "A Rage Greater Than Grief," *Atlantic Monthly*, May 1967. Jackie enrolling Caroline at the Convent of the Sacred Heart School on East 91st Street was reported in "Caroline Enters a School in City," *New York Times*, September 16, 1964. Bobby's urging to "cheer up" at the Justice Department was described in "The Family in Mourning," *Time*, December 6, 1963. Jacqueline Kennedy's undated poem "Meanwhile in Massachusetts Jack Kennedy dreamed . . ." was contained in the JPK papers at the JFK Presidential Library. Jacqueline Kennedy's 1967 letter to Mary Ryan about visiting the Kennedy Homestead was provided to the author for review by Patrick Grennan and Mary Ann Ryan during interviews with them. Jackie's marriage to Onassis and the church's reaction was discussed in Christopher P. Andersen, *Jackie after Jack*; David E. Koskoff, *Joseph P. Kennedy: A Life and Times*; and John Henry Cutler, *Cardinal Cushing of Boston*.

Chapter Thirty-Four: The Awful Grace of God

Robert Kennedy's 1964 speech to the Friendly Sons of Ireland, including the recitation of the poem about Owen Roe O'Neill, was recalled in Edwin O. Guthman, *We Band of Brothers*; Edwin Guthman and Jeffrey Shulman, eds., *Robert Kennedy: In His Own Words*; and in author's interview with Guthman. Manchester's anecdote about the poem was described in William R. Manchester, *One Brief Shining Moment: Remembering Kennedy*. RFK escorting Jackie to his brother's graveside where she leaves a sprig of shamrocks was described in "Shamrock Left at Kennedy Grave," *New York Times*, March 18, 1964. LBJ's speech to the Friendly Sons in New York was reported in Felix Belair Jr., "President Addresses Friendly Sons of St. Patrick," *New York Times*, March 18, 1964. The racist response to a NAACP float in Boston's St. Patrick's Day parade was also recorded in the same issue of the *Times*. Robert Kennedy's request to his older children to express the significance of their uncle's death to the United States was recalled by Michael Kennedy in "Robert Kennedy—Tribute," *People*, June 6, 1988, as were quotes in this chapter from Adam Walinsky, Anthony Lewis and Michael Novak. William vanden Heuval's quote came from Robert S. Bird, "At Home with the Heir Apparent," *Saturday Evening Post*, August 25, 1967. Pierre Salinger's recollection of the Florida football game was in Tom Mathews, "Remembering Bobby," *Newsweek*, May 9, 1988. RFK as "too Catholic, too physical, too combative" came from Jack Newfield, *Robert Kennedy—A Memoir*. Roy Cohn's near fisticuffs with RFK on the McCarthy Senate Committee was recounted in Roy Cohn, *McCarthy*, 1968. RFK's claim that his brother told Jackie that "Lyndon Johnson was incapable of telling the truth" came from RFK's oral history at the Kennedy library, as did the long exchange about LBJ's alleged theories of "divine retribution" at play in the JFK assassination. In the 1964 Senate election, the opposition of James Baldwin, I.F. Stone and Gore Vidal regarding Kennedy and his characterization as an "Irish Roy Cohn" was reported in Jack Newfield, "The Bobby Phenomenon," *Nation*, November 14, 1966. The observations of Jimmy Breslin and John V. Lindsay were recorded in Jimmy Breslin, "The Music Is Different," *New York Herald Tribune*, October 18, 1964. RFK's "kind of moral righteousness, rooted in a primitive Catholicism" was recalled in Richard Goodwin, *Remembering America*, Boston: Little, Brown, 1988. The comment of Herman Badillo and Manfred Ohrenstein came from C. David Heymann, *RFK: A Candid Biography of Robert F. Kennedy*. RFK as a "tribune for the underclass" was described in Arthur M. Schlesinger Jr., *Robert Kennedy and His Times*. The Kennedys tracing "the same narrative arc as their church" came from James Carroll, "The Catholic Side of Camelot," *Boston Globe*, December 30, 1997. Guthman's recollections were from interview with author as were those expressed by Joe Gargan and Kathleen Kennedy Townsend. RFK description as "so pure Irish" came from Murray Kempton, "Pure Irish—Robert F. Kennedy," *New Republic*, February 15, 1964, while Kempton's "piece of faith" comment was quoted in Schlesinger's *Robert Kennedy and His Times*. RFK's quote about "the innocent suffer—how can that be possible and God be just" was mentioned in Evan Thomas, *Robert Kennedy: His Life*. RFK's view of liberals as "too soft" was described in David Halberstam, "Ask Not What Ted Sorensen Can Do for You," *Harper's*, November 1969. RFK's comment about the *Times* ("their idea of a good story is 'More nuns leave convents than ever before.'") was quoted in Jack Newfield, *Robert Kennedy: A Memoir*.

Chapter Thirty-Five: The Politics of Outsiders

Robert Kennedy's trip to South Africa and his reaction to it was described in Evan Thomas, *Robert Kennedy: His Life*; Arthur M. Schlesinger Jr., *Robert Kennedy and His Times*; John Henry Cutler, *Cardinal Cushing of Boston*; "Robert Kennedy Recalled," *National Catholic Reporter*, July 3, 1998; and commented upon in "Scaling Mt. Kennedy," Hendrik Hertzberg, *New Yorker*, November 20, 2000. The letter-writer questioning the often-told "No Irish need Apply" anecdote used by the Kennedys was detailed in James W. Hilty, *Robert Kennedy, Brother Protector*. RFK reinventing the JFK legacy into "the buried spirit of radical discontent" was from Murray Kempton, "The Emperor's Kid Brother," *Esquire*, July 1968. RFK's efforts with Chavez and the farm workers were described in Jack Newfield, "The Bobby Phenomenon," *Nation*, November 14, 1966; "Kennedy on Latin America," *Commonweal*, June 3, 1966; Murray Kempton, "His Catholic Conscience," *Newsday*, June 3, 1993; and the oral history of Cesar Chavez for the Kennedy library. The *Times's* 1964 review of *A Nation of Immigrants* noting that "John Kennedy was always aware that he was part of the migration" came from "Books of the Times," *New York Times*, October 8, 1964. RFK raising the immigration issue in the 1964 Senate campaign was detailed in C.P. Trussell, "New Alien Quotas," *New York Times*, July 23, 1964; "Kennedy Pledges Aid to Northeast," *New York Times*, September 16, 1964; "Kennedy Assails Immigration Curb," *New York Times*, October 6, 1964; and "Goldwater Scored on Minority Attack," *New York Times*, October 10, 1964. The effort by the surviving Kennedy brothers to pass the 1965 Immigration Act was recorded in "President Ask Ending of Quotas for Immigrants," *New York Times*, January 14, 1965, an editorial "I lift My

Lamp," *New York Times*, January 14, 1965; "Kennedy Predicts Approval," *New York Times*, June 11, 1965; "Immigration Law Praised by DAR," *New York Times*, September 15, 1964; "Kennedy Backs Immigration Bill," *New York Times*, September 21, 1965; and Cabell Phillips, "Immigration Bill Passes Senate...," *New York Times, September 23, 1965. The long-term consequences of the 1965 bill were discussed in "Out of Control Immigration," *Foreign Affairs*, Sept–Oct 2000. Sen. Edward M. Kennedy's comments about the 1965 immigration legislation and its impact were in written response to the author's questions to him. Nicholas De B. Katzenbach's exchange with Sen. Sam Erving was described in Andrew Kopkind, "New Immigration Policy," *New Republic*, February 27, 1965. "Nativism is far from dead in the United States" was cited in Robert H. Amundson, "Breakthrough in Immigration," *America*, January 29, 1966; and Ernest Van Den Haag's comments were in "More Immigration?" *National Review*, September 21, 1965. RFK's attendance at Cardinal Spellman's funeral and his remark ("all the way up to Absalom, Absalom") was recalled in Jack Newfield, *Robert Kennedy: A Memoir*. Spellman's reference to the Vietnam conflict as "Christ's war" was cited in "Spellman's View on War Called Outrageous...," *New York Times*, February 5, 1967. The church's Declaration on Religious Liberty as well as the twenty-six representatives from American Catholic universities issuing a 1967 "declaration of independence" from the American hierarchy were described in Eric O. Hanson, *Catholic Church in World Politics*. RFK's admission regarding fault about Vietnam was repeated in Ronald Steel, *In Love with Night*. RFK's speech at Marymount concerning bombing of North Vietnam was recalled in Jack Newfield, *Robert Kennedy: A Memoir*. RFK's biblical reference "To the Vietnamese, however, it must often seem the fulfillment of the prophecy of Saint John the Divine" was recorded in Douglas Ross, *Robert F. Kennedy: Apostle of Change*. RFK writing down remark by Camus about evil and comparison to St. Augustine was mentioned in Arthur M. Schlesinger Jr., *Robert Kennedy and His Times*. Goodwin's observation of Eugene McCarthy as "a reverential Catholic but not in the way most Irish are Catholic" appeared in Richard Goodwin, *Remembering America*. RFK's dislike of Gene McCarthy (who "felt he should have been the first Catholic President just because he knew more St. Thomas Aquinas than my brother") was recalled in Jack Newfield, *Robert Kennedy: A Memoir*. McCarthy's reaction to RFK's entry into 1968 race was in Tom Wicker, "Kennedy to Make 3 Primary Races; Attacks Johnson," *New York Times, March 17, 1968. Michael Novak's noticed differences between Bobby Kennedy and Gene McCarthy were described in Jean Stein and George Plimpton, *American Journey: The Times of Robert Kennedy*. "Bobby had an inferiority complex" came from author's interview with McCarthy. RFK's view of himself as "pure Shanty Irish" comes from Jack Newfield, *Robert Kennedy: A Memoir*. The angry response at the St. Patrick Day parade among some Irish to RFK's candidacy was in Murray Schumach, "Kennedy Parades to Mixed Chorus," *New York Times*, March 17, 1968. Kempton's telegram to Ted Kennedy was recalled in Richard Goodwin, *Remembering America*. POAU's criticism of RFK and McCarthy on their failure to take an "unequivocal" stand on separation of church and state was recalled in John Tracy Ellis, *American Catholicism*. Against Nixon in a proposed 1968 race, the Harris poll says Bobby only gets 42 percent of the Protestant vote as reported by Jack Newfield, "The Bobby Phenomenon," *Nation*, November 14, 1966. RFK's comment "The deprived if you like, they are for me" was recorded in Murray Kempton, "The Emperor's Kid Brother," *Esquire*, July 1968. Arthur M. Schlesinger recalls Jackie's fear that "they'll do to him what they did to Jack" was in Jean Stein and George Plimpton, *American Journey: The Times of Robert Kennedy*. RFK's view that "Tragedy is a tool for the living to gain wisdom, not a guide by which to live" comes from his speech at Kansas State University as recalled in "Robert Kennedy Recalled," *National Catholic Reporter*, July 3, 1998. The racial and ethnic breakdown of the 1968 California primary results were in Lawrence E. Davies, "New Yorker Captures Lead Over McCarthy in Late Tabulation," *New York Times*, June 5, 1968, a story eclipsed by news of RFK's assassination in the same late editions. Romain Gary's recollection of RFK conversation appeared in Associated Press, "French Writer Recalls Kennedy Premonition," *New York Times*, June 6, 1968. Hosea Williams's comment came from Jean Stein and George Plimpton, *American Journey: The Times of Robert Kennedy*. RFK's comment "that fellow Harvey Lee...Lee Harvey; he set something loose in this country" was reported in Jeff Greenfield, "RFK: The Politics That Might Have Been," *New Yorker*, June 5, 1978. The scene inside the hotel after RFK was shot was described in Jack Newfield, *Robert Kennedy: A Memoir*. Archbishop Terence J. Cooke's eulogy for RFK was quoted in Conrad Cherry, "Two American Sacred Ceremonies: Their Implications for the Study of Religion in America," *American Quarterly*, Winter 1969; "the terrible culminating hour of all the dreaded apprehensions of almost five years" was in Norman Cousins, "Impression's At St. Patrick's," *Saturday Review*, June 22, 1968. Ethel Kennedy's instructions about the Mass were recorded in Jean Stein and George Plimpton, *American Journey: The Times of Robert Kennedy*, which also included the recollections of Frank Mankiewicz, Michael Harrington, Geraldine Brooks Joseph Alsop of the funeral train ride. "Family was clearly the leit-motif" came from "Saturday June 8 in Manhattan . . . ," *America*, June 22, 1968. Calls for Teddy to assume his brother's mantle in the 1968 campaign included an editorial in the *Nation*, June 17, 1968. Tom Hayden's thoughts of the stigmata were in "Robert Kennedy—Tribute," *People,* June 6, 1988.

Further details and context were provided by "Dogged by Fate," *Nation*, June 17, 1968; Marshall Frady,"The Transformation of Bobby Kennedy," *New York Review of Books*, October 12, 1978; "Notes and Comment," *New Yorker*, August 3, 1968; Peter Lisagor, "Portrait of a Man Emerging from Shadows," *New York Times Magazine,* July 19, 1964; Anthony Lewis, "What Drives Bobby Kennedy," *New York Times Magazine,* April 7, 1963; Garry Wills, "The Kennedys in the King Years," *New York Review of Books*, November 10, 1988; Michael Barone, "We've Been Here Before," AEI Lecture Series, October 4, 1999; Alan Wolfe, "Liberalism and Catholicism," *American Prospect,* January 31, 2000; James Carroll, "The Catholic Side of Camelot," *Boston Globe*, December 30, 1997; Ronald Steel, "The Kennedy Fantasy," *New York Review of Books*, November 19, 1970; Martin Merzer, "Remembering RFK," *Orange County Register*, June 6, 1993; "Senator Kennedy Crosses the Color Line," *Commonweal*, July 22, 1966; Murray Kempton, "Remembering RFK," *Newsday*, March 11, 1993; "Mortalized," *New Yorker*, February 13, 1971.

Chapter Thirty-Six: The Ghosts of Camelot

Don DeLillo's comment appeared in Vince Passaro, "Dangerous Don DeLillo," *New York Times*, May 19, 1991. Judith Campbell Exner's comments were in Seymour Hersh, *The Dark Side of Camelot.* "The Exner account was a sort of triple whammy" was from Tom Wicker, "Kennedy Without End, Amen," *Esquire*, June 1977. Theodore White said Jackie Kennedy "regarded me as one of Kennedy's 'scholar' friends rather than an 'Irish' or 'swinging' friend" in Theodore H. White, *In Search of History.* "He was a story-book President" described in James Reston, "What Was Killed Was Not only the President," *New York Times Magazine*, November 15, 1964. The public's identification with JFK image was analyzed in Henry Fairlie, "Camelot Revisited," *Harper's*, January 1973. Tom Wicker's discussion of the press's relationship with JFK, as well as his own conversation with Richard Scammon about the significance of the 1960 election, was mentioned in Tom Wicker, "Kennedy Without End, Amen," *Esquire*, June 1977. Wicker's admission that "Bobby Kennedy was an easy man to fall in love with... if you were a reporter, and too many people did" was cited in "Mortalized," *New Yorker*, February 13, 1971. Sander Vanocur of NBC was sent a January 31, 1961, letter from Joe Kennedy suggesting the loss of an "exclusive" interview with Jackie Kennedy if favorable coverage wasn't provided, contained in the JPK papers of the Kennedy presidential library. Schlesinger's criticism of ethnocentricity was in Arthur M. Schlesinger Jr., *The Disuniting of America: Reflections on a Multicultural Society.* The ritual-like telling of the Kennedy Camelot story as a "passion play" was observed in Gore Vidal, "The Holy Family," *Esquire*, April 1967. The Ralph Ginsburg case was discussed in C. David Heymann, *RFK: A Candid Biography.* RFK's comment about "one Senator from the South who had a Negro mistress" could be found on page 311 of his oral history for the JFK Presidential Library. Jackie Kennedy's marriage to Onassis and the church's reaction was detailed in John Henry Cutler, *Cardinal Cushing of Boston*; Laurence Leamer, *The Kennedy Women*; David E. Koskoff, *Joseph P. Kennedy: A Life and Times*; and Christopher P. Andersen, *Jackie after Jack.* Cushing's views on birth control and John Rock were desribed in John Henry Cutler, *Cardinal Cushing of Boston.* JFK's opposition to government policy of encouraging birth control was attributed to the church and Catholic power in "Church and State," *New Republic*, January 25, 1960. A presidential commission on the status of women, started by Kennedy, would call in 1968 for repeal of restrictive abortion laws, described in Karen O'Connor, *No Neutral Ground? Abortion Politics in an Age of Absolutes.* The Kennedys' varying views on abortion were discussed in Laurence Leamer, *The Kennedy Women*; and in the author's interviews with Kathleen Kennedy Townsend. RFK's 1967 encounter with Father Joe DiMaggio at Skidmore College was recounted in Jack Newfield, *Robert Kennedy: A Memoir.* JFK giving Catholics a sense of "arrival" was recalled in Richard John Neuhaus, *The Catholic Moment.* RFK's statement after Ted's plane goes down "there are more of us than there is trouble" came from Marshall Frady, "The Transformation of Bobby Kennedy," *New York Review of Books*, October 12, 1978. The so-called "Kennedy curse" was refuted in Theodore C. Sorensen, "RFK: A Personal Memoir," *Saturday Review*, June 22, 1968. Ted Kennedy's televised Chappaquiddick speech raising and denying the spectre of "whether some awful curse did actually hang over all the Kennedys . . ." was quoted in "The Ghost of Charisma Past," *Esquire*, February 1972. Further discussion about tragic fate and the Kennedys was found in Andrew Greeley, "Leave John Kennedy in Peace," *Christian Century*, November 21, 1973, and Robert F. Drinan, "Grieving We Find Comfort..." *National Catholic Reporter*, July 30, 1999.

Chapter Thirty-Seven: Last Hurrahs

Sen. Edward Kennedy's part in Boston's busing debate during the 1970s was detailed in Thomas H. O'Connor, *The Boston Irish: A Political History*; Adam Clymer, *Edward M. Kennedy: A Biography*; James MacGregor Burns, *Edward Kennedy and the Camelot Legacy*; and particularly Ronald P. Formisano, *Boston Against Busing: Race, Class, and Ethnicity in the 1960s and 1970s*. Ted's comment "Let them say what they want about our people—and we have many faults—they cannot say we are not loyal to our chieftain" was quoted in Clymer's book. Joe Kennedy scolding Morrissey for presuming a judgeship would be "marked" for him was contained in a June 3, 1960, letter in the JPK papers at the JFK Presidential Library. Ted's comment on the Morrissey judgeship—"It's the only thing my father ever asked of me"—was reported in "Is Loyalty Enough?" *Newsweek*, October 18, 1965. Other coverage included "LBJ and Edward Kennedy: Their Nominee Under Fire," *U.S. News and World Report*, October 11, 1965; Arthur Krock's column in *New York Times*, October 1, 1965; and "One for Old Joe," *Newsweek*, October 11, 1965. Ted singing the Irish songs at Ken O'Donnell's wedding was described in Theodore H. White, *In Search of History*. Tubridy's comments were from her oral history and reflected in the author's interview in Dublin. "Ulster is becoming England's Vietnam" came from "Northern Ireland: Off the Deep End," *Time*, November 1, 1971. Ted Kennedy's encouraging telegram to John Hume, leader of the protesting Catholics, that they were not alone was recalled in Paul Routledge, *John Hume: A Biography*. Further details and context were provided by Charles Carlton, *Bigotry and Blood: Documents on the Ulster Troubles*; Edward M. Kennedy, "Ulster Is an International Issue," *Foreign Policy*, September 1973; John Hume, *A New Ireland: Politics, Peace and Reconciliation*; and J. Bowyer Bell, *The Irish Troubles: A Generation of Violence, 1967–1992*. The Four Horsemen are described in Clymer's biography and "The IRA's Angels," *Newsweek*, May 18, 1981. "The smart thing for Ted Kennedy to do is to get out of politics and take care of the kids" was from John Henry Cutler, *Cardinal Cushing of Boston*. "We all know he might be assassinated," Rose says in Lenore Hershey, "Mrs. Kennedy," *Ladies Home Journal*, May 1972. "Because of, uh, what, uh, happened to my brothers, nobody close to you will advise you" came from Ann Taylor Fleming, "The Kennedy Mystique," *New York Times Magazine*, June 17, 1979. The optimistic appeal of a Kennedy campaign was mentioned in Richard Reeves, "The Inevitability of Teddy," *Esquire*, February 13, 1979. Nostalgia as a campaign issue was cited in Joe Klein, "Camelot Collapsing," *New Yorker*, December 24, 1979; and Michael Kramer, "Brooklyn to Teddy: No Irish Need Apply," *New Yorker*, January 28, 1980. Rostenkowski and other Illinois Democrats expressed their views in Edward Walsh, "Chicago Catholics: No Longer a Reliable Voting Bloc," *Washington Post*, February 2, 1980. Ted Kennedy's speech at the 1980 Democratic National Convention was desribed in Pete Hamill, "A Brief, Shining Moment," *New Yorker*, August 25, 1980.

Chapter Thirty-Eight: A Matter of Faith

Rose Kennedy's quote about religious faith came from Lenore Hershey, "Mrs. Kennedy," *Ladies Home Journal*, May 1972. Cushing's talk about tragedy and faith with Rose Kennedy ("If I collapsed, the morale of the family would be lowered") was in John Henry Cutler, *Cardinal Cushing of Boston*. Monsignor Jeremiah O'Mahoney's description of Rose Kennedy's faith recalled in Randy Schultz, "Matriarch of an American Dynasty," *Palm Beach Post*, January 23, 1995. Rose Kennedy's rebuttal to *Times* columnist James Reston, who wrote that JFK did not believe in his Roman Catholic religion, was detailed in Liz Smith, "What Ever Happened to the Kennedys?" *Ladies Home Journal*, January 1977. Ted defined "the family" as the engine of power for the

Kennedys in Ann Taylor Fleming, "The Kennedy Mystique," *New York Times Magazine,* June 17, 1979. Rose was as "zealous" in bringing up the grandchildren as she was with her own children's well-being, described in Edward Kennedy, "My Mother, Rose Kennedy," *Ladies Home Journal,* December 1975. Joseph P. Kennedy II's "desolation" after his father's death was recalled in "Excerpt from the Eulogy," *Cape Cod Times,* January 4, 1998. JFK Jr. criticism of "poster boys for bad behavior" was first cited in his *George* magazine and later recalled in Peter Collier, "A Kennedy Apart," *National Review,* August 9, 1999. "His marriage vow to be faithful had not been honestly made" came from Adam Clymer, *Edward M. Kennedy: A Biography.* Sheila Rauch's dispute over annulment was detailed in Laurence Leamer, *The Kennedy Women.* Ted Kennedy's views on abortion were discussed in Peter Steinfels, "Beliefs," *New York Times,* March 4, 2000; and Clymer's biography. The rise of conservative power after Vatican II was discussed in Alan Wolfe, "Liberalism and Catholicism," *American Prospect,* January 31, 2000. Kennedy's support for Geraldine Ferraro in 1984 was detailed in Eric O. Hanson, *The Catholic Church in World Politics.* Kennedy's meeting with Jerry Falwell was recounted in David Espo, "Kennedy Preaches to Fundamentalist's Flock," Associated Press, October 4, 1983. Kathleen Kennedy Townsend's comments were from her interview with the author; Laurence Leamer, *The Kennedy Women;* and from a speech at the Kennedy Presidential Library in 2000. Robert F. Kennedy Jr.'s comments were in the introduction to Michael Padden, *May the Road Rise to Meet You.* Ted Kennedy's comments about no priests in the family was mentioned in Robert F. Drinan, "Grieving We Find Comfort," *National Catholic Reporter,* July 30, 1999.

Chapter Thirty-Nine: Looking Backward and Forward

"When the Irish came to America . . ." Kathleen Kennedy Townsend's comments from author's interview. RFK's delight that "the Irish legacy has percolated down through my bloodlines" came from Michael Padden, *May the Road Rise to Meet You.* Rep. Patrick Kennedy's speech in Dublin about racism and Irish history came from "Patrick Kennedy Warns on Evils of Racism," *Irish Times,* April 16, 1998. Bridget Dirrane was mentioned in Michael Finlan, "100 Years on, Islander Is Still Praying for Peace," *Irish Times,* November 16, 1994. The story of Paul Hill and his involvement with the Kennedy family was recounted in Tim Pat Coogan, *The Troubles: Ireland's Ordeal 1966–1996 and the Search for Peace;* and Robert Kee, *Trial and Error: The Maguires, the Guildford Pub Bombings and British Justice.* Further coverage that yielded details and further context came from Adam Cohen, "Bobby and Ethel's Brood: The Weight of Legacy," *Time,* January 12, 1998; George Howe Colt, "The Kennedys Third Generation," *Life,* Summer 1997; Andrew Pierce, "Well-Connected Priest Who Knows the Power of the Press," *Times of London,* September 13, 1995; "Paul Hill," *60 Minutes,* CBS News, July 3, 1994; Larry King, "Fifteen Years for a Crime He Didn't Commit," *Larry King Live,* June 14, 1994, Nick Pryer, "Scum, As Kennedy Clan Fly In to Aid Terror Man," *Evening Standard,* February 23, 1994; "Blair Apologises to Guildford Four," *BBC Online,* June 6, 2000; J.D. Podolsky, "In the Name of the Son," *People,* February 14, 1994; Geordie Grieg, "How One of the Guildford Four Met and Fell in Love with a Kennedy," *Evening Standard,* January 19, 1993; "'Family Ties' Paul Hill, Kennedy Kin Fight Murder Rap," *Day One / ABC News,* February 28, 1994; John Edwards, "In the Name of the Family," *London Daily Mail,* February 24, 1994; Ben Macintyre, "The Meddling Kennedys," *Times of London,* March 1, 1994; Kevin Cullen, "You Only Live Twice," *Independent (London),* January 30, 1994. Vitriolic coverage of the Kennedys in the British press was typified by Martin Walker, "Downhill with Ted," *Manchester Guardian (Weekly),* December 1, 1991. Jean Kennedy Smith's appointment as U.S. ambassador to Ireland was recalled in the author's interviews with Jean Kennedy Smith, Elizabeth Shannon and by Sen. Edward Kennedy in written response to the author's questions. "It sort of developed as a wisp of a thought" was quoted in Lawrence Leamer, *The Kennedy Women.* Further details and context about Smith's arrival was derived from Conor O'Clery, *Daring Diplomacy: Clinton's Secret Search for Peace in Ireland;* Adam Clymer, *Edward M. Kennedy: A Biography;* and Laura Blumenfeld, "The Envoy's Bloodlines," *Washington Post,* August 31, 1995. Jean Kennedy Smith's visit to Dunganstown was recalled in author's interviews with Mary Ann Ryan and Patrick Grennan.

Chapter Forty: Principles of Peace

The opening quote is from President Kennedy's June 28, 1963, speech to the Irish Parliament, in which he paraphrased from William Butler Yeats's poem, "The Three Marching Songs." Gerry

Adams's comments are from the author's interview with him in Letterkenny, County Donegal, Republic of Ireland, and subsequent telephone interview with Adams from New York. Further details of the conversation between Adams and Vice President Al Gore were detailed in Tim Pat Coogan, *The Troubles: Ireland's Ordeal 1966–1996 and the Search for Peace;* and Conor O'Clery, *Daring Diplomacy: Clinton's Secret Search for Peace in Ireland.* Jean Kennedy Smith's "hint of melancholy about her" was described in Kevin Cullen, "A Kennedy Leaves Her Mark on Ireland," *Boston Globe,* July 2, 1998. Also see, John Burns, "It's That Clan Again," *Sunday Times of London,* June 27, 1993. "We took vacations" was from the author's conversation with Jean Kennedy Smith. Smith recollections of her mother were in Laura Blumenfeld, "A Green Light at the White House," *Washington Post,* March 18, 1995. John Hume's long-time friendship with the Kennedys was mentioned in Paul Routledge, *John Hume: A Biography;* and John Hume, *A New Ireland: Politics, Peace and Reconciliation,* with foreword by Sen. Edward M. Kennedy. "I saw the suffering this woman was experiencing" was from a profile of Jean Kennedy Smith in Niall O'Dowd, "Irish American of the Year," *Irish America,* April 30, 1995. "I knew John was talking to him and I didn't see any downside to it, frankly" was from author's talk with Smith. Gerry Adams's background was detailed in Tim Pat Coogan, *The Troubles;* Tim Pat Coogan, *The IRA: A History;* Terry Golway, *For the Cause of Liberty: A Thousand Years of Ireland's Heroes;* and Gerry Adams, *Before the Dawn: An Autobiography.* Adams's arrival in Boston with Sen. Edward Kennedy was reported in Kevin Cullen, "Sinn Fein Campaign Embraces Boston," *Boston Globe,* September 25, 1994. The dispute with Smith over the Adams's visa was detailed in Richard Gilbert, "Dissent in Dublin," *Foreign Service Journal,* July 1996. President Clinton's initial instruction to his new ambassador to Ireland were cited in the author's interview with Smith. Albert Reynolds's comments about the Kennedys came from Laura Blumenfeld, "The Envoy's Bloodlines," *Washington Post,* August 31, 1995. Clinton's biographer suggested the photo symbolized "a transference of politics" for the future president, while another Irish journalist quipped that it appeared "a laying of hands" of one American chieftain to another in David Maraniss, *First in His Class.* Frank Mankiewicz's observation about Clinton's affinity with the Kennedys and the JFK legacy was reported in Kathy Lewis, "An Invitation from Jackie," *Dallas Morning News,* August 25, 1993. Clinton's statement "I've always been conscious of being Irish" came from Conor O'Cleary, "Bill O'Clinton," *Irish Times,* November 25, 1995. "There was huge protestation" was from the author's interview with Adams. Niall O'Dowd's recollections were also from an interview. The comments of former U.S. Ambassador to Great Britain Raymond Seitz, and the resulting controversy, were reported in "Seitz Attack Threat to Peace, Says Kennedy," *Irish Independent,* January 20, 1998; and Kevin Cullen, "A Kennedy Leaves Her Mark in Ireland," *Boston Globe,* July 2, 1998. Kathleen Kennedy Townsend's recollection of her trip to Ireland with Clinton were from an interview. Further details about Clinton and the Kennedys came from Michael Cox, "The War That Came In from the Cold: Clinton and the Irish Question," *World Policy Journal,* March 22, 1999; Anne Brennan, "Handshake Launches Lifelong Connection with the Kennedys," *Cape Cod Times,* August 6, 2000; Christopher Ogden, "With Help from Their Friends," *Time,* April 20, 1998; as well as Clinton's remarks on October 23, 2000, in Lowell, Massachusetts, where he said "Whatever I have accomplished as President, so much of it would never have been possible if Ted Kennedy wasn't there every single step of the way." The comments of Irish President Mary McAleese were contained in Maol Muire Tynan, "Kennedy Smith Given Honorary Citizenship," *Irish Times,* July 27, 1998. Amb. Smith sharing a laugh with Pat Kennedy was recalled in Kevin Cullen, "A Kennedy Leaves Her Mark in Ireland," *Boston Globe,* July 2, 1998. Smith's appearance at a County Wexford commemoration of the battles of 1798 was described in Roisin de Rossa, "1798–1998: The Pikes Are Carried Again," *An Phoblacht/Republican News,* August 27, 1998. Sen. Edward Kennedy said his family's personal history was "certainly a factor" in efforts by Jean Kennedy Smith and himself to bring about peace in Northern Ireland, based on his written response to the author. Ted Kennedy's comments about the suffering in Ulster and recalling his father's letter was derived from a 1998 speech at the University of Ulster in Derry entitled, "Northern Ireland—A View from America."

Chapter Forty-One: Legacies

John F. Kennedy Jr.'s comment after working briefly with Mother Teresa's group came from Elaine Lafferty, "The Promise of Camelot Beckoned," *Irish Times,* July 19, 1999. Pierre Salinger's recollection was from a United Press International dispatch from July 1999. The interview with Gerry Adams was contained in John Kennedy, "Gerry Adams's Last Shot," *George*, August 1997. Kennedy's trip to Belfast was recalled by Richard McAuley in an interview. "Like many Irish-Americans, they have a very strong sense of their Irishness" was Gerry Adams's assessment of the Kennedys during an interview. News coverage of JFK Jr.'s fatal 1999 crash included the comments of Mike Barnicle and Doris Kearns Goodwin in Tom Brokaw and Katie Couric, "An American Tragedy," transcript from NBC News, July 23, 1999. Orrin Hatch's comment and other postulating about the fate of the Kennedy was in Rick Hampson, "Greek Saga Seems to Hit Famous Irish Clan," *USA Today*, July 21, 1999. After the JFK Jr. crash, Ted Kennedy denies any existence of a Kennedy curse in "Sen. Kennedy talks about his grief," Associated Press, *Cape Cod Times*, May 3, 2000. Sen. Kennedy's eulogy for his nephew was repeated in numerous accounts, including N.R. Kleinfield, "Recalling JFK Jr.'s Promise," *New York Times*, July 24, 1999. The memorial Mass at old St. Patrick's in lower Manhattan was described in Richard Pyle, "Kennedy Relatives Prepare for Mass," Associated Press, July 23, 1999. The long-term impact of the 1965 Immigration Act was cited in James Goldsborough, "Out of Control Immigration," *Foreign Affairs,* September–October 2000. Sen. Kennedy's retrospective view of the 1965 immigration bill's impact, as well as the comparison of conditions for today's undocumented workers to those faced by his Irish immigrant ancestors, was in a written response to the author. Financial details of the $30 million Joseph P. Kennedy Foundation were provided by publicly available IRS Form 990s documents filed by the group and examined by the author. Tim Russert recalled his Irish Catholic community's reaction to JFK's 1960 victory in Niall O'Dowd, "Meet the Best: Tim Russert of NBC," *Irish America*. Sen. Joseph Lieberman's recollection of the same event was recalled his May 14, 2001, speech at the John F. Kennedy Library. Kathleen Kennedy Townsend's analogy about Galileo was from the author's interview. Details of the 2000 Democratic National Convention came from Mike Feinsilber, "Kennedys Celebrate the Party's Liberal Legacy," Associated Press, August 16, 2000.

Selected Bibliography

Adams, Gerry. "*Free Ireland: Towards a Lasting Peace*," Dingle, Co. Kerry: Brandon, 1995.

____. *Before the Dawn: An Autobiography*, London: Heinemann: in association with Brandon Book Publishers, 1996.

____. *An Irish Voice: The Quest for Peace*, Dingle, Co. Kerry: Mount Eagle, 1997.

____. *An Irish Journal*," Dingle, Co. Kerry: Brandon, 2001.

Andersen, Christopher P. "*Jack and Jackie: Portrait of an American Marriage*, New York: William Morrow, 1996.

____. *Jackie after Jack: Portrait of the Lady*, New York: William Morrow, 1998.

Beatty, Jack. *The Rascal King: The Life and Times of James Michael Curley, 1874–1958*, New York: Addison-Wesley, 1992.

Bell, J. Bowyer. *The Irish Troubles: A Generation of Violence, 1967–1992*, New York: St. Martin's Press, 1993.

Beran, Michael Knox. *The Last Patrician: Bobby Kennedy and the End of American Aristocracy*, New York: St. Martin's Press, 1998.

Bernstein, Irving. *Promises Kept: John F. Kennedy's New Frontier*, New York: Oxford University Press, 1991.

Beschloss, Michael R. *Kennedy and Roosevelt: The Uneasy Alliance*, foreword by James McGregor Burns, New York: Norton, 1980.

____. *The Crisis Years: Kennedy and Khrushchev, 1960–1963*, New York: Edward Burlingame Books, 1991.

____. *Taking Charge: The Johnson White House Tapes, 1963–1964*, edited and with commentary by Michael R. Beschloss, New York: Simon & Schuster, 1997.

____. *Reaching for Glory: Lyndon Johnson's Secret White House Tapes, 1964–1965*, edited and with commentary by Michael Beschloss, New York: Simon & Schuster, 2001.

Blair, Joan, and Clay Blair Jr. *The Search for JFK,* New York: Berkley Pub. Corp.: distributed by Putnam, 1976.

Blanshard, Paul. *American Freedom and Catholic Power*, Boston: Beacon Press, 1949.

____. *The Irish and Catholic Power: An American Interpretation*, Boston: Beacon Press, 1953.

Blet, Pierre. *Pius XII and the Second World War According to the Archives of the Vatican*, Paulist, 2001.

Bradlee, Benjamin C. *Conversations with Kennedy,* New York: W.W. Norton, 1975.

Branch, Taylor. *Parting The Waters: America in the King Years, 1954–63,* New York: Simon and Schuster, 1988.

Breen, Dan. *My Fight for Irish Freedom,* Dublin: Anvil Books, 1981.

Brennan, John F., Rev. *The Evolution of Everyman: Ancestral lineage of John F. Kennedy,* Dundalk: Dundalgan Press, 1968.

Brinkley, Alan. *Voices of Protest: Huey Long, Father Coughlin and the Great Depression,* New York: Alfred A. Knopf, 1982.

Burner, David. *John F. Kennedy and a New Generation,* edited by Oscar Handlin, Boston: Little, Brown, 1988.

Burns, James MacGregor. *John Kennedy: A Political Profile,* New York: Harcourt, Brace and World, Inc., 1961.

____. *Edward Kennedy and the Camelot Legacy,* New York: Norton, 1976.

Cahill, Thomas. *Pope John XXII W.W.,* New York: Penguin, 2002.

Callan, Louise. *The Society of the Sacred Heart in North America,* London: Longmans, Green and Co., 1937.

Cameron, Gail. *Rose: A Biography of Rose Fitzgerald Kennedy,* New York: Putnam, 1971.

Carlton, Charles. *Bigotry and Blood: Documents on the Ulster Troubles,* Chicago: Nelson-Hall, 1977.

Carroll, James. *Constantine's Sword: The Church and the Jews: A History,* Boston: Houghton Mifflin, 2001.

Carson, Claybourne, ed., *The Autobiography of Martin Luther King Jr.,* New York: Intellectual Properties Management in association with Warner Books, 1998.

Cecil, David. *The Young Melbourne.* New York: Bobbs-Merrill, 1939.

Chomsky, Noam. *Rethinking Camelot: JFK, the Vietnam War, and U.S. Political Culture,* Boston: South End Press, 1993.

Churchill, Winston. *Their Finest Hour: The Second World War.* Boston: Houghton Mifflin, 1949.

Clinch, Nancy Gager. *The Kennedy Neurosis,* with a foreword by Bruce Mazlish, New York: Grosset & Dunlap, 1973.

Clymer, Adam. *Edward M. Kennedy: A Biography,* New York: Morrow, 1999.

Cogley, John. *A Canterbury Tale: Experiences,* Seabury Press, Crossroads Press, 1976.

Cohn, Roy. *McCarthy,* New York: New American Library, 1968.

Collier, Peter, and David Horowitz. *The Kennedys: An American Drama,* New York: Summit Books, 1984.

Considine, Bob. *It's All News To Me—A Reporter's Deposition,* New York: Meredith Press, 1967.

Conway, Bertrand L. *The Question Box,* with preface by Francis Cardinal Spellman, Paulist Press, 1961; multiple editions dating back to early 1900s.

Coogan, Tim Pat. *Michael Collins: A Biography,* London: Hutchinson, 1990.

____. *De Valera: Long Fellow, Long Shadow,* London: Hutchinson, 1993.

____. *The IRA,* London: HarperCollins, 1995.

____. *The Troubles: Ireland's Ordeal 1966–1995 and the Search for Peace,* London: Hutchinson, 1995.

____. *Wherever Green Is Worn: The Story of the Irish Diaspora,* London: Hutchinson, 2000.

Cooney, John. *The American Pope: The Life and Times of Francis Cardinal Spellman,* New York: Times Books, 1984.

Cornell, Thomas C., and James H. Forest, eds., *A Penny a Copy,* New York: MacMillan Co., 1968.

Cornwell, John. *Hitler's Pope: The Secret History of Pius XII,* New York: Viking, 1999.

Cronin, Sean. *Washington's Irish Policy, 1916–1986: Independence, Partition, Neutrality,* Dublin: Anvil; St. Paul, Minn.: Irish Books and Media, 1987.

Crosby, Donald F. *God, Church and Flag: Senator Joseph R. McCarthy and the Catholic Church, 1950–1957,* Chapel Hill: University of North Carolina Press, 1978.

Curran, Thomas J. *Xenophobia and Immigration, 1820–1930,* Boston: Twayne Publishers, 1975.

Cutler, John Henry. *Honey Fitz: Three Steps to the White House; The Life and Times of John F. (Honey Fitz) Fitzgerald,* Indianapolis: Bobbs-Merrill, 1962.

_____. *Cardinal Cushing of Boston,* New York: Hawthorn Books, 1970.

Davis, Jay, ed. *The Kennedy Reader,* Indianapolis: Bobbs-Merrill Co., 1967.

Davis, John H. *The Kennedys: Dynasty and Disaster, 1848–1983,* New York: McGraw-Hill, 1984.

Davis, Kenneth S. *FDR: Into the Storm 1937–1940: A History,* New York: Random House, 1993.

De Bréadún, Deaglán. *The Far Side of Revenge: Making Peace in Northern Ireland,* Doughcloyne, Wilton, Cork: Collins, 2001.

Dever, Joseph. *Cushing of Boston: A Candid Portrait,* Boston: Bruce Humphries Publishers, 1965.

Diner, Hasia R. *Erin's Daughters in America: Irish Immigrant Women in the Nineteenth Century,* Baltimore: Johns Hopkins University Press, 1983.

Dinneen, Joseph F. *The Purple Shamrock: The Honorable James Michael Curley of Boston.* New York, Norton, 1949.

_____. *The Kennedy Family,* Boston: Little, Brown, 1960.

DuBois, W.E. B. *Dusk of Dawn,* New York: Harcourt Brace, 1940.

Dwyer, T. Ryle. *Strained Relations: Ireland at Peace and the USA at War 1941–45,* Dublin: Gill and Macmillan; Totowa, N.J.: Barnes & Noble, 1988.

Ellis, John Tracy. *American Catholicism,* Chicago: University of Chicago Press, 1956.

Erie, Steven P. *Rainbow's End: Irish-Americans and the Dilemmas of Urban Machine Politics, 1840–1985,* Berkeley: University of California Press, 1988.

Fairlie, Henry. *The Kennedy Promise; The Politics of Expectation,* Garden City, N.Y.: Doubleday, 1973.

Fay, Paul B. *The Pleasure of His Company,* New York: Harper & Row, 1966.

Fenton, John H. *Salt of the Earth: An Informal Portrait of Richard Cardinal Cushing,* New York: Coward-McCann, 1965.

FitzGerald, Frances. *Fire in the Lake: The Vietnamese and the Americans in Vietnam,* New York: Vintage Books, 1973.

Forbes, H. A. Crosby, and Henry Lee. *Massachusetts Help to Ireland during the Great Famine,* with a foreword by Richard Cardinal Cushing. Milton, Mass.: Captain Robert Bennet Forbes House, 1967.

Formisano, Ronald P. *Boston Against Busing: Race, Class, and Ethnicity in the 1960s and 1970s,* University of North Carolina Press, 1991.

Foster, R. F. *Modern Ireland 1600–1972,* New York: Penquin Books, 1989.

Fraser, Antonia. *Cromwell, The Lord Protector,* New York: Knopf, 1973.

Fuchs, Lawrence H. *John F. Kennedy and American Catholicism,* New York: Meredith Press, 1967.

Gallagher, Thomas. *Paddy's Lament,* New York: Harcourt Trade Publishers, 1982.

Gannon, Robert I., S.J. *The Cardinal Spellman Story,* Garden City, N.Y.: Doubleday & Co., 1962.

Gardner, Gerald. *All the Presidents' Wits: The Power of Presidential Humor,* New York: Beech Tree Books, 1986.

Gellman, Irwin F. *The Contender,* New York: The Free Press, 1999.

Gleeson, Dermot. *The Last Lords of Ormond,* Dublin: Sheed & Ward, 1938.

Goldfarb, Ronald L. *Perfect Villains, Imperfect Heroes: Robert F. Kennedy's War against Organized Crime,* New York: Random House, 1995.

Golway, Terry. *For the Cause of Liberty: A Thousand Years of Ireland's Heroes,* New York: Simon and Schuster, 2000.

Goodwin, Doris Kearns. *The Fitzgeralds and the Kennedys,* New York: Simon and Schuster, 1987.

Goodwin, Richard. *Remembering America,* Boston: Little, Brown, 1988.

Greeley, Andrew M. *The American Catholic,* New York: Basic Books, 1977.

_____. *The Irish-Americans: The Rise to Money and Power,* New York: Harper & Row, 1981.

Guthman, Edwin O. *We Band of Brothers,* New York: Harper & Row, 1971.

Guthman, Edwin, and Jeffrey Shulman, eds. *Robert Kennedy: In His Own Words,* New York: Bantam, 1988.

Halberstam, David. *The Unfinished Odyssey of Robert Kennedy*, New York: Random House, 1969.

_____. *The Best and the Brightest*, New York: Random House, 1972.

Hamilton, Nigel. *JFK: Reckless Youth*, New York: Random House, 1992.

Handlin, Oscar. *Boston's Immigrants, 1790–1865: A Study in Acculturation*, Cambridge: Harvard University Press; London: H. Milford, Oxford University Press, 1941.

_____. *The Uprooted; The Epic Story of the Great Migrations that Made the American People*, New York: Grosset & Dunlap, 1957.

_____. *Al Smith and his America*, Boston: Little, Brown, 1958.

_____. *Immigration as a Factor in American History*, Englewood Cliffs, N.J.: Prentice-Hall, 1959.

_____. *A Pictorial History of Immigration*, New York: Crown Publishers, 1972.

Hanson, Eric O. *The Catholic Church in World Politics*, Princeton, N.J.: Princeton University Press, 1987.

Harris, Ruth-Ann M., et al. ed., *The Search for Missing Friends, Vol. 1–5, Boston: New England Historic Genealogical Society, 1989–1995*.

Hastings, Selina. *Evelyn Waugh: A Biography*, Boston: Houghton Mifflin, 1994.

Herman, Arthur. *Joseph McCarthy: Re-Examining the Life and Legacy of America's Most Hated Senator*, New York: Free Press, 1999.

Hersh, Burton. *The Education of Edward Kennedy—A Family Biography*, New York: Morrow, 1972.

Hersh, Seymour M. *The Dark Side of Camelot*, Boston: Little, Brown, 1997.

Heymann, C. David. *A Woman Named Jackie*, New York: Carol Communications, 1989.

_____. *RFK: A Candid Biography of Robert F. Kennedy*, New York: Dutton, 1998.

Higham, Charles. *Rose: The Life and Times of Rose Fitzgerald Kennedy*, New York: Pocket Books, 1995.

Higham, John. *Strangers in the Land: Patterns of American Nativism, 1860–1925*, New York: Atheneum, 1978.

Hilty, James W. *Robert Kennedy, Brother Protector*, Philadelphia: Temple University Press, 1997.

Hoffmann, Joyce. *Theodore H. White and Journalism as Illusion*, Columbia: University of Missouri Press, 1995.

Hume, John. *A New Ireland: Politics, Peace and Reconciliation*, with foreword by Sen. Edward M. Kennedy, Boulder, Colo.: Roberts Rinehart Publishers, 1996.

Ignatiev, Noel. *How the Irish Became White*, New York: Routledge, 1995.

Jaffee, Frederick S., Barbara L. Lindheim and Philip R. Lee, *Abortion Politics: Private Morality and Public Policy*, New York: McGraw-Hill, 1981.

Johnson, Paul. *Pope John XXIII*, Boston: Little, Brown, 1974.

Kee, Robert. *The Green Flag: The Turbulent History of the Irish National Movement*, New York: Delacorte Press, 1972.

_____. *Trial and Error: The Maguires, the Guildford Pub Bombings and British Justice*, London: Hamish Hamilton, 1986.

_____. *Ireland: A History*, London: Abacus, 1995.

Kennedy, Caroline. *Profiles in Courage for Our Time*, introduced and edited by Caroline Kennedy, New York: Hyperion, 2002.

Kennedy, Edward M. *Words Jack Loved*, privately printed, quoted from Library of Congress copy, 1977.

Kennedy, John F. *A Nation of Immigrants*, New York: Harper & Row, 1986, revised edition of 1958 original, with 1964 introduction by Robert F. Kennedy and new preface by John P. Roche.

_____., ed. *As We Remember Joe*, Cambridge, Mass., Privately printed [at the] University Press, 1945.

Kennedy, John F. *Profiles in Courage*, New York: Harper, 1956.

Kennedy, John, with Deirdre Henderson, ed. *Prelude to Leadership: The European Diary of John F. Kennedy, Summer 1945*, introduction by Hugh Sidey, Washington, DC: Regnery Pub.; Lanham, MD: Distributed to the trade by National Book Network, 1995.

Kennedy, Robert F. *The Enemy Within*, New York: Harper & Row, 1960.

Kennedy, Robert F. *To Seek A Newer World*, Garden City, N.Y.: Doubleday, 1967.

Kennedy, Robert F. *Thirteen Days: A Memoir of the Cuban Missile Crisis,* foreword by Arthur Schlesinger, Jr., New York: W.W. Norton, 1999, c1971.

Kennedy, Rose Fitzgerald. *Times to Remember,* Garden City, N.Y.: Doubleday, 1974.

Hennessy, Maurice N. *I'll Come Back in the Springtime: John F. Kennedy and the Irish,* New York: Washburn, 1966.

Kessler, Ronald. *The Sins of the Father: Joseph P. Kennedy and the Dynasty He Founded,* New York: Warner Books, 1996.

Kinsella, Anna. *County Wexford in the Famine Years,* Duffry Press, Enniscorthy, 1995.

Klein, Edward. *Just Jackie: Her Private Years,* New York: Ballantine Books, 1998.

Koestenbaum, Wayne. *Jackie under My Skin: Interpreting an Icon,* New York: Farrar, Straus and Giroux, 1995.

Koskoff, David E. *Joseph P. Kennedy: A Life and Times,* Englewood Cliffs, N.J.: Prentice-Hall, 1974.

Krock, Arthur. *Memoirs: Sixty Years On the Firing Line,* New York: Funk and Wagnalls, 1968.

Lasky, Victor. *J. F. K.: The Man and the Myth,* New York: Macmillan, 1963.

Laxton, Edward. *The Famine Ships: The Irish Exodus to America,* New York: Henry Holt & Co., 1997.

Leamer, Laurence. *The Kennedy Women: The Saga of an American Family,* New York: Villard Books, 1994.

_____. *The Kennedy Men: 1901–1963: The Laws of the Father,* New York: W. Morrow, 2001.

Lerner, Max. *Ted and the Kennedy Legend: A Study in Character and Destiny,* New York: St. Martin's Press, 1980.

Lincoln, Abraham, *Speeches and Writings, 1832–1858,* New York: Viking Press, 1989.

Lovat, Laura Lister Fraser, Lady. *Maurice Baring: A Postscript,* New York: Sheed & Ward, 1948.

Lowe, Jacques. *The Kennedy Legacy : A generation Later,* photographs and captions by Jacques Lowe; text by Wilfrid Sheed; design by Ken Harris, New York: Viking Penguin, 1988.

Lukas, J. Anthony. *Common Ground: A Turbulent Decade in the Lives of Three American Families,* New York: Knopf, 1985.

MacManus, Seumas, ed. *The Four Winds of Eirinn: Poems by Ethna Carbery,* Dublin: M. H. Gill and Son, Ltd., 1906.

Mahoney, Richard D. *Sons & Brothers: The Days of Jack and Bobby Kennedy,* New York: Arcade Pub., Distributed by Time Warner Trade Pub., 1999.

Manchester, William R.. *Death of a President,* New York: Harper and Row, 1967.

_____. *One Brief Shining Moment : Remembering Kennedy,* Boston: Little, Brown, 1983.

Maraniss, David. *First in His Class,* New York: Simon and Schuster, 1995.

Martin, Ralph G. *A Hero for Our Time: An Intimate Story of the Kennedy Years,* New York: Macmillan, 1983.

_____. *Seeds of destruction: Joe Kennedy and His Sons,* New York: G.P. Putnam's Sons, 1995.

Massa, Mark S. *Catholics and American Culture: Fulton Sheen, Dorothy Day and the Notre Dame Football Team,* New York: Crosswood Pub. Co., 1999.

Matthews, Christopher. *Kennedy & Nixon: The Rivalry that Shaped Postwar America,* New York: Simon & Schuster, 1996.

McCarthy, Joe. *The Remarkable Kennedys,* New York: Dial Press, 1960.

McDonald, Henry. *Trimble,* London: Bloomsbury, 2000.

McSorley, Richard T. *The More, the Merrier: The Story of a Mother of Fifteen Children,* Washington: Georgetown University Press, 1963.

McTaggart, Lynne. *Kathleen Kennedy, Her Life and Times,* Garden City, N.Y.: Dial Press, 1983.

Miller, Kerby A. *Emigrants and Exiles,* Cambridge: Oxford University Press, 1985.

Miller, William D. *A Harsh and Dreadful Love: Dorothy Day and the Catholic Worker Movement,* New York: W.W. Norton, 1973.

Mitchell, Arthur. *JFK and his Irish heritage,* Dublin, Ireland: Moytura Press, 1993.

Mitchell, George J. *Making Peace,* New York: Alfred A. Knopf, 1999.

Morgan, Ted. *FDR: A Biography,* New York: Simon and Schuster, 1986.

Morris, Charles R. *American Catholic: The Saints and Sinners Who Built America's Most Powerful Church*, New York: Times Books, 1997.

Murphy, Paul I. *La Popessa*, New York: Warner Book, 1983.

Murray, John Courtney. *We Hold These Truths,* New York: Sheed & Ward, 1960.

Navasky, Victor S. *Kennedy Justice*, New York: Atheneum, 1971.

Neuhaus, Richard John. *The Catholic Moment: The Paradox of the Church in Post-Modern World*, San Francisco: Harper and Row, 1990.

Newfield, Jack. *Robert Kennedy—A Memoir*, New York: Dutton, 1969.

O'Brien, David J. *American Catholics and Social Reform: The New Deal Years*, New York: Oxford University Press, 1968.

O'Clery, Conor. *The Greening of the White House: The Inside Story of How America Tried to Bring Peace to Ireland*, Dublin: Gill & Macmillan, 1996; the American edition was named *Daring Diplomacy: Clinton's Secret Search for Peace in Ireland*.

O'Connell, William. *Recollections of Seventy Years*, Boston: Houghton Mifflin, 1934.

O'Connor, Karen. *No Neutral Gound? Abortion Politics in an Age of Absolutes*, Boulder, Colo.: Westview Press, 1996.

O'Connor, Thomas H. *The Boston Irish: A Political History*, Boston: Northeastern University Press, 1995.

_____. *Boston Catholics: A History of the Church and Its People*, Boston: Northeastern University Press, 1998.

O'Donnell, Kenneth P., and David F. Powers, with Joe McCarthy. *Johnny, We Hardly Knew Ye; Memories of John Fitzgerald Kennedy*, New York: Pocket Books, 1973.

Oppenheimer, Jerry. *The Other Mrs. Kennedy: Ethel Skakel Kennedy: An American Drama of Power, Privilege, and Politics,* New York: St. Martin's Press, 1994.

Oshinsky, David. *A Conspiracy So Immense: The World of Joseph McCarthy*, New York: The Free Press, 1983.

O'Toole, James M. *Militant and Triumphant: William Henry O'Connell and the Catholic Church in Boston, 1859–1944,* Notre Dame: University of Notre Dame Press, 1992.

Padden, Michael, Robert Sullivan and Robert F. Kennedy. *May the Road Rise to Meet You— Everything You Need to Know About Irish American History*, New York: Plume/NAL, 1999.

Parmet, Herbert S. *Jack: The Struggles of John F. Kennedy,* New York: Dial Press, 1980.

_____. *JFK, The Presidency of John F. Kennedy*, New York: Dial Press, 1983.

Pearce, Joseph. *Literary Converts: Spiritual Inspiration in An Age of Unbelief*, San Francisco: Ignatius Press, 2000.

Perret, Geoffrey. *Jack: A Life Like No Other*, New York: Random House, 2001.

Potter, George W. *To the Golden Door; The Story of the Irish in Ireland and America*, Boston: Little, Brown, 1960.

Pottker, Janice. *Janet and Jackie: The Story of a Mother and her Daughter, Jacqueline Kennedy Onassis*, New York: St. Martin's Press, 2001.

Rachlin, Harvey. *The Kennedys: A Chronological History, 1823–present*, New York: World Almanac; Distributed in the U.S. by Ballantine Books, 1986.

Rainie, Harrison. *Growing Up Kennedy: The Third Wave Comes of Age*, New York: Putnam, 1983.

Reedy, George E. *From the Ward to the White House: The Irish in American Politics*, New York: C. Scribner; Toronto: Collier Macmillan Canada, 1991.

Reeves, Richard. *President Kennedy: Profile of Power*, New York: Simon & Schuster, 1993.

Renehan, Edward. *The Kennedys At War, 1937–1945*, New York: Doubleday, 2002.

Roosevelt, James. *My Parents: A Differing View,* Chicago: Playboy Press, 1976.

Ross, Douglas. *Robert F. Kennedy: Apostle of Change*, New York: Trident Press, 1968.

Routledge, Paul. *John Hume: A Biography*, New York: HarperCollins, 1997.

Ryan, Dennis P. *Beyond the Ballot Box: A Social History of the Boston Irish, 1845–1917,* Madison, N.J.: Fairleigh Dickinson University Press, 1983.

Salinger, Pierre. *P.S., A Memoir,* New York: St. Martin's Press, 1995.

Schlesinger, Arthur M., Jr. *The Age of Roosevelt,* Boston, Houghton Mifflin, 1957.

_____. *Kennedy or Nixon; Does It Make any Difference?* New York: Macmillan, 1960.

_____. *A Thousand Days; John F. Kennedy in the White House,* Boston: Houghton Mifflin, 1965.

_____. *Robert Kennedy and His Times,* Boston: Houghton Mifflin, 1978.

_____. *The Disuniting of America: Reflections on a Multicultural Society,* Knoxville, Tenn.: Whittle Direct Books, 1991.

Searls, Hank. *The Lost Prince; Young Joe, The Forgotten Kennedy; The Story of the Oldest Brother,* New York: World Pub. Co., 1969.

Shannon, William V. *The American Irish,* New York: MacMillan, 1963.

_____. *The Heir Apparent: Robert Kennedy and the Struggle for Power,* New York: Macmillan, 1967.

Sheehan, Neil. *A Bright Shining Lie: John Paul Vann and America in Vietnam,* New York: Random House, 1988.

Sherrill, Robert. *The Last Kennedy,* New York: Dial Press, 1976.

Shesol, Jeff. *Mutual Contempt: Lyndon Johnson, Robert Kennedy, and the Feud that Defined a Decade,* New York: W.W. Norton, 1997.

Shorter, Edward. *The Kennedy Family and the Story of Mental Retardation,* Philadelphia: Temple University Press, 2000.

Slayton, Robert A. *Empire Statesman: The Rise and Redemption of Al Smith,* New York: Free Press, 2001.

Smith, Amanda. *Hostage to Fortune: The Letters of Joseph P. Kennedy,* New York: Viking, 2001.

Solomon, Barbara Miller. *Ancestors and Immigrants, A Changing New England Tradition,* Cambridge: Harvard University Press, 1956.

Sorensen, Theodore C. *Kennedy,* New York: Harper & Row, 1965.

_____. *The Kennedy Legacy,* New York: Macmillan, 1969.

Stannard, Martin. *Evelyn Waugh,* New York: Norton, 1987.

Steel, Ronald. *In Love with Night: The American Romance with Robert Kennedy.* New York: Simon & Schuster, 2000.

Stein, Jean. *American Journey; The Times of Robert Kennedy.* Interviews by Jean Stein. Edited by George Plimpton. New York: Harcourt Brace Jovanovich, 1970.

Strober, Gerald S., and Deborah H. *Let Us Begin Anew : An Oral History of the Kennedy Presidency,* New York: HarperCollinsPublishers, 1993.

Swanson, Gloria. *Swanson on Swanson,* New York: Random House, 1980.

Thomas, Evan. *Robert Kennedy: His Life,* New York: Simon & Schuster, 2000.

Thompson, Lawrance, and R.H. Winnick. *Robert Frost: The Later Years, 1938–1963,* New York: Holt, Rinehart and Winston, 1976.

Thompson, Robert E. *Robert F. Kennedy; The Brother Within,* Thompson and Hortense Myers, New York: Macmillan, 1962.

vanden Heuvel, William J. *On His Own: Robert F. Kennedy, 1964–1968,* vanden Heuvel and Milton Gwirtzman, Garden City, N.Y.: Doubleday, 1970.

Whalen, Richard J. *The Founding Father; The Story of Joseph P. Kennedy,* New York: New American Library, 1964.

Whalen, Thomas J. *Kennedy versus Lodge: The 1952 Massachusetts Senate Race,* foreword by Robert Dallek, Boston: Northeastern University Press, 2000.

White, Theodore H. *The Making of the President, 1960,* New York: Atheneum Publishers, 1961.

_____. *In Search of History: A Personal Adventure.* New York: Warner Books, 1978.

Whyte, Robert. *Journey of an Irish Coffin Ship,* ed. James Mangan, Cork, Ireland: Mercier Press, 1994.

Wicker, Tom. *Kennedy Without Tears, The Man Beneath the Myth,* foreword by Arthur Krock, New York: Morrow, 1964.

Williamson, Chilton, Jr. *The Immigration Mystique,* New York: Basic Books, 1996.

Wills, Garry. *The Kennedy Imprisonment: A Meditation on Power*, Boston: Little, Brown, 1982.

_____. *Papal Sin Structures of Deceit*, Doubleday, 2001.

Wilson, David A. *United Irishmen, United States: Immigrant Radicals in the Early Republic*, Ithaca: Cornell University Press, 1998.

Wofford, Harris. *Of Kennedys and Kings: Making Sense of the Sixties*, New York: Farrar, Straus, Giroux, 1980.

Woodham Smith, Cecil Blanche Fitz Gerald. *The Great Hunger: Ireland 1845–1849*, New York: Harper & Row, 1962.

Zuccotti, Susan. *Under His Very Windows: The Vatican and the Holocaust in Italy*, New Haven, Conn.: Yale University Press, 2000.

Bylined Articles in Newspapers, Periodicals and Journals

Allen, Henry. "Waiting for the Phoenix to Stir; Arthur Schlesinger, Tender of Liberalism and Its Heroes," *Washington Post*, October 20, 1978.

Alsop, Joseph. "Question of Bigotry," *New Republic*, April 25 and May 2, 1960.

_____. "The Legacy of John F. Kennedy," *Saturday Evening Post*, November 21, 1964.

Alsop, Stewart. "Battle of Wisconsin," *Saturday Evening Post*, April 2, 1960.

Amundson, Robert H. "Breakthrough in Immigration," *America*, January 29, 1966.

Anderson, Jack. Nixon Is Linked to Billy Graham," *Washington Post,* September 12, 1960.

Baker, Russell. "Kennedy in Race," *New York Times*, Janaury 3, 1960.

Barone, Michael. "We've Been Here Before," AEI Lecture Series, October 4, 1999.

Beatty, Jack. "Grand Expectations: The United States, 1945–1974—A Book Review," *Atlantic Monthly*, September 1996.

Behan, D. "Hail to the O'Chief," *Life*, June 21, 1963.

Belair, Felix Jr. "President Addresses Friendly Sons of St. Patrick," *New York Times,* March 18, 1964.

Bennett, John C., Stanley Lowell and William Clancy. "A Protestant Look At American Catholicism," *Christianity and Crisis*, 1958.

Bergquist, Laura. "The Rise of the Brothers Kennedy," *Look*, August 6, 1957.

_____. "A Lonely Summer for Jacqueline," *Look*, November 17, 1964.

Bird, Robert S. "At Home with the Heir Apparent," *Saturday Evening Post,* August 25, 1967.

Black, Chris. "In Washington, March 17 Is Weeklong Affair," *Boston Globe,* March 16, 1997.

Blanshard, Paul. "One-Sided Diplomacy," *Atlantic*, January 1952.

Blumenfeld, Laura. "A Green Light at the White House," *Washington Post*, March 18, 1995.

_____. "The Envoy's Bloodlines," *Washington Post*, August 31, 1995.

Blumenthal, Sidney. "Ted Kennedy: No Regrets As the Torch Is Passed," *Washington Post*, July 19, 1988.

Booker. Simeon. "What Negroes Can Expect from Kennedy," *Ebony*, January 1961.

_____. "How JFK Surpassed Abraham Lincoln," *Ebony*, February 1964.

Bradlee, Benjamin. "Front Runner," *Newsweek*, March 28, 1960.

Breen, Bill. "Irish and Illegal In America," *Christian Science Monitor*, March 23, 1989.

Brennan, Anne. "Handshake Launches Lifelong Connection with the Kennedys," *Cape Cod Times*, August 6, 2000.

Breslin, Jimmy. "Still They Come to the Hillside: Arlington National Cemetery," *Saturday Evening Post*, November 21, 1964.

_____. "The Music Is Different," *New York Herald Tribune*, October 18, 1964.

Brewer, Sam Pope. "Spellman Hailed at Rome Airport On His Arrival for Consistory," *New York Times*, January 15, 1946.

Broder, David S. "It Was a Family Picnic, Touched by Eloquence and Poignancy," *Washington Post*, October 21, 1979.

Brogran, D. W. "The Catholic Politician," *Atlantic,* August 1962.

Brozan, Nadine. "Chronicle," *New York Times,* July 2, 1993.

Buckley, William F., Jr. "Decline of Mr. Kennedy?" *National Review,* August 13, 1963.

Burns, John. "It's That Clan Again," *Sunday Times of London,* June 27, 1993.

Cardenas, Jose. "State's 1st Chavez Day Marked; Ethel Kennedy Joins Children in Downtown LA," *Los Angeles Times,* March 31, 2001.

Carroll, James. "The Catholic Side of Camelot," *Boston Globe,* December 30, 1997.

_____. "A Theologian Who Took Up the Torch in the Quest for World Peace," *Boston Globe,* February 23, 1999.

_____. "People of the Church Must Take It Back," *Boston Globe,* January 22, 2002.

Cherry, Conrad. "Two American Sacred Ceremonies: Their Implications for the Study of Religion in America," *American Quarterly,* Winter 1969.

Cogley, John. "Catholic for President?" *Commonweal,* March 27 and April 10, 1959.

_____. "Sauce for the Goose: Senator Kennedy Before the Council of Methodist Bishops," *Commonweal,* May 8, 1959.

_____. "Kennedy the Catholic," *Commonweal,* January 10, 1964.

Cohen, Adam. "Bobby and Ethel's Brood: The Weight of Legacy," *Time,* January 12, 1998.

Collier, Peter. "A Kennedy Apart," *National Review,* August 9, 1999.

Colt, George Howe. "The Kennedys' Third Generation," *Life,* Summer 1997.

Connelly, Tony. "J.F.K.'s Emigre Spirit Lives On in Ireland," *United Press International,* November 22, 1993.

Coogan, Tim Pat. "Sure and It's County Kennedy Now," *New York Times Magazine,* June 23, 1963.

Cousins, Norman. "Impressions At St. Patrick's," *Saturday Review,* June 22, 1968.

_____. "The Improbable Triumvirate," *Saturday Review,* October 30, 1971.

Cox, Michael. "The War that Came In from the Cold: Clinton and the Irish Question," *World Policy Journal,* March 22, 1999.

Cullen, Kevin. "Sinn Fein Campaign Embraces Boston," *Boston Globe,* September 25, 1994.

_____. "You Only Live Twice," *Independent (London),* January 30, 1994.

_____. "A Kennedy Leaves Her Mark in Ireland," *Boston Globe,* July 2, 1998.

Cunningham, Peter. "Fantasy Property—The Duke of Devonshire's Irish Summer House," *Independent (London),* May 10, 1998.

Dalin, David G. "Pius XII and the Jews," *Weekly Standard,* February 26, 2001.

Daniel, Clifton. "Totalitarian Rule Unwanted, Churchill Tells Free Europe," *New York Times,* May 14, 1945.

Davies, Lawrence E. "New Yorker Captures Lead Over McCarthy in Late Tabulation," *New York Times,* June 5, 1968.

Davis, Mark. "Public Service at Small Manhattan Church," *Philadelphia Inquirer,* July 22, 1999.

Davison, Peter. "Reverberations of the Irish Boom," *Atlantic Monthly,* November 2001.

de Rossa, Roisin. "1798–1998: The Pikes Are Carried Again," *An Phoblacht/Republican News,* August 27, 1998.

Di Liberto, James. "Civil Disobedience," *Hoya of Georgetown University,* January 21, 2000.

Dionne, E. J., Jr. "The Pope's Guardian of Orthodoxy," *New York Times,* November 24, 1985.

Doerr, Edd. "Vatican Interests versus the Public Interest; The Political Power of the Catholic Church," *Humanist,* September 1993.

Downie, Leonard, Jr. "Clergy Hopes Papal Visit Will Invigorate Ireland's Church," *Washington Post,* September 24, 1979.

Drinan, Robert F. "Grieving We Find Comfort," *National Catholic Reporter,* July 30, 1999.

Edwards, John. "In the Name of the Family, A New Court of Kennedys; Dynasty Out in Force for Appeal by their Guildford-In-Law," *Daily Mail (London),* February 24, 1994.

Epstein, Joseph. "Maurice Baring & the Good High-Brow," *New Criterion,* October 1992.

Espo, David. "Kennedy Preaches to Fundamentalist's Flock," Associated Press, October 4, 1983.

Fairlie, Henry. "Camelot Revisited," *Harper's*, January 1973.

Feinsilber, Mike. "Kennedys Celebrate the Party's Liberal Legacy," Associated Press, August 16, 2000.

Finlan, Michael. "100 years on, Islander Is Still Praying for Peace," *Irish Times*, November 16, 1994.

Finney, John W. "Democrats List 5 as Extremists," *New York Times*, September 17, 1960.

_____. "Jesuit Rules Out Church Control Over a President," *New York Times*, September 28, 1960.

Fleming, Anne Taylor. "The Kennedy Mystique," *New York Times Magazine*, June 17, 1979.

Fleming, T. J. "Kennedy the Catholic," *Nation*, June 8, 1964.

Fogarty, Gerald P. "The American Catholic Tradition of Dialogue," *America*, October 26, 1996.

Frady, Marshall. "The Transformation of Bobby Kennedy," *New York Review of Books*, October 12, 1978.

Frazier, Nancy. "Viet Prelate Excommunicated," *Chicago Catholic*, April 15, 1983.

Fuchs, Lawrence H. "Catholic as President?" *America*, September 13, 1958.

Garland, Russell. "Profile: Patrick J. Kennedy No longer a Newcomer," *Providence Journal-Bulletin*, October 16, 1996.

Getler, Michael. "The Pedigreed President; Genealogists Say Reagan Is Descended From Irish King," *Washington Post*, May 28, 1984.

Gibbons, Russell W. "The Real Christianity of John F. Kennedy," *St. Joseph Magazine*, April 1965.

Gilbert, Richard. "Dissent in Dublin," *Foreign Service Journal*, July 1996.

Goldman, Peter. "Brother-in-Law," *Newsweek*, January 26, 1976.

Goldsborough, James. "Out of Control Immigration," *Foreign Affairs*, September–October, 2000.

Goodman, Walter. "Striking Changes in the Way Protestant and Catholics Feel about Each Other," *Redbook*, March 1964.

Gorney, Cynthia. "Sirhan," *Washington Post*, August 20, 1979.

Greeley, Andrew M. "Leave John Kennedy in Peace," Christian Century, November 21, 1973.

_____. "Going Their Own Way," *New York Times*, October 10, 1982.

Greenfeld, Jeff. "RFK: The Politics That Might Have Been," *New Yorker*, June 5, 1978.

Grieg, Geordie. "How One of the Guildford Four Met and Fell in Love with a Kennedy," *Evening Standard*, January 19, 1993.

Gruson, Sydney. "Dublin Acclaims Kennedy As One Returning Home," *New York Times*, June 27, 1963.

_____. "Kennedy Praises Ireland as Model to Small Nations," *New York Times*, June 29, 1963.

Guttman, Robert J. "Jean Kennedy Smith: America's Activist Ambassador," *Europe*, July/August 1996.

Halberstam, David. "Ask Not What Ted Sorensen Can Do for You," *Harper's*, November 1969.

Hamill, Pete. "A Brief, Shining Moment," *New Yorker*, August 25, 1980.

_____. "JFK: The Real Thing," *New Yorker*, November 28, 1988.

_____. "The Sweet Words That Will Win An Irish Peace," *Newsday*, September 7, 1994.

_____. "Book Review," *National Review*, August 2000.

Hampson, Rick. "Greek Saga Seems to Hit Famous Irish Clan," *USA Today*, July 21, 1999.

Hauser, Thomas. "The Last Word: John F. Kennedy; An Appreciation," *Irish America*, January 31, 2002.

Hebblethwaite, Peter. "Politics in the Purple Kingdom: The Derailment of Vatican II," *National Catholic Reporter*, December 10, 1993.

Hersey, John. "Survival," *New Yorker*, June 17, 1944.

Hershey, Lenore. "Mrs. Kennedy," *Ladies Home Journal*, May 1972.

Hertzberg, Hendrik. "Scaling Mt. Kennedy," *New Yorker*, November 20, 2000.

Hill, Gladwin. "Religion Remains Big Issue in Texas," *New York Times*, November 3, 1960.

_____. "Morton Blames Rivals," *New York Times*, November 6, 1960.

Hittinger, Russell. "The Catholic Theology of John Courtney Murray," *Weekly Standard*, January 4, 1999.

Hoffman, B. H. "What It's Like to Marry a Kennedy," *Ladies Home Journal,* October 1962.

Hughes, Ken. "JFK and the Fall of Diem," *Boston Globe Magazine,* October 24, 1999.

Hughes, Philip, Msgr. "The Catholic Pioneers," *Atlantic,* August 1962.

Ingram, T. Robert. "The Blanshard Book," *Atlantic,* Feb 1950.

Johnson, G.W. "Religious Issue," *New Republic,* March 9, 1959.

Johnson, Haynes. "Bob—Looking Back on RFK: We Miss His Humor, His Humanity," *Washington Post,* June 7, 1978.

Johnson, Sherman E. "Paul Blanshard and the Church," *Atlantic,* August 1951.

Jones, Arthur. "McSorley and His Famous Friend Go Way Back; Georgetown University's Richard McSorley," *National Catholic Reporter,* July 28, 1995.

Jordan, Mary. "Minister Waging War for Peace and Justice; For Longtime Activist McSorley, Gulf Crisis Is Another Call to Battle," *Washington Post,* January 7, 1991.

Kempton, Murray. "Pure Irish—Robert F. Kennedy," *New Republic,* February 15, 1964.

_____. "Sorensen's Kennedy," *Atlantic Monthly,* October 1965.

_____. "A Rage Greater Than Grief," *Atlantic Monthly,* May 1967.

_____. "The Emperor's Kid Brother," *Esquire,* July 1968.

_____. "Ashes of the Kennedy Legend," *Newsday,* June 5, 1991.

_____. "Remembering RFK," *Newsday,* March 11, 1993.

_____. "His Catholic Conscience," *Newsday,* June 3, 1993.

Kempton, Murray, and James Ridgeway. "Romans," *New Republic,* December 7, 1963.

Kennedy, Edward M. "Ulster Is an International Issue," *Foreign Policy,* September 1973.

_____. "My Mother, Rose Kennedy," *Ladies Home Journal,* December 1975.

Kennedy, Eugene Cullen. "Catholicism's Chernobyl; Destruction Results When Hierarchs Practice Unquestioning Loyalty," *Chicago Tribune,* April 30, 2002.

Kennedy, Jacqueline Lee (Bouvier). "Memoir," *Look,* November 17, 1964.

_____. "Words JFK Loved Best," *Look,* November 17, 1964.

Kennedy, John. "Gerry Adams's Last Shot," *George,* August, 1997.

Kennedy, John F. "De Valera Aims to Unite Ireland," *New York Journal American,* July 29, 1945.

_____. "War in Indochina," *Vital Speeches,* May 1, 1954.

_____. "Foreign Policy Is the People's Business," *New York Times Magazine,* August 8, 1954.

_____. "Statement on U.S. Immigration Policy," *Congressional Digest,* January 1956.

_____. "America's Stake in Vietnam," *Vital Speeches,* August 1, 1956.

_____. "Moral Imperative," *Vital Speeches,* July 1, 1963.

_____. "Strategies of Peace," *Vital Speeches,* July 1, 1963.

_____. "Visit to Ireland," *Department of State Bulletin,* July 22, 1963.

_____. "A Nation of Immigrants—excerpt," *New York Times Magazine,* August 4, 1963.

_____. "President Recommends Revision of Immigration Laws," *Department of State Bulletin,* August 19, 1963.

_____. "With Clean Hands and a Clear Conscience: Excerpt from 'A Nation of Immigrants,'" *Saturday Evening Post,* October 3, 1964.

Kennedy, Robert F. "Look Behind the Russian Smiles," *U.S. News and World Report,* October 21, 1955.

_____. "Soviet Brand of Colonialism," *New York Times Magazine,* April 8, 1956.

Kenney, Michael. "Cache of Letters Offers Glimpse of the Private Cushing," *Boston Globe,* August 1, 1995.

King, Larry. "Fifteen Years for a Crime He Didn't Commit," *Larry King Live,* CNN, June 14, 1994.

King, Steven. "The Kennedys' Irish Connection," *Belfast Telegraph,* July 22, 1999.

Klein, Joe. "Camelot Collapsing," *New York,* December 24, 1979.

Knebel, Fletcher. "Democratic Forecast: A Catholic in 1960," *Look,* March 3, 1959.

_____. "The Bishops vs. Kennedy," *Look,* May 23, 1961.

Kopkind, Andrew. "New Immigration Policy," *New Republic,* February 27, 1965.

Kornblut, Anne E., and Alex Canizares. "A Kennedy's Anti-Castro Bent, Patrick's View Seen Tied to Rights, JFK," *Boston Globe*, April 13, 2000.

Kotkin, Joel. "Movers & Shakers; Immigrants Revive Dying Neighborhoods," *Reason*, December 1, 2000.

Kramer, Michael. "Brooklyn to Teddy: No Irish Need Apply," *New York*, January 28, 1980.

Krikorian, Mark. "Get Tight: Now More than Ever, Immigration Should Be Curtailed," *National Review*, March 25, 2002.

Kurkjian, Stephen. "Kennedy Won't Enter '90 Race for Governor; Announces Separation from Wife of 10 Years," *Boston Globe*, March 11, 1989.

Lader, L. "His Excellency, Joseph P. Kennedy, the United States Ambassador to the Court of St. James, Requests the Pleasure of Your—," *Esquire*, September 21, 1961.

Lafferty, Elaine. "The Promise of Camelot Beckoned," *Irish Times*, July 19, 1999.

Lawler, Philip F. "The End of the Irish Century," *Catholic World Report,* January 1996, later reprinted in *National Catholic Reporter.*

Lewis, Anthony. "What Drives Bobby Kennedy," *New York Times Magazine*, April 7, 1963.

Lewis, Kathy. "An Invitation from Jackie," *Dallas Morning News*, August 25, 1993.

Libit, Howard, and Sarah Koenig. "Support of Women Voters for Townsend Lukewarm; Gender: The Lieutenant Governor Leads, a poll Shows, but not by as Much as Expected," *Baltimore Sun*, November 2, 2002.

Lippmann, Walter. "Change of Course: President's Commitment to the Negro," *Newsweek*, July 8, 1963.

Lisagor, Peter. "Portrait of a Man Emerging from Shadows," *New York Times Magazine*, July 19, 1964.

Lunn, Arnold. "The Catholics of Great Britain," *Atlantic*, October 1944.

Maas, Peter. "Kennedy Women," *Look*, October 14, 1960.

MacIntyre, Ben. "The Meddling Kennedys," *Times of London*, March 1, 1994.

MacPherson, Myra. "The Hurrah! Kennedy Victory: Something to Cheer About; The Kennedy Bandwagon in Victory: Grins, Gratitude & the Battles Ahead," *Washington Post*, March 27, 1980.

Mailer, Norman. "Evening With Jackie Kennedy," *Esquire*, July 1962.

———. "On Kennedy and Existential Politics," *Esquire,* November 1963.

Manning, R. "Someone the President Can Talk To," *New York Times* Magazine, May 28, 1961.

March, William. "Democrats Celebrate Legacies," *Tampa Tribune*, August 16, 2000.

Markoe, Lauren. "Irish Prime Minister, Kennedys Bond; Political Clan Very Popular in Ireland," *Patriot Ledger (Quincy, MA)*, December 17, 1997.

Martin, Harold H. "The Amazing Kennedys," *Saturday Evening Post*, September 7, 1957.

Mathews, Tom. "Remembering Bobby," *Newsweek*, May 9, 1988.

McCabe, Ian. "JFK Raised the Issue of Partition," *Irish Times*, January 6, 1993.

McCarthy, Colman. "The McSorley Connection," *Washington Post*, October 16, 1992.

McCarthy, Joe. "Jack Kennedy," *Look*, October 13, 27 and November 10, 1959.

McGreevy, John T. "Thinking on One's Own: Catholicism in the American Imagination— 1928–1960," *Journal of American History*, June 1997.

McGrory, Mary. "Another Member of the Family," *America*, June 30, 1962.

———. "With Blessings Like These, Counting Sheep Is More Effective," *Washington Post*, November 24, 1983.

———. "In the Game of The Father," *Washington Post*, July 17, 1994.

Mclynn, Frank. "A Far from Pious World View, Welcomes A Biography Which Reveals the Shameful History Of the Wartime Pope," *Herald (Glasgow)*, September 23, 1999.

Mead, Margaret. "New Role for Jacqueline Kennedy?" *Redbook*, June 1964.

Merton, Thomas. "Nuclear War and Christian Responsibility, *Commonweal*, February 9, 1962.

Merzer, Martin. "Remembering RFK," *Orange County Register*, June 6, 1993.

Miller, Helen Hill. "A Catholic for President?" *New Republic*, November 18, 1957.

Morgan, E.P. "Kennedy and the Catholic Issue," *Reporter,* January 21, 1960.

Morrow, Lance. "The Rise and Fall of Anti-Catholicism," *Time*, October 15, 1979.

Moseley, Ray. "Protestant Firebrand Vows Victory on 'Evil Day'; At 72, Ian Paisley, a Formidable Foe," *Chicago Tribune*, May 21, 1998.

Mulligan, Hugh A. "A Prickly Jewel In the Papal Crown," Associated Press, September 26, 1979.

Neal, Steve. "JFK Still Is Standard for Nation's Leaders," *Chicago Sun-Times,* July 21, 1999.

Neville, Robert. "The Pope and the Vatican," *Look*, March 17, 1959.

Newfield, Jack. "The Bobby Phenomenon," *Nation*, November 14, 1966.

Nicholson, Jim. "A Brief History of U.S-Holy See Relations," *30 Giorni Magazine*, November 2002.

Niebuhr, Reinhold. "Catholics and the State," *New Republic*, October 17, 1960.

O Cathaoir, Brendan. "Kennedy Told Not to Mention Partition on Irish Visit," *Irish Times*, January 3, 1994.

O'Connell, Shaun. "Goodbye to All That: The Rise and Demise of Irish America," *New England Journal of Public Policy*, Spring/Summer 1993.

O'Connor, James V. "Leaders & Success—Irish King Brian Boru," *Investor's Business Daily*, March 17, 1999.

O Corrain, Donnchadh. "The Unstoppable Boru Remembered as a Martyr," *Sunday Times of London,* March 21, 1999.

O'Donnell, Bill. "White House Conference—Beyond St. Patrick's Day," *Boston Irish,* July 1, 1995.

O'Dowd, Niall. "Irish American of the Year: A Very Special Envoy," *Irish America*, April 30, 1995.

———. "Irish America Mourns JFK Jr.," *Irish Voice*, July 27, 1999.

Ogden, Christopher. "With Help from Their Friends," *Time*, April 20, 1998.

O'Hanlon, Ray. "Irish once again pin hopes on a Kennedy; Letter from New York," *The Irish News,* May 14, 2002.

———. Immigration Is on the Holiday Hit List; Letter From New York," *Irish News*, July 30, 2002.

Oliphant, Thomas. "Revisiting JFK's '52 Race," *Boston Globe*, March 27, 2000.

O'Toole, Fintan. "Broken Dreams: 20 Years on De Valera's Legacy Is Being Derided," *Irish Times*, August 26, 1995.

Passaro, Vince. "Dangerous Don DeLillo," *New York Times*, May 19, 1991.

Paulson, Michael. "Cushing, FBI linked—Files Show J. Edgar Hoover Cultivated Friendship with Cardinal in '50s, '60s," *Boston Globe*, April 13, 2000.

Pearson, Drew. "Texas Repeats 1928 Campaign," *Nashville Tennessean*, August 23, 1960.

Phillips, Cabell. "Case History Of a Senate Race," *New York Times Magazine*, October 26, 1952.

———. "How to Be a Presidential Candidate," *New York Times Magazine,* July 13, 1958.

———. "Immigration Bill Passes Senate..." *New York Times,* September 23, 1965.

Pierce, Andrew. "Well-Connected Priest Who Knows Power of the Press," Times Newspapers Limited, *Times of London*, September 13, 1995.

Podolsky, J.D. "In the Name of the Son; Out of Prison, His Tumultuous Life Story Now a Movie,
 · Gerry Conlon Finally Puts His Father's Ghost to Rest," *People,* February 14, 1994.

Pollitt, Katha. "Abortion in American History," *Atlantic Monthly,* May 1997.

Powell, Stewart. "Why Kennedy Legend Lives On," *U.S. News & World Report*, July 23, 1979.

Pryer, Nick. "Scum As Kennedy Clan Fly In To Aid Terror Case Man," *Evening Standard*, February 23, 1994.

Pyle, Richard. "Kennedy Relatives Prepare for Mass," Associated Press, July 23, 1999.

Reddy, Patrick. "Immigration: The Real Kennedy Legacy," *Public Perspective*, The Roper Center for Public Opinion Research, October/Novembe, 1998.

Reeves, Richard. "The Inevitability of Teddy," *Esquire*, February 13, 1979.

Reid, T.R. "Minding the Store; Despite Fond Memories of 1980 Race, Kennedy Content To Skip This Campaign," *Washington Post*, April 16, 1984.

Reid, T. R., and Marjorie Hyer. "The Catholic Church in America; Lacking The 'Benefit' of State Aid, the Church Struggled and Prospered," *Washington Post*, October 7, 1979.

Reston, James. "Party's Debate on Kennedy Takes Note of Catholic Vote," *The New York Times*, January 3, 1960.

_____. "Dallas," *New York Times*, September 14, 1960.

_____. "What Was Killed Was Not Only the President but the Promise," *New York Times Magazine*, November 15, 1964.

Rimer, Sara. "THE 1994 CAMPAIGN: MASSACHUSETTS; 'Perfect Anti-Kennedy' Opposes the Senator," *New York Times*, October 25, 1994.

Roberts, Paul Craig. "Cultural Pressures Undoing Our Unity," *Washington Times*, February 26, 2001.

Roddy, Joseph. "Irish Origins of a President," *Look*, March 14, 1961.

_____. "Pope John: The Astonishing Catholic Pontiff," *Look*, July 2, 1963.

_____. "Ireland: The Kennedy Cult: They Cried the Rain Down that Night," *Look*, November 17, 1964.

Roosevelt, Eleanor. "On My Own," *Saturday Evening Post*, March 8, 1958.

Rovere, Richard H. "Letter from Washington," *New Yorker*, November 19, 1960.

_____. "Our Far-Flung Correspondents: Journal of a Psuedo-Event," *New Yorker*, July 13, 1963.

Russell, Francis. "Why Massachustetts Loves the Kennedys," *National Review*, August 11, 1970.

Rynne, Xavier. "Letter from Vatican City," *New Yorker*, January 18, 1964.

Schindehette, Susan, and Jane Sims Podesta. "Taking Aim: RFK's Daughter Kathleen Kennedy Townsend Targets Guns as she Campaigns in Sniper-Terrorized Maryland," *People*, November 4, 2002.

Schlesinger, Arthur, Jr. "Liberalism and Catholicism," *American Prospect*, March 13, 2000.

Schultz, Randy. "Matriarch of an American Dynasty," *Palm Beach Post*, January 23, 1995.

Schumach, Murray. "Kennedy Parades to Mixed Chorus," *New York Times*, March 17, 1968.

Sesno, Frank. "Irish Memorial Mass Pays Tribute to John F. Kennedy Jr.," *CNN LIVE EVENT/ SPECIAL*, Transcript # 99072201V54, July 22, 1999.

Shales, Tom. The Networks Blink and Miss the Best Parts," *Washington Post*, August 16, 2000.

Shaw, David. "The Pope and the Press: Too Much Sensationalism, Too Little Substance?" *Los Angeles Times*, April 18, 1995.

Sherrill, Robert. "Camelot Again," *New York Times*, July 27, 1980.

Shribman, David M. "For JFK, A Wide Embrace," *Boston Globe*, March 20, 2001.

Sidey, Hugh. "Joe Kennedy's Feelings about His Son," *Life*, Decmber 19, 1960.

_____. "What the Ks Really Told Each Other," *Life*, June 16, 1961.

_____. "Back Door No Longer," *Time*, October 15, 1979.

Smith, Alfred E. "American Catholic," *Atlantic Monthly*, May 1927.

Smith, Hugh. "De Valera Defends His Neutrality; Makes 'Allowances' for Churchill," *New York Times*, May 17, 1945.

_____. "DeValera Defends Honor for Hitler," *New York Times*, July 20, 1945.

Smith, Liz. "What Ever Happened to the Kennedys?" *Ladies Home Journal*, January 1977.

Sorensen, Theodore C. "RFK: A Personal Memoir," *Saturday Review*, June 22, 1968.

Steel, Ronald. "The Kennedy Fantasy," *New York Review of Books*, November 19, 1970.

Stegner, Wallace. "Who Persecutes Boston?" *Atlantic*, July 1944.

Steinem, Gloria. "Mrs. Kennedy at the Moment," *Esquire*, October 1964.

Steinfels, Peter. "Beliefs," *New York Times*, May 3, 1997.

_____. "Beliefs: Given the Presidential Campaign Hubbub, One Would Think Anti-Catholicism Owed Its Existence to Bob Jones University. It Doesn't." *New York Times*, March 4, 2000.

Sterling, Claire. "Vatican and Kennedy," *Reporter*, October 27, 1960.

Tolischus, Otto D. "Roosevelt Victory Foreseen in Reich," *New York Times*, November 4, 1936.

Trussell, C.P. "New Alien Quotas," *New York Times*, July 23, 1964.

Tynan, Maol Muire. "Kennedy Smith Given Honorary Citizenship," *Irish Times,* July 27, 1998.

Van Den Haag, Ernest. "More Immigration?" *National Review,* September 21, 1965.

Vidal, Gore. "The Holy Family," *Esquire,* April 1967.

Wald, Matthew L. "Many Seek O'Neill Seat, But Only One Is A Kennedy," *New York Times,* August 18, 1986.

Walker, Martin. "Downhill with Ted," *Manchester Guardian (Weekly),* December 1, 1991.

Walsh, Edward. "Chicago Catholics: No Longer a Reliable Voting Bloc," *Washington Post,* February 2, 1980.

Ward, Barbara. "The Pope of the Dialogue," *Atlantic,* September 1963.

White, Theodore H. "For President Kennedy: An Epilogue," *Life,* December 6, 1963.

Wicker, Tom "Ireland Prepares for Kennedy Visit Thursday," *New York Times,* June 23, 1963.

———. "Kennedy Sees the Cousin Who Didn't Catch the Boat," *New York Times,* June 28, 1963.

———. "Kennedy Without Tears," *Esquire,* June 1964.

———. "Kennedy to Make 3 Primary Races; Attacks Johnson," *New York Times,* March 17, 1968.

———. "Kennedy Without End, Amen," *Esquire,* June 1977.

Wicklein, John. "Vast Anti-Catholic Drive Slated Before Election," *New York Times,* October 16, 1960.

———. "Anti-Catholic Groups Closely Cooperate in Mail Campaign to Defeat Kennedy," *New York Times,* October 17, 1960.

———. "Campaign Issues: Effect of Anti Catholic Sentiment Is Weighed as Factor at the Polls," *New York Times,* November 3, 1960.

Wills, Garry. "Why We Regard Ourselves As Set Apart as a Nation," *U.S. News and World Report,* July 26, 1982.

———. "The Kennedys in the King Years," *New York Review of Books,* November 10, 1988.

Wolfe, Alan. "Liberalism and Catholicism," *American Prospect,* January 31, 2000.

Woodham-Smith, Cecil. "Ireland's Hunger, England's Fault?" *Atlantic,* January, 1963.

Unbylined Articles and Research Material

"A Compendium of Curious Coincidences," *Time,* August 21, 1964.

"A Debut into a Burgeoning Family," *Life,* April 21, 1958.

"After the Election," *Commonweal,* November 18, 1960.

"Aftermath of the Kennedy Statement," *Commonweal,* March 20, 1959.

"Amazing Story of Joseph Kennedy," *U.S. News and World Report,* January 1, 1962.

"Amazing Kennedys," *Reader's Digest,* November 1957.

"And President Kennedy Enjoys Every Minute," *Irish Press,* June 28, 1963.

"Attack on Catholics," *New York Times,* February 11, 1960.

"Birth Control Issue," *Time,* December 7, 1959.

"Blair Apologises to Guildford Four," BBC News Online: UK: Northern Ireland, Tuesday June 6, 2000.

"Blauvelt Campaign: Reports of a Previous Marriage by President Kennedy," *Newsweek,* September 24, 1962.

"Both Sides of the Catholic Issue," *U.S. News and World Report,* September 26, 1960.

"Campaign Issues," *New York Times,* November 3, 1960.

"Can A Catholic Win?" *Time,* May 18, 1959.

"Cardinal Cushing Remembers: 'Twice, I Saw Jack Kennedy Cry'," *Look,* November 17, 1964.

"Cardinal Visits FDR," *New York Daily News,* November 6, 1936.

"Caroline Enters a School in City," *New York Times,* September 16, 1964.

"Catholic for President?" *Commonweal,* March 6, 1959.

"Catholic Opposed," *New York Times,* April 9, 1960.

"Catholicism in the U.S.," *Time*, August 21, 1964.

"Catholics and Others," *America*, January 28, 1961.

"Catholics and the State," *New Republic*, October 17, 1960.

"Church and Mr. Kennedy," *Commonweal*, February 9, 1962.

"Church and the President," *America*, January 13, 1962.

"Church and State," *New Republic*, January 25, 1960.

"Coughlin Quits Air, Suspends His Union, Saying Farewell," *New York Times*, November 8, 1936.

"Doctor Describes Illness of Pope," *New York Times*, October 12, 1958.

"Dogged by Fate," *Nation*, June 17, 1968.

"Dr. Ricardo Galeazzi-Lisi Dies; Sold Deathbed Story of Pius XII," Associated Press, November 17, 1968.

"Economy Slipping," *New York Times*, October 31, 1960.

"Ethel Kennedy and Her Children," *Life*, November 10, 1961.

"Excerpt from the Eulogy," *Cape Cod Times*, January 4, 1998.

"Family Man with a Big New Job to Do," *Life*, November 21, 1960.

"Family Ties—Paul Hill, Kennedy Kin Fight Murder Rap," *Day One ABC*, February 28, 1994.

"First Lady At the Vatican," *America*, March 24, 1962.

"Former Hub Mayor Dead," *Boston Post*, October 3, 1950.

"French Writer Recalls Kennedy Premonition," *New York Times*, June 6, 1968.

"Goldwater Scored on Minority Attack," *New York Times*, October 10, 1964.

"Harvard, Six; Irish, Six," *America*, December 9, 1961.

"High Point In A Notable Week: Christening of John F. Kennedy's Son," *Life*, December 19, 1960.

"I Am Not the Catholic Candidate for President," *U.S. News and World Report*, May 2, 1960.

"I Lift My Lamp," *New York Times*, January 14, 1965.

"Immigration Law Praised by DAR," *New York Times*, September 15, 1964.

"In Her Time of Trial," *Newsweek*, December 9, 1963.

"In Their Own Words," *Dallas Morning News*, November 21, 2000.

"Inaugural Address—President John F. Kennedy, Washington, D.C., January 20, 1961," John Fitzgerald Kennedy Library, Boston, Massachusetts.

"Ireland—Lifting the Green Curtain," *New York Times Magazine*, July 12, 1963.

"Irish American of the Year 1997: Senator Edward Kennedy; Leading the Cause of Ireland," *Irish America*, April 30, 1997.

"Is Kennedy in Political Trouble at Home?" *U.S. News and World Report*, July 8, 1963.

"Is Loyalty Enough?" *Newsweek*, October 18, 1965.

"J.F.K. as Theologian," *Christian Century*, May 8, 1963.

"J.F.K.: Chipper at 46, Pointing to '64," *Newsweek*, June 3, 1963.

"J.F.K. to the Vatican," *America*, June 1, 1963.

"John Jr.," *Time*, December 5, 1960.

"Kennedy Accepts Invitation," *New York Times*, September 9, 1960.

"Kennedy Assails Immigration Curb," *New York Times*, October 6, 1964.

"Kennedy and Baldwin: The Gulf," *Newsweek*, June 3, 1963.

"Kennedy and the Clergy," *Newsweek*, January 22, 1962.

"Kennedy Assures Texas Ministers of Independence," *New York Times*, September 13, 1960.

"Kennedy Backs Immigration Bill," *New York Times*, September 21, 1965.

"Kennedy Faces Southern Battle, *New York Times,* September 8, 1960.

"Kennedy Hailed by Bobby Soxers," *New York Times*, April 21, 1960.

"Kennedy Living: Homes of the Kennedy Clan," *Time*, September 1, 1961.

"Kennedy on Latin America," *Commonweal*, June 3, 1966.

"Kennedy Pledges Aid to Northeast," *New York Times*, September 16, 1964.

"Kennedy Predicts Approval," *New York Times*, June 11, 1965.

"Kennedy Runs True to Form," *Dallas Morning News*, September 7, 1960.

"Kennedy Visits Convent to See Cousin, a Nun," *New York Times*, June 28, 1963.
"Kennedy vs. A McCormack Again," *U.S. News and World Report*, March 19, 1962.
"Kennedy's Irish Kin," *Life*, July 1963.
"Kennedy's Trip—The Mood and the Flavor," *New York Times*, June 30, 1963.
"Kennedy's Worry: Is the Solid South Lost in '64?" *U.S. News and World Report,* October 28, 1963.
"L.B.J. and Edward Kennedy: Their Nominee Under Fire," *U.S. News and World Report*, October 11, 1965.
"Liberalism and Catholicism," *American Prospect*, March 13, 2000.
"Life Goes Courting With A U.S. Senator," *Life*, July 20, 1953.
"L'Osservatore on Politics," *Commonweal*, June 3, 1960.
"Man of the Year—Pope John XXIII," *Time*, January 4, 1963.
"Massachusetts on Trial," *Saturday Evening Post*, June 5, 1965.
"May God Forgive Dallas," *Newsweek*, December 9, 1963.
"May the Angels, Dear Jack, Lead You Into Paradise," *Newsweek*, December 9, 1963.
"More than a Brother," *Time*, February 16, 1962.
"Mortalized," *New Yorker*, February 13, 1971.
"Nixon Previews Campaign," *The New York Times,* January 28, 1960.
"Northern Ireland—A View from America," address by Sen. Edward Kennedy, Tip O'Neill Memorial Lecture, University of Ulster, Magee College, Incor, Guildhall, Derry, Northern Ireland, January 9, 1998.
"Northern Ireland: Off the Deep End," *Time*, November 1, 1971.
"Notes and Comment," *New Yorker*, August 3, 1968.
"Now a New Worry for Kennedy: The White Vote in '64," *U.S. News and World Report,* September 9, 1963.
"Obituary of Dowager Duchess of Devonshire," *The Daily Telegraph*, December 27, 1988.
"On Questioning Catholic Candidates," *America*, March 7, 1959.
"One for Old Joe," *Newsweek*, October 11, 1965.
"Origins," *New Yorker*, June 15, 1963.
"Out of Control Immigration," *Foreign Affairs*, Sept–Oct 2000.
"Pacelli Lunches With Roosevelt," *New York Times*, November 6, 1936.
"Paul Hill—Irishman Fights to Clear Conviction," *60 Minutes*, CBS News, July 3, 1994.
"Peale Criticized," *New York Times*, September 9, 1960.
"Pius Doctor Is Barred From Practice in Italy," Associated Press, *New York Times*, December 13, 1958.
"P.O.A.U. Defends Kennedy Against Bias Charges," *Christian Century*, May 16, 1962.
"Politics: JFK's Vost Votes," *Newsweek*, October 21, 1963.
"Pope's Strength Is Ebbing, Vatican Bulletin Indicates," *New York Times*, February 6, 1954.
"Portrait—Robert Kennedy," *New York Times Magazine*, March 6, 1955.
"Power of the Kennedy Brothers," *U.S. News and World Report*, July 16, 1962.
"President Ask Ending of Quotas for Immigrants," *New York Times*, January 14, 1965.
"President Vows a Return to Erin," *New York Times*, June 30, 1963.
"President's Wife Received by Pope," *New York Times,* March 11, 1962.
"Pride of the Clan," *Time*, July 11, 1960.
"Priest Sees Bias as Bad as 1928," *New York Times*, September 10, 1960.
"Protestant Unit Wary on Kennedy," *New York Times*, September 8, 1960.
"Protestants in Politics," *New Republic*, September 19, 1960.
"Reality and the American Dream," *Commonweal*, July 8, 1960.
"Recalling JFK Jr.'s Promise," N.R. Kleinfield, *New York Times*, July 24, 1999.
"Religion and Politics," *Time*, August 22, 1960.
"Religion in the Campaign," *Des Moines Register*, September 17, 1960.
"Remarks by Caroline Kennedy to the Democratic National Convention in Los Angeles," Associated Press, August 15, 2000.

"Rev. Martin D'Arcy, A Jesuit Philosopher Dies in London at 88," *New York Times*, February 19, 1951.

"Robert Kennedy Recalled," *National Catholic Reporter*, July 3, 1998.

"Robert Kennedy—Tribute," *People*, June 6, 1988.

"Roman Catholics: Clear It with the Vatican," *Time*, September 20, 1963.

"Rose-Colored Glasses," *Time*, April 22, 1974.

"Rose Kennedy at 76," *America*, November 18, 1967.

"Saturday June 8 in Manhattan . . . ," *America*, June 22, 1968.

"Seitz Attack Threat to Peace, Says Kennedy," *Irish Independent*, January 20, 1998.

"Sen. Kennedy Talks about His Grief," *Cape Cod Times*, May 3, 2000.

"Senator Kennedy and His Critics," *Commonweal*, March 20, 1959.

"Senator Kennedy and the Chapel," *Commonweal*, January 29, 1960.

"Senator Kennedy Crosses the Color Line," *Commonweal*, July 22, 1966.

"Shamrock Left at Kennedy Grave," *New York Times*, March 18, 1964.

"Spellman's View on War Called Outrageous..." *New York Times*, February 5, 1967.

"Tattling About the Dead Now a National Pastime," *Washington Post*, October 12, 1978.

"Test of Religion," *Time*, September 26, 1960.

"Texas Repeats 1928 Campaign," *Nashville Tennessean*, August 23, 1960.

"The Cold War, Episode 11—Vietnam," *CNN*, December 1998.

"The Competent American," *Look*, November 17, 1964.

"The Family in Mourning," *Time*, December 6, 1963.

"The Ghost of Charisma Past," *Esquire*, February 1972.

"The IRA's Angels," *Newsweek*, May 18, 1981.

"The Kennedy Homestead," *Newsweek*, July 1, 1963.

"The Kennedys," [videorecording], a co-production of *WBGH/Boston and Thames Television*, London; Alexandria, Va.: PBS Video, 1992.

"The Kennedys and Their Son at Christening," *Life*, December 19, 1960.

"The Long Road from Prison to High Society," BBC News Online, Tuesday, June 6, 2000.

"The Lost Children of Camelot," *Scottish Daily Record & Sunday Mail*, November 21, 1998.

"The Papacy—Vatican Revolutionary," *Time*, June 7, 1963.

"Third Degree for Catholics," *America*, March 14, 1959.

"3 Sisters Put Questions to Kennedy in Telecast," *Washington Post*, November 8, 1960.

"Truman Accuses GOP of Bigotry," *New York Times,* September 6, 1960.

"Truman Hails Nixon on Religious Issue," *New York Times,* September 15, 1960.

"Two Presidents Greet 2,000 Guests," *Irish Press*, June 28, 1963.

"Vatican and U.S.: Closer Ties?" *U.S. News and World Report*, July 15, 1963.

"Vatican City Official Clipper Bound to U.S.," *New York Times*, September 4, 1943.

"Wanted to Stay in Office," *Dallas Morning News*, October 30, 1960.

"What Drives Bobby Kennedy," *New York Times Magazine*, April 7, 1963.

"When Kennedy Died: Psychogical Impact," *Newsweek*, September 14, 1964.

"When Kennedy Went 'Home' to Ireland," *U.S. News and World Report*, July 8, 1963.

"Will Kennedy Run for President?" *Liberty*, May 21, 1938.

"Will the Religious Issue Stop Kennedy in '60?" *U.S. News and World Report,* September 7, 1959.

"Why We Regard Ourselves as Set Apart as a Nation—A Conversation With Garry Wills," *U.S. News and World Report*, July 26, 1982.

"Young Man Now Really On His Way: West Virginia Landslide," *Life*, May 23, 1960.

"Youth Writes Anti-Catholic Pamphlet," *Minneapolis Sunday Tribune*, September 11, 1960.

About the Author

THOMAS MAIER is an award-winning author and investigative journalist. His most recent work, *Dr. Spock: An American Life*, was selected as one of the top ten nonfiction books of 1998 by the *Boston Globe* and as a "Notable Book of the Year" by the *New York Times*. Excerpts appeared in *Newsweek*, *U.S. News and World Report*, and it was condensed as a *Reader's Digest* book. Maier also appeared on NBC's "Today" show, C-Span's BookTV, and served as consultant and on-air commentator for a documentary about Dr. Spock's life, jointly produced by the BBC and A&E's "Biography." A paperback version was published in spring 2003 by Basic Books to mark Dr. Spock's 100th birthday.

Maier's 1994 book, *Newhouse: All the Glitter, Power and Glory of America's Richest Media Empire and the Secretive Man Behind It*, won the Frank Luther Mott Award by the National Honor Society in Journalism and Mass Communication as best media book of the year. Excerpts appeared in the *Columbia Journalism Review*, *Worth*, the *IRE Journal* and the *London Telegraph* magazine. An updated trade paperback of *Newhouse*, published by Johnson Books, was picked by *Entertainment Weekly* as one of the top ten "must reads" for the 1997 summer season.

Since 1984, Maier has been a writer for *Newsday* in New York, and previously worked at the *Chicago Sun-Times*. He has won several national and regional honors, including the national Society of Professional Journalists' top reporting prize in 1987 for an expose on police misconduct. In 2002, Maier received the first-place prize from the International Consortium of Investigative Journalists for his reporting from El Salvador on the plight of immigrant workers. He also testified before a U.S. Senate labor subcommittee examining the immigrant issue, and won honors from Columbia University for his "outstanding" coverage on race and ethnicity.

At the Columbia University Graduate School of Journalism, Maier won the John M. Patterson Prize for television documentary making and his documentary, *The Mob, the Merchants and the Fulton Fish Market*, was broadcast by WNET/Channel 13. He later received a John McCloy Journalism Fellowship to Europe, which is awarded by the Columbia Journalism School and the American Council on Germany. He received a bachelor's degree in political science from Fordham University, and for three years, he taught journalism as an adjunct professor at Hofstra University.

Maier lives on Long Island with his wife, Joyce McGurrin, and their three sons, Andrew, Taylor and Reade, for whom this book is dedicated.

Index